Medical English Literature Reading
of Common Clinical Diseases

临床常见疾病
医学英语文献阅读

● 主　编　马志方　晋建华　王斌全

● 副主编　岳颖莱　王东文

● 编　者（按姓氏笔画排序）

土　锐　王小兵　王晓飞　付永良　刘宏业

刘晓东　闫小挺　许召良　李　丹　李春辉

李袁飞　杨　慧　闵国文　张　伟　张　瑾

张海利　岳　亮　郝　斌　茹　峰　高　妍

高宏飞　魏　亮

人民卫生出版社

图书在版编目（CIP）数据

临床常见疾病医学英语文献阅读 / 马志方，晋建华，王斌全主编. —北京：人民卫生出版社，2014

ISBN 978-7-117-19107-4

Ⅰ. ①临…　Ⅱ. ①马…②晋…③王…　Ⅲ. ①常见病－诊疗－英语－阅读教学－医学院校 - 教学参考资料　Ⅳ. ①H319.4

中国版本图书馆 CIP 数据核字（2014）第 109631 号

| 人卫社官网　www.pmph.com | 出版物查询，在线购书 |
| 人卫医学网　www.ipmph.com | 医学考试辅导，医学数据库服务，医学教育资源，大众健康资讯 |

临床常见疾病　医学英语文献阅读

主　　编：马志方　晋建华　王斌全
出版发行：人民卫生出版社（中继线 010-59780011）
地　　址：北京市朝阳区潘家园南里 19 号
邮　　编：100021
E - mail：pmph @ pmph.com
购书热线：010-59787592　010-59787584　010-65264830
印　　刷：保定市中画美凯印刷有限公司
经　　销：新华书店
开　　本：710×1000　1/16　印张：42
字　　数：870 千字
版　　次：2014 年 8 月第 1 版　2024 年 3 月第 1 版第 11 次印刷
标准书号：ISBN 978-7-117-19107-4/R·19108
定　　价：90.00 元
打击盗版举报电话：010-59787491　E-mail：WQ @ pmph.com
（凡属印装质量问题请与本社市场营销中心联系退换）

随着时代发展,高等医学教育国际化的步伐正在加快,对医学生的培养要求也越来越高。英语水平是反映学生综合素质的重要方面,医学英语是高等医学院校学生的必修课程之一,需要长期地系统地学习。医学本科生、研究生和低年资住院医师在见习、实习阶段要接触很多临床专业的常见病,如果在这一期间同步进行专业外语的学习,可以提高学习兴趣,掌握相对全面的基本专业外语。通过阅读本书可以学习临床各专业常见100个典型疾病的概念、诊断和治疗原则,快速掌握相关英文的关键词汇和口语表达,是医学生从公共英语过渡到专业英文文献的桥梁教材。

本书编写特点是:①精心挑选临床上最常见的100个病种,涵盖面广;②以疾病的概念、临床表现、诊断和治疗原则为主线,简明扼要;③以问答的形式串联相关内容,采用通俗化的语言,便于理解和掌握;④在每个疾病后附有关键词汇和主要短语的中英文注释。

本书由山西医科大学第一临床医学院教务处策划,并组织一批青年骨干教师以及高年级研究生进行编写,同时还邀请外校英语专业教师参与编写和校对。为了体现英文教材纯正的英语表达,部分内容参阅了 WebMD 和 Wikipedia 等国外医学网站内容。由于编写时间和水平有限,书中难免有不足之处,欢迎各位读者批评指正。

编 者

Contents
目 录

Section One: Surgical Disease

第一部分 外科疾病

1 ——— Appendicitis
阑　尾　炎

What is appendicitis?

Appendicitis is an inflammation of the appendix, a 3 1/2-inch-long tube of tissue that extends from the large intestine. No one is absolutely certain what the function of the appendix is. One thing we do know: We can live without it, without apparent consequences.

Appendicitis is a medical emergency that requires prompt surgery to remove the appendix. Left untreated, an inflamed appendix will eventually burst, or perforate, spilling infectious materials into the abdominal cavity. This can lead to peritonitis, a serious inflammation of the abdominal cavity's lining (the peritoneum) that can be fatal unless it is treated quickly with strong antibiotics.

Sometimes a pus-filled abscess (infection that is walled off from the rest of the body) forms outside the inflamed appendix. Scar tissue then "walls off" the appendix from the rest of the abdomen, preventing infection from spreading. An abscessed appendix is a less urgent situation, but unfortunately, it can't be identified without surgery. For this reason, all cases of appendicitis are treated as emergencies, requiring surgery.

In the U.S., one in 15 people will get appendicitis. Although it can strike at any age, appendicitis is rare under age 2 and most common between ages 10 and 30.

What causes appendicitis?

Appendicitis occurs when the appendix becomes blocked, often by stool, a foreign body, or cancer. Blockage may also occur from infection, since the appendix swells in response to any infection in the body.

What are the symptoms of appendicitis?

The classic symptoms of appendicitis include:
- Dull pain near the navel or the upper abdomen that becomes sharp as it moves to the lower right abdomen. This is usually the first sign.
- Loss of appetite

3

- Nausea and/or vomiting soon after abdominal pain begins
- Abdominal swelling
- Fever of 99-102 degrees Fahrenheit
- Inability to pass gas

Almost half the time, other symptoms of appendicitis appear, including:

- Dull or sharp pain anywhere in the upper or lower abdomen, back, or rectum
- Painful urination
- Vomiting that precedes the abdominal pain
- Severe cramps
- Constipation or diarrhea with gas

If you have any of the mentioned symptoms, seek medical attention immediately since timely diagnosis and treatment is very important. Do not eat, drink, or use any pain remedies, antacids, laxatives, or heating pads, which can cause an inflamed appendix to rupture.

How is appendicitis diagnosed?

Diagnosing appendicitis can be tricky. Symptoms of appendicitis are frequently vague or extremely similar to other ailments, including gallbladder problems, bladder or urinary tract infection, Crohn's disease, gastritis, intestinal infection, and ovary problems.

The following tests are usually used to make the diagnosis:

- Abdominal exam to detect inflammation
- Urine test to rule out a urinary tract infection
- Rectal exam
- Blood test to see if your body is fighting infection
- CT scans and/or ultrasound

How is appendicitis treated?

Surgery to remove the appendix, which is called an appendectomy, is the standard treatment for appendicitis.

If appendicitis is even suspected, doctors tend to err on the side of safety and quickly remove the appendix to avoid its rupture. If the appendix has formed an abscess, you may have two procedures: one to drain the abscess of pus and fluid, and a later one to remove the appendix.

Appendectomy: What to Expect

Antibiotics are given before an appendectomy to fight possible peritonitis. General anesthesia is usually given, and the appendix is removed through a 4-inch incision or by laparoscopy. If you have peritonitis, the abdomen is also irrigated and drained of pus.

Within 12 hours of surgery you may get up and move around. You can usually return to normal activities in two to three weeks. If surgery is done with a laparoscope (a thin telescope-like instrument for viewing inside the abdomen), the incision is smaller and recovery is faster.

After an appendectomy, call your doctor if you have:

- Uncontrolled vomiting
- Increased pain in your abdomen
- Dizziness/feelings of faintness
- Blood in your vomit or urine
- Increased pain and redness in your incision
- Fever
- Pus in the wound

Can appendicitis be prevented?

There is no way to prevent appendicitis. However, appendicitis is less common in people who eat foods high in fiber, such as fresh fruits and vegetables.

中英文注释

关键词汇

appendectomy [ˌæp(ə)n'dektəmi] n. 阑尾切除术

blocked [blɔkt] adj. 堵塞

burst [bə:st] v. 破裂

fever ['fi:və] n. 发热

inflammation [ˌinflə'meiʃən] n. 炎症

laparoscope ['læpərəuskəup] n. 腹腔镜

perforate ['pə:fəreit] v. 穿孔

peritonitis [ˌperitə'naitis] n. 腹膜炎

pus [pʌs] n. 脓, 浓汁

主要短语

abdominal swelling 腹胀

high in fiber 富含纤维

lower right abdomen 右下腹

loss of appetite 食欲缺乏

medical emergency 医疗急症

rule out 排除

付永良　马志方

2 Bowel Obstruction, Ileus (Paralytic Ileus)
肠梗阻，麻痹性肠梗阻

Bowel Obstruction
肠 梗 阻

What is a bowel obstruction?

A bowel obstruction happens when either your small or large intestine is partly or completely blocked. The blockage prevents food, fluids, and gas from moving through the intestines in the normal way. The blockage may cause severe pain that comes and goes.

This topic covers a blockage caused by tumors, scar tissue, or twisting or narrowing of the intestines. It does not cover ileus, which most commonly happens after surgery on the belly (abdominal surgery).

What causes a bowel obstruction?

Tumors, scar tissue (adhesions), or twisting or narrowing of the intestines can cause a bowel obstruction. These are called mechanical obstructions.

In the small intestine, scar tissue is most often the cause. Other causes include hernias and Crohn's disease, which can twist or narrow the intestine, and tumors, which can block the intestine. A blockage also can happen if one part of the intestine folds like a telescope into another part, which is called intussusception.

In the large intestine, cancer is most often the cause. Other causes are severe constipation from a hard mass of stool, and narrowing of the intestine caused by diverticulitis or inflammatory bowel disease.

What are the symptoms of bowel obstruction?

Symptoms include:
- Cramping and belly pain that comes and goes. The pain can occur around or below the belly button.

- Vomiting.
- Bloating.
- Constipation and a lack of gas, if the intestine is completely blocked.
- Diarrhea, if the intestine is partly blocked.

Go to hospital right away if your belly pain is severe and constant. This may mean that your intestine's blood supply has been cut off or that you have a hole in your intestine. This is an emergency.

How is a bowel obstruction diagnosed?

Your doctor may do:

- Check your belly for tenderness and bloating.
- Your symptoms and other digestive problems you've had.
- An abdominal X-ray, which can find blockages in the small and large intestines.
- A CT scan of the belly, which helps your doctor see whether the blockage is partial or complete.

How is it treated?

Most bowel obstructions are treated in the hospital.

In the hospital, the doctor will give the patient medicine and fluids through a vein (IV). To help the patient stay comfortable, the doctor may place a tiny tube called a nasogastric (NG) tube through your nose and down into your stomach. The tube removes fluids and gas and helps relieve pain and pressure. The patient will not be given anything to eat or drink.

Most bowel obstructions are partial blockages that get better on their own. Some people may need more treatment. These treatments include using liquids or air (enemas) or small mesh tubes (stents) to open up the blockage.

Surgery is almost always needed when the intestine is completely blocked or when the blood supply is cut off. You may need a colostomy or an ileostomy after surgery. The diseased part of the intestine is removed, and the remaining part is sewn to an opening in the skin. Stool passes out of the body through the opening and collects in a disposable colostomy bag.

If the blockage was caused by another health problem, such as diverticulitis, the blockage may come back if the patient don't treat that health problem.

中英文注释

关键词汇

adhesion [əd'hiːʒ(ə)n] n. 粘连

bloating ['bləʊtiŋ] adj. 腹胀

blockage ['blɒkidʒ] n. 堵塞

colostomy [kə'lɒstəmi] n. 结肠造口术

cramping ['kræmpiŋ] n. 绞痛

diverticulitis [ˌdaivətikjʊ'laitis] n. 憩室炎

enema ['enimə] n. 灌肠剂

ileostomy [ˌili'ɒstəmi] n. 回肠造口术

intussusception [ˌintəsə'sepʃ(ə)n] n. 肠套叠

nasogastric [ˌneizəu'gæstrik] n. 鼻胃管

vomiting ['vɒmitiŋ] v. 呕吐

主要短语

a lack of gas 不排气

bowel obstruction 肠梗阻

get better 好转

scar tissue 瘢痕组织

Ileus(Paralytic Ileus)
肠梗阻(麻痹性肠梗阻)

What is ileus?

Ileus is a condition where bowel movement stops for a period of time. It often occurs after surgery on the abdomen. The stomach and the small bowel recover usually within 24 hours after surgery. However, the large intestine takes much longer to recover, sometimes up to 72 hours. This then leads to a backing up of the bowel contents at the level of the colon.

What causes ileus?

In addition to postoperative causes, ileus also results from intraperitoneal or retroperitoneal inflammation (eg, appendicitis, diverticulitis, perforated duodenal ulcer), retroperitoneal or intra-abdominal hematomas (eg, ruptured abdominal aortic aneurysm, lumbar compression fracture), metabolic disturbances (eg, hypokalemia), or drugs (eg, opioids, anticholinergics, sometimes Ca^{2+} channel blockers). Ileus sometimes occurs in association with renal or thoracic disease (eg, lower rib fractures, lower lobe pneumonias).

Gastric and colonic motility disturbances after abdominal surgery are common. The small bowel is typically least affected, with motility and absorption returning to normal within hours after surgery. Stomach emptying is usually impaired for about 24 h or more. The colon is often most affected and may remain inactive for 48 to 72 h or more.

What are the symptoms of ileus?

Swelling of the bowel, abdominal pain and vomiting of dark bowel contents with a fecal smell are common signs and symptoms of ileus. Blood poisoning (toxemia) and dehydration may also be present. If neglected, ileus can cause shock and pus to form in the infected area (sepsis). Upon examination, the physician will fail to hear the normal bowel sounds in the abdomen. Swollen bowel loops can be seen on X-rays of the abdomen.

How is a ileus diagnosed?

Clinical evaluation

Sometimes X-rays

The most essential task is to distinguish ileus from intestinal obstruction. In both conditions, X-rays show gaseous distention of isolated segments of intestine. In postoperative ileus, however, gas may accumulate more in the colon than in the small bowel. Postoperative accumulation of gas in the small bowel often implies development of a complication (eg, obstruction, peritonitis). In other types of ileus, X-ray findings are similar to obstruction; differentiation can be difficult unless clinical features clearly favor one or the other. Water-soluble contrast studies may help differentiate.

How is ileus treated?

Ileus is treated through decompression therapy, which involves providing continuous suctioning through a tube hooked up to a vacuum machine. Food intake is restricted until the bowel sounds reappear and the patient passes gas. The potassium level is monitored as a low potassium level could also contribute to the ileus. Intravenous fluids are given to treat dehydration. When the patient starts to pass gas, their diet is gradually built up from fluids to a full diet over a period of three days.

Treatment involves continuous nasogastric suction, NPO status, IV fluids and electrolytes, a minimal amount of sedatives, and avoidance of opioids and anticholinergic drugs. Maintaining an adequate serum K level (> 4 mEq/L [> 4 mmol/L]) is especially important. Ileus persisting > 1 week probably has a mechanical obstructive cause, and laparotomy should be considered. Sometimes colonic ileus can be relieved by colonoscopic decompression; rarely, cecostomy is required. Colonoscopic decompression is helpful in treating pseudo-obstruction (Ogilvie syndrome), which consists of apparent obstruction at the splenic flexure, although no cause can be found by contrast enema or colonoscopy for the failure of gas and feces to pass this point. Some clinicians use IV neostigmine.

中英文注释

关键词汇

dehydration [ˌdiːhaiˈdreiʃən] n. 脱水

distention [disˈtenʃən] n. 膨胀，扩张

enema [ˈenimə] n. 灌肠剂

hematoma [ˌhiːməˈtəʊmə] n. 血肿

intraperitoneal [ˈintrəˌperitəʊˈniːəl] adj. 腹膜内的

obstipation [ˌɒbstiˈpeiʃ(ə)n] n. 顽固性便秘

peritonitis [ˌperitəˈnaitis] n. 腹膜炎

postoperative [pəʊstˈɒpərətiv] adj. 术后

retroperitoneal [ˌretroˌperitnˈiəl] adj. 腹膜后的

sepsis [ˈsepsis] n. 败血症

toxemia [tɒkˈsiːmiə] n. 毒血症

主要短语

bowel loops 肠袢

bowel movement 肠蠕动

bowel sounds 肠鸣音

continuous nasogastric suction 持续胃肠减压

channel blockers 钙离子拮抗剂

decompression therapy 减压疗法

splenic flexure 结肠脾曲

付永良　马志方

3 Gallstones
胆 结 石

Gallstones form in the gallbladder, a small organ located under the liver. The gallbladder aids in the digestive process by storing bile and secreting it into the small intestine when food enters. Bile is a fluid produced by the liver and is made up of several substances, including cholesterol, bilirubin, and bile salts.

What are gallstones?

Gallstones are pieces of solid material that form in the gallbladder. These stones develop because cholesterol and pigments in bile sometimes form hard particles.

The two main types of gallstones are:

- **Cholesterol stones:** Usually yellow-green in color, approximately 80% of gallstones are cholesterol stones.
- **Pigment stones:** These stones are smaller and darker and are made up of bilirubin.

What causes gallstones?

Several factors may come together to create gallstones, including:

- Genetics
- Body weight
- Decreased motility (movement) of the gallbladder
- Diet

Gallstones can form when there is an imbalance in the substances that make up bile. For instance, cholesterol stones may develop as a result of too much cholesterol in the bile. Another cause may be the inability of the gallbladder to empty properly.

Pigment stones are more common in people with certain medical conditions, such as cirrhosis (a liver disease in which scar tissue replaces healthy liver tissue) or blood diseases such as sickle cell anemia.

What are the risk factors for gallstones?

Risk factors for getting gallstones include:

- **Genetics.** If other people in your family have had gallstones, you are at increased risk of developing gallstones.
- **Obesity.** This is one of the biggest risk factors. Obesity can cause a rise in cholesterol and can also keep the gallbladder from emptying completely.
- **Estrogen.** Estrogen can increase cholesterol and reduce gallbladder motility. Women who are pregnant or who take birth control pills or hormone replacement therapy have higher levels of estrogen and may be more likely to develop gallstones.
- **Ethnic background.** Certain ethnic groups, including Native Americans and Mexican-Americans, are more likely to develop gallstones.
- **Gender and age.** Gallstones are more common among women and older people.
- **Cholesterol drugs.** Some cholesterol-lowering drugs increase the amount of cholesterol in bile, which may increase the chances of developing cholesterol stones.
- **Diabetes.** People with diabetes tend to have higher levels of triglycerides (a type of blood fat), which is a risk factor for gallstones.
- **Rapid weight loss.** If a person loses weight too quickly, his or her liver secretes extra cholesterol, which may lead to gallstones. Also, fasting may cause the gallbladder to contract less.

What are the symptoms of gallstones?

Gallstones often don't cause symptoms. Those that don't are called "silent stones." A person usually learns he or she has gallstones while being examined for another illness.

When symptoms do appear, they may include:
- Pain in the upper abdomen and upper back. The pain may last for several hours.
- Nausea
- Vomiting
- Other gastrointestinal problems, including bloating, indigestion and heartburn, and gas

How are gallstones diagnosed?

If the doctor suspects you have gallstones, he or she will do a physical exam and may perform various other tests, including the following:
- **Blood tests:** Blood tests may be given to check for signs of infection or obstruction and/or to rule out other conditions.
- **Ultrasound:** This procedure produces images of various parts of the body and

can be used to identify gallstones.

- **CAT scan:** This test uses specialized X-rays to create cross-section images of organs and body tissues.
- **Cholescintigraphy (HIDA scan):** This test can determine whether the gallbladder is contracting correctly. A radioactive material is injected into the patient and makes its way to the gallbladder. The technician can then observe the movement of the gallbladder.
- **Endoscopic ultrasound:** This test combines ultrasound and endoscopy to look for gallstones.
- **Endoscopic retrograde cholangiopancreatography (ERCP):** The doctor inserts an endoscope through the patient's mouth down to the small intestine and injects a dye to allow the bile ducts to be seen. The doctor can then remove gallstones that have moved into the ducts.

How are gallstones treated?

Gallstones are usually treated with surgery to take out the gallbladder. The traditional operation is called an open cholecystectomy. A newer procedure, called laparoscopic cholecystectomy, is less invasive, has fewer complications, and is used more often.

- **Laparoscopic cholecystectomy:** During this procedure, instruments, a light, and a camera are passed through several small incisions in the abdomen. The surgeon views the inside of the body by looking at a video monitor. This procedure is used in approximately 80% of gallbladder removals. After the surgery, the patient spends the night in the hospital.
- **Open cholecystectomy:** This is a more invasive procedure in which the surgeon makes incisions in the abdomen to remove the gallbladder. The patient stays in the hospital for a few days after the surgery.

If gallstones are in the bile ducts, endoscopic retrograde cholangiopancreatography may be used to find and remove them before or during gallbladder surgery.

Are there any nonsurgical treatments for gallstones?

If you have a medical condition and the doctor feels you shouldn't have gallstone surgery, he or she may prescribe the medications Actigall or Chenix. These drugs work by dissolving cholesterol stones. Mild diarrhea is a side effect of both medications.

The downside of using either medication is that you may have to take it for years to completely dissolve the stones. In addition, the stones may come back after you stop taking the drug.

中英文注释

关键词汇

bile [bail] n. 胆汁

bilirubin [ˌbiliˈruːbin] n. 胆红素

cholesterol [kəˈlestərɒl] n. 胆固醇

cirrhosis [siˈrəʊsis] n. 肝硬化

estrogen [ˈestrədʒən] n. 雌性激素

gallbladder [ˈgɔːlˌblædə] n. 胆囊

genetics [dʒiˈnetiks] n. 遗传

nausea [ˈnɔːsiə; -z-] n. 恶心

obesity [ə(ʊ)ˈbiːsiti] n. 肥胖

triglyceride [traiˈglisəraid] n. 甘油三酯

vomiting [ˈvɔmitiŋ] v. 呕吐

主要短语

bile salts 胆盐

body weight 体重

cholesterol stones 胆固醇结石

endoscopic ultrasound 超声内镜

endoscopic retrograde cholangiopancreatography (ERCP) 内窥镜逆行胆管造影

laparoscopic cholecystectomy 腹腔镜胆囊切除术

open cholecystectomy 开腹胆囊切除术

pigment stones 胆色素结石

sickle cell anemia 镰状细胞贫血

the digestive process 消化过程

付永良　马志方

4

Gastric Perforation
胃 穿 孔

Another name for Gastric Perforation is Perforated Ulcer.

What is a perforated ulcer?

A person with a perforated ulcer has a hole in the wall of the stomach, small intestine, or esophagus, caused by peptic ulcer disease. The perforated ulcer allows food and blood to leak into the abdomen. The food or blood causes severe inflammation of the inside of the abdomen, called peritonitis.

What are the causes of perforated ulcer?

- Peptic ulcer disease
- Zollinger-Ellison syndrome
- Gastrointestinal bleeding
- Peritonitis

What are the symptoms of a perforated ulcer?

Symptoms of a perforated ulcer include severe abdominal pain, abdominal swelling, abdominal tenderness, nausea, vomiting, and fever.

Abdominal pain:
- Pain is usually severe
- Pain often starts abruptly
- Pain worsens with movement
- Pain usually occurs all over the abdomen, rather than in one region
- Lower abdominal pain
- Upper abdominal pain
- Pain may radiate to the back

Abdominal tenderness:
- Right lower abdominal tenderness
- Left lower abdominal tenderness
- Right upper abdominal tenderness

- Left upper abdominal tenderness
- Upper abdominal tenderness
- Lower abdominal tenderness
- Abdominal swelling
- Back pain
- Nausea
- Vomiting
- Hiccups
- Fever
- Chills
- Constipation
- Faintness
- Fainting
- Fatigue
- Difficulty breathing
- Rapid pulse

How is perforated ulcer diagnosed?

- On X-rays, free gas/air may be visible in the abdominal cavity.
- The perforation can often be visualised using computed tomography.
- White blood cells are often elevated.
- Visible signs can occasionally include a ridged abdomen on palpation.

How does the doctor treat a perforated ulcer?

Treatment for a perforated ulcer requires surgery to repair the hole in the stomach, intestine, or esophagus.

Below from: Primary Surgery, Volume One: Non-trauma, Chapter 5. The surgery of the stomach

non-operative treatment for a perforated peptic ulcer indications.

- A perforation which appears to have sealed itself already, as shown by diminished pain and improved abdominal signs.
- Heart or lung disease, which increases the surgical and anaesthetic risks.
- The patient who is admitted after a day or two and is almost moribund with diffuse peritonitis. Non-operative treatment may be best, because it is unlikely that he would have survived so long with an open perforation.

contraindications.

- An uncertain diagnosis.

- The absence of really good nursing by day and night.
- The seriously ill patient, with a short history, whose only hope is vigorous resuscitation and an urgent laparotomy. If you do decide that such a patient is 'not fit for surgery', wait to do so until vigorous resuscitation has failed [md] don't make the decision when he is first admitted.

method.

Give him morphine 5 to 10 mg intravenously. As soon as this has had time to act, pass a large tube and empty his stomach. When it is empty, pass as wide a radio-opaque nasogastric tube as he will tolerate. Take him to the X-ray department and take AP erect films of his chest and lower abdomen. These should show that there are no fluid levels in his stomach, and that the tube is well placed. If not, adjust it and take more films. Look for subdiaphragmatic gas to confirm the diagnosis.

Back in the ward, ask a nurse to aspirate his stomach every 15 minutes initially. Set up an intravenous drip, and monitor his pulse and blood pressure hourly.

He is progressing well if:

- His pain eases, so that he does not need more analgesics.
- Another erect film 12 hours later (optional) shows no fluid level, and no increase in the gas under his diaphragm. Continue to ''suck and drip him' for 4 or 5 days, until his abdomen is no longer tender and rigid, and his bowel sounds return.
- If pain persists, or the gas under his diaphragm increases, operate.

laparotomy for a perforated peptic ulcer equipment. A general set. Several litres of warm saline. Two assistants make upper abdominal surgery easier.

PREPARATION. Pass a nasogastric tube and aspirate his stomach. He will have lost much fluid into his peritoneal cavity, so correct at least part of his fluid loss before you operate. If he is dehydrated or hypotensive, give him 1 to 3 litres of fluid rapidly. If more than 12 hours have elapsed since he perforated, he will need even more. Operate soon, but not before you have resuscitated him. He has not bled, so he does not need blood.

perioperative antibiotics. are only indicated in late cases with peritonitis.

anaesthesia.

- General anaesthesia with good relaxation.
- If this is contraindicated because of lung disease, do an intercostal block, from T6 to T11.

Premedicate him with intravenous morphine, and palpate his abdomen when this has taken effect. If his rigidity is generalized, morphine will make little difference if he has a perforation, but if he has appendicitis, rigidity will now be localized to his right iliac fossa.

incision. Make a midline or upper right paramedian incision. The escape of gas as you incise his peritoneum confirms the diagnosis.

Initial examination will probably show a pool of exudate under his liver, with food and fluid everywhere, and an inflamed peritoneum. The fluid may be odourless and colourless with yellowish flecks, or bile-stained if it is pure bile, he has biliary peritonitis. If you see patches of fat necrosis, he has acute pancreatitis. If there is no fluid or little fluid, push a swab on a holder beside his ascending colon towards his caecum. If you withdraw it soaked with fluid, this suggests a perforation. Draw his stomach and transverse colon downwards: you may see flecks of fibrin, and perhaps pieces of food.

To expose his stomach and duodenum place a self- retaining retractor in the wound. Place a moist abdominal pack on the greater curvature of his stomach. Draw this downwards, and ask your assistant to hold it; at the same time ask him to hold the patient's liver upwards with a deep retractor. Put an abdominal pack between the retractor and his liver to protect it. If necessary, get the help of a second assistant.

Suck away any fluid, looking carefully to see where it is coming from.

Search for a small (1 to 10 mm or more) circular hole on the anterior surface of his duodenum, looking as if it has just been drilled out. Feel it. The tissues around it will be oedematous, thickened, scarred, and friable. If his duodenum is normal, look at his stomach, especially its lesser curve. If the hole is small, there may be more to feel than to see. Sometimes, a gastric ulcer is sealed off by adhesions to the liver. Remember that a gastric ulcer may be malignant: consider biopsy.

If his stomach is adherent to his liver, separate it.

Open his lesser sac through his lesser omentum. Feel the posterior surface of his stomach. An ulcer high up posteriorly may be difficult to find. Feel carefully.

If his stomach and duodenum are normal, feel gently downwards towards his appendix. If there is a mass or it is obviously inflamed, close the midline incision and make a gridiron one. Two smaller incisions are better than one huge one.

To close the perforation, use 2/0 chromic catgut on an atraumatic needle to bring its edges together with 1 to 3 deep stitches. If the tissue is so rigid that the stitches cut out, you may be able to reduce the size of the hole with loose sutures, or by using a purse string suture. Always sew omentum over the perforation, by bringing up a fold of greater omentum. A hole so plugged is unlikely to leak.

Wash out his peritoneal cavity. This is absolutely critical, and may be more important than closing the hole. Tip a litre of warm saline into his peritoneal cavity, spread it well, and then suck it out again. Repeat this several times, and try to wash out every possible recess in his upper abdomen. Mop the upper surface of his liver. Instil tetracycline 1 g in a litre of of saline and leave it in. This may be unnecessary if you operate within 6 hours of the perforation.

further procedures. If:

● his general condition is good, and you are operating early (within 6 to 8 hours of a duodenal, or particularly a gastric perforation).

● he has severe ulcer disease (uncontrollable symptoms, or a previous bleed or perforation).

you are experienced, consider doing a vagotomy and gastroenterostomy. Otherwise, proceed to close his abdomen.

closure. Close his abdomen securely with non-absorbable sutures in a single layer, because it is particularly likely to burst. Don't insert drains.

postoperatively. Nurse him sitting up in a high Fowler's position. He will breathe more easily, he will be less likely to have chest complications, and any exudate will gravitate downwards. Continue with nasogastric suction and intravenous fluids. Replace gastric aspirate with 0.9% saline. If he is likely to get lung complications, chest physiotherapy is vital.

中英文注释

关键词汇

fainting ['feintiŋ] n. v. 昏厥

gastroenterostomy ['gæstrəu,entə'rɔstəmi] n. 胃肠造口吻合术

inflammation [inflə'meiʃ(ə)n] n. 炎症

laparotomy [,læpə'rɒtəmi] n. 剖腹探查术

malignant [mə'lignənt] n. 恶变

nausea ['nɔ:siə; –z–] n. 恶心

radiate ['reidieit] v. 放射，辐射

tenderness ['tendənəs] n. 疼痛，压痛

vagotomy [vei'gɒtəmi] n. 迷走神经切断术

vomiting ['vɔmitiŋ] v. 呕吐

主要短语

abdominal pain 腹痛

abdominal swelling 腹胀

biliary peritonitis 胆汁性腹膜炎

diffuse peritonitis 弥漫性腹膜炎

intercostal block 肋间神经阻滞

lesser sac 小网膜囊
perforated ulcer 穿孔性溃疡
rapid pulse 脉速
subdiaphragmatic gas 膈下游离气体

付永良　马志方

5　Pancreatitis
胰　腺　炎

Your pancreas is a large gland behind your stomach and close to your duodenum. The pancreas secretes powerful digestive enzymes that enter the small intestine through a duct. These enzymes help you digest fats, proteins, and carbohydrates. The pancreas also releases the hormones insulin and glucagon into the bloodstream. These hormones play an important part in metabolizing sugar.

Pancreatitis is a rare disease in which the pancreas becomes inflamed. Damage to the gland occurs when digestive enzymes are activated and begin attacking the pancreas. In severe cases, there may be bleeding into the gland, serious tissue damage, infection, and cysts. Enzymes and toxins may enter the bloodstream and seriously injure organs, such as the heart, lungs, and kidney.

There are two forms of pancreatitis. The acute form occurs suddenly and may be a severe, life-threatening illness with many complications. Usually, the patient recovers completely. If injury to the pancreas continues, such as when a patient persists in drinkingalcohol, a chronic form of the disease may develop, bringing severe pain and reduced functioning of the pancreas that affects digestion and causes weight loss.

What is acute pancreatitis?

An estimated 50,000 to 80,000 cases of acute pancreatitis occur in the United States each year. This disease occurs when the pancreas suddenly becomes inflamed and then gets better. Some patients have more than one attack but recover fully after each one. Most cases of acute pancreatitis are caused either by alcohol abuse or by gallstones. Other causes may be use of prescribed drugs, trauma or surgery to the abdomen, or abnormalities of the pancreas or intestine. In rare cases, the disease may result from infections, such as mumps. In about 15 percent of cases, the cause is unknown.

What are the symptoms of acute pancreatitis?

Acute pancreatitis usually begins with pain in the upper abdomen that may last for a few days. The pain is often severe. It may be constant pain, just in the abdomen, or it may reach to the back and other areas. The pain may be sudden and intense, or it may begin as a mild pain that is aggravated by eating and slowly grows worse. The abdomen may be swollen and very tender. Other symptoms may include nausea, vomiting, fever, and an increased pulse rate. The person often feels and looks very sick.

About 20 percent of cases are severe. The patient may become dehydrated and have low blood pressure. Sometimes the patient's heart, lungs, or kidneys fail. In the most severe cases, bleeding can occur in the pancreas, leading to shock and sometimes death.

How is acute pancreatitis diagnosed?

If your doctor thinks you have pancreatitis, he or she will ask questions about your medical history and do a physical exam along with lab and imaging tests.

Two blood tests that measure enzymes are used to diagnose an attack of pancreatitis. These tests are:

- Serum amylase. An increase of amylase in the blood usually indicates pancreatitis.
- Serum lipase. Sudden (acute) pancreatitis almost always raises the level of lipase in the blood.

Other blood tests may be done, such as:

- A complete blood count (CBC). The number of white blood cells rises during an attack of pancreatitis, sometimes dramatically.
- Liver function tests. Increases in liver enzymes, particularly of alanine aminotransferase and alkaline phosphatase, can be a sign of sudden pancreatitis caused by gallstones.
- Bilirubin. The level of bilirubin in the blood may increase if the common bile ductis blocked.

Imaging tests that may be done include:

- CT scan with contrast dye. A CT scan can help rule out other causes of abdominal pain, determine whether tissue is dying (pancreatic necrosis), and find complications such as fluid around the pancreas, blocked veins, and obstructed bowels.
- Abdominal ultrasound. This test can locate gallstones. It also can show an enlarged common bile duct.
- MRI. Sometimes an MRI is used to look for signs of pancreatitis. It provides information similar to that of a CT endoscopic retrograde cholangiopancreatogram (ERCP). This procedure allows the doctor to see the structure of the common bile duct, other bile ducts, and the pancreatic duct. ERCP is the only diagnostic test that also can be used to treat narrow areas (strictures) of the bile ducts and

remove gallstones from the common bile duct.

- Endoscopic ultrasound. In this form of ultrasound, a probe attached to a lighted scope is placed down the throat and into the stomach. Sound waves show images of organs in the abdomen.
- Magnetic resonance cholangiopancreatogram (MRCP). This form of MRI can detect gallstones in the common bile duct. This test is not available everywhere.

If the doctor is not sure whether your pancreatic tissue is infected, he or she may use a needle to take some fluid from the inflamed area. The fluid is then tested for organisms that can cause infection.

In severe, chronic pancreatitis, a stool analysis may be done to look for fat in stools, which is a sign that you may not be getting enough nutrition. This happens when the pancreas no longer produces the enzymes you need to digest fat.

What is the treatment for acute pancreatitis?

The treatment a patient receives depends on how bad the attack is. Unless complications occur, acute pancreatitis usually gets better on its own, so treatment is supportive in most cases. Usually the patient goes into the hospital. The doctor prescribes fluids by vein to restore blood volume. The kidneys and lungs may be treated to prevent failure of those organs. Other problems, such as cysts in the pancreas, may need treatment too.

Sometimes a patient cannot control vomiting and needs to have a tube through the nose to the stomach to remove fluid and air. In mild cases, the patient may not have food for 3 or 4 days but is given fluids and pain relievers by vein. An acute attack usually lasts only a few days, unless the ducts are blocked by gallstones. In severe cases, the patient may be fed through the veins for 3 to 6 weeks while the pancreas slowly heals.

Antibiotics may be given if signs of infection arise. Surgery may be needed if complications such as infection, cysts, or bleeding occur. Attacks caused by gallstones may require removal of the gallbladder or surgery of the bile duct. Surgery is sometimes needed for the doctor to be able to exclude other abdominal problems that can simulate pancreatitis or to treat acute pancreatitis. When there is severe injury with death of tissue, an operation may be done to remove the dead tissue.

After all signs of acute pancreatitis are gone, the doctor will determine the cause and try to prevent future attacks. In some patients the cause of the attack is clear, but in others further tests need to be done.

What if the patient has gallstones?

Ultrasound is used to detect gallstones and sometimes can provide the doctor with an idea of how severe the pancreatitis is. When gallstones are found, surgery is usually needed to remove them. When they are removed depends on how severe the pancreatitis is. If it is mild, the gallstones often can be removed within a week or so. In more severe cases, the patient may wait a month or more, until he improves, before the stones are removed. The CAT (computer axial tomography) scan may also be used to find out what is happening in and around the pancreas and how severe the problem is. This is important information that the doctor needs to determine when to remove the gallstones.

After the gallstones are removed and inflammation subsides, the pancreas usually returns to normal. Before patients leave the hospital, they are advised not to drink alcohol and not to eat large meals.

What is chronic pancreatitis?

Chronic pancreatitis has many causes but 70 to 80 percent of cases are due to chronic alcohol abuse. It may develop after only one acute attack, especially if the ducts of the pancreas become damaged. Damage to the pancreas from drinking alcohol may cause no symptoms for many years, and then the patient suddenly has an attack of pancreatitis. It is more common in men than women and often develops between 30 and 40 years of age. In other cases, pancreatitis may be inherited. Inherited forms appear to be due to abnormalities of the pancreas enzymes that cause the enzymes to autodigest the pancreas.

In the early stages, the doctor cannot always tell whether the patient has acute or chronic disease. The symptoms may be the same. Patients with chronic pancreatitis tend to have three kinds of problems: pain, malabsorption of food leading to weight loss, or diabetes.

Some patients do not have any pain but most do. Pain may be constant in the back and abdomen, and for some patients, the pain attacks are disabling. In some cases, the abdominal pain goes away as the condition advances. Doctors think this happens because pancreatic enzymes are no longer being made by the pancreas.

Patients with this disease often lose weight, even when their appetite and eating habits are normal. This occurs because the body does not secrete enough pancreatic enzymes to break down food, so nutrients are not absorbed normally. Poor digestion leads to loss of fat, protein, and sugar into the stool. Diabetes may also develop at this stage if the insulin-producing cells of the pancreas (islet cells) have been damaged.

How is chronic pancreatitis diagnosed?

Diagnosis may be difficult but is aided by a number of new techniques. Pancreatic function tests help the physician decide if the pancreas still can make enough digestive enzymes. The doctor can see abnormalities in the pancreas using several techniques (ultrasonic imaging, endoscopic retrograde cholangiopancreatography (ERCP), and the CAT scan). In more advanced stages of the disease, when diabetes and malabsorption (a problem due to lack of enzymes) occur, the doctor can use a number of blood, urine, and stool tests to help in the diagnosis of chronic pancreatitis and to monitor the progression of the disorder.

How is chronic pancreatitis treated?

The doctor treats chronic pancreatitis by relieving pain and managing the nutritional and metabolic problems. The patient can reduce the amount of fat and protein lost in stools by cutting back on dietary fat and taking pills containing pancreatic enzymes. This will result in better nutrition and weight gain. Sometimes insulin or other drugs must be given to control the patient's blood sugar.

In some cases, surgery is needed to relieve pain by draining an enlarged pancreatic duct. Sometimes, part or most of the pancreas is removed in an attempt to relieve chronic pain.

Patients must stop drinking, adhere to their prescribed diets, and take the proper medications in order to have fewer and milder attacks.

中英文注释

关键词汇
cyst [sist] n. 囊肿
digest [dai'dʒest; di-] vi/vt. 消化
enzyme ['enzaim] n. 酶
fever ['fiːvə] n/vi. 发热
gallstone ['gɔːlstəʊn] n. 胆结石
glucagon ['gluːkəg(ə)n; -gɒn] n. 胰高血糖素
insulin ['insjʊlin] n. 胰岛素
metabolize [mi'tæbəlaiz] vi/vt. 代谢
mumps [mʌmps] n. 流行性腮腺炎
pancreas ['pæŋkriəs] n. 胰腺
vomiting ['vɒmitiŋ] vi. 呕吐

主要短语
abdominal ultrasound 腹部超声
alcohol abuse 酗酒

chronic pancreatitis 慢性胰腺炎
digestive enzyme 消化酶
endoscopic retrograde cholangiopancreatogram (ERCP) 内镜逆行性胆胰管造影术
serum amylase 血清淀粉酶

付永良　马志方

Ulcers

消化性溃疡

What is a peptic ulcer?

A peptic ulcer is a break in the inner lining of the esophagus, stomach, or duodenum. A peptic ulcer of the stomach is called a gastric ulcer; of the duodenum, a duodenal ulcer; and of the esophagus, an esophageal ulcer. Peptic ulcers occur when the lining of these organs is corroded by the acidic digestive (peptic) juices which are secreted by the cells of the stomach. A peptic ulcer differs from an erosion because it extends deeper into the lining of the esophagus, stomach, or duodenum and excites more of an inflammatory reaction from the tissues that are eroded.

What are the causes of peptic ulcers?

For many years, excess acid was believed to be the major cause of ulcer disease. Accordingly, the emphasis of treatment was on neutralizing and inhibiting the secretion of stomach acid. While acid is still considered necessary for the formation of ulcers, the two most important initiating causes of ulcers are infection of the stomach by a bacterium called "Helicobacter pyloricus" (H. pylori) and chronic use of anti-inflammatory medications, commonly referred to as nonsteroidal anti-inflammatory drugs (NSAIDs), including aspirin. Cigarette smoking also is an important cause of ulcer formation as well as failure of ulcer treatment.

Infection with H. pylori is very common, affecting more than a billion people worldwide. Infection usually persists for many years, leading to ulcer disease in 10% to 15% of those infected. it is estimated that currently only 20% of ulcers are associated with the bacterium. While the mechanism by which H. pylori causes ulcers is complex, elimination of the bacterium by antibiotics has clearly been shown to heal ulcers and prevent the recurrence of ulcers.

NSAIDs are medications used for the treatment of arthritis and other painful inflammatory conditions in the body. Aspirin, ibuprofen (Motrin), naproxen (Naprosyn), and etodolac (Lodine) are a few of the examples of this class of medications. Prostaglandins are substances which are important in helping the linings of the esophagus, stomach, and duodenum to resist damage by the acidic digestive juices of the stomach. NSAIDs cause ulcers by interfering with prostaglandins in the stomach.

Cigarette smoking not only causes ulcers, but it also increases the risk of complications from the ulcers such as ulcer bleeding, stomach obstruction, and perforation. Cigarette smoking also is a leading cause of failure of treatment for ulcers.

Contrary to popular belief, alcohol, coffee, colas, spicy foods, and caffeine have no proven role in ulcer formation. Similarly, there is no conclusive evidence to suggest that life stresses or personality types contribute to ulcer disease.

What are the symptoms of a peptic ulcer?

Symptoms of ulcer disease are variable. Many ulcer patients experience minimal indigestion, abdominal discomfort that occurs after meals, or no discomfort at all. Some complain of upper abdominal burning or hunger pain one to three hours after meals or in the middle of the night. These symptoms often are promptly relieved by food or antacids that neutralize stomach acid. The pain of ulcer disease correlates poorly with the presence or severity of active ulceration. Some patients have persistent pain even after an ulcer is almost completely healed by medication. Others experience no pain at all. Ulcers often come and go spontaneously without the individual ever knowing that they are present unless a serious complication (like bleeding or perforation) occurs.

How are peptic ulcers diagnosed?

The diagnosis of an ulcer is made by either a barium upper gastrointestinal X-ray (upper GI series) or an upper gastrointestinal endoscopy (EGD or esophagogastroduodenoscopy). The barium upper GI X-rayis easy to perform and involves no risk (other than exposure to radiation) or discomfort. Barium is a chalky substance that is swallowed. It is visible on X- rays, and allows the outline of the stomach to be seen on X-rays; however, barium X-rays are less accurate and may miss ulcers in up to 20% of the time.

An upper gastrointestinal endoscopy is more accurate than X-rays, but involves sedation of the patient and the insertion of a flexible tube through the mouth to inspect the esophagus, stomach, and duodenum. Upper endoscopy has the added advantage of having the capability of removing small tissue samples (biopsies) to test for H. pylori infection. Biopsies are also examined under a microscope to exclude a cancerous ulcer. While virtually all duodenal ulcers are benign, gastric ulcers can occasionally be cancerous. Therefore, biopsies often are performed on gastric ulcers to exclude cancer.

What is the treatment for peptic ulcers?

The goal of ulcer treatment is to relieve pain, heal the ulcer, and prevent complications. The first step in treatment involves the reduction of risk factors (NSAIDs and cigarettes). The next step is medications.

Antacids neutralize existing acid in the stomach. Antacids such as Maalox, Mylanta, and Amphojel are safe and effective treatments. However, the neutralizing action of these agents is short-lived, and frequent dosing is required. Magnesium containing antacids, such as Maalox and Mylanta, can cause diarrhea, while aluminum containing agents like Amphojel can cause constipation. Ulcers frequently return when antacids are discontinued.

H2 blockers

Studies have shown that a protein released in the stomach called histamine stimulates gastric acid secretion. Histamine antagonists (H2 blockers) are drugs designed to block the action of histamine on gastric cells and reduce the production of acid. While H2 blockers are effective in ulcer healing, they have a limited role in eradicating H. pylori without antibiotics. Therefore, ulcers frequently return when H2 blockers are stopped.

Generally, H2 blockers are well tolerated and have few side effects even with long term use. In rare instances, patients report headache, confusion, lethargy, or hallucinations. Chronic use of cimetidine may rarely cause impotence or breast swelling. Both cimetidine and ranitidine can interfere with the body's ability to handle alcohol. Patients on these drugs who drink alcohol may have elevated blood alcohol levels. These drugs may also interfere with the liver's handling of other medications like phenytoin (Dilantin), warfarin (Coumadin), and theophylline. Frequent monitoring and adjustments of the dosages of these medications may be needed.

Proton-pump inhibitors (PPIs)

Proton-pumpinhibitors: omeprazole (Prilosec), lansoprazole (Prevacid), pantoprazole (Protonix), esomeprazole (Nexium), and rabeprazole (Aciphex) are more potent than H2 blockers in suppressing acid secretion. The different proton-pump inhibitors are very similar in action and there is no evidence that one is more effective than the other in healing ulcers. While proton-pump inhibitors are comparable to H2 blockers in effectiveness in treating gastric and duodenal ulcers, they are superior to H2 blockers in treating esophageal ulcers. Esophageal ulcers are more sensitive than gastric and duodenal ulcers to minute amounts of acid. Therefore, more complete acid suppression accomplished by proton-pump inhibitors is important for esophageal ulcer healing.

Proton-pump inhibitors are well tolerated. Side effects are uncommon; they include headache, diarrhea, constipation, nausea and rash. Interestingly, proton-pump inhibitors do not have any effect on a person's ability to digest and absorb nutrients. Proton-pump inhibitors have also been found to be safe when used long term, without serious adverse health effects. Although they may promote loss of bone (osteoporosis) and low magnesium levels, both of these side effects are easily identified and treated.

Sucralfate (Carafate) and misoprostol (Cytotec)

Sucralfate (Carafate) and misoprostol (Cytotec) are agents that strengthen the gut lining against attacks by acidic digestive juices. Sucralfate coats the ulcer surface and promotes healing. Sucralfate has very few side effects. The most common side effect is constipation and the interference with the absorption of other medications. Misoprostol is a prostaglandin-like substance commonly used to counteract the ulcerogenic effects of NSAIDs. Studies suggest that misoprostol may protect the stomach from ulceration among people who take NSAIDs chronically. Diarrhea is a common side effect. Misoprostol can cause miscarriages when given to pregnant women, and should be avoided by women of childbearing age.

H. pylori treatment

Many people harbor H. pylori in their stomachs without ever having pain or ulcers. It is not completely clear whether these patients should be treated with antibiotics. More studies are needed to answer this question. Patients with documented ulcer disease and H. pylori infection should be treated for both the ulcer and the H. pylori. H. pylori can be very difficult to completely eradicate. Treatment requires a combination of several antibiotics, sometimes in combination with a proton-pump inhibitor, H2 blockers, or Pepto-Bismol. Eradication of H. pylori prevents the return of ulcers (a major problem with all other ulcer treatment options). Elimination of this bacteria also may decrease the risk of developing gastric cancer in the future. Treatment with antibiotics carries the risk of allergic reactions, diarrhea, and sometimes severe antibiotic-induced colitis (inflammation of the colon).

Diet

There is no conclusive evidence that dietary restrictions and bland diets play a role in ulcer healing. No proven relationship exists between peptic ulcer disease and the intake of coffee and alcohol. However, since coffee stimulates gastric acid secretion, and alcohol can cause gastritis, moderation in alcohol and coffee consumption is recommended.

What are the complications of peptic ulcer?

Patients with ulcers generally function quite comfortably. Some ulcers probably heal even without medications (though they probably recur as well). Therefore, the major problems resulting from ulcers are related to ulcer complications. Complications include bleeding, perforation, and obstruction of the stomach.

Patients with ulcer bleeding may report passage of black tarry stools (melena), weakness, a sense of passing out upon standing (orthostatic syncope), and vomiting blood (hematemesis). Initial treatment involves rapid replacement of lost blood intravenously, usually with fluids. Patients with persistent or severe bleeding may require blood transfusions. An endoscopy is performed to establish the site of bleeding and to stop active ulcer bleeding with the aid of specialized endoscopic instruments.

Perforation through the stomach leads to the leakage of stomach contents into the abdominal (peritoneal) cavity, resulting in acute peritonitis (infection of the abdominal cavity). These patients report a sudden onset of extreme abdominal pain, which is worsened by any type of motion. Abdominal muscles become rigid and board-like. Urgent surgery usually is required. A duodenal ulcer that has perforated can burrow into adjacent organs such as the pancreas or behind the abdomen and into the back. An esophageal ulcer that perforates can cause severe inflammation of the tissues that surround it and the heart, and those that lie between the lungs (mediastinitis).

If an ulcer occurs in the narrow outlet from the stomach, it can obstruct the flow of stomach contents into the duodenum. Duodenal ulcers sometimes also may obstruct the flow of intestinal contents. Patients with obstruction often report increasing abdominal pain, vomiting of undigested or partially digested food, diminished appetite, and weight loss. The obstruction usually occurs at or near the pylorus that separates the stomach from the duodenum. Endoscopy is useful in establishing the diagnosis of obstruction from an ulcer and excluding gastric cancer as the cause of the obstruction. In some patients, gastric obstruction can be relieved by suction of the stomach contents with a tube for 72 hours, along with intravenous anti-ulcer medications, such as cimetidine (Tagamet) and ranitidine (Zantac). Patients with persistent obstruction require surgery.

Peptic ulcer summary

With modern treatment, patients with ulcer disease can lead normal lives without lifestyle changes or dietary restrictions. Cigarette smokers have been found to have more complications from ulcers and treatment failure. Eradication of the bacteria H. pylori not only heals ulcers but also prevents the recurrence of ulcer disease.

中英文注释

关键词汇

cimetidine [saiˈmetiˌdiːn] n. 西咪替丁

complications [ˌkɔmpliˈkeiʃəns] n. 并发症

indigestion [indiˈdʒestʃ(ə)n] n. 消化不良

peptic [ˈpeptik] n. 消化器官；adj. 有助消化的

perforation [ˌpɜːfəˈreiʃn] n. 穿孔

recurrence [riˈkʌrəns] n. 复发

swallow [ˈswɒləʊ] vi/vt. 吞咽

stomach [ˈstʌmək] n. 胃

主要短语

acute peritonitis 急性腹膜炎

abdominal discomfort 腹部不适

allergic reactions 过敏反应，致敏反应

bland diets 清淡饮食

cancerous ulcer 癌性溃疡

inflammatory reaction 炎性反应

peptic ulcer 消化性溃疡

proton-pump inhibitors 质子泵抑制剂

付永良　马志方

7 Benign Prostatic Hyperplasia (BPH)
良性前列腺增生症

What is BPH?

Benign prostatic hyperplasia (BPH) is an enlarged prostate gland. The prostate gland surrounds the urethra, the tube that carries urine from the bladder out of the body. As the prostate gets bigger, it may squeeze or partly block the urethra. This often causes problems with urinating.

What causes BPH?

Benign prostatic hyperplasia (BPH) is probably a normal part of the aging process in men, caused by changes in hormone balance and cell-growth factors. Genetics may also play a role. This is especially true for severe BPH requiring surgery in men younger than 60.

Men who are older than 50 have a higher chance of developing BPH. But why some men have more severe symptoms than others is not known.

What are the symptoms of BPH?

Many men with benign prostatic hyperplasia (BPH) have no symptoms. When symptoms (known as lower urinary tract symptoms, or LUTS) occur, they may range from mild and barely noticeable to serious and disruptive. The amount of prostate enlargement is not always related to the severity of the symptoms. Some men with only slight enlargement have serious symptoms, and some men with a great deal of enlargement have few symptoms.

Your symptoms may become worse during cold weather or as a result of physical or emotional stress.

Some medicines can make your symptoms worse. These include over-the-counter cold medicines such as diphenhydramine (Benadryl, for example), pseudoephedrine (such as Sudafed), oxymetazoline spray (such as Afrin), and prescription medicines such as antidepressants, water pills (diuretics), testosterone (gels, implants, or injections), and pain medicines (narcotics).

The symptoms of BPH may involve problems emptying the bladder or problems with bladder storage.

Symptoms related to bladder emptying include:

- Difficulty starting a urine stream (hesitancy and straining).
- Decreased strength of the urine stream (weak flow).
- Dribbling after urination.
- Feeling that the bladder is not completely empty.
- An urge to urinate again soon after urinating.
- Pain during urination (dysuria).

Symptoms related to bladder storage include:

- Waking at night to urinate (nocturia).
- Frequent urination.
- A sudden, uncontrollable urge to urinate.

These symptoms are not always related to prostate enlargement and can be caused by other conditions. BPH symptoms are often balanced between the two types of symptoms. If symptoms come on rapidly, or if you have more of one type of symptom than the other type, you may have another condition. Other conditions that may cause similar symptoms include urinary tract infections, prostatitis, prostate cancer, diabetes, heart failure, and neurologic diseases.

What increases your risk?

Men who are older than 50 have a higher risk of developing BPH.

The hormone testosterone, which is produced mainly by the testicles, is necessary in order for BPH to develop. Men who have their testicles removed before puberty never develop BPH. Men who have their testicles removed after puberty (but before they have symptoms of BPH) rarely develop BPH.

A family history of BPH may increase your risk for needing treatment for this condition, especially if a relative needed treatment before age 60.

A vasectomy does not increase your risk of BPH.

How is BPH diagnosed?

The doctor will first want to make sure that your urination problem is caused by BPH and not by something else. This can usually be determined from your medical history, a physical exam that focuses on the urinary tract, a urinalysis, and a blood test. A neurological exam should also be done to determine whether your symptoms are related to a problem with the nerves to the bladder. A questionnaire such as the American Urological Association (AUA) symptom index may be used to evaluate how bothersome your symptoms are. It is not used to diagnose BPH.

Tests that are often done

- A digital rectal exam checks the size and firmness of the prostate. The size of the prostate does not always determine the severity of the symptoms. A man with only a small degree of prostate enlargement may have more severe symptoms than a man with more enlargement.
- A urinalysis and urine culture check for a urinary tract infection that might be the cause of the symptoms.
- A blood creatinine test checks how well your kidneys are working.
- A prostate-specific antigen (PSA) test helps check for prostate cancer, which can cause the same symptoms as BPH.

Tests that are used as needed

If the patients' symptoms are moderate to severe, additional tests, called urodynamic studies, may be done.

- Post-void residual urine test (PVR) measures the amount of urine left in the bladder after urination. This test is done using ultrasound or a small tube (catheter) put into the bladder through the urethra.
- Pressure flow studies measure pressure in the bladder while urinating. They may help distinguish between urinary symptoms caused by obstruction, such as BPH, and those caused by a problem affecting the bladder muscles or nerves.
- Cystometrogram measures the bladder's pressure, compliance, and capacity during urinary storage. This may include a uroflowmetry test, which measures how fast the urine flows out of the bladder.

Tests that may be done

The following tests may be done if the patients have complications of BPH or if there is a need to look for other causes of the symptoms.

- Ultrasound uses sound waves to check the size and structure of the kidneys, bladder, and prostate. A small device called a transducer is inserted into the rectum (transrectal ultrasound) to evaluate the prostate.
- Cystoscopy allows the doctor to look inside the urethra and bladder. This may allow the doctor to see the extent of blockage of the urethra caused by an enlarged prostate and estimate its severity.
- Intravenous pyelogram (IVP) uses X-rays to show the function of the kidneys and the flow of urine from the kidneys to the bladder.
- Spiral (helical) computed tomography (CT) scan uses X-rays to make detailed pictures of structures inside the body. These scanners can check for an enlarged prostate gland, blockage, and urine flow from the kidneys.

Early Detection

There is no routine screening test for prostate enlargement. But it may be detected during other screening tests that are regularly done to check for prostate or rectal cancer, such as the digital rectal exam and prostate-specific antigen (PSA) test.

How is BPH treated?

Benign prostatic hyperplasia (BPH) cannot be cured, so treatment focuses on reducing your symptoms. Treatment is based on how severe your symptoms are, how much they bother you, and whether you have complications.

Deciding how to treat BPH is greatly influenced by how bothersome your symptoms are. The American Urological Association (AUA) symptom index is an interactive questionnaire that can help you tell how bad your symptoms are and measure how well your treatment is working. This questionnaire ranks the severity of your symptoms on a numerical scale. The higher the number, the more you are bothered by your symptoms and the more aggressive you may want to be in your treatment.

Initial treatment

The American Urological Association (AUA) makes the following treatment recommendations for benign prostatic hyperplasia (BPH) based on how bad your symptoms are.

- Symptoms that are mild or that do not bother you (AUA score of 0 to 7) may be best treated by watchful waiting. This means you may make small changes to your lifestyle to control your symptoms, but you do not take medicines or have surgery. You have regular checkups to be sure your symptoms are not getting worse.

- The treatment of moderate to severe symptoms (AUA score of 8 or more) depends on how much you are bothered by them. If the symptoms are not greatly affecting your quality of life, you may choose watchful waiting or treatment with medicine. If the symptoms are bothersome or you want more aggressive treatment, you may be offered surgery or less invasive therapies, such as transurethral microwave therapy (TUMT) or transurethral needle ablation (TUNA).

- Severe symptoms, such as ongoing inability to urinate, bladder stones, kidney damage, or ongoing blood in your urine, should be treated with surgery.

There are some things you can do that may help reduce how much BPH affects your quality of life.

- Do not try to rush your urination. Try to relax while using the bathroom.
- Spread your fluid intake throughout the day. Limit fluid intake in the evening if you often wake up at night to urinate.

- If possible, avoid medicines that make your symptoms worse.
- Consider trying an herbal therapy for BPH, such as saw palmetto or beta-sitosterol. Talk with your doctor before starting any herbal therapy.

Medications

Medicines are sometimes used to help relieve bothersome, moderate to severe urination problems caused by benign prostatic hyperplasia (BPH). If you stop using medicine, the symptoms will usually return.

The American Urological Association (AUA) symptom index is an interactive questionnaire that can help you determine how bad your urinary symptoms are and check how well your treatment is working. But the most important thing in deciding whether to use medicines is not your AUA score but how much the symptoms bother you and affect your quality of life. A high score on the AUA does not necessarily mean you need medicines.

In general, the side effects of the most commonly used medicines are minor. And the side effects stop when you stop taking the medicine.

Medication Choices

- Alpha-blockers, such as terazosin (Hytrin), relieve symptoms within a few weeks but do not stop the process of prostate enlargement.
- 5-alpha reductase inhibitors, such as dutasteride (Avodart) or finasteride (Proscar), may reduce the size of an enlarged prostate but may take 6 months or more to show any effect on symptoms.
- Using a combination of an alpha-blocker with a 5-alpha reductase inhibitor may help your symptoms more than either medicine alone.

What to think about?

Alpha-blockers and 5-alpha reductase inhibitors affect different prostate tissues. How much your symptoms improve may depend on which tissue is contributing most to your symptoms. None of these medicines will work for everyone.

Alpha-blockers may help symptoms caused by a blockage at the opening to the bladder. With this type of obstruction, you may have a hard time starting to urinate, and you may have a weak urine stream. Alpha-blockers relax the smooth muscle tissue in the prostate and the opening to the bladder. This muscle tissue must relax to allow urine to flow.

5-alpha reductase inhibitors can reduce the size of your prostate and can slow the rate of enlargement. Men with smaller prostates see less benefit than those with larger prostates. Men who have only slightly enlarged prostates usually find alpha-blockers more helpful.

5-alpha reductase inhibitors may cause you to have less desire to have sex (decreased libido).

If you have difficulty urinating because of benign prostatic hyperplasia (BPH), you probably will not need surgery unless you:

- Cannot urinate. If you cannot urinate, you will need catheterization. In catheterization, a tube is passed up the penis into the bladder and urine is drained. Half of these men will be able to urinate again after catheterization. Those who do not improve may need surgery.
- Have a partial blockage in your urethra that is causing repeated urinary tract infections, bladder stones, or bladder damage.
- You have blood in your urine that is not getting better and is causing other problems such as clots that make it hard to urinate.
- Have kidney damage.

If you have no complications but have symptoms that bother you or if other treatment has not worked, you may choose to have surgery. In this case, think about:

- How bad your symptoms are.
- How much you expect the surgery to improve your symptoms.
- How you feel about the risk of developing a complication because of the surgery.

Surgery Choices

Surgery that does not require an incision through the skin is usually used. The surgical instruments are passed up the urinary opening in the penis to the location of the prostate. This is described as a transurethral surgery of the prostate.

Transurethral resection of the prostate (TURP) is the surgery for benign prostatic hyperplasia that has been studied the most. It is the surgery that is used the most to treat symptoms of BPH. All other surgeries are compared to TURP. In TURP, part of the prostate is removed.

Some of the other surgeries that have been studied and compared to TURP include:

- Transurethral incision of the prostate (TUIP), in which incisions are made in the prostate that cause it to press less on the urethra.
- Laser therapy (transurethral laser coagulation and transurethral laser vaporization), in which a laser is used to make incisions in or remove a portion of the prostate.
- Transurethral microwave therapy (TUMT), in which microwave energy is used to destroy a portion of the prostate through heating.
- Transurethral needle ablation (TUNA), in which a heated needle is used to destroy a portion of the prostate.

In most cases, these treatments have been studied for only a few years, so their long-term effectiveness is not yet known. There are also some other surgeries.

The oldest surgical method to treat BPH is an open prostatectomy, in which an incision is made through the skin to reach the prostate. Doctors use this method less often now, but it is still preferred if the prostate is very large.

Surgery is the most reliable way to relieve symptoms. But surgery may not relieve all your symptoms. And it puts you at risk for certain surgical complications, including erection problems (erectile dysfunction). Other complications include the inability to control the release of urine (urinary incontinence) and ejaculation of semen into the bladder instead of out through the penis (retrograde ejaculation). The complication depends on which type of surgery is used.

Men who have severe symptoms often notice great improvement in the quality of life following surgery. Men whose symptoms are mild may find that surgery does not greatly improve quality of life, and they may want to think carefully before deciding to have surgery to treat BPH.

If you have decided to have surgery, or if there are clear medical reasons to have surgery, the best surgical option depends on the size and shape of your prostate and the experience of the surgeon.

- Transurethral resection of the prostate (TURP) is the most common surgery for BPH.
- Other types of surgery have fewer risks and a shorter recovery period than TURP. But they may not work as well to stop symptoms. And you may need more treatment or surgery in the future.

中英文注释

关键词汇

bladder ['blædə] n. 膀胱

block [blɒk] vt. 阻止；阻塞；限制

bothersome ['bɒðəsəm] adj. 麻烦的；令人讨厌的

catheter ['kæθitə] n. 导管；导尿管；尿液管

catheterization [ˌkæθitəri'zeʃən] n. 导管插入，尿管插入

clot [klɒt] n. 血块

complication [kɒmpli'keiʃ(ə)n] n. 并发症

desire [di'zaiə] n. 欲望；要求；性欲

disruptive [dis'rʌptiv] adj. 破坏的；分裂性的

diuretics [ˌdaijuə'retiks] n. 利尿剂，利尿药

dribble ['dribl] n. 漏泄；v. 滴下；尿滴沥

dysuria [dis'jʊəriə] n. 排尿困难

ejaculation [i,dʒækjʊ'leiʃ(ə)n] n. 射精

erection [i'rekʃ(ə)n] n. 阴茎勃起

genetics [dʒi'netiks] n. 遗传学

kidney ['kidni] n. 肾脏

hesitancy ['hezit(ə)nsi] n. 踌躇，犹豫

hormone ['hɔ:məun] n. 激素；荷尔蒙；性激素

hyperplasia [,haipə'pleiziə] n. [病理]增生；畸形生长

hypertrophy [hai'pɜ:trəfi] n. [病理]肥大；过度增大

laser ['leizə] n. 激光

libido [li'bi:dəʊ] n. 性欲；生命力

nocturia [nɔk'tjuəriə] n. 夜尿症；遗尿症

penis ['pi:nis] n. [解剖]阴茎

prostate ['prɒsteit] n. [解剖]前列腺

prostatectomy [,prɒstə'tektəmi] n. 前列腺切除术

prostatitis [,prɒstei'taitis] n. [泌尿]前列腺炎

puberty ['pju:bəti] n. 青春期

questionnaire [,kwestʃə'neə] n. 问卷；调查表

semen ['si:mən] n. 精液；精子

squeeze [skwi:z] vt. 挤；紧握 vi. 压榨

testicle ['testikəlz] n. 睾丸

testosterone [te'stɒstərəun] n. [生化]睾酮，睾丸素

ultrasound ['ʌltrəsaʊnd] n. 超声；超音波

urethra [jʊ'ri:θrə] n. [解剖]尿道

urinate ['jʊərineit] vi. 排尿，撒尿，小便

urinalysis [jʊəri'nælisis] n. 验尿；尿分析

urological [jʊ'rɑlədʒi] adj. 泌尿道的；泌尿科学的

vasectomy [və'sektəmi] n. [泌尿]输精管切除术

主要短语

alpha-blocker α受体阻滞剂

American Urological Association (AUA) 美国泌尿外科学会

benign prostatic hyperplasia (BPH) 良性前列腺增生症

bladder stones 膀胱结石

digital rectal exam (DRE) 直肠指检

erectile dysfunction (ED) 勃起功能障碍

5-alpha reductase inhibitors 5-α还原酶抑制剂

heart failure 心力衰竭

herbal therapy 中药治疗

intravenous pyelogram (IVP) 静脉肾盂造影

lower urinary tract symptoms(LUTS) 下尿路症状

medical history 病史

prostate-specific antigen (PSA) 前列腺特异性抗原

post-void residual urine test (PVR) 残余尿量测定

retrograde ejaculation 逆行射精

risk factors 危险因素

side effects 副作用

spiral (helical) computed tomography (CT) scan 螺旋 CT 扫描

transrectal ultrasound (TRUS) 经直肠超声

transurethral incision of the prostate (TUIP) 经尿道前列腺切开术

transurethral microwave thermotherapy (TUMT) 经尿道微波热疗术

transurethral needle ablation of the prostate (TUNA) 经尿道前列腺针刺消融术

transurethral resection of the prostate (TURP) 经尿道前列腺电切术

urinary tract infections 尿路感染

urinary incontinence 尿失禁；遗尿

watchful waiting 观察等待

岳　亮　马志方

8 Kidney Stones
肾 结 石

What are kidney stones?

Kidney stones are made of salts and minerals in the urine that stick together to form small "pebbles." They are usually painless while they remain in the kidney, but they can cause severe pain as they travel through the ureters (narrow tubes that connect the kidneys and the bladder) to exit the body during urination.

There are four main types of kidney stones, and they can be as small as grains of sand or as large as a golf ball. Kidney stones occur most often in adults and are rare in children.

What cause kidney stones?

Kidney stones may form when the normal balance of water, salts, minerals, and other substances found in urine changes. How this balance changes determines the type of kidney stone you have. Most kidney stones are calcium-type. They form when the calcium levels in your urine change.

Factors that change your urine balance include:

- Not drinking enough water. When you don't drink enough water, the salts, minerals, and other substances in the urine can stick together and form a stone. This is the most common cause of kidney stones.
- Medical conditions. Many medical conditions can affect the normal balance and cause stones to form. Examples include gout and inflammatory bowel disease, such as Crohn's disease.

More commonly, kidney stones can run in families, as stones often occur in family members over several generations.

In rare cases, a person forms kidney stones because the parathyroid glands produce too much of a hormone, which leads to higher calcium levels and possibly calcium kidney stones.

What are the symptoms of kidney stones?

Kidney stones form in the kidney. If they stay in the kidney, they typically do not cause pain. When they travel out of the body through the tubes of the urinary tract (including the ureters, which connect the kidney to the bladder, or the urethra, which leads outside the body), their movement may cause:

- No symptoms, if the stone is small enough.
- Sudden, severe pain that gets worse in waves. Stones may cause intense pain in the back, side, abdomen, groin, or genitals. People who have had a kidney stone often describe the pain as "the worst pain I've ever had."
- Feeling sick to the stomach (nausea) and vomiting.
- Blood in the urine (hematuria), which can occur either with stones that stay in the kidney or with those that travel through the ureters.
- Frequent and painful urination, which may occur when the stone is in the ureter or after the stone has left the bladder and is in the urethra. Painful urination may occur when a urinary tract infection is also present.
- Conditions with similar symptoms include appendicitis, hernias, ectopic pregnancy, and prostatitis.

How are kidney stones diagnosed?

The patient's first diagnosis of kidney stones often occurs when he see the doctor or go to an emergency room because he is in great pain. The doctor or an emergency medicine specialist will ask the patient questions and examine him. After the patient passes a stone, the doctor may give him another exam to find out whether he is likely to get kidney stones again.

Tests to diagnose kidney stones

The doctor may do one or more of the following tests to help diagnose kidney stones, see where the stones are located, and find out if they are causing or may cause damage to the urinary tract

- A noncontrast spiral computed tomography (CT) scan is the preferred test for kidney stones. It is a special type of CT scan that moves in a circle.
- An intravenous pyelogram (IVP) is an X-ray test that can show the size, shape, and position of the urinary tract, including the kidneys and ureters. See an IVP of a kidney stone
- A retrograde pyelogram may be done if the IVP or CT scan does not provide a diagnosis.
- Urinalysis and urine cultures test your urine. An abdominal X-ray (KUB) gives

a picture of the kidneys, the bladder, and the tubes that connect the kidneys to the bladder (ureters).

- An ultrasound exam of the kidneys (ultrasonogram) is the preferred test for pregnant women.

Tests to find out the type of stone

Determining the type of the patient's kidney stone will help with treatment decisions and measures to prevent stones from forming again. Tests include:

- A medical history and physical exam.
- Stone analysis.
- Blood chemistry screen, to measure kidney function, levels of calcium, uric acid, phosphorus, electrolytes, and other substances that may have caused the stone to form.
- Urine collection for 24 hours, to measure volume, pH, calcium, oxalate, uric acid, and other substances that may have caused the stone to form. This is a test the patient may do at home.

How are they treated?

For small stones, most people don't need any treatment other than taking pain medicine and drinking enough fluids.

Treatment for your first stone

If the doctor thinks the stone can pass on its own, and if you feel you can deal with the pain, he or she may suggest home treatment, including:

- Using pain medicine. Nonprescription medicine, such as nonsteroidal anti-inflammatory drugs (NSAIDs), may relieve your pain. Your doctor can prescribe stronger pain medicine if needed.
- Drinking enough fluids. You'll need to keep drinking water and other fluids when you are passing a kidney stone.

The doctor may prescribe medicine to help your body pass the stone. To learn more, see Medications.

If your pain is too severe, if the stones are blocking the urinary tract, or if you also have an infection, your doctor will probably suggest a medical procedure, such as lithotripsy, or surgery to deal with the stone.

Medicine to help pass stones

Medicine you can buy without a prescription, such as nonsteroidal anti-inflammatory drugs (NSAIDs), may relieve your pain while you pass a stone.

Your doctor may also prescribe medicine to help your body pass the stone. Alpha-blockers have been shown to help kidney stones pass more quickly with very few side effects. Ask your doctor if these medicines can help you.

Medicine to prevent stones

Which medicine you take depends on the type of stones you have.

Calcium stones

Calcium stones are the most common kind ofkidney stone. To prevent them, you may take:

- Thiazides.
- Potassium citrate.
- Orthophosphate.

Uric acid stones

About 5 to 10 out of 100 kidney stones are made of uric acid, a waste product that normally exits the body in the urine. To prevent these types of stones, you may take:

- Potassium citrate.
- Sodium bicarbonate.
- Allopurinol.

Cystine stones

A very small number of stones are made of a chemical called cystine. Medicines to prevent them include:

- Potassium citrate.
- Penicillamine.
- Tiopronin.
- Captopril.

Struvite stones

Some struvite stones (staghorn calculi) form because of frequent kidney infections. If you have a struvite stone, you will most likely need antibiotics to cure the infection and help prevent new stones from forming. You may need surgery to remove the stone. Urease inhibitors may be used to prevent struvite stones.

Surgery

Surgery is rarely needed to treat kidney stones. Surgery is only needed when the kidney stone is very large, caused by an infection (staghorn calculi), blocking the flow of urine out of the kidney, or causing other problems like severe bleeding.

- In percutaneous nephrolithotomy or nephrolithotripsy, the surgeon makes a small cut in your back. He or she then puts a hollow tube into your kidney and either removes (lithotomy) or breaks up and removes (lithotripsy) the stone. This surgery may be used if other procedures do not work or if you have a very large stone. See a picture of nephrolithotomy.

- In open surgery, the surgeon makes a cut in your side or stomach to reach the kidneys. He or she removes the stone.

If your kidney stones were caused by a problem with your parathyroid gland, your doctor may suggest surgery to remove a parathyroid gland or glands (parathyroidectomy). This can help prevent future kidney stones.

Other treatments

Other treatments for kidney stones are much more common than surgery. You may need one of these treatments if your pain is very bad, your stone is blocking the urinary tract, or you have an infection. Your options include:

- Extracorporeal shock wave lithotripsy (ESWL). ESWL uses shock waves that pass easily through the body but are strong enough to break up a kidney stone. This is the most commonly used medical procedure for treating kidney stones. See a picture of ESWL

- Ureteroscopy. The surgeon passes a very thin viewing tool (ureteroscope) up the urinary tract to the stone's location, and then he or she uses tools to remove the stone or break it up for easier removal. You may need a small, hollow tube (ureteral stent) placed in the ureter to keep it open for a short time and drain urine and any stone pieces. This procedure is often used for stones that have moved from the kidney to the ureter. See a picture of ureteroscopy

Whether these treatments will work for you will depend on the size of the stone, its location in the urinary tract, and your overall health.

How can you prevent kidney stones?

After you have had kidney stones, you are more likely to have them again. You can help prevent them by drinking plenty of water, enough so that your urine is light yellow or clear like water, about 8 to 10 glasses of water a day. You may have to eat less of certain foods. Your doctor may also give you medicine that helps prevent stones from forming.

中英文注释

关键词汇

allopurinol [ˌælə(ʊ)'pjʊərinɒl] n. 别嘌呤醇

appendicitis [əˌpɛndə'saitis] n. 阑尾炎

captopril ['kæptəpril] n. 甲巯丙脯酸

dehydrated [ˌdiː'haidreitid] adj. 脱水的

electrolytes [i'lektrəˌlaits] n. 电解质

gauze [gɔz] n. 纱布；薄纱

gout [gaʊt] n. 痛风

groin [grɔin] n. 腹股沟

hernia ['hɜːniə] n. 疝气

lithotripsy ['liθəˌtripsi] n. 碎石术

nephrolithotomy [ˌnefrəuli'θɔtəmi] n. 肾切开取结石术

oxalate ['ɑksəˌlet] n. 草酸；草酸盐

orthophosphate [ˌɔːθəʊ'fʊsfeit] n. 正磷酸盐

parathyroidectomy [ˌpærəˌθairɔi'dɛktəmi] n. 甲状旁腺切除术

pebble ['pɛbl] n. 卵石

penicillamine [ˌpɛni'siləˌmin] n. 青霉胺

phosphorus ['fɑsfərəs] n. 磷

ureteroscope [jʊəriːtə'rəskəʊp] n. 输尿管镜

ureteroscopy [jʊəriːtə'rəskəpi] n. 输尿管镜检查术

主要短语

abdominal X-ray (KUB) 腹部平片

alpha-blocker α-受体阻滞剂

Crohn's disease 克罗恩病

calcium stone 含钙结石

cystine stone 胱氨酸结石

ectopic pregnancy 宫外孕

extracorporeal shock wave lithotripsy (ESWL) 体外冲击波碎石术

inflammatory bowel disease 炎症性肠病

nonsteroidal anti-inflammatory drugs (NSAIDs) 非甾体类抗炎药

parathyroid glands 甲状旁腺

potassium citrate 柠檬酸钾

percutaneous nephrolithotomy 经皮肾镜取石术

retrograde pyelogram 逆行肾盂造影

rib cage 胸腔

sodium bicarbonate 碳酸氢钠

struvite stone 感染性结石

staghorn calculi 鹿角形结石

uric acid stone 尿酸结石

茹 峰 马志方

Pneumothorax

气　　胸

9

What is a pneumothorax?

A pneumothorax is a buildup of air in the space between the lung and the chest wall (pleural space). As the amount of air in this space increases, the pressure against the lung causes the lung to collapse. This prevents your lung from expanding properly when you try to breathe in, causing shortness of breath and chest pain.

A pneumothorax may become life-threatening if the pressure in your chest prevents the lungs from getting enough oxygen into the blood.

What causes a pneumothorax?

A pneumothorax is usually caused by an injury to the chest, such as a broken rib or puncture wound. It may also occur suddenly without an injury.

A pneumothorax can result from damage to the lungs caused by conditions such as chronic obstructive pulmonary disease (COPD), asthma, cystic fibrosis, and pneumonia. Spontaneous pneumothorax can also occur in people who don't have lung disease. This happens when an air-filled blister (bleb) on the lung ruptures and releases air into the pleural space.

People who smoke cigarettes are much more likely to develop a pneumothorax than those who don't. Also, the more you smoke, the greater your chances of having a pneumothorax.

What are the symptoms of pneumothorax?

Symptoms depend on the size of the pneumothorax. In minor cases, you may not realize you have a pneumothorax. In more severe cases, symptoms will develop rapidly and may lead to shock.

Symptoms may include:
- Shortness of breath (dyspnea), which may be mild to severe, depending on how much of the lung is collapsed.
- Sudden, severe, and sharp chest pain on the same side as the collapsed lung.

48

Symptoms may become worse with altitude changes (such as flying in an airplane or going underground or underwater).

How is a pneumothorax diagnosed?

A pneumothorax usually is diagnosed through a physical exam and a chest X-ray. The doctor may also perform blood tests to measure the level of oxygen in your blood.

A computed tomography (CT) scan or ultrasound may be needed to diagnose the severity of your condition and help plan your treatment.

How is it treated?

A minor pneumothorax may only require observation by the doctor; in some cases, oxygen may be given (through a mask). More serious cases are treated by inserting a needle or a chest tube into the chest cavity. Both of these procedures relieve the pressure on the lung and allow it to re-expand.

Surgery may be needed if the original treatment does not work or if the pneumothorax returns.

What are the chances that a pneumothorax will return?

If you have had one pneumothorax, you have an increased risk for another. Nearly all recurrences happen within 2 years of the first pneumothorax. If you smoke, quitting smoking can reduce your risk of another pneumothorax.

中英文注释

关键词汇

collapse [kə'læps] n. 萎陷
dyspnea [disp'niə] n. 呼吸困难
mask [mɑ:sk] n. 面罩
pleural [pluərəl] adj. 胸膜的
pneumothorax [nju:'məuniə] n. 气胸
pneumonia [nju:'məuniə] n. 肺炎
shock [ʃɒk] n. 休克

主要短语

chest wall　胸壁
chronic obstructive pulmonary disease (COPD)　慢性阻塞性肺疾病
cystic fibrosis　囊性纤维化
computed tomography (CT)　计算机断层扫描

pleural space 胸膜腔
puncture wound 刺伤
quitsmoking 戒烟
shortness of breath 气促，气短
spontaneous pneumothorax 自发性气胸

张　伟　马志方

10 Fractures Basics
骨 折 基 础

What is a fracture?

A fracture is the medical term for a broken bone.

The main categories are displaced, non-displaced, open, and closed. Displaced and non-displaced fractures refer to the way the bone breaks.

In a displaced fracture, the bone snaps into two or more parts and moves so that the two ends are not lined up straight. If the bone is in many pieces, it is called a comminuted fracture. In a non-displaced fracture, the bone cracks either part or all of the way through, but does move and maintains its proper alignment. Fractures are common; the average person has two during a lifetime. They occur when the physical force exerted on the bone is stronger than the bone itself.

Your risk of fracture depends, in part, on your age. Broken bones are very common in childhood, though children's fractures are generally less complicated than fractures in adults. As you age, your bones become more brittle and you are more likely to suffer fractures from falls that would not occur when you were young.

There are many types:

- A closed fracture is when the bone breaks but there is no puncture or open wound in the skin. An open fracture is one in which the bone breaks through the skin; it may then recede back into the wound and not be visible through the skin. This is an important difference from a closed fracture because with an open fracture there is a risk of a deep bone infection.

Some fracture types are:

- Greenstick fracture: an incomplete fracture in which the bone is bent. This type occurs most often in children.
- Transverse fracture: a fracture at a right angle to the bone's axis.
- Oblique fracture: a fracture in which the break has a curved or sloped pattern.
- Comminuted fracture: a fracture in which the bone fragments into several pieces.
- An impacted fracture is one whose ends are driven into each other. This is

commonly seen in arm fractures in children and is sometimes known as a buckle fracture. Other types of fracture are pathologic fracture, caused by a disease that weakens the bones, and stress fracture, a hairline crack.

- Other types of fracture are pathologic fracture, caused by a disease that weakens the bones, and stress fracture.
- The severity of a fracture depends upon its location and the damage done to the bone and tissue near it. Serious fractures can have dangerous complications if not treated promptly; possible complications include damage to blood vessels or nerves and infection of the bone (osteomyelitis) or surrounding tissue. Recuperation time varies depending on the age and health of the patient and the type of fracture. A minor fracture in a child may heal within a few weeks; a serious fracture in an older person may take months to heal.

What are the symptoms of a broken bone?

Signs and symptoms of a broken bone include:
- Swelling or bruising over a bone.
- Deformity of an arm or leg.
- Pain in the injured area that gets worse when the area is moved or pressure is applied.
- Loss of function in the injured area.
- In open fractures, bone protruding from the skin.
- Fractures are usually caused by a fall, blow, or other traumatic event.

Pathologic fractures are those caused by disease (such as cancer) that weakens the bones and can occur with little or no trauma. Osteoporosis, a disorder in which the bones thin and lose strength as they age, causes 1.5 million fractures each year in the U.S.—especially in the hip, wrist, and spine.

How is a fracture diagnosed?

Doctors can usually recognize most fractures by examining the injury and taking X-rays.

Sometimes an X-ray will not show a fracture. This is especially common with some wrist fractures, hip fractures (especially in older people), and stress fractures. In these situations, your doctor may perform other tests, such as a computed tomography (CT) scan, magnetic resonance imaging (MRI), or a bone scan.

In some cases, such as a possible wrist fracture with an initially normal X-ray, your doctor may apply a splint to immobilize the area and order a second X-ray 10 to 14 days later.

Occasionally, even after the fracture diagnosis has been made, you may need other tests (such as a CT scan, MRI, or angiogram, a special X-ray of blood vessels) to determine whether other tissues around the bone have been damaged.

If your doctor suspects a skull fracture, he or she will probably skip plain X-rays altogether and proceed directly to a CT scan, which will diagnose the fracture and any more important related injuries inside the skull, such as bleeding around the brain.

What are the treatments for a fracture?

A fracture often requires emergency treatment at a hospital. An example of a minor fracture that may not require emergency care is a fracture of the tip of a toe. If you think that bones may be broken in the back, neck, or hip, do not move the person; instead, call for emergency medical assistance. If the person is in shock (faint, pale, or breathing shallowly), call for emergency help, lay the person down, and raise his or her legs about 8to 12 inches unless you think leg bones may be broken.

In other cases, you may call for assistance or transport the person to the emergency room. Before transporting the person, protect the injured area to avoid further damage. For broken arm or leg bones, put a splint (made of wood, plastic, metal, or another rigid material padded with gauze) against the area to prevent movement; wrap the splint to the area using gauze. If there is bleeding, apply pressure to stop bleeding before splinting, then elevate the fracture.

Fractured bones must be set in their proper place and held there in order to heal properly. Setting a bone is called "reduction." Repositioning bone without surgery is "closed reduction." Most fractures in children are treated with closed reduction. Serious fractures may require open reduction—repositioning using surgery. In some cases, devices such as pins, plates, screws, rods, or glue are used to hold the fracture in place. Open fractures must also be cleaned thoroughly to avoid infection.

After setting, most fractures are immobilized with a cast, splint, or, occasionally, traction to reduce pain and help healing. In most cases, medication is limited to painkillers to reduce pain. In open fractures, antibiotics are administered to prevent infection. Rehabilitation begins as soon as possible, even if the bone is in a cast. This promotes blood flow, healing, maintenance of muscle tone, and helps prevent blood clots and stiffness.

After the cast or splint is removed, the area around the fracture usually is stiff for several weeks with swelling and bumps. In children, increased hair on the arms and legs due to irritation of the hair follicles from the cast can occur. With fractured legs, there may be a limp. Symptoms generally disappear within a few weeks.

If you have broken a bone, once the cast or splint is removed you should gradually begin using the area again. It may take another four to six weeks for the bone to regain past strength. Ask your doctor what activity type and intensity is safe for you, based on your fracture and overall health. Exercising in a swimming pool is generally a good way to rehabilitate bones.

中英文注释

关键词汇

angiogram ['ændʒiəugræm] n.（心）血管造影

antibiotic [ˌæntibai'ɔtik] n. 抗生素

cast [kæst] n. 管型石膏

faint ['feint] adj. 虚弱的

fracture ['fræktʃə] n. 骨折

gauze [gɔ:z] n. 医用纱布

immobilize [i'məubilaiz] vt. 使固定

painkiller ['pein,kilə] n. 止痛药

pale [peil] adj. 苍白的

reduction [ri'dʌkʃən] n. 复位

rehabilitation ['ri:hə,bili'teiʃən] n. 功能锻炼

reposition [ˌri:pə'ziʃən] n. 复位术；vt. 使（骨骼、器官等）复位

shock [ʃɔk] n. 休克

splint [splint] n.（固定骨折等用的）夹板

stiffness ['stifnis] n. 僵硬

swelling ['sweliŋ] n. 肿胀

traction ['trækʃən] n. 牵引术

主要短语

blood clot 血栓

bone scan 骨扫描

breathing shallowly 呼吸表浅

closed fracture 闭合性骨折

closed reduction 闭合复位术

comminuted fracture 粉碎性骨折

computed tomography (CT) scan 计算机断层扫描

displaced fracture 移位性骨折

emergency room 急诊室

greenstick fracture 青枝骨折

hair follicle 毛囊

impacted fracture 嵌入骨折

magnetic resonance imaging (MRI) 磁共振成像

muscle tone 肌张力

oblique fracture 斜形骨折

open fracture 开放性骨折

open reduction 切开复位术

pathologic fracture 病理性骨折

stress fracture 应力性骨折

transverse fracture 横形骨折

高宏飞　马志方

11 Colles' Fracture
桡骨远端骨折

What is Colles' fracture?

A Colles' fracture—or distal radius fracture—is often called a "broken wrist." Technically, it's a break in the larger of the two bones in your forearm. The bone breaks on the lower end, close to where it connects to the bones of the hand on the thumb side of the wrist.

Colles' fractures are very common; they're the most frequently broken bone in the arm. In the United States, one out of every 10 broken bones is a broken wrist.

What causes Colles' fracture?

Usually, these injuries result from falling onto an outstretched arm or getting hit on the wrist.

Broken wrists are common in people who play contact sports, as well as skiers, inline skaters, and bikers. People with osteoporosis or thinning of the bones are at particularly high-risk for wrist fractures. But they can happen to anyone who takes a fall or gets hit.

In more serious cases, the following may occur:
- The break extends into the wrist joint.
- A piece of broken bone breaks through the skin.
- The bone is broken in multiple places.
- Ligaments may be torn.
- These types of broken wrists may be harder to treat.

What are the symptoms of Colles' fracture?

Symptoms of a broken wrist can include:
- Pain, especially when flexing the wrist
- Tenderness
- Swelling
- Bruising
- Deformity of the wrist, causing it to look crooked and bent.

Occasionally, a broken wrist can affect the nerves or blood flow. You should go to the emergency room if:

- Your wrist is in great pain.
- Your wrist, arm, or hand is numb.
- Your fingers are pale.

What's the treatment for a broken wrist?

If the broken wrist is not in the correct position to heal, the doctor may need to reset it. This can be pretty painful so it's usually done with anesthesia. However, painkillers will help afterward.

The patient will probably also need:

A splint, which you might use for a few days to a week while the swelling goes down. If a splint is used initially, a cast is usually put on about a week later.

A cast, which you might need for six to eight weeks or longer, depending on how bad the break is. (You might need a second cast if the first one gets too loose after the swelling goes away.)

Regular X-rays to make sure your wrist is healing normally.

You will probably also want to:

Elevate your wrist on a pillow or the back of a chair above the level of your heart for the first few days. This will ease pain and swelling.

Ice the wrist. Do this for 20-30 minutes every three to four hours for two to three days. Be careful to keep the splint or cast dry while icing.

Take over-the-counter painkillers. Ask your doctor about nonsteroidal anti-inflammatory drugs (NSAIDs), like ibuprofen, naproxen, or aspirin. They can help with pain and swelling. However, these drugs have side effects, such as an increased risk of bleeding and ulcers. They should be used only occasionally unless your doctor specifically says otherwise, as this may delay healing.

Practice stretching and strengthening exercises of the fingers, elbow, and shoulder if your doctor recommends them.

Most of the time, these treatments will be enough. But sometimes, people with a broken wrist need surgery. Your doctor might suggest this if the bone is not likely to heal well in a cast. Sometimes, pins, plates, screws, or other devices are needed to hold the bone in place so it can mend.

When will broken wrist feel better?

Of course, what you really want to know is when you can get back in the game after breaking your wrist. There's no easy answer.

Here are some things to keep in mind during recovery from a broken wrist:

It might take eight weeks or longer for your wrist to heal. More severe breaks may not fully mend for six months. You and your doctor will decide when you are fully recovered.

Don't rush back into your activity too soon. If you start working out before your wrist is healed, you could cause more serious damage.

You may still have discomfort and stiffness in your wrist for months, or even years, after the injury.

Follow your doctor's instructions for taking care of your cast. Remember that casts cannot get wet.

See your doctor if the pain or swelling keeps getting worse after you get a cast or if you experience numbness in your fingers.

How can I prevent a broken wrist?

A broken wrist is tough to prevent, since it usually happens during an accidental fall. But it can help to use wrist guards during risky sports, like inline skating. Sometimes, a broken wrist can indicate osteoporosis, especially in women. Talk to your doctor about your risk factors for osteoporosis and fractures. There are steps you can take to improve your bone health.

中英文注释

关键词汇

anesthesia [ˌænisˈθiːziə] n. 麻醉

aspirin [ˈæsprin] n. 阿司匹林

crooked [ˈkrukid] adj. 弯曲的

deformity [diˈfɔːməti] n. 畸形

ibuprofen [ˌaibjuˈprəuf(ə)n] n. 布洛芬

ligament [ˈligəmənt] n. 韧带

numb [nʌm] adj. 麻木的

osteoporosis [ˌɔstiəupəˈrəusis] n. 骨质疏松（症）

painkiller [ˈpeinkilə] n. 止痛药

reset [ˌriˈset] v. 复位

splint [splint] n. 夹板；vt. 用夹板固定

tenderness [ˈtendənəs] n. 压痛

ulcer [ˈʌlsə] n. 溃疡

主要短语

blood flow 血流

Colles' Fracture 桡骨远端骨折，Colles 骨折
nonsteroidal anti-inflammatory drugs (NSAIDs) 非甾体类抗炎药
over-the-counter 非处方的
physical exam 体格检查
side effects 副作用
wrist guards 护腕
wrist joint 腕关节

高宏飞　马志方

12 Osteomyelitis
骨 髓 炎

What is osteomyelitis?

Osteomyelitis is a bone infection, usually caused by bacteria, that can be either acute or chronic. This disorder usually occurs as a result of an infection in one part of the body that is transported through the bloodstream to a bone in a distant location. Among children and teens, the long bones of the legs and arms are most frequently affected. In adults, osteomyelitis most often affects the vertebrae of the spine and/or the hips.

Osteomyelitis is an infection of the bone, a rare but serious condition. Bones can become infected in a number of ways: Infection in one part of the body may spread into the bone, or an open fracture that exposes bone to may get infected.

What causes osteomyelitis?

In children, the long bones are usually affected. In adults, the vertebrae and the pelvis are most commonly affected.

Acute osteomyelitis almost invariably occurs in children. When adults are affected, it may be because of compromised host resistance due to debilitation, intravenous drug abuse, infectious root-canaled teeth, or other disease or drugs (e.g., immunosuppressive therapy).

Osteomyelitis is a secondary complication in 1–3% of patients with pulmonary tuberculosis. In this case, the bacteria, in general, spread to the bone through the circulatory system, first infecting thesynovium (due to its higher oxygen concentration) before spreading to the adjacent bone. In tubercular osteomyelitis, the long bones and vertebrae are the ones that tend to be affected.

Staphylococcus aureus is the organism most commonly isolated from all forms of osteomyelitis.

Bloodstream-sourced osteomyelitis is seen most frequently in children, and nearly 90% of cases are caused by Staphylococcus aureus. In infants, S. aureus, Group B streptococci (most common) and Escherichia coliare commonly isolated; in children from one to 16 years of age, S. aureus, Streptococcus pyogenes, and Haemophilus influenzae are common. In some subpopulations, including intravenous drug users and splenectomized patients, Gram-negative bacteria, including enteric bacteria, are significant pathogens.

The most common form of the disease in adults is caused by injury exposing the bone to local infection. Staphylococcus aureus is the most common organism seen in osteomyelitis, seeded from areas of contiguous infection. But anaerobes and Gram-negative organisms, including Pseudomonas aeruginosa, E. coli, and Serratia marcescens, are also common. Mixed infections are the rule rather than the exception.

Systemic mycotic (fungal) infections may also cause osteomyelitis. The two most common are Blastomyces dermatitidis and Coccidioides immitis.

In osteomyelitis involving the vertebral bodies, about half the cases are due to S. aureus, and the other half are due to tuberculosis (spread hematogenously from the lungs). Tubercular osteomyelitis of the spinewas so common before the initiation of effective antitubercular therapy, it acquired a special name, Pott's disease.

Following laboratory analysis of clinical data and studied literature, we can say that the bone pathological changes are induced by several interrelated mechanisms the drug components, produced clandestinely. The Burkholderia cepacia complex has been implicated in vertebral osteomyelitis in intravenous drug users.

Who gets osteomyelitis?

Only two out of every 10,000 people get osteomyelitis. The condition affects children and adults, although in different ways. Certain conditions and behaviors that weaken the immune system increase a person's risk for osteomyelitis, including:

- Diabetes (most cases of osteomyelitis stem from diabetes)
- Sickle cell disease
- HIV or AIDS
- Rheumatoid arthritis
- Intravenous drug use
- Alcoholism
- Long-term use of steroids
- Bone surgery, including hip and knee replacements, also increase the chance for infection to invade a bone.
- Osteomyelitis in Children and Adults

  In children, osteomyelitis is usually acute. Acute osteomyelitis comes on quickly, is easier to treat, and overall turns out better than chronic osteomyelitis. In children, osteomyelitis usually shows up in arm or leg bones.

  In adults, osteomyelitis can be either acute or chronic. People with diabetes,

HIV, or peripheral vascular disease are more prone to chronic osteomyelitis, which persists or recurs, despite treatment. Whether chronic or acute, osteomyelitis often affects an adult's pelvis or vertebrae of the spine. It can also occur in the feet, especially in a person with diabetes.

What are the symptoms of osteomyelitis?

Acute osteomyelitis develops rapidly over a period of seven to 10 days. The symptoms for acute and chronic osteomyelitis are very similar and include:

- Fever, irritability, fatigue
- Nausea
- Tenderness and swelling around the affected bone
- Lost range of motion
- Osteomyelitis in the vertebrae makes itself known through severe back pain, especially at night.

How is it diagnosed?

Diagnosis of osteomyelitis is often based on radiologic results showing a lytic center with a ring of sclerosis. Culture of material taken from a bone biopsy is needed to identify the specific pathogen; alternative sampling methods such as needle puncture or surface swabs are easier to perform, but do not produce reliable results.

Factors that may commonly complicate osteomyelitis are fractures of the bone, amyloidosis, endocarditis, or sepsis.

How is osteomyelitis treated?

Figuring out if a person has osteomyelitis is the first step in treatment. It's also surprisingly difficult. Doctors rely on X-rays, blood tests, and bone scans to get a picture of what's going on. They also need to determine the type of organism, typically bacteria, causing the infection so they can prescribe the right medication.

Treatment focuses on stopping infection in its tracks and preserving as much function as possible. Most people with osteomyelitis are treated with antibiotics, surgery, or both.

Antibiotics help bring the infection under control and often make it possible to avoid surgery. People with osteomyelitis usually get antibiotics for several weeks through an IV, and then switch to a pill form.

More serious or chronic osteomyelitis requires surgery to remove the infected tissue and bone. Osteomyelitis surgery prevents the infection from spreading further or getting so bad that amputation is the only remaining option.

How to prevent osteomyelitis?

The best way to prevent osteomyelitis is to keep things clean. If you or your child has a cut, especially a deep cut, wash it completely. Flush out any open wound under running water for five minutes, then bandage it in sterile bandages.

If you have chronic osteomyelitis, make sure your doctor knows about your medical history so you can work together to keep the condition under control. If you have diabetes, pay close attention to your feet and contact your doctor at the first sign of infection.

The sooner you treat osteomyelitis, the better. In cases of acute osteomyelitis, early treatment prevents the condition from becoming a chronic problem that requires ongoing treatment. Besides the pain and inconvenience of repeated infections, getting osteomyelitis under control early provides the best chance for recovery.

中英文注释

关键词汇

alcoholism ['ælkəhɔlizəm] n. 酗酒

amputation [,æmpju'teiʃən] n. 截肢

anaerobe [æ'nɛərəub] n. 厌氧菌

bacteria [bæk'tiəriə] n. [复数] 细菌

debilitation [di,bili'teiʃən] n. 衰弱

diabetes [,daiə'biːtiːz] n. 糖尿病

fungal ['fʌŋgəl] adj. 真菌的

hematogenous [,hemə'tɔdʒinəs] adj. 血源性

irritability [,iritə'biləti] n. 应激性

mycotic [mai'kɔtik] adj. 霉菌的

organism ['ɔːgənizəm] n. 微生物

osteomyelitis ['ɔstiəu,maiə'laitis] n. 骨髓炎

pathogen ['pæθədʒən] n. 病原体

sclerosis [skliə'rəusis] n. 硬化症

splenectomize [spli'nektəmaiz] vt. 切除脾

sterile ['sterail] adj. 无菌的

steroid ['sterɔid] n. 类固醇

synovium [si'nəuviəm; sai-] n. 滑膜

vertebrae ['vəːtibriː] n. 椎骨

主要短语

antitubercular therapy 抗结核的治疗

back pain 背痛

blastomyces dermatitidis 皮炎芽生菌

blood test 验血

bloodstream-sourced osteomyelitis 血源性骨髓炎

burkholderia cepacia complex, Bcc 洋葱伯克氏菌群

circulatory system 循环系统

coccidioides immitis 粗球孢子菌

E. Coli 大肠杆菌

enteric bacteria 肠道细菌

escherichia coli 大肠杆菌，大肠埃希菌

gram-negative bacteria 革兰氏阴性菌

group B streptococci 乙（B）型链球菌

haemophilus influenzae 流感嗜血杆菌

hip and knee replacements 髋关节和膝关节置换

immune system 免疫系统

immunosuppressive therapy 免疫抑制疗法

intravenous drug abuse 静脉注射吸毒

intravenous drug users 静脉注射吸毒者

needle puncture 穿刺

peripheral vascular disease 周围性血管疾病

pott's disease 脊椎结核病

pseudomonas aeruginosa 铜绿假单胞菌

pulmonary tuberculosis 肺结核

rheumatoid arthritis 类风湿关节炎

serratia marcescens 黏质沙雷菌

sickle cell disease 镰状细胞病

staphylococcus aureus (S. Aureus) 金黄色葡萄球菌

streptococcus pyogenes 化脓性链球菌

surface swabs 表面拭子

tubercular osteomyelitis 结核性骨髓炎

高宏飞　马志方

13 — Cerebral Aneurysm
脑 动 脉 瘤

What is cerebral aneurysm?

A cerebral aneurysm occurs at a weak point in the wall of a blood vessel (artery) that supplies blood to the brain. Because of the flaw, the artery wall bulges outward and fills with blood. This bulge is called an aneurysm. An aneurysm can rupture, spilling blood into the surrounding body tissue. A ruptured cerebral aneurysm can cause permanent brain damage, disability, or death.

A cerebral aneurysm can occur anywhere in the brain. Aneurysms can have several shapes. The saccular aneurysm, once called a berry aneurysm, resembles a piece of fruit dangling from a branch. Saccular aneurysms are usually found at a branch in the blood vessel where they balloon out by a thin neck. Saccular cerebral aneurysms most often occur at the branch points of large arteries at the base of the brain. Aneurysms may also take the form of a bulge in one wall of the artery—a lateral aneurysm—or a widening of the entire artery—a fusiform aneurysm.

Some aneurysms may have a genetic link and run in families. The genetic link has not been completely proven and a pattern of inheritance has not been determined. Some studies seem to show that first-degree relatives of people who suffered aneurysmal subarachnoid hemorrhage (SAH) are more likely to have aneurysms themselves. These studies reported that such immediate family members were four times more likely to have aneurysms than the general population. Other studies do not confirm these findings. Better evidence links aneurysms to certain rare diseases of the connective tissue. These diseases include Marfan syndrome, pseudoxanthoma elasticum, Ehlers-Danlos syndrome, and fibromuscular dysplasia. Polycystic kidney disease is also associated with cerebral aneurysms.

These diseases are also associated with an increased risk of aneurysmal rupture. Certain other conditions raise the risk of rupture, too. Most aneurysms that rupture are a half-inch or larger in diameter. Size is not the only factor, however, because smaller aneurysms also rupture. Cigarette smoking, excessive alcohol consumption, and recreational drug use (for example, use of cocaine) have been linked with an increased risk. The role, if any, of high blood pressure has not been determined. Some studies have implicated high blood pressure in aneurysm formation and rupture, but people with normal blood pressure also experience aneurysms and SAH. High blood pressure may be a risk factor but not the most important one. Pregnancy, labor, and delivery also seem to increase the possibility that an aneurysm might rupture, but not all doctors agree. Physical exertion and use of oral contraceptives are not suspected causes for aneurysmal rupture.

What causes cerebral aneurysm?

For unruptured aneurysm

Studies have shown a strong link to family history. If an immediate family member has suffered an aneurysm, you are 4 times more likely to have one as well. The genetic link is not completely understood and studies are underway to determine if there is a pattern of inheritance. The most important inherited conditions associated with aneurysms include Ehlers-Danlos IV, Marfan's syndrome, neurofibromatosis NF1, and polycystic kidney disease.

For ruptured aneurysm

Risk factors for aneurysmal SAH currently being studied are smoking, high blood pressure, alcohol, genetic (family inherited), atherosclerosis, oral contraceptives, and lifestyle.

Risk Factors

Are you at risk for cerebral aneurysm?

- Risk factors that doctors and researchers believe contribute to t Smoking
- High blood pressure or hypertension
- Congenital resulting from inborn abnormality in artery wall
- Family history of brain aneurysms
- Age over 40
- Gender, women compared with men have an increased incidence of aneurysms at a ratio of 3:2
- Other disorders: Ehlers-Danlos Syndrome, Polycystic Kidney Disease, Marfan Syndrome, and Fibromuscular Dysplasia (FMD)
- Presence of an arteriovenous malformation (AVM)
- Drug use, particularly cocaine
- Infection
- Tumors
- Traumatic head injury

Risk factors that doctors and researchers believe contribute to the rupture of brain aneurysms:

- Smoking
- High blood pressure or hypertension

What are symptoms of cerebral aneurysm?

Most aneurysms go unnoticed until they rupture. However, 10-15% of unruptured cerebral aneurysms are found because of their size or their location. Common warning signs include symptoms that affect only one eye, such as an enlarged pupil, a drooping eyelid, or pain above or behind the eye. Other symptoms are a localized headache, unsteady gait, a temporary problem with sight, double vision, or numbness in the face.

Some aneurysms bleed occasionally without rupturing. Symptoms of such an aneurysm develop gradually. The symptoms include headache, nausea, vomiting, neck pain, black-outs, ringing in the ears, dizziness, or seeing spots.

Eighty to ninety percent of aneurysms are not diagnosed until after they have ruptured. Rupture is not always a sudden event. Nearly 50% of patients who have aneurysmal SAH also experience "the warning leak phenomenon." Persons with warning leak symptoms have sudden, atypical headaches that occur days or weeks before the actual rupture. These headaches are referred to as sentinel headaches. Nausea, vomiting, and dizziness may accompany sentinel headaches. Unfortunately, these symptoms can be confused with tension headaches or migraines, and treatment can be delayed until rupture occurs.

When an aneurysm ruptures, most victims experience a sudden, extremely severe headache. This headache is typically described as the worst headache of the victim's life. Nausea and vomiting commonly accompany the headache. The person may experience a short loss of consciousness or prolonged coma. Other common signs of a SAH include a stiff neck, fever, and a sensitivity to light. About 25% of victims experience neurological problems linked to specific areas of the brain, swelling of the brain due to fluid accumulation (hydrocephalus), or seizure.

How is cerebral aneurysm diagnosed?

For Unruptured Aneurysm

Most people find out they have an unruptured aneurysm by chance (incidental) during a scan for some other medical problem. If you are experiencing symptoms and your primary care doctor suspects an aneurysm, you may be referred to a neurosurgeon. The doctor will learn as much about your symptoms, current and previous medical problems, current medications, family history, and perform a physical exam. Diagnostic tests are used to help determine the aneurysm's location, size, type, and involvement with other structures.

- **CT Scans and Unruptured Aneurysm Diagnosis**

Computed Tomography Angiography (CTA) scan is a noninvasive X-ray to review the anatomical structures within the brain to detect blood in or around the brain. A newer technology called CT angiography involves the injection of contrast into the blood stream to view the arteries of the brain. This type of test provides the best pictures of blood vessels through angiography and soft tissues through CT.

- **Angiogram for Unruptured Aneurysm**

Angiogram is an invasive procedure, where a catheter is inserted into an artery and passed through the blood vessels to the brain. Once the catheter is in place, a contrast dye is injected into the bloodstream and the X-ray images are taken.

- **MRI to Diagnose Unruptured Aneurysm**

Magnetic resonance imaging (MRI) scan is a noninvasive test, which uses a magnetic field and radio-frequency waves to give a detailed view of the soft tissues of your brain. An MRA (Magnetic Resonance Angiogram) is the same non-invasive study, except it is also an angiogram, which means it also examines the blood vessels, as well as the structures of the brain.

- **For ruptured aneurysm**

When a patient is brought to the emergency room with a suspected ruptured aneurysm, doctors will learn as much as possible about his or her symptoms, current and previous medical problems, medications, and family history. A physical exam will be performed. Diagnostic tests will help determine the source of the bleeding.

- **CT Scans and Ruptured Aneurysm Diagnosis**

Computed Tomography (CT) scan is a noninvasive X-ray that provides images of anatomical structures within the brain. It is especially useful to detect blood in or around the brain. A newer technology called CT angiography (CTA) involves the injection of contrast into the blood stream to view the arteries of the brain. CTA provides the best pictures of blood vessels (through angiography) and soft tissues (through CT).

- **Lumbar Puncture to Diagnose Ruptured Aneurysm**

Lumbar puncture is an invasive procedure in which a hollow needle is inserted into the subarachnoid space of the spinal canal to detect blood in the cerebrospinal fluid (CSF). The doctor will collect 2 to 4 tubes of CSF.

- **Angiogram for Ruptured Aneurysm**

Angiogram is an invasive procedure in which a catheter is inserted into an artery and passed through the blood vessels to the brain. Once the catheter is in place, contrast dye is injected into the bloodstream and X-rays are taken.

- ● **MRI to Diagnose Ruptured Aneurysm**

Magnetic Resonance Imaging (MRI) scan is a noninvasive test that uses a magnetic field and radio-frequency waves to give a detailed view of the soft tissues of the brain. An MRA (Magnetic Resonance Angiogram) is the same non-invasive study, except that it is also an angiogram, which means it examines the blood vessels in addition to structures of the brain.

How is it treated?

For unruptured aneurysm

Deciding how, or even if, to treat an unruptured aneurysm involves weighing the risks of rupture versus the risks of treatment. The risk of aneurysm rupture is about 1% but may be higher or lower depending on the size and location of the aneurysm; however, when a rupture occurs there is a 50% risk of death. Risk factors for rupture include smoking, high blood pressure, alcohol, genetic factors (family inherited), atherosclerosis (hardening of the arteries), oral contraceptives, and lifestyle. Other factors such as the size and location of the aneurysm, overall health of the patient, and medical history must also be considered. Generally, the larger the aneurysm, the higher risk of rupture. Also, aneurysms in the posterior circulation (basilar, vertebral and posterior communicating arteries) have a higher risk of rupture. The neurosurgeon will discuss with you all the options and recommend a treatment that is best for your individual case.

Observation

Sometimes the best treatment may be to simply watch and reduce your risk of rupture (quit smoking, control high blood pressure). Aneurysms that are small, unruptured, and asymptomatic may be observed with imaging scans every year until the growth or symptoms necessitate surgery. Observation may be the best option for patients with other health conditions.

- ● **Surgical clipping**

The most common treatment for an aneurysm is direct surgical clipping. Using general anesthesia, an opening is made in the skull, called a craniotomy. The brain is gently retracted so that the artery with the aneurysm may be located. A small clip is placed across the neck of the aneurysm to block the normal blood flow from entering the aneurysm. The clip is made of titanium and remains on the artery permanently.

- ● **Artery occlusion and bypass**

If surgical clipping is not possible or the artery is too damaged, the surgeon may completely block (occlude) the artery that has the aneurysm. The blood flow is detoured (bypassed) around the occluded section of artery by inserting a vessel graft. The graft is a small artery, usually taken from your leg, that is connected above and below the blocked artery so that blood flow is rerouted (bypassed) through the graft.

A bypass can also be created by detaching a donor artery from its normal position on one end, redirecting it to the inside of the skull, and connecting it above the blocked artery. This is called a STA-MCA (superficial temporal artery to middle cerebral artery) bypass.

● **Endovascular coiling**

In contrast to surgery, another form of treatment is endovascular coiling. This is performed in the angiography suites of the radiology department by a neuro interventionalist and sometimes requires general anesthesia. In a coiling procedure, a catheter is inserted into an artery in the groin and then passed through the blood vessels to the aneurysm. The doctor guides the catheter through the bloodstream while watching a fluoroscopy (a type of X-ray) monitor. Through the catheter, the aneurysm is packed with material, either platinum coils or balloons, that prevents blood flow into the aneurysm. Since coiling is a relatively new procedure, follow-up angiograms are performed periodically to confirm the aneurysm is still occluded and not growing larger.

For ruptured aneurysm

Treatment may include lifesaving measures, symptom relief, repair of the bleeding aneurysm, and complication prevention. For 10 to 14 days following an aneurysm rupture, the patient will remain in the neuroscience intensive care unit (NSICU), where doctors and nurses can watch closely for signs of renewed bleeding, vasospasm, hydrocephalus, and other potential complications.

● **Medication**

Pain medication will be given to alleviate headache, anticonvulsant medication may be prescribed to prevent or treat seizures, and a vasodilator will be prescribed to prevent vasospasm. Blood pressure is lowered to reduce further bleeding and to control intracranial pressure.

● **Surgery**

Determining the best surgical treatment for a ruptured aneurysm involves many factors, such as the size, location, and type of aneurysm as well as the overall health of the patient and their medical history.

  ● Surgical clipping: an opening is made in the skull, called a craniotomy, to locate the aneurysm. A small clip is placed across the "neck" of the aneurysm to block the normal blood flow from entering. The clip is made of titanium and remains on the artery permanently.

- Endovascular coiling: is performed during an angiogram in the radiology department and sometimes requires general anesthesia. A catheter is inserted into an artery in the groin and then passed through the blood vessels to the aneurysm. Through the catheter, the aneurysm is packed with platinum coils or acrylic glue, which prevents blood flow into the aneurysm.
- Artery occlusion and bypass: if surgical clipping is not possible or the artery is too damaged, the surgeon may completely block (occlude) the artery that has the aneurysm. The blood flow is detoured (bypassed) around the occluded section of artery by inserting a vessel graft. The graft is a small artery, usually taken from your leg, that is connected above and below the blocked artery so that blood flow is rerouted (bypassed) through the graft.

A bypass can also be created by detaching a donor artery from its normal position on one end, redirecting it to the inside of the skull, and connecting it above the blocked artery.

中英文注释

关键词汇

aneurysm ['ænjə,rizəm] n. 动脉瘤

angiography [,ændʒi'agrəfi] n. 血管造影

basilar ['bæsələ˞] adj.（尤指颅骨）基部的，底部的

bypass ['bai,pæs] n. 旁路

dizziness ['dizinəs] n. 头昏眼花

hydrocephalus [,haidro'sɛfələs] n. 脑水肿，脑积水

vasospasm ['vezo,spæzəm] n. 血管痉挛

主要短语

anticonvulsant medication　抗惊厥药

Computed Tomography Angiography (CTA)　CT 血管造影

double vision　复视

Ehlers Danlos Syndrome　埃勒斯 - 当洛综合征

endovascular coiling　血管内栓塞

fibromuscular dysplasia　纤维肌性发育不良

lumbar puncture　腰椎穿刺

Magnetic Resonance Imaging (MRI)　磁共振成像

Magnetic Resonance Angiogram (MRA)　磁共振血管造影

Marfan Syndrome　马方综合征

middle cerebral artery　大脑中动脉

neurofibromatosis NF1 神经纤维瘤病 1 型
neurointerventionalist 神经介入专家
pseudoxanthoma elasticum 弹性假黄色瘤
saccular aneurysm 囊状动脉瘤
subarachnoid hemorrhage (SAH) 蛛网膜下出血
superficial temporal artery 颞浅动脉
surgical clipping 手术夹闭

刘晓东

14 Intracerebral Hemorrhage

脑 出 血

What is intracerebral hemorrhage?

Intracranial hemorrhage is bleeding within the skull cavity (cranium) that usually progresses rapidly and often results in permanent brain damage and death. All bleeding within the skull is called intracranial bleeding, whether the bleeding occurs within the brain itself (intracerebral hemorrhage) or in the area between the brain and the skull (epidural, subdural, and subarachnoid hemorrhage).

A cerebral hemorrhage is an intra-axial hemorrhage; that is, it occurs within the brain tissue rather than outside of it. The other category of intracranial hemorrhage is extra-axial hemorrhage, such as epidural, subdural, and subarachnoid hematomas, which all occur within the skull but outside of the brain tissue. There are two main kinds of intra-axial hemorrhages: intraparenchymal hemorrhage and intraventricular hemorrhages. As with other types of hemorrhages within the skull, intraparenchymal bleeds are a serious medical emergency because they can increase intracranial pressure, which if left untreated can lead to coma and death. The mortality rate for intraparenchymal bleeds is over 40%.

Intracerebral hemorrhage accounts for 8-13% of all strokes and results from a wide spectrum of disorders. Intracerebral hemorrhage is more likely to result in death or major disability than ischemic stroke or subarachnoid hemorrhage. Intracerebral hemorrhage and accompanying edema may disrupt or compress adjacent brain tissue, leading to neurological dysfunction. Substantial displacement of brain parenchyma may cause elevation of intracranial pressure (ICP) and potentially fatal herniation syndromes.

Predilection sites for intracerebral hemorrhage include the basal ganglia (40-50%), lobar regions (20-50%), thalamus (10-15%), pons (5-12%), cerebellum (5-10%), and other brainstem sites (1-5%).

High blood pressure, atherosclerosis (buildup of plaque in artery walls), and amyloid angiopathy (protein deposits in artery walls) can weaken blood vessel walls. Aneurysms, which are bulges in weakened areas, can form when blood vessels are damaged or they can be present at birth. Arteriovenous malformations, which are abnormal connections between arteries and veins that may be present at birth, are another vascular abnormality that can be a site of cerebral hemorrhage.

What causes intracerebral hemorrhage?

The most common cause of a brain hemorrhage is elevated blood pressure. Over time, elevated blood pressure can weaken arterial walls and lead to rupture. When this occurs, blood collects in the brain leading to symptoms of a stroke. Other causes of hemorrhage include aneurysm — a weak spot in the wall of an artery — which then balloons out and may break open. Arteriovenous malformations (AVM) are abnormal connections between arteries and veins and are usually present from birth and can cause brain hemorrhage later in life. In some cases, people with cancer who develop distant spread of their original cancer to their brain (metastatic disease) can develop brain hemorrhages in the areas of brain where the cancer has spread. In elderly individuals, amyloid protein deposits along the blood vessels can cause the vessel wall to weaken leading to a hemorrhagic stroke. Cocaine or drug abuse can weaken blood vessels and lead to bleeding in the brain. Some prescription drugs can also increase the risk of brain hemorrhage.

There are several risk factors and causes of Intracerebral Hemorrhage. The most common include:

- **High blood pressure.** This chronic condition can, over a long period of time, weaken blood vessel walls. Untreated high blood pressure is a major preventable cause of brain hemorrhages.
- **Head trauma.** Injury is the most common cause of bleeding in the brain for those younger than age 50.
- **Aneurysm.** This is a weakening in a blood vessel wall that swells. It can burst and bleed into the brain, leading to a stroke.
- **Blood vessel abnormalities.** (Arteriovenous malformations) Weaknesses in the blood vessels in and around the brain may be present at birth and diagnosed only if symptoms develop.
- **Amyloid angiopathy.** This is an abnormality of the blood vessel walls that sometimes occurs with aging and high blood pressure. It may cause many small, unnoticed bleeds before causing a large one.
- **Blood or bleeding disorders.** Hemophilia and sickle cell anemia can both contribute to decreased levels of blood platelets.
- **Liver disease.** This condition is associated with increased bleeding in general.
- **Brain tumors.**

You may be able to lower your risk of cerebral hemorrhage by:

- Controlling your blood pressure
- Eating a healthy diet
- Exercising regularly
- Quitting smoking
- Taking precautions against falling
- Using safety devices such as helmets and seatbelts when necessary

What are symptoms of intracerebral hemorrhage?

Symptoms of cerebral hemorrhage are related to their location. Some can interfere with function of parts of the body, some can interfere with sensation, and some can interfere with thought processes.

Although headache is frequently associated with bleeding in the brain, it is not always present. Most often, the symptoms associated with a brain hemorrhage are dependent on the particular area of the brain that is involved. If the bleeding is in the part of the brain associated with vision, there may be problems seeing. Problems with balance and coordination, weakness on one side, numbness, or sudden seizure may occur. The speech center for many people is located in the left side of the brain and bleeding into this area may cause marked speech disturbances. If the bleeding is in the lower brain (brainstem), where most of the automatic body functions are regulated, a patient may become unresponsive or go into a coma. Additionally, sometimes symptoms of brain hemorrhage may come on very abruptly and rapidly worsen. Alternatively, the symptoms may progress slowly over many hours or even days.

Common symptoms of cerebral hemorrhage

- Change in level of consciousness or alertness such as passing out or unresponsiveness
- Difficulty swallowing
- Difficulty with thinking, talking, comprehension, writing or reading
- Loss of vision or changes in vision
- Numbness or weakness
- Paralysis
- Seizures
- Severe headache

Serious symptoms that might indicate a life-threatening condition

- Change in level of consciousness or alertness such as passing out or unresponsiveness
- Change in mental status or sudden behavior change such as confusion, delirium,

lethargy, hallucinations or delusions

- Garbled or slurred speech or inability to speak
- Paralysis or inability to move a body part
- Seizure
- Sudden change in vision, loss of vision, or eye pain
- Trauma to the head
- Worst headache of your life

How is intracerebral hemorrhage diagnosed?

- **History:** The individual with an intracranial hemorrhage is often unconscious or dazed or otherwise unable to give a complete medical history. The physician may need to rely on those who were with the individual when the event occurred, as well as friends or family members, to provide information about the individual's current and past medical conditions and diseases. In this case, the history may be inaccurate or incomplete for past injuries, illnesses, surgical procedures, and current treatment of existing chronic diseases.

  Individuals with intracerebral hemorrhage may have a history of hypertension, diabetes, or treatment with anticoagulants. Symptoms of hemorrhage typically come on during the day and include progressive deterioration in consciousness (50% of cases), nausea and vomiting (40% to 50% of cases), headache (40% of cases), seizures (6% to 7% of cases), weakness or paralysis on one side (including face, arm, and leg), slurred speech, difficulty expressing themselves in words (expressive aphasia) or understanding speech (receptive aphasia), disturbances in eye movement, difficulty swallowing (dysphagia), or respiratory depression.

- **Physical exam:** The examiner may observe changes in the individual's mental status and level of consciousness that may range from clouding of consciousness, confusion, lethargy, obtundation, and stupor to coma. Strength testing may reveal weakness or paralysis on one side. The individual may vomit and have seizures. Speech may be disturbed. Elevated pressure inside the cranium (intracranial pressure [ICP]), and thus in the brain and CSF, may result in pupils that appear unequal in size and react sluggishly to light. If the individual's neurological status is deteriorating rapidly, the examiner must make a quick diagnosis of the type of trauma or hemorrhage based on the most prominent signs and symptoms, so surgical intervention can proceed.

- **Tests:** Computed tomography (CT) is the standard diagnostic tool to quickly determine the presence of skull fractures and bleeding within the skull. If the

CT is negative for bleeding, lumbar puncture is performed to determine if blood is present in the CSF. Magnetic resonance imaging (MRI) is not used in the acute phase of injury but is useful after the initial 48 hours to assess the extent of injury to the brain. If a ruptured aneurysm is suspected, a complete vascular study (arteriography) of the carotid and cerebral arteries helps pinpoint the location of the ruptured aneurysm. An angiography may also be performed if subarachnoid hemorrhage is suspected. Additional diagnostic tests may include an electrocardiogram (ECG), chest X-ray, urinalysis, and blood studies (complete blood count [CBC], prothrombin time [PT], erythrocyte sedimentation rate [ESR], blood glucose, electrolytes, and blood type). A diagnosis of subdural hemorrhage/hematoma may require additional tests because symptoms are similar to those of many other diseases and conditions.

How is it treated?

Immediate medical treatment for acute intracranial hemorrhages includes maintaining the airway; assisting respiration if needed; regulating body temperature, blood oxygen level, and blood pressure; establishing intravenous (IV) access to replace fluids and maintain a constant blood sugar level; controlling external bleeding; monitoring ICP; and stabilizing the cervical spine until cervical fracture is ruled out. Maintaining an acceptable ICP with corticosteroids and diuretics is mandatory so that further brain injury does not occur. Setting respiratory parameters so that breaths occur frequently and deeply (hyperventilation) decreases carbon dioxide levels, which lowers intracranial pressure. Once the individual's condition stabilizes, treatment focuses on maintaining the status quo and treating underlying medical conditions and diseases.

Medication

- Antihypertensive therapy in acute phases. The AHA/ASA and EUSI guidelines (American Heart Association/American Stroke Association guidelines and the European Stroke Initiative guidelines) have recommended antihypertensive therapy to stabilize the mean arterial pressure at 110 mmHg. One paper showed the efficacy of this antihypertensive therapy without worsening outcome in patients of hypertensive intracerebral hemorrhage within 3 hours onset.
- Giving Factor VIIa within 4 hours limits the bleeding and formation of a hematoma. However, it also increases the risk of thromboembolism.
- Mannitol is effective in acutely reducing raised intracranial pressure.
- Acetaminophen may be needed to avoid hyperthermia, and to relieve headache.
- Frozen plasma, vitamin K, protamine, or platelet transfusions are given in case of a coagulopathy.

- Fosphenytoin or other anticonvulsant is given in case of seizures or lobar hemorrhage.
- H2 antagonists or proton pump inhibitors are commonly given for stress ulcer prophylaxis, a condition somehow linked with ICH
- Corticosteroids, in concert with antihypertensives, reduces swelling.

Surgery

- Surgery is required if the hematoma is greater than 3 cm (1 in), if there is a structural vascular lesion or lobar hemorrhage in a young patient.
- A catheter may be passed into the brain vasculature to close off or dilate blood vessels, avoiding invasive surgical procedures.
- Aspiration by stereotactic surgery or endoscopic drainage may be used in basal ganglia hemorrhages, although successful reports are limited.

Other treatment

- Tracheal intubation is indicated in patients with decreased level of consciousness or other risk of airway obstruction.
- IV fluids (Intravenous therapy) are given to maintain fluid balance, using normotonic rather than hypotonic fluids.

中英文注释

关键词汇

aneurysm ['ænjʊriz(ə)m] n.动脉瘤

arteriography [ɑːˌtiəri'ɒɡrəfi] n.动脉造影

atherosclerosis [ˌæθərəʊskliə'rəʊsis; –sklə–] n.动脉粥样硬化

coagulopathy [kəuˌægju'lɔpəθi] n.凝血障碍

consciousness ['kɒnʃəsnis] n.意识

corticosteroids [ˌkɔːtikəus'tirɔid] n.皮质激素，类固醇

electrocardiogram [iˌlektrəʊ'kɑːdiəgræm] n.心电图

lethargy ['leθədʒi] n.昏睡，嗜睡

mannitol ['mænitɒl] n.甘露醇

numbness ['nʌmnəs] n.麻木，麻痹

seizures ['siːʒə] n.癫痫发作

subarachnoid [ˌsʌbə'ræknɔid] adj.蛛网膜下的

thalamus ['θæləməs] n.丘脑

thromboembolism [ˌθrɒmbəʊ'embəliz(ə)m] n.血栓栓塞

主要短语

amyloid angiopathy 淀粉样脑血管病

arteriovenous malformations 动静脉畸形

basal ganglia 基底节

difficulty swallowing 吞咽困难

extra-axial hemorrhage 额外轴向出血

hemorrhagic stroke 出血性卒中

high blood pressure 高血压

intracranial pressure 颅内压

intraparenchymal hemorrhage 脑实质内出血

intraventricular hemorrhages 脑室出血

mortality rate 死亡率

respiratory depression 呼吸抑制

刘晓东

15. Subarachnoid Hemorrhage (SAH)
蛛网膜下腔出血

What is SAH?

A subarachnoid hemorrhage (SAH) is an abnormal and very dangerous condition in which blood collects beneath the arachnoid mater, a membrane that covers the brain. This area, called the subarachnoid space, normally contains cerebrospinal fluid. The accumulation of blood in the subarachnoid space can lead to stroke, seizures, and other complications. Additionally, subarachnoid hemorrhages may cause permanent brain damage and a number of harmful biochemical events in the brain. A subarachnoid hemorrhage and the related problems are frequently fatal.

Subarachnoid hemorrhages are classified into two general categories: traumatic and spontaneous. Traumatic refers to brain injury that might be sustained in an accident or a fall. Spontaneous subarachnoid hemorrhages occur with little or no warning and are frequently caused by ruptured aneurysms or blood vessel abnormalities in the brain.

Traumatic brain injury is a critical problem in the United States. According to annual figures compiled by the Brain Injury Association, approximately 373,000 people are hospitalized, more than 56,000 people die, and 99,000 survive with permanent disabilities due to traumatic brain injuries. The leading causes of injury are bicycle, motorcycle, and automobile accidents, with a significant minority due to accidental falls, and sports and recreation mishaps.

Exact statistics are not available on traumatic subarachnoid hemorrhages, but several large clinical studies have found an incidence of 23%~39% in relation to severe head injury. Furthermore, subarachnoid hemorrhages have been described in the medical literature as the most common brain injury found during autopsy investigations of head trauma.

Spontaneous subarachnoid hemorrhages are often due to an aneurysm (a bulge or sac-like projection from a blood vessel) which bursts. Arteriovenous malformations (AVMs), which are abnormal interfaces between arteries andveins, may also rupture and release blood into the subarachnoid space. Both aneurysms and AVMs are associated with weak spots in the walls of blood vessels and account for approximately 60% of all spontaneous subarachnoid hemorrhages. The rest may be attributed to other causes, such as cancer or infection, or are of unknown origin.

In industrialized countries, it is estimated that there are 6.5-26.4 cases of spontaneous subarachnoid hemorrhage per 100,000 people annually. Certain factors raise the risk of suffering a hemorrhage. Aneurysms are acquired over a person's lifetime and are rarely a factor in subarachnoid hemorrhage before age 20. Conversely, arteriovenous malformation (AVM) are present at birth. In some cases, there may be a genetic predisposition for aneurysms or AVMs. Other factors that have been implicated, but not definitively linked to spontaneous subarachnoid hemorrhages, include atherosclerosis, cigarette use, extreme alcohol consumption, and the use of illegal drugs, such as cocaine. The exact role of high blood pressure is somewhat unclear, but since it does seem linked to the formation of aneurysms, it may be considered an indirect risk factor.

What causes SAH?

In 85% of cases of spontaneous SAH, the cause is rupture of a cerebral aneurysm—a weakness in the wall of one of the arteries in the brain that becomes enlarged. They tend to be located in the circle of Willis and its branches. While most cases of SAH are due to bleeding from small aneurysms, larger aneurysms (which are less common) are more likely to rupture.

In 15%~20% of cases of spontaneous SAH, no aneurysm is detected on the first angiogram. About half of these are attributed to non-aneurysmal perimesencephalic hemorrhage, in which the blood is limited to the subarachnoid spaces around the midbrain (i.e. mesencephalon). In these, the origin of the blood is uncertain. The remainder are due to other disorders affecting the blood vessels (such as arteriovenous malformations), disorders of the blood vessels in the spinal cord, and bleeding into various tumors. Cocaine abuse and sickle cell anemia (usually in children) and, rarely, anticoagulant therapy, problems with blood clotting and pituitary apoplexy can also result in SAH.

Subarachnoid blood can be detected on CT scanning in as many as 60% of people with traumatic brain injury. Traumatic SAH (tSAH) usually occurs near the site of a skull fracture or intracerebral contusion. It usually happens in the setting of other forms of traumatic brain injury and has been linked with a poorer prognosis. It is unclear, however, if this is a direct result of the SAH or whether the presence of subarachnoid blood is simply an indicator of severity of the head injury and the prognosis is determined by other associated mechanisms.

Risk Factors

Are you at risk for SAH?

Risk factors for a subarachnoid hemorrhage include:

Aneurysm in a vessel outside the brain.

- Aneurysm in the chest
- Aneurysm in the abdomen
- Cerebral aneurysm
- Cerebral arteriovenous malformation
- Diabetes
- Family history of subarachnoid hemorrhage

Fibromuscular dysplasia:

An arterial disease of unknown cause that affects the arteries of young to middle-aged women. Commonly affected arteries include the carotid arteries in the neck and the renal arteries in the kidneys.

- Heart disease
- Ehlers Danlos syndrome type 4
- Neurofibromatosis type 1
- High cholesterol
- Hypertension
- Obesity
- Polycystic kidney disease
- Smoking

What are symptoms of SAH?

Headache is usually severe, peaking within seconds. Loss of consciousness may follow, usually immediately but sometimes not for several hours. Severe neurologic deficits may develop and become irreversible within minutes or a few hours. Sensorium may be impaired, and patients may become restless. Seizures are possible. Usually, the neck is not stiff initially unless the cerebellar tonsils herniate. However, within 24h, chemical meningitis causes moderate to marked meningismus, vomiting, and sometimes bilateral extensor plantar responses. Heart or respiratory rate is often abnormal. Fever, continued headaches, and confusion are common during the first 5 to 10 days. Secondary hydrocephalus may cause headache, obtundation, and motor deficits that persist for weeks. Rebleeding may cause recurrent or new symptoms.

How is SAH diagnosed?

When a patient is brought to the emergency room with an SAH, doctors will learn as much as possible about his or her symptoms, current and previous medical problems, medications, and family history. A physical exam will be performed. Diagnostic tests will help determine the source of the bleeding.

CT Scans and SAH Diagnosis

Computed Tomography (CT) is a noninvasive X-ray that provides detailed images of anatomical structures within the brain. It is especially useful to detect blood in or around the brain. A newer technology called CT angiography (CTA) involves the injection of contrast into the blood stream to view the arteries of the brain. CTA provides the best pictures of blood vessels (through angiography) and soft tissues (through CT).

Lumbar Puncture to Diagnose SAH

Lumbar puncture is an invasive procedure in which a hollow needle is inserted into the subarachnoid space of the spinal canal to detect blood in the cerebrospinal fluid (CSF). The doctor will collect 2 to 4 tubes of CSF. If the CT scan does not show evidence of bleeding but the patient symptoms are typical for SAH, a lumbar puncture may be performed.

Angiogram for SAH

Angiogram is an invasive procedure in which a catheter is inserted into an artery and passed through the blood vessels to the brain. Once the catheter is in place, contrast dye is injected into the bloodstream and X-ray images are taken.

MRI to Diagnose SAH

Magnetic resonance imaging (MRI) scan is a noninvasive test that uses a magnetic field and radio-frequency waves to give a detailed view of the soft tissues of the brain. An MRA (Magnetic Resonance Angiogram) is the same non-invasive study, except that it is also an angiogram, which means it examines the blood vessels in addition to structures of the brain.

How is it treated?

Treatment for SAH varies, depending on the underlying cause of the bleeding and the extent of damage to the brain. Treatment may include lifesaving measures, symptom relief, repair of the bleeding vessel, and complication prevention.

For 10 to 14 days following SAH, the patient will remain in the neuroscience intensive care unit (NSICU), where doctors and nurses can watch closely for signs of renewed bleeding, vasospasm, hydrocephalus, and other potential complications.

SAH Medication

Pain medication will be given to alleviate headache, and anticonvulsant medication may be given to prevent or treat seizures.

SAH Surgery

If the SAH is from a ruptured aneurysm, surgery may be performed to stop the bleeding. Options include:

- Surgical clipping: an opening in the skull (craniotomy) is made to locate the aneurysm. A small titanium clip is placed across the neck of the aneurysm to stop blood flow from entering.
- Endovascular coiling: a catheter is inserted into an artery in the groin during an angiogram. The catheter is advanced through the blood stream to the aneurysm. Platinum coils or liquid glue (Onyx) are packed into the aneurysm to stop blood flow from entering.

Controlling hydrocephalus for SAH

Clotted blood and fluid buildup in the subarachnoid space may cause hydrocephalus and increase intracranial pressure. Blood pressure is lowered to reduce further bleeding and to control intracranial pressure. Excess cerebrospinal fluid (CSF) and blood can be removed with 1) a lumbar drain, which is inserted into the subarachnoid space of the spinal canal in the lower back, or 2) a ventricular drain, which is inserted into the ventricles of the brain.

Controlling vasospasm for SAH

Five to 10 days after an SAH, the patient may develop vasospasm. Vasospasm narrows the artery and reduces blood flow to the region of the brain that the artery feeds. Vasospasm occurs in 70% of patients after SAH. Of these, 30% have symptoms that require treatment.

A patient in the NSICU will be monitored for signs of vasospasm, which include weakness in an arm or leg, confusion, sleepiness, or restlessness. Transcranial doppler (TCD) ultrasounds are preformed routinely to monitor for vasospasm. TCDs are used to measure the blood flow through the arteries. This test can show which arteries are in spasm as well as the severity. To prevent vasospasm, patients are given the drug nimodipine while in the hospital. Additionally, these following therapy are used:

- Hypertension: involves increasing the blood pressure to force blood through the narrowed arteries.
- Hypervolemia: involves increasing IV fluids to make more blood volume.
- Hemodilution: involves making the blood thin and watery so that it flows more easily through narrowed arteries.

If vasospasm is severe, patients may require an injection of medication directly into the artery to relax and stop the spasm. This is done through a catheter during an angiogram. Sometimes balloon angioplasty is used to stretch open the artery.

中英文注释

关键词汇

abdomen ['æbdəmən,æb'domən] n. 下腹；腹腔

aneurysm ['ænjə,rizəm] n. 动脉瘤

arachnoid [ə'ræknɔid] n. 蛛网膜；adj. 蛛网状的，蛛网膜的

atherosclerosis [,æθərosklə'rosis] n. 动脉粥样硬化

catheter ['kæθitə-] n. 导尿管，尿液管，导管

hemodilution [,hi:məudai'ljuʃən] n. 血液稀释

intracranial [,intrə'kreniəl] n. 头颅内的，颅骨内的

ischemia [i'skimiə] n. 缺血

meningitis [,mɛnin'dʒaitis] n. 脑膜炎

obesity [o'bisiti] n. 肥胖；肥胖症

sensorium [sɛn'sɔriəm, -'sor-] n. 感觉中枢，感觉器官

traumatic [traʊ'mætik] adj. 外伤的；创伤的；治外伤的

vasospasm ['vezo,spæzəm] n. 血管痉挛

主要短语

anticonvulsant medication 抗惊厥药

arteriovenous malformation (AVM) 动静脉畸形

cerebrospinal fluid (CSF) 脑脊髓液

Ehlers Danlos Syndrome 埃勒斯 - 当洛综合征

fibromuscular dysplasia 纤维肌性发育不良

high cholesterol 高胆固醇

polycystic kidney disease 多囊性肾病

plantar responses 跖反射

subarachnoid hemorrhage (SAH) 蛛网膜下出血

spinal cord 脊髓

tonsils herniate 扁桃体疝

surgical clipping 手术夹闭

transcranial doppler 经颅多普勒

刘晓东

16 Blepharoptosis
眼 睑 下 垂

What is blepharoptosis?

Blepharoptosis is the drooping of the upper lid margin to a position that is lower than normal. The drooping may be worse after being awake longer, when the individual's muscles are tired. If severe enough and left untreated, the drooping eyelid can cause other conditions, such as amblyopia or astigmatism. This is why it is especially important for this disorder to be treated in children at a young age, before it can interfere with vision development.

What causes blepharoptosis and its classification?

Blepharoptosis may be due to a myogenic, neurogenic, aponeurotic, mechanical or traumatic cause and it usually occurs isolated, but may be associated with various other conditions, like immunological, degenerative, or hereditary disorders, tumors, or infections. Depending upon the cause it can be classified into congenital ptosis and acquired ptosis.

Congenital ptosis

The vast majority of congenital ptosis is due to the levator muscle hypoplasia, or its control motor nerve oculomotor nerve (CN III) abnormalities or dysfunction. A small number of cases is due to the outer and medial horn of levator aponeurosis or the superior transverse ligament (Whitanall's) is too tight, or too much fiber adhesion to posterior wall of the orbital septum, thus limiting the movement of the levator muscle.

Congenital ptosis is more common in bilateral than unilateral, some patients have a family history. Ptosis can occur in isolation, may also be accompanied by other eye muscle paralysis or paresis, one of the most common is the superior rectus muscle palsy or inferior oblique muscle dysfunction.

Congenital ptosis can also be associated with ocular abnormalities: coexistent strabismus and amblyopia, Marcus Gunn's jaw-winking syndrome, blepharophimosis syndrome (triad of ptosis, telecanthus and phimosis of lid fissure), congenital anophthalmos or microphthalmos, and coexistent eyelid hamartoma, such as neurofibromas, hemangiomas or lymphangiomas.

Acquired ptosis

Four types of acquired ptosis are divided: myogenic ptosis, traumatic ptosis, neurogenic and mechanical ptosis.

- myogenic ptosis

Myogenic ptosis can be divided to involutional myopathic and chronic progressive external ophthalmoplegia. The former which is also called senile ptosis, is the most common type. The levator aponeurosis is attached to the anterior tarsus, dermal attachments are maintained and therefore the supratarsal creases rises. Levator function is usually good. The other is chronic progressive external ophthalmoplegia, caused by the progressive muscular dystrophy affecting the extraocular muscles and levator, 5% of cases involve the facial and oropharyngeal muscles.

- traumatic ptosis

Traumatic ptosis is more common in unilateral. Upper eyelid lacerations, cuts, forceps injury, post-traumatic upper eyelid scar or edema, can lead to the levator muscle function diminished or disappeared.

- neurogenic ptosis

Neurogenic ptosis is a result of the oculomotor nerve lesions. The nature of the lesion may be a developmental abnormalities, trauma, cancer, inflammation, vascular disease and endocrine or metabolic diseases. This ptosis can exist alone, but most of them associated with other extraocular muscle paralysis, or abnormal collection of pupil movement. It is one of the signs of nervous system diseases.

- mechanical ptosis

Mechanical ptosis is caused by eyelid tumors, such as neurofibroma, hemangioma, lymphatic tumor and severe trachoma, which can increase the weight of the upper eyelid.

Evluation of blepharoptosis

Pre-operative check-ups and correct judgment of the cause, type and extent of ptosis, are the basement of surgical method selection, the estimate of surgical results and the prevention of some kind of complications that may arise.

- determination of the degree of ptosis

Looking straight head, the upper eyelid covering the edge of the cornea is more than 2 mm, can be diagnosed blepharoptosis.

Compare with contralateral side if unilateral, the height difference of palpebral fissure is the amount of drooping. Normal eyelid margin is in the right middle horizontal line between the upper edge of pupil and the upper edge of cornea, which covers the cornea 1.5 -2 mm. To bilateral ptosis, displayed eyelid is located on the edge of the pupil, the droop is about 1-2mm, known as mild ptosis; upper eyelid covered 1/3 of the pupil, the droop is approximately 3-4mm, called moderate ptosis; such as eyelid edge whereabouts to the center of the pupil horizontal lines, sagging about 4mm or more, said severe ptosis.

- the levator muscle strength determination

Suppress thumb to supraorbital eyebrows to exclude levator role of frontalis muscle. Ask the patient gaze down, put a millimeter ruler in front of the face, zero point alignment on the lid margin, and the patient is then asked to look up as far as possible, the lid margin increase from the bottom up. Measure from extreme downward gaze to extreme upward gaze while immobilizing the brow, more than 10 mm is good, 5-10 mm is fair, and the poor is less than 5 mm.

- the superior rectus function test

The patient is asked to rotate eyeballs in all directions, and then close their eyes. Make eyelids open with your fingers to check whether the eyeballs rotate upward. If there is no turn, compared to the lack of Bellphenomenon, and it is not appropriate for ptosis corrective surgery because of postoperative exposure keratitis possibility. If surgery is necessary, the amount of correction should be conservative as far as possible, to reduce or eliminate lagophthalmos.

- exclude myasthenia gravis

For blepharoptosis patients with Honer syndrome, as well as Marcus Gunn's jaw-winking syndrome, levator muscle should first be cut off and then correct the drooping, or else the symptoms would aggravate.

How is blepharoptosis treated?

For congenital ptosis, since the palpebra frontalis covering some or all of the visual axis, the patients tend to frown and raise up their eyebrows to get rid of the interference, increasing and deepening the forehead wrinkles, even cervical spine deformities, thus congenital ptosis should be early corrected in principle. Early surgery could prevent amblyopia in children. If Marcus Gunn's jaw-winking syndrome exists, consider surgery only if the drooping was still obvious after puberty. If more than 10 mm of levator excursion (excellent), aponeurotic surgery or Müllerectomy is needed; if 5~10 mm of excursion (moderate), then levator resection or advancement; if 0~5 mm of excursion (poor), then need frontalis suspension. For those coexisted with microphthalmos, inner canthus epicanthus correction and outer canthus open angioplasty should first be made, six months before the correction of ptosis. For myogenic ptosis, the follow-up treatment should be postponed to 6 to 12 months later, allowing for recovery of myoneural dysfunction, resolution of edema and softening of scar. Blepharoptosis can also occur after cataract surgery from dehiscence of levator aponeurosis. For oculomotor nerve palsy caused ptosis, surgery could be operated only after the condition is in stable for 6 months. Accompanied by other external ophthalmoplegia or diplopia, diplopia should be corrected before surgery. Myasthenia gravis ptosis is not a contraindication for surgery if the myasthenia gravis is not progressive and the ptosis degree is fixed.

Fasanella-servat procedure

Conjunctival approach to excise tarsus, Muller's muscle, and conjunctiva should be considered only when levator function is excellent with minimal ptosis. Avoid external incision — therefore unable to alter supratarsal crease somewhat less predictable than external approaches. Resection of tarsus can result in postoperative floppy lid with lid peaking and eversion.

Mustarde's split-level approach

Anterior resection of skin, conjunctival resection of tarsus and conjunctiva, retention of levator and Muller's muscle.

Levator aponeurosis advancement

Useful for mild to moderate ptosis.

Amenable to monitored anaesthesia technique.

Technique:

- Incise skin at desired supratarsal fold.
- Expose orbital septum and distal levator aponeurosis beneath orbicularis fibers.
- Incise septum and retract the preaponeurotic fat to expose the aponeurosis, which can be identified by the vertically oriented vessels on its superior surface.
- Incise distal aponeurosis at the superior tarsal border, and dessect it free from Muller's muscle.
- Place a central-lifting suture: double-arm 6-0 suture passed into superior tarsus and levator aponeurosis; tarsus will need to be recentered in cases of temporal displacement.
- If levator excursion is 8-10 mm, then upper lid should be slightly lower than the upper limbus after advancement; if 6-8 mm, then it should be at the limbus; if 4-6 mm, then slightly higher than limbus.
- Additional medial and lateral sutures are placed.

Perfomsupratarsal crease fixation—"anchor blepharoplasty" or resection of orbicularis.

Externl levator resection

Best used when levator function is fair

Sacrificies the viable levator muscle

Levator reinsertion

Only useful in true levator dehiscence, which is likely only after trauma

Involves resuturing the dehisced end to the tarsus

Frontalis suspension

● Required if levator function poor (congenital cases. Neurogenic cases)

● Can give 1 cm of excursion; good result in straightforward gaze; gives lagophthalmos while asleep, which requires ointment or nighttime patching.

● Incorporates a sling (fascia lata, temporalis fascia, homograft fascia, silicone strips, Gore-Tex) from frontalis to lid.

● For unilateral congenital cases, bilateral suspension performed to improve symmetry.

● Non-surgical modalities like the use of "crutch" glasses or special Scleral contact lenses to support the eyelid may also be used.

Ptosis that is caused by a disease will improve if the disease is treated successfully.

Complications

Ptosis surgery has many complications, according to the incidence from high to low order are as follows: undercorrection, overcorrection, excessive lagophthalmos, corneal exposure or keratitis, dry-eye syndrome, eyelid contour abnormality, temporal overcorrection, eyelid crease asymmetry, eyelash ptosis or lash abnormalities, entropion or ectropion/eversion of the upper lid, extraocular muscle imbalance, conjunctival prolapse.

中英文注释

关键词汇

amblyopia [æmbli'əʊpiə] n. 弱视

anophthalmos ['ænəfθælməʊz] n. 无眼畸形

aponeurotic [ˌæpənju'rɔtik] adj. 腱膜的

astigmatism [ə'stigmətiz(ə)m] n. 散光

blepharoptosis [ˌblefərə'tɔsis] n. 眼睑下垂

conjunctiva [kən'dʒʌŋ(k)tivə] n. 结膜

dehiscence [di'hisəns] n. 裂开

diplopia [di'pləʊpiə] n. 复视

hamartoma [hæmə'təʊmə] n. 错构瘤

hemangiomas [hiˌmændʒi'əʊmə] n. 血管瘤

keratitis [kerə'taitis] n. 角膜炎

lagophthalmos [lægɒf'θælmɒs] n. 睑裂闭合不全

lymphangiomas [limˌfændʒiˈəumə] n. 淋巴管瘤

mechanical [miˈkænikəl] adj. 机械的

microphthalmos [maikrəfˈθælməuz] n. 小眼畸形

myasthenia [maiəsˈθiːniə] n. 肌无力

myogenic [maiə(ʊ)ˈdʒenik] adj. 肌原性的

neurofibromas [njʊərə(ʊ)faiˈbrəumə] n. 纤维神经瘤

neurogenic [njʊərə(ʊ)ˈdʒenik] adj. 神经性的；起源于神经组织的

ophthalmoplegia [ɔfˌθælməˈpliːdʒiə, ɔp-] n. 眼肌麻痹

pupil [ˈpjupəl] n. 瞳孔

senile [ˈsiːnail] adj. 高龄的

tarsus [ˈtɑːsəs] n. 睑板

trachoma [trəˈkəumə] n. 沙眼

主要短语

acquired ptosis 获得性上睑下垂

Blepharophimosis Syndrome 睑裂狭小综合征

congenital ptosis 先天性上睑下垂

levator muscle 提上睑肌

levator aponeurosis 提上睑肌腱膜

Marcus Gunn's Jaw-winking Syndrome 上颌瞬目综合征

myasthenia gravis 重症肌无力

oculomotor nerve (CN III) 动眼神经（第 3 对脑神经）

orbital septum 眶隔

superior transverse ligament (Whitanall's ligament) 上横韧带（Whitanall 韧带）

supratarsal crease 重睑

triad of ptosis, telecanthus and phimosis of lid fissure 上睑下垂、内眦距离过宽、睑裂闭锁三联征

王小兵

17 Cleft Lip
唇　裂

What is cleft lip?

Cleft lip is a variation of a type of clefting congenital deformity caused by abnormal facial development during gestation. It is the non-fusion of the body's natural structures that form before birth. Approximately 1 in 700 children born have a cleft lip or a cleft palate or both. In decades past, the condition was sometimes referred to as harelip, based on the similarity to the cleft in the lip of a hare, but that term is now generally considered to be offensive.

Clefts can also affect other parts of the face, such as the eyes, ears, nose, cheeks, and forehead. In 1976, Paul Tessier described fifteen lines of cleft. Most of these craniofacial clefts are even rarer and are frequently described as Tessier clefts using the numerical locator devised by Tessier.

A cleft lip or palate can be successfully treated with surgery, especially so if conducted soon after birth or in early childhood.

What causes cleft lip?

The development of the face is coordinated by complex morphogenetic events and rapid proliferative expansion, and is thus highly susceptible to environmental and genetic factors, rationalising the high incidence of facial malformations. During the first six to eight weeks of pregnancy, the shape of the embryo's head is formed. Five primitive tissue lobes grow:

- one from the top of the head down towards the future upper lip; (Frontonasal Prominence)
- two from the cheeks, which meet the first lobe to form the upper lip; (Maxillar Prominence)
- and just below, two additional lobes grow from each side, which form the chin and lower lip. (Mandibular Prominence)

If these tissues fail to meet, a gap appears where the tissues should have joined (fused). This may happen in any single joining site, or simultaneously in several or all of them. The resulting birth defect reflects the locations and severity of individual fusion failures.

The upper lip is formed earlier than the palate, from the first three lobes named a to c above. Formation of the palate is the last step in joining the five embryonic facial lobes, and involves the back portions of the lobes b and c. These back portions are called palatal shelves, which grow towards each other until they fuse in the middle. This process is very vulnerable to multiple toxic substances, environmental pollutants, and nutritional imbalance. The biologic mechanisms of mutual recognition of the two cabinets, and the way they are glued together, are quite complex and obscure despite intensive scientific research.

Genetics

Genetic factors contributing to cleft lip and cleft palate formation have been identified for some syndromic cases, but knowledge about genetic factors that contribute to the more common isolated cases of cleft lip/palate is still patchy.

Many clefts run in families, even though in some cases there does not seem to be an identifiable syndrome present, possibly because of the current incomplete genetic understanding of midfacial development.

Many genes are known to play a role in craniofacial development and are being studied through the FaceBase initiative for their part in clefting. These genes are AXIN2, BMP4, FGFR1, FGFR2, FOXE1, IRF6, MAFB (gene), MMP3, MSX1, MSX2 (Msh homeobox 2), MSX3, PAX7, PDGFC, PTCH1, SATB2, SOX9, SUMO1 (Small ubiquitin-related modifier 1), TBX22, TCOF (Treacle protein), TFAP2A, VAX1, TP63, ARHGAP29, NOG, NTN1, WNT genes, and locus 8q24.

Environment

Environmental influences may also cause, or interact with genetics to produce, orofacial clefting. In humans, fetal cleft lip and other congenital abnormalities have been linked to maternal hypoxia, as caused by e.g. maternal smoking, maternalalcohol abuse or some forms of maternal hypertension treatment. Other environmental factors that have been studied include: seasonal causes (such as pesticide exposure); maternal diet and vitamin intake; retinoids — which are members of the vitamin A family; anticonvulsant drugs; alcohol; cigarette use; nitrate compounds; organic solvents; parental exposure to lead; and illegal drugs (cocaine, crack cocaine, heroin, etc.).

What are symptoms of cleft lip?

If the cleft does not affect the palate structure of the mouth it is referred to as cleft lip. Cleft lip is formed in the top of the lip as either a small gap or an indentation in the lip (partial or incomplete cleft) or it continues into the nose (complete cleft). Lip cleft can occur as a one sided (unilateral) or two sided (bilateral). It is due to the failure of fusion of the maxillary and medial nasal processes (formation of the primary palate).

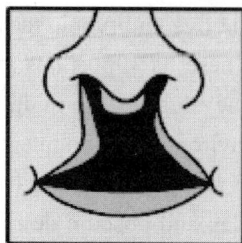

Bilateral complete   Unilateral complete   Unilateral incomplete

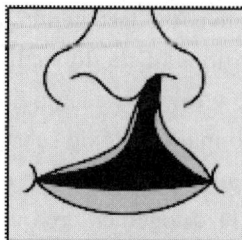

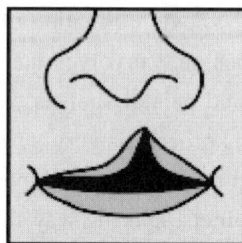

A mild form of a cleft lip is a microform cleft. A microform cleft can appear as small as a little dent in the red part of the lip or look like a scar from the lip up to the nostril. In some cases muscle tissue in the lip underneath the scar is affected and might require reconstructive surgery. It is advised to have newborn infants with a microform cleft checked with a craniofacial team as soon as possible to determine the severity of the cleft.

Psychosocial

Most children who have their clefts repaired early enough are able to have a happy youth and social life. Having a cleft palate/lip does not inevitably lead to a psychosocial problem. However, adolescents with cleft palate/lip are at an elevated risk for developing psychosocial problems especially those relating to self-concept, peer relationships and appearance. Adolescents may face psychosocial challenges but can find professional help if problems arise. A cleft lip may impact an individual's self-esteem, social skills and behavior. Self-concept may be adversely affected by the presence of a cleft lip and or cleft palate, particularly among girls.

Research has shown that during the early preschool years (ages 3–5), children with cleft lip and or cleft palate tend to have a self-concept that is similar to their peers without a cleft. However, as they grow older and their social interactions increase, children with clefts tend to report more dissatisfaction with peer relationships and higher levels of social anxiety. Experts conclude that this is probably due to the associated stigma of visible deformities and possible speech impediments. Children who are judged as attractive tend to be perceived as more intelligent, exhibit more positive social behaviors, and are treated more positively than children with cleft lip and or cleft palate. Children with clefts tend to report feelings of anger, sadness, fear, and alienation from their peers, but these children were similar to their peers in regard to "how well they liked themselves."

Complications

A baby being fed using a customized bottle. The upright sitting position allows gravity to help the baby swallow the milk more easily. Cleft may cause problems with feeding, ear disease, speech and socialization. Due to lack of suction, an infant with a cleft may have trouble feeding. An infant with a cleft palate will have greater success feeding in a more upright position. Gravity will help prevent milk from coming through the baby's nose if he/she has cleft palate. Gravity feeding can be accomplished by using specialized equipment, such as the Haberman Feeder, or by using a combination of nipples and bottle inserts like the one shown, is commonly used with other infants. A large hole, crosscut, or slit in the nipple, a protruding nipple and rhythmically squeezing the bottle insert can result in controllable flow to the infant without the stigma caused by specialized equipment.

Individuals with cleft also face many middle ear infections which may eventually lead to hearing loss. The eustachiantubes and external ear canals may be angled or tortuous, leading to food or other contamination of a part of the body that is normally self-cleaning. Hearing is related to learning to speak. Babies with palatal clefts may have compromised hearing and therefore, if the baby cannot hear, it cannot try to mimic the sounds of speech. Thus, even before expressive language acquisition, the baby with the cleft palate is at risk for receptive language acquisition. Because the lips and palate are both used in pronunciation, individuals with cleft usually need the aid of a speech therapist.

How is cleft lip diagnosed?

Traditionally, the diagnosis is made at the time of birth by physical examination. Recent advances in prenatal diagnosis have allowed obstetricians to diagnose facial clefts in utero.

How is it treated?

Cleft lip and palate is very treatable; however, most children with a form of clefting are monitored by a cleft palate team or craniofacial team through young adulthood. Care can be lifelong. Treatment can differ between individual cases depending on the type and severity of the cleft, and a series of treatment are needed.

Primary cleft lip repair

3 months of age is standard

Goals:

● Reconstruction of phitrum, Cupid's bow, and tubercle

- Functional muscle reconstruction
- Symmetry
- Minimal scarring

Primary cleft nasal repair

- Performed at time of primary lip repair (3 months)
- Release and repositioning of cleft nasal components and alar cartilages successfully integrated into primary lip repair without significant growth impairment

Columellar lengthening (bilateral cleft lip)

12-24 months of age

May be performed at time of palate repair

Alveolar cleft repair

Gingivoperiosteoplasty

- Gingivoperiosteoplasty is the primary closure of alveolar cleft by advancing bilateral mucoperiosteal flaps; it is performed at the time of primary cleft lip repair.
- Presurgical orthopedics are usually needed to narrow cleft and align segments so that primary repair is technically feasible.
- Of patients who underwent nasoalveolar molding and gingivoperiosteoplasty, 60% did not require secondary bone grafting.

Primary alveolar bone grafting (before 2 years of age)

Rib grafts is placed under mucosal flaps in upper buccal sulcus.

Multiple studies report associated growth impairment.

Modified techniques that limit dissection and avoid the use of vomerine flaps reportedly have improved dental outcomes without growth impairment.

Secondary bone grafting

Early secondary: 2-5 years old

Secondary: 5-16 years old

Late secondary: > 16 years old

Repair of secondary cleft lip deformities

Optimal timing depends on the severity of the deformity and its effect on the psychosocial development of the patient. Most commonly performed during:

- Preschool: when developing peer interation
- Adolescence: optimal results after cessation of facial growth

Common deformities that require correction:

- White roll deformities
- Deficient vermilion (whistle deformity)

- Buccal sulcus deformity
- Short lip
- Long lip (bilateral cleft)
- Tight lip

Repair of secondary cleft lip nasal deformity

Preschool age

Risk of growth disturbance with septoplasty

May result in bulbous tip in adolescence because of accumulation of fibrofatty tissue and scar

Adolescence

Definitive osteoplastic rhinoplasty and septoplasty after cessation of facial growth

Orthognathic surgery

Treatment of maxillary hypoplasia with Le Fort I advancement during adolescence

中英文注释

关键词汇

alveolar [æl'viələ] adj. 齿槽的

craniofacial [ˌkreiniə'feiʃəl] adj. 颅面的

embryonic [ˌembri'ɔnik] adj. 胚胎的

gestation [dʒe'steiʃ(ə)n] n. 怀孕；妊娠期

gingivoperiosteoplasty [d'ʒigivəupri:əusti:əuplæs] n. 牙龈骨膜成形术

harelip [heə'lip] n. 兔唇；[口腔] 唇裂

morphogenetic [ˌmɔ:fəudʒi'netik] adj. 有关形态发生的

mucoperiosteal [mu:kəupri:əus'tel] adj. 黏膜骨膜的

nasoalveolar [nə'səulviələ] adj. 鼻牙槽的

nitrate ['naitreit] n. 硝酸盐

obstetricians [ˌɒbstə'triʃ(ə)n] n. 产科医师

orthognathic [əθəg'næθik] n. 正颌学的

orthopedics [ˌɔ:θə'pi:diks] n. 矫形术

retinoids [riti'nɔidz] n. 类视黄醇

septoplasty [septəup'læsti] n. 鼻中隔成形术

tubercle ['tju:bək(ə)l] n. 结节

主要短语

Cupid's bow　唇弓

frontonasal prominence　额鼻突

maxillar prominence　上颌突

mandibular Prominence 下颌突
mucosal flap 黏膜瓣
prenatal diagnosis 产前诊断

王小兵

18

Microtia

小　耳　症

What is microtia?

Microtia is a congenital deformity where the pinna (external ear) is underdeveloped. A completely undeveloped pinna is referred to as anotia. Because microtia and anotia have the same origin, it can be referred to asmicrotia-anotia. Microtia can be unilateral (one side only) or bilateral (affecting both sides). Microtia occurs in 1 out of about 8,000–10,000 births. In unilateral microtia, the right ear is most commonly affected. It may occur as a complication of taking Accutane (isotretinoin) during pregnancy.

What causes microtia?

Variabale degrees of penetrance of the gene responsible for hypoplasia account for the different sizes of microtic remnants seen. Even with extremely small microtic remnants, a lobular component is almost present, although vertically oriented and superiorly displaced.

Anotia, the severest of ear deformities, is extremely rare and probably represents complete failure of development of the auricular helix through a lack of mesenchymal proliferation. Other severe form of microtia probably represent arrests in embryonic development occurring at approximately 6-8 weeks of gestation. Less extreme forms of microtia are likely the result of embryonic accidents at a later stage, around the third month of fetal development.

What are symptoms of microtia?

Classification

Many attempts have been made to classify microtia based on embryologic development and severity of deformity.

Current system (Nagata, Tanzer) divides categories based on surgical correction of the deformity.

- Anotia: absence of auricular tissue
- Lobular type: remnant ear with lobule and helix but without concha, acoustic

meatus, or tragus.
- Conchal type: remnant ear and lobule with concha, acoustic meatus, and tragus.
- Small conchal type: remnant ear and lobule with small indentation of concha.
- Atypical microtia: cases that do not fall into the previous categories.

Associated conditions

Atresia of the cartilaginous or bony external canal is commonly associated with microtia. The atresia ranges from complete absence to several degrees of narrowing, blind pouches, or tracts. In Tanzer's series all patients had some deformity of the ear canal, middle ear, or both, and 50% had overt evidence of the first and second branchial arch syndrome (hemifacial microsomia).

Studies suggest that isolated microtia may represent the mildest phenotypic expression of hemifacial microsomia. In addition, there is increasing evidence that hemifacial microsomia, Goldenhar's syndrome, and oculoauriculovertebral dysplasia (OAV) are variants of the same condition, with a phenotypic spectrum of severity including various degrees of microtia.

How is microtia diagnosed?

There are four grades of microtia:

Grade I: A less than complete development of the external ear with identifiable structures and a small but present external ear canal.

Grade II: A partially developed ear (usually the top portion is underdeveloped) with a closed (stenotic) external ear canal producing a conductive hearing loss.

Grade III: Absence of the external ear with a small peanut-like vestige structure and an absence of the external ear canal and ear drum. Grade III microtia is the most common form of microtia.

Grade IV: Absence of the total ear or anotia.

How is it treated?

The goal of medical intervention is to provide the best form and function to the underdeveloped ear.

Hearing

Typically, testing is first done to determine the quality of hearing. This can be done as early as in the first two weeks with a BAER test (Brain Auditory Evoked Response Test). At age 5–6, CT or "CAT Scans" of the middle ear can be done to elucidate its development and clarify which patients are appropriate candidates for surgery to improve hearing. For younger individuals, this is done under sedation.

The hearing loss associated with congenital **aural atresia** is a conductive hearing loss—hearing loss caused by inefficient conduction of sound to the inner ear. Essentially, children with aural atresia have hearing loss because the sound cannot travel into the (usually) healthy inner ear—there is no ear canal, no eardrum, and the small ear bones (malleus/hammer, incus/anvil, and stapes/stirrup) are underdeveloped. "Usually" is in parentheses because rarely, a child with atresia also has a malformation of the inner ear leading to a sensorineural hearing loss (as many as 19% in one study). Sensorineural hearing loss is caused by a problem in the inner ear, the cochlea. Sensorineural hearing loss is not correctable by surgery, but properly fitted and adjusted hearing amplification (hearing aids) generally provide excellent rehabilitation for this hearing loss. If the hearing loss is severe to profound in both ears, the child may be a candidate for a cochlear implant (beyond the scope of this discussion).

Unilateral sensorineural hearing loss was not generally considered a serious disability by the medical establishment before the nineties; it was thought that the afflicted person was able to adjust to it from birth. In general, there are exceptional advantages to gain from an intervention to enable hearing in the microtic ear, especially in bilateral microtia. Children with untreated unilateral sensorineural hearing loss are more likely to have to repeat a grade in school and/or need supplemental services than their peers.

Children with unilateral sensorineural hearing loss often require years of speech therapy in order to learn how to enunciate and understand spoken language. What is truly unclear, and the subject of an ongoing research study, is the effect of unilateral conductive hearing loss (in children with unilateral aural atresia) on scholastic performance. If atresia surgery or some form of amplification is not used, special steps should be taken to ensure that the child is accessing and understanding all of the verbal information presented in school settings. Recommendations for improving a child's hearing in the academic setting include preferential seating in class, an FM system (the teacher wears a microphone, and the sound is transmitted to a speaker at the child's desk or to an ear bud or hearing aid the child wears), a bone conducting hearing aid, or conventional hearing aids. Age for BAHA implantation depends on whether you are in Europe (18 months) or the US (age 5). Until then it is possible to fit a Baha on a softband.

It is important to note that not all children with aural atresia are candidates for atresia repair. Candidacy for atresia surgery is based on the hearing test (audiogram) and CT scan imaging. If a canal is built where one does not exist, minor complications can arise from the body's natural tendency to heal an open wound closed. Repairing aural atresia is a very detailed and complicated surgical procedure which requires an expert in atresia repair. While complications from this surgery can arise, the risk of complications is greatly reduced when using a highly experienced otologist. Atresia patients who opt for surgery will temporarily have the canal packed with gelatin sponge and silicone sheeting to prevent closure. It must be stressed that many surgeons believe that ear canal reconstruction is unnecessary and overcomplicated and that very good hearing is possible with modern hearing aids which can be hidden under the skin.

In cases where a later surgical reconstruction of the external ear of the child might be possible, positioning of the Baha implant is critical. It may be necessary to position the implant further back than usual to enable successful reconstructive surgery – but not so far as to compromise hearing performance. If the reconstruction is ultimately successful, it is easy to remove the percutaneous BAHA abutment. If the surgery is unsuccessful, the abutment can be replaced and the implant re-activated to restore hearing.

Related conditions

Aural atresia is the underdevelopment of the middle ear and canal and usually occurs in conjunction with microtia. Atresia occurs because patients with microtia may not have an external opening to the ear canal, though. However, the cochlea and other inner ear structures are usually present. The grade of microtia usually correlates to the degree of development of the middle ear. Microtia is usually isolated, but may occur in conjunction with hemifacial microsomia, Goldenhar Syndrome or Treacher-Collins Syndrome. It is also occasionally associated with kidney abnormalities (rarely life-threatening), and jaw problems, and more rarely, heart defects and vertebral deformities.

External ear

For auricular reconstruction, there are several different options:

Rib Cartilage Graft Reconstruction: This surgery may be performed by specialists in the technique. It involves sculpting the patient's own rib cartilage into the form of an ear. Because the cartilage is the patient's own living tissue, the reconstructed ear continues to grow as the child does. This surgery varies from two to four stages depending on the surgeon's preferred method. The major advantage of this surgery is that the patient's own tissue is used for the reconstruction.

Timing of surgery

Middle ear and auricular reconstructive procedures are planned jointly by the otologist and the plastic surgeon, and the timing of the surgery takes into account the hearing status of the patient as well as cosmetic considerations with its psychological sequelae. As plastic surgeons, we will focus on factors that determine the appropriate time for reconstructing the external ear, namely (a) rate at with costal cartilage develops; (b) risk of the child's becoming a target of ridicule; and (c) corresponding size between the fabricated framework and the normal ear.

It is generally agreed that by about age 6 affected children become targets of ridicule by their peers. At that age the child is aware of being different and is motivated to conform, which will make him/her more cooperative with the surgery and the restrictions it entails. Before age 6 there may not be sufficient rib cartilage to build an ear framework of the proper vertical dimension and horizontal projection. The ear reaches approximately 85% of its full size by age 6, 90% by age 9, and 95% by age 14. Approximately 88%-94% of the adult ear width is reached in the first year of life, and girl's ears grow faster than boys'. With respect to ear length, the figure is 75% by the end of year 1 and 93% by age 10. The ear continues to grow longer over the next decade, although for practical purposes the ear is considered to be almost fully developed at age 6. According to the facts above, the generally recommended time for surgery is 6-7 age.

Reconstruct the ear using a polyethylene plastic implant (also called Medpor): This is a 1–2 stage surgery that can start at age 3 and can be done as an outpatient without hospitalization. Using the porous framework, which allows the patient's tissue to grow into the material and the patient's own tissue flap, a new ear is constructed in a single surgery. A small second surgery is performed in 3–6 months if needed for minor adjustments. This surgery should only be performed by experts in the techniques involved.

Ear Prosthesis: An auricular (ear) prosthesis is custom made by an anaplastologist to mirror the other ear. Prosthetic ears can appear very realistic. They require a few minutes of daily care. They are typically made of silicone, which is colored to match the surrounding skin and can be attached using either adhesive or with titanium screws inserted into the skull to which the prosthetic is attached with a magnetic or bar/clip type system. These screws are the same as the BAHA (bone anchored hearing aid) screws and can be placed simultaneously. The biggest advantage over any surgery is having a prosthetic ear that allows the affected ear to appear as normal as possible to the natural ear. The biggest disadvantage is the daily care involved and knowing that the prosthesis is not real.

Complications

The possible complications of microtia surgery are as follows:skin loss, infection, hematoma, chest wall donor site complications such as pneumothorax, atelectasis, hypertrophic scar.

中英文注释

关键词汇
abutment [ə'bʌtmənt] n. 邻接

accutane ['ækjuːtein] n.（青春痘特效药）异维甲酸

anotia [æ'nəutə] n. 无耳，无耳畸形

atresia [eit'riːziə] n. 闭锁畸形

concha ['kɒŋkə] n. 外耳，耳甲

cochlea ['kɒkliə] n. 耳蜗

hypoplasia [,haipəʊ'pleizjə] n. 发育不全

isotretinoin [aisətriti'nɔin] n. 异维甲酸

lobular ['lɔbjulə] adj. 有小叶的

microtia ['maikrətiːə] n. 小耳症

mesenchymal [mes'eŋkiməl] adj. 间叶细胞的

percutaneous [,pɜːkjuː'teiniəs] adj. 经由皮肤的

pinna ['pinə] n. 耳廓

polyethylene [,pɒli'eθəliːn] n. 聚乙烯

prosthesis [prɒs'θiːsis] n. 假体

scholastic [skə'læstik] adj. 学术的

tragus ['treigəs] n. 耳屏

主要短语

acoustic meatus 听道

auricular helix 耳轮

ear bones:malleus/hammer, incus/anvil, stapes/stirrup 耳骨：锤骨，砧骨，镫骨

ear drum 耳鼓膜

hemifacial microsomia 半侧面部发育不良

王小兵

19 — Scar

瘢　痕

What is scar?

Scars are areas of fibrous tissue that replace normal skin after injury. A scar results from the biological process of wound repair in the skin and other tissues of the body. Thus, scarring is a natural part of the healing process. With the exception of very minor lesions, every wound results in some degree of scarring. An exception to this is animals with regeneration, which do not form scars and the tissue will grow back exactly as before.

Scar tissue is the exact same protein (collagen) as the tissue that it replaces, but the fiber composition of the protein is different; instead of a random basket weave formation of the collagen fibers found in normal tissue, in fibrosis the collagen cross-links and forms a pronounced alignment in a single direction. This collagen scar tissue alignment is usually of inferior functional quality to the normal collagen randomised alignment. For example, scars in the skin are less resistant to ultraviolet radiation, and sweat glands and hair follicles do not grow back within scar tissues. A myocardial infarction, commonly known as a heart attack, causes scar formation in the heart muscle, which leads to loss of muscular power and possibly heart failure. However, there are some tissues (e.g. bone) that can heal without any structural or functional deterioration.

What causes scar?

If a wound becomes covered with epithelial tissue within two weeks, minimal collagen will be deposited and no scar will form. Generally, if a wound takes longer than three to four weeks to become covered, a scar will form. Deep second-degree burns heal with scarring and hair loss. Sweat glands do not form in scar tissue, which impairs the regulation of body temperature.

The scar is a result of the body's repair mechanism after injury in many tissues.

Any injury does not become a scar until the wound has completely healed; this can take many months, or years in the worst pathological cases, such as keloids. To begin to patch the damage, a clot is created; the clot is the beginning process that results in a provisional matrix. In the process, the first layer is a provisional matrix and is not scar. Over time, the wounded body tissue then over expresses collagen inside the provisional matrix to create a collagen matrix. This collagen over expression continues and crosslinks the fiber arrangement inside the collagen matrix, making the collagen dense. This densely packed collagen, morphing into an inelastic whitish collagen scar wall, blocks off cell communication and regeneration; as a result, the new tissue generated will have a different texture and quality than the surrounding unwounded tissue. This prolonged collagen-producing process results in a fortuna scar.

The scarring is created by fibroblast proliferation, a process that begins with a reaction to the clot.

To mend the damage, fibroblasts slowly form the collagen scar. The fibroblast proliferation is circular and cyclically, the fibroblast proliferation lays down thick, whitish collagen inside the provisional and collagen matrix, resulting in the abundant production of packed collagen on the fibers giving scars their uneven texture. Over time, the fibroblasts continue to crawl around the matrix, adjusting more fibers and, in the process, the scarring settles and becomes stiff. This fibroblast proliferation also contracts the tissue. In unwounded tissue, these fibers are not over expressed with thick collagen and do not contract.

The fibroblast involved in scarring and contraction is the myofibroblast, which is a specialized contractile fibroblast. These cells express a-smooth muscle actin (a-SMA).

The myofibroblasts are absent in the first trimester in the embryonic stage; damage then heals scar free; small incisional or excision wounds less than 2 mm also heal without scarring; and in adult unwounded tissues where the fibroblast in itself is arrested; however, the myofibroblast is found in massive numbers in adult wound healing which heals with a scar. The myofibroblasts make up a high proportion of the fibroblasts proliferating in the postembryonic wound at the onset of healing. In the rat model, for instance, myofibroblasts can constitute up to 70% of the fibroblasts, and is responsible for fibrosis on tissue. Generally, the myofibroblasts disappear from the wound within 30 days, but can stay around in pathological cases in hypertrophy, such as keloids.

Prolonged inflammation, as well as the fibroblast proliferation can occur. Redness that often follows an injury to the skin is not a scar, and is generally not permanent (see wound healing). The time it takes for this redness to dissipate may, however, range from a few days to, in some serious and rare cases, a few years.

Scars form differently based on the location of the injury on the body and the age of the person who was injured. The worse the initial damage is, the worse the scar will generally be.

　　Skin scars occur when the dermis (the deep, thick layer of skin) is damaged. Most skin scars are flat and leave a trace of the original injury that caused them.

　　Wounds allowed to heal secondarily tend to scar worse than wounds from primary closure.

What are the symptoms of scar?

　　All scarring is composed of the same collagen as the tissue it has replaced, but the composition of the scar tissue, compared to the normal tissue, is different. Scars differ from other scars in the amounts of collagen overexpressed. Labels have been applied to the differences in overexpression. Two of the most common types are hypertrophic and keloid scarring, both of which experience excessive stiff collagen bundled growth overextending the tissue, blocking off regeneration of tissues. Another form is atrophic scarring (sunken scarring), which also has an overexpression of collagen blocking regeneration. This scar type is sunken, because the collagen bundles do not overextend the tissue. Stretch marks (striae) are regarded as scars by some.

Hypertrophic scars

　　Hypertrophic scars occur when the body overproduces collagen, which causes the scar to be raised above the surrounding skin. Hypertrophic scars take the form of a red raised lump on the skin. They usually occur within 4 to 8 weeks following wound infection or wound closure with excess tension and/or other traumatic skin injuries.

Keloid scars

　　Keloid scars are a more serious form of hypertrophic scarring, because they can grow indefinitely into large, tumorous (although benign) neoplasms. Hypertrophic scars are often distinguished from keloid scars by their lack of growth outside the original wound area, but this commonly taught distinction can lead to confusion. Keloid scars are all hypertrophic, but "only a small percentage of hypertrophic scars" are keloid.

　　Keloid scars can occur on anyone, but they are most common in dark-skinned people. They can be caused by surgery, accident, acne or, sometimes, body piercings. In some people, keloid scars form spontaneously. Although they can be a cosmetic problem, keloid scars are only inert masses of collagen and therefore completely harmless and not cancerous. However, they can be itchy or painful in some individuals. They tend to be most common on the shouldersand chest. Hypertrophic scars and its subset keloids tend to be more common in wounds closed by secondary intention.

Atrophic scars

　　An atrophic scar takes the form of a sunken recess in the skin, which has a pitted appearance. These are caused when underlying structures supporting the skin, such as fat or muscle, are lost. This type of scarring is often associated with acne, chickenpox, other diseases [especially Staphylococcus (or MRSA) infection], surgery, or accidents.

Stretch marks

Stretch marks (technically called striae) are also a form of scarring. These are caused when the skin is stretched rapidly (for instance during pregnancy, significant weight gain, or adolescent growth spurts), or when skin is put under tension during the healing process, (usually near joints). This type of scar usually improves in appearance after a few years.

Elevated corticosteroid levels are implicated in striae development.

How is it treated?

Early and effective treatment of acne scarring can prevent severe acne and the scarring that often follows. High melanin levels and either African or Asian ancestry may make adverse scarring more noticeable. As of 2004 no prescription drugs for the treatment or prevention of scars were available.

Collagen Induction Therapy

Collagen induction therapy (CIT) is an aesthetic medical procedure that involves repeatedly puncturing the skin with tiny, sterile needles. Typically, this is done with a specialized device called a microneedling device. CIT is often referred to as "microneedling" or "skin needling" in media and literature.

Chemical peels

Chemical peels are chemicals which destroy the epidermis in a controlled manner, leading to exfoliation and the alleviation of certain skin conditions, including superficial acne scars. Various chemicals can be used depending upon the depth of the peel, and caution should be used, particularly for dark-skinned individuals and those individuals susceptible to keloid formation or with active infections.

Filler injections

Filler injections of collagen or Artefill can be used to raise atrophic scars to the level of surrounding skin. Risks vary based upon the filler used, and can include temporary improvement, further disfigurement, and allergic reaction.

Dermabrasion

Dermabrasion involves the removal of the surface of the skin with special equipment, and usually involves a local anaesthetic.

Laser treatment

Nonablative lasers, such as the 585 nm pulsed dye laser, 1064 nm and 1320 nm Nd:YAG, or the 1540 nm Er: Glass are used as the standard laser therapy for hypertrophic scars and keloids. This therapy smooths the epidermis via contact cooling.

Multiple sessions are usually required for a significant reduction in redness and improvement in the texture and pliability of hypertrophic scars and keloids.

Ablative lasers such as the carbon dioxide laser or Er:YAG offer the best results for atrophic and acne scars. Like dermabrasion, ablative lasers work by destroying the epidermis to a certain depth. Healing times for ablative therapy are much longer and the risk profile is greater compared to nonablative therapy; however, nonablative therapy offers only minor improvements in cosmetic appearance of atrophic and acne scars.

Radiotherapy

Low-dose, superficial radiotherapy is sometimes used to prevent recurrence of severe keloid and hypertrophic scarring. It is thought to be effective despite a lack of clinical trials, but only used in extreme cases due to the perceived risk of long-term side effects.

Semiocclusive ointments and pressure dressing

Silicone scar treatments are commonly used in preventing scar formation and improving existing scar appearance. The effectiveness and safety of silicone sheeting for the treatment and prevention of scars is supported by an abundance of clinical studies.

Semiocclusive, silicone-based ointments are used to speed healing and reduce the appearance of scars, and likely work in a similar manner as silicone scar sheets.

Pressure dressings are commonly used in managing burn and hypertrophic scars, although supporting evidence is lacking. These involve elastic materials or gauze to apply pressure to the area. For large scars and particularly large burns, pressure garments may be worn. They are believed to work by applying constant pressure to surface blood vessels, and eventually causing scars to flatten and become softer. Retrospective and ultrasonic studies since the 1960s have supported their use, but the only randomized clinical trial found no statistically significant difference in wound healing. Care providers commonly report improvements, however, and pressure therapy has been effective in treating ear keloids. The general acceptance of the treatment as effective may prevent it from being further studied in clinical trials.

Steroids

Under medical supervision, a long-term course of corticosteroid injections into the scar may help flatten and soften the appearance of keloid or hypertrophic scars.

The steroid is injected into the scar itself; since very little is absorbed into the blood stream, side effects of this treatment are minor. However, it does cause thinning of the scar tissue so it does carry risks when injected into scars caused by operations into ruptured tendons. This treatment is repeated at four- to six-week intervals.

Topical steroids are ineffective.

Surgery

Scar revision is a process of cutting the scar tissue out. After the excision, the new wound is usually closed up to heal byprimary intention, instead of secondary intention. Deeper cuts need a multilayered closure to heal optimally, otherwise depressed or dented scars can result.

Surgical excision of hypertrophic or keloid scars is often associated to other methods, such as pressotherapy or silicone gel sheeting. Lone excision of keloid scars, however, shows a recurrence rate close to 45%. A clinical study is currently ongoing to assess the benefits of a treatment combining surgery and laser-assisted healing in hypertrophic or keloid scars.

Vitamins

Research shows the use of vitamin E and onion extract (sold as Mederma) as treatments for scars is ineffective. Vitamin E causes contact dermatitis in up to 33% of users and in some cases it may worsen scar appearance. But Vitamin C and some of its esters fade the dark pigment associated with some scars.

中英文注释

关键词汇

dermatitis [ˌdɜːməˈtaitis] n. 皮炎

dissipate [ˈdisipeit] v. 消散

exfoliation [eksˌfəuliˈeiʃən] n. 表皮脱落

hypertrophic [ˌhaipəˈtrɔfik] adj. 肥厚的

melanin [ˈmelənin] n. 黑色素

neoplasm [ˈniːə(ʊ)plæz(ə)m] n. 肿瘤

nonablative [nʌnˈæblətiv] adj. 非剥离性

striae [stˈraiiː] n. 条纹

sunken [ˈsʌŋkən] adj. 凹陷的

主要短语

allergic reaction 变态反应

atrophic scars 萎缩性瘢痕

collagen matrix 胶原基质

epithelial tissue 上皮组织

hair follicles 毛囊

hypertrophic scars 增生性瘢痕

keloid scars 瘢痕疙瘩

myocardial infarction 心肌梗死

sweat glands 汗腺
sunken scarring 凹陷性瘢痕
ultraviolet radiation 紫外辐射

王小兵

20 — Vascular Anomalies

血 管 畸 形

What is vascular anomalies?

A vascular anomaly is a kind of birthmark caused by a disorder of the vascular development, although it is not always present at birth. A vascular anomaly is a localized defect in blood vessels that can affect each part of the vasculature (capillaries, arteries, veins, lymphatics or a combination of these). These defects are characterized by an increased number of vessels and vessels that are both enlarged and sinuous. Some vascular anomalies are congenital and therefore present at birth, others appear within weeks to years after birth and others are acquired by trauma or during pregnancy. Inherited vascular anomalies are also described and often present with a number of lesions that increase with patients' age. Vascular anomalies can also be a part of a syndrome and, occasionally, they can be acquired by trauma. The estimated prevalence of vascular anomalies is 4.5%. Vascular anomalies can occur throughout the whole body (skin, bone, liver, intestines, i.e.), but in 60% of patients vascular anomalies are localized in the head and neck region.

How is vascular anomalies classified?

Vascular anomalies can present in various ways. Vascular anomalies that are situated deep below the skin, appear blue and are often called cavernous. Superficial vascular anomalies appear as red-coloured stains and are associated with vascular anomalies affecting the dermis. Historically, vascular anomalies have been labeled with descriptive terms, according to the food they resembled (port wine, strawberry, cherry, salmon patch). This imprecise terminology has caused diagnostic confusion, blocked communication and even caused incorrect treatment, as it does not differentiate between various vascular anomalies.

However, in 1982, Mulliken introduced a classification that replaced these descriptive terms and gave direction to the management of various vascular anomalies. This classification, based on clinical features, natural history and cellular characteristics, divides vascular anomalies into two groups: hemangiomas and vascular malformations.

Although the appearance of both hemangiomas and vascular malformations can resemble, there are important differences between both.

How is hemangiomas classified and treated?

Hemangiomas are the most common tumors in infants, occurring in 1-2%. Prevalence is even higher (10%) in premature infants of very low birth weight. Vascular tumors are characterized by overgrowth of normal vessels, which show increased endothelial proliferation. It can be present at birth, but often appears within a couple of weeks after birth or during infancy. There are different kinds of vascular tumors, but the 4 most common types are: infantile hemangioma, congenital hemangioma, kaposiform hemangioendothelioma and pyogenic granuloma.

Infantile Hemangioma
What is infantile hemangioma?

Infantile hemangioma (IH) is the most common vascular tumor. It is a benign tumor, which occurs in 4%-5% of Caucasian infants, but rarely in dark skinned infants. It occurs in 20% of low weight premature infants and 2.2 to 4.5 times more frequently in females. IH most commonly presents in the head and neck regio (60%), but also involves the trunk and extremities. One third of these lesions is present at birth as a telangiectatic stain or ecchymotic area. During the first four weeks of life, 70% to 90% appear. Lesions that are situated beneath the skin may not appear until 3 to 4 months of age, when the tumor is large enough. During the first 9 months, IH undergoes rapidly growth, which is faster than the growth of the child. This is called the proliferating phase. After 9 months, the growth of the tumor will decrease and equal the growth of the child for about 3 months. After 12 months, the tumor will start to involute and might even disappear. Involution occurs in one-third of patient by the age of 3 years, in 50% by the age of 5 years and in 72% by the age of 7 years. Involution may result in residual telangiectasis, pallor, atrophy, textural changes and sometimes fibrofatty residuum. Since 90% of IH is small, localized and asymptomatic, treatment mainly consists of observation and awaiting until involution is complete. IH can be treated with corticosteroids, which accelerate involution: in 95% of patients, growth is stabilized and 75% of tumors decrease in size.

How is infantile hemangioma treated?

Intralesional corticosteroids are most effective, but may require additional injections, as the effect is only temporarily. Systemic corticosteroids may cause lost of side-effects and are only used in problematic IH, which is too large to treat with intralesional injections. During the proliferating phase, the tumor is highly vascular. Patients who undergo operative treatment during this period, are at risk for blood loss. Moreover, surgery during this phase, often leads to an inferior aesthetic outcome. However, patients may require intervention during childhood, because 50% of IH leave residual fibrofatty tissue, redundant skin, or damaged structures after involution. Waiting until involution is completed, ensures that the least amount of fibro fatty residuum and excess skin is resected, giving the smallest possible scar. Another option for treatment in the pulsed-dye laser. After involution residual telangiectasias can be treated with laser therapy.

Congenital Hemangioma
What is congenital hemangioma?

Congenital hemangioma can be distinguished from infantile hemangioma because it is fully developed at birth. It forms during prenatal life and has reached its maximal size at birth. Congenital hemangioma can even be diagnosed in utero by prenatal ultrasound. Unlike IH, CH is more common in the extremities, has an equal sex distribution, and is solitary, with an average diameter of 5cm. It commonly presents in the head and neck and in the lower extremities. Congenital hemangioma are divided into 2 subgroups: the rapidly involuting congenital hemangiomas (RICHs) and the non-involuting congenital hemangiomas (NICHs).

The rapidly involuting congenital hemangioma, RICH, presents at birth as a solitary raised tumor with a central depression, scar, or ulceration surrounded by a rim of pallor. It is noted for its involution, which typically begins several weeks after birth and is completed no later than 14 months of age. After regression RICH may cause a residual deformity, such as atrophic skin and subcutaneous tissue. It mainly affects the limbs (52%), but also the head and neck region (42%) and the trunk (6%).

The non-involuting congenital hemangioma, NICH, presents as a solitary, well-circumscribed reddish-pink to purple plaque with central telangiectasia and hypopigmented rim. In contrast to RICH, NICH does not involute and rarely ulcerates. It persists into late childhood and can even mimic a vascular malformation by growing commensurately with the child. Although NICH can resemble RICH in its external appearance, it can be differentiated from RICH by a greater elevation and coarse telangiectases. It mainly affects the head and neck region (43%), but also the limbs (38%) and the trunk (19%).

How is congenital hemangioma treated?

Surgical resection for congenital hemangiomas is rarely needed, because RICH undergoes postnatal regression and NICH is benign and often asymptomatic. Resection may be indicated to improve the appearance of the affected area, as long as the surgical scar is less noticeable than the lesion. Other indications are problematic ulcers with persistent bleeding or chronic infection. Although most NICH lesions are non-problematic and do not cause significant deformity, the threshold for resection of NICH is lower, because it neither involutes, nor responds to pharmacotherapy. RICH tumors are observed until involution is completed. Involuted RICH may leave behind atrophic tissue, which can be reconstructed with autologous grafts. It is often best to postpone excision until regression is complete. There are effective pharmacologic treatments, which include intralesional corticosteroid injection, systemic corticosteroid injection, interferon α-2a or α-2b and angiogenic inhibitors. The use of corticosteroids leads to accelerated regression in 30%, stabilization of growth in 40%, lightening of color and softening of the tumor. However, 30% shows minimal or no response. Another drug treatment is interferon α-2a or α-2b. It is often used for patients who did not respond to corticosteroids. Although the response rate is much slower, it has been successful for 80% of children treated. The most serious side effect of interferon is a spastic diplegia. Other therapeutic options are embolization and pulsed-dye laser, which improves residual telangiectasis in RICH and in NICH.

Kaposiform Hemangioendothelioma
What is kaposiform hemangioendothelioma?

Kaposiform hemangioendothelioma (KHE) is a rare vascular neoplasm that is locally aggressive but without metastatic potential. It occurs particularly in the skin, deep soft tissue, retroperitoneum, mediastinum, and rarely in bone. Although lesions occur solitary, they often involve large areas of the body, such as the head/neck region (40%), trunk (30%), or extremity (30%). Usually, it is present at birth as a flat, reddish-purple, tense and edematouslesion. Although half of lesions are congenital, 58% of KHE develop during infancy, 32% between age 1 and 10 years (32%) and 10% after 11 years of age. Moreover, adult onset has been described too with mainly males being affected. Both sexes are affected equally in children. Lesions are often greater than 5 cm in diameter and can cause visible deformity and pain. During early childhood, KHE may enlarge and after 2 years of age, it may partially regress. Though, it usually persists longterm. In addition, 50% of patients suffer from coagulopathy due to thrombocytopenia (<25,000/mm3), presenting with petechiae and bleeding. This is called the Kasabach-Meritt Phenomenon, which is caused by trapping of platelets and other clotting factors within the tumor. Kasabach-Meritt Phenomenon is less likely in patients with lesions less than 8 cm. As two-thirds of adult-onset KHE tumors are less than 2 cm, KHE in adults is rarely associated with Kasabach-Meritt Phenomenon. Patients with KHE and Kasabach-Meritt Phenomenon present with. Most KHE tumors are diffuse involving multiple tissue planes and important structures. Resection of KHE is thus often difficult.

How is it treated?

Treatment of kaposiform hemangioendothelioma is therefore medical. The primary drug is interferon alfa, which is successful in 50% of children. Another option is vincristine, which has lots of side-effects, but has a response rate of 90%. Drug therapy is often used in shrinking the tumor and treating the coagulopathy. However, many of these kaposiform hemangioendotheliomas do not completely regress and remain as a much smaller asymptomatic tumor. However, KHE still has a high mortality rate of 30%. Although complete surgical removal with a large margin has the best reported outcome, it is usually not done because of the risk of bleeding, extensiveness, and the anatomic site of the lesion. Operative management may be possible for small or localized lesions. Removal of larger areas also may be indicated for symptomatic patients or for patients who have failed farmacotherapy. Resection is not required for lesions that are not causing functional problems, because KHE is benign and because resection could cause deformity.

Pyogenic granuloma
What is pyogenic granuloma?

Pyogenic granuloma, also known as lobular capillary hemangioma, is a small benign vascular tumor that primarily involves the skin (88.2%) and mucous membranes. Pyogenic granuloma appears as a red macule that grows rapidly, turns into a papule and eventually becomes pedunculated, being attached to a narrow stalk. The average diameter of these lesions is 6.5 mm. Although these lesions are small, they are often complicated by bleeding, crusting and ulceration. Microscopically, pyogenic granulomas are characterized by vascular proliferation amidst granulation tissue and chronic inflammatory infiltrate. Pyogenic granulomas are rarely congenital. It commonly develops in infants: 42.1% develops within the first 5 years of life. This vascular tumor is twice as common in males as in females and 25% of lesions seem to be associated with trauma, an underlying cutaneous condition, pregnancy, hormonal alterations and medications. Pyogenic granulomas can also arise within a capillary malformation. Of all pyogenic granulomas, 62% is distributed on the head or neck, occurring mainly on the cheek and in the oral cavity. Lesions on the face may cause visible deformity.

How is it treated?

Numerous treatment methods have been described for pyogenic granuloma. Lesions involving the reticular dermis, may be out of the reach of pulsed-dye laser, cautery or shave excision and therefore have a recurrence rate of 43.5%. Definitive management requires full-thickness skin excision. Other options arecurrettage or laser therapy. Furthermore, thorough curettage and cauterization are often used for small lesions and full-thickness excision for larger lesion.

How is vascular malformations classified and treated?

Vascular malformation is a collective term for different disorders of the vasculature (errors in vascular development). It can be a disorder of the capillaries, arteries, venes and lymphs or a disorder of a combination of these (lesions were named based on the primary vessel that was malformed). A vascular malformation consists of a clew of deformed vessels, due to an error in the vascular development (dysmorphogenesis). However, endothelial turnover is stable in these defects. Congenital vascular malformations are always present at birth, although they are not always visible. In contrast to vascular tumors, vascular malformations do not have a growth phase, nor an involution phase. Vascular malformations tend to grow proportionately with the child. Vascular malformations never regress, but persist throughout life. Vascular malformations can be divided in slow-flow vascular malformations, fast-flow vascular malformations and complex-combined vascular malformations.

Slow-flow vascular malformations

Capillary malformation (also known as port-wine stain): Capillary malformations are flat, reddish lesions that typically affect the skin, mostly around the head and the neck, who darken with age, contrary to birthmarks such assalmon patch, Nevus simplex or vascular stain, who lighten or disappear within the first few years of life. Capillary malformations are 11% of the vascular malformations. Syndromes associated with capillary malformations are: Sturge-Weber syndrome and Klippel-Trenaunay syndrome. Capillary malformations can be treated with IPL-(Intensed-pulsed-light)-therapy or surgical reduction.

Venous malformation is a bluish lesion compressible on palpation, the masses enlarge with physical activity or a dependent position. The bluish lesion is caused by dilated venous channels. Venous malformations can be painful in the morning due to stasis and microthrombi within the veins. Venous malformations' localization is usually in the head and neck. Venous malformations are the most common vascular anomaly, they are 40% of all vascular malformations Venous malformation can be treated with sclerotherapy and surgical reduction.

Lymphatic malformation is a benign growth of the lymphatic system. They result from a blockage or defect of the lymphatic vessels as they are forming. 28% of all vascular malformations consists of lymphatic malformations. Lymphatic malformations can be treated with sclerotherapy and surgical reduction.

Fast flow vascular malformtations

All fast flow malformations are malformations with an arterial type in it. Contain about 14% of the vascular malformations.

Arterial malformation

Arteriovenous fistula (AVF): a lesion with a direct transition in fistulas between an artery and a vein.

Arteriovenous malformation: a lesion with a direct connection between an artery and a vein, without an intervening capillary bed, but with an interposed nidus of dysplastic vascular channels in between.

Combined-complex vascular malformations

a combination of various vascular malformations. They are complex because they're a combination of two different types of vessels.

CVM: capillary venous malformation

CLM: capillary lymphatic malformation

LVM: lymphatic venous malformation

CLVM: capillary lymphatic venous malformation. CLVM is associated with Klippel-Trenaunay syndrome

AVM-LM: arteriovenous malformation- lymphatic malformation

CM-AVM: capillary malformation- arteriovenous malformation

Surgery is always operated to treat arteriovenous malformations. The procedure of treatment is as follows:

- Preoperative medical management of any underlying coagulation defect secondary to thrombotic consumption
- Preoperativeembolization followed by surgical resection within 72 hours
- Wide local excision because recurrence rates are very high
- Use of ischemic suture techniques, hypotensive anaesthesia, and even cardiopulmonary bypass control bleeding
- Post-excisional reconstruction with flaps often necessary

中英文注释

关键词汇

asymptomatic [əˌsimptə'mætik; ei-] adj. 无症状的

atrophic [æ'trɔfik] adj. 萎缩的

caucasian [kɔː'keiziən] n. 高加索人

cautery ['kɔːt(ə)ri] n. 烧灼

cavernous ['kævənəs] adj. 洞穴状的

coagulopathy [kəu,ægju'lɔpəθi] n. 凝血障碍

commensurately [kə'menʃərət] adv. 相当的，成比例的

ecchymotic [,eki'məʊsis] adj. 瘀斑的

ecchymosis [,eki'məʊsis] n. 瘀斑

granulation [,grænjʊ'leiʃən] n. 粗糙，使成粒状

hemangioendotheliomas [hi,mændʒiəu'endəu,θiːli'əumə] n. 血管内皮瘤

hypopigmented [haipʊpig'məntid] adj. 色素减少的

lobular ['lɔbjulə] adj. 有小叶的

mucous ['mjuːkəs] adj. 黏液的

petechiae [pi'tekiiː] n. 瘀点

postnatal ['pəʊst'neitl] adj. 出生后的

sclerotherapy [skliərəʊ'ðerəpi] n. 硬化疗法

sinuous ['sinjuəs] adj. 弯曲的

telangiectatic [telædʒi:k'tætik] adj. 毛细血管扩张的

telangiectasia [te,lændʒiek'teiziə] n. 毛细管扩张

thrombocytopenia [,θrɒmbə(ʊ),saitə(ʊ)'piːniə] n. 血小板减少（症）

主要短语

congenital hemangioma　先天性血管瘤

infantile hemangioma　婴儿性毛细血管瘤

kaposiform hemangioendothelioma　卡波西样血管内皮瘤

pyogenic granuloma　脓性肉芽肿

王小兵

Section Two: Internal Disease

第二部分　内科疾病

21 Arrhythmia (Heart Rhythm Disorders)
心 律 失 常

The primary function of the heart is to supply blood and nutrients to the body. The regular beating, or contraction, of the heart moves the blood throughout the body. Each heartbeat is controlled by electrical impulses traveling through the heart. In the normal heart these electrical impulses occur in regular intervals. When something goes wrong with the heart's electrical system, the heart does not beat regularly. The irregular beating results in a rhythm disorder, or arrhythmia.

The electrical system regulating heartbeat consists of two main areas of control and a series of conducting pathways, similar to the electrical wiring in a house.

- The sinoatrial, or SA, node is located in the right atrium. It is the source and main control and is the source of each heartbeat. The SA node responds to the body's overall need for blood and increases the heart rate when necessary, such as during exercise, emotional excitement, or illness such as fever. The SA node is sometimes called the "natural pacemaker" of the heart.
- Electrical impulses leave the SA node and travel through special conducting pathways in the heart to the other area of control, the atrioventricular (AV) node. The AV node provides a pathway for impulses from the atria to the ventricles. It also creates a delay in conduction from the atria to the ventricle. This causes the atria to contract first and allow the ventricles to fill with blood before they contract themselves.
- The delay ensures proper timing so that the lower chambers have time to fill completely before they contract.
- Normally, the heart beats 60-100 times a minute. This state is called "normal sinus rhythm" or "normal rhythm." Depending upon the needs of the body, it may beat faster (sinus tachycardia) due to stress or slower (sinus bradycardia) such as during sleep.

What are arrhythmias?

Arrhythmias are abnormalities of the heartbeat. There are many types of arrhythmias, and they are classified by where they begin, (the atria, AV node, or the

123

ventricles). Generally speaking, those that do not originate from the ventricles are called supraventricular arrhythmias while those that come from the ventricles are called ventricular arrhythmias.

The following are some of the more commonly encountered arrhythmias, starting with the supraventricular arrhythmias.

- Premature atrial contractions (sometimes called PACs, APCs, or premature supraventricular contractions): PACs are an extra heart beat arising from the atria, outside of the SA node, that causes the heart to contract earlier than expected. This is a very common occurrence in all ages and usually is not serious.

- Supraventricular tachycardia, or paroxysmal SVT: SVTs are regular, rapid heartbeats resulting from abnormal electrical impulses above the ventricle (usually the atria or the AV node).

- Sick sinus syndrome: This syndrome is characterized by irregular firing of the SA node resulting in both slower and faster-than-normal heart rates.

- Atrial fibrillation: A common condition caused by electrical impulses discharged at a rapid rate from many different areas of the atria. It usually causes a fast and irregular heartbeat.

- Atrial flutter: A condition caused by a rapid discharge of abnormal electrical impulses from the right atrium. Typically, the right atrium fires at a rate of 300 beats per minute, but only every other beat is conducted through the AV node, meaning that the ventricular rate is classically 150 beats per minute.

Arrhythmias arising in the ventricle are more likely to be found in people with more serious heart disease but may also be found in healthy individuals.

Premature ventricular complex, or PVCs: This abnormal electrical impulse arises from the ventricle, causing the heart to beat earlier than expected. Usually, the heart returns to its normal rhythm right away.

Ventricular tachycardia: Fast and usually regular impulses come from the ventricles and cause a very rapid heart rate. This is usually a life-threatening tachycardia and needs immediate medical attention and potentially treatment with an electrical shock or defibrillation.

Ventricular fibrillation: Electrical impulses arise from the ventricles in a fast and disordered sequence. The resulting uncoordinated contractions cause the heart to lose its ability to beat and pump blood. The condition usually causes fainting and collapse, and is fatal if not treated immediately.

Arrhythmias can be frightening, but in many cases, especially in younger patients with normal underlying hearts, they are not life threatening and can be effectively treated with medications.

Supraventricular arrhythmias are very common in middle-aged and elderly adults. The older you get, the more likely you are to experience an arrhythmia, especially atrial fibrillation.

Many supraventricular arrhythmias are temporary and not serious, especially if no underlying heart disease is present. These arrhythmias are a response to normal activities or emotions.

Even if an arrhythmia has a serious underlying cause, the arrhythmia itself may not be dangerous. The underlying problem can often be treated effectively.

What causes heart rhythm disorders?

Among individuals without known heart disease, arrhythmias are generally random, isolated occurrences that do not carry any significance. However, a discussion with a doctor is advised.

A variety of heart diseases cause arrhythmias. Heart disease can refer to patients with coronary artery disease, heart valve problems, heart failure, or disorders with heart conduction or high blood pressure. Remember, however, that having an arrhythmia does not necessarily mean that you have heart disease. Arrhythmias have many causes; sometimes the cause of an arrhythmia is never determined.

Sometimes, conditions other than heart disease may cause or aggravate arrhythmias. These conditions include the following:

- Infection or fever
- Physical or emotional stress
- Diseases such as anemia or thyroid disease
- Drugs and other stimulants, such as caffeine, tobacco, alcohol, cocaine, amphetamines, and certain over-the-counter and prescription medications
- Certain arrhythmias can be inherited as well

What are the symptoms of heart rhythm disorders?

Many arrhythmias cause no or minimal symptoms. Other people, however, can actually feel the arrhythmia when it happens.

Common symptoms include the following:

- Palpitations, feeling "skipped beats"
- Thumping or fluttering in the chest
- Sensation of the heart racing

In addition, some can experience the following:

- Feeling faint or tired

- Light-headedness or passing out (syncope)
- Shortness of breath
- Chest pain or discomfort

On the other hand, people may feel many of the sensations described above and have no arrhythmias whatsoever. These may be due to anxiety, stress, or other causes besides an abnormal heartbeat.

Most people have noticed their heart racing, a fluttering in the chest, or a sensation that the heart skipped a beat. If this happens once, or infrequently, with no other symptoms, it is usually not serious. However, any questions or concerns should be discussed with a health care provider. The health care provider should also be notified if a recommended treatment does not alleviate the symptoms.

More serious symptoms should be evaluated immediately at the nearest hospital emergency department. These symptoms include:

- Any unexplained shortness of breath
- Light-headedness or feeling faint
- Feeling that the heart is beating too slowly or too quickly
- Chest pain with any of these symptoms

How are rhythm disorders diagnosed?

Evaluation of heart rhythm disorders requires a discussion of symptoms and a physical exam with a health care provider.

In addition, an electrocardiogram (ECG) is mandatory to establish the exact type of arrhythmia. If the rhythm disturbance is present while the ECG is being recorded, the problem can be identified immediately. Otherwise, more specialized testing may be required. A 24-hour (or longer) recording of the heartbeat is often necessary to detect any rhythm problem that occurs daily but not constantly.

However, if the arrhythmia is even more infrequent, an event recorder may be used. These vary from hand-held machines that are activated by the patient whenever he or she feels symptoms, to some that are placed surgically under the skin and left there for up to one year.

An ultrasound of the heart, called an echocardiogram, is often used for an evaluation of the structure and function of the heart. In more serious cases, a test using electrodes placed inside the heart, called an electrophysiologic study (EPS), may be recommended to determine further management.

How are heart rhythm disorders treated?

The treatment of heart rhythm disorders varies depending on the presence or absence of symptoms, how frequent the arrhythmia occurs, and the seriousness of any underlying heart condition. The treatment may range from medication to more advanced surgical procedures, such as an internal implanted cardiac defibrillator (ICD). Sometimes no treatment is necessary. At times, simple or specialized pacemakers may be required to control arrhythmias.

A detailed discussion of the tests and treatment options should be done with the health care provider.

Medications for Heart Rhythm Disorders

The choice and use of medications depends on the specific type of heart rhythm disorder you have.

Follow-Up for Heart Rhythm Disorders

Follow-up for a heart rhythm disorder is usually done with the primary care provider and often with a heart specialist. The patient is monitored for effectiveness of treatment, recurrence of symptoms or arrhythmia, side effects of medication, additional routine testing, and overall condition. For those requiring pacemakers, follow-up on a regular basis is mandatory.

中英文注释

关键词汇

aggravate ['ægrəveit] vt. 加重, 恶化

alleviate [ə'li:vieit] vt. 减轻, 缓和

arrhythmia [ə'riθmiə] n. 心律不齐, 心律失常

fainting ['fentiŋ] n. 晕厥

mandatory ['mændətɔri] adj. 强制的, 命令的

palpitation [ˌpælpi'teʃnz] n. 心悸, 颤动

sinoatrial [ˌsainəu'etriəl] n. 窦房的

syncope ['siŋkəpi] n. 晕厥

主要短语

atrial fibrillation 心房纤颤

atrial flutter 心房扑动

atrioventricular node 房室结

conducting pathways 传导通路

electrical defibrillation 电除颤

electro physiologic study (EPS) 电生理学研究

emergency department 急诊科

implanted cardiac defibrillator (ICD) 植入心脏除颤器

normal sinus rhythm 正常窦性心律
premature atrial contractions 房性期前收缩
premature ventricular complex 室性期前收缩
sick sinus syndrome 病态窦房结综合征
sinus bradycardia 窦性心动过缓
sinus tachycardia 窦性心动过速
supraventricular tachycardia 室上性心动过速
ventricular fibrillation 室颤
ventricular tachycardia 室性心动过速

张 伟 马志方

22. Coronary Artery Disease (CAD)
冠 心 病

Coronary artery disease, also called coronary heart disease, or simply, heart disease, is the No. 1 killer in America, affecting more than 13 million Americans.

Heart disease is a result of plaque buildup in a person's arteries, which blocks blood flow and heightens the risk for heart attack and stroke.

What is coronary artery disease?

Heart disease is a result of plaque buildup in a person's coronary arteries — a condition called atherosclerosis — that leads to blockages. The arteries, which start out smooth and elastic, become narrow and rigid, restricting blood flow to the heart. The heart becomes starved of oxygen and the vital nutrients it needs to pump properly.

What causes coronary artery disease?

From a young age, cholesterol-laden plaque can start to deposit in the blood vessel walls. As you get older, the plaque burden builds up, inflaming the blood vessel walls and raising the risk of blood clots and heart attack. The plaques release chemicals that promote the process of healing but make the inner walls of the blood vessel sticky. Then, other substances, such as inflammatory cells, lipoproteins, and calcium that travel in your bloodstream start sticking to the inside of the vessel walls.

Eventually, a narrowed coronary artery may develop new blood vessels that go around the blockage to get blood to the heart. However, during times of increased exertion or stress, the new arteries may not be able to supply enough oxygen-rich blood to the heart muscle.

In some cases, a blood clot may totally block the blood supply to the heart muscle, causing heart attack. If a blood vessel to the brain is blocked, usually from a blood clot, an ischemic stroke can result. If a blood vessel within the brain bursts, most likely as a result of uncontrolled hypertension (high blood pressure), a hemorrhagic stroke can result.

What is ischemia?

Cardiac ischemia occurs when plaque and fatty matter narrow the inside of an artery to a point where it cannot supply enough oxygen-rich blood to meet your heart's needs. Heart attack can occur - with or without chest pain and other symptoms.

Ischemia is most commonly experienced during:

- Exercise or exertion
- Eating
- Excitement or stress
- Exposure to cold

Coronary artery disease can progress to a point where ischemia occurs even at rest. And ischemia can occur without any warning signs in anyone with heart disease, although it is more common in people with diabetes.

What are the symptoms of coronary artery disease?

The most common symptom of coronary artery disease is angina, or chest pain. Angina can be described as a heaviness, pressure, aching, burning, numbness, fullness, squeezing or painful feeling. It can be mistaken for indigestion or heartburn. Angina is usually felt in the chest, but may also be felt in the left shoulder, arms, neck, back, or jaw.

Other symptoms that can occur with coronary artery disease include:

- Shortness of breath
- Palpitations (irregular heart beats, skipped beats, or a "flip-flop" feeling in your chest)
- A faster heartbeat
- Weakness or dizziness
- Nausea
- Sweating

How is coronary artery disease diagnosed?

To find out if one person has or is at risk for coronary artery disease, the doctor will do a physical exam and check his risk based on his health and risk factors.

You may then have several different kinds of tests to check your risk for getting heart disease. If your doctor thinks you have heart disease, you will need more tests to make sure.

Tests to measure your risk for coronary artery disease

The main tests your doctor uses to check your risk for getting heart disease include:

- Blood pressure. High blood pressure increases your risk for heart disease.
- Cholesterol (a blood test). High cholesterol increases your risk for heart disease.

Your doctor will use your blood pressure, cholesterol, and other risk factors such as your age and if you smoke, to know your risk of heart disease. If you know your blood pressure and cholesterol levels, you can check your risk for a heart attack.

Other tests may help your doctor find out your risk for heart disease, especially when they are considered along with your other risk factors. But these tests are not helpful for everyone. Such tests may include:

- C-reactive protein (CRP) test. High CRP levels are linked to higher risk for heart disease.
- Coronary calcium scan. This test uses a special kind of X-ray to check for buildup of calcium in the heart's arteries. The result is a number, or score. If you have a high score, you may need more tests to check for heart disease or to find out how bad it is. For more information, see.

Sometimes doctors schedule routine tests because they think that's what patients expect. But experts say routine heart tests can be a waste of time and money. See the topic Heart Tests: When Do You Need Them?

Tests to diagnose coronary artery disease

If your doctor thinks you may have heart disease, you will need some tests to make sure. Most often, the first tests include:

- An electrocardiogram (EKG or ECG).
- A chest X-ray.
- Blood tests.
- An exercise electrocardiogram. This is also called a "stress test."

Other tests may include:

- Cardiac perfusion scan. This test shows if you have enough blood flow to the heart.
- Echocardiogram and stress echocardiogram. This test uses ultrasound to see areas of poor blood flow in the heart. It can also check how well your heart is working after a heart attack. The test can help your doctor find out how much blood your heart is pumping during each heartbeat (ejection fraction).
- Coronary angiogram. This is an X-ray test that creates pictures of the blood flow through your coronary arteries. It allows your doctor to see any blockage or narrowing of the artery. It's done using a soft, thin tube (catheter) that is put in a blood vessel in the arm or groin and gently moved into the heart. For more information, see the topic.
- CT angiogram. CT (computed tomography) angiograms use X-rays to get detailed pictures of the heart and its blood vessels.

How is coronary artery disease treated?

Treatment for coronary artery disease involves making lifestyle changes, taking medications, possibly undergoing invasive and/or surgical procedures, and seeing your cardiologist for regular checkups.

- **Reduce your risk factors.** If you smoke, quit. Avoid high-cholesterol foods and adopt a low-fat, low-salt diet. Keep your blood sugar in control if you have diabetes. Exercise more to maintain a healthy weight (but talk to your doctor before you starting an exercise program).
- **Medications.** If making lifestyle changes isn't enough to control your heart disease, medications may be needed to help your heart work more efficiently and receive more oxygen-rich blood. The drugs you are on depend on you and your specific heart problem.
- **Surgery and other procedures.** Common procedures to treat coronary artery disease include balloon angioplasty (PTCA), stent placement, and coronary artery bypass surgery. All of these procedures increase blood supply to your heart, but they do not cure coronary heart disease. You will still need to decrease your risk factors to prevent future disease.

Doctors are also studying several innovative ways to treat heart disease. Here are a couple of the more promising ones:

- **Angiogenesis.** This involves giving substances, such as stem cells and other genetic material, through the vein or directly into damaged heart tissue to trigger the growth of new blood vessels to bypass the clogged ones.
- **EECP (Enhanced External Counterpulsation).** Patients who have chronic angina but are not helped by nitrate medications or who do not qualify for various surgeries and procedures may find relief with EECP. The outpatient procedure involves using treatment cuffs placed on the legs that inflate and deflate, increasing the blood supply that feeds coronary arteries.

What to do if you have a coronary emergency?

Learn to recognize your heart disease symptoms and the situations that cause them. Call your doctor if you begin to have new symptoms or if they become more frequent or severe. If you or someone you are with experiences chest discomfort, especially if there is shortness of breath, heart palpitations, dizziness, a fast heart beat, nausea or sweating, don't wait longer than a few minutes to call 911 for help.

If you have angina and have been prescribed nitroglycerin, call your doctor or have someone take you to the nearest emergency room if pain persists after taking two doses (taken at five-minute intervals) or after 15 minutes.

Emergency personnel may tell you to chew an aspirin to help break up a possible blood clot, if there is not a medical reason for you to avoid aspirin.

Lifestyle and Your Heart

If you smoke, quit. You should also get in the habit of exercising, because exercise strengthens the heart and blood vessels, reduces stress, and has been shown to reduce blood pressure while also boosting HDL (good) cholesterol levels. Numerous studies done in recent decades indicate that drinking alcohol in moderation may actually reduce the risk of heart disease. But more than one drink a day, or a few drinks per week, is not recommended.

For many people, learning to relax can help prevent and treat heart disease. While success varies from person to person, stress-reduction techniques have been shown to moderate high blood pressure, heart arrhythmias, and emotional responses such as anxiety, anger, and hostility that have been linked to coronary heart disease, angina, and heart attack. The choice of relaxation technique is up to you. Some that have proved beneficial are meditation, progressive relaxation, yoga, and biofeedback training.

Nutrition, Diet, and Your Heart

Even modest changes in diet and lifestyle can significantly reduce the risk of heart disease. Being overweight, especially in the mid-section, can lead to high blood pressure and diabetes. If you are 20% or more over the ideal weight for your age, height, and sex, you put a strain on your heart's ability to pump blood efficiently. Although lowering sodium, cholesterol and saturated fat consumption are important for lowering blood pressure and reducing the risk of coronary heart disease, equally vital is increasing intake of fresh fruits and vegetables, whole unprocessed high-fiber grains, and vegetarian sources of fats and proteins (as from fish, nuts, seeds, soy-based items, avocados, etc.).

中英文注释

关键词汇

alcohol ['ælkəhɒl] n. 酒精，乙醇

angina [æn'dʒainə] n. 心绞痛；咽喉痛；咽峡炎

angiogenesis [ˌændʒiə(ʊ)'dʒenisis] n. 血管生成；血管再生术

atherosclerosis [ˌæθərəʊsklə'rəʊsis] n. 动脉粥样硬化；动脉硬化

biofeedback [baiəʊ'fiːdbæk] n. 生物反馈

boosting [buːst] vt. 促进；增加；支援

calcium ['kælsiəm] n. 钙

cardiologist ['kardi'alədʒist] n. 心脏病学家；心脏病科医师

cholesterol [kə'lestərɒl] n. 胆固醇

coronary ['kɒr(ə)n(ə)ri] adj. 冠的；冠状的；

deposit [di'pɒzit] n. 沉淀物；vt. 使沉积；存放；vi. 沉淀

echocardiogram [ˌɛko'kɑrdiəˌgræm] n. 超声波心动图，心回波图

elastic [i'læstik] adj. 有弹性的；灵活的；易伸缩的；n. 松紧带；橡皮圈

electrocardiogram(EKG or ECG) [iˌlektrəʊ'kɑːdiəgræm] n. 心电图

emergency [i'mɜːdʒ(ə)nsi] n. 紧急情况；突发事件；非常时刻；adj. 紧急的

groin [grɒin] n. 腹股沟

heartburn ['hɑːtbɜːn] n. 心痛，妒忌；[内科]胃灼热

ischemic [i'skemik] adj. 缺血性的；局部缺血的

lipoproteins [ˌlipəʊ'prəʊtin] n. 脂蛋白

numbness ['nʌmnəs] n. 麻木；麻痹

palpitations [ˌpælpi'teʃnz] n. 心悸

perfusion [pɚ'fjʊʒən] n. 灌注；充满

plaque [plæk; plɑːk] n. 血小板

rigid ['ridʒid] adj. 严格的；僵硬的，死板的；坚硬的；精确的

saturated ['sætʃəreitid] adj. 饱和的；渗透的；深颜色的；v. 使渗透，使饱和（saturate 的过去式）

sodium ['səʊdiəm] n. 钠（11 号元素，符号 Na）

squeeze [skwiːz] vt. 挤；紧握；勒索；vi. 压榨；n. 压榨；紧握；拥挤

starve [stɑːv] vi. 饿死；挨饿；渴望；vt. 使饿死；使挨饿

sticky ['stiki] adj. 黏的；黏性的

stroke [strəʊk] n. 中风

vegetarian [vedʒi'teəriən] n. 素食者；食草动物；adj. 素食的

yoga ['jəʊgə] n. 瑜伽；瑜伽术

主要短语

balloon angioplasty 气囊血管成形术；球囊成形术

coronary artery disease 冠状动脉疾病；冠心病

C-reactive protein (CRP) C 反应蛋白

EECP (Enhanced External Counterpulsation) 增强型体外反搏

ejection fraction 射血分数；射出分率

HDL (high density lipoprotein) 高密度脂蛋白

PTCA (Percutaneous Transluminal Coronary Angioplasty) 经皮腔内冠状动脉成形术

stent placement 支架植入

岳　亮　马志方

23 Hypertension/High Blood Pressure

高 血 压 病

What is high blood pressure?

High blood pressure, also known as hypertension, is the most common cardiovascular disease.

Blood pressure refers to the force of blood pushing against artery walls as it courses through the body. Like air in a tire or water in a hose, blood fills arteries to a certain capacity. Just as too much air pressure can damage a tire or too much water pushing through a garden hose can damage the hose, high blood pressure can threaten healthy arteries and lead to life-threatening conditions such as heart disease and stroke.

Hypertension is the leading cause of stroke and a major cause of heart attack. In the U.S. alone, more than 30% of American adults have high blood pressure.

If you have high blood pressure, you'll probably find out about it during a routine checkup. Or, you may have noticed a problem while taking your own blood pressure. Be sure to see your doctor for a definite diagnosis, and take the opportunity to learn what you can do to bring your blood pressure under control.

How is blood pressure measured?

A blood pressure reading appears as two numbers. The first and higher of the two is a measure of systolic pressure, or the pressure in the arteries when the heart beats and fills them with blood. The second number measures diastolic pressure, or the pressure in the arteries when the heart rests between beats.

Normal blood pressure rises steadily from about 90/60 at birth to about 120/80 in a healthy adult. If someone were to take your blood pressure immediately after you'd delivered a speech or jogged five miles, the reading would undoubtedly seem high. This is not necessarily cause for alarm: It's natural for blood pressure to rise and fall with changes in activity or emotional state.

It's also normal for blood pressure to vary from person to person, even from one area of your body to another. But when blood pressure remains consistently high, talk with your doctor about treatment. Consistently high blood pressure forces the heart to work far beyond its capacity. Along with injuring blood vessels, hypertension can damage the brain, eyes, and kidneys.

People with blood pressure readings of 140/90 or higher, taken on at least two occasions, are said to have high blood pressure. If the pressure remains high, your doctor will probably begin treatment. People with blood pressure readings of 200/130 or higher need treatment immediately. People with diabetes are treated if their blood pressure rises above 130/80, because they already have a high risk of heart disease.

Researchers identified people with blood pressures slightly higher than 120/80 as a category at high risk for developing hypertension. This condition is called pre-hypertension and affects an estimated 50 million American men and women. Pre-hypertension is now known to increase the likelihood of damage to arteries and the heart, brain, and kidneys, so many doctors are now recommending early treatment, though there is no evidence that this helps in the long run.

Even so, many people with high blood pressure don't realize they have the condition. Indeed, hypertension is often called "the silent killer" because it rarely causes symptoms, even as it inflicts serious damage to the body. Left untreated, high blood pressure can lead to vision problems, as well as to heart attack, stroke, and other potentially fatal conditions, including kidney failure.

Hypertension may also lead to heart failure, a common but disabling condition that can cause breathing problems. Patients who have very high blood pressure are said to have malignant hypertension, with a diastolic pressure usually exceeding 130 or a systolic pressure above 200. Malignant hypertension is a dangerous condition that may develop rapidly and cause organ damage quickly. It requires immediate medical attention.

Fortunately, high blood pressure can be controlled effectively. The first step is to have your blood pressure checked regularly.

Who are more likely to get hypertension?

High blood pressure is more likely in people who:
- Have a family history of high blood pressure, heart disease, or diabetes
- Are African-American
- Are over age 55
- Are overweight
- Are not physically active
- Drink excessively
- Smoke
- Eat foods high in saturated fats or salt

● Use certain medications such as NSAIDs (ibuprofen, aspirin, e.g.), decongestants, and illicit drugs such as cocaine

What causes high blood pressure?

Essential Hypertension

In as many as 95% of reported high blood pressure cases in the U.S., the underlying cause cannot be determined. This type of high blood pressure is called essential hypertension.

Though essential hypertension remains somewhat mysterious, it has been linked to certain risk factors. High blood pressure tends to run in families and is more likely to affect men than women. Age and race also play a role. In the U.S., blacks are twice as likely as whites to have high blood pressure, although the gap begins to narrow around age 44. After age 65, black women have the highest incidence of high blood pressure.

Essential hypertension is also greatly influenced by diet and lifestyle. The link between salt and high blood pressure is especially compelling. People living on the northern islands of Japan eat more salt per capita than anyone else in the world and have the highest incidence of essential hypertension. By contrast, people who add no salt to their food show virtually no traces of essential hypertension.

Many people with high blood pressure are "salt sensitive", meaning that anything more than the minimal bodily need for salt is too much for them and increases their blood pressure. Other factors that have been associated with essential hypertension include obesity; diabetes; stress; insufficient intake of potassium, calcium, and magnesium; lack of physical activity; and chronic alcohol consumption.

Secondary Hypertension

When a direct cause for high blood pressure can be identified, the condition is described as secondary hypertension. Among the known causes of secondary hypertension, kidney disease ranks highest. Hypertension can also be triggered by tumors or other abnormalities that cause the adrenal glands (small glands that sit atop the kidneys) to secrete excess amounts of the hormones that elevate blood pressure. Birth control pills — specifically those containing estrogen — and pregnancy can boost blood pressure, as can medications that constrict blood vessels.

What are symptoms & types of hypertension?

Are there hypertension symptoms? What are the complications of high blood pressure? Learn about hypertension, its symptoms, complications, and types.

Symptoms

One of the most dangerous aspects of hypertension is that you may not know that you have it. In fact, nearly one-third of people who have high blood pressure don't know it. The only way to know if your blood pressure is high is through regular checkups. This is especially important if you have a close relative who has high blood pressure.

If your blood pressure is extremely high, there may be certain symptoms to look out for, including:

- Severe headache
- Fatigue or confusion
- Vision problems
- Chest pain
- Difficulty breathing
- Irregular heartbeat
- Blood in the urine
- Pounding in your chest, neck, or ears

If you have any of these symptoms, see a doctor immediately. You could be having a hypertensive crisis that could lead to a heart attack or stroke.

Untreated hypertension can lead to serious diseases, including stroke, heart disease, kidney failure and eye problems.

What are warning signs of hypertension?

Hypertensive Crisis

In most cases, there are no clear warning signs of high blood pressure, but blood pressure can become dangerously high and threaten your organs and your life.

Types

What is malignant hypertension?

Malignant hypertension is extremely high blood pressure that develops suddenly and rapidly and causes some type of organ damage. "Normal" blood pressure is below 120/80. A person with malignant hypertension has a blood pressure that's typically above 180/120. It's considered a hypertensive emergency and should be treated as a medical emergency.

What causes malignant hypertension?

In many people, high blood pressure is the main cause of malignant hypertension. Missing doses of blood pressure medications can also cause it. In addition, there are certain medical conditions that can cause it. They include:

- Collagen vascular disease, such as scleroderma
- Kidney disease

- Spinal cord injuries
- Tumor of the adrenal gland
- Use of certain medications, including birth control pills and monoamine oxidase inhibitors (MAOIs)
- Use of illegal drugs, such as cocaine

Who's at risk for malignant hypertension?

Malignant hypertension is rare. About 1% of people who have a history of high blood pressure develop this life-threatening condition.

You are at greater risk of developing it if you are a man, African-American, or someone of lower economic status. Poor access to health care increases the risk.

What are the symptoms of malignant hypertension?

The main symptoms of malignant hypertension are a rapidly increasing blood pressure of 180/120 or higher and signs of organ damage. Usually the damage happens to the kidneys or the eyes.

Other symptoms depend on how the rise in blood pressure affects your organs. A common symptom is bleeding and swelling in the tiny blood vessels in the retina. The retina is the layer of nerves that line the back of the eye. It senses light and sends signals to the brain through the optic nerve, which can also be affected by malignant hypertension. When the eye is involved, malignant hypertension can cause changes in vision.

Other symptoms of malignant hypertension include:

- Blurred vision
- Chest pain (angina)
- Difficulty breathing
- Dizziness
- Numbness in the arms, legs, and face
- Severe headache
- Shortness of breath

In rare cases, malignant hypertension can cause brain swelling, which leads to a dangerous condition called hypertensive encephalopathy. Symptoms include:

- Blindness
- Changes in mental status
- Coma
- Confusion
- Drowsiness

- Headache that continues to get worse
- Nausea and vomiting
- Seizures

High blood pressure, in general, makes it difficult for kidneys to filter wastes and toxins from the blood. It is a leading cause of kidney failure. Malignant hypertension can cause your kidneys to suddenly stop working properly. If this happens, the condition is called malignant nephrosclerosis.

How is malignant hypertension diagnosed?

A diagnosis of malignant hypertension is based on blood pressure readings and signs of acute organ damage.

If you have symptoms of malignant hypertension, the doctor will:

- Recheck your blood pressure and listen to your heart and lungs for abnormal sounds.
- Examine your eyes to check for damage to the blood vessels of the retina and swelling of the optic nerve.
- Order blood and urine tests that may include:
- Blood urea nitrogen (BUN) and creatinine levels, which increase if you have kidney damage.
- Blood clotting tests.
- Blood sugar (glucose) level.
- Complete blood count.
- Sodium and potassium levels.
- Urinalysis to check for blood, protein, or abnormal hormone levels related to kidney problems.

Additional blood tests may be needed, depending on the result of the tests listed above.

The doctor will also ask for imaging tests, including:

- Echocardiogram to check heart function and blood flow through the heart.
- Electrocardiogram (ECG) to check the heart's electrical function.
- Chest X-ray to look at the shape and size of the heart structures and to detect fluid in the lungs.
- Other imaging tests to evaluate the kidneys and their arteries.

How is malignant hypertension treated?

Malignant hypertension is a medical emergency and needs to be treated in a hospital, often in an intensive care unit. The doctor will consider your symptoms and overall health when deciding what treatment plan is best for you. The goal of treatment is to carefully lower your blood pressure within a matter of minutes.

You will receive blood pressure medicines through an IV, which is the quickest way to treat extremely high blood pressure. Once blood pressure is at a safe level, the medications may be switched to oral forms. If you develop kidney failure, you may need kidney dialysis.

Other treatments depend on your specific symptoms and possible causes of the malignant hypertension.

What are complications of malignant hypertension?

Untreated, malignant hypertension causes death. Complications of malignant hypertension include:

- Aortic dissection, which is a sudden rupture of the main blood vessel leaving the heart.
- Coma.
- Fluid in the lungs, called pulmonary edema.
- Heart attack.
- Heart failure.
- Stroke.
- Sudden kidney failure.

Immediate medical treatment decreases your chances for life-threatening complications.

What is secondary hypertension?

In about 10% of people, high blood pressure is caused by another disease (this is called secondary hypertension). In such cases, when the root cause is treated, blood pressure usually returns to normal or is significantly lowered. These causes include the following conditions:

- Chronic kidney disease
- Sleep apnea
- Tumors or other diseases of the adrenal gland
- Coarctation of the aorta — A narrowing of the aorta that you are born with that can cause high blood pressure in the arms
- Pregnancy
- Use of birth control pills
- Alcohol addiction
- Thyroid dysfunction

In the other 90% of cases, the cause of high blood pressure is not known (primary hypertension). Although the specific cause is unknown, certain factors are recognized as contributing to high blood pressure.

Factors That Can't Be Changed

- Age: The older you get, the greater the likelihood that you will develop high blood pressure, especially systolic, as your arteries get stiffer. This is largely due to arteriosclerosis, or "hardening of the arteries."
- Race: African Americans have high blood pressure more often than whites. They develop high blood pressure at a younger age and develop more severe complications sooner.
- Family history (heredity): The tendency to have high blood pressure appears to run in families.
- Sex: Generally men have a greater likelihood of developing high blood pressure than women. This likelihood varies according to age and among various ethnic groups.

What is renal hypertension?

Renal hypertension, also called renovascular hypertension, is elevated blood pressure caused by kidney disease. It can usually be controlled by blood pressure drugs. Some people with renal hypertension can be helped by angioplasty, stenting, or surgery.

What are causes of renal hypertension?

Renal hypertension is caused by a narrowing in the artery that delivers blood to the kidney. One or both kidneys' arteries may be narrowed. This is a condition called renal artery stenosis.

When the kidneys receive a low blood flow, they act as if the low flow is due to dehydration. So they respond by releasing hormones that stimulate the body to retain sodium and water. Blood vessels fill with additional fluid, and blood pressure goes up.

The narrowing in one or both renal arteries is most often caused by atherosclerosis, or hardening of the arteries. This is the same process that leads to many heart attacks and strokes. A less common cause of the narrowing is fibromuscular dysplasia. This is a condition in which the structure of the renal arteries develops abnormally for unclear reasons.

What are symptoms of renal hypertension?

Renal hypertension usually causes no symptoms. The narrowing in the arteries can't be felt. Unless it's dangerously high, high blood pressure causes no symptoms either. Symptoms of severely elevated blood pressure include:

- Headache
- Confusion
- Blurry or double vision
- Bloody (pink-colored) urine
- Nosebleed

The vast majority of people with renal hypertension never experience these (or any) symptoms. High blood pressure is dangerous partly because there are no symptoms, so organ damage can occur slowly without being recognized.

Renal hypertension can cause chronic kidney disease. This is a slow decline in kidney function. Until the condition is well advanced, chronic kidney disease also causes no symptoms.

Because there are usually no symptoms, a doctor may suspect renal hypertension when someone has uncontrolled high blood pressure despite multiple medications or has unexplained chronic kidney disease.

What are treatments for renal hypertension?

Medications are used first to try to control high blood pressure in renal hypertension. The most important blood pressure medications to treat renal hypertension include:

- ACE inhibitors (angiotensin converting enzyme inhibitors). These include lisinopril, captopril, benazepril, ramipril, and others.
- ARBs (angiotensin II receptor blockers). Examples include valsartan, losartan, candesartan, and olmesartan.

For most people with renal hypertension due to renal artery narrowing, medications can effectively control blood pressure. More than one blood pressure drug is often needed, however.

In some people with renal hypertension due to narrowing of the renal artery, even taking three or more medications every day cannot adequately control blood pressure. In these situations, a procedure to improve blood flow to the kidneys can often help.

Possible procedures include the following.

Angioplasty. A doctor threads a catheter through a large artery in the groin and advances it into the renal artery. A balloon is then inflated for a few moments. This widens the artery and improves blood flow.

Stenting. During angioplasty, a wire-mesh stent can be expanded inside the renal artery. The stent stays in place. This keeps the artery open after the balloon is removed. In general, stenting is more effective than angioplasty at improving blood flow to the kidney.

Surgery. A surgeon can bypass the narrowed renal artery by sewing a healthy blood vessel next to it. Surgery is generally considered only when angioplasty and stenting are not possible.

These procedures are similar to those used to improve blood flow in the heart in people with coronary artery disease.

What are complications of hypertension?

High Blood Pressure and Atherosclerosis

One of the most serious health problems related to untreated high blood pressure, atherosclerosis contributes to coronary artery disease. Learn about symptoms, diagnoses, and treatment of atherosclerosis.

Stroke and Hypertension

A stroke occurs when blood flow to an area in the brain is cut off and people who have hypertension are four to six times more likely to have a stroke. Stay safe: Learn your risk factors and the warning signs of stroke and what to do in a stroke emergency.

Hypertension and Heart Disease

Heart disease is the No. 1 cause of death associated with hypertension. Learn more about related heart conditions, their diagnoses, and treatment.

Kidney Disease and Hypertension

Hypertension is a major cause of kidney disease and kidney failure. There are symptoms to watch for — and treatment options. Learn more.

High Blood Pressure and Eye Disease

Untreated hypertension can affect your eyesight, causing damage to the blood vessels in the retina. Known as hypertensive retinopathy, learn more about this condition and its prevention.

High Blood Pressure and Diabetes

Hypertension is a risk factor for the development and worsening of many diabetes complications, and likewise having diabetes increases your risk of developing high blood pressure. Learn more about how these two conditions affect one another.

Preeclampsia: High Blood Pressure and Pregnancy

High blood pressure can be a sign of preeclampsia, a pregnancy-related problem that can become life-threatening. Learn what you need to know.

Metabolic Syndrome and High Blood Pressure

Metabolic syndrome is a group of health problems which include too much fat around the waist, elevated blood pressure, elevated blood sugar, and more — all increasing your risk of heart attack, stroke, and diabetes. Find out more about metabolic syndrome here.

High Blood Pressure and Erectile Dysfunction

High blood pressure by itself can lead to erectile dysfunction. But some drugs for treating high blood pressure can actually be the cause as well. Find out more about why high blood pressure is a major cause of erection problems.

Side Effects of High Blood Pressure Medications

This article lists the side effects that may be caused by each type of high blood pressure drug.

How is hypertension diagnosed?

Diagnosing hypertension is important. Learn how doctors test for high blood pressure and even see a photo of how the test is done.

Diagnosis

Diagnosing High Blood Pressure

Hypertension, or high blood pressure, is often called a "silent disease" because you usually don't know that you have it. There may be no symptoms or signs. Nonetheless, it damages the body and eventually may cause problems like heart disease.

Therefore, it's important to regularly monitor your blood pressure, especially if it has ever been high or above the "normal" range, or if you have a family history of hypertension. Because hypertension can cause heart disease, you may also need to be tested for heart disease.

Measuring Blood Pressure

You can get your blood pressure measured by a health care provider, at a pharmacy, or you can purchase a blood pressure monitor for your home.

Blood pressure is most often measured with a device known as a sphygmomanometer, which consists of a stethoscope, arm cuff, dial, pump, and valve.

Blood pressure is measured in two ways: systolic and diastolic.

- Systolic blood pressure is the maximum pressure during a heartbeat.
- Diastolic blood pressure is the lowest pressure between heartbeats.

Blood pressure is measured in millimeters of mercury (mm Hg) and is written systolic over diastolic (for example, 120/80 mm Hg, or "120 over 80"). According to the most recent guidelines, a normal blood pressure is less than 120/80 mm Hg. Hypertension is blood pressure that is greater than 140/90, while prehypertension consists of blood pressure that is 120 to 139/80 to 89.

Blood pressure may increase or decrease, depending on your age, heart condition, emotions, activity, and the medications you take. One high reading does not mean you have high blood pressure. It is necessary to measure your blood pressure at different times, while you are resting comfortably for at least five minutes. To make the diagnosis of hypertension, at least three readings that are elevated are usually required.

In addition to measuring your blood pressure, your doctor will ask about your medical history (whether you've had heart problems before), assess your risk factors (whether you smoke, have high cholesterol, diabetes, etc.), and talk about your family history (whether any members of your family have had high blood pressure or heart disease).

Your doctor will also conduct a physical exam. As part of this exam, he or she may use a stethoscope to listen to your heart for any abnormal sounds and your arteries for a whooshing or swishing sound that may indicate that the artery may be partially blocked. Your doctor may also check the pulses in your arm and ankle to determine if they are weak or even absent.

If you're diagnosed with high blood pressure, your doctor may recommend other tests, such as:

- Electrocardiogram (EKG or ECG): A test that measures the electrical activity, rate, and rhythm of your heartbeat via electrodes attached to your arms, legs, and chest. The results are recorded on graph paper.
- Echocardiogram: This is a test that uses ultrasound waves to provide pictures of the heart's valves and chambers so the pumping action of the heart can be studied and measurement of the chambers and wall thickness of the heart can be made.

How is it treated?

Hypertension Treatment

High blood pressure, is dangerous because it can lead to strokes, heart attacks, heart failure, or kidney disease. The goal of hypertension treatment is to lower high blood pressure and protect important organs, like the brain, heart, and kidneys from damage. Treatment for hypertension has been associated with reductions in stroke (reduced an average of 35%-40%), heart attack (20%-25%), and heart failure (more than 50%), according to research.

High blood pressure is classified as:
- Normal blood pressure: less than 120/80
- Prehypertension: 120-139/80-89
- Hypertension: greater than 140/90
- Stage 1 Hypertension:140-159/90-99
- Stage 2 Hypertension: 160 or greater/100 or greater

All patients with blood pressure readings greater than 120/80 should be encouraged to make lifestyle modifications, such as eating a healthier diet, quitting smoking, and getting more exercise. Treatment with medication is recommended to lower blood pressure to less than 140/90. For patients who have diabetes or chronic kidney disease the recommended blood pressure is less than 130/80.

Treating high blood pressure involves lifestyle changes and possibly drug therapy.

Lifestyle Changes to Treat High Blood Pressure

A critical step in preventing and treating high blood pressure is a healthy lifestyle. You can lower your blood pressure with the following lifestyle changes:

- Losing weight if you are overweight or obese.
- Quitting smoking.
- Eating a healthy diet, including the DASH diet (eating more fruits, vegetables, and low fat dairy products, less saturated and total fat).
- Reducing the amount of sodium in your diet to less than 1,500 milligrams a day if you have high blood pressure. Healthy adults need to limit their sodium intake to no more 2,300 milligrams a day (about 1 teaspoon of salt).
- Getting regular aerobic exercise (such as brisk walking at least 30 minutes a day, several days a week).
- Limiting alcohol to two drinks a day for men, one drink a day for women.
- In addition to lowering blood pressure, these measures enhance the effectiveness of high blood pressure drugs.
- Drugs to Treat High Blood Pressure
- There are several types of drugs used to treat high blood pressure, including:
- Angiotensin-converting enzyme (ACE) inhibitors
- Angiotensin II receptor blockers (ARBs)
- Diuretics
- Beta-blockers
- Calcium channel blockers
- Alpha-blockers
- Alpha-agonists
- Renin inhibitors
- Combination medications

Diuretics are often recommended as the first line of therapy for most people who have high blood pressure.

However, your doctor may start a medicine other than a diuretic as the first line of therapy if you have certain medical problems. For example, ACE inhibitors are often a choice for a people with diabetes. If one drug doesn't work or is disagreeable, other types of drugs are available.

If your blood pressure is more than 20/10 points higher than it should be, your doctor may consider starting you on two drugs or placing you on a combination drug.

High blood pressure treatment follow-Up

After starting high blood pressure drug therapy, you should see your doctor at least once a month until the blood pressure goal is reached. Once or twice a year, your doctor will check the level of potassium in your blood (diuretics can lower this, and ACE inhibitors and ARBs may increase this) and other electrolytes and BUN/creatinine levels (to check the health of the kidneys).

After the blood pressure goal is reached, you should continue to see your doctor every three to six months, depending on whether you have other diseases such as heart failure.

High Blood Pressure and Smoking

Did you know that smoking and heart disease are related? Or that smoking increases blood pressure? Most people associate cigarette smoking with breathing problems and lung cancer. But people who smoke are more also likely to develop hypertension and heart disease.

About 30% of all deaths from heart disease in the U.S. are directly related to cigarette smoking. That's because smoking is a major cause of coronary artery disease, especially in younger people.

A person's risk of heart attack greatly increases with the number of cigarettes he or she smokes and the longer a person smokes, the greater their risk of heart attack. People who smoke a pack of cigarettes a day have more than twice the risk of heart attack than non-smokers. Women who smoke and also take birth control pills increase several times their risk of heart attack, stroke, and peripheral vascular disease.

Hypertension and Stress

Stress is a normal part of life. But too much stress can lead to emotional, psychological, and even physical problems — including heart disease, high blood pressure, chest pains, or irregular heart beats.

Reducing stress can help lower high blood pressure.

High blood pressure drugs

Your doctor has hundreds of different high blood pressure drugs to choose from. These medications work in a variety of ways to lower blood pressure.

Calcium Channel Blockers

Calcium channel blockers are drugs used to lower blood pressure. They work by slowing the movement of calcium into the cells of the heart and blood vessel walls, which makes it easier for the heart to pump and widens blood vessels.

ACE Inhibitors

Angiotensin converting enzyme (ACE) inhibitors are high blood pressure drugs that widen or dilate your blood vessels to improve the amount of blood your heart pumps and lower blood pressure.

Angiotensin II Receptor Blockers (ARBs)

Angiotensin II receptor blockers (ARBs) have the same effects as ACE inhibitors, another type of blood pressure drug, but work by a different mechanism.

Diuretics (Water Pills)

For high blood pressure, diuretics, commonly known as "water pills," help your body get rid of unneeded water and salt through the urine. Getting rid of excess salt and fluid helps lower blood pressure and can make it easier for your heart to pump.

Beta-Blockers

Beta-blockers are drugs used to treat high blood pressure. They block the effects of the sympathetic nervous system on the heart.

Omega-3 Fish Oil Supplements

In the past 10 years, many Americans have turned to omega-3 fish oil supplements. Dietary fish and fish oil supplements have benefits for healthy people and also those with heart disease.

中英文注释

关键词汇

angioplasty [ˌændʒioˈplæsti] n. 血管成形术

arteriosclerosis [ɑːˌtiəriəʊskliəˈrəʊsis] n. 动脉硬化

cardiovascular [ˌkɑːdiəʊˈvæskjʊlə] adj. 心血管的

creatinine [kriˈætiniːn] n. 肌酐

diabetes [ˌdaiəˈbiːtiːz] n. 糖尿病；多尿症

dehydration [ˌdiːhaiˈdreiʃən] n. 脱水

diuretic [ˌdaijʊ(ə)ˈretik] n. 利尿剂

edema [iˈdiːmə] n. 水肿

hypertension [haipəˈtenʃ(ə)n] n. 高血压；过度紧张

nephrosclerosis [ˈnefrəʊˌskliəˈrəʊsis] n. 肾硬化，肾硬变

preeclampsia [ˌpriiˈklæmpsiə] n. 子痫前期；惊厥前期

retina [ˈretinə] n. 视网膜

scleroderma [ˌskliərəˈdʒːmə] n. 硬皮病

sphygmomanometer [ˌsfigməʊməˈnɒmitə] n. 血压计

stethoscope [ˈsteθəskəʊp] vt. 用听诊器诊断 n. 听诊器

stroke [strəʊk] n. 中风；脑卒中

主要短语

Adrenalglands 肾上腺

aerobic exercise 有氧运动

aortic dissection 主动脉夹层

artery walls 动脉壁

birthcontrolpills 避孕药

bloodureanitrogen (BUN) 血尿素氮

brainswelling 脑水肿

collagenvasculardisease 胶原血管病

diastolicpressure 舒张压

erectile dysfunction (ED) 勃起功能障碍

essentialhypertension 原发性高血压；特发性高血压

fibromuscular dysplasia 肌纤维发育不良；纤维肌性发育不良

hypertensivecrisis 高血压危象

hypertensiveencephalopathy 高血压性脑病；高血压脑病

hypertensive retinopathy 高血压性视网膜病变

intensive care unit (ICU) 特护病房；重症监护病房

kidney dialysis 肾透析

malignanthypertension 恶性高血压

metabolic syndrome 代谢综合征

opticnerve 视神经

pre-hypertension 高血压前期

renovascular hypertension 肾血管性高血压

saturatedfats 饱和脂肪酸

secondaryhypertension 继发性高血压

sleep apnea 睡眠呼吸暂停；睡眠呼吸暂停症

systolicpressure 收缩压

thyroid dysfunction 甲状腺功能不全

许召良　马志方

24   Heart Failure
心 力 衰 竭

Heart failure affects about 5 million Americans. Roughly 550,000 people are diagnosed with heart failure each year. It is the leading cause of hospitalization in people older than 65.

What is heart failure?

Heart failure does not mean the heart has stopped working. Rather, it means that the heart's pumping power is weaker than normal. With heart failure, blood moves through the heart and body at a slower rate, and pressure in the heart increases. As a result, the heart cannot pump enough oxygen and nutrients to meet the body's needs. The chambers of the heart respond by stretching to hold more blood to pump through the body or by becoming more stiff and thickened. This helps to keep the blood moving for a short while, but in time, the heart muscle walls weaken and are unable to pump as strongly. As a result, the kidneys respond by causing the body to retain fluid (water) and sodium. If fluid builds up in the arms, legs, ankles, feet, lungs, or other organs, the body becomes congested, and congestive heart failure is the term used to describe the condition.

What causes heart failure?

Heart failure is caused by many conditions that damage the heart muscle, including:
- **Coronary artery disease.** Coronary artery disease (CAD), a disease of the arteries that supply blood and oxygen to the heart, causes decreased blood flow to the heart muscle. If the arteries become blocked or severely narrowed, the heart becomes starved for oxygen and nutrients.
- **Heart attack.** A heart attack may occur when a coronary artery becomes suddenly blocked, stopping the flow of blood to the heart muscle and damaging it. All or part of the heart muscle becomes cut off from its supply of oxygen. A heart attack can damage the heart muscle, resulting in a scarred area that does not function properly.

151

- **Cardiomyopathy.** Damage to the heart muscle. Causes include artery or blood flow problems, infections, and alcohol and drug abuse.
- **Conditions that overwork the heart.** Conditions including high blood pressure, heart valve disease, thyroid disease, kidney disease, diabetes, or heart defects present at birth can all cause heart failure. In addition, heart failure can occur when several diseases or conditions are present at once.

What are the types of heart failure?

Systolic dysfunction (or systolic heart failure) occurs when the heart muscle doesn't contract with enough force, so there is less oxygen-rich blood that is pumped throughout the body.

Diastolic dysfunction (or diastolic heart failure) occurs when the heart contracts normally, but the ventricle — the main pumping chamber — does not relax properly, reducing the amount of blood that can enter the heart and raising blood pressure in the lungs.

A test called the ejection fraction (EF) is used measure how well your heart pumps with each beat to help determine if systolic or diastolic dysfunction is present. The ejection fraction is a measure of the percentage of blood that your heart pumps out with each beat. Your doctor can discuss which condition you have.

In patients with systolic heart failure, the ejection fraction is less than 40%. Imaging studies such as an echocardiogram (heart ultrasound) show the heart is enlarged and pumps out less than a normal amount of blood with each beat.

In contrast, patients with diastolic heart failure usually have a normal ejection fraction, normal heart pumping capability, but an echocardiogram shows that the heart does not fill up with blood properly during the heart relaxation phase that occurs between beats.

Stages of Heart Failure

In 2001, the American Heart Association (AHA) and American College of Cardiology (ACC) developed the "Stages of Heart Failure." These stages, which were updated in 2005, will help you understand that heart failure is often a progressive condition and can worsen over time. They will also help you understand why a new medication was added to your treatment plan and may help you understand why lifestyle changes and other treatments are needed.

The stages classified by the AHA and ACC are different than the New York Heart Association (NYHA) clinical classifications of heart failure that rank patients as class I-II-III-IV, according to the degree of symptoms or functional limits. Ask your doctor what stage of heart failure you are in.

Check the table below to see if your therapy matches what the AHA and ACC recommend. Note that you cannot go backward in stage, only forward.

The table below outlines a basic plan of care that may or may not apply to you, based on the cause of your heart failure and your special needs. Ask your doctor to explain therapies that are listed if you do not understand why you are or are not receiving them.

Stage	Definition of Stage	Usual Treatments
Stage A	People at high risk of developing heart failure (pre-heart failure), including people with: High blood pressure Diabetes Coronary artery disease Metabolic syndrome History of cardiotoxic drug therapy History of alcohol abuse History of rheumatic fever Family history of cardiomyopathy	• Exercise regularly. • Quit smoking. • Treat high blood pressure. • Treat lipid disorders. • Discontinue alcohol or illegal drug use. • An angiotensin converting enzyme inhibitor (ACE inhibitor) or an angiotensin II receptor blocker (ARB) is prescribed if you've had coronary artery disease or if you have diabetes, high blood pressure, or other vascular or cardiac conditions. • Beta-blockers may be prescribed if you have high blood pressure or if you've had a previous heart attack
Stage B	People diagnosed with systolic left ventricular dysfunction but who have never had symptoms of heart failure (pre-heart failure), including people with: Prior heart attack Valve disease Cardiomyopathy The diagnosis is usually made when an ejection fraction of less than 40% is found during an echocardiogram test	• Treatment methods above for Stage A apply. • All patients should take an angiotensin converting enzyme inhibitor (ACE inhibitors) or angiotensin II receptor blocker (ARB). • Beta-blockers should be prescribed for patients after a heart attack. • An aldosterone inhibitor may be prescribed if the symptoms continue while on good doses of beta blockers and ACE/ARB medications. • Surgery options for coronary artery repair and valve repair or replacement (as appropriate) should be discussed. • If appropriate, surgery options should be discussed for patients who have had a heart attack

Continue

Stage	Definition of Stage	Usual Treatments
Stage C	Patients with known systolic heart failure and current or prior symptoms. Most common symptoms include: Shortness of breath Fatigue Reduced ability to exercise	• Treatment methods above for Stage A apply. • All patients should take an angiotensin converting enzyme inhibitor (ACE inhibitors) and beta-blockers. • African-American patients may be prescribed a hydralazine/nitrate combination if symptoms persist. • Diuretics (water pills) and digoxin may be prescribed if symptoms persist. • An aldosterone inhibitor may be prescribed when symptoms remain severe with other therapies. • Restrict dietary sodium (salt) • Monitor weight • Restrict fluids (as appropriate) • Drugs that worsen the condition should be discontinued. • As appropriate, cardiac resynchronization therapy (biventricular pacemaker) may be recommended. • An implantable cardiac defibrillator (ICD) may be recommended
Stage D	Patients with systolic heart failure and presence of advanced symptoms after receiving optimum medical care	• Treatment methods for Stages A, B, & C apply. • Patient should be evaluated to determine if the following treatments are available options: heart transplant, ventricular assist devices, surgery options, research therapies, continuous infusion of intravenous inotropic drugs, and end-of-life (palliative or hospice) care

What are symptoms of heart failure?

You may not have any heart failure symptoms, or the symptoms may be mild to severe. Symptoms can be constant or can come and go. Heart failure symptoms are related to the changes that occur to your heart and body, and the severity depends on how weak your heart is. The symptoms can include:

- **Congested lungs.** A weak heart causes fluid to back up in the lungs. This can cause shortness of breath with exercise or difficulty breathing at rest or when lying flat in bed. Lung congestion can also cause a dry, hacking cough or wheezing.
- **Fluid and water retention.** A weak heart pumps less blood to your kidneys and causes fluid and water retention, resulting in swollen ankles, legs, and abdomen (called edema) and weight gain. This can also cause an increased need to urinate during the night as your body attempts to get rid of this excess fluid. Bloating in your stomach may cause a loss of appetite or nausea.
- **Dizziness, fatigue, and weakness.** Less blood to your major organs and muscles makes you feel tired and weak. Less blood to the brain can cause dizziness or confusion.
- **Rapid or irregular heartbeats.** The heart beats faster to pump enough blood to the body. This can cause a fast or irregular heartbeat.

If you have heart failure, you may have one or all of these symptoms or you may have none of them. In addition, your symptoms may not be related to how weak your heart is; you may have many symptoms but your heart function may be only mildly weakened. Or you may have a more severely damaged heart but have few symptoms.

How is heart failure diagnosed?

To diagnose heart failure, your doctor will first ask you questions about your symptoms and medical history. Your doctor will want to know:

- If you have any other health conditions such as diabetes, kidney disease, angina, high blood pressure, or other heart problems.
- If you smoke.
- If you drink alcohol and how much you drink.

What medications are you taking.

Your doctor will also perform a complete physical exam. Your doctor will look for signs of heart failure as well as any other illnesses that may have caused your heart to weaken.

Your doctor may also order tests to determine the cause and severity of your heart failure. These include:

- **Blood tests.** Blood tests are used to evaluate kidney and thyroid function as well as to check cholesterol levels and the presence of anemia. Anemia is a blood disorder that occurs when there is not enough hemoglobin (the substance in red blood cells that enables the blood to transport oxygen through the body) in a person's blood.

- **B-type natriuretic peptide (BNP) blood test .** BNP is a substance secreted from the heart in response to changes in pressure that occur when heart failure develops and worsens. The level of BNP in the blood increases when heart failure symptoms worsen, and decreases when the heart failure condition is stable. The BNP level in a person with heart failure — even someone whose condition is stable — is higher than in a person with normal heart function.

- **Chest X-ray.** Chest X-ray shows the size of your heart and whether there is fluid build-up around the heart and lungs.

- **Echocardiogram.** This test (often called an "echo") shows a graphic outline of the heart's movement. During an echo, a wand is placed on the surface of your chest. This wand sends ultrasound waves that provide pictures of the heart's valves and chambers so the pumping action of the heart can be studied. Echo is often combined with Doppler ultrasound and color Doppler to evaluate blood flow across the heart's valves.

- **Ejection fraction (EF).** A normal EF is generally between 55% and 75%, which means that over half of the blood volume is pumped out of the heart with each beat. Heart failure may occur as the result of a low EF (called systolic heart failure), or from another cause, such as a valve disorder or from diastolic dysfunction. People with diastolic dysfunction can have a normal EF.

- **Electrocardiogram (EKG or ECG).** ECG records the electrical impulses traveling through the heart. During the test, small, flat, sticky patches called electrodes are placed on your chest. The electrodes are attached to an electrocardiograph monitor (ECG) that charts your heart's electrical activity on graph paper. Your doctor will also be interested in determining your ejection fraction, or EF. This is a measurement of how much blood is pumped out of the heart with each heartbeat.

- **Stress test.** The patient's heart is "stressed" by walking on a treadmill or by medications that increase the pumping of the heart. It helps determine if someone may have clogged heart arteries.

- **Cardiac catheterization.** This is an invasive test which measures whether you have clogged heart arteries (coronary artery disease).

- **CT coronary angiogram.** This is a noninvasive test which uses X-ray and intravenous contrast dye to determine whether you have coronary artery disease.

- **Cardiac MRI.** This less commonly used test helps your doctor understand whether you have abnormalities of the heart muscle itself or of the tissues surrounding the heart (pericardium).

How is heart failure treated?

Today there are more options available to treat heart failure than ever before. Regular medications and lifestyle changes coupled with careful monitoring is the first line of treatment. As the condition progresses, centers specializing in the treatment of heart failure can offer more advanced treatment options, such as surgery.

What drugs are used to treat heart failure?

Taking your heart failure medications as prescribed is one of the most important things you can do to manage your condition. The more you know about your medications and how they work, the easier it will be for you to stay on track.

Common types of drugs used to treat heart failure include:

- Angiotensin II receptor blockers (ARBs)
- Beta-blockers
- Digoxin
- Diuretics
- Blood vessel dilators
- Potassium or magnesium
- Aldactone Inhibitors
- Calcium channel blockers
- Heart pump medication

What surgical procedures are used to treat heart failure?

Surgery is aimed at stopping further damage to the heart and improving the heart's function. Procedures used include:

- **Bypass surgery:** The most common surgery for heart failure is bypass surgery to route blood around a blocked heart artery.
- **Left ventricular assist device (LVAD):** The LVAD helps your heart pump blood throughout your body. It allows you to be mobile, sometimes returning home to await a heart transplant.
- **Heart valve surgery:** As heart failure progresses, the heart valves that normally help direct the flow of blood through the heart to the rest of the body may no longer completely close, allowing blood to "leak" backward. The valves can be repaired or replaced.
- **Infarct exclusion surgery (Modified Dor or Dor Procedure):** When a heart attack occurs in the left ventricle (left lower pumping chamber of the heart), a scar forms. The scarred area is thin and can bulge out with each beat (an

aneurysm). A heart surgeon can remove the dead area of heart tissue or the aneurysm.

● **Heart transplant:** A heart transplant is considered when heart failure is so severe that it does not respond to all other therapies.

中英文注释

关键词汇

ankle ['æŋk(ə)l] n. 踝关节

aldosterone [æl'dɒstərəʊn] n. 醛固酮

angina [æn'dʒainə] n. 心绞痛

cardiomyopathy [ˌkɑːdiəʊmai'ɒpəθi] n. 心肌病

cholesterol [kə'lestərɒl] n. 胆固醇

diuretic [ˌdaijʊ(ə)'retik] n. 利尿剂；adj. 利尿的

edema [i'diːmə] n. 水肿

hemoglobin [ˌhiːməʊ'gləʊbin] n. 血红蛋白

hospice ['hɒspis] n. 养老院

pacemaker ['peismeikə] n. 起搏器

palliative ['pæliətiv] adj. 缓和的，姑息性的

主要短语

alcohol and drug abuse 酒精及药物滥用

angiotensin converting enzyme inhibitor (ACE inhibitor) 血管紧张素转换酶抑制剂

angiotensin II receptor blocker (ARB) 血管紧张素 II 受体阻断剂

blood vessel dilators 血管扩张剂

B-type natriuretic peptide (BNP) B 型钠尿肽

calcium channel blockers 钙通道阻滞剂

congested lungs 肺充血

congestive heart failure 充血性心力衰竭

coronary artery disease (CAD) 冠心病

CT coronary angiogram 冠脉 CT 造影

diastolic dysfunction 舒张功能不全

ejection fraction (EF) 射血分数

heart attack 心脏病发作

heartfailure 心衰

heart valve surgery 心脏瓣膜手术

implantable cardiac defibrillator (ICD) 植入式心脏除颤器

left ventricular assist device (LVAD) 左心室辅助装置
left ventricular dysfunction 左心室功能不全
retain fluid (water) and sodium 水钠潴留
rheumatic fever 风湿热
systolic dysfunction 舒张功能不全
systolic heart failure 收缩性心衰

张　伟　马志方

25

Acute Respiratory Distress Syndrome (ARDS)
急性呼吸窘迫综合征

What is acute respiratory distress syndrome (ARDS)?

Acute respiratory distress syndrome (ARDS) is a lung problem. It happens when fluid builds up in the lungs, causing breathing failure and low oxygen levels in the blood. ARDS is life-threatening, because it keeps organs like the brain and kidneys from getting the oxygen they need to work.

ARDS is a rapidly developing, life-threatening condition in which the lung is injured to the point where it can't properly do its job of moving air in and out of the blood. ARDS occurs most often in people who are being treated for another serious illness or injury. Most of the time, people who get ARDS are already in the hospital for another reason.

Doctors first recognized the syndrome in 1967, when they came across 12 people who developed sudden breathing problems and rapid lung failure. All of them had similar patchy spots on their chest X-rays.

At first, the condition was called adult respiratory distress syndrome, so people would not confuse it with a similar type of lung distress seen in infants. But because ARDS can also occur in children aged 1 and older, doctors now refer to it as acute respiratory distress syndrome. Acute means sudden or new.

ARDS may also be called acute lung injury, noncardiac pulmonary edema, and increased-permeability pulmonary edema. In the past it was also called stiff lung, wet lung, and shock lung.

According to the National Heart Lung and Blood Institute, about 190,000 people in the U.S. develop ARDS each year. About 40% of people (4 out of 10) who get ARDS don't survive it. That means that 60% of people (6 out of 10) survive.

What causes ARDS?

ARDS can occur when a major injury or extreme inflammation somewhere in the body damages the small blood vessels including those in the lungs. As a result, the lungs are unable to fill with air and can't move enough oxygen into the bloodstream.

The lung damage can be direct or indirect.

Conditions that can directly injure the lungs and possibly lead to ARDS include:

- Breathing in smoke or poisonous chemicals
- Breathing in stomach contents while throwing up (aspiration)
- Near drowning
- Pneumonia
- Severe acute respiratory syndrome (SARS), a lung infection

Conditions that can indirectly injure the lungs and possibly lead to ARDS include:

- Bacterial blood infection (sepsis)
- Drug overdose
- Having many blood transfusions
- Heart-lung bypass
- Infection or irritation of the pancreas (pancreatitis)
- Severe bleeding from a traumatic injury (such as a car accident)
- Severe hit to the chest or head

The conditions that have most commonly been linked to ARDS include sepsis, traumatic injury, and lung infections such as pneumonia. However, it's important to note that not everyone who has these conditions develops ARDS. Doctors are not sure why some people develop ARDS and others do not.

What are the symptoms of ARDS?

Symptoms of ARDS come on suddenly, usually within hours or days of the event that initially caused injury to the lung.

ARDS is defined by three main signs and symptoms:

- Rapid breathing
- Feeling like you can't get enough air in your lungs
- Low oxygen levels in your blood, which can lead to organ failure and symptoms such as rapid heart rate, abnormal heart rhythms, confusion, and extreme tiredness

Other symptoms can occur, depending on the event that caused the ARDS. For example, if pneumonia is causing the ARDS, symptoms may also include chest pain and fever.

ARDS mostly occurs about 72 hours after the trigger, such as an injury (trauma, burns, aspiration, massive blood transfusion, drug/alcohol abuse) or an acute illness (infectious pneumonia, sepsis, acute pancreatitis).

ARDS is characterized by:

- Acute onset

- Bilateral infiltrates on chest radiograph sparing costophrenic angles
- Pulmonary artery wedge pressure < 18mmHg (obtained by pulmonary artery catheterization), if this information is available; if unavailable, then lack of clinical evidence of left atrial hypertension
- If $PaO_2:FiO_2$ < 300mmHg (40kPa) acute lung injury (ALI) is considered to be present
- If $PaO_2:FiO_2$ < 200mmHg (26.7kPa) acute respiratory distress syndrome (ARDS) is considered to be present

The $PaO_2:FiO_2$ ratios above refer to the gradient between the inspired oxygen level and the oxygen that is present in the blood. The lower the ratio, the less inspired oxygen is getting into the blood, and so the worse the patient's condition — so ARDS represents a more severe progression of disease from ALI by these diagnostic criteria.

Since ARDS is an extremely serious condition which requires invasive forms of therapy it is not without risk. Complications to be considered are:

- **Pulmonary:** barotrauma (volutrauma), pulmonary embolism (PE), pulmonary fibrosis, ventilator-associated pneumonia (VAP).
- **Gastrointestinal:** hemorrhage (ulcer), dysmotility, pneumoperitoneum, bacterial translocation.
- **Cardiac:** arrhythmias, myocardial dysfunction.
- **Renal:** acute renal failure (ARF), positive fluid balance.
- **Mechanical:** vascular injury, pneumothorax (by placing pulmonary artery catheter), tracheal injury/stenosis (result of intubation and/or irritation by endotracheal tube.
- **Nutritional:** malnutrition (catabolic state), electrolyte deficiency.

To summarize and simplify, ARDS is an acute (rapid onset) syndrome (collection of symptoms) that affects the lungs widely and results in a severe oxygenation defect, but is not due to heart failure. ARDS is a medical emergency. The severe loss of oxygen can rapidly lead to death without prompt treatment.

How is ARDS diagnosed?

There is no test to definitively diagnose ARDS. The doctor will perform a physical exam and listen to your heart and lungs using a stethoscope. If one has ARDS, the doctor will hear abnormal breathing sounds, such as wheezing or crackles.

If one have low blood oxygen levels, his skin and lips may be a bluish color. An arterial blood gas test is done to check the oxygen level in his blood. Low blood oxygen levels can be a sign of ARDS.

Other tests that are done to help diagnose ARDS include:

- Chest X-ray to check for fluid in the air spaces in your lungs
- Complete blood count and other blood tests to look for signs of infection
- Sputum culture to see if bacteria or fungi are present in a sample of mucus that you coughed up from your lungs
- Lung CT scan to look for fluid in the lungs, signs of pneumonia, or other lung problems
- Heart tests are also done to rule out heart failure as the cause. Heart failure can cause fluid buildup in the lungs

Four main criteria for ARDS:

- Acute onset
- Chest X-Ray: Bilateral diffuse infiltrates of the lungs
- No cardiovascular lesion
- No evidence of left atrial hypertension: PaO_2/FiO_2 ratio equal to or less than 200mmHg.

The criteria for diagnosis of Acute Lung Injury (ALI) are similar except that PaO_2/FiO_2 ratio is <300mmHg.

To assess the severity of ARDS, the Murray scoring system is used, which takes into account the chest X-ray, the PaO_2/FiO_2 ratio, the positive end-expiratory pressure, and lung compliance.

How is ARDS treated?

Most people who develop ARDS are very sick and already in the hospital. A person who has ARDS is admitted to the hospital's intensive care unit (ICU). There is no specific treatment for ARDS. The goal is to support breathing and allow the patient's lungs to heal. This involves the use of a breathing machine (mechanical ventilator) and supplemental oxygen. Researchers continue to study new ways to provide patients oxygen. A study by the National Heart Lung and Blood Institute found that smaller puffs of air from a mechanical ventilator lowered the death rate and allowed a patient to be off the machine for more days.

The possibilities of non-invasive ventilation are limited to the very early period of the disease or, better, to prevention in individuals at risk for the development of the disease (atypical pneumonias, pulmonary contusion, major surgery patients).

It's also very important to treat the underlying cause of the ARDS. For example, if there is a bacterial infection, antibiotics will be prescribed. The patient will also be given fluids and nutrients through an IV or feeding tube. The fluid balance will be carefully monitored to make sure fluid does not build up in the lungs.

Treatment of the underlying cause is imperative, as it tends to maintain the ARDS picture.

Appropriate antibiotic therapy must be administered as soon as microbiological culture results are available. Empirical therapy may be appropriate if local microbiological surveillance is efficient. More than 60% ARDS patients experience a (nosocomial) pulmonary infection either before or after the onset of lung injury.

The origin of infection, when surgically treatable, must be operated on. When sepsis is diagnosed, appropriate local protocols should be enacted.

Commonly used supportive therapy includes particular techniques of mechanical ventilation and pharmacological agents whose effectiveness with respect to the outcome has not yet been proven. It is now debated whether mechanical ventilation is to be considered mere supportive therapy or actual treatment, since it may substantially affect survival.

Survivors of ARDS have an increased risk of lower quality of life, persistent cognitive impairment, depression and posttraumatic stress disorder.

Mechanical ventilation

The overall goal is to maintain acceptable gas exchange and to minimize adverse effects in its application. Three parameters are used: PEEP (positive end-expiratory pressure, to maintain maximal recruitment of alveolar units), mean airway pressure (to promote recruitment and predictor of hemodynamic effects) and plateau pressure (best predictor of alveolar overdistention).

Conventional therapy aimed at tidal volumes (Vt) of 12-15 ml/kg. Recent studies have shown that high tidal volumes can overstretch alveoli resulting in volutrauma (secondary lung injury). Low tidal volumes (Vt) may cause hypercapnia and atelectasis due to their inherent tendency to increase physiologic shunt. Physiologic dead space cannot change as it is ventilation without perfusion. A shunt is perfusion without ventilation.

Airway pressure release ventilation

It is often said that no particular ventilator mode is known to improve mortality in airway pressure release ventilation (APRV). Well documented advantages to APRV ventilation include: decreased airway pressures, decreased minute ventilation, decreased dead-space ventilation, promotion of spontaneous breathing, almost 24 hour a day alveolar recruitment, decreased use of sedation, near elimination of neuromuscular blockade, optimized arterial blood gas results, mechanical restoration of FRC (functional residual capacity), a positive effect on cardiac output (due to the negative inflection from the elevated baseline with each spontaneous breath), increased organ and tissue perfusion and potential for increased urine output secondary to increased renal perfusion.

A patient with ARDS, on average, spends between 8 and 11 days on a mechanical ventilator; APRV may reduce this time significantly and conserve valuable resources.

Positive end-expiratory pressure

Positive end-expiratory pressure (PEEP) is used in mechanically-ventilated patients with ARDS to improve oxygenation. In ARDS, three populations of alveoli can be distinguished. There are normal alveoli which are always inflated and engaging in gas exchange, flooded alveoli which can never, under any ventilatory regime, be used for gas exchange, and atelectatic or partially flooded alveoli that can be "recruited" to participate in gas exchange under certain ventilatory regimens. The recruitablealveoli represent a continuous population, some of which can be recruited with minimal PEEP, and others which can only be recruited with high levels of PEEP. An additional complication is that some or perhaps most alveoli can only be opened with higher airway pressures than are needed to keep them open. Hence the justification for maneuvers where PEEP is increased to very high levels for seconds to minutes before dropping the PEEP to a lower level. Finally, PEEP can be harmful. High PEEP necessarily increases mean airway pressure and alveolar pressure. This in turn can damage normal alveoli by overdistension resulting in DAD.

A compromise between the beneficial and adverse effects of PEEP is inevitable.

Prone position

Distribution of lung infiltrates in acute respiratory distress syndrome is non-uniform. Repositioning into the prone position (face down) might improve oxygenation by relieving atelectasis and improving perfusion. However, although the hypoxemia is overcome there seems to be no effect on overall survival.

Fluid management

Several studies have shown that pulmonary function and outcome are better in patients that lost weight or pulmonary wedge pressure was lowered by diuresis or fluid restriction.

Corticosteroids

A study has found significant improvement in ARDS using modest doses of corticosteroids. But high dose steroid therapy has no effect on ARDS when given within 24 hours of the onset of illness. This was a study involving a small number of patients in one center. A recent study demonstrated that they are not efficacious in ARDS. The benefit of steroids in late ARDS may be explained by the ability of steroids to promote breakdown and inhibit fibrosis.

Nitric oxide

Inhaled nitric oxide (NO) potentially acts as selective pulmonary vasodilator. Rapid binding to hemoglobin prevents systemic effects. It should increase perfusion of better ventilated areas. There are no large studies demonstrating positive results. Therefore its use must be considered individually.

The outlook for patients with ARDS

The survival rate for people with ARDS has improved in recent years, although doctors aren't sure why. Some people who get ARDS make a full recovery, but others have lasting lung damage and long-term breathing problems.

The following factors have been associated with a poor prognosis:

- Active cancer
- Advanced age
- Bacteria blood infection (sepsis)
- Being African-American
- Long-term alcohol abuse
- Long-term liver disease
- HIV infection
- Multiple organ failure
- Organ transplant

It can take many months or even years to recover from ARDS. Some people are very tired and weak after being on a breathing machine, and still have some shortness of breath after going home from the hospital. Pulmonary rehabilitation is an important part of recovery. Such therapy teaches patients how to exercise their lungs and become active again. Support groups and counseling can also be helpful.

中英文注释

关键词汇

alveoli [æl'viəlai] n. 肺泡

atelectasis [ˌæti'lektəsis] n. 肺不张

barotrauma [ˌbærə'trɔːmə] n. 气压伤

bloodstream ['blʌdˌstriːm] n. 血流

crackle ['kræk(ə)l] n. 爆裂声

diuresis [ˌdaijʊ(ə)'riːsis] n. 利尿

fungi ['fʌŋgai] n. 真菌

gastrointestinal [ˌgæstroin'tɛstinl] adj. 胃肠的

hemodynamic [ˌhɛmodai'næmik] n. 血液动力学的

hypoxemia [ˌhaipɑk'simiə] n. 血氧不足；低氧血症

parameter [pə'ræmitə] n. 参数

permeability [pɜːmiə'biliti] n. 渗透性

pneumonia [njuːˈməʊniə] n. 肺炎

pneumoperitoneum [ˈnjuːməˌperitəˈniəm] n. 气腹

pneumothorax [ˌnjuːmə(ʊ)ˈθɔːræks] n. 气胸

sepsis [ˈsepsis] n. 败血症

tracheostomy [ˌtrekiˈɑstəmi] n. 气管造口术

vasodilator [ˌveizəʊdaiˈleitə] n. 血管舒张药

wheezing [hwiz] n. 哮喘，气喘

主要短语

acute lung injury (ALI) 急性肺损伤

acute renal failure (ARF) 急性肾功能衰竭

acute respiratory distress syndrome (ARDS) 急性呼吸窘迫综合征

airway pressure release ventilation(APRV) 气道压力释放通气

arterial blood gas test 动脉血气分析

costophrenic angles 肋膈角

functional residual capacity(FRC) 功能残气量

mechanical ventilation 机械通气

nitric oxide (NO) 一氧化氮

PaO2:FiO2 ratios 动脉血氧分压（PaO$_2$）/吸入氧分数值（FiO$_2$）

positive end-expiratory pressure (PEEP) 呼气末正压通气

posttraumatic stress disorder 创伤后应激障碍

pulmonary artery wedge pressure 肺动脉楔压

pulmonary fibrosis 肺纤维化

severe acute respiratory syndrome (SARS) 严重急性呼吸系统综合征; 非典型肺炎

sputum culture 痰培养

tidal volumes (Vt) 潮气量

ventilator-associated pneumonia (VAP) 呼吸机相关性肺炎

李 丹

26 Asthma
哮　喘

What is asthma?

Asthma is a chronic disease of the airways that makes breathing difficult. With asthma, there is inflammation of the air passages that results in a temporary narrowing of the airways that carry oxygen to the lungs. This results in asthma symptoms, including coughing, wheezing, shortness of breath, and chest tightness. Some people refer to asthma as "bronchial asthma."

Even though there are seemingly miraculous treatments for asthma symptoms, asthma is still a serious — even dangerous — disease that affects more than 25 million Americans and causes nearly 2 million emergency room visits ever year.

In each of the following sections, there are in-depth articles that link to the topics. Be sure to read each health topic so you have a greater understanding of asthma and how it is diagnosed and treated.

There are three major features of asthma:

- Airway obstruction. During normal breathing, the bands of muscle that surround the airways are relaxed, and air moves freely. But in people with asthma, allergy-causing substances and environmental triggers make the bands of muscle surrounding the airways tighten, and air cannot move freely. Less air causes a person to feel short of breath, and the air moving through the tightened airways causes a whistling sound known as wheezing.
- Inflammation. People with asthma have red and swollen bronchial tubes. This inflammation is thought to contribute greatly to the long-term damage that asthma can cause to the lungs. And, therefore, treating this inflammation is key to managing asthma in the long run.
- Airway irritability. The airways of people with asthma are extremely sensitive. The airways tend to overreact and narrow due to even the slightest triggers such as pollen, animal dander, dust, or fumes.

Adult-Onset Asthma

Asthma may occur at any age, although it's more common in younger individuals (under age 40).

People who have a family history of asthma have an increased risk of developing the disease. Allergies and asthma often occur together. Smoking with asthma, a dangerous combination, is still seen commonly.

However, anyone can develop asthma at any time, and adult-onset asthma happens frequently. If you have adult-onset asthma, your doctor will instruct you in using the asthma inhalers and other asthma medications to prevent further breathing problems.

What are the symptoms of asthma?

Asthma is characterized by inflammation of the bronchial tubes with increased production of sticky secretions inside the tubes. People with asthma experience symptoms when the airways tighten, inflame, or fill with mucus. Common asthma symptoms include:

- Coughing, especially at night
- Wheezing
- Shortness of breath
- Chest tightness, pain, or pressure

Still, not every person with asthma has the same symptoms in the same way. You may not have all of these symptoms, or you may have different symptoms at different times. Your asthma symptoms may also vary from one asthma attack to the next, being mild during one and severe during another.

Some people with asthma may go for extended periods without having any symptoms, interrupted by periodic worsening of their symptoms called asthma attacks. Others might have asthma symptoms every day. In addition, some people may only have asthma during exercise or asthma with viral infections like colds.

Mild asthma attacks are generally more common. Usually, the airways open up within a few minutes to a few hours. Severe attacks are less common but last longer and require immediate medical help. It is important to recognize and treat even mild asthma symptoms to help you prevent severe episodes and keep asthma under better control.

Know the Early Symptoms of Asthma

Early warning signs are changes that happen just before or at the very beginning of an asthma attack. These signs may start before the well-known symptoms of asthma and are the earliest signs that your asthma is worsening.

In general, these signs are not severe enough to stop you from going about your daily activities. But by recognizing these signs, you can stop an asthma attack or prevent one from getting worse. Early warning signs of asthma include:

- Frequent cough, especially at night

- Losing your breath easily or shortness of breath
- Feeling very tired or weak when exercising
- Wheezing or coughing after exercise
- Feeling tired, easily upset, grouchy, or moody
- Decreases or changes in lung function as measured on a peak flow meter
- Signs of a cold or allergies (sneezing, runny nose, cough, nasal congestion, sore throat, and headache)
- Trouble sleeping

If you have early warning signs or symptoms of asthma, you should take more asthma medication as described in your asthma action plan.

Know the Symptoms of an Asthma Attack

An asthma attack is the episode in which bands of muscle surrounding the airways are triggered to tighten. This tightening is called bronchospasm. During the attack, the lining of the airways becomes swollen or inflamed and the cells lining the airways produce more and thicker mucus than normal.

All of these factors — bronchospasm, inflammation, and mucus production — cause symptoms such as difficulty breathing, wheezing, coughing, shortness of breath, and difficulty performing normal daily activities. Other symptoms of an asthma attack include:

- Severe wheezing when breathing both in and out
- Coughing that won't stop
- Very rapid breathing
- Chest pain or pressure
- Tightened neck and chest muscles, called retractions
- Difficulty talking
- Feelings of anxiety or panic
- Pale, sweaty face
- Blue lips or fingernails

The severity of an asthma attack can escalate rapidly, so it's important to treat these asthma symptoms immediately once you recognize them.

Without immediate treatment, such as with your asthma inhaler or bronchodilator, your breathing will become more labored. If you use a peak flow meter at this time, the reading will probably be less than 50%.

As your lungs continue to tighten, you will be unable to use the peak flow meter at all. Gradually, your lungs will tighten so there is not enough air movement to produce wheezing. This is sometimes called the "silent chest," and it is an ominous sign. You need to be transported to a hospital immediately. Unfortunately, some people interpret the disappearance of wheezing as a sign of improvement and fail to get prompt emergency care.

If you do not receive adequate asthma treatment, you will eventually be unable to speak and will develop a bluish coloring around your lips. This color change, known as cyanosis, means you have less and less oxygen in your blood. Without aggressive treatment for this asthma emergency, you will lose consciousness and eventually die.

If you are experiencing an asthma attack, follow the "Red Zone" or emergency instructions in your asthma action plan immediately. These symptoms occur in life-threatening asthma attacks. You need medical attention right away.

Know the Asthma Symptoms in Children

Asthma affects as many as 10% to 12% of children in the United States and is the leading cause of chronic illness in children. For unknown reasons, the incidence of asthma in children is steadily increasing. While asthma symptoms can begin at any age, most children have their first asthma symptoms by age 5.

Not all children with asthma wheeze. Chronic coughing with asthma may be the only obvious sign, and a child's asthma may go unrecognized if the cough is attributed to recurrent bronchitis.

Know About Unusual Asthma Symptoms

Not everyone with asthma has the usual symptoms of cough, wheezing, and shortness of breath. Sometimes individuals have unusual asthma symptoms that may not appear to be related to asthma. Some "unusual" asthma symptoms may include the following:

- rapid breathing
- sighing
- fatigue
- inability to exercise properly (called exercise-induced asthma)
- difficulty sleeping or nighttime asthma
- anxiety
- difficulty concentrating
- chronic cough without wheezing

Also, asthma symptoms can be mimicked by other conditions such as bronchitis, vocal cord dysfunction, and even heart failure.

It's important to understand your body. Talk with your asthma doctor and others with asthma. Be aware that asthma may not always have the same symptoms in every person.

Know Why Infections Trigger Asthma Symptoms

Sometimes a virus or bacterial infection is an asthma trigger. For instance, you might have a cold virus that triggers your asthma symptoms. Or your asthma can be triggered by a bacterial sinus infection. Sinusitis with asthma is common.

It's important to know the signs and symptoms of respiratory tract infections and to call your health care provider immediately for diagnosis and treatment. For instance, you might have symptoms of increased shortness of breath, difficulty breathing, or wheezing with a bronchial infection. In people who don't have asthma, the bronchial infection may not trigger the same debilitating symptoms. Know your body and understand warning signs that an infection might be starting. Then take the proper medications as prescribed to rid the infection and regain control of your asthma and health.

Your doctor or asthma specialist plays the first and most significant role in helping you get control of your asthma. Not only does your doctor serve as the one who can accurately diagnose and prescribe treatment for your asthma, your doctor may become a close, dependable friend who can give you support when your concerns turn into ongoing worries and anxieties.

At the initial exam, your doctor will obtain a detailed medical history, including any information on asthma symptoms, how you feel, known asthma and allergy triggers, your activity level and diet, your home and work environment, and family history. During this evaluation, it is important that you talk openly with your doctor about your asthma symptoms and triggers. Some questions you might consider beforehand include:

- Shortness of breath
- Wheezing, possibly triggered by allergies, a cold, sinus infection, or bronchitis
- Frequent cough or just coughing at night
- Severe wheezing when breathing both in and out
- Rapid breathing
- Chest pain or pressure
- Difficulty talking
- Feelings of anxiety or panic
- Pale, sweaty face
- Blue lips or fingernails

How is asthma diagnosed?

After talking with you about your asthma symptoms and possible asthma triggers, your doctor will do a physical exam, laboratory testing, and other possible asthma tests. This will allow you to have a firm understanding of your breathing problems and will be the basis for the suggested plan of asthma treatment.

Your doctor may use one or more of the following asthma tests in diagnosing asthma. These tests are used to assess your breathing and to monitor the effectiveness of asthma treatment.

Spirometry a lung (or pulmonary) function test that measures how much air you can exhale. This asthma test confirms the presence of airway obstruction that improves with treatment, which is very characteristic of asthma, and can accurately measure the degree of lung function impairment. This test can also monitor your response to asthma medications and is recommended for adults and children over age 5.

Peak Flow Testing a self-assessment you can do at home to evaluate lung function. The peak expiratory flow rate (PEFR) provides a reliable objective measure of airway function. Your doctor will go over how to use a peak flow meter, which involves taking a deep breath and blowing out as hard as you can. Peak flow is the highest airflow velocity that you can achieve. When done accurately, a drop in the peak flow measurement reflects an obstruction in your airways. While peak flow is less accurate than office spirometry for monitoring of lung function, peak flow monitoring at home can help you manage your symptoms at home and help indicate when an asthma attack may be approaching.

Chest X-Ray while not routinely required, if there are symptoms that may be caused by another condition such as pneumonia, your doctor may want to do a chest X-ray. Or, if your asthma treatment is not working as well as it should, a chest X-ray may help to clarify the problem.

How is asthma treated?

If you or a loved one has asthma, you should know about the most effective asthma treatments for short-term relief and long-term control. Understanding asthma treatments will enable you to work with your asthma doctor to confidently manage your asthma symptoms daily. When you do have an asthma attack or asthma symptoms, it's important to know when to call your doctor or asthma specialist to prevent an asthma emergency. Be sure to read all the in-depth articles that link to topics within each of the following sections. By doing so, you will gain new insight into asthma and how it's treated.

Asthma Medications

Asthma medications can save your life — and let you live an active life in spite of your asthma. There are two basic types of drugs used in asthma treatment.

Steroids and Other Anti-Inflammatory Drugs

Anti-inflammatory drugs, particularly inhaled steroids, are the most important treatment for most people with asthma. These lifesaving medications prevent asthma attacks and work by reducing swelling and mucus production in the airways. As a result, the airways are less sensitive and less likely to react to asthma triggers and cause asthma symptoms.

Bronchodilators and Asthma

Bronchodilators relieve the symptoms of asthma by relaxing the muscles that can tighten around the airways. This helps to open up the airways.

Short-acting bronchodilator inhalers are often referred to as rescue inhalers and are used to quickly relieve the cough, wheeze, chest tightness, and shortness of breath caused by asthma. They may also be used prior to exercise for people with exercise-induced asthma. These should not be used daily in the routine treatment of asthma. If you need to use a short-acting bronchodilator as a rescue inhaler more than twice a week, then your asthma is not optimally controlled. Ask your doctor about improving your asthma controller medication.

Long-acting bronchodilators are used in combination with inhaled steroids for control of asthma symptoms or when someone has ongoing asthma symptoms despite treatment with a daily inhaled steroid. Long-acting bronchodilators are never used alone as long-term therapy for asthma.

Asthma Inhalers

Asthma inhalers are the most common and effective way to deliver asthma drugs to the lungs. They are available in different types that require different techniques for use. Some inhalers deliver one medication and others contain two different medications.

Asthma Nebulizer

If you're having difficulty using small inhalers, your doctor may prescribe an asthma nebulizer, also known as a breathing machine. The asthma nebulizer uses a mouthpiece or mask and is typically used for infants, small children, older adults, or anyone who has difficulty using inhalers with spacers. The nebulizer changes asthma medications from a liquid to a mist, so that they can be more easily inhaled into the lungs. This takes a few more minutes than using inhalers.

Prednisone and Asthma Attacks

If you have a serious asthma attack (exacerbation), your doctor may prescribe a short course of oral corticosteroids. When used orally for less than two weeks, the side effects of corticosteroids are only temporary, but when used for many months, these side effects can be serious and permanent. After the severe symptoms of your asthma attack have been successfully treated and controlled, your doctor will work with you to minimize your need for prednisone in the future. Faithfully taking an inhaled corticosteroid every day is the most commonly successful method to do this.

中英文注释

关键词汇

allergy ['ælɚdʒi] n. 过敏症

asthma ['æzmə] n. 哮喘

bronchospasm ['brɔŋkəspæzəm] n. 支气管痉挛

cyanosis [ˌsaiə'nosis] n. 发绀

debilitate [di'biliteit] vt. 使衰弱，使虚弱

escalate ['eskəleit] vi/vt. 逐步增强

exacerbation [ekˌsæsə'beiʃən] n. 恶化

exhale [ɛks'hel] vi. 呼气，呼出

fume [fjum] n/vi. 熏，烟气

grouchy ['graʊtʃi] adj. 不高兴，不满的

incidence ['insidəns] n. 发病率

inhale [in'hel] vi. 吸入，吸气

irritability [ˌirətə'biləti] n. 过敏性，兴奋性

mimicked [mimikt] v. 模仿

miraculous [mi'rækjələs] adj. 不可思议的

mist [mist] n. 薄雾

moody ['mudi] adj. 郁郁寡欢的

nebulizer ['nɛbjəˌlaizɚ] n. 喷雾剂，喷雾器

ominous ['amɪnəs] adj. 预兆的；不吉利的

optimally ['əptəməli] adv. 最佳；最适宜地

panic ['pænik] n. 恐慌，惊恐

pollen ['palən] n. 花粉

prednisone ['prednizəʊn] n. 强的松

sinusitis [ˌsainə'saitis] n. 鼻窦炎

spirometry [spai'rɔmitri] n. 肺活量测定法

主要短语

airway irritability 气道应激性，气道过敏性

airway obstruction 气道梗阻

bronchial asthma 支气管哮喘

bronchodilator 支气管扩张剂

peak expiratory flow rate (PEFR) 最大呼气流速

vocal cord 声带

张　伟　马志方

Chronic Obstructive Pulmonary Disease (COPD)

27

慢性阻塞性肺疾病

What is COPD?

COPD, or chronic obstructive pulmonary disease, is a long-term lung disease that refers to both chronic bronchitis and emphysema.

What causes COPD?

COPD is most often caused by smoking. Most people with COPD are long-term smokers, and research shows that smoking cigarettes increases the risk of getting COPD:

- Out of every 100 long-term smokers, about 15 to 20 get COPD with symptoms. That means that about 80 to 85 out of 100 do not get COPD with symptoms.
- Some studies show that up to half of long-term smokers older than age 60 get COPD.
- Smoking both tobacco and marijuana increases the risk of COPD more than smoking either one.

COPD is often a mix of two diseases: chronic bronchitis and emphysema. Both of these diseases are caused by smoking. Although you can have either chronic bronchitis or emphysema, people more often have a mixture of both diseases.

Chronic bronchitis

Almost all people with chronic bronchitis are, or have been, tobacco smokers. Over time, tobacco smoke and other lung irritants can lead to inflammation in the airways of the lungs (bronchial tubes). As a result, the airways produce more mucus than they normally would. Inflammation and excess mucus cause coughing and narrow the airways. It is hard to breathe through the narrow airways, so you feel short of breath.

Long-term (chronic) mucus production and inflammation over many years may lead to permanent lung damage and may make it more likely that you will get lung infections.

Emphysema

In emphysema, tobacco smoke and other irritants can damage the elastic fibers in the lungs. These stretchy strands of tissue are needed for normal lung function. They

176

allow the lung tissue to stretch when you breathe in and help pull the lungs back to their normal size and shape as you breathe out. When the elastic fibers are damaged:

- The tiny air sacs (alveoli) at the end of the bronchial tubes are damaged. These air sacs are where the blood exchanges carbon dioxide (a by-product of metabolism) for oxygen. When air sacs are damaged or destroyed, their walls break down and the sacs become larger. These large air sacs move less oxygen into the blood. After air sacs are destroyed, they cannot be replaced.
- The smaller airways in the lungs (bronchioles) tend to collapse when you breathe out, trapping air in the alveoli. As a result, oxygen-rich air has trouble entering the air sacs. And carbon dioxide has a harder time getting out of the lungs.

See pictures of bronchitis and emphysema.

In chronic bronchitis, exposure to tobacco smoke and other lung irritants over time can lead to inflammation in the airways that deliver air into the lungs (bronchial tubes). As a result, the airways produce more mucus than they would normally. Inflammation and extra mucus reduce air flow and cause coughing. Mucus production and inflammation over many years may lead to progressive and permanent lung damage.

Emphysema is a long-term (chronic) lung disease. In emphysema, the tiny air sacs (alveoli) at the end of the airways in the lungs are damaged. When the air sacs are damaged or destroyed, their walls break down and the sacs become larger. These larger air sacs move less oxygen into the blood. This causes difficulty breathing or shortness of breath that gets worse over time. After air sacs are destroyed, they cannot be replaced.

Emphysema is a form of chronic obstructive pulmonary disease (COPD). It is usually caused by smoking. A rare type of emphysema is caused by the lack of a substance in the lungs called alpha1-antitrypsin. This type of emphysema is usually inherited.

Other causes

Other possible causes of COPD include:

- Long-term exposure to lung irritants such as industrial dust and chemical fumes.
- Preterm birth that leads to lung damage (neonatal chronic lung disease).
- Inherited factors (genes), including alpha-1 antitrypsin deficiency, a rare condition in which your body may not be able to make enough of a protein (alpha-1 antitrypsin) that helps protect the lungs from damage. People who have this disorder and who smoke generally start to have symptoms of emphysema in their 30s or 40s. Those who have this disorder but do not smoke generally start to have symptoms in their 80s.

What are the symptoms of COPD?

When you have COPD:

- You have a cough that won't go away.
- You often cough up mucus.
- You are often short of breath, especially when you exercise.

COPD exacerbation

Many people with COPD have attacks called flare-ups or exacerbations (say "egg-ZASS-er-BAY-shuns"). This is when your usual symptoms quickly get worse and stay worse. A COPD flare-up can be dangerous, and you may have to go to the hospital.

Symptoms include:

- Coughing up more mucus than usual.
- A change in the color or thickness of that mucus.
- More shortness of breath than usual.

These attacks are most often caused by infections-such as acute bronchitis and pneumonia-and air pollution.

Work with your doctor to make a plan for dealing with a COPD flare-up. If you are prepared, you may be able to get it under control. Try not to panic if you start to have one. Quick treatment at home may help you manage serious breathing problems.

The stages of COPD

The stages of COPD are often defined according to your symptoms plus a measure of how well your lungs work, called your "lung function".

In the following symptoms lists, lung function FEV1 is a test result that shows how fast you can breathe air out of your lungs. FEV1 stands for forced expiratory volume in 1 second.

FEV1 can be measured by machines called spirometers. The test result is reported as a percentage of normal. In other words, an FEV1 of 100% means the lungs are working normally; 80% is less than normal; 30% is very much less than normal.

Here is how the stages of COPD are described by the Global Initiative for Chronic Obstructive Lung Disease.

- Mild COPD (stage 1)

  Usually, but not always, a chronic cough that often brings up mucus from the lungs

  Lung function FEV1 of 80% of normal or higher
- Moderate COPD (stage 2)

  Chronic cough with a lot of mucus

  Shortness of breath, especially with exercise

  An occasional COPD flare-up

  Lung function FEV1 of 50% to 79%
- Severe COPD (stage 3)

  Chronic cough with a lot of mucus

Shortness of breath

Fatigue and a reduced ability to exercise

Repeated and sometimes severe COPD flare-ups

Lung function FEV1 of 30% to 49%

- Very severe COPD (stage 4)

Chronic cough with a lot of mucus

Severe shortness of breath

Weight loss

Blue skin color, especially in the lips, fingers, and toes (called cyanosis)

Fluid buildup in the legs and feet (called edema)

Life-threatening COPD flare-ups

Lung function FEV1 of less than 30%, or of less than 50% along with chronic respiratory failure (a condition caused by carbon dioxide that stays in the lungs)

Conditions with similar symptoms

Conditions with symptoms similar to COPD include:

- Heart failure.
- Coronary artery disease.
- Asthma. Some people with COPD may have asthma too. But the two conditions differ in a number of ways, including how old you are when you get the disease and what triggers an attack.
- Cystic fibrosis.
- Pulmonary fibrosis.
- Bronchiectasis.

How to diagnose COPD?

To diagnose COPD, do the following tests:

- **Medical history and physical exam.** These will give your doctor important information about your health.
- **Lung function tests.** These measure the amount of air in your lungs and the speed at which air moves in and out. Spirometry is the most important of these tests.
- **Chest X-ray.** This helps rule out other conditions with similar symptoms, such as lung cancer.

Tests done as needed

- **Arterial blood gas test.** This test measures how much oxygen, carbon dioxide, and acid is in your blood. It helps your doctor decide whether you need oxygen treatment.
- **Oximetry.** This test measures the oxygen saturation in the blood. It can be

useful in finding out whether oxygen treatment is needed, but it provides less information than the arterial blood gas test.

- **Electrocardiogram (ECG, EKG) or echocardiogram.** These tests may find certain heart problems that can cause shortness of breath.
- **Transfer factor for carbon monoxide.** This test looks at whether your lungs have been damaged, and if so, how much damage there is and how bad your COPD might be.

Tests rarely done

- A test to measure levels of **alpha-1 antitrypsin**, or **ATT**. ATT is a protein your body makes that helps protect the lungs. People whose bodies don't make enough ATT are more likely to get emphysema.
- A **CT scan**. This gives doctors a detailed picture of the lungs.

Regular checkups

Because COPD is a disease that keeps getting worse, it is important to schedule regular checkups with your doctor. Checkups may include:

- Spirometry.
- Arterial blood gas test.
- X-rays or ECGs.

Tell your doctor about any changes in your symptoms and whether you have had any flare-ups. Your doctor may change your medicines based on your symptoms.

Early detection

The sooner COPD is diagnosed, the sooner you can take steps to slow down the disease and keep your quality of life for as long as possible. Screening tests help your doctor diagnose COPD early, before you have any symptoms.

Talk to your doctor about COPD screening if you:

- Are a smoker or ex-smoker.
- Have had serious asthma symptoms for a long time, which have not improved with treatment.
- Have a family history of emphysema.
- Have a job where you are exposed to a lot of chemicals or dust.

The U.S. Preventive Services Task Force (USPSTF) does not recommend COPD screening for adults who are not at high risk of developing COPD.

How is it treated?

Although COPD cannot be cured, it can be managed. The goals of treatment are to:

- Slow down the disease by avoiding tobacco smoke and air pollution.
- Limit your symptoms, such as shortness of breath.

- Increase your activity level.
- Improve your overall health.
- Prevent and treat flare-ups. A flare-up, or exacerbation, is when your symptoms quickly get worse and stay worse.

Many people are able to manage their COPD well enough to take part in their usual daily activities, hobbies, and family events.

Initial treatment

At first, treatment for COPD helps you breathe better and slow the disease. Much of the treatment includes things you do for yourself:

- **Quit smoking.** This is so important. And it's never too late. No matter how long you have had COPD or how serious it is, quitting smoking will help slow down the disease and improve your quality of life. Today's medicines offer lots of help for people who want to quit. You will double your chances of quitting even if medicine is the only treatment you use to quit, but your odds get even better when you combine medicine and other quit strategies, such as counseling.
- **Stay active.** If you stay active, you may have less shortness of breath, have a better attitude about your life and the disease, and be less likely to feel depressed or isolated from friends and family. Exercise improves shortness of breath and will help you be more active.

Medications

Medicine for COPD is used to:

- Reduce shortness of breath.
- Control coughing and wheezing.
- Prevent COPD flare-ups, also called exacerbations, or keep the flare-ups you do have from being life-threatening.

Most people with COPD find that medicines make breathing easier.

Some COPD medicines are used with devices called inhalers or nebulizers. Most doctors recommend using spacers with inhalers. It's important to learn how to use these devices correctly. Many people don't, so they don't get the full benefit from the medicine.

Surgery

Lung surgery is rarely used to treat COPD. Surgery is never the first treatment choice and is only considered for people who have severe COPD that has not improved with other treatment.

Surgery Choices

- Lung volume reduction surgery: Removes part of one or both lungs, making room for the rest of the lung to work better. It is used only for severe emphysema.

- Lung transplant: Replaces a sick lung with a healthy lung from a person who has just died.
- Bullectomy: Removes the part of the lung that has been damaged by the formation of large, air-filled sacs called bullae. This surgery is rarely done.

中英文注释

关键词汇

alveoli [æl'viəlai] n. 肺泡

antitrypsin ['ænti'tripsin] n. 抗胰蛋白酶

bronchiectasis [ˌbrɒŋki'ektəsis] n. 支气管扩张

bronchiole ['brɒŋkiəʊl] n. 细支气管

emphysema [ˌemfi'si:mə] n. 气肿；肺气肿

exacerbation [ekˌsæsə'beiʃən] n. 恶化；激怒；

irritant ['irit(ə)nt] n. 刺激物，刺激剂

marijuana [ˌmæri'hwɑ:nə] n. 大麻；大麻毒品

mucus ['mju:kəs] n. 黏液

neonatal [ˌni:ə(ʊ)'neit(ə)l] adj. 新生的；初生的

preterm [pri:'tɜ:m] n. 早产，早产婴儿

spirometer [spai'rɒmitə] n. 呼吸量计；肺活量计

主要短语

bronchial tube 支气管

chronic bronchitis 慢性支气管炎

chronic obstructive pulmonary disease (COPD) 慢性阻塞性肺病

cystic fibrosis 囊胞性纤维症

elastic fibers 弹性纤维

forced expiratory volume 用力呼气量；强力呼气容积

oxygen saturation 氧饱和；氧饱和度

pulmonary fibrosis 肺纤维化

许召良　马志方

28 ———————— Pneumonia
肺　　炎

What is pneumonia?

Pneumonia is a lung infection that can make you very sick. You may cough, run a fever, and have a hard time breathing. For most people, pneumonia can be treated at home. It often clears up in 2 to 3 weeks. But older adults, babies, and people with other diseases can become very ill. They may need to be in the hospital.

One can get pneumonia in his daily life, such as at school or work. This is called community-associated pneumonia. One can also get it when he is in a hospital or nursing home. This is called healthcare-associated pneumonia. It may be more severe because he already is ill.

What causes pneumonia?

Viruses, bacteria, or (in rare cases) parasites or other organisms can cause pneumonia.
- In most cases, the specific organism (such as bacteria or virus) cannot be identified even with testing. When an organism is identified, it is usually the bacteria streptococcus pneumoniae.
- Many types of bacteria may cause pneumonia. Pneumonia caused by mycoplasma pneumoniae is sometimes mild and called "walking pneumonia".
- Viruses, such as influenza A (the flu virus) and respiratory syncytial virus (RSV) can cause pneumonia.

In people with impaired immune systems, pneumonia may be caused by other organisms, including some forms of fungi, such as Pneumocystis jiroveci (formally called Pneumocystis carinii). This fungus frequently causes pneumonia in people who have AIDS. Some doctors may suggest an HIV test if they think that pneumocystis jiroveci is causing the pneumonia.

How do you get pneumonia?

You may get pneumonia:
- After you breathe infected air particles into your lungs.

- After you breathe certain bacteria from your nose and throat into your lungs. This generally occurs during sleep.
- During or after a viral upper respiratory infection, such as a cold or influenza (flu).
- As a complication of a viral illness, such asmeasles or chickenpox
- If you breathe large amounts of food, gastric juices from the stomach, or vomit into the lungs (aspiration pneumonia). This can happen when you have had a medical condition that affects your ability to swallow, such as a seizure or a stroke.
- A healthy person's nose and throat often contain bacteria or viruses that cause pneumonia. Pneumonia can develop when these organisms spread to your lungs while your lungs are more likely to be infected. Examples of times when this can happen are during or soon after a cold or if you have a long-term (chronic) illness, such as chronic obstructive pulmonary disease (COPD).
- You can get pneumonia in your daily life, such as at school or work (community-associated pneumonia) or when you are in a hospital or nursing home (healthcare-associated pneumonia). Treatment may differ in healthcare-associated pneumonia, because bacteria causing the infection in hospitals may be different from those causing it in the community. This topic focuses on community-associated pneumonia.

What are the symptoms?

Bacterial pneumonia

Symptoms of pneumonia caused by bacteria in otherwise healthy people younger than 65 usually come on suddenly. They often start during or after an upper respiratory infection, such as the flu or a cold. Symptoms may include:

- Cough, often producing mucus, also called sputum, from the lungs. Mucus may be rusty or green or tinged with blood.
- Fever, which may be less common in older adults.
- Shaking, "teeth-chattering" chills, one time only or many times.
- Fast, often shallow, breathing and the feeling of being short of breath.
- Chest wall pain that is often made worse by coughing or breathing in.
- Fast heartbeat.
- Feeling very tired or weak.
- Nausea and vomiting.
- Diarrhea.

Nonbacterial pneumonia

Symptoms of pneumonia not caused by bacteria may come on gradually and are often not as bad or as obvious as symptoms of bacterial pneumonia. Many people don't know that they have nonbacterial pneumonia, because they don't feel sick. But symptoms may include:

- Fever.
- Cough.
- Shortness of breath.
- Little mucus when you cough.

When symptoms are mild, your doctor may call your condition "walking pneumonia."

In older adults and children

Older adults may have different, fewer, or milder symptoms, such as having no fever or having a cough with no mucus (a dry or nonproductive cough). The major sign of pneumonia in older adults may be a change in how clearly they think (confusion or delirium) or when a lung disease they already have gets worse.

In children, symptoms may depend on age:

- In infants younger than 1 month of age, symptoms may include having little or no energy (lethargy), feeding poorly, grunting, or having a fever.
- In children, symptoms of pneumonia are often the same as in adults. Your doctor will look for signs such as cough and a breathing rate over 60 breaths a minute.

Some conditions with symptoms similar to pneumonia include bronchitis, COPD, and tuberculosis.

How is pneumonia diagnosed?

The doctor will usually diagnose pneumonia with:

- Medical history.
- A physical exam.
- A chest X-ray, which is almost always done to check for changes in the lungsthat may mean pneumonia and to look for other causes of your symptoms. But an X-ray does not always show whether you have pneumonia, especially if it is done when you first get sick. In some cases, the X-ray results may:
- Suggest the type of organism (bacterial, viral, or fungal) causing pneumonia.
- Show complications of pneumonia.
- Show conditions that may occur with pneumonia, such as fluid in the chest cavity or a collapsed lung.
- Reveal another condition, such as heart failure, lung cancer, or acute bronchitis.

Other tests

The need for more tests often depends on how severe your symptoms are, your age, and your overall health. In general, the sicker you are, the more tests you will have. This is especially true for older adults and infants.

- **Mucus test.** If you are very ill, have severe shortness of breath, or have a condition that increases your risk (such as asthma or COPD), your doctor may test your mucus. Tests include a Gram stain and a sputum culture.
- **Rapid urine test.** This test can identify some bacteria that cause pneumonia. This can help guide treatment for pneumonia.
- **HIV test.** In people who have impaired immune systems, pneumonia may be caused by other organisms, including some forms of fungi, such as pneumocystis jiroveci (formally called pneumocystis carinii). This fungus often causes pneumonia in people who have AIDS. Some doctors may suggest an HIV test if they think that pneumocystis jiroveci is causing the pneumonia.

If you have severe pneumonia, you may need other tests, including tests to check for complications and to find out how well your immune system is working.

How is it treated?

Doctors use antibiotics to treat pneumonia caused by bacteria, the most common cause of the condition. Antibiotics have a high cure rate for pneumonia.

Your doctor will choose your antibiotic based on a number of things, including your age, your symptoms and how severe they are, and whether you need to go to the hospital. The number of days you take antibiotics depends on your general health, how serious your pneumonia is, and the type of antibiotic you are taking.

Most people see some improvement in symptoms in 2 to 3 days. Unless you get worse during this time, your doctor usually will not change your treatment for at least 3 days.

Getting started on antibiotics soon after getting pneumonia may help recovery.

If there is no improvement or if your symptoms get worse, you may need a culture and a sensitivity test. These tests help identify the organism that is causing your symptoms. These tests also help your doctor find out whether the bacteria is resistant to the antibiotic.

If you do not need to go to the hospital for pneumonia, it is not usually necessary to identify the organism causing the pneumonia before starting treatment. If you do go to the hospital, you will probably have some testing to identify the bacteria.

You likely will not have to go to the hospital unless you:

- Are older than 65.
- Have other health problems, such as COPD, heart failure, asthma, diabetes, long-term (chronic) kidney failure, or chronic liver disease.

- Cannot care for yourself or would not be able to tell anyone if your symptoms got worse.
- Have severe illness that reduces the amount of oxygen getting to your tissues.
- Have chest pain caused by inflammation of the lining of the lung (pleurisy) so you are not able to cough up mucus effectively and clear your lungs.
- Are being treated outside a hospital and are not getting better (such as your shortness of breath not improving).
- Are not able to eat or keep food down, so you need to take fluids through a vein (intravenous).

Viral pneumonia

Pneumonia also can be caused by viruses, such as those that cause the flu andchickenpox (varicella). Antibiotics do not work to treat pneumonia caused by a virus.

- At this time, there is no proven medicine to treat pneumonia caused by the flu virus. Home treatment, such as rest and taking care of your cough, is the only treatment.
- Varicella pneumonia, which is rare, can be treated with antiviral medicine.

How can you prevent pneumonia?

If you are 65 or older, you smoke, or you have a heart or lung problem, you may want to get a pneumococcal vaccine. It may not keep you from getting pneumonia. But if you do get pneumonia, you probably won't be as sick.

You can also lower your chances of getting pneumonia by staying away from people who have the flu, colds, measles, or chickenpox. You may get pneumonia after you have one of these illnesses. Wash your hands often. This helps prevent the spread of viruses and bacteria that may cause pneumonia.

中英文注释

关键词汇

bacteria [bæk'tiriə] n. 细菌
bronchitis [brɒŋ'kaitis] n. 支气管炎
chickenpox ['tʃikinpɑks] n. 水痘
diarrhea [ˌdɑlə'rlə] n. 痢疾，腹泻
grunt [grʌnt] n. 呼噜声
influenza [influ'enzə] n. 流行性感冒
lethargy ['leθədʒi] n. 昏睡
measle ['mi:zl] n. 麻疹

mycoplasma [ˌmaɪkə(ʊ)ˈplæzmə] n. 支原体

mucus [ˈmjukəs] n. 黏痰

parasite [ˈpærəsaɪt] n. 寄生虫

particle [ˈpɑrtɪkl] n. 颗粒物

pneumococcal [ˌnjuːməˈkɒkəl] n. 肺炎球菌

pneumonia [njuːˈməʊnɪə] n. 肺炎

tinge [tɪndʒ] n. 淡色，些许味道

tuberculosis [tjʊˌbɜːkjʊˈləʊsɪs] n. 肺结核，结核病

vaccine [vækˈsin] n. 疫苗

virus [ˈvaɪrəs] n. 病毒

主要短语

aspiration pneumonia 吸入性肺炎

community-associated pneumonia 社区获得性肺炎

gram stain 革兰氏染色

healthcare-associated pneumonia 护理相关性肺炎

nausea and vomiting 恶心呕吐

pneumocystis jiroveci 肺孢子虫

respiratory syncytial virus (RSV) 呼吸道合胞病毒

sputum culture. 细菌培养

streptococcus pneumonia 肺炎双球菌

upper respiratory infection 上呼吸道感染

viral pneumonia 病毒性肺炎

张 伟 马志方

29 Respiratory Failure

呼 吸 衰 竭

What is respiratory failure?

Respiratory failure (lung failure) is a condition in which the level of oxygen in the blood becomes dangerously low or the level of carbon dioxide becomes dangerously high.

- Conditions that block the airways, damage lung tissue, weaken the muscles that control breathing, or decrease the drive to breathe may cause lung failure.
- People may be very short of breath, have a bluish coloration to the skin, and be confused or sleepy.
- Doctors use blood tests to detect low levels of oxygen or high levels of carbon dioxide in the blood.
- Oxygen is given.
- Sometimes people need the help of a machine to breathe until the underlying problem can be treated.

Respiratory failure is a medical emergency that can result from long-standing, progressively worsening lung disease or from severe lung disease that develops suddenly, such as the acute respiratory distress syndrome.

What causes respiratory failure?

Almost any condition that affects breathing or the lungs can lead to respiratory failure. Certain disorders, such as hypothyroidism or sleep apnea, can decrease the unconscious reflex that drives people to breathe. An overdose of opioids or alcohol also can decrease the drive to breathe by causing profound sedation. Obstruction of the airways, injury to the lung tissues, damage to the bones and tissues around the lungs, and weakness of the muscles that normally inflate the lungs are also common causes. Respiratory failure can occur if blood flow through the lungs becomes abnormal, as happens in pulmonary embolism (see Pulmonary Embolism (PE): Pulmonary Embolism). This disorder does not stop air from moving in and out of the lungs, but without blood flow to a portion of the lungs, oxygen is not properly extracted from the air.

189

What are the symptoms of respiratory failure?

Respiratory failure causes insufficient oxygenation or ventilation and can cause a number of symptoms, which can be severe.

Common symptoms of respiratory failure

Respiratory failure is accompanied by a number of symptoms including:

- Bluish coloration of the lips or fingernails
- Confusion or loss of consciousness
- Fainting or change in level of consciousness or lethargy
- Fatigue
- Irregular heart rate (arrhythmia)
- Rapid breathing (tachypnea) or shortness of breath

Serious symptoms that might indicate a life-threatening condition

In some cases, respiratory failure can be life threatening. Seek immediate medical care (call 120) if you, or someone you are with, have any of these life-threatening symptoms including:

- Bluish coloration of the lips or fingernails
- Change in level of consciousness or alertness, such as passing out or unresponsiveness
- Rapid heart rate (tachycardia)
- Respiratory or breathing problems, such as shortness of breath, difficulty breathing, labored breathing, wheezing, not breathing, or choking

How is it diagnosed?

A doctor may suspect respiratory failure because of the symptoms and physical examination findings. A blood test done on a sample taken from an artery confirms the diagnosis when it shows a dangerously low level of oxygen or a dangerously high level of carbon dioxide. Chest X-rays and other tests are done to determine the cause of respiratory failure.

Type 1

Type 1 respiratory failure is defined as hypoxia without hypercapnia, and indeed the P_aCO_2 may be normal or low. It is typically caused by a ventilation/perfusion (V/Q) mismatch; the volume of air flowing in and out of the lungs is not matched with the flow of blood to the lungs. The basic defect in type 1 respiratory failure is failure of oxygenation characterized by:

P_aO_2	low (< 60 mmHg (8.0 kPa))
P_aCO_2	normal or low (<50 mmHg (6.7 kPa))
$P_{A-a}O_2$	increased

This type of respiratory failure is caused by conditions that affect oxygenation such as:

- Parenchymal disease (V/Q mismatch)
- Diseases of vasculature and shunts: right-to-left shunt, pulmonary embolism
- Interstitial lung diseases: ARDS, pneumonia, emphysema

Type 2

The basic defect in type 2 respiratory failure is characterized by:

P_aO_2	decreased (< 60 mmHg (8.0 kPa))
P_aCO_2	increased (> 50 mmHg (6.7 kPa))
$P_{A-a}O_2$	normal
pH	decreased

Type 2 respiratory failure is caused by inadequate ventilation; both oxygen and carbon dioxide are affected. Defined as the build up of carbon dioxide levels (P_aCO_2) that has been generated by the body. The underlying causes include:

- Increased airways resistance (chronic obstructive pulmonary disease, asthma, suffocation)
- Reduced breathing effort (drug effects, brain stem lesion, extreme obesity)
- A decrease in the area of the lung available for gas exchange (such as in chronic bronchitis).
- Neuromuscular problems (GB syndrome, myasthenia gravis, motor neurone disease)
- Deformed (kyphoscoliosis), rigid (ankylosing spondylitis), or flail chest

How is respiratory failure treated?

Treatment for respiratory failure begins with seeking medical care from your health care provider. The goals of treatment for respiratory failure are to increase oxygenation and improve ventilation. Treatment depends on the severity of the respiratory failure and the cause. Acute respiratory failure treatment will address the underlying cause and include ventilation and oxygenation as needed. Treatment for chronic respiratory failure may be administered at home. Exacerbation of chronic respiratory failure by infection may require hospitalization, and treatment may include oxygenation and ventilator support. Bronchodilators may improve airway patency.

Respiratory failure treatment options

Multiple options are available for the treatment of respiratory failure. Examples include:

- Antibiotics for respiratory infections
- Bilevel positive airway pressure (BiPAP)
- Bronchodilators, including anticholinergics, such as tiotropium (Spiriva), or beta agonists, such as albuterol (Proventil)
- Continuous positive airway pressure (CPAP)
- Inhaled steroid medications to decrease inflammation
- Lung transplant, in rare cases
- Mechanical ventilation, if oxygen therapy if not sufficient to increase blood oxygen levels
- Oxygen therapy to increase blood oxygen levels
- Tracheostomy, a hole made in the front of the neck to help you breathe

What are the potential complications of respiratory failure?

Complications of untreated respiratory failure can be serious, even life threatening in some cases. You can help minimize your risk of serious complications by following the treatment plan you and your health care professional design specifically for you. Complications of respiratory failure include:

- Heart failure
- Myocardial infarction (heart attack)
- Organ failure or dysfunction
- Pneumonia
- Respiratory arrest
- Shock

中英文注释

关键词汇

emphysema [ˌemfˈsiːmə] n. 肺气肿

exacerbation [eksˌæsə(ː)beiʃən] n. 加重、恶化

hypercapnia [ˌhaipə(ː)ˈkæpniə] n. 高碳酸血症

hypoxia [haiˈpɔksiə] n. 缺氧

lethargy [ˈleθədʒiː] n. 嗜睡

oxygenation [ˌɔksidʒiˈneiʃən] n. 氧合作用

suffocation [ˌsʌfəˈkeiʃən] n. 窒息

tachycardia [ˌtækiˈkɑːdiə] n. 心动过速

tracheostomy [ˌtræki'ɔstəmi] n. 气管造口术
ventilation [ˌventl'eiʃən] n. 通气，换气

主要短语

acute respiratory distress syndrome(ARDS) 急性呼吸窘迫综合征
chronic obstructive pulmonary disease(COPD) 慢性阻塞性肺病
flail chest 连枷胸
irregular heart rate 心律不齐
loss of consciousness 意识丧失
pulmonary embolism 肺动脉栓塞
respiratory failure 呼吸衰竭
sleep apnea 睡眠呼吸暂停

李袁飞　马志方

30 ——————— Pulmonary Embolism
肺 栓 塞

What is deep vein thrombosis and pulmonary embolism?

Deep vein thrombosis (DVT) is a condition wherein a blood clot forms in a vein of the deep system. DVT can occur anywhere in the body, but are most frequently found in the deep veins of the legs, thighs, and pelvis. They may infrequently arise from the upper extremities usually because of trauma, or from an indwelling catheter (tubing) or device.

A thrombosis in a deep vein is a much more serious problem than one in a superficial vein, because a piece of the clot can break off and travel through the deep veins back to the heart, and eventually be pumped by the heart into the arteries of the lung. When this happens, the condition is called pulmonary embolism (PE). Pulmonary embolisms occur in 30% of people with DVT, and cause 60,000 deaths annually, many of them unrecognized and labeled as heart attacks.

Pulmonary embolism is the sudden blockage of a major blood vessel (artery) in the lung, usually by a blood clot. In most cases, the clots are small and are not deadly, but they can damage the lung. But if the clot is large and stops blood flow to the lung, it can be deadly. Quick treatment could save the patient's life or reduce the risk of future problems.

PE is a serious condition that can:
- Damage part of the patient's lung because of a lack of blood flow to his lung tissue. This damage may lead to pulmonary hypertension (increased pressure in the pulmonary arteries). Cause low oxygen levels in his blood.
- Damage other organs in his body because of a lack of oxygen.
- If a blood clot is large, or if there are many clots, PE can cause death.

The exact number of people affected by DVT and PE isn't known. Estimates suggest these conditions affect 300,000 to 600,000 people in the United States each year. If left untreated, about 30 percent of patients who have PE will die. Most of those who die do so within the first few hours of the event.

The good news is that a prompt diagnosis and proper treatment can save lives and help prevent the complications of PE.

What causes pulmonary embolism?

In most cases, pulmonary embolism is caused by a blood clot in the leg that breaks loose and travels to the lungs. A blood clot in a vein close to the skin is not likely to cause problems. But having blood clots in deep veins (deep vein thrombosis) can lead to pulmonary embolism. Almost all blood clots that cause pulmonary embolism are formed in the deep leg veins. Clots also can form in the deep veins of the arms or pelvis. More than 300,000 people each year have deep vein thrombosis or a pulmonary embolism. Other things can block an artery, such as tumors, air bubbles, amniotic fluid, or fat that is released into the blood vessels when a bone is broken. But these are rare.

In rare cases, pulmonary embolism may be caused by other substances, include:
- Small masses of infectious material.
- Fat, which can be released into the bloodstream after some types of bone fractures, surgery, trauma, or severe burns.
- Air bubbles from trauma, surgery, or medical procedures.
- Amniotic fluid from normal or complicated pregnancy and childbirth (very rare).
- Tumors caused by rapidly growing cancer cells.
- Foreign substances-such as a catheter that can break off during a medical procedure, talc, mercury, iodine, cotton, or the growth of tapeworm larvae.

If a large blood clot blocks the artery in the lung, blood flow may be completely stopped, causing sudden death. A smaller clot reduces the blood flow and may cause damage to lung tissue. But if the clot dissolves on its own, it may not cause any major problems. Blood clots that cause pulmonary embolism may dissolve on their own. But if you have had pulmonary embolism, you have an increased risk of a repeat episode if you do not receive treatment. If pulmonary embolism is diagnosed promptly, treatment with anticoagulant medicines (usually heparin and warfarin) may prevent new blood clots from forming.

Having multiple episodes of pulmonary embolism can severely reduce blood flow through the lungs and heart. Over time, this increases blood pressure in the lungs (pulmonary hypertension), eventually leading to right-sided heart failure and possibly death.

What increases your risk of pulmonary embolism?

Having a blood clot in the deep vein of your leg and having a previous pulmonary embolism are the two greatest risk factors for pulmonary embolism. Risk factors for developing clots include having slowed blood flow, abnormal clotting, and a blood vessel injury.

When blood does not circulate normally, clots are more likely to develop. Reduced circulation may result from:

- Long-term bed rest, such as if you are confined to bed after an operation, injury, or serious illness.
- Traveling and sitting for a long time, especially when traveling long distances by airplane.
- Leg paralysis. When you use your muscles, the muscles contract, and that squeezes the blood vessels in and around the muscles. The squeezing helps the blood move back toward the heart. Paralysis can reduce circulation because the muscles can't contract.
- Abnormal clotting.

Some people have blood that clots too easily or too quickly. People with this problem are more likely to form larger clots that can break loose and travel to the lungs. Conditions that may cause increased clotting include:

- Inherited factors. Some people have an inherited tendency to develop blood clots that can lead to pulmonary embolism.
- Cancer.
- Heart failure.
- Serious burns.
- Severe infections.
- Use of birth control pills or other medicines that contain estrogen or estrogen-like hormones, such as those some women take for hormone replacement therapy during menopause.
- Heavy smoking.
- Injury to the blood vessel wall.

Blood is more likely to clot in veins and arteries shortly after they are injured. Injury to a vein can be caused by:

- Recent surgery that involved the legs, hips, belly, or brain.
- A tube (catheter) placed in a large vein of the body (central venous catheter).

Other risk factors include:

- Pregnancy. A woman's risk for developing blood clots increases both during pregnancy and shortly after delivery.
- Age. As people get older (especially older than age 70), they are more likely to develop blood clots.
- Weight. Being overweight increases the risk for developing clots.
- Not taking anticoagulant medicine as prescribed.

What are symptoms of pulmonary embolism?

Symptoms of pulmonary embolism usually begin suddenly. Reduced blood flow to one or both lungs can cause shortness of breath and a rapid heart rate. Inflammation of the tissue covering the lungs and chest wall (pleura) can cause sharp chest pain.

The symptoms of pulmonary embolism may include:

- Shortness of breath that may occur suddenly.
- Sudden, sharp chest pain that may become worse with deep breathing or coughing.
- Rapid heart rate.
- Rapid breathing.
- Sweating.
- Anxiety.
- Coughing up blood or pink, foamy mucus.
- Fainting.
- Heart palpitations.
- Signs of shock.

Pulmonary embolism may be hard to diagnose because its symptoms may occur with or are similar to other conditions, such as a heart attack, a panic attack, or pneumonia. Also, some people with pulmonary embolism do not have symptoms.

Complications of pulmonary embolism may include:

- Cardiac arrest and sudden death.
- Shock.
- Abnormal heart rhythms.
- Death of part of the lung, called pulmonary infarction.
- A buildup of fluid (pleural effusion) between the outside lining of the lungs and the inner lining of the chest cavity.
- Paradoxical embolism.
- Pulmonary hypertension.

How is pulmonary embolism diagnosed?

Diagnosing pulmonary embolism is difficult because there are so many other medical conditions that can cause similar symptoms, such as a heart attack or an anxiety attack.

Diagnosis depends on an accurate and thorough medical history and ruling out other conditions. We need to know the symptoms and risk factors for pulmonary embolism, such as having recent surgery or having a prior history or family history of blood clots. This information, combined with a careful physical exam, will point to the initial tests that are best suited to diagnose a deep vein thrombosis or pulmonary embolism.

Tests that are often done if you have shortness of breath or chest pain include:

- **A chest X-ray.** Results may rule out an enlarged heart or pneumonia as a cause of your symptoms. If the chest X-ray is normal, you may need further testing.
- **Electrocardiogram (EKG, ECG).** The electrical activity of the heart is recorded with this test. EKG results will help rule out a possible heart attack.
- **Arterial blood gas analysis.** A sudden drop in the blood oxygen level may suggest a pulmonary embolism.

Further testing may include:

- **D-dimer.** A D-dimer blood test measures a substance that is released when a blood clot breaks up. D-dimer levels are usually high in people with pulmonary embolism.
- **Spiral (helical) computed tomography.** This test is used commonly in most hospitals to check for pulmonary embolism.
- **Ventilation-perfusion scanning.** This test scans for abnormal blood flow through the lungs after a radioactive tracer has been injected and you breathe a radioactive gas.
- **Pulmonary angiogram.** A pulmonary angiogram (also called a pulmonary arteriogram) is the most accurate way to diagnose pulmonary embolism. This test is not available at some smaller hospitals and is more invasive than other testing.
- **Computed tomography (CT) angiogram.** A CT angiogram uses a special dye and a series of X-rays to produce pictures of blood vessels. It can be done to look for a pulmonary embolism or for a blood clot that may cause a pulmonary embolism.
- **Doppler ultrasound.** A Doppler ultrasound test uses reflected sound waves to determine whether a blood clot is present in the large veins of the legs.
- **Echocardiogram.** This test detects abnormalities in the size or function of the heart's right ventricle, which may be a sign of pulmonary embolism.
- **Magnetic resonance imaging (MRI).** This test may be used to view clots in the deep veins and lungs.

If you are diagnosed with pulmonary embolism, other tests can help guide treatment and suggest how well you will recover. These tests may include:

- A blood test to check the level of the hormone brain natriuretic peptide (BNP). Higher levels of BNP mean your heart is under increased stress.

● A blood test to look at the level of the protein troponin. Higher levels of troponin can mean there is damage to your heart muscle.

How is it treated?

Treatment of pulmonary embolism focuses on preventing future pulmonary embolism by using anticoagulant medicines. Anticoagulants prevent existing blood clots from growing larger and help prevent new ones from developing.

If symptoms are severe and life-threatening, immediate and sometimes aggressive treatment is needed. Aggressive treatment may include thrombolytic medicines, which can dissolve a blood clot quickly but also increase the risk of severe bleeding. Another option for life-threatening, large pulmonary embolism is surgical removal of the clot, called an embolectomy. This surgery is only available at a few large hospitals.

Some people may also benefit from having a vena cava filter inserted into the large central vein of the body. This filter can help prevent blood clots from reaching the lungs. It is used when anticoagulants are not an option, when clots form despite anticoagulant use, or when there is an increased risk of death or a severely restricted lifestyle if another pulmonary embolism occurs.

Medications

Medicines can help prevent repeated episodes of pulmonary embolism by preventing new blood clots from forming or preventing existing clots from getting larger.

Anticoagulants

Anticoagulants are prescribed when pulmonary embolism is diagnosed or strongly suspected. Normally, when an injury that causes bleeding occurs, the body sends out signals that cause the blood to clot at the wound. The clot naturally breaks down as the wound heals. A person who is prone to abnormal clotting has an imbalance between clot formation and clot breakdown. Anticoagulants prevent the production of certain proteins that are needed for blood to clot. Although anticoagulants can prevent new clots from forming and prevent existing clots from getting larger, they do not break up or dissolve existing blood clots. Heparin and warfarin are the two main types of anticoagulants used to treat pulmonary embolism.

Heparin

Heparin is an anticoagulant given by injection. It immediately affects the clotting system in your body. Oral anticoagulant medicine (warfarin) takes longer to start working.

Low-molecular-weight heparin (LMWH) as initial treatment is usually preferred because it can be given as an injection once or twice a day, and it may be given at home, which allows you to leave the hospital earlier. Blood tests are not usually needed to monitor LMWH's clotting effect.

Unfractionated heparin is another form that can be used. It is given in the hospital. Unfractionated heparin is usually given continuously through your vein (intravenously, or IV), but it can also be given as an injection under the skin. Frequent blood tests are used to monitor the clotting effects of this medicine.

Warfarin (such as Coumadin)

Warfarin is an anticoagulant that is taken in pill form. It is usually started while a person is still being treated with heparin because it takes several days for warfarin to build up to a level that's effective. When the warfarin is at a proper level, heparin is stopped and treatment with warfarin continues.

Typically, warfarin is given for at least 3 months after pulmonary embolism to reduce the risk of having another blood clot. Treatment with anticoagulants may continue throughout your life if the risk of having another pulmonary embolism remains high.

Because warfarin can increase the risk of birth defects, pregnant women with a risk of developing blood clots are limited to taking heparin.

Safety with anticoagulant medicine

When you take anticoagulants, you need to take extra steps to avoid bleeding problems.

Heparin. If you take heparin:

- Prevent injuries.
- Prevent medicine interactions.

Warfarin. If you take warfarin:

- Get regular blood tests.
- Prevent falls and injuries.
- Eat a steady diet, and pay attention to foods that contain vitamin K.
- Tell your doctors about all other medicines and vitamins that you take.

Thrombolytics

Clot-dissolving (thrombolytic) medicines are not commonly used to treat pulmonary embolism. Although they can quickly dissolve a blood clot, thrombolytics also greatly increase the risk of serious bleeding. They are occasionally used to treat a life-threatening pulmonary embolism.

Surgery

Surgical removal of a clot is called an embolectomy. Surgery increases the risk of forming new blood clots that can cause another pulmonary embolism. So this type of treatment for pulmonary embolism is rarely used. It is considered for people who can't have other kinds of treatment or those whose clot is so dangerous that they can't wait for medicine to work. An embolectomy also may be an option for a person whose condition is stable but who shows signs of significant reduced blood flow in the pulmonary artery.

Other Treatment

Some people cannot take anticoagulant medicines, or they continue to develop blood clots despite taking the medicines. If surgery or medicines are not options, other methods of preventing pulmonary embolism may be considered, such as a vena cava filter.

If you have recently had a major stroke, surgery, or active internal bleeding, you usually cannot take anticoagulant or thrombolytic medicines. A vena cava filter may help to reduce the risk of another pulmonary embolism in this case.

A vena cava filter may be inserted in the large central vein that passes through the abdomen and returns blood from the body to the heart (vena cava). This filter can prevent blood clots in the leg or pelvic veins from traveling to the lungs and heart. These filters may be permanent or removable.

Studies have shown that vena cava filters help prevent pulmonary embolism. But they may be most effective when combined with anticoagulant therapy.

Vena cava filters are not recommended as the first treatment for pulmonary embolism. But they may be considered if you:

- Continue to have pulmonary embolism despite taking anticoagulant medicine.
- Cannot take anticoagulants because of bleeding risk.
- Have an increased risk of death or a severely restricted lifestyle should another pulmonary embolism occur.
- Vena cava filters may benefit people who have had a pulmonary embolism surgically removed (embolectomy) if another pulmonary embolism would likely be fatal or severely limit a person's lifestyle.
- Vena cava filters can cause serious health problems if they break or become blocked with one or more blood clots.
- Vena cava filters have not been shown to lower the death rate in people with pulmonary embolism.

What can we do to prevent pulmonary embolism?

Daily use of anticoagulant medicines may help prevent recurring pulmonary embolism by stopping new blood clots from forming and stopping existing clots from growing.

The risk of forming another blood clot is highest in the weeks after the first episode of pulmonary embolism. This risk decreases over time. But the risk remains high for months and sometimes years, depending upon what caused the pulmonary embolism. People with recurrent blood clots and/or pulmonary embolism may have to take anticoagulants daily for the rest of their lives. Anticoagulant medicines also are often used for people who are not active due to illness or injury, or people who are having surgery on the legs, hips, belly, or brain.

Other preventive methods may also be used, such as:

- Exercise. Keep blood moving in your legs by pointing your toes up toward your head so that your calves are stretched, then relaxing. Repeat. This exercise is especially important when you are sitting for long periods of time, for example, on long driving trips or airplane flights.

- Get up out of bed as soon as possible after an illness or surgery. It is very important to get moving as soon as you are able. If you cannot get out of bed, do the leg exercises described above every hour to keep the blood moving through your legs.

- Quit smoking. This is especially important if you are using any medicines that contain estrogen, such as birth control pills.

- Wear compression stockings to help prevent leg deep vein thrombosis if you are at increased risk for this condition.

- If you are already at high risk for pulmonary embolism or deep vein thrombosis, talk to your doctor before taking a long flight or car trip. Ask if you need to take any special precautions to prevent blood clots during travel.

中英文注释

关键词汇

anticoagulant [ˌæntikəʊˈægjʊl(ə)nt] n.[助剂]抗凝剂；adj. 抗凝的

childbirth [ˈtʃail(d)bɜːθ] n. 分娩

embolectomy [ˌembəˈlektəmi] n.[外科]栓子切除术

foamy [ˈfəʊmi] adj. 泡沫的；起泡沫的；全是泡沫的

heparin [ˈhepərin] n.[生化]肝素

inherited [inˈheritid] adj. 遗传的；继承权的；通过继承得到的

intravenously [ˌintrəˈviːnəsli] adv. 静脉注射地；通过静脉

iodine [ˈaiədiːn; –ain; –in] n. 碘；碘酒

menopause [ˈmenəpɔːz] n. 更年期；活动终止期

mercury [ˈməkjəri] n. 水银；水银柱；精神

palpitations [pælpiˈteiʃ(ə)n] n.[内科]心悸；跳动；颤动

paralysis [pə'rælisis] n. 麻痹；无力；停顿

pelvis ['pelvis] n. 骨盆

pleura ['pluərə] n.［解剖］胸膜；［解剖］肋膜

thigh [θai] n. 大腿，股

thrombolytic [ˌθrɔmbəu'litik] n. 溶解血栓剂；adj. 溶解血栓的

thrombosis [θrɒm'bəusis] n.［病理］血栓形成；血栓症

troponin ['trɒpənin] n.［生化］肌钙蛋白

venous ['vi:nəs] adj. 静脉的；有脉纹的

ventricle ['ventrik(ə)l] n. 室；心室；脑室

warfarin ['wɔ:fərin] n. 华法林

主要短语

amniotic fluid 羊水

brain natriuretic peptide (BNP) 脑钠肽

D-dimer D- 二聚体

deep vein thrombosis 深静脉血栓形成

low-molecular-weight heparin (LMWH) 低分子肝素

pulmonary embolism 肺栓塞

tapeworm larvae 绦虫幼虫

李　丹

31 — Pulmonary Heart Disease
肺源性心脏病

What is pulmonary heart disease?

Heart disease resulting from a lung (pulmonary) disorder. A complication of lung disorders where the blood flow into the lungs is slowed or blocked causing increased lung pressure. The right side of the heart has to pump harder to push against the increased pressure and this can lead to enlargement of the heart muscle and other problems. Ultimately, congestive heart failure of the right side of the heart can result. Other chronic lung conditions that can cause pulmonary heart disease are pulmonary hypertension, cystic fibrosis and advanced emphysema.

What causes pulmonary heart disease?

To research the causes of Pulmonary heart disease, consider researching the causes of these diseases that may be similar, or associated with Pulmonary heart disease:
- Atrial septal defect
- Ventricular septal defect
- Patent ductus arteriosus
- Pulmonary hypertension
- Transposition for great vessels

What are the symptoms of pulmonary heart disease?

The list of signs and symptoms mentioned in various sources for Pulmonary heart disease includes the 9 symptoms listed below:
- Shortness of breath
- Shortness of breath on exertion
- Syncope
- Dyspnoea
- Chest pain
- Tachycardia
- Tachypnoea

- Fatigue
- Weight loss

Heart and circulatory disorders exhibit symptoms such as breathlessness during exertion or at rest, swollen ankles, chest pain, palpitations, dizziness and pain. However, many other health problems, some of them minor, can also cause these symptoms.

Dizziness and Fainting

Most attacks of dizziness, where an individual feels unsteady and lightheaded for a few seconds, are harmless. However, recurrent attacks of dizziness may be due to a heart or circulatory problem.

Fainting is due to a lack of oxygen reaching the brain. Fainting is usually harmless and is often the result of standing for a long time in a hot or stuffy atmosphere. Sometimes fainting is due to over stimulation of the vagus nerve, which helps control the heart rate, or results from severe pain or a sudden shock. According to the National Heart Lung and Blood Institute, dizziness and feeling lightheaded often advances to fainting, as the disease gets progressively worse. Anyone who faints during exercise should have the cause investigated immediately; it could be a symptom of something more serious.

Breathlessness

Breathlessness is common during strenuous exercise because the heart and other muscles require more oxygen. According to the Cleveland Clinic, breathlessness when a person is resting or doing non-strenuous exercise may be a symptom of pulmonary heart disease. The heart becomes less efficient at pumping blood through the lungs. This results in breathlessness, because the lungs cannot maintain an adequate supply of oxygen to the circulation and because fluid accumulates in the lungs because of inefficient circulation.

Chest Pain and Palpitations

A strained muscle, a broken rib, a trapped nerve, emotional stress or irritation of the esophagus are all associated with short-term chest pain, which is common. In some people, the pain continues or worsens over time and can be the result of a heart condition such as angina, a heart attack or pericarditis.

Palpitations are fluttering or thumping sensations in the chest or neck that make you aware of your own heartbeat. According to the Cleveland Clinic, some individuals suffer palpitations when they are anxious, others when they feel relaxed and rested, but in advanced stages of pulmonary heart disease, palpitations can be a strong throbbing sensation in the chest. An ectopic heartbeat, an isolated, irregular beat, can cause palpitations, but it is not usually due to heart disease or disorder. If an individual suffers with chest pain and palpitations, which seem to be getting progressively worse or more frequent, it may be a symptom of pulmonary heart disease

Swollen Ankles

Swelling of the ankles is an indication of fluid retention in the tissues. According to the Mayo Clinic, one of several causes is heart disease and heart failure, in which the heart's ventricles do not empty properly. Blood retained in the right ventricle causes a buildup of blood causing an increase in pressure throughout the circulatory system, forcing fluid out into the surrounding tissues. The ankles, in particular, will swell because the effect of gravity pulls the fluid down into the lower extremities.

How is it treated?

The treatment of pulmonary heart disease largely rests with treating the underlying cause and supportive measures. Oxygen therapy may slow progression. Right heart failure secondary to pulmonary pathology should be treated similarly to congestive heart failure. Vasodilators such as the calcium channel blockers may be particularly useful in reducing the pressure of the pulmonary circulation.

Drugs/Products Used in the Treatment of This Disease:

- Dilzem (Diltiazem hydrochloride)
- Felodur ER (Felodipine)
- Glyceryl Trinitrate for Injection (DBL) (Glyceryl trinitrate)
- Imdur Durules (Isosorbide mononitrate)
- Nifecard (Nifedipine)
- Norvasc (Amlodipine besylate)

中英文注释

关键词汇

breathlessness ['breθləsnəs] n. 呼吸急促

dyspnoea [dis'pni:ə] n. 呼吸困难

lightheaded ['lait'hedid] adj. 头晕眼花的

oxygen ['ɒksidʒ(ə)n] n. 氧气

palpitations [,pælpi'teʃnz] n. 心悸

swollen ['swəʊlən] adj. 肿胀的

syncope ['siŋkəpi] n. 晕厥

主要短语

congestive heart failure 充血性心力衰竭

fluid retention 液体潴留

heart attack 心脏病发作

heart rate 心率
lower extremities 下肢
pulmonary hypertension 肺动脉高压
vagus nerve 迷走神经

李袁飞　马志方

32

Tuberculosis

肺 结 核

What is tuberculosis?

Tuberculosis (TB) is an infection caused by slow-growing bacteria that grow best in areas of the body that have lots of blood and oxygen. That is why it is most often found in the lungs. This is called pulmonary TB. But TB can also spread to other parts of the body, which is called extrapulmonary TB.

TB was once a widespread disease. It was virtually wiped out with the help of antibiotics developed in the 1950s, but the disease has resurfaced in potent new forms — multidrug-resistant TB and extensively drug-resistant TB. According to the World Health Organization, more than 8.8 million people worldwide are infected with tuberculosis, and almost 1.6 million people per year die from tuberculosis. Today, these new and dangerous forms of the disease — resistant to some of the commonly used drug treatments — have created a public health crisis in many large cities worldwide. If one person has TB — in its active or latent state — he must seek medical treatment.

Most people who are exposed to TB never develop symptoms because the bacteria can live in an inactive form in the body. But if the immune system weakens, such as in people with HIV or elderly adults, TB bacteria can become active. In their active state, TB bacteria cause death of tissue in the organs they infect. Active TB disease can be fatal if left untreated.

Tuberculosis is either latent or active:

- Latent TB means that one patient has the TB bacteria in his body, but his body is defenses (immune system) are keeping it from turning into active TB. This means that he don't has any symptoms of TB right now and can't spread the disease to others. If he has latent TB, it can become active TB.
- Active TB means that the TB bacteria are growing and causing symptoms. If his lungs are infected with active TB, it is easy to spread the disease to others.

Because the bacteria that cause tuberculosis are transmitted through the air, the disease can be contagious. Infection is most likely to occur if one patient is exposed to someone with TB on a day-to-day basis, such as by living or working in close quarters with someone who has the active disease. Even then, because the bacteria generally stay latent (inactive) after they invade the body, only a small number of people infected with TB will ever have the active disease. The remaining will have what's called latent TB infection — they show no signs of infection and won't be able to spread the disease to others, unless their disease becomes active. Because these latent infections can eventually become active, even people without symptoms should receive medical treatment. Medication can help get rid of the inactive bacteria before they become active.

What causes TB?

Pulmonary TB (in the lungs) is contagious. It spreads when a person who has active TB breathes out air that has the TB bacteria in it and then another person breathes in the bacteria from the air. An infected person releases even more bacteria when he or she does things like cough or laugh.

Tuberculosis (TB) develops when Mycobacterium tuberculosis bacteria are inhaled into the lungs. The infection usually stays in the lungs. But the bacteria can travel through the bloodstream to other parts of the body (extrapulmonary TB).

Latent TB

An initial (primary) infection can be so mild that you don't even know you have an infection. In a person who has a healthy immune system, the body usually fights the infection by walling off (encapsulating) the bacteria into tiny capsules called tubercles. The bacteria remain alive but cannot spread to surrounding tissues or other people. This stage is called latent TB, and most people never go beyond it.

If a person's immune system becomes unable to prevent the bacteria from growing, the TB becomes active. Of people who have latent TB, 5% (1 person out of 20) will develop active TB within 2 years after the initial infection. Another 5% of people who have latent TB will develop active TB at some point in their lives.

Active TB

Active TB in the lungs (pulmonary TB) is contagious. TB spreads when a person who has active disease exhales air that contains TB-causing bacteria and another person inhales the bacteria from the air. These bacteria can remain floating in the air for several hours. Coughing, sneezing, laughing, or singing releases more bacteria than breathing. In general, after 2 weeks of treatment with antibiotics, you cannot spread an active pulmonary TB infection to other people.

Skipping doses of medicine can delay a cure and cause a relapse. In these cases, you may need to start treatment over. Relapses usually occur within 6 to 12 months after treatment. Not taking the full course of treatment also allows antibiotic-resistant strains of the bacteria to develop, making treatment more difficult.

Without treatment, active TB can cause serious complications, such as:

- Pockets or cavities that form in the lungs. These damaged areas may cause bleeding in the lungs or may become infected with other bacteria and form pockets of pus (abscesses).
- A hole that forms between nearby airways in the lungs.
- Difficulty breathing because of blocked airways.
- TB can be fatal if it is not treated.
- Active TB outside the lungs.

Active TB in parts of the body other than the lungs (extrapulmonary TB) is not spread easily to other people. You take the same medicines that are used to treat pulmonary TB. You may need other treatments depending on where in your body the infection is growing and how severe it is.

Who is most at risk for TB?

Some people are more likely than others to get TB. This includes people who:

- Have HIV or another illness that weakens the immune system.
- Have close contact with someone who has active TB, such as living in the same house as someone who is infected with TB.
- Care for a patient who has active TB, such as doctors or nurses.
- Live or work in crowded places, such as prisons, nursing homes, or homeless shelters, where other people may have active TB.
- Have poor access to health care, such as homeless people and migrant farm workers.
- Abuse drugs or alcohol.
- Travel to or were born in places where untreated TB is common, such as Latin America, Africa, Asia, Eastern Europe, and Russia.

It is important for people who are at a high risk for getting TB to get tested once or twice every year.

What are the symptoms of TB?

The symptoms of tuberculosis range from no symptoms (latent tuberculosis) to symptoms of active disease. In fact, you may not even be aware that you have a latent TB infection until it's revealed through a skin test, perhaps during a routine checkup.

If one has latent tuberculosis (TB), he do not has symptoms and cannot spread the disease to others. If he have active TB, he do has symptoms and can spread the disease to others. Which specific symptoms he has will depend on whether his TB infection is in his lungs (the most common site) or in another part of his body (extrapulmonary

TB). Symptoms of active TB in the lungs begin gradually and develop over a period of weeks or months. One patient may has one or two mild symptoms and not even know that he has the disease. There are other conditions with symptoms similar to TB, such as pneumonia and lung cancer.

Symptoms of active TB in the lungs:

- A cough with thick, cloudy, and sometimes bloody mucus from the lungs (sputum) for more than 2 weeks.
- Night sweats and a slight fever.
- Fatigue and weakness.
- Loss of appetite and unexplained weight loss.
- Shortness of breath and chest pain.

Symptoms of an active TB infection outside the lungs:

Symptoms of TB outside the lungs (extrapulmonary TB) vary widely depending on which area of the body is infected. For example, back pain can be a symptom of TB in the spine, or your neck may get swollen when lymph nodes in the neck are infected.

Most of the time when people are first infected with TB, the disease is so mild that they don't even know they have it. People with latent TB don't have symptoms unless the disease becomes active.

How is TB diagnosed?

The active tuberculosis (TB) in the lungs (pulmonary TB) is diagnosed by using a medical history and physical exam, and by checking his symptoms (such as an ongoing cough, fatigue, fever, or night sweats). Doctors usually find latent TB by doing a tuberculin skin test. During the skin test, a doctor or nurse will inject TB antigens under his skin. If he has TB bacteria in his body, within 2 days he will get a red bump where the needle went into his skin. The test can't tell when he became infected with TB or if it can be spread to others.

To find pulmonary TB, doctors test a sample of mucus from the lungs (sputum) to see if there are TB bacteria in it. Doctors sometimes do other tests on sputum and blood or take a chest X-ray to help find pulmonary TB.

To find extrapulmonary TB, doctors can take a sample of tissue (biopsy) to test. Or one might get a CT scan or an MRI so the doctor can see pictures of the inside of his body.

Diagnosing active TB in the lungs

- **Sputum culture.** Testing mucus from the lungs (sputum culture) is the best way to diagnose active TB. But a sputum culture can take 1 to 8 weeks to provide results.

- **Sputum cytology.**
- **Chest X-ray.** A chest X-ray usually is done if he has:

A positive tuberculin skin test (also called a TB skin test, PPD test, or Mantoux test).

Symptoms of active TB, such as a persistent cough, fatigue, fever, or night sweats.

An uncertain reaction to the tuberculin skin test because of a weakened immune system, or to a previous bacille Calmette-Guerin (BCG) vaccination.

  - **Rapid sputum test.** This test can provide results within 24 hours. This test is done only when a person is strongly suspected of having TB.

Diagnosing latent TB in the lungs

A tuberculin skin test will show if he has ever had a TB infection. See a picture of a tuberculin skin test.

Rapid blood tests help detect latent TB. They can help diagnose TB when results from a tuberculin skin test are uncertain. These tests also can tell if a person who has had a BCG vaccination has a TB infection. A rapid test requires only one visit to the doctor or clinic, instead of two visits as required for the tuberculin skin test. Rapid blood tests are also called interferon-gamma release assays (IGRAs).

Diagnosing TB outside the lungs

Diagnosing TB in other parts of the body (extrapulmonary TB) requires more testing. Tests include:

  - **Biopsy.** A sample of the affected area is taken out and sent to a lab to look for TB-causing bacteria.
  - **Urine culture.** This test looks for TB infection in the kidneys (renal TB).
  - **Cerebrospinal fluid test.** A sample of fluid around the spine is taken to look for a TB infection in the brain (TB meningitis).
  - **CT scan.** This test is used to diagnose TB that has spread throughout the body (miliary TB) and to detect lung cavities caused by TB.
  - **MRI.** This test looks for TB in the brain or the spine.

Tests during TB treatment

During treatment, a sputum culture is done once a month-or more often-to make sure that the antibiotics are working. You may have a chest X-ray at the end of treatment to use as a comparison in the future.

You may have tests to see if TB medicines are harming other parts of your body. These tests may include:

Liver function tests

Eye tests, especially if you are taking ethambutol for TB treatment.

Hearing tests, especially if you are taking streptomycin for TB treatment.

How is it treated?

Treatment is recommended for anyone with a skin test that shows a TB infection, and is especially important for people who:

- Are known to or are likely to be infected with the human immunodeficiency virus (HIV).
- Have close contact with a person who has active TB.
- Have a chest X-ray that suggests a TB infection and have not had a complete course of treatment.
- Inject illegal drugs.
- Have medical conditions or take medicines that weaken the immune system.
- Have had a tuberculin skin test within the past 2 years that did not show a TB infection but now a new test indicates an infection.

Medications

The antibiotics can kill the TB bacteria. These medicines are given to everyone who has TB, including infants, children, pregnant women, and people who have a weakened immune system. Treatment for TB depends on whether it is active or latent.

Latent TB Infection

If you're infected with TB but don't have the active disease, your doctor will go over your risk factors for developing active TB and will discuss your treatment options. An antibiotic called isoniazid (INH) is often prescribed to help prevent the dormant infection from becoming active.

Your doctor will likely give you a daily or twice weekly dose of isoniazid and evaluate you regularly to ensure that you're tolerating the drug without major side effects. The risks of taking INH increase with age. In addition, your doctor may recommend vitamin B6 (pyridoxine) to prevent specific side effects of INH.

Most people with latent TB are treated with only one antibiotic that they take for 9 months. This reduces their risk for getting active TB.

When treating latent TB, experts recommend:

- Using one medicine to kill the TB bacteria and prevent active TB. The standard treatment is isoniazid taken for 9 months. For people who cannot take isoniazid for 9 months, sometimes a 6-month treatment program is done.
- Treatment with rifampin for 4 months. This is an acceptable alternate treatment, especially for people who have been exposed to bacteria that is resistant to isoniazid.

Active TB Disease

Most of the time, doctors combine four antibiotics to treat active TB to help prevent resistant bacteria from emerging in your body. You may be taking a combination of antibiotics that may include isoniazid, rifampin, pyrazinamide, or ethambutol for 6 to 12 months. It is important to take the medicine for active TB for at least 6 months. Almost all people are cured if they take their medicine just like their doctors say to take it. If tests still show an active TB infection after 6 months, then treatment continues for another 2 or 3 months. Because active TB disease can be fatal if left untreated, regular monitoring and treatment by a doctor are crucial.

When treating active TB, health experts recommend:

- Using more than one medicine to prevent multidrug-resistant TB. The standard treatment begins with four medicines given for 2 months.
- Continuing treatment for 4 to 9 months or longer if needed. The number of medicines used during this time depends on the results of sensitivity testing.
- Using directly observed therapy (DOT). This means visits with a health professional who watches you every time you take your medicine. A cure for TB requires you to take all doses of the antibiotics. These visits ensure that people follow medicine instructions, which is helpful because of the long treatment course for TB.
- Trying a different combination of medicines if the treatment is not working because of drug resistance (when tests show that TB-causing bacteria are still active).
- Using different treatment programs for people infected with the human immunodeficiency virus (HIV), people infected with TB bacteria that are resistant to one or more medicines, pregnant women, and children.

Multidrug-Resistant TB

A form of TB, called multidrug-resistant TB, is caused by strains of the tuberculosis bacteria that, through mutation, have developed the ability to resist two or more antibiotic drugs. Worldwide, almost half a million people develop this form of TB annually, and about 150,000 die from this disease.

An even newer form of TB, called extensively drug-resistant TB, resists almost all TB treatments. Fortunately, this form of TB is still relatively rare. Most cases of TB are still highly treatable if the patient follows the full course of antibiotic treatment. For people who have multidrug-resistant TB, treatment may continue for as long as 24 months.

Extrapulmonary TB

TB disease that occurs in parts of your body other than the lungs (extrapulmonary

TB) usually is treated with the same medicines and for the same length of time as active TB in the lungs (pulmonary TB). But TB throughout the body (miliary TB) or TB that affects the brain or the bones and joints in children may be treated for at least 12 months.

If you miss doses of your medicine, or if you stop taking your medicine too soon, your treatment may fail or have to go on longer. You may have to start your treatment over again. This can also cause the infection to get worse or may lead to an infection that is resistant to antibiotics. This is much harder to treat. Taking all of the medicines is especially important for people who have an impaired immune system. They may be at an increased risk for a relapse because the original TB infection was never cured.

TB can only be cured if you take all the doses of your medicine. A doctor or nurse may have to watch you take it to make sure that you never miss a dose and that you take it the proper way. You may have to go to the doctor's office every day. Or a nurse may come to your home or work. This is called direct observational treatment. It helps people follow all of the instructions and keep up with their treatment, which can be complex and take a long time. Cure rates for TB have greatly improved because of this type of treatment. If active TB is not treated, it can damage your lungs or other organs and can be deadly. You can also spread TB by not treating an active TB infection.

Corticosteroid medicines also may be given in some severe cases to reduce inflammation. They may be helpful for children at risk of central nervous system problems caused by TB and for people who have conditions such as high fever, TB throughout the body (miliary TB), pericarditis, or peritonitis.

Surgery

Surgery is rarely used to treat tuberculosis (TB). But it may be used to treat extensively drug-resistant TB (XDR-TB) or to treat complications of an infection in the lungs or another part of the body.

Surgery is used to:
- Repair lung damage, such as serious bleeding that cannot be stopped any other way, or repeated lung infections other than TB.
- Remove a pocket of bacteria that cannot be killed with long-term medicine treatment.

Surgery has a high success rate, but it also has a risk of complications, which may include infections other than TB and shortness of breath after surgery.

Surgery for TB outside the lungs

Surgery sometimes may be needed to remove or repair organs damaged by TB in parts of the body other than the lungs (extrapulmonary TB) or to prevent other rare complications, such as:

- TB infection of the brain (TB meningitis). The doctor may surgically place a tube (shunt) that drains excess fluid from the brain to prevent a buildup of pressure that can further damage the brain.
- TB infections of the heart (TB pericarditis). The surgeon may partially remove or repair the infected sac around the heart.
- TB infection of the kidneys (renal TB). The surgeon may need to either remove the patient's infected kidney or repair the kidney or other parts of the urinary system.
- TB infection of the joints. One patient may need surgery to repair damaged areas of his spine or joints (orthopedic surgery).

What can we do to prevent TB?

Active TB is very contagious. The World Health Organization (WHO) estimates that one-third of the world's population is infected with the bacteria that cause TB.

To avoid getting an active TB infection:

- Do not spend long periods of time in stuffy, enclosed rooms with anyone who has active TB until that person has been treated for at least 2 weeks.
- Use protective measures, such as face masks, if you work in a facility that cares for people who have untreated TB.
- If you live with someone who has active TB, help and encourage the person to follow treatment instructions.
- A TB vaccine (Bacille Calmette-Guerin, or BCG) is used in many countries to prevent TB. But this vaccination is almost never used in the United States because:

The risk of getting TB is low in the U.S.

The vaccine is not effective in adults who receive it.

The BCG vaccine may cause a tuberculin skin test to indicate a TB infection even if a person is not infected with TB. This complicates the use of the tuberculin skin test to check people for TB.

中英文注释

关键词汇

abscess ['æbsis; –ses] n. 脓肿；脓疮；vi. 形成脓肿

appetite ['æpitait] n. 食欲；嗜好

cerebrospinal [ˌseribrə(ʊ)'spain(ə)l] adj. [解剖] 脑脊髓的

contagious [kən'teidʒəs] adj. 感染性的；会蔓延的

cytology [sai'tɒlədʒi] n. 细胞学

ethambutol [e'θæmbjʊtɒl] n.［药］乙胺丁醇片（一种抗结核药）

isoniazid (INH) [ˌaisə(ʊ)'naiəzid] n. 异烟肼（抗结核药）

latent ['leit(ə)nt] adj. 潜在的；潜伏的；隐藏的

meningitis [ˌmenin'dʒaitis] n. 脑膜炎

mycobacterium [ˌmaikəubæk'tiəriəm] n. 分枝杆菌；［微］分枝杆菌属

pericarditis [ˌperikɑ:'daitis] n.［内科］心包炎

peritonitis [ˌperitə'naitis] n.［内科］腹膜炎

pneumonia [nju:'məʊniə] n. 肺炎

pulmonary ['pʌlmən(ə)ri] adj. 肺的；有肺的；肺状的

pyrazinamide [ˌpirə'zinəmaid] n.［药］吡嗪酰胺

rifampin [rai'fæmpin] n.（美）利福平（抗生素类药，等于 rifampicin）

sputum ['spju:təm] n.［生理］痰；唾液

streptomycin [ˌstreptə(ʊ)'maisin] n.［药］［微］链霉素

swollen ['swəʊlən] adj. 肿胀的，浮肿的

tuberculin [tjʊ'bɜ:kjulin] n.［免疫］结核菌素

tuberculosis [tjʊˌbɜ:kjʊ'ləʊsis] n. 肺结核；结核病

vaccination [ˌvæksi'neiʃən] n. 接种疫苗；种痘

主要短语

BCG (Bacillus Calmette - Guerin) 卡介苗

human immunodeficiency virus (HIV) 人体免疫缺损病毒

lymph node 淋巴结

miliary TB 粟粒性肺结核

multidrug-resistant TB 多重抗药性结核病

night sweat 夜间盗汗

skin test 皮肤反应测验

TB meningitis 结核性脑膜炎

World Health Organization (WHO) 世界卫生组织

李 丹

33

Cirrhosis of the Liver
肝 硬 化

What is Cirrhosis of the liver?

Cirrhosis of the liver is characterized by abnormal structure and function of the liver. The diseases that lead to cirrhosis do so because they injure and kill liver cells, and the inflammation and repair that is associated with the dying liver cells causes scar tissue to form. The liver cells that do not die multiply in an attempt to replace the cells that have died. This results in clusters of newly-formed liver cells (regenerative nodules) within the scar tissue.

What causes cirrhosis of the liver?

There are many causes of cirrhosis. They include chemicals (such as alcohol, fat, and certain medications), viruses, toxic metals (such as iron and copper that accumulate in the liver as a result of genetic diseases), and autoimmuneliver disease in which the body's immune system attacks the liver.

- Alcohol is a very common cause of cirrhosis, particularly in the Western world. The development of cirrhosis depends upon the amount and regularity of alcohol intake. Chronic, high levels of alcohol consumption injure liver cells. Thirty percent of individuals who drink daily at least eight to sixteen ounces of hard liquor or the equivalent for fifteen or more years will develop cirrhosis. Alcohol causes a range of liver diseases; from simple and uncomplicated fatty liver (steatosis), to the more serious fatty liver with inflammation (steatohepatitis or alcoholic hepatitis), to cirrhosis.

- Nonalcoholic fatty liver disease (NAFLD) refers to a wide spectrum of liver diseases that, like alcoholic liver disease, ranges from simple steatosis, to nonalcoholic steatohepatitis (NASH), to cirrhosis. All stages of NAFLD have in common the accumulation of fat in liver cells. The term nonalcoholic is used because NAFLD occurs in individuals who do not consume excessive amounts of alcohol, yet, in many respects, the microscopic picture of NAFLD is similar to what can be seen in liver disease that is due to excessive alcohol. NAFLD is associated with a condition called insulin resistance, which, in turn, is associated with the metabolic syndrome and diabetes mellitus type 2. NAFLD is the most common liver disease in the United States and is responsible for 24% of all liver disease. In fact, the number of livers that are transplanted for NAFLD-related cirrhosis is on the rise.

- Cryptogenic cirrhosis (cirrhosis due to unidentified causes) is a common reason for liver transplantation. It is termed cryptogenic cirrhosis because for many years doctors have been unable to explain why a proportion of patients developed cirrhosis. Doctors now believe that cryptogenic cirrhosis is due to NASH (nonalcoholic steatohepatitis) caused by long standing obesity, type 2 diabetes, and insulinresistance. The fat in the liver of patients with NASH is believed to disappear with the onset of cirrhosis, and this has made it difficult for doctors to make the connection between NASH and cryptogenic cirrhosis for a long time. One important clue that NASH leads to cryptogenic cirrhosis is the finding of a high occurrence of NASH in the new livers of patients undergoing liver transplant for cryptogenic cirrhosis. Finally, a study from France suggests that patients with NASH have a similar risk of developing cirrhosis as patients with long standing infection with hepatitis C virus. However, the progression to cirrhosis from NASH is thought to be slow and the diagnosis of cirrhosis typically is made in patients in their sixties.

- Chronic viral hepatitis is a condition where hepatitis B or hepatitis Cvirus infects the liver for years. Most patients with viral hepatitis will not develop chronic hepatitis and cirrhosis. For example, the majority of patients infected with hepatitis A recover completely within weeks, without developing chronic infection. In contrast, some patients infected with hepatitis B virus and most patients infected with hepatitis C virus develop chronic hepatitis, which, in turn, causes progressive liver damage and leads to cirrhosis, and, sometimes, liver cancers.

- Inherited (genetic) disorders result in the accumulation of toxic substances in the liver which lead to tissue damage and cirrhosis. Examples include the abnormal accumulation of iron (hemochromatosis) or copper (Wilson's disease). In hemochromatosis, patients inherit a tendency to absorb an excessive amount of iron from food. Over time, iron accumulation in different organs throughout the body causes cirrhosis, arthritis, heart muscle damage leading to heart failure, and testicular dysfunction causing loss of sexual drive. Treatment is aimed at preventing damage to organs by removing iron from the body through bloodletting (removing blood). In Wilson disease, there is an inherited abnormality in one of the proteins that controls copper in the body. Over time, copper accumulates in the liver, eyes, and brain. Cirrhosis, tremor, psychiatric disturbances and otherneurological difficulties occur if the condition is not treated early. Treatment is with oral medication that increases the amount of copper that is eliminated from the body in the urine.

- Primary biliary cirrhosis (PBC) is a liver disease caused by an abnormality of the immune system that is found predominantly in women. The abnormal immunity in PBC causes chronic inflammation and destruction of the small bile ducts within the liver. The bile ducts are passages within the liver through which bile travels to the intestine. Bile is a fluid produced by the liver that contains substances required for digestion and absorption of fat in the intestine, as well as other compounds that are waste products, such as the pigment bilirubin. (Bilirubin is produced by the breakdown of hemoglobin from old red blood cells.). Along with the gallbladder, the bile ducts make up the biliary tract. In PBC, the destruction of the small bile ducts blocks the normal flow of bile into the intestine. As the inflammation continues to destroy more of the bile ducts, it also spreads to destroy nearby liver cells. As the destruction of the hepatocytes proceeds, scar tissue (fibrosis) forms and spreads throughout the areas of destruction. The combined effects of progressive inflammation, scarring, and the toxic effects of accumulating waste products culminates in cirrhosis.

- Primary sclerosing cholangitis (PSC) is an uncommon disease found frequently in patients with ulcerative colitis. In PSC, the large bile ducts outside of the liver become inflamed, narrowed, and obstructed. Obstruction to the flow of bile leads to infections of the bile ducts and jaundice and eventually causes cirrhosis. In some patients, injury to the bile ducts (usually as a result of surgery) also can cause obstruction and cirrhosis of the liver.

- Autoimmune hepatitis is a liver disease caused by an abnormality of the immune system that is found more commonly in women. The abnormal immune activity in autoimmune hepatitis causes progressive inflammation and destruction of liver cells (hepatocytes), leading ultimately to cirrhosis.

- Infants can be born without bile ducts (biliary atresia) and ultimately develop cirrhosis. Other infants are born lacking vital enzymes for controlling sugars that leads to the accumulation of sugars and cirrhosis. On rare occasions, the absence of a specific enzyme can cause cirrhosis and scarring of the lung (alpha 1 antitrypsin deficiency).

- Less common causes of cirrhosis include unusual reactions to some drugs and prolonged exposure to toxins, as well as chronic heart failure (cardiac cirrhosis). In certain parts of the world (particularly Northern Africa), infection of the liver with a parasite (schistosomiasis) is the most common cause of liver disease and cirrhosis.

What are symptoms of cirrhosis of the liver?

Individuals with cirrhosis may have few or no symptoms and signs of liver disease. Some of the symptoms may be nonspecific, that is, they don't suggest that the liver is their cause. Some of the more common symptoms and signs of cirrhosis include:

- Yellowing of the skin (jaundice) due to the accumulation of bilirubin in the blood
- Fatigue
- Weakness
- Loss of appetite
- Itching
- Easy bruising from decreased production of blood clotting factors by the diseased liver.

How is cirrhosis of the liver diagnosed?

The single best test for diagnosing cirrhosis is biopsy of the liver. Liver biopsies, however, carry a small risk for serious complications, and, therefore, biopsy often is reserved for those patients in whom the diagnosis of the type of liver disease or the presence of cirrhosis is not clear. The possibility of cirrhosis may be suggested by the history, physical examination, or routine testing. If cirrhosis is present, other tests can be used to determine the severity of the cirrhosis and the presence of complications. Tests also may be used to diagnose the underlying disease that is causing the cirrhosis. The following are some examples of how doctors discover, diagnose and evaluate cirrhosis.

In taking a patient's history, the physician may uncover a history of excessive and prolonged intake of alcohol, a history of intravenous drug abuse, or a history of hepatitis. These pieces of information suggest the possibility of liver disease and cirrhosis.

- Patients who are known to have chronic viral hepatitis B or C have a higher probability of having cirrhosis.
- Some patients with cirrhosis have enlarged livers and/or spleens. A doctor can often feel (palpate) the lower edge of an enlarged liver below the right rib cage and feel the tip of the enlarged spleen below the left rib cage. A cirrhotic liver

also feels firmer and more irregular than a normal liver.

- Some patients with cirrhosis, particularly alcoholic cirrhosis, have small red spider-like markings (telangiectasias) on the skin, particularly on the chest, that are made up of enlarged, radiating blood vessels. These spider telangiectasias also can be seen in individuals without liver disease, however.
- Jaundice (yellowness of the skin and of the whites of the eyes due to elevated bilirubin in the blood) is common among patients with cirrhosis, but jaundice can occur in patients with liver diseases without cirrhosis and other conditions such as hemolysis (excessive break down of red blood cells).
- Swelling of the abdomen (ascites) and/or the lower extremities (edema) due to retention of fluid is common among patients with cirrhosis though other diseases can cause them commonly, e.g., congestive heart failure.
- Patients with abnormal copper deposits in their eyes or certain types of neurologic disease may have Wilson's disease, a genetic disease in which there is abnormal handling and accumulation of copper throughout the body, including the liver, that can lead to cirrhosis.
- Esophageal varices may be found unexpectedly during upper endoscopy (EGD), and they strongly suggesting cirrhosis.
- Computerized tomography (CT or CAT) or magnetic resonance imaging (MRI) scans and ultrasound examinations of the abdomen done for reasons other than evaluating the possibility of liver disease may unexpectedly detect enlarged livers, abnormally nodular livers, enlarged spleens, and fluid in the abdomen that suggest cirrhosis.
- Advanced cirrhosis leads to a reduced level of albumin in the blood and reduced blood clotting factors due to the loss of the liver's ability to produce these proteins. Thus, reduced levels of albumin in the blood or abnormal bleeding suggest cirrhosis.
- Abnormal elevation of liver enzymes in the blood (such as ALT and AST) that are obtained routinely as part of yearly health examinations suggests inflammation or injury to the liver from many causes as well as cirrhosis.
- Patients with elevated levels of iron in their blood may have hemochromatosis, a genetic disease of the liver in which iron is handled abnormally and which leads to cirrhosis.
- Auto-antibodies (antinuclear antibody, anti-smooth muscle antibody and anti-mitochondrial antibody) sometimes are detected in the blood and may be a clue to the presence of autoimmune hepatitis or primary biliary cirrhosis, both of which can lead to cirrhosis.

- Liver cancer (hepatocellular carcinoma) may be detected by CT and MRI scans or ultrasound of the abdomen. Liver cancer most commonly develops in individuals with underlying cirrhosis.
- If there is an accumulation of fluid in the abdomen, a sample of the fluid can be removed using a long needle. The fluid then can be examined and tested. The results of testing may suggest the presence of cirrhosis as the cause of the fluid.

How is it treated?

Treatment of cirrhosis includes: ① preventing further damage to the liver; ② treating the complications of cirrhosis; ③ preventing liver cancer or detecting it early and liver transplantation.

Preventing further damage to the liver

- Consume a balanced diet and one multivitamin daily. Patients with PBC with impaired absorption of fat soluble vitamins may need additional vitamins D and K.
- Avoid drugs (including alcohol) that cause liver damage. All patients with cirrhosis should avoid alcohol. Most patients with alcohol induced cirrhosis experience an improvement in liver function with abstinence from alcohol. Even patients with chronic hepatitis B and C can substantially reduce liver damage and slow the progression towards cirrhosis with abstinence from alcohol.
- Avoid nonsteroidal anti-inflammatory drugs (NSAIDs, e.g., ibuprofen). Patients with cirrhosis can experience worsening of liver and kidney function with NSAIDs.
- Eradicate hepatitis B and hepatitis C virus by using anti-viral medications. Not all patients with cirrhosis due to chronic viral hepatitis are candidates for drug treatment. Some patients may experience serious deterioration in liver function and/or intolerable side effects during treatment. Thus, decisions to treat viral hepatitis have to be individualized, after consulting with doctors experienced in treating liver diseases (hepatologists).
- Remove blood from patients with hemochromatosis to reduce the levels of iron and prevent further damage to the liver. In Wilson's disease, medications can be used to increase the excretion of copper in the urine to reduce the levels of copper in the body and prevent further damage to the liver.
- Suppress the immune system with drugs such as prednisone andazathioprine (Imuran) to decrease inflammation of the liver in autoimmune hepatitis.
- Treat patients with PBC with a bile acid preparation, ursodeoxycholic acid

(UDCA), also called ursodiol (Actigall). Results of an analysis that combined the results from several clinical trials showed that UDCA increased survival among PBC patients during 4 years of therapy. The development of portal hypertension also was reduced by the UDCA. It is important to note that despite producing clear benefits, UDCA treatment primarily retards progression and does not cure PBC. Other medications such as colchicine and methotrexate also may have benefit in subsets of patients with PBC.

● Immunize patients with cirrhosis against infection with hepatitis A and B to prevent a serious deterioration in liver function. There are currently no vaccines available for immunizing against hepatitis C.

Treating the complications of cirrhosis

● Edema and ascites. Retention of salt and water can lead to swelling of the ankles and legs (edema) or abdomen (ascites) in patients with cirrhosis. Doctors often advise patients with cirrhosis to restrict dietary salt (sodium) and fluid to decrease edema and ascites. The amount of salt in the diet usually is restricted to 2 grams per day and fluid to 1.2 liters per day. In most patients with cirrhosis, however, salt and fluid restriction is not enough, and diuretics have to be added.

● Diuretics are medications that work in the kidneys to promote the elimination of salt and water into the urine. A combination of the diureticsspironolactone (Aldactone) and furosemide can reduce or eliminate the edema and ascites in most patients. During treatment with diuretics, it is important to monitor the function of the kidneys by measuring blood levels ofblood urea nitrogen (BUN) and cretonne to determine if too much diuretic is being used. Too much diuretic can lead to kidney dysfunction that is reflected in elevations of the BUN and creatinine levels in the blood.

● Sometimes, when the diuretics do not work (in which case the ascites is said to be refractory), a long needle or catheter is used to draw out the ascitic fluid directly from the abdomen, a procedure called abdominal paracentesis. It is common to withdraw large amounts (liters) of fluid from the abdomen when the ascites is causing painful abdominal distension and/or difficulty breathing because it limits the movements of the diaphragms.

● Another treatment for refractory ascites is a procedure called transjugular intravenous portosystemic shunting (TIPS, see below).

● Bleeding from varices. If large varices develop in the esophagus or upper stomach, patients with cirrhosis are at risk for serious bleeding due to rupture of these varices. Once varices have bled, they tend to rebleed and the probability that a patient will die from each bleeding episode is high (30%-

35%). Therefore, treatment is necessary to prevent the first (initial) bleeding episode as well as rebleeding. Treatments include medications and procedures to decrease the pressure in the portal vein and procedures to destroy the varices.

- Propranolol (Inderal), a beta blocker, is effective in lowering pressure in the portal vein and is used to prevent initial bleeding and rebleeding from varices in patients with cirrhosis. Another class of oral medications that lowers portal pressure is the nitrates, for example, isosorbide dinitrate (Isordil). Nitrates often are added to propranolol if propranolol alone does not adequately lower portal pressure or prevent bleeding.
- Octreotide (Sandostatin) also decreases portal vein pressure and has been used to treat variceal bleeding.
- During upper endoscopy (EGD), either sclerotherapy or band ligation can be performed to obliterate varices and stop active bleeding and prevent rebleeding. Sclerotherapy involves infusing small doses of sclerosing solutions into the varices. The sclerosing solutions cause inflammation and then scarring of the varices, obliterating them in the process. Band ligation involves applying rubber bands around the varices to obliterate them. (Band ligation of the varices is analogous to rubber banding of hemorrhoids.) Complications of sclerotherapy include esophageal ulcers, bleeding from the esophageal ulcers, esophageal perforation, esophageal stricture (narrowing due to scarring that can cause dysphagia), mediastinitis (inflammation in the chest that can cause chest pain), pericarditis (inflammation around the heart that can cause chest pain), and peritonitis (infection in the abdominal cavity). Studies have shown that band ligation may be slightly more effective with fewer complications than sclerotherapy.
- Transjugular intrahepatic portosystemic shunt (TIPS) is a non-surgical procedure to decrease the pressure in the portal vein. TIPS is performed by a radiologist who inserts a stent (tube) through a neck vein, down the inferior vena cava and into the hepatic vein within the liver. The stent then is placed so that one end is in the high pressure portal vein and the other end is in the low pressure hepatic vein. This tube shunts blood around the liver and by so doing lowers the pressure in the portal vein and varices and prevents bleeding from the varices. TIPS is particularly useful in patients who fail to respond to beta blockers, variceal sclerotherapy, or banding. (TIPS also is useful in treating patients with ascites that do not respond to salt and fluid restriction and diuretics.) TIPS can be used in patients with cirrhosis to prevent variceal bleeding while the patients are waiting for liver transplantation. The most

common side effect of TIPS is hepatic encephalopathy. Another major problem with TIPS is the development of narrowing and occlusion of the stent, causing recurrence of portal hypertension and variceal bleeding and ascites. The estimated frequency of stent occlusion ranges from 30%-50% in 12 months. Fortunately, there are methods to open occluded stents. Other complications of TIPS include bleeding due to inadvertent puncture of the liver capsule or a bile duct, infection, heart failure, and liver failure.

- A surgical operation to create a shunt (passage) from the high-pressure portal vein to veins with lower pressure can lower blood flow and pressure in the portal vein and prevent varices from bleeding. One such surgical procedure is called distal splenorenal shunt (DSRS). It is appropriate to consider such a surgical shunt for patients with portal hypertension who have early cirrhosis. (The risks of major shunt surgery in these patients is less than in patients with advanced cirrhosis.) During DSRS, the surgeon detaches the splenic vein from the portal vein, and attaches it to the renal vein. Blood then is shunted from the spleen around the liver, lowering the pressure in the portal vein and varices and preventing bleeding from the varices.

Hepatic encephalopathy

Patients with an abnormal sleep cycle, impaired thinking, odd behavior, or other signs of hepatic encephalopathy usually should be treated with a low protein diet and oral lactulose. Dietary protein is restricted because it is a source of the toxic compounds that cause hepatic encephalopathy. Lactulose, which is a liquid, traps the toxic compounds in the colon. Consequently, they cannot be absorbed into the blood stream and cause encephalopathy. To be sure that adequate lactulose is present in the colon at all times, the patient should adjust the dose to produce 2-3 semiformed bowel movements a day. (Lactulose is alaxative, and the adequacy of treatment can be judged by loosening or increasing frequency of stools.) If symptoms of encephalopathy persist, oral antibiotics such as neomycin or metronidazole (Flagyl), can be added to the treatment regimen. Antibiotics work by blocking the production of the toxic compounds by the bacteria in the colon.

Hypersplenism

The filtration of blood by an enlarged spleen usually results in only mild reductions of red blood cells (anemia), white blood cells (leukopenia) and platelets (thrombocytopenia) that do not require treatment. Severe anemia, however, may require blood transfusions or treatment witherythropoietin or epoetin alfa (Epogen, Procrit), hormones that stimulate the production of red blood cells. If the numbers of white blood cells are severely reduced, another hormone called granulocyte-colony stimulating factor is available to increase the numbers of white blood cells. An example of one such factor is filgrastim (Neupogen).

No approved medication is available yet to increase the number of platelets. As a necessary precaution, patients with low platelets should not use aspirin or other nonsteroidal antiinflammatory drugs (NSAIDS) since these drugs can hinder the function of platelets. If a low number of platelets is associated with significant bleeding, transfusions of platelets usually should be given. Surgical removal of the spleen (called splenectomy) should be avoided, if possible, because of the risk of excessive bleeding during the operation and the risk of anesthesia in advanced liver disease.

Spontaneous bacterial peritonitis (SBP)

Patients suspected of having spontaneous bacterial peritonitis usually will undergo paracentesis. Fluid that is removed is examined for white blood cells and cultured for bacteria. Culturing involves inoculating a sample of the ascites into a bottle of nutrient-rich fluid that encourages the growth of bacteria, thus facilitating the identification of even small numbers of bacteria. Blood and urine samples often are obtained as well for culturing because many patients with spontaneous bacterial peritonitis also will have infection in their blood and urine. In fact, many doctors believe that infection may have begun in the blood and the urine and spread to the ascitic fluid to cause spontaneous bacterial peritonitis. Most patients with spontaneous bacterial peritonitis are hospitalized and treated with intravenous antibiotics such as ampicillin, gentamycin, and one of the newer generation cephalosporin. Patients usually treated with antibiotics include:

- Patients with blood, urine, and/or ascites fluid cultures that contain bacteria.
- Patients without bacteria in their blood, urine, and ascitic fluid but who have elevated numbers of white blood cells (neutrophils) in the asciticfluid (>250 neutrophils/cc). Elevated neutrophil numbers in ascitic fluid often means that there is bacterial infection. Doctors believe that the lack of bacteria with culturing in some patients with increased neutrophils is due either to a very small number of bacteria or ineffective culturing techniques.

Spontaneous bacterial peritonitis is a serious infection. It often occurs in patients with advanced cirrhosis whose immune systems are weak, but with modern antibiotics and early detection and treatment, the prognosis of recovering from an episode of spontaneous bacterial peritonitis is good.

In some patients oral antibiotics (such as Cipro or Septra) can be prescribed to prevent spontaneous bacterial peritonitis. Not all patients with cirrhosis and ascites should be treated with antibiotics to prevent spontaneous bacterial peritonitis, but some patients are at high risk for developing spontaneous bacterial peritonitis and warrant preventive treatment:

- Patients with cirrhosis who are hospitalized for bleeding varices have a high risk of developing spontaneous bacterial peritonitis and should be started on antibiotics early during the hospitalization to prevent spontaneous bacterial peritonitis

- Patients with recurring episodes of spontaneous bacterial peritonitis

- Patients with low protein levels in the ascitic fluid (Ascitic fluid with low levels of protein is more likely to become infected)

Prevention and early detection of liver cancer

Several types of liver disease that cause cirrhosis are associated with a particularly high incidence of liver cancer, for example, hepatitis B and C, and it would be useful to screen for liver cancer since early surgical treatment or transplantation of the liver can cure the patient of cancer. The difficulty is that the methods available for screening are only partially effective, identifying at best only 50% of patients at a curable stage of their cancer. Despite the partial effectiveness of screening, most patients with cirrhosis, particularly hepatitis B and C, are screened yearly or every six months with ultrasound examination of the liver and measurements of cancer-produced proteins in the blood, e.g. alpha fetoprotein.

Liver transplantation

Cirrhosis is irreversible. Many patients' liver function will gradually worsen despite treatment and complications of cirrhosis will increase and become difficult to treat. Therefore, when cirrhosis is far advanced, liver transplantation often is the only option for treatment. Recent advances in surgical transplantation and medications to prevent infection and rejection of the transplanted liver have greatly improved survival after transplantation. On average, more than 80% of patients who receive transplants are alive after five years. Not everyone with cirrhosis is a candidate for transplantation. Furthermore, there is a shortage of livers to transplant, and there usually is a long (months to years) wait before a liver for transplanting becomes available. Therefore, measures to retard the progression of liver disease and treat and prevent complications of cirrhosis are vitally important.

中英文注释

关键词汇

ascites [ə'saiti:z] n. 腹水

bile [bail] n. 胆汁

bilirubin [ˌbili'ru:bin] n. 胆红素

edema [i'di:mə] n. 水肿

gallbladder ['gɔ:l,blædə] n. 胆囊

itching ['itʃiŋ] n. 瘙痒

jaundice ['dʒɔ:ndis] n. 黄疸

telangiectasias [te,lændʒiek'teiziə] n. 毛细血管扩张

主要短语

autoimmune hepatitis 自身免疫性肝炎

cirrhosis of the Liver 肝硬化

chronic viral hepatitis 慢性病毒性肝炎

cryptogenic cirrhosis 隐源性肝硬化

enlarged spleen 脾肿大

esophageal varices 食管静脉曲张

liver transplantation 肝移植

nonalcoholic fatty liver disease (NAFLD) 非酒精性脂肪肝

primary biliary cirrhosis 原发胆汁性肝硬化

primary sclerosing cholangitis (PSC) 原发硬化性胆管炎

spider telangiectasias 蜘蛛痣

spontaneous bacterial peritonitis 特发性细菌性腹膜炎

李袁飞

34   Crohn's Disease (CD)

克 罗 恩 病

What is Crohn's disease?

Crohn's disease is a lifelong inflammatory bowel disease (IBD). Parts of the digestive system get swollen and have deep sores called ulcers. Crohn's disease usually is found in the last part of the small intestine and the first part of the large intestine. But it can develop anywhere in the digestive tract, from the mouth to the anus.

What causes Crohn's disease?

The cause of Crohn's disease is unknown. This disease may result from an abnormal response by the body's immune system to normal intestinal bacteria. Disease-causing bacteria and viruses also may play a role.

Crohn's disease can run in families, so some people may be more likely than others to develop the condition when exposed to something that triggers an immune reaction. Environmental factors may also play a role in causing this disease.

What are the symptoms of Crohn's disease?

The main symptoms of Crohn's disease include:

- **Abdominal pain.** The pain often is described as cramping and intermittent, and the abdomen may be sore when touched. Abdominal pain may turn to a dull, constant ache as the condition progresses.
- **Diarrhea.** Some people may have diarrhea 10 to 20 times a day. They may wake up at night and need to go to the bathroom. Crohn's disease may cause blood in stools, but not always.
- **Loss of appetite.**
- **Fever.** In severe cases, fever or other symptoms that affect the entire body may develop. A high fever may mean that you have a complication involving infection, such as an abscess.
- **Weight loss.** Ongoing symptoms, such as diarrhea, can lead to weight loss.
- **Anemia.** Some people with Crohn's disease develop anemia because of low

iron levels caused by bloody stools or the intestinal inflammation itself.

People with Crohn's disease also may have:

- Sores in the mouth.
- Nutritional deficiencies, such as lowered levels of vitamin B12, folic acid, iron, and fat-soluble vitamins, because the intestines may not be able to absorb nutrients from food.
- Bowel obstruction.
- Signs of disease in or around the anus. These may include:
  - Abnormal tunnels or openings called fistulas that sometimes form between organs. These develop because Crohn's disease causes inflammation and ulcers in the deep layers of the intestinal wall. Fistulas may form between parts of the intestine or between the intestine and another organ such as the bladder, vagina, or skin. A fistula may be the first sign of Crohn's disease.
  - Pockets of infection (abscesses).
  - Small tears in the anus (anal fissures).
  - Skin tags that may resemble hemorrhoids. These are caused by inflamed skin.

Because there is some immune system involvement, one patient also may has symptoms outside the digestive tract, such as joint pain, eye problems, a skin rash, or liver disease.

Other conditions with symptoms similar to Crohn's disease include diverticulitis and ulcerative colitis.

How is Crohn's disease diagnosed?

Crohn's disease is diagnosed through a medical history and physical exam, imaging tests to look at the intestines, and laboratory tests.

Crohn's disease can be difficult to diagnose. The disease may go undiagnosed for years because symptoms usually develop gradually and the same part of the intestine is not always involved. Other diseases can also have the same symptoms as Crohn's disease. But Crohn's disease tends to cause the intestine to have a cobblestone appearance, which can help doctors diagnose it. The pattern results from the repeated formation and healing of sores (ulcers) in the intestine.

Tests used to diagnose Crohn's disease include:

- **Flexible sigmoidoscopy or colonoscopy,** in which a lighted viewing instrument is used to look at the inside of the colon. In general, colonoscopy is the preferred test because it can be used to examine the entire colon. Sigmoidoscopy reaches only the last part of the colon.

- **Abdominal X-ray,** which provides a picture of possible obstruction in the abdomen.
- **Upper gastrointestinal (UGI) series** with small-bowel follow-through to examine all of the small intestine. In this test the doctor examines the upper and part of the middle portions of the digestive tract. After you swallow a "shake" made of a white liquid (barium) and water, continuous X-rays (fluoroscopy) are taken to track the movement of the barium through the esophagus, stomach, and the small intestine. A video monitor displays the images.
- **Upper gastrointestinal endoscopy,** which allows your doctor to look at the interior lining of your esophagus, stomach, and duodenum with a thin, flexible imaging instrument called an endoscope.
- **Barium enema,** a test that allows the doctor to examine the large intestine (colon). For a barium enema, a white liquid (barium) is inserted through the rectum into the colon. The barium outlines the inside of the colon so that it can be more clearly seen on an X-ray.
- **Computed tomography (CT) scan,** which uses X-rays to produce detailed pictures of structures inside the body. A CT enterography may be done. This type of CT scan looks specifically at your small intestine for signs of Crohn's disease.
- **Magnetic resonance imaging (MRI),** which uses a magnetic field and pulses of radio wave energy to provide pictures of organs and structures inside the body.
- **Standard blood tests and urine tests,** which may be used to check for anemia, inflammation, or malnutrition. Depending on the symptoms, an erythrocyte sedimentation rate (ESR, or sed rate) or C-reactive protein (CRP) blood test may be done to look for infection or inflammation.
- **A biopsy** of a sample of tissue from the lining of the intestine, collected during sigmoidoscopy or colonoscopy, can be used to confirm the diagnosis of Crohn's disease. A biopsy also may be done to find out whether a tumor is present. Multiple biopsies for cancer screening are often done in people who have had Crohn's disease of the colon or rectum for 8 years or more. Bowel biopsies are painless (other than the potential discomfort of the scope procedure) and remove only a tiny piece of tissue.
- **A stool analysis** is often done, depending on symptoms, to look for blood, signs of bacterial infection, malabsorption, parasites, or the presence of white blood cells. This test can be used to distinguish Crohn's disease from irritable bowel syndrome (IBS), which is a less serious condition that sometimes has similar symptoms.

Other exams and tests that may also be used to evaluate Crohn's disease include:

- **Video capsule endoscopy (VCE),** in which one swallow a tiny camera that records its trip through his digestive tract by sending images to a recording device that he wears on a belt. The doctor later examines the images by downloading them from the recording device. The camera passes out of his body in stool within 10 to 48 hours. VCE is particularly useful in examining the small intestine, which is difficult to see with other endoscopic tests.
- **Small bowel enteroscopy,** which uses a longer, lighted flexible tube with a tiny camera that sends pictures of the small intestine to a video screen. This helps the doctor look at the small intestine. The doctor can also take small samples (biopsy) of the tissue.
- **Blood tests** to find antibody, which can sometimes help the doctor tell if he has Crohn's disease or ulcerative colitis. These tests include anti-neutrophil cytoplasmic antibody with perinuclear staining (pANCA), anti-Saccharomyces cerevisiae antibody (ASCA), and outer membrane porin C (Omp C).

How is it treated?

The main treatment for Crohn's disease is medicine to stop the inflammation in the intestine and medicine to prevent flare-ups and keep you in remission. A few people have severe, persistent symptoms or complications that may require a stronger medicine, a combination of medicines, or surgery. The type of symptoms one has and how bad they are will determine the treatment he need.

Initial treatment

Mild symptoms may respond to an antidiarrheal medicine such as loperamide (Imodium, for example), which slows or stops the painful spasms in your intestines that cause symptoms.

For mild to moderate symptoms, your will probably take:

- Aminosalicylates (such as sulfasalazine or mesalamine). These medicines help manage symptoms for many people who have Crohn's disease.
- Antibiotics (such as ciprofloxacin ormetronidazole). These may be tried if aminosalicylates are not helping. They are also used to treat fistulas and abscesses.
- Corticosteroids (such as budesonide orprednisone). These may be given by mouth for a few weeks or months to control inflammation. But corticosteroids have serious side effects, such as high blood pressure, osteoporosis, and increased risk of infection.
- Medicines that suppress the immune system (called immunomodulator

medicines), such as azathioprine or mercaptopurine. One may take these if the medicines listed above do not work, if his symptoms come back when he stop taking corticosteroids, or if his symptoms come back often, even with treatment.

● Biologics (such as infliximab or adalimumab). One patient can try these medicines if he has not had success with other medicines for Crohn's disease. In some cases, these medicines are tried before some of the other medicines that are listed above. They are also used to treat fistulas.

Severe symptoms may be treated with corticosteroids given through a vein (intravenous, IV) or biologics. With severe symptoms, the first step is to control the disease. When your symptoms are gone, you will be asked to start taking one of the medicines listed above to keep you symptom-free (in remission).

Ongoing treatment

Ongoing treatment is designed to find a medicine or combination of medicines that keeps Crohn's disease in remission.

How do one patient cope with Crohn's disease?

Having Crohn's disease can be stressful. The disease affects every part of your life. Seek support from family and friends to help you cope. Get counseling if you need it.

Many people with inflammatory bowel diseases look to alternative treatments to improve their well-being. These treatments have not been proved effective for Crohn's disease, but they may help you cope. They include massage, supplements such as vitamins D and B12, and herbs like aloe and ginseng.

中英文注释

关键词汇

abdomen ['æbdəmen] n. 腹部；下腹；腹腔

abscess ['æbsis] n. 脓肿；脓疮

anemia [ə'niːmiə] n. 贫血；贫血症

anus ['einəs] n. 肛门

ciprofloxacin [,siprəu'flɔksəsin] n. 环丙沙星；氟哌酸

cobblestone ['kɒbl,stəun] n. 鹅卵石；圆石

diverticulitis [,daivətikjʊ'laitis] n. 憩室炎

duodenum [,djuːə'diːnəm] n. 十二指肠

esophagus [iː'sɔfəgəs] n. 食管；食道

hemorrhoids ['hemərɔidz] n. 痔疮

malabsorption [,mæləb'sɔːpʃən] n. 吸收不良，吸收障碍

stomach ['stʌmək] n. 胃；腹部；胃口

sulfasalazine [ˌsʌlfəˈsæləzin] n. 柳氮磺胺吡啶

swollen ['swəulən] adj. 肿胀的，浮肿的

主要短语

bowel obstruction 肠梗阻

C-reactive protein (CRP) C 反应蛋白

erythrocyte sedimentation rate (ESR, or sed rate) 红细胞沉降率

flexible sigmoidoscopy 软式乙状结肠镜

李袁飞

35

Hemorrhage of Digestive Tract (Gastrointestinal Bleeding)

消化道出血

What is gastrointestinal bleeding?

Gastrointestinal bleeding or gastrointestinal hemorrhage describes every form of hemorrhage (loss of blood) in the gastrointestinal tract, from the pharynx to the rectum. It can be roughly divided into two clinical syndromes: upper gastrointestinal bleeding and lower gastrointestinal bleeding. Upper gastrointestinal (GI) bleeding refers to hemorrhage in the upper gastrointestinal tract. The anatomic cut-off for upper GI bleeding is the ligament of Treitz, which connects the fourth portion of the duodenum to the diaphragm near the splenic flexure of the colon.

What causes gastrointestinal bleeding?

Gastrointestinal bleeding has diverse causes, and a medical history, as well as physical examination, generally distinguishes between the main forms. The degree of bleeding can range from nearly undetectable to acute, massive, life-threatening bleeding. People are usually stratified into having either variceal or non-variceal sources of upper GI hemorrhage, as the two have different treatment algorithms and prognosis.

The causes for upper GI hemorrhage include the following:
- Esophageal causes
- Esophageal varices
- Esophagitis
- Esophageal cancer
- Esophageal ulcers
- Mallory-Weiss tear

Gastric causes:
- Gastric ulcer
- Gastric cancer
- Gastritis
- Gastric varices

- Gastric antral vascular ectasia
- Dieulafoy's lesions
- Duodenal causes
- Duodenal ulcer
- Vascular malformation, including aorto-enteric fistulae. Fistulae are usually secondary to prior vascular surgery and usually occur at the proximal anastomosis at the third or fourth portion of the duodenum where it is retroperitoneal and near the aorta. Hematobilia, or bleeding from the biliary tree
- Hemosuccus pancreaticus, or bleeding from the pancreatic duct
- Severe superior mesenteric artery syndrome

What are symptoms of gastrointestinal bleeding?

Gastrointestinal bleeding can range from microscopic bleeding, where the amount of blood is such that it can only be detected by laboratory testing, to massive bleeding where bright red blood is passed and hypovolemia and shock may develop. Blood that is digested may appear black rather than red, resulting in "coffee ground" vomitus or stool.

How is gastrointestinal bleeding diagnosed?

Upper gastrointestinal
Laboratory testing

Recommended laboratory blood testing includes: cross matching blood, hemoglobin, hematocrit, platelets, coagulation time, and electrolytes. If the ratio of blood urea nitrogen to creatinine is greater than 30 the source is more likely from the upper GI tract.

Imaging

A CT angiography is useful for determining the exact location of the bleeding within the gastrointestinal tract.

The diagnosis of upper GI bleeding is assumed when hematemesis is documented. In the absence of hematemesis, an upper source for GI bleeding is likely in the presence of at least two factors among: black stool, age < 50 years, and blood urea nitrogen/creatinine ratio 30 or more. In the absence of these findings, consider a nasogastric aspirate to determine the source of bleeding. If the aspirate is positive, an upper GI bleed is greater than 50%, but not high enough to be certain. If the aspirate is negative, the source of a GI bleed is likely lower. The accuracy of the aspirate is improved by using the Gastroccult test.

Lower gastrointestinal

Lower gastrointestinal bleeding, commonly abbreviated LGIB, refers to any form of bleeding in the lower gastrointestinal tract. LGIB is a common ailment seen at emergency departments. It presents less commonly than upper gastrointestinal bleeding (UGIB). It is estimated that UGIB accounts for 100–200 per 100,000 cases versus 20–27 per 100,000 cases for LGIB. Approximately 85% of lower gastrointestinal bleeding involves the colon, 10% are from bleeds that are actually upper gastrointestinal bleeds, and 3–5% involve the small intestines. The mortality rate for LGIB is between 2–4%.

The following are possible diagnosis of a LGIB:

- Hemorrhoids are a common occurrence; however, rarely they have been known to rupture and result in a massive hemorrhage. Causes for this include frequent or chronic constipation, straining to have a bowel movement, diets low in fiber, and pregnancy. It may present with small amounts of bright red bleeding.
- Anal fissures
- Rectal foreign bodies
- Ulcerative colitis
- Crohn's disease
- Pseudomembranous colitis
- Infectious diarrhea
- Radiation colitis
- Diverticulosis
- Mesenteric ischemia
- colonic polyps
- colon cancer

Evaluations will most often be conducted by either a clinic triagenurse, emergency department nurse, and/or a physician or other clinician. The initial assessment will include the appearance of the individual, their vital signs, and mental status. A patient history will help reveal a disposition or history of LGIBs or potential differential diagnosis.

Orthostatic vital signs are often used as an indicator of hypovolemia.

Laboratory test will also help give indications of a LGIB. Hemoglobin, hematocrit, and platelets are very good physical signs of hypovolemia or blood loss anemia. Partial thromboplastin time (PTT) and INR will also help determine the body's current ability to clot.

Aspiration of the stomach contents by way of a nasogastric tube (NG tube) will help differentiate between either a UGIB and a LGIB. A negative presence of blood will help to rule out an UGIB.

Differential diagnosis

A differential diagnosis is a systematic method used to identify unknowns. With the use of a differential diagnosis, physicians or other clinicians begin to rule out what the illness is not to narrow the diagnosis of the specific disease process, as with a lower gastrointestinal bleed.

Diverticulosis, Angiodysplasia, Infectious Colitis, Ischemic Colitis, Inflammatory Bowel Disease, Neoplasms, Radiation Telangiectasia and Proctitis, and NSAID Enteropathy and Colopathy are the causes of LGIB in adults.

The most common cause of massive bleeding in pediatric patients is Meckels Diverticulum. Anorectal disease (hemorrhoids and fissures) causes less severe bleeding in pediatric patients.

Diagnostic approach

Diagnosis is often based on direct observation of blood in the stool or vomit. This can be confirmed with a fecal occult blood test. Differentiating between upper and lower bleeding in some cases can be difficult. The severity of an upper GI bleed can be judged based on the Blatchford score or Rockall score. The Rockall score is the more accurate of the two. AS of 2008 there is no scoring system useful for lower GI bleeds.

Clinical

Gastric aspiration and or lavage, where a tube is inserted into the stomach via the nose in an attempt to determine if there is blood in the stomach, if negative does not rule out an upper GI bleed but if positive is useful for ruling one in. Clots in the stool indicate a lower GI source while melana stools an upper one.

How is it treated?

The initial focus is on resuscitation beginning with airway management and fluid resuscitation using either intravenous fluids and or blood. A number of medications may improve outcomes depending on the source of the bleeding.

Peptic ulcers

Based on evidence from people with other health problems crystalloid and colloids are believed to be equivalent for peptic ulcer bleeding. Proton pump inhibitors may reduce mortality in those with severe disease as well as the risk of re-bleeding and the need for surgery among this group. In those with less severe disease and where endoscopy is rapidly available, they are of less immediate clinical importance. The evidence for the inhibition of fibrinolysis with tranexamic acid is insufficient to recommend its use. Somatostatin and octreotide, while recommended for varicial bleeding, have not been found to be of general use for non varicial bleeds.

Variceal bleeding

For initial fluid replacement colloids or albumin is preferred in people with cirrhosis. Medications typically include octreotide or, if not available, vasopression and nitroglycerin to reduce portal pressures. Terlipressin appears to be more effective than octreotide, but it is not available in many areas of the world. This is in addition to endoscopic banding or sclerotherapy for the varicies. If this is sufficient then beta blockers and nitrates may be used for the prevention of re-bleeding. If bleeding continues then balloon tamponade with a Sengstaken-Blakemore tube or Minnesota tube may be used in an attempt to mechanically compress the varicies. This may then be followed by a transjugular intrahepatic portosystemic shunt. In those with cirrhosis antibiotics decrease the chance of re bleeding, shorten the length of time spent in hospital, and decrease mortality. Octreotide reduces the need for blood transfusions and may decrease mortality. No trials of vitamin K have been conducted.

Blood products

The evidence for benefit of blood transfusions in GI bleed is poor with some evidence finding harm. In those in shock O-negative packed red blood cells are recommended. If large amounts of pack red blood cells are used additional platelets and fresh frozen plasma (FFP) should be administered to prevent coagulopathies. In alcoholics FFP is suggested before confirmation of a coagulopathy due to presumed blood clotting problems. Some evidence supports holding off on blood transfusions in those who have ahemoglobin greater than 7 to 8 g/dL and only moderate bleeding. If the INR is greater than 1.5 to 1.8 correction with fresh frozen plasma or prothrombin complex may decrease mortality. Evidence of a harm or benefit of recombinant activated factor VII in those with liver diseases and gastrointestinal bleeding is not determined. A massive transfusion protocol may be used, but there is a lack of evidence for this indication.

Procedures

The Blakemore esophageal balloon used for stopping esophageal bleeds if other measures have failed.

The benefits versus risks of placing a nasogastric tube in those with upper GI bleeding are not determined. Endoscopy within 24 hours is recommended, in addition to medical management. A number of endoscopic treatments may be used, including: epinephrine injection, band ligation, sclerotherapy, and fibrin glue depending on what is found. Prokinetic agents such as erythromycin before endocopy can decrease the amount of blood in the stomach and thus improve the operators view. They also decrease the amount of blood transfusions required. Early endoscopy decreases hospital and the amount of blood transfusions needed. A second endoscopy within a day is routinely recommended by some but by others only in specific situation. Proton pump inhibitors, if they have not been started earlier, are recommended in those in whom high risk signs for bleeding are found. High and low dose PPIs appear equivalent at this point. It is also recommended that people with high risk signs are kept in hospital for at least 72 hours. Those at low risk of re-bleeding may begin eating typically 24 hours following endoscopy. If other measures fail or are not available, esophageal balloon tamponade may be attempted. While there is a success rate up to 90%, there are some potentially significant complications including aspiration and esophageal perforation.

Colonoscopy is useful for the diagnosis and treatment of lower GI bleeding. A number of techniques may be employed including: clipping, cauterizing, and sclerotherapy. Preparation for colonoscopy takes a minimum of six hours which in those bleeding briskly may limit its applicability. Surgery, while rarely used to treat upper GI bleeds, is still commonly used to manage lower GI bleeds by cutting out the part of the intestines that is causing the problem. Angiographic embolization may be used for both upper and lower GI bleeds. transjugular intrahepatic portosystemic shunting (TIPS) may also be considered.

中英文注释

关键词汇

ailment ['eilm(ə)nt] n. 疾病，小病

angiodysplasia [æŋgi:əʊdisp'leiziə] n. 血管发育不良

angiography [ˌændʒi'ɒgrəfi] n. 血管造影术

creatinine [kri'ætini:n] n. 肌酐

electrolytes [i'lektrəˌlaits] n. 电解质

enteropathy [ˌentə'rɒpəθi] n. 肠下垂

hematemesis [ˌhi:mə'temisis] n. 呕血，咯血

hematocrit ['hemətəʊkrit] n. 红细胞压积

hemoglobin [ˌhi:məʊ'gləʊbin] n. 血红蛋白

hemorrhoids ['hemərɔidz] n. 痔疮；

hypovolemia ['haipəʊvə'li:miə] n. 血容量减少；血容量过低

lavage ['lævidʒ] vt. 灌洗；洗胃

platelets ['pleitlits] n. 血小板

resuscitation [riˌsʌsi'teiʃən] n. 复苏；

somatostatin [ˌsəʊmətə'stætin] n. 生长抑素

vomitus ['vɒmitəs] n. 呕吐物

主要短语

blood urea nitrogen 血尿素氮

coagulation time 凝血时间

fecal occult blood test 大便潜血实验

mesenteric ischemia 肠系膜缺血

nasogastric tube 经鼻胃管

proton pump inhibitors 质子泵抑制剂

pseudomembranous colitis 假膜性结肠炎

radiation colitis 放射性肠炎

transjugular intrahepatic portosystemic shunt 经颈静脉肝内门体分流术

variceal bleeding 静脉曲张破裂出血

李袁飞

36 ───────── Ulcerative Colitis

溃疡性结肠炎

Ulcerative colitis and Crohn's disease are the most common types of inflammatory bowel disease. Ulcerative colitis affects only the colon and rectum. Crohn's disease can affect any part of the digestive tract.

What is ulcerative colitis?

Ulcerative colitis is a disease that causes inflammation and sores (ulcers) in the lining of the large intestine (colon). It usually affects the lower section (sigmoid colon) and the rectum. But it can affect the entire colon. In general, the more of the colon that's affected, the worse the symptoms will be.

The disease can affect people of any age. But most people who have it are diagnosed before the age of 30.

What causes ulcerative colitis?

The exact cause of ulcerative colitis is unclear, but researchers suspect the immune system is involved. In people with UC, immune cells may react abnormally to bacteria in the digestive tract. It is not known whether this triggers the condition or is a result of it. Doctors are confident that the disease is not caused by stress or diet, although these factors can make the symptoms worse.

What are the symptoms of ulcerative colitis?

The symptoms of ulcerative colitis may include:
- Diarrhea or rectal urgency. Some people may have diarrhea 10 to 20 times a day. The urge to go to the bathroom may wake you up at night.
- Rectal bleeding. The disease usually causes bloody diarrhea and mucus. You also may have rectal pain and an urgent need to empty your bowels.
- Belly pain, often described as cramping. Your belly may be sore when touched.
- Constipation. This symptom may develop depending on what part of the colon is affected. Constipation is much less common than diarrhea.
- Loss of appetite.

- Fever. In severe cases, fever or other symptoms that affect the entire body may develop.
- Weight loss. Ongoing symptoms, such as diarrhea, can lead to weight loss.
- Too few red blood cells (anemia). Some people get anemia because of low iron levels caused by bloody stools or intestinal inflammation.

Other conditions with symptoms similar to ulcerative colitis include Crohn's disease, diverticulitis, irritable bowel syndrome (IBS), and colon cancer.

Ulcerative colitis symptoms may come and go. During remission, you may have no discomfort at all. This period can last for months or years, but the symptoms eventually return. Not knowing when symptoms will flare can add to the stress of the disease and make it difficult to come up with an effective treatment plan.

How is ulcerative colitis diagnosed?

Ulcerative colitis can be fairly easy to diagnose, because it normally affects only the colon and rectum. And it usually causes an obvious change in daily bowel habits, such as frequent stools with blood or mucus.

The doctors may:

- Conduct a medical history and physical exam.
- Look inside your colon and rectum with flexible sigmoidoscopy or colonoscopy. The doctor uses a small, lighted scope to look inside the intestine. In general, colonoscopy is preferred because it can be used to see the entire colon. Both procedures can be used to take a sample (biopsy) of intestinal tissue. Biopsies are collected during sigmoidoscopy or colonoscopy to see if you have ulcerative colitis. A biopsy also may be done to look for cancer.

Other exams and tests that may be used include:

- **Abdominal X-ray.** It provides a picture of the inside of the abdomen.
- **Barium enema.** It allows the doctor to examine the colon.
- **Computed tomography (CT) scan or MRI.** These provide detailed pictures of the inside of the body.
- **Stool analysis** (including a test for blood in the stool). This test looks for blood, signs of bacterial infection, parasites, or white blood cells.
- **Blood and urine tests to check for anemia, inflammation, or malnutrition.** erythrocyte sedimentation rate (ESR, or sed rate) or a C-reactive protein (CRP) blood test may be done to look for infection or inflammation.

Some people have symptoms of inflammatory bowel disease (IBD), but neither Crohn's disease nor ulcerative colitis can be diagnosed. These people have a form of IBD called indeterminate colitis. Doctors believe that it has features of both Crohn's disease and ulcerative colitis.

How is it treated?

Treatment for ulcerative colitis depends mainly on how bad the disease is. It usually includes medicines and changes in diet. A few people have symptoms that are long-lasting and severe, in some cases requiring more medicines or surgery.

You may need to treat other problems, such as anemia or infection. Treatment in children and teens may include taking nutritional supplements to restore normal growth and sexual development.

If you don't have any symptoms or if your disease is not active (in remission), you may not need treatment. But your doctor may suggest that you take medicines to keep the disease in remission.

If you do have symptoms, they usually can be managed with medicines to put the disease in remission. It often is easier to keep the disease in remission than to treat a flare-up.

Mild symptoms

Mild symptoms may respond to:

- Antidiarrheal medicines.
- Enemas or suppositories that contain medicine.
- Aminosalicylates. These medicines relieve inflammation in the intestines. They are also taken to keep the disease in remission.
- Steroid medicines. It is taken for a few weeks to control active disease.
- Changes in your diet.

Moderate to severe symptoms

These symptoms usually require steroid medicines to control inflammation. The dose you need may be higher than that needed to treat mild symptoms. When inflammation goes away, you will take aminosalicylates to keep the condition in remission.

Severe symptoms also may be treated with:

- Immunomodulator medicines or cyclosporine. These strong medicines suppress the immune system to prevent inflammation.
- Biologics. They block the inflammatory response in your body and help reduce the inflammation in your colon. They may be used if other medicines don't control your symptoms.
- Surgery. Removal of the large intestine (colon) cures ulcerative colitis. But surgery may not cure all of the problems that the condition can cause in other areas of the body, such as the liver and joints. Surgery also is done to treat problems such as bleeding or toxic megacolon.

中英文注释

关键词汇

colonoscopy [ˌkəʊləˈnɒskəpi] n. 结肠镜检查

constipation [ˌkɔnstiˈpeiʃən] n. 便秘

intestine [inˈtestin] n. 肠

malnutrition [ˌmælnjuːˈtriʃən] n. 营养不良

mucus [ˈmjuːkəs] n. 黏液

remission [riˈmiʃən] n. 缓解

ulcer [ˈʌlsə] n. 溃疡

主要短语

barium enema 钡灌肠

digestive tract 消化道

erythrocyte sedimentation rate 红细胞沉降率, 血沉

inflammatory bowel disease (IBD) 炎症性肠病

irritable bowel syndrome (IBS) 肠应激综合征

loss of appetite 食欲减退

sigmoid colon 乙状结肠

toxic megacolon 中毒性巨结肠

ulcerative colitis 溃疡性结肠炎

李袁飞

37

Nephrotic Syndrome
肾病综合征

What is nephrotic syndrome?

Nephrotic syndrome is a sign that your kidneys are not working right. One patient has nephrotic syndrome if he has high levels of protein in his urine, low levels of protein in the blood, and high cholesterol.

Nephrotic syndrome is not a disease. It is a warning that something is damaging his kidneys. Without treatment, that problem could cause kidney failure. So it's important to get treatment right away.

Nephrotic syndrome can occur at any age. But it is most common in children between the ages of 18 months and 8 years.

What causes nephrotic syndrome?

Nephrotic syndrome is caused by damage to the tiny blood vessels in the kidney that filter waste and excess water from the blood.

Many conditions and diseases can cause nephrotic syndrome, including:

- Minimal change disease (also called nil disease), a type of kidney disease. The cause of minimal change disease is unknown. But this disease causes most of the cases of nephrotic syndrome in children.
- Membranous glomerulopathy and focal segmental glomerulosclerosis, which are two other diseases of the kidney. Both of these diseases affect the glomeruli. The glomeruli help filter waste out of your blood. In focal segmental glomerulosclerosis, some of the parts of the glomeruli have scar tissue. This can affect how they filter the blood. In membranous glomerulopathy, the tissue wall (membrane) that separates blood and urine and acts as a filter in your kidney becomes thickened and damaged.
- Diabetes and lupus. Diabetes is the most common cause of nephrotic syndrome in adults.
- Infections, such as HIV, hepatitis B, or hepatitis C.
- Cancer.

- Medicines, such as nonsteroidal anti-inflammatory drugs, penicillamine, gold therapy, or captopril.
- Illegal drugs, such as heroin.
- Conditions such as preeclampsia, chronic graft rejection following an organ transplant, and allergic reactions to bee stings.
- Unknown (idiopathic) factors.

What are the symptoms of nephrotic syndrome?

Many people who have nephrotic syndrome do not have any noticeable physical symptoms. When symptoms are present, they can include:

- Swelling in the tissues around the eyes (periorbital edema) or in the feet or ankles (peripheral edema). This is the most common early symptom of nephrotic syndrome in both children and adults.
- Shortness of breath caused by fluid buildup in the lungs (pulmonary edema). Adults older than 65 may be misdiagnosed with heart failure.
  Children are often thought to have allergies.
- Dry skin.
- Swelling of the scrotum (scrotal edema), which may cause a cord in the testicles (testicular torsion).

Signs of nephrotic syndrome in blood and urine tests can include:

- Protein in the urine (proteinuria).
- Low protein (albumin) in the blood.
- High cholesterol and triglyceride levels.
- Low blood levels of iron and vitamin D.

How is nephrotic syndrome diagnosed?

In addition to a medical history and physical exam, other tests to diagnose nephrotic syndrome include:

- A 24-hour urine collection, which measures the total amount of protein in the urine collected over 24 hours. You will be diagnosed with nephrotic syndrome if you have more than 3 grams of protein in your urine.
- Blood test for albumin. Lower levels of albumin in the blood can cause fluid to collect in the ankles, lungs, or abdomen.
- Creatinine and creatinine clearance. Results of these tests give information on how well your kidneys are working.
- Blood profile tests to measure the amount of protein, cholesterol, and sugar (glucose) in the blood.

- Kidney ultrasound to look at the kidneys. This exam can rule out other causes of your symptoms.

One may need other tests before treatment for nephrotic syndrome begins. These include:

- A test for varicella (chickenpox) antibodies.
- A bone density scan.

In adults, testing usually includes:

- Serum protein electrophoresis (SPEP).
- Antinuclear antibodies (ANA).
- Antibody tests for systemic lupus erythematosus.
- C3 and C4 complement, proteins normally found in the blood.
- Tests for hepatitis B, hepatitis C, and HIV.

Unless nephrotic syndrome is clearly caused by diabetes, a kidney biopsy is usually done to find the cause. Children do not usually have abiopsy.

How is it treated?

Treatment for nephrotic syndrome depends on the cause and the age of the person who has the condition. Medicines, changes in diet, and care for other conditions, such as diabetes or high blood pressure, are all possible treatments for this syndrome. These treatments may reverse, slow, or prevent further kidney damage.

Most children who have nephrotic syndrome do well with treatment and have a normal life expectancy.

Doctors define complete recovery as living without symptoms or treatment for more than 2 years.

Initial treatment

Treatment of nephrotic syndrome depends on the cause of the disease and may include:

- Corticosteroids, such as prednisone or prednisolone, to reduce swelling.
- Diuretics to reduce fluid build up in the body (edema) and to help with reducing sodium, potassium, and water. Fluid reduction should occur slowly to avoid further kidney damage and low blood pressure.
- Medicines, such as angiotensin-converting enzyme (ACE) inhibitors andangiotensin II receptor blockers (ARBs), to reduce the amount of protein lost in the urine, lower blood pressure, and slow the progress of the disease.
- In rare cases, salt-free albumin given through a vein (IV). Albumin helps remove extra fluid from the tissues.

First treatments can last from 6 to 15 weeks, often longer in adults. Depending on how severe your symptoms are or whether they return, ongoing treatment may be needed for months to years, or even for the rest of your life.

Ongoing treatment

Ongoing treatment for nephrotic syndrome and complications of the disease include:

- Daily or alternate-day prednisone, if nephrotic syndrome returns.
- Cyclophosphamide, cyclosporine, or mycophenolate mofetil, when treatment with corticosteroids is not successful.
- Steps to lower blood pressure, including medicine, a healthier diet, and exercise. Untreated high blood pressure increases your risk for stroke or heart attack. For more information, see the topics High Blood Pressure, Coronary Artery Disease, and Stroke.
- Changes in diet to replace nutrients lost through the urine, reduce fluid buildup in the body, and reduce the risk of complications. Some doctors prescribe a diet that limits protein, salt (sodium), and fats but is high in carbohydrates. The amount of protein allowed may vary, depending on your condition.
- Anticoagulants, such as warfarin (Coumadin) or heparin, to treat blood clots if they form.
- Early treatment of infections with antibiotics.
- Vaccinations with a pneumococcal vaccine, chickenpox (varicella) vaccine, and a yearly flu shot. Vaccination is not recommended until nephrotic syndrome has responded to treatment with corticosteroids.
- Calcium and vitamin D supplements to protect your bones and help preventosteoporosis during long-term corticosteroid treatment (for example, prednisone).

One may need emotional support during treatment for nephrotic syndrome. If he or his child has nephrotic syndrome and he is having a hard time handling treatment or the severity of his child's condition, it may help to talk with a doctor or seek counseling.

Treatment if the condition gets worse

Sometimes treatment for nephrotic syndrome is unsuccessful. If this occurs, you may develop chronic kidney disease. Your doctor may recommend that you beginhemodialysis, peritoneal dialysis, or consider a kidney transplant. For more information, see the topic Chronic Kidney Disease.

Clinical trials are ongoing to test more effective medicines for the treatment of steroid-resistant (relapsing) nephrotic syndrome. If treatment has not successfully controlled your nephrotic syndrome, ask your doctor about clinical trials. To take part in a clinical trial, you may need to travel to a large treatment center.

中英文注释

关键词汇

albumin ['ælbjʊmin] n. 白蛋白, 清蛋白

allergic [ə'lɜːdʒik] adj. 对…过敏的

captopril ['kæptəpril] n. 甲巯丙脯酸, 卡托普利

chickenpox ['tʃikinpɑks] n. 水痘

cholesterol [kə'lestərɒl] n. 胆固醇

creatinine [kri'ætiniːn] n. 肌酐

cyclophosphamide [ˌsaiklə'fɑsfə,maid] n. 环磷酰胺

cyclosporine [ˌsaiklə'spɔrin] n. 环孢霉素

diuretics [ˌdaijʊ'rɛtik] n. 利尿剂

glomeruli [glɔ'merjulai] n. 小球, 肾小球

glomerulopathy [gləʊme'rjulɒpəsi] n. 肾小球疾病

hemodialysis [ˌhiːmədai'ælisis] n. 血液透析（复数 hemodialyses）

heroin ['herəuin] n. 海洛因, 吗啡

idiopathic [ˌidiə(ʊ)'pæθik] adj. 先天的, 病因不明的, 特发的, 自发的

nephrotic [ni'frotik] adj. 肾病的

nonsteroidal [nɔn'stərɔidəl] adj. 非甾类化合物的, 非类固醇的

osteoporosis [ˌɒstiəʊpə'rəusis] n. 骨质疏松症

periorbital ['pɛrə,prɑktɔl] adj. 眶周的; 眶骨膜的

potassium [pə'tæsiəm] n. 钾（符号 K）

prednisone ['prednizəun] n. 强的松（肾上腺皮质激素）

preeclampsia [ˌpriiˈklæmpsiə] n. 子痫前期; 惊厥前期

scrotum ['skrəutəm] n. 阴囊[复数 scrotums 或 scrota]

segmental [seg'ment(ə)l] adj. 部分的

sodium ['səudiəm] n. 钠（符号 Na）

triglyceride [trai'glisəraid] n. 甘油三酸酯

ultrasound ['ʌltrəsaund] n. 超声, 超音波

varicella [ˌværi'selə] n. 水痘

主要短语

angiotensin-converting enzyme (ACE) 血管紧张素转化酶

alternate-day 隔日

antinuclear antibodies (ANA) 抗核抗体

bone density 骨密度

coronary artery 冠状动脉

creatinine clearance 肌酐清除率
focal segmental glomerulosclerosis 局灶性节段性肾小球硬化
hepatitis B 乙型肝炎
kidney failure 肾衰竭
membranous glomerulopathy 膜性肾小球病
nephrotic syndrome 肾病综合征
periorbital edema 眶周水肿
peritoneal dialysis 腹膜透析
pulmonary edema 肺水肿
testicular torsion 扭曲

张 瑾 马志方

38

Type 2 Diabetes
2 型糖尿病

What is type 2 diabetes?

Type 2 diabetes, once called non-insulin dependent diabetes, is the most common form of diabetes, affecting 90% to 95% of the 26 million Americans with diabetes.

Type 2 diabetes, once called adult-onset diabetes, is the most common form of diabetes, affecting 90% to 95% of the 13 million men with diabetes.

What are causes of Type 2 Diabetes?

Diabetes is a number of diseases that involve problems with the hormone insulin. While not everyone with type 2 diabetes is overweight, obesity and lack of physical activity are two of the most common causes of this form of diabetes.

Type 2 diabetes prevention is possible by adopting some healthy lifestyle habits and paying attention to specific preventable diabetes complications associated with this disease.

Maintaining a healthy diet is important for everyone, but it is especially important for people with diabetes.

What are the symptoms of type 2 diabetes?

Very often, people with type 2 diabetes will have no symptoms. When symptoms of type 2 diabetes occur, they can vary from person to person and may include:
- Increased thirst
- Increased hunger (especially after eating)
- Dry mouth
- Nausea and occasionally vomiting
- Frequent urination
- Fatigue (weak, tired feeling)
- Blurred vision
- Numbness or tingling of the hands or feet
- Frequent infections of the skin, urinary tract or vagina

● Sores that are slow to heal

Rarely, a person may be diagnosed with type 2 diabetes after presenting to the hospital in a diabetic coma.

How is type 2 diabetes diagnosed?

Type 2 Diabetes Screening

Type 2 diabetes is a common and serious disease in the United States and worldwide. However, it's thought that one-third of those with type 2 diabetes are unaware that they have this serious illness.

Diabetes Testing

If he experiences symptoms of severe increased thirst, frequent urination, unexplained weight loss, increased hunger, tingling of his hands or feet — the doctor may run a test for diabetes.

Oral Glucose Tolerance Test

Though not routinely used anymore, the oral glucose tolerance test (OGTT) is the gold standard for making the diagnosis of type 2 diabetes.

The Hemoglobin A1c (HbA1c) Test for Diabetes

The hemoglobin A1c test — also called HbA1c, glycated hemoglobin test, or glycohemoglobin — is an important blood test used to determine how well your diabetes is being controlled.

To diagnose type 2 diabetes, your health care provider will first check for abnormalities in your blood (high blood glucose level) during a random fasting blood test or through a screening test known as the 2 hour glucose tolerance test. Or you may get a blood test called a hemoglobin A1C that reflects your average blood sugar for the past 2 to 3 days. In addition, he or she may look for glucose or ketone bodies in your urine.

What are complications associated with type 2 diabetes?

If your type 2 diabetes isn't well controlled, there are a number of serious or life-threatening problems you may experience, including:

● **Retinopathy.** People with type 2 diabetes may already have abnormalities in the eyes related to the development of diabetes. Over time more and more people who initially do not have eye problems related to the disease will develop some form of eye problem. It is important to control not only sugars but blood pressure and cholesterol to prevent progression of eye disease. Fortunately, the vision loss isn't significant in most.

● **Kidney damage.** The risk of kidney disease increases over time, meaning the longer you have diabetes the greater your risk. This complication carries significant risk of serious kidney failure if not diagnosed and treated early.

● **Poor blood circulation and nerve damage.** Damage to the blood vessels can lead to increased risk of stroke and heart attack as well as peripheral artery disease. Damage to nerves and hardening of the arteries leads to decreased sensation and poor blood circulation in the feet. This can lead to increased infections and an increased risk of ulcers which heal poorly and can in turn significantly raises the risk of amputation. Damage to nerves may also lead to digestive problems, such as nausea, vomiting, and diarrhea.

How is type 2 diabetes treated?

weight loss surgery and type 2 diabetes

Increasingly, weight loss surgery is being used as a tool to manage type 2 diabetes. That's because controlling diabetes and managing the related health risks is directly related to losing weight.

natural remedies for type 2 diabetes

Diabetes treatment can include many elements, including traditional medications, alternative medicine, and natural remedies.

non-insulin diabetes injectables

Today, metformin is the first drug doctors usually recommend for people with type 2 diabetes who need to take medication.

oral diabetes medications

Oral diabetes medications — diabetes pills — help control blood sugar levels in people whose bodies still produce some insulin (the majority of people with type 2 diabetes).

your diabetes care team

If you have diabetes, you likely have a care team that includes a primary care doctor, dietitian, diabetes educator, eye doctor, foot doctor, dentist, and possibly an exercise trainer.

Insulin

diabetes treatment with insulin

When used as a medication, it is derived from either pork (porcine), beef (no longer available in the U.S.), or is genetically made to be identical to human insulin.

inhaled insulin

Inhaled insulin is another option that's been considered. Although it's possible to make inhaled insulin, there are no inhaled insulin drugs on the market.

giving yourself an insulin shot for diabetes

For those with diabetes, an insulin shot delivers medicine into your subcutaneous tissue — the tissue between your skin and muscle.

diabetic shock and insulin reactions

The symptoms of diabetic shock may seem mild at first. But they should not be ignored.

Type 2 Diabetes and the insulin pump

If you have type 2 diabetes and take insulin, you may want to ask your doctor about the insulin pump.

Complications

Type 2 diabetes and sleep

People who have diabetes often have poor sleep habits, including difficulty falling asleep or staying asleep.

diabetic coma in type 2 diabetes

Diabetic coma — also known as hyperglycemic hyperosmolar nonketotic syndrome — is a serious complication that can happen to a person with diabetes who is ill or whose body is stressed.

diabetes, insulin overdose, and other complications

Cold sweats, trembling hands, intense anxiety, a general sense of confusion — no, it's not the night before final exams. These are the signs of low blood sugar or hypoglycemia.

diabetes and heart disease

If you have diabetes, it's important to understand your heart disease risk and what you can do to lower it.

stroke and diabetes

If you have diabetes, it's important to understand your increased risk of stroke.

diabetes and infection

Diabetes can slow down your body's ability to fight infection. High blood sugar (glucose) leads to high levels of sugar in your body's tissues, allowing bacteria to grow and infections to develop more quickly.

diabetic nephropathy

Diabetic nephropathy — kidney disease that results from diabetes — is the number one cause of kidney failure. Almost a third of people with diabetes develop diabetic nephropathy.

diabetes and inflammation

Inactivity and obestiy increase the risk for diabetes, but exactly how is unclear. Recent research suggests that inflammation inside the body plays a role in the development of type 2 diabetes.

中英文注释

关键词汇

amputation [ˌæmpjʊˈteiʃən] n. 截肢；切断（术）

blurred [blɜːd] adj. 模糊不清的；被弄污的

cholesterol [kəˈlestərɒl] n. [生化]胆固醇

coma [ˈkəʊmə] n. [医]昏迷

confusion [kənˈfjuːʒ(ə)n] n. 混淆，混乱；困惑

diabetes [ˌdaiəˈbiːtiːz] n. 糖尿病；多尿症

diarrhea [ˌdaiəˈriə] n. 腹泻，痢疾

dietitian [daiəˈtiʃ(ə)n] n. (美)营养学家；饮食学家

digestive [daiˈdʒestiv; di–] adj. 消化的；助消化；n. 助消化药

hemoglobin [ˌhiːməʊˈgləʊbin] n. [生化]血红蛋白（等于 haemoglobin）；血红素

hyperglycemic [ˌhaipəglaiˈsiːmiə] adj. 高血糖的；血糖过多的

injectables [inˈdʒektəbl] n. 血管注射剂；adj. 可注射的

insulin [ˈinsjʊlin] n. [生化][药]胰岛素

intense [inˈtens] adj. 强烈的；紧张的；非常的；热情的

juvenile [ˈdʒuːvənail] adj. 青少年的；幼稚的 n. 青少年；少年读物

nephropathy [nəˈfrapəθi] n. [泌尿]肾病

numbness [ˈnʌmnəs] n. 麻木；麻痹

obesity [ə(ʊ)ˈbiːsiti] n. 肥大，肥胖

peripheral [pəˈrif(ə)r(ə)l] adj. 外围的；次要的

prevention [priˈvenʃn] n. 预防；阻止；妨碍

remedies [ˈremidi] vt. 补救；治疗；纠正；n. 补救；治疗；赔偿

retinopathy [ˌretinˈɔpəθiˌ –ˈnɔp–] n. [眼科]视网膜病

screening [ˈskriːniŋ] n. 筛选

sore [sɔː] adj. 疼痛的，痛心的；n. 溃疡，痛处

stroke [strəʊk] n. 中风

subcutaneous [ˌsʌbkjuːˈteiniəs] adj. 皮下的；皮下用的

tingling [ˈtiŋgliŋ] n. 麻刺感；发出叮当声

trembling [trembliŋ] n. 发抖；战栗；担心；adj. 发抖的；战栗的；哆嗦的

vagina [vəˈdʒainə] n. [解剖]阴道

主要短语

blood circulation 血液循环

blood sugar 血糖

gold standard 金标准

glycated hemoglobin test 糖化血红蛋白检测

ketone bodies 酮体

Oral Glucose Tolerance Test [医] 口服葡萄糖耐量试验

urinary tract 尿路；泌尿道

岳　亮　马志方

39 · Hyperthyroidism, Hypothyroidism
甲状腺功能亢进和甲状腺功能减低

Hyperthyroidism
甲状腺功能亢进

What is hyperthyroidism?

Hyperthyroidism means your thyroid makes too much thyroidhormone. Your thyroid is a gland in the front of your neck. It controls your metabolism, which is how your body turns food into energy. It also affects your heart, muscles, bones, and cholesterol.

Having too much thyroid hormone can make a lot of things in your body speed up. You may lose weight quickly, have a fast heartbeat, sweat a lot, or feel nervous and moody. Or you may have no symptoms at all. While your doctor is doing a test for another reason, he or she may discover that you have hyperthyroidism.

What causes hyperthyroidism?

Graves' disease is the most common cause of hyperthyroidism. Graves' diseasecauses the thyroid gland to make too much thyroid hormone. Graves' disease, like many thyroid problems, often runs in families.

Other common causes include:

- Thyroid nodules. Thyroid nodules are abnormal growths in the thyroid gland that can make too much thyroid hormone. For more information, see the topic Thyroid Nodules.
- Thyroiditis. Thyroiditis occurs when your body makes antibodies that damage your thyroid gland. You can also get thyroiditis from a viral or bacterial infection. At first, thyroiditis may cause your thyroid levels to rise as hormone leaks out from the damaged gland. Later, levels may be low (hypothyroidism) until the gland repairs itself.

Uncommon causes of hyperthyroidism include tumors or eating foods or taking

259

medicines that contain large amounts of iodine.

Hyperthyroidism can occur at any age but rarely affects children. It affects women more often than men. Graves' disease is the most common cause of hyperthyroidism.

What are the symptoms of hyperthyroidism?

One may has hyperthyroidism if he:

- Feel nervous, moody, weak, or tired.
- Have hand tremors, or have a fast or irregular heartbeat, or have trouble breathing even when you are resting.
- Feel very hot, sweat a lot, or have warm, red skin that may be itchy.
- Have frequent and sometimes loose bowel movements.
- Have fine, soft hair that is falling out.
- Lose weight even though you are eating normally or more than usual.

Also, some women have irregular menstrual cycles or stop having periods altogether. And some men may develop enlarged breasts.

The symptoms of hyperthyroidism are not the same for everyone. Your symptoms will depend on how much hormone your thyroid gland is making, how long you have had the condition, and your age. If you are older, it's easy to mistakenly dismiss your symptoms as normal signs of aging.

Specific symptoms of Graves' disease

People with Graves' disease often have additional symptoms, including:

- Goiter, which is an enlarged, painless thyroid gland.
- Thickened nails that lift off the nail beds.
- Pretibial myxedema, which is lumpy, reddish, thick skin on the front of the shins and sometimes on top of the feet.
- Clubbing (fingers with wide tips).
- Graves' ophthalmopathy, which causes bulging, reddened eyes, among other symptoms.

Complications

Graves' ophthalmopathy is a possible complication of hyperthyroidism. It can occur before, after, or at the same time as your symptoms of hyperthyroidism. People with Graves' ophthalmopathy develop eye problems, including bulging, reddened eyes, sensitivity to light, and blurring or double vision. People who smoke are more likely to develop Graves' ophthalmopathy.

If you have Graves' ophthalmopathy, it may temporarily get worse if you have radioactive iodine treatment. On the other hand, it may get better if you take antithyroid medicine.

If you do not treat your hyperthyroidism, you may:

- Lose weight because your body's metabolism is faster.
- Have heart problems such as rapid heart rate, atrial fibrillation, and heart failure.
- Have trouble replacing calcium and other minerals in your bones, which can lead to osteoporosis.

In rare cases, hyperthyroidism can cause a life-threatening condition called thyroid storm, which happens when the thyroid gland releases large amounts of thyroid hormones in a short period of time.

How is hyperthyroidism diagnosed?

The doctor will ask questions about one patient's medical history, do a physical exam, and order medical tests to diagnose hyperthyroidism.

If the doctor thinks he may has hyperthyroidism, he may order:

- A thyroid-stimulating hormone (TSH) test, which is a blood test that measures your levels of TSH. If your TSH level is low, your doctor will want to do more tests.
- Thyroid hormone tests, which are blood tests to measure your levels of two types of thyroid hormones, called T_3 and T_4. If your thyroid hormone levels are high, you have hyperthyroidism.

When he is being treated for hyperthyroidism, the doctor will test his TSH and thyroid hormones several times a year to see how well his treatment is working.

After he is diagnosed with hyperthyroidism, the doctor may also want to do:

- An antithyroid antibody test to see if you have the kind of antibodies that attack thyroid tissue. This test can help diagnose Graves' disease and autoimmune thyroiditis.
- A radioactive thyroid scan and radioactive iodine uptake tests, which use radiation and a special camera to find out the cause of your hyperthyroidism.

If you have Graves' ophthalmopathy, your doctor may also do an ultrasound, MRI, or a CT scan to look more closely at your eyes.

Early detection

It is not clear whether people who do not have any risk factors and who do not have any symptoms of hyperthyroidism need to be tested regularly for thyroid problems. The American Thyroid Association recommends that adults, particularly women, be screened for thyroid problems every 5 years, beginning at age 35. The U.S. Preventive Services Task Force does not think there is enough evidence to recommend either for or against regular thyroid testing. Talk to your doctor about whether you need to be tested for thyroid problems.

How is it treated?

There are three treatments for hyperthyroidism. Antithyroid medicine and radioactive iodine are the ones doctors use most often. In rare cases, surgery may be done. Hyperthyroidism can lead to more serious problems. So even if your symptoms are not bothering you, you still need treatment.

The kind of treatment you have depends on your age, what is causing your hyperthyroidism, how much thyroid hormone your body is making, and other medical conditions you may have. Each kind of treatment has benefits and risks. Discuss the benefits and risks of each kind of treatment with your doctor. For some people, more than one kind of treatment may be needed.

Initial treatment

Initial treatment for hyperthyroidism usually is antithyroid medicine or radioactive iodine therapy. If you have a lot of symptoms, your doctor may recommend you take antithyroid medicine first to help you feel better. Then you can decide whether to have radioactive iodine therapy.

- Antithyroid medicines work best if you have mild hyperthyroidism, if this is the first time you are being treated for Graves' disease, if you are younger than 50, or if your thyroid gland is only swollen a little bit (small goiter).
- Radioactive iodine is often recommended if you have Graves' disease and are older than 50, or if you have thyroid nodules (toxic multinodular goiter) that are releasing too much thyroid hormone. Radioactive iodine is not used if:
  - You are pregnant or you want to become pregnant within 6 months of treatment.
  - You are breast-feeding.
  - You have thyroiditis or another kind of hyperthyroidism that is often temporary.

If you have symptoms such as a fast heartbeat, tremors, sweating, nervousness, or dry eyes, you may take some additional medicines to treat those symptoms.

Surgery is not usually part of initial treatment. You may need surgery if your thyroid gland is so big that you have a hard time swallowing or breathing. Or you may need surgery if a single large thyroid nodule is releasing too much thyroid hormone.

Ongoing treatment

During and after treatment for hyperthyroidism, you will have regular blood tests to check your levels of thyroid-stimulating hormone (TSH). You will also have regular thyroid hormone tests to check your levels of hormones called T_4 and T_3. These tests are a good way to know how well your treatment is working. If your symptoms do not go away after your initial treatment, you may need to repeat the treatment or try a different treatment.

- If you have Graves' disease and have been taking antithyroid medicine but your hyperthyroidism has not improved, you can continue to take antithyroid medicine or you can try radioactive iodine therapy.
- If you have lots of side effects from antithyroid medicines and radioactive iodine is not an option for you, you may need surgery to remove all or part of your thyroid gland (thyroidectomy).

Sometimes treatment cures your hyperthyroidism but may cause hypothyroidism. Hypothyroidism is the opposite of hyperthyroidism-instead of making too much thyroid hormone, your body is now making too little thyroid hormone. Hypothyroidism is most common after treatment with radioactive iodine. But it can also occur after surgery and sometimes after taking antithyroid medicine.

Be sure to call your doctor if you start to gain weight, feel tired, or feel cold more often than usual. These symptoms may mean you have hypothyroidism and you need to take a different medicine called thyroid hormone medicine.

Treatment if the condition gets worse

If radioactive iodine or antithyroid medicines are not working well, you may need:

- Another treatment of radioactive iodine.
- Surgery to remove all or part of your thyroid gland (thyroidectomy).

After treatment with radioactive iodine, you may develop hypothyroidism (too little thyroid hormone). Call your doctor if you have any of the symptoms of hypothyroidism such as gaining weight, feeling tired, or feeling cold more often than usual. If you do have hypothyroidism, you may need to take thyroid hormone medicine for the rest of your life. For more information, see the topic Hypothyroidism.

中英文注释

主要词汇

abnormal [əb'nɔːm(ə)l] adj. 反常的，不规则的，变态的

goiter ['gɒitə] n. 甲状腺肿

hyperthyroidism [ˌhaipə'θairɒidiz(ə)m] n. 甲状腺功能亢进

hypothyroidism [ˌhaipəʊ'θairɒidiz(ə)m] n. 甲状腺功能减退

iodine ['aiədiːn; –ain; –in] n. 碘，碘酒

menstrual ['menstrʊəl] adj. 月经的，月经周期的，一月一次的

nodule ['nɒdjuːl] n. 小结，小瘤，结节

ophthalmopathy [ˌɔfθæl'mɔpəθi] n. 眼病

thyroid ['θairɒid] n. 甲状腺，甲状软骨，甲状腺素

thyroiditis [ˌθairɒi'daitis] n. 甲状腺炎

tremor ['tremə] n. 震动，颤抖

主要短语

antithyroid medicine 抗甲状腺药物

Graves' disease 原发性甲状腺功能亢进，Graves 病

Graves' ophthalmopathy Graves 眼病

life-threatening 威胁生命的

menstrual cycle 月经周期

pretibial myxedema 胫前黏液性水肿

thyroid-stimulating hormone (TSH) 促甲状腺激素

thyroid storm 甲状腺危象

toxic multinodular goiter 毒性多结节性甲状腺肿，结节性甲状腺肿

Hypothyroidism
甲状腺功能减低

What is hypothyroidism?

Hypothyroidism, also called underactive thyroid disease, is a common disorder. With hypothyroidism, your thyroid gland does not make enough thyroid hormone.

The thyroid gland is located in the front lower part of your neck. Hormones released by the gland travel through your bloodstream and affect nearly every part of your body, from your heart and brain, to your muscles and skin.

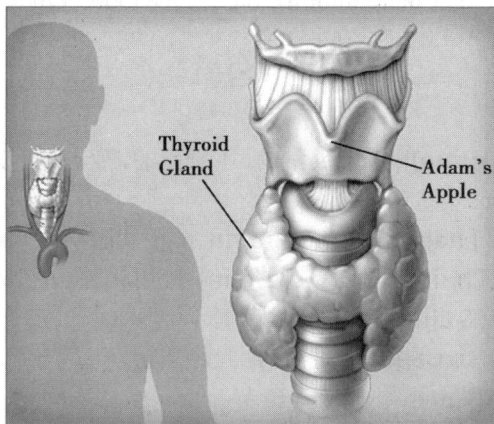

The thyroid controls how your body's cells use energy from food, a process called metabolism. Among other things, your metabolism affects your body's temperature, your heartbeat, and how well you burn calories. If you don't have enough thyroid hormone, your body processes slow down. That means your body makes less energy, and your metabolism becomes sluggish.

What causes hypothyroidism?

The most common cause of hypothyroidism is Hashimoto's thyroiditis. "Thyroiditis" is an inflammation of the thyroid gland. Hashimoto's thyroiditis is an autoimmune disorder. With Hashimoto's, your body produces antibodies that attack and destroy the thyroid gland. Thyroiditis may also be caused by a viral infection.

Other causes of hypothyroidism include:

Radiation therapy to the neck area. Treating certain cancers, such as lymphoma, requires radiation to the neck. Radiation damages the cells in the thyroid. This makes it more difficult for the gland to produce hormone.

Radioactive iodine treatment. This treatment is commonly prescribed to people who have an overactive thyroid gland, a condition known as hyperthyroidism. However, radiation destroys the cells in the thyroid gland. This usually leads to hypothyroidism.

Use of certain medications. Certain medicines to treat heart problems, psychiatric conditions, and cancer can sometimes affect the production of thyroid hormone. These include amiodarone (Cordarone), lithium, interferon alpha, and interleukin-2.

Thyroid surgery. Surgery to remove the thyroid will lead to hypothyroidism. If only part of the thyroid is removed, the remaining gland may still be able to produce enough hormone for the body's needs.

Too little iodine in the diet. The thyroid needs iodine to produce thyroid hormone. Your body doesn't make iodine, so you need to get it through your diet. Iodized table salt is rich in iodine. Other food sources of iodine include shellfish, saltwater fish, eggs, dairy products, and seaweed. Iodine deficiency is rare in the U.S.

Pregnancy. The reason isn't clear, but sometimes, inflammation of the thyroid occurs after pregnancy. This is called postpartum thyroiditis. Women with this condition usually have a severe increase in thyroid hormone levels followed by a sharp drop in thyroid hormone production. Most women with postpartum thyroiditis will regain their normal thyroid function.

Problems with the thyroid at birth. Some babies may be born with a thyroid gland that did not develop correctly or does not work properly. This type of hypothyroidism is called congenital hypothyroidism. Most hospitals in the U.S. screen babies at birth for this disease.

Pituitary gland damage or disorder. Rarely, a problem with the pituitary gland can interfere with the production of thyroid hormone. The pituitary gland makes a hormone, called thyroid-stimulating hormone (TSH), which tells your thyroid how much hormone it should make and release.

Disorder of the hypothalamus. An extremely rare form of hypothyroidism can occur if the hypothalamus in the brain does not produce enough of a hormone called TRH. TRH affects the release of TSH from the pituitary gland.

Primary hypothyroidism is caused by a problem with the thyroid gland itself.

Secondary hypothyroidism occurs when another problem interferes with the thyroid's ability to produce hormones. For example, the pituitary gland and hypothalamus produce hormones that trigger the release of thyroid hormone. A problem with one of these glands can make your thyroid underactive.

Sometimes, an underactive thyroid that results from a problem with the hypothalamus is called tertiary hypothyroidism.

Who is at risk for hypothyroidism?

Women, particularly older women, are more likely to develop hypothyroidism than men. You are also more likely to develop hypothyroidism if you have a close family member with an autoimmune disease. Other risk factors include:

- Race (being white or Asian)
- Age (growing older)
- Prematurely graying hair
- Autoimmune disorders such as type 1 diabetes, multiple sclerosis, rheumatoid arthritis, celiac disease, Addison's disease, pernicious anemia, or vitiligo
- Bipolar disorder
- Down syndrome
- Turner syndrome

What are the symptoms of hypothyroidism?

Symptoms of hypothyroidism may be vague and can often mimic other conditions. They may include:

- Changes in the menstrual cycle
- Constipation
- Depression
- Dry hair and hair loss
- Dry skin
- Fatigue
- Greater sensitivity to cold
- Slow heart rate
- Swelling of the thyroid gland (goiter)

- Unexplained weight gain
- Carpal tunnel syndrome

Babies with hypothyroidism may have no symptoms. If symptoms do occur, they can include:

- Cold hands and feet
- Constipation
- Extreme sleepiness
- Hoarse cry
- Little or no growth
- Low muscle tone (floppy infant)
- Persistent jaundice (yellowing of the skin and whites of the eyes)
- Poor feeding habits
- Puffy face
- Stomach bloating
- Swollen tongue

Make an appointment with your health care provider if you or your baby has any of these symptoms. It is important to note that these symptoms can be due to other medical conditions.

How is hypothyroidism diagnosed?

If you have symptoms of hypothyroidism, your doctor will order blood tests to check hormone levels. These may include:

- Thyroid-stimulating hormone (TSH)
- T_4 (thyroxine)

Lower-than-normal T_4 levels usually mean you have hypothyroidism. However, some people may have increased TSH levels while having normal T_4 levels. This is called subclinical (mild) hypothyroidism. It is believed to be an early stage of hypothyroidism.

If your test results or physical exam of the thyroid are abnormal, your doctor may order a thyroid ultrasound, or thyroid scan, to check for nodules or inflammation.

How is hypothyroidism treated?

If you have hypothyroidism, your doctor will prescribe a synthetic (man-made) thyroid hormone T_4. You take this pill every day. Certain other medications can interfere with how your body absorbs synthetic thyroid hormone. Make sure you doctor knows about all the medicines, herbs, and supplements you take, including over-the-counter products.

You will need regular blood tests to check your thyroid hormone levels. Your doctor may need to adjust your medication dose from time to time.

Complications of hypothyroidism

Untreated, hypothyroidism may cause:

- Heart problems
- Infertility
- Joint pain
- Obesity

Thyroid problems in a pregnant woman can affect the developing baby. During the first three months of pregnancy, the baby receives all thyroid hormone from its mother. If the mother has hypothyroidism, the baby does not get enough thyroid hormone. This can lead to problems with mental development.

Extremely low levels of thyroid hormone can cause a life-threatening condition called myxedema. Myxedema is the most severe form of hypothyroidism. A person with myxedema can lose consciousness or go into a coma. The condition can also cause the body temperature to drop very low, which can cause death.

中英文注释

主要词汇

amiodarone [ˌæmiəu'dærəu] n. 胺碘酮

autoimmune [ˌɔ:təʊi'mju:n] adj. 自身免疫的；自体免疫的

calorie ['kæləri] n. 卡路里（热量单位）

celiac ['si:liæk] adj. 腹腔的

coma ['kəʊmə] n. 昏迷

congenital [kən'dʒenit(ə)l] adj. 先天的

herbs [hə:bs] n. 药草，草本植物

hypothalamus [ˌhaipə(ʊ)'θæləməs] n. 下丘脑

infertility [ˌinfə'tiliti] n. 不毛，不肥沃，贫瘠，不孕症

interleukin [ˌintə'lu:kin] n. 白介素

lithium ['liθiəm] n. 锂（符号 Li）

lymphoma [lim'fəʊmə] n. 淋巴瘤

multiple ['mʌltipl] adj. 多重的，多样的

myxedema [ˌmiksə'di:mə] n. 黏液腺瘤，黏液水肿

obesity [ə(ʊ)'bi:siti] n. 肥大，肥胖

pituitary [pi'tju:it(ə)ri] n. 垂体 adj. 脑垂体的，脑垂体分泌失调引起的

prematurely ['premətʃəli] adv. 过早地；早熟地

psychiatric [ˌsaiki'ætrik] adj. 精神病学的，精神病治疗的
radiation [reidi'eiʃ(ə)n] n. 辐射，放射
sluggish ['slʌgiʃ] adj. 迟钝的，迟缓的
synthetic [sin'θetik] adj. 合成的，人造的
thyroiditis [ˌθairɒi'daitis] n. 甲状腺炎
vitiligo [ˌviti'laigəʊ] n. 白癜风

主要短语

Hashimoto's thyroiditis 桥本氏甲状腺炎
interferon alpha α- 干扰素
postpartum thyroiditis 产后甲状腺炎
pituitary gland 脑垂体
rheumatoid arthritis 风湿性关节炎
tertiary hypothyroidism 三发性甲状腺功能减低
TRH 促甲状腺素释放激素

张　瑾　晋建华

40

Rheumatoid Arthritis

类风湿性关节炎

What is rheumatoid arthritis?

Arthritis is a general term that means inflammation in a joint. Joint inflammation is characterized by redness, warmth, swelling, and pain within the joint.

Rheumatoid arthritis is a type of chronic arthritis that typically occurs in joints on both sides of the body (such as hands, wrists, or knees). This symmetry helps distinguish rheumatoid arthritis from other types of arthritis. In addition to affecting the joints, rheumatoid arthritis may occasionally affect the skin, eyes, lungs, heart, blood, or nerves.

Rheumatoid arthritis is an autoimmune disorder that affects about 1% of the U.S. population. While it is two to three times more common in women than in men, men tend to be more severely affected when they get it. It usually occurs in middle age; however, young children and the elderly also can develop rheumatoid arthritis.

What causes rheumatoid arthritis?

The exact cause of rheumatoid arthritis is unknown, but it is thought to be due to a combination of genetic, environmental, and hormonal factors. With rheumatoid arthritis, something seems to trigger the immune system to attack the joints and sometimes other organs. Some theories suggest that a virus or bacteria may alter the immune system, causing it to attack the joints. Other theories suggest that smoking may lead to the development of rheumatoid arthritis.

Research hasn't completely determined exactly what role genetics plays in rheumatoid arthritis. However, some people do seem to have a genetic or inherited factor that increases their chance of developing rheumatoid arthritis.

What are the symptoms of rheumatoid arthritis?

Rheumatoid arthritis (RA) is a chronic (long-term) disease. Rheumatoid arthritis symptoms can come and go, and each person with RA is affected differently. Some people have long periods of remission. Their rheumatoid arthritis is inactive, and they have few or no symptoms during this time. Other people might have near-constant rheumatoid arthritis symptoms for months at a stretch.

Although rheumatoid arthritis can involve different parts the body, joints are always affected. When the disease acts up, joints become inflamed. Inflammation is the body's natural response to infection or other threats, but in rheumatoid arthritis inflammation occurs inappropriately and for unknown reasons.

Rheumatoid arthritis and joint inflammation

Joint inflammation is a hallmark of rheumatoid arthritis. That includes:

- Stiffness. The joint is harder to use and might have a limited range of motion. "Morning stiffness" is one of the hallmark symptoms of rheumatoid arthritis. While many people with other forms of arthritis have stiff joints in the morning, it takes people with rheumatoid arthritis more than an hour (sometimes several hours) before their joints feel loose.
- Swelling. Fluid enters into the joint and it becomes puffy; this also contributes to stiffness.
- Pain. Inflammation inside a joint makes it sensitive and tender. Prolonged inflammation causes damage that also contributes to pain.
- Redness and warmth. The joints may be somewhat warmer and more pink or red than neighboring skin.

Which joints does RA affect? The hands are almost always affected, although literally any joint can be affected with rheumatoid arthritis symptoms: knees, wrists, neck, shoulders, elbows, even the jaw. Joints are usually affected in a symmetrical pattern — the same joints on both sides of the body.

Rheumatoid arthritis symptoms That affect the entire body

Rheumatoid arthritis can affect many areas of the body. These effects all result from the general process of inflammation, leading to a wide variety of symptoms of rheumatoid arthritis:

- Fatigue
- Malaise (feeling ill)
- Loss of appetite, which can lead to weight loss
- Muscle aches

These feelings have been compared to having the flu, although they are usually less intense and longer lasting.

Rheumatoid arthritis may affect other areas of your body. Involvement of multiple areas of the body occurs is more common with moderate to severe rheumatoid arthritis.

Rheumatoid nodules are bumps under the skin that most often appear on the elbows. Sometimes they are painful.

Lung involvement, due to either damage to the lungs or inflammation of the lining around the lungs, is common but usually causes no symptoms. If shortness of breath develops, it can be treated with drugs that reduce inflammation in the lungs.

Rheumatoid arthritis can even affect a joint in your voice box or larynx (cricoarytenoid joint), causing hoarseness.

Rheumatoid arthritis can cause inflammation in the lining around the heart, but it usually has no symptoms. If symptoms do develop, it may cause shortness of breath or chest pain. In addition, people with rheumatoid arthritis are more likely to develop clogged arteries in their heart, which can lead to chest pain and heart attack.

The eyes are affected in less than 5% of people with rheumatoid arthritis. When the eyes are affected, symptoms can include red, painful eyes or possibly dry eyes.

When you have symptoms of rheumatoid arthritis, early and aggressive treatment can help prevent further symptoms as well as stop progression of rheumatoid arthritis.

How does rheumatoid arthritis affect the body?

Once the immune system is triggered, immune cells migrate from the blood into the joints and joint-lining tissue, called synovium. There the immune cells produce inflammatory substances that cause irritation, wearing down of cartilage (cushioning material at the end of bones), and swelling and inflammation of the joint lining. As the cartilage wears down, the space between the bones narrows. If the condition worsens, the bones could rub against each other.

Inflammation of the joint lining causes excessive fluid with the joint. As the lining expands, it may erode the adjacent bone, resulting in bone damage.

All of these factors cause the joint to become very painful, swollen, and warm to the touch.

How is rheumatoid arthritis diagnosed?

The diagnosis of rheumatoid arthritis is based on a combination of factors, including:

- The specific location and symmetry of painful joints, especially the hand joints
- The presence of joint stiffness in the morning
- Presence of bumps and nodules under the skin (rheumatoid nodules)
- Results of X-ray tests that suggest rheumatoid arthritis
- Positive results of a blood test called the rheumatoid factor as well as other blood tests

Most, but not all, people with rheumatoid arthritis have the rheumatoid-factor (RF) antibody in their blood. Rheumatoid factor may sometimes be present in people who do not have rheumatoid arthritis (other diseases can also cause the rheumatoid factor to be produced in the blood). Therefore, the diagnosis of rheumatoid arthritis is based on a combination of joint abnormalities, as well as test results.

A newer, more specific blood test for rheumatoid arthritis is thecylic citrulline antibody test, also called anti-CCP. The presence of anti-CCP antibodies suggests a tendency toward a more aggressive form of rheumatoid arthritis.

People with rheumatoid arthritis may have mild anemia. Blood tests may also reveal an elevated erythrocyte sedimentation rate (ESR) or elevated C-reactive protein (CRP) levels, which are markers of inflammation.

Some people with rheumatoid arthritis may also have a positive antinuclear antibody test (ANA), which indicates the presence of an autoimmune disorder — whether it is rheumatoid arthritis or another autoimmune disease.

How is rheumatoid arthritis treated?

There are many different ways to treat rheumatoid arthritis. Treatments include medications, rest and exercise, and surgery to correct damage to the joint.

The type of treatment will depend on several factors, including the person's age, overall health, medical history, and severity of the arthritis.

Rheumatoid arthritis medications

There are many rheumatoid arthritis medications available to decrease joint pain, swelling, and inflammation. Some of these drugs prevent or minimize the progression of the disease.

Drugs that offer relief of arthritis symptoms (joint pain, stiffness, and swelling) include:

- Anti-inflammatory painkiller drugs, such as aspirin, ibuprofen, or naproxen
- Topical (applied directly to the skin) pain relievers
- Corticosteroids, such as prednisone
- Narcotic pain relievers

There are also many strong medications called disease-modifying anti-rheumatic drugs (DMARDs), which work by interfering with or suppressing the immune system's attack on the joints. They include:

- Plaquenil (originally used to treat malaria)
- Immune suppression drugs, such as methotrexate, Imuran, and Cytoxan
- Biologic treatments, such as Enbrel, Humira, Remicade, Orencia, Rituxan, and Xeljanz
- Other drugs, such as Azulfidine and Arava

Why are rest and exercise important for rheumatoid arthritis?

A balance of rest and exercise is important in treating rheumatoid arthritis. During flare-ups (worsening of joint inflammation), it is best to rest the joints that are inflamed. This may be accomplished by the temporary use of a cane or joint splints.

When joint inflammation is decreased, guided exercise programs are necessary to maintain flexibility of the joints and to strengthen the muscles that surround the joints. Range-of-motion exercises should be done regularly to maintain joint mobility.

When is surgery necessary for rheumatoid arthritis?

If joint pain and inflammation become truly unbearable or joints simply refuse to function, some people choose joint replacement surgery. Today, joint replacement is commonly done on the hips and knees and sometimes the shoulders. Surgery can dramatically improve pain and mobility and is typically done after age 50 since artificial joints tend to wear down after 15 to 20 years.

Some joints, such as the ankles, don't respond well to artificial replacement and do better with joint fusion.

Physical and occupational therapy for rheumatoid arthritis

Physical and occupational therapy are key components of any rheumatoid arthritis treatment plan.

Physical therapists focus on helping you be able to keep moving around. They can help you design an exercise plan, teach you the appropriate use of heat and ice, perform therapeutic massage, and even provide motivation and encouragement.

Occupational therapists help you keep doing things you are used to doing every day. They can evaluate your daily activities, determine what you may be doing to stress your joints, and teach you easier ways to accomplish daily activities. They can also determine which assistive devices can help you throughout the day.

Can rheumatoid arthritis be cured?

Although there isn't a cure for rheumatoid arthritis, early, aggressive treatment has been shown to help prevent disability.

中英文注释

主要词汇

abnormality [ˌæbnɔːˈmæliti] n. 畸形, 异常情况

alter [ˈɔːltə; ˈɒl-] vt. 改变, 更改

ankle [ˈæŋk(ə)l] n. 踝关节, 踝

arthritis [ɑːˈθraitis] n. 关节炎

azulfidine n. 柳氮磺胺吡啶

cartilage [ˈkɑːt(i)lidʒ] n. 软骨

cytoxan n. 环磷酰胺

disability [disəˈbiliti] n. 残疾，病残，缺陷

dramatically [drəˈmætikəli] adv. 戏剧地，引人注目地

erode [iˈrəud] vt. 腐蚀，侵蚀

fatigue [fəˈtiːg] n. 疲劳，疲乏

flu [fluː] n. 流感

hoarseness [ˈhorsnəs] n. 嘶哑，刺耳

humira n. 阿达木单抗

ibuprofen [ˌaibjuːˈprəuf(ə)n] n. 布洛芬

imuran n. 硫唑嘌呤 (azathioprine) 制剂的商品名

jaw [dʒɔː] n. 颌，颚；下颌

larynx [ˈlæriŋks] n. 喉，喉头

malaise [mæˈleiz] n. 不舒服，心神不安

malaria [məˈleəriə] n. 疟疾，瘴气

massage [ˈmæsɑːʒ; məˈsɑːʒ; -dʒ] n. 按摩，揉

methotrexate [ˌmeθəˈtrekseit; ˌmiːθə-] n. 甲氨蝶呤

migrate [maiˈgreit; ˈmaigreit] vi. 移动，移植

naproxen [nəˈprɔksin] n. 萘普生，甲氧萘丙酸

narcotic [nɑːˈkɒtik] n. 麻醉药；镇静剂

prolonged [prəˈlɒŋd] adj. 延长的，拖延的，持续很久的

rheumatic [ruˈmætik] n. 风湿病；adj. 风湿病的，风湿病引起的

stiffness [ˈstifnis] n. 僵硬，坚硬，不自然，顽固

symmetrical [siˈmetrik(ə)l] adj. 匀称的，对称的

symmetry [ˈsimitri] n. 对称（性），整齐，匀称

synovium [siˈnəuviəm, sai-] n. 滑膜

tender [ˈtendə] adj. 柔软的，脆弱的

wrist [rist] n. 手腕，腕关节

主要短语

c-reactive protein (CRP) c反应蛋白 (CRP)

cricoarytenoid joint 环杓关节

disease-modifying anti-rheumatic drugs 抗风湿药物

erythrocyte sedimentation rate(ESR) 红细胞沉降率

immune suppression drugs 免疫抑制药物

inherited factor 遗传因素
morning stiffness 晨僵
near-constant 几乎不停的
rheumatic arthritis 风湿性关节炎
rheumatoid factor 类风湿因子

张 瑾 马志方

41
Systemic Lupus Erythematosus (SLE)
系统性红斑狼疮

What is systemic lupus erythematosus, or lupus?

Lupus is the common name for systemic lupus erythematosus, also called SLE. Lupus is an autoimmune disease, which means that the body's natural defense system (immune system) attacks its own tissues instead of attacking foreign substances like bacteria and viruses. This causes inflammation. Inflammation causes swelling, pain, and tissue damage throughout the body. If you develop severe lupus, you may have problems with your kidneys, heart, lungs, nervous system, or blood cells.

Although some people with lupus have only mild symptoms, the disease is lifelong and can become severe. But most people can control their symptoms and prevent severe damage to their organs. They do this by seeing their doctors often for checkups, getting enough rest and exercise, and taking medicines.

This topic focuses on systemic lupus erythematosus (SLE), the most common and most serious type of lupus. But there are four other types of lupus: discoid or cutaneous lupus, drug-induced systemic lupus, neonatal lupus, and subacute cutaneous lupus.

What causes lupus?

The exact cause of lupus is not known. Experts believe that some people are born with certain genes that affect how the immune system works and that they are more likely to get lupus. Then a number of other factors can trigger lupus attacks. These include viral infections, including the virus that causes mononucleosis, and sunlight.

Although these things can trigger lupus, they may affect one person but not another person.

What are the symptoms of lupus?

Lupus improves at times, and worsens at others. Symptoms of lupus include:
- Profound fatigue
- Low-grade fever
- Severe joint pain and muscle aches

277

- Skin rash on the face or body
- Extreme sun sensitivity
- Weight loss
- Mental confusion and seizures
- Chest pain on taking a deep breath
- Nose, mouth, or throat sores
- Enlarged lymph nodes
- Poor circulation in fingers and toes
- Bald patches and hair loss

How is lupus diagnosed?

Lupus can be hard to recognize, sometimes taking weeks to years to diagnose. Lupus affects different people in different ways, and it can take time to develop the symptoms that suggest this disease. Your doctor will record your medical history and perform a physical exam, checking for the presence of certain criteria to help diagnose lupus. These criteria are used to separate lupus from other similar diseases. A person with 4 of these 11 conditions can be classified as having lupus. These conditions may be present all at once, or they may appear in succession over a period of time.

Classification criteria for systemic lupus erythematosus:

- Butterfly (malar) rash on cheeks
- Rash on face, arms, neck, torso (discoid rash)
- Skin rashes that result from exposure to sunlight or ultraviolet light (photosensitivity)
- Mouth or nasal sores (ulcers), usually painless
- Joint swelling, stiffness, pain involving two or more joints (arthritis)
- Inflammation of the membranes surrounding the lungs (pleuritis) or heart (pericarditis)
- Abnormalities in urine, such as increased protein in the urine or clumps of redblood cells or kidney cells, called cell casts, in the urine
- Nervous system problems, such as seizures or psychosis, without known cause
- Problems with the blood, such as reduced numbers of red blood cells (anemia), platelets, or white blood cells
- Laboratory tests indicating increased autoimmune activity (antibodies against normal tissue)
- Positive antinuclear antibody (ANA) test

Initial diagnosis and disease monitoring

If you have physical signs of lupus and a positive ANA test result, further testing may not be necessary. If your doctor feels that further testing is necessary to clarify your diagnosis, you may have one or more of the following tests:

- Other antibody blood tests
- Complement test
- Erythrocyte sedimentation rate (ESR, or sed rate) or C-reactive protein (CRP)
- Complete blood count (CBC)
- Urinalysis
- Lupus anticoagulant test, such as a partial thromboplastin time test

Evaluating possible organ damage

As part of ongoing treatment for lupus, you may have a:

- Urinalysis to check for protein and cells, signs of possible kidney problems.
- Kidney biopsy, if your doctor sees signs of kidney inflammation. This test may help to determine the best treatment for you. Only a small number of people with lupus need a kidney biopsy.

To evaluate other possible causes of symptoms, imaging tests are sometimes done, depending on which organ systems are involved. Imaging tests include computed tomography (CT) scan, echocardiogram, magnetic resonance imaging (MRI), and X-rays.

How is it treated?

Lupus is unpredictable and thus difficult to control, but close self-monitoring and proper treatment usually helps. There are a number of treatment options now available:

- For milder cases, nonsteroidal anti-inflammatory drugs (NSAIDs), such as aspirinor ibuprofen, can help relieve joint pain.
- Stubborn rashes and more severe joint pain may respond to hydroxychloroquine. The drug also helps to reduce the number of lupus flares.
- A short course of corticosteroids, sometimes called simply "steroids," reduces inflammation and is recommended for flare-ups.
- People with active, autoantibody-positive lupus may benefit from Benlysta (belimumab) in addition to standard drug therapy. The drug targets a protein involved in B cell development and reduces the number of abnormal B cells thought to be a problem in lupus. B cells are responsible for making the autoantibodies that cause lupus.
- Mild skin rashes can be treated with over-the-counter corticosteroid creams. Some rashes may require prescription steroid creams, steroid injections, or drugs such as hydroxychloroquine.
- Antidepressants and mild anti-anxiety drugs can help with the sleeping problems that frequently accompany lupus.

- Cyclophosphamide or mycophenylate, drugs that suppress the immune system, may be used for severe cases of lupus that cause kidney damage or affect the brain.

Nutrition and supplements

Proper nutrition is important for people with lupus. A diet low in fat and high in essential fatty acids, with plenty of vegetables, fruits, and whole grains, promotes general health and may decrease pain. Fatty, deep-water fish — such as sardines, salmon, tuna, mackerel, and trout — or fish oil capsules may lessen joint pain. Talk to a nutritionist to create a personalized eating plan.

Taking a daily multivitamin, while not a substitute for a healthy and balanced diet, helps ensure that you get the nutrients you need.

Rest and exercise

Rest eases the fatigue of lupus. But it's just as important to get appropriate exercise, particularly swimming and walking. Exercise increases muscle strength, eases joint stiffness, helps control weight, and helps in the prevention of bone loss. It also reduces stress and improves your outlook on life. Work with your doctor to create a fitness program well suited to your needs and abilities.

中英文注释

主要词汇

antidepressant [ˌæntidiˈpres(ə)nt] n. 抗抑郁剂

bald [bɔːld] adj. 秃顶的

criteria [kraiˈtiəriə] n. 标准，条件（criterion 的复数）

cutaneous [kjuˈteiniəs] adj. 皮肤的，侵犯皮肤的

hydroxychloroquine [haiˌdrɔksiˈklɔːrəkwiːn] n. 羟化氯喹

lupus [ˈluːpəs] n. 狼疮

mononucleosis [ˌmɒnə(ʊ)njuːkliˈəʊsis] n. 单核细胞增多症

neonatal [ˌniːə(ʊ)ˈneit(ə)l] adj. 新生的，初生的

pericarditis [ˌperikɑːˈdaitis] n. 心包炎

pleuritis [pluəˈraitis] n. 胸膜炎

prescription [priˈskripʃ(ə)n] n. 药方；指示

psychosis [saiˈkəʊsis] n. 精神病

rheumatology [ˌruːməˈtɒlədʒi] n. 风湿病学

salmon [ˈsæmən] n. 鲑鱼

sardine [sɑːˈdiːn] n. 沙丁鱼

seizures [ˈsiːʒə] n. 癫痫，痉挛

specialist [ˈspeʃəlist] n. 专家，专科医生

tuna ['tjuːnə] n. 金枪鱼
urinalysis [ˌjʊəri'nælisis] n. 验尿；尿分析

主要短语
antinuclear antibody (ANA) 抗核抗体 (ANA)
lymph node 淋巴结
nonsteroidal anti-inflammatory drugs (NSAIDs) 非甾体类抗炎药
systemic lupus erythematosus(SLE) 系统性红斑狼疮
ultraviolet light 紫外线

张　瑾　马志方

42

Anemia

贫　血

What is anemia?

Anemia is a condition that develops when your blood lacks enough healthy red blood cells or hemoglobin. Hemoglobin is a main part of red blood cells and binds oxygen. If you have too few or abnormal red blood cells, or your hemoglobin is abnormal or low, the cells in your body will not get enough oxygen. Symptoms of anemia — like fatigue — occur because organs aren't getting what they need to function properly.

What causes anemia?

There are more than 400 types of anemia, which are divided into three groups:

- Anemia caused by blood loss
- Anemia caused by decreased or faulty red blood cell production
- Anemia caused by destruction of red blood cells

Anemia caused by blood loss

Red blood cells can be lost through bleeding, which can occur slowly over a long period of time, and can often go undetected. This kind of chronic bleeding commonly results from the following:

- Gastrointestinal conditions such as ulcers, hemorrhoids, gastritis (inflammation of the stomach), and cancer
- Use of nonsteroidal anti-inflammatory drugs (NSAIDS) such as aspirinor ibuprofen, which can cause ulcers and gastritis
- Menstruation and childbirth in women, especially if menstrual bleeding is excessive and if there are multiple pregnancies

Anemia caused by decreased or faulty red blood cell production

With this type of anemia, the body may produce too few blood cells or the blood cells may not function correctly. In either case, anemia can result. Red blood cells may be faulty or decreased due to abnormal red blood cells or the a lack of minerals and vitamins needed for red blood cells to work properly. Conditions associated with these causes of anemia include the following:

- Sickle cell anemia
- Iron-deficiency anemia
- Vitamin deficiency
- Bone marrow and stem cell problems
- Other health conditions

Sickle cell anemia is an inherited disorder that affects African-Americans. Red blood cells become crescent-shaped because of a genetic defect. They break down rapidly, so oxygen does not get to the body's organs, causing anemia. The crescent-shaped red blood cells also get stuck in tiny blood vessels, causing pain.

Iron-deficiency anemia

It occurs because of a lack of the mineral iron in the body. Bone marrow in the center of the bone needs iron to make hemoglobin, the part of the red blood cell that transports oxygen to the body's organs. Without adequate iron, the body cannot produce enough hemoglobin for red blood cells. The result is iron-deficiency anemia. This type of anemia can be caused by:

- An iron-poor diet, especially in infants, children, teens, vegans, and vegetarians
- The metabolic demands of pregnancy and breastfeeding that deplete a woman's iron stores
- Menstruation
- Frequent blood donation
- Endurance training
- Digestive conditions such as Crohn's disease or surgical removal of part of the stomach or small intestine
- Certain drugs, foods, and caffeinated drinks

Vitamin-deficiency anemia may occur when vitamin B12 and folate are deficient. These two vitamins are needed to make red blood cells. Conditions leading to anemia caused by vitamin deficiency include:

- Megaloblastic anemia: Vitamin B12 or folate or both are deficient
- Pernicious anemia: Poor Vitamin B12 absorption caused by conditions such as Crohn's disease, an intestinal parasite infection, surgical removal of part of the stomach or intestine, or infection with HIV
- Dietary deficiency: Eating little or no meat may cause a lack Vitamin B12, while overcooking or eating too few vegetables may cause a folate deficiency
- Other causes of vitamin deficiency: pregnancy, certain medications, alcohol abuse, intestinal diseases such as tropical sprue and celiac disease

During early pregnancy, sufficient folic acid can prevent the fetus from developing neural tube defects such as spina bifida.

Bone marrow and stem cell problems may prevent the body from producing enough red blood cells. Some of the stem cells found in bone marrow develop into red blood cells. If stem cells are too few, defective, or replaced by other cells such as metastatic cancer cells, anemia may result. Anemia resulting from bone marrow or stem cell problems include:

- Aplastic anemia occurs when there's a marked reduction in the number of stem cells or absence of these cells. Aplastic anemia can be inherited, can occur without apparent cause, or can occur when the bone marrow is injured by medications, radiation, chemotherapy, or infection.
- Thalassemia occurs when the red cells can't mature and grow properly. Thalassemia is an inherited condition that typically affects people of Mediterranean, African, Middle Eastern, and Southeast Asian descent. This condition can range in severity from mild to life-threatening; the most severe form is called Cooley's anemia.
- Lead exposure is toxic to the bone marrow, leading to fewer red blood cells. Lead poisoning occurs in adults from work-related exposure and in children who eat paint chips, for example. Improperly glazed pottery can also taint food and liquids with lead.

Anemia associated with other conditions usually occur when there are too few hormones necessary for red blood cell production. Conditions causing this type of anemia include the following:

- Advanced kidney disease
- Hypothyroidism
- Other chronic diseases, such as cancer, infection, lupus, and rheumatoid arthritis

Anemia caused by destruction of red blood cells

When red blood cells are fragile and cannot withstand the routine stress of the circulatory system, they may rupture prematurely, causing hemolytic anemia. Hemolytic anemia can be present at birth or develop later. Sometimes there is no known cause. Known causes of hemolytic anemia may include:

- Inherited conditions, such as sickle cell anemia and thalassemia
- Stressors such as infections, drugs, snake or spider venom, or certain foods
- Toxins from advanced liver or kidney disease
- Inappropriate attack by the immune system (called hemolytic disease of the newborn when it occurs in the fetus of a pregnant woman)
- Vascular grafts, prosthetic heart valves, tumors, severe burns, chemical exposure, severe hypertension, and clotting disorders

- In rare cases, an enlarged spleen can trap red blood cells and destroy them before their circulating time is up

What are the symptoms of anemia?

The symptoms of anemia vary according to the type of anemia, the underlying cause, and any underlying health problems, such as hemorrhage, ulcers, menstrual problems, or cancer. Specific symptoms of those problems may be noticed first.

The body also has a remarkable ability to compensate for early anemia. If your anemia is mild or has developed over a long period of time, you may not notice any symptoms.

Symptoms common to many types of anemia include the following:
- Easy fatigue and loss of energy
- Unusually rapid heart beat, particularly with exercise
- Shortness of breath and headache, particularly with exercise
- Difficulty concentrating
- Dizziness
- Pale skin
- Leg cramps
- Insomnia

Other symptoms are associated with specific forms of anemia.

Anemia caused by iron deficiency

People with an iron deficiency may experience these symptoms:
- A hunger for strange substances such as paper, ice, or dirt (a condition called pica)
- Upward curvature of the nails, referred to as koilonychias
- Soreness of the mouth with cracks at the corners

Anemia caused by vitamin B12 deficiency

People whose anemia is caused by a deficiency of Vitamin B12 may have these symptoms:
- A tingling, "pins and needles" sensation in the hands or feet
- Lost sense of touch
- A wobbly gait and difficulty walking
- Clumsiness and stiffness of the arms and legs
- Dementia
- Hallucinations, paranoia, and schizophrenia

Anemia caused by chronic lead poisoning

Chronic lead poisoning may lead to these symptoms:
- A blue-black line on the gums referred to as a lead line

- Abdominal pain
- Constipation
- Vomiting

Anemia caused by chronic red blood cell destruction

Anemia caused by chronic red blood cell destruction may include these symptoms:

- Jaundice (yellow skin and eyes)
- Brown or red urine
- Leg ulcers
- Failure to thrive in infancy
- Symptoms of gallstones

Sickle cell anemia

Symptoms of sickle cell anemia may include:

- Fatigue
- Susceptibility to infection
- Delayed growth and development in children
- Episodes of severe pain, especially in the joints, abdomen, and limbs

Anemia caused by sudden red blood cell destruction

Symptoms of anemia caused by sudden red blood cell destruction may include:

- Abdominal pain
- Brown or red urine
- Jaundice (yellow skin)
- Small bruises under the skin
- Seizures
- Symptoms of kidney failure

Call the doctor if the patient notice any of these signs or symptoms of anemia:

- Persistent fatigue, breathlessness, rapid heart rate, pale skin, or any other symptoms of anemia
- Poor diet or inadequate dietary intake of vitamins and minerals
- Very heavy menstrual periods
- Symptoms of an ulcer, gastritis, hemorrhoids, or colorectal cancer
- Concern about environmental exposure to lead
- A hereditary anemia runs in your family and you would like genetic counseling before having a child

For women considering pregnancy, the doctor will likely recommend that she begin taking supplements, especially folate, even before conception. These supplements benefit both mother and baby.

How is it diagnosed?

To diagnose anemia, the doctor will likely ask the patient about his medical history, perform a physical exam, and order blood tests.

The patients can help by providing detailed answers about their symptoms, family medical history, diet, medications they take, alcohol intake, and ethnic background. The doctor will look for symptoms of anemia and other physical clues that might point to a cause.

There are basically three different causes of anemia: blood loss; decreased or faulty red blood cell production; or destruction of red blood cells.

Blood tests will not only confirm the diagnosis of anemia, but also help point to the underlying condition. Tests might include:

- Complete blood count (CBC), which determines the number, size, volume, and hemoglobin content of red blood cells
- Blood iron level and your serum ferritin level, the best indicators of your body's total iron stores
- Levels of vitamin B12 and folate, vitamins necessary for red blood cell production
- Special blood tests to detect rare causes of anemia, such as an immune attack on your red blood cells, red blood cell fragility, and defects of enzymes, hemoglobin, and clotting
- Reticulocyte count, bilirubin, and other blood and urine tests to determine if you have a hemolytic anemia, where your red blood cells have a shortened life span.

Only in rare cases will a doctor need to remove a sample of bone marrow to determine the cause of your anemia.

What are the treatments for anemia?

The doctor will not treat anemia until the underlying cause has been established. The treatment for one type of anemia may be both inappropriate and dangerous for another type of anemia.

Anemia caused by blood loss

If you suddenly lose a large volume of blood, you may be treated with fluids, a blood transfusion, oxygen, and possibly iron to help your body build new red blood cells. Chronic blood loss is treated by identifying the source of bleeding, stopping the bleeding, and, if necessary, providing treatment for iron-deficiency anemia.

Anemia caused by decreased red blood cell production

The type of treatment the patient receive depends on the cause of decreased red blood cell production.

Anemia caused by iron deficiency

Without adequate iron, the body is unable to produce normal red blood cells. In young women, iron deficiency anemia can result from heavy menstrual bleeding. Non-menstruating women or men who develop iron deficiency need to have a colon exam (colonoscopy or barium enema) to help identify the source of chronic bleeding.

With iron deficiency anemia, your doctor will probably recommend iron supplements that contain the ferrous form of iron, which your body can absorb easily. Timed-release iron supplements are not a good choice for most people, because iron is primarily absorbed in the upper part of the digestive tract. If you use iron supplements, remember the following cautions:

- Always consult with the doctor before taking iron supplements. Excess iron intake can be harmful. Symptoms of iron overload include fatigue, vomiting, diarrhea, headache, irritability, heart disease, and joint problems.

- Iron supplements — like all supplements and any medication — should be kept out of the reach of children. Iron poisoning is the most common cause of accidental poisoning in young children. Eating even a few tablets can prove fatal in a matter of hours. Symptoms of poisoning in a child include dizziness, confusion, nausea, vomiting, and diarrhea. Seek medical help immediately.

- Watch for side effects. You may need to continue taking iron supplements for up to one year. Taking iron supplements with food can help prevent common side effects, which may include nausea, diarrhea, constipation, and stomach pain. Let the doctor know if the patient continue to have side effects. Different formulations are available.

- Watch for drug interactions. Tell the doctor if you are being treated for another condition. For example, calcium supplements interfere with iron absorption, so it is best to take them at different times of the day.

- Your doctor may also recommend that you increase the amount of iron in your diet. Good dietary sources of iron include red meat, beans, egg yolk, whole-grain products, nuts, and seafood. Many processed foods and milk are also reinforced with iron.

- Your doctor will monitor your red blood cell counts, including hematocrit, hemoglobin, and ferritin levels, during treatment. If your anemia doesn't improve with iron supplements, your doctor will look for some other underlying cause. In rare cases, your doctor may prescribe iron injections or give you iron intravenously (through a needle in the vein). In extremely rare cases of life-threatening iron-deficiency anemia, treatment may involve a blood transfusion.

Anemia caused by vitamin B12 and folate deficiency

Treatment depends on the cause of the deficiency. If your body stores are depleted of vitamin B12, your doctor will most likely prescribe vitamin B12 injections and may also recommend high doses of B12 supplements or a B12 nasal spray. There is a good chance that many of the symptoms of deficiency will improve once the body is provided with the needed B12.

Most people with vitamin B12 deficiency have a permanent inability to absorb vitamin B12 and will need injections every one to three months or pills daily for the rest of their lives.

Some forms of gastric bypass surgery are associated with deficiencies of iron, vitamin B12, and other nutrients typically absorbed in the part of the stomach that is bypassed.

Your doctor may also recommend that you increase the amount of vitamin B12 in your diet. Good dietary sources of vitamin B12 are meat, liver, and kidney; fish, oysters, and clams; and milk, cheese, and eggs.

If you have a folate deficiency, your doctor will prescribe folate supplements, and may recommend you increase the amount of folate in your diet. Good dietary sources of folate include fresh fruits, green leafy vegetables, and cruciferous vegetables (cauliflower, broccoli, and brussels sprouts); liver and kidney; dairy products; and whole grain cereals. Vegetables should be eaten raw or lightly cooked.

Anemia caused by problems of the bone marrow and stem cells.

This anemia tends to be more persistent and difficult to treat. The treatments for hereditary anemias, such as thalassemia or sickle cell disease, vary widely and depend on the specific condition and the severity of symptoms. Some anemias will not require any treatment, while others may require repeated transfusions and other aggressive measures. Although aplastic anemia will occasionally go into spontaneous remission, people with this disorder generally require bone marrow transplantation.

Anemia caused by chronic disease

It is best to treat the underlying condition whenever possible. Anemia caused by chronic kidney disease or following chemotherapy can be treated with an injection of recombinant human erythropoietin. Erythropoietin is a hormone that stimulates the production of red blood cells in the bone marrow.

Anemia caused by increased red blood cell destruction

The treatment of hemolytic anemia will be tailored to the underlying cause. Mild cases of hemolytic anemia may not require any treatment at all. If an offending environmental agent can be identified — a chemical, for example — exposure to this agent should stop immediately. People with hemolytic anemia may need surgery to replace faulty heart valves, remove a tumor, or repair abnormal blood vessels.

Supportive treatment — like intravenous fluids and pain medication — will often be given. A blood transfusion may be necessary in some cases. Steroids can halt the body's immune attack on its own red blood cells. Certain damaging factors can be removed from the blood by a treatment called plasmapheresis.

If hemolytic anemia persists despite treatment, your doctor may recommend splenectomy — surgical removal of the spleen — as a last resort. Most people can lead a normal life without their spleen.

Longstanding hemolytic anemia can cause gallstones to develop from the by-products of red blood cell destruction. Gallbladder surgery may be necessary for symptomatic gallstones. A type of hemolytic anemia that occurs more commonly in children is associated with kidney damage, and dialysis may be necessary. In extremely rare cases, bone marrow transplantation may be the only solution for certain types of hemolytic anemia.

Sickle cell anemia

Occasionally, children with sickle cell disease who have an appropriate donor may be cured by a bone marrow transplant. Alternatively, a drug called hydroxyurea appears to stimulate the formation of an alternate form of hemoglobin that isn't susceptible to the sickling, and may be used to reduce the frequency of bone pain. The bone pain can usually be eased with pain medications and the anemia may require transfusions.

Lead poisoning is treated by discontinuing exposure to lead and administering a drug that binds and draws lead out of the body.

中英文注释

关键词汇

anemia [ə'niːmiə] n. 贫血；贫血症

bilirubin [ˌbili'ruːbin] n. 胆红素

breastfeeding ['brestˌfiːdiŋ] n. 母乳哺育

breathlessness ['breθlisnis] n. 呼吸急促

constipation ['kɑnstə'peʃən] n. 便秘

dementia [di'menʃə] n. 痴呆

erythropoietin [iˌriθropɔi'itin] n. 红细胞生成素

gastritis [gæ'straitis] n. 胃炎

gastrointestinal [ˌgæstroin'tɛstinl] adj. 胃肠的

hemoglobin [ˌhɛmo'globin] n. 血红蛋白

hemorrhoids ['hɛməˌrɔidz] n. 痔疮

hydroxyurea [haiˌdrɒksi'juəriə] n. 羟基脲

inherited [in'heritid] n. 遗传的
irritability [iritə'biliti] n. 过敏性
jaundice ['dʒɔ:ndis] n. 黄疸
koilonychias [,kɔiləu'nikiə] n. 凹甲
paranoia [,pærə'nɔiə] n. 偏执狂，妄想狂
schizophrenia [skitsə'friniə] n. 精神分裂症
vegetarian [vedʒi'teəriən] n. 素食者

主要短语

blood donation　献血
celiac disease　乳糜泻；脂泻病
complete blood count (CBC)　全部血球数
Cooley's anemia.　地中海贫血
crohn's disease　克罗恩病
folic acid　叶酸
gastric bypass surgery　胃分流术
genetic counseling　遗传咨询，基因咨询
inherited disorder　遗传病
iron-deficiency anemia　缺铁性贫血
lead poisoning　铅中毒
leg cramps　腿痛性痉挛
megaloblastic anemia　巨幼红细胞性贫血
nonsteroidal anti-inflammatory drugs (NSAIDS)　非甾体抗炎药
pernicious anemia　恶性贫血
pins and needles　手脚发麻
prosthetic heart valves　人工心脏瓣膜
reticulocyte count　网织红细胞计数
serum ferritin　血清铁蛋白
severe burns　重度烧伤
shortness of breath　气促；呼吸浅短
sickle cell anemia　镰状细胞贫血
spontaneous remission　自动缓解
supportive treatment　支持性治疗
vascular grafts　人造血管
vitamin deficiency　维生素缺乏

王　锐　马志方

Aplastic Anemia
再生障碍性贫血

What is aplastic anemia?

Aplastic anemia is a disease in which the bone marrow, and the blood stem cells that reside there, are damaged. This causes a deficiency of all three blood cell types: red blood cells (anemia), white blood cells (leukopenia), and platelets (thrombocytopenia).

It occurs most commonly in the teens and twenties, and also among the elderly.

The definitive diagnosis is by bone marrow biopsy; normal bone marrow has 30%~70% blood stem cells, but in aplastic anemia, these cells are mostly gone and replaced by fat.

Aplastic anemia is treated with immunosuppressive drugs, typically either anti-lymphocyte globulin or anti-thymocyte globulin, combined with corticosteroids and cyclosporine, with a response rate of about 70%; this indicates that aplastic anemia has an auto-immune component. Stem cell transplant is also used, especially for patients < 30 years.

What causes aplastic anemia?

Aplastic anemia can be caused by exposure to chemicals, drugs, radiation, infection, immune disease, and heredity; in about half the cases, the cause is unknown.

Many drugs are associated with aplasia mainly according to case reports, but at a very low probability. As an example, chloramphenicol treatment is followed by aplasia in less than one in 40,000 treatment courses, and carbamazepine aplasia is even more rare.

Exposure to ionizing radiation from radioactive materials or radiation-producing devices is also associated with the development of aplastic anemia. Marie Curie, famous for her pioneering work in the field of radioactivity, died of aplastic anemia after working unprotected with radioactive materials for a long period of time; the damaging effects of ionizing radiation were not then known.

Aplastic anemia is present in up to 2% of patients with acute viral hepatitis.

One known cause is an autoimmune disorder in which white blood cells attack the bone marrow.

Short-lived aplastic anemia can also be a result of parvovirus infection. In humans, the P antigen (also known as globoside) is the cellular receptor for parvovirus B19 virus that causes erythema infectiosum (fifth disease) in children. Parvovirus causes complete cessation of red blood cell production. In most cases, this goes unnoticed, as red blood cells live on average 120 days, and the drop in production does not significantly affect the total number of circulating red blood cells. In people with conditions where the cells die early (such as sickle cell disease), however, parvovirus infection can lead to severe anemia.

In some animals, aplastic anemia may have other causes. For example, in the ferret (Mustela putorius furo), it is caused by estrogen toxicity, because female ferrets are induced ovulators, so mating is required to bring the female out of heat. Intact females, if not mated, will remain in heat, and after some time the high levels of estrogen will cause the bone marrow to stop producing red blood cells.

How is it diagnosed?

The condition needs to be differentiated from pure red cell aplasia. In aplastic anemia, the patient has pancytopenia (i.e., anemia, neutropenia and thrombocytopenia) resulting in decrease of all formed elements. In contrast, pure red cell aplasia is characterized by reduction in red cells only. The diagnosis can only be confirmed on bone marrow examination. Before this procedure is undertaken, a patient will generally have had other blood tests to find diagnostic clues, including a complete blood count, renal function andelectrolytes, liver enzymes, thyroid function tests, vitamin B_{12} and folic acid levels.

The following tests aid in determining differential diagnosis for aplastic anemia:
- Bone marrow aspirate and biopsy: to rule out other causes of pancytopenia (i.e. neoplastic infiltration or significant myelofibrosis)
- History of iatrogenic exposure to cytotoxic chemotherapy: can cause transient bone marrow suppression
- X-rays, computed tomography (CT) scans, or ultrasound imaging tests: enlarged lymph nodes (sign of lymphoma), kidneys and bones in arms and hands (abnormal in Fanconi anemia)
- Chest X-ray: infections
- Liver tests: liver diseases
- Viral studies: viral infections
- Vitamin B_{12} and folate levels: vitamin deficiency
- Blood tests for paroxysmal nocturnal hemoglobinuria

- Test for antibodies: immune competency

How is it treated?

Treating immune-mediated aplastic anemia involves suppression of the immune system, an effect achieved by daily medicine intake, or, in more severe cases, a bone marrow transplant, a potential cure. The transplanted bone marrow replaces the failing bone marrow cells with new ones from a matching donor. The multipotent stem cells in the bone marrow reconstitute all three blood cell lines, giving the patient a new immune system, red blood cells, and platelets. However, besides the risk of graft failure, there is also a risk that the newly created white blood cells may attack the rest of the body ("graft-versus-host disease").

Medical therapy of aplastic anemia often includes a short course of antithymocyte globulin (ATG) orantilymphocyte globulin (ALG) and several months of treatment with a cyclosporin to modulate the immune system. Mild chemotherapy with agents such as cyclophosphamide and vincristine may also be effective. Antibody therapy, such as ATG, targets T-cells, which are believed to attack the bone marrow. Steroids are generally ineffective, though are often used to combat serum sickness caused by ATG use.

One prospective study involving cyclophosphamide was terminated early due to a high incidence of mortality, due to severe infections as a result of prolonged neutropenia.

In the past, before the above treatments became available, patients with low leukocyte counts were often confined to a sterile room or bubble (to reduce risk of infections), as in the case of Ted DeVita.

Acquired aplastic anemia

It is a rare disorder involving severe failure of the bone marrow to produce new blood cells. Acquired aplastic anemia means that the condition was not present at birth but developed during the persons lifetime. The condition may be caused by such things as autoimmune reactions, radiation and certain drugs, chemicals or viral infections.

The list of signs and symptoms mentioned in various sources for Acquired Aplastic Anemiaincludes the 20 symptoms listed below:

- Reduced level of red blood cells
- Reduced level of white blood cells
- Reduced level of platelets
- Easy bruising
- Bleeding problems
- Frequent infections
- Tiredness

- Irregular heartbeat
- Fatigue
- Dizziness
- Shortness of breath
- Pallor
- Headache
- Pulsating noise in ears
- Bleeding gums
- Nose bleeds
- Heavy menstrual periods
- Prolonged menstrual periods
- Blood blisters in mouth
- Petechiae

Idiopathic Aplastic Anemia

中英文注释

关键词汇

aplasia [ə'pleʒə] n. 发育不全

globulin ['glɑbjəlin] n. 球蛋白；血球素

iatrogenic [ai‚ætrə'dʒɛnik] adj. 医源性的

leukocyte ['lju:kəʊsait] n. 白细胞

leukopenia [lʊkə'piniə] n. 白细胞减少症

lymphocyte ['limfə'sait] n. 淋巴细胞

neutropenia [njʊtrə'piniə] n. 嗜中性白血球减少症

palpitation [pælpə'teʃən] n. 心悸；跳动

pancytopenia ['pæn‚saitə'pi:niə] n. 全血细胞减少症

petechiae [pi'tekii:] n. 瘀点，出血点

thrombocytopenia [θrɑmbə‚saitə'piniə] n. 血小板减少（症）

thymocyte ['θaiməsait] n. 胸腺细胞

主要短语

antithymocyte globulin (ATG) 抗胸腺细胞球蛋白

aplastic anemia 再生障碍性贫血

autoimmune disorder 自身免疫紊乱

bone marrow biopsy 骨髓活检

cytotoxic chemotherapy 细胞毒药物治疗

immunosuppressive drug 免疫抑制药

irregular heartbeat 不规则心跳

liver enzymes 肝酶

menstrual periods 月经期

paroxysmal nocturnal hemoglobinuria (PNH) 阵发性睡眠性血红蛋白尿症

pure red cell aplasia 纯红细胞再生障碍

thyroid function 甲状腺功能

土 锐 马志方

44 Leukemia

白 血 病

What is leukemia?

Leukemia is cancer of the blood cells. It starts in the bone marrow, the soft tissue inside most bones. Bone marrow is where blood cells are made.

When you are healthy, your bone marrow makes:

- White blood cells, which help your body fight infection.
- Red blood cells, which carry oxygen to all parts of your body.
- Platelets, which help your blood clot.

When you have leukemia, the bone marrow starts to make a lot of abnormal white blood cells, called leukemia cells. They don't do the work of normal white blood cells, they grow faster than normal cells, and they don't stop growing when they should.

Over time, leukemia cells can crowd out the normal blood cells. This can lead to serious problems such as anemia, bleeding, and infections. Leukemia cells can also spread to the lymph nodes or other organs and cause swelling or pain.

Are there different types of leukemia?

There are several different types of leukemia. In general, leukemia is grouped by how fast it gets worse and what kind of white blood cell it affects.

- It may be acute or chronic. Acute leukemia gets worse very fast and may make you feel sick right away. Chronic leukemia gets worse slowly and may not cause symptoms for years.
- It may be lymphocytic or myelogenous. Lymphocytic (or lymphoblastic) leukemia affects white blood cells called lymphocytes. Myelogenous leukemia affects white blood cells called myelocytes.

The four main types of leukemia are:

- Acute lymphoblastic leukemia, or ALL.
- Acute myelogenous leukemia, or AML.
- Chronic lymphocytic leukemia, or CLL.
- Chronic myelogenous leukemia, or CML.

297

In adults, chronic lymphocytic leukemia (CLL) and acute myelogenous leukemia (AML) are the most common leukemias. In children, the most common leukemia isacute lymphoblastic leukemia (ALL). Childhood leukemias also include acute myelogenous leukemia (AML) and other myeloid leukemias, such as chronic myelogenous leukemia (CML) and juvenile myelomonocytic leukemia (JMML).

There are less common leukemias, such as hairy cell leukemia. There are also subtypes of leukemia, such as acute promyelocytic leukemia (a subtype of AML).

What causes leukemia?

Experts do not yet know what causes leukemia.

A risk factor is anything that raises your chance of getting a disease. Risk factors for some types of leukemia include:

- Smoking and tobacco use.
- Being exposed to large amounts of radiation.
- Being exposed to certain chemicals in the workplace.
- Past chemotherapy or radiation for anothercancer. (This is rare, and not all chemotherapies raise your leukemia risk.)

Most people who get leukemia do not have any risk factors.

Most types of leukemia do not seem to run in families. But in some cases chronic lymphocytic leukemia (CLL) does. There are also certain genetic conditions, like Down syndrome, that can make acute myelogenous leukemia (AML) more likely.

What are the symptoms of leukemia?

Symptoms of leukemia depend on how much the cancer has grown and may include:

- Fevers and night sweats.
- Frequent or unusual infections.
- Weakness and fatigue.
- Headaches.
- Bruising of the skin and bleeding from the gums or rectum.
- Bone pain.
- Joint pain.
- Swelling in the belly or pain on the left side of the belly or in the left shoulder from a swollen spleen.
- Swollen lymph nodes in the armpit, neck, or groin.
- Decreased appetite and weight loss because you feel full and don't want to eat.

The chronic forms of leukemia often cause no symptoms until much later in the disease.

How is leukemia diagnosed?

If your doctor suspects leukemia, he or she will ask about your medical history. Your doctor also will check for enlarged lymph nodes in your neck, underarm, or groin. He or she will also examine you to see if your liver or spleen is enlarged.

Your doctor will order blood tests, such as a complete blood count (CBC) and abloood profile. These provide important information about the cells in your blood. They are used to look into symptoms such as fatigue, weakness, fever, bruising, orweight loss.

If your blood work points to possible leukemia, your doctor will want to find out what kind you might have. Your treatment plan will depend on the specific kind of leukemia that you have.

- A blood test is usually enough to find signs of chronic lymphocytic leukemia (CLL).
- A bone marrow aspiration and biopsy is the key to diagnosing most leukemias.

Tests that look closely at unusual cells, chromosomes, or proteins on cells can show what type or subtype of leukemia you have. These tests can help guide treatment. Sometimes they can help your doctor and you know whether your leukemia is likely to go into remission or come back. In some cases, the tests can predict survival rates.

These tests include:

- A test that looks for certain changes in the cell chromosomes from a sample of blood or bone marrow (cytogenetic analysis).
- A test that compares cancer cells to normal blood cells to find the specific kind of leukemia (immunophenotyping).
- A test to look for genes that are "turned on" in several subtypes of leukemia, such as acute promyelocytic leukemia. This test is called a reverse transcription-polymerase chain reaction test, or RT-PCR.

Your doctor may also order other tests, including:

- Chest X-rays, to find out if leukemia or an infection is the cause of lung problems such as persistent coughing, coughing up blood, chest pain, or difficulty breathing.
- CT scan of the head, chest, and belly, to find out whether leukemia has spread there.
- Lumbar puncture, to find out whether leukemia cells are in your cerebrospinal fluid (CSF).
- MRI of the brain, to look into symptoms such as confusion, paralysis, numbness, vision problems, vertigo, or headaches. Those symptoms could mean the leukemia has spread to the brain.

Also, a biopsy of a lymph node or other tissues may be done to look for cancer cells.

How is it treated?

The goal of treatment for leukemia is to destroy the leukemia cells and allow normal cells to form in your bone marrow. Treatment decisions are based on the kind of leukemia you have, its stage, and your age and general health.

Treatment for acute leukemia

Chemotherapy is the use of drugs to fight cancer. It is the usual treatment for acute leukemia. For most people, that means receiving drugs in stages:

- The goal of induction is to kill leukemia cells in the blood and bone marrow to induce remission. During remission, there are no signs or symptoms of leukemia.
- The goal of consolidation is to kill any leukemia cells that may be present even though they don't show up in tests. If these cells regrow, they could cause a relapse.
- The goal of maintenance also is to prevent any remaining leukemia cells from growing. This may be done using lower doses of chemotherapy than those used during induction or consolidation. This is only used in people with ALL and a few rare forms of AML.

Some types of acute leukemia spread to the brain and spinal cord. Regular chemotherapy cannot reach those areas, because your body puts up a special barrier to protect them. A different way of giving chemotherapy, calledintrathecal chemotherapy, treats these areas by injecting the drugs directly into your spinal canal to attack any leukemia cells there.

Radiation therapy uses high doses of radiation, such as X-rays, to destroy cancer cells. Radiation is usually given from a machine outside the body that directs radiation to the cancer (external radiation). Radiation is also used to treat acute leukemia that has spread to the brain and spinal cord.

Stem cell transplant may be part of the treatment plan for people who have high-risk acute leukemia. Most stem cell transplants for leukemia are allogeneic, meaning the stem cells are donated by someone else. The goal of a transplant is to destroy all the cells in your bone marrow, including the leukemia cells, and replace them with new, normal cells.

Treatment if acute leukemia gets worse

Sometimes leukemia gets worse in spite of treatments. Sometimes it gets better, or "goes into remission." Sometimes it comes back, or "relapses." Even when that happens, there are several treatments that may help to cure the leukemia or help you live longer:

- Stem cell transplant . Donated cells from a "matched" donor can rebuild your supply of normal blood cells and your immune system.
- Chemotherapy. Sometimes medicines or doses that are different from those used during your initial chemotherapy can help.

Clinical trials . People who have leukemia may enter a research program when they first start treatment or if the leukemia is not getting better. These programs test new ways to treat the disease.

Treatment of chronic leukemia

Chronic lymphocytic leukemia (CLL)

Chronic lymphocytic leukemia is not always treated right away. It usually gets worse more slowly than acute leukemia.

Treatment choices for CLL include:

- Watchful waiting. CLL usually gets worse very slowly, and you may have no symptoms for some time. You and your doctor may decide to hold off on treatment for a while. During this time your doctor will watch you carefully.
- Radiation therapy. Radiation may be used to destroy cancer cells. It also may be used to shrink swollen lymph nodes or a swollen spleen. Sometimes radiation is used on the whole body to prepare for a bone marrow transplant.
- Chemotherapy. Chemotherapy is the use of medicines that attack cancer cells. Many medicines are available to fight leukemia and help you live longer.
- Surgery. If the spleen starts destroying red blood cells and platelets, it may need to be removed. This operation is called a splenectomy.
- Targeted therapy with a monoclonal antibody. These antibodies can kill cancer cells, stop their growth, or keep them from spreading.

When you have CLL, your body is not able to fight infections very well. You and your doctor need to watch for any signs of infections, such as pneumonia or yeast infections. Early treatment of these and other infections will help you live longer. You can sometimes prevent certain infections or keep from getting very sick by getting a flu shot or a pneumonia vaccine. Your doctor also may give you antibiotics to prevent infection while you are being treated for leukemia.

Chronic myelogenous leukemia (CML)

Chronic myelogenous leukemia is treated right away.

Treatment choices for CML include:

- Targeted therapy with a tyrosine kinase inhibitor, such as imatinib or dasatinib, is the first treatment used for CML.
- Chemotherapy. Chemotherapy is the use of medicines that attack cancer cells. Many medicines are available to fight leukemia and help you live longer.

- Biological therapy. This is the use of special medicines that improve your body's natural defenses against cancer.
- High-dose chemotherapy with stem cell transplant. After chemotherapy is completed, stem cells that were previously donated and frozen are thawed and infused.
- Donor lymphocyte infusion (DLI). This is a treatment that may be used after a stem cell transplant. With DLI, a person is given more of their donor's white blood cells (lymphocytes).
- Surgery. If the spleen starts destroying red blood cells and platelets, it may need to be removed. This operation is called a splenectomy.

Leukemia in children

Treatments for children who have leukemia are not the same as treatments for adults who have leukemia. Children may respond and react to treatments in ways that are different from how adults respond. Also, after the leukemia has been treated, children may need to be monitored for treatment side effects that may appear months or years later.

中英文注释

关键词汇

allogeneic [ˌæIədʒiˈniik] adj. 同种异体的

armpit [ˈɑːmpit] n. 腋窝

bruising [ˈbruːziŋ] n. 挫伤

chromosome [ˈkroməsom] n. 染色体

headache [ˈhedeik] n. 头痛

leukemia [lʊˈkimiə] n. 白血病

lymphocytic [ˌlimfəˈsaitik] adj. 淋巴细胞的

myelogenous [ˌmaiəˈlɒdʒənəs] adj. 骨髓性的

platelets [ˈpleitlits] n. 血小板

pneumonia [njuːˈməʊniə] n. 肺炎

rectum [ˈrɛktəm] n. 直肠

spleen [spliːn] n. 脾脏

splenectomy [spliˈnektəmi] n. 脾切除术

vaccine [vækˈsin] n. 疫苗

主要短语

acute lymphoblastic leukemia, or ALL 急性成淋巴细胞性白血病

acute myelogenous leukemia, or AML. 急性骨髓性白血病

bone marrow 骨髓

cerebrospinal fluid (CSF) 脑脊液

chronic lymphocytic leukemia, or CLL. 慢性淋巴细胞白血病

chronic myelogenous leukemia, or CML. 慢性髓细胞性白血病

complete blood count (CBC) 全部血球计数

cytogenetic analysis 细胞遗传学分析

hairy cell leukemia 毛细胞白血病

immunophenotyping 免疫表型

lymph nodes 淋巴结

monoclonal antibody 单克隆抗体

myelomonocytic leukemia (JMML) 慢性骨髓单核细胞性白血病

night sweats 盗汗；夜间盗汗

transcription-polymerase chain reaction test, or RT-PCR 聚合酶链反应

tyrosine kinase inhibitor 酪氨酸激酶抑制剂

土 锐 马志方

45 ─────────────── Lymphoma
淋 巴 瘤

The lymphatic system is a network of nodes (knots of tissue) connected by vessels that drain fluid and waste products from the body. The lymph nodes act as tiny filters, straining out foreign and cells.

The lymphatic system also is involved in producing important white blood cells called lymphocytes that help protect you against various infections caused by bacteria, viruses, and fungi. When the lymphatic system is fighting an active infection, you may notice that some of your lymph nodes and tissue in the area of the infection become swollen and tender. This is the body's normal reaction to infection.

Lymphoma occurs when the lymph node cells or the lymphocytes begin to multiply uncontrollably, producing malignant cells that have the abnormal ability to invade other tissues throughout your body.

The two main types of lymphoma are Hodgkin lymphoma and non-Hodgkin lymphoma, which are classified by certain unique characteristics of the cancer cells.

Non-Hodgkin Lymphoma (NHL)

What is NHL?

NHL is cancer of the lymphatic system, which is part of the immune system. The lymphatic system is found throughout the body. When you have this disease, cells in the lymphatic system either grow without control or do not die as cells normally do.

There are many types of NHL. Sometimes they are grouped as:
- Aggressive lymphomas, which are also called intermediate-grade and high-grade lymphomas. These cancers tend to grow and spread quickly and cause severe symptoms.
- Nonaggressive lymphomas, which are also called indolent or low-grade lymphomas. These tend to grow and spread quite slowly and cause few symptoms.

NHL is different from Hodgkin's lymphoma.

NHL can start almost anywhere in the body. It may start in a single lymph node, a group of lymph nodes, or an organ such as the spleen. NHL can spread to almost any part of the body, including the liver and bone marrow.

Treatment can cure some people and may allow others to live for years. How long you live depends on the type of NHL you have and how early it's diagnosed.

What causes NHL?

The cause of NHL is unknown. The incidence of NHL has continued to increase over the years. When a person has NHL, abnormal rapid cell growth occurs. This abnormal growth may need a "trigger" to start, such as an infection or exposure to something in your environment. There is also a link between NHL and problems with the immune system. NHL is not contagious and is not caused by injury.

What are the symptoms of NHL?

Symptoms of NHL include:

- A painless swelling of the lymph nodes in the neck, underarm, or groin. This is the most common symptom.
- Fever not caused by another health problem.
- Night sweats.
- Extreme fatigue.
- Weight loss you can't explain.
- Itchy skin.
- Reddened patches on the skin.
- A cough or shortness of breath.
- Pain in the belly or back.

How is NHL diagnosed?

If NHL is suspected, your doctor will ask about your medical history and perform a physical exam. This exam includes checking for enlarged lymph nodes in your neck, underarm, and groin.

A tissue sample (biopsy) is needed to make a diagnosis. A biopsy for non-Hodgkin's lymphoma is usually taken from a lymph node, but other tissues may be sampled as well.

A bone marrow aspiration and biopsy is usually done to find out if lymphoma cells are present in the bone marrow.

Your doctor may also order other tests, including:

- Blood tests, such as a chemistry screen to measure the levels of several substances in the blood and a CBC (complete blood count) to provide information about the kinds and numbers of cells in the blood.
- A chest X-ray to provide a picture of organs and structures within the chest, including the heart and lungs, the blood vessels of the chest, and the thin sheet of muscle (diaphragm) that separates the chest cavity from the abdominal cavity.
- A CT scan (computed tomography) or MRI (magnetic resonance imaging) to provide detailed pictures of the organs and structures in the chest, abdomen, and pelvis.
- PET scan (positron emission tomography) to show areas of increased metabolicactivity. Metabolic activity refers to all of the chemical processes that take place in the body, such as using sugars for energy. Metabolic activity is generally high in cancer cells.
- Lab tests, such as flow cytometry, that check the types of cells in a biopsy sample. These tests help your doctor find out the type of lymphoma.
- Lumbar puncture (also called a spinal tap) to find out whether lymphoma cells are in the fluid (cerebrospinal fluid, or CSF) surrounding your brain and spinal cord.
- Multigated acquisition (MUGA) scan, which is a type of cardiac blood pool scan. A cardiac blood pool scan shows how well your heart is pumping blood to the rest of your body. A MUGA scan can show whether your heart is strong enough to tolerate certain types of chemotherapy, like doxorubicin.

Early Detection

At this time, there are no special tests recommended for early detection of NHL. The best strategy for early diagnosis is to see your doctor if you develop signs or symptoms of NHL.

How is it treated?

Different types of treatment are used for different types of NHL. Treatment of NHL depends on:

- The stage of the disease.
- The type of lymphoma. The kind of treatment you have will depend on whether you have B-cell or T-cell lymphoma and whether it is fast-growing or slow-growing.
- The size of the tumor, where the lymphoma is located, and what organs are involved.

- Your general health.
- Whether you have had lymphoma in the past (recurrent disease). Although lymphoma that has come back (recurred) may be controlled, it often is not curable.

Initial treatment

Treatment recommendations that may be appropriate when you are first diagnosed with NHL include:

- Watchful waiting (surveillance), a period of time after the diagnosis of some types of NHL when you are not receiving treatment but are still being watched closely by your doctor. Watchful waiting gives as good or better results than more aggressive treatment for some types of NHL, such as advanced low-grade indolent lymphoma.
- Radiation therapy, which is often the treatment of choice for early-stage, indolent NHL. Radiation therapy may be used alone or combined with other treatment options for more advanced NHL.
- Chemotherapy, which kills cancer cells or stops them from dividing. The way chemotherapy is given depends on the type and stage of cancer. This may include taking it by mouth or having it injected into a vein or muscle. Or chemotherapy may be placed directly into the spine, an organ, or into the belly.
- Monoclonal antibody therapy. This is a cancer treatment that uses specialantibodies that attach to cancer cells and destroy them without harming normal cells. Examples include rituximab (Rituxan) and alemtuzumab (Campath).

If you have recently been diagnosed with NHL, you may experience a lot of emotions. Most people experience some denial, anger, and grief. Other people may have fewer emotions. There is no "normal" or "right" way to react to a diagnosis of lymphoma. There are many steps you can take to help with your emotional reactions. You may find that talking with family and friends helps you with your emotions. Some people may find that spending time alone is what they need.

If your reaction is interfering with your ability to make decisions about your health, it is important to talk with your doctor. Your cancer treatment center may offer psychological or financial services. You may also contact your local chapter of the American Cancer Society to help you find a support group. Talking with other people who may have had similar feelings can be very helpful

You may use home treatment to help you manage the side effects that may happen with NHL or its treatment.

Ongoing treatment

Schedule regular follow-up examinations with your doctor after you have been treated for NHL. Follow-up care is an important part of the overall treatment plan. During regular follow-up care:

- You will probably be seen about every 3 months for the first year and then less often the next year or two. After that, you will only need a checkup each year if you have had no relapse.
- Changes in health can be discussed with your doctor. To monitor your health, your doctor may obtain lab tests, such as a chemistry screen and CBC, and imaging tests, such as a chest X-ray or CT scan.

Report to your doctor any problems you have, as soon as they appear. If you are having a problem, you may need to make some new appointments.

Treatment if the condition gets worse

You may be offered the following treatment options if your disease progresses:

- Radiation therapy may be used alone or in combination with other treatments if NHL recurs. Targeted radiation therapy uses monoclonal antibodies to deliver radiation directly to lymphoma cells.
- Chemotherapy often effectively treats recurrent NHL. Sometimes a person may take one type of chemotherapy for several cycles and later be switched to different medicines if the first medicines are no longer working.
- Stem cell transplant is often used to treat recurrent lymphoma. Stem celltransplant may be offered as part of standard treatment or in a clinical trial. Talk with your doctor to see if a clinical trial may be available for your type of recurrent disease.
- Biological therapy may be used to treat recurrent lymphoma.

Hodgkin lymphoma

What is Hodgkin lymphoma?

Hodgkin lymphoma, also known as Hodgkin's disease, is a type of lymphoma, a cancer of the lymphatic system. Hodgkin disease is most common in two different age groups: young adults (ages 15 to 35) and older adults (over age 50). It is somewhat more common in males than females, and more common in Caucasians than in African-Americans. Because of progress in treating Hodgkin lymphoma, most people with a diagnosis of Hodgkin lymphoma will be long-time survivors.

What causes Hodgkin lymphoma?

The exact cause of Hodgkin lymphoma is not known, but the following have been implicated:

- Viruses: The Epstein-Barr virus, the same virus that causes infectious mononucleosis (mono), has been implicated as a cause of Hodgkin lymphoma. The presence of the genome of this virus is seen in 20%-80% of Hodgkin lymphoma tumors.
- Familial: Same-sex siblings and an identical twin of a person with Hodgkin lymphoma are at high risk of developing the disease. Children with a parent who has Hodgkin is also at an increased risk.
- Environment: Fewer siblings, early birth order, single-family homes, and fewer playmates are associated with an increased risk of developing Hodgkin lymphoma — possibly due to a lack of exposure to bacterial and viral infections at an early age.

What are the symptoms of Hodgkin lymphoma?

Symptoms of Hodgkin lymphoma may include:
- Painless swelling of one or more lymph nodes, without a recent infection
- Symptoms stemming from pressure of swollen lymph nodes on nearby organs or structures. They may include a cough, shortness of breath, abdominal pain and/or swelling, a Horner's syndrome (a neurological problem affecting the face and eyes, due to damage to nerves in the neck), nerve pain, and leg swelling
- Fever, either persistent or alternating with periods of normal temperatures, for 14 consecutive days or longer. These fevers usually occur twice daily, usually in the late afternoon and early evening, and rarely are greater than 102 degrees Farenheit
- Pain in lymph nodes or abdomen after drinking alcohol
- Drenching night sweats and/or chills lasting for 14 consecutive days or longer
- Unintentional weight loss (more than 10% over six months)
- Bone pain
- Increased susceptibility to infections
- Total body itching

The symptoms of fever, chills, night sweats, and weight loss, occur in 30% of people with Hodgkin lymphoma, usually older adults. These symptoms are usually associated with a more advanced, and more aggressive, disease, with a poorer prognosis. The presence of these symptoms require extra staging studies, such as a bone marrow aspiration and biopsy.

Call Your Doctor About Hodgkin Lymphoma If:
- You notice one or more painless, swollen lymph nodes and you have not had a recent infection

- You develop an unexplained fever, either persistent or interspersed with periods of normal temperature, for 14 consecutive days or longer
- You regularly awaken at night drenched in sweat, for at least 14 consecutive days
- You begin to lose weight unintentionally
- You have unexplained abdominal pain or swelling
- You develop an unexplained cough, shortness of breath, or wheezing
- You have unexplainable, severe itching of your skin
- You begin to contract more frequent infections

How is it diagnosed?

The diagnosis of Hodgkin lymphoma can only be made by a tissue biopsy — cutting a tissue sample for examination. If you have an enlarged, painless lymph node that your doctor suspects may be due to Hodgkin lymphoma, tissue will be taken for biopsy or the entire node will be removed. The diagnosis of Hodgkin lymphoma can be confirmed if a type of cell, called a Reed-Sternberg cell, is seen.

If a biopsy reveals that you do have Hodgkin lymphoma, you may need additional tests to determine the extent, or stage, of the disease. Tests include blood tests, chest X-ray, computed tomography (CT) scans of the chest, abdomen and pelvis, and possibly the neck, and a PET scans. Magnetic resonance imaging (MRI) scans, bone scans, spinal tap (lumbar puncture), and bone marrow studies are useful under special circumstances.

These tests will confirm the stage of the disease and the best type of therapy to pursue.

What are the stages of Hodgkin lymphoma?

The outlook and treatment of Hodgkin depends on the stage it is in, or how widespread the disease. The stages are:
- Stage I. Hodgkin lymphoma is found in only one lymph node area or structure (such as the spleen).
- Stage II. Hodgkin lymphoma is found in two or more lymph node areas on the same side of the diaphragm (the muscle beneath the lungs that moves up and down to help you breathe).
- Stage III. Hodgkin lymphoma is in lymph nodes on both sides of the diaphragm, or the cancer cells may also have extended to an area or organ adjacent to the lymph node and/or to the spleen.
- Stage IV. Hodgkin lymphoma has spread to one or more organs outside the lymphatic system, such as the bone marrow or liver.

Refractory or recurrent Hodgkin lymphoma.

Refractory disease is the term used when the disease does not respond to initial therapy. Recurrent disease means that Hodgkin lymphoma has come back after it has been treated. This may occur shortly after treatment or, less commonly, years later.

What is the treatment for Hodgkin lymphoma?

The goal of treatment for Hodgkin is to eradicate the lymphoma cells with as little damage as possible to normal cells, in order to limit the side effects of treatment. Talk with your doctor about any treatment-related side effects you experience.

The most common treatment for Hodgkin lymphoma is chemotherapy (drugs). Radiation therapy's use as a treatment has diminished over time.

Patients with Hodgkin lymphoma that is resistant to treatment or returns after initial treatment may need autologous stem cell transplantation. In this procedure, higher doses of chemotherapy and/or total body irradiation are applied in an effort to destroy Hodgkin lymphoma cells that have survived standard therapy. As a side effect, the higher doses of therapy are likely to destroy normal blood and bone marrow cells. Therefore, normal bone marrow stem cells are taken from the patient's bloodstream before they undergo chemotherapy or radiation. The stem cells are then frozen and saved and returned to your body intravenously after your treatment in order to repopulate the bone marrow.

A new drug, Adcetris (brentuximabvedotin), is designed to treat patients whose lymphoma has progressed after treatment with bone marrow stem cell transplantation or those who have had two chemotherapy treatments and are not eligible for transplant. It's the first new drug approved to treat Hodgkin lymphoma in nearly 35 years.

中英文注释

关键词汇
fungi ['fʌŋgi:] n. 真菌
lymphatic [lim'fætik] adj. 淋巴的；含淋巴的
lymphocyte ['limfə(ʊ)sait] n. 淋巴细胞
wheeze [wi:z] vt. vi. 喘息

主要短语
biological therapy 生物疗法
flow cytometry 流式细胞术
Hodgkin lymphoma 霍奇金淋巴瘤
itchy skin 皮肤瘙痒

lumbar puncture 腰椎穿刺
malignant cells 恶性细胞
monoclonal antibody 单克隆抗体
non-Hodgkin lymphoma 非霍奇金淋巴瘤
positron emission tomography 正电子放射断层造影术
radiation therapy 放射治疗
spinal tap 脊椎穿刺

王 锐 马志方

46

Purpura
紫　癜

What is purpura?

Purpura (from Latin: *purpura*, meaning "purple") is the appearance of red or purple discolorations on the skin that do not blanch on applying pressure. They are caused by bleeding underneath the skin usually secondary to vasculitis or dietary deficiency of vitamin C (scurvy). Purpura measure 0.3–1 cm (3–10 mm), whereas petechiae measure less than 3 mm, and ecchymoses greater than 1 cm.

This is common with typhus and can be present with meningitiscaused by meningococcal meningitis or septicaemia. In particular, meningococcus (*Neisseria meningitidis*), a Gram-negative diplococcus organism, releases endotoxin when it lyses. Endotoxin activates the Hageman factor (clotting factor XII), which causes disseminated intravascular coagulation (DIC). The DIC is what appears as a rash on the affected individual.

Purpura are a common and nonspecific medical sign; however, the underlying mechanism commonly involves one of the following:

Platelet disorders (Thrombocytopenic purpura)

- Primary thrombocytopenic purpura
- Secondary thrombocytopenic purpura
- Post-transfusion purpura

Vascular disorders (nonthrombocytopenic purpura)

- Microvascular injury, as seen in senile (old age) purpura, when blood vessels are more easily damaged
- Hypertensive states
- Deficient vascular support
- Vasculitis, as in the case of Henoch Schönlein purpura

Coagulation disorders

- Disseminated intravascular coagulation (DIC)
- Scurvy (vitamin C deficiency) - defect in collagen synthesis due to lack of hydroxylation of procollagen results in weakened capillary walls and cells

313

Meningococcemia

Cocaine use with concomitant use of the one-time chemotherapy drug and now veterinary deworming agentlevamisole is added predominantly by South American cocaine traffickers to cocaine because it dilutes, cuts it, and supposedly makes it cheaper prolonging the high. This chemical combination can cause purpura of the ears, face, trunk, or extremities, sometimes needing reconstructive surgery.

There are also cases of psychogenic purpura described in the medical literature, some claimed to be due to "autoerythrocyte sensitization". Other studiessuggest the local (cutaneous) activity of TPA can be increased in psychogenic purpura, leading to substantial amounts of localized plasmin activity, rapid degradation of fibrin clots, and resultant bleeding. Petechial rash is also characteristic of a rickettsialinfection.

Henoch-Schonlein Purpura (HSP)

What is HSP?

It is a disease involving inflammation of small bloodvessels. It most commonly occurs in children. The inflammation causes blood vessels in the skin, intestines, kidneys, and joints to start leaking. The main symptom is a rash with numerous small bruises, which have a raised appearance, over the legs or buttocks.

Although HSP can affect people at any age, most cases occur in children between the ages of 2 and 11. It is more common in boys than girls. Adults with HSP are more likely to have more severe disease compared to children.

HSP usually ends after four to six weeks — sometimes with recurrence of symptoms over this period, but with no long-term consequences. If organs such as the kidneys and intestines are affected, treatment is often needed and it is important to have regular follow-up to prevent serious complications.

What causes HSP?

The exact cause of HSP is not known. The body's immune system is believed to play a role in targeting the blood vessels involved. An abnormal immune response to an infection may be a factor in many cases. Approximately two-thirds of the cases of HSP occur days after symptoms of an upper respiratory tract infection develop.

Some cases of HSP have been linked to vaccinations for typhoid, cholera, yellow fever, measles, or hepatitis B; foods, drugs, chemicals, and insect bites. Some experts also say that HSP is associated with the colder weather of fall and winter.

What are symptoms of HSP?

The classic symptoms of HSP are rash, joint pain and swelling, abdominal pain, and/or related kidney disease, including blood in urine. Before these symptoms begin, patients may have two to three weeks of fever, headache, and muscular aches and pains. Rarely, other organs, such as the brain, heart, or lungs, may be affected.

Here are some key details about the symptoms of HSP:

- **Rash.** The rash usually appears in all patients with HSP. The initial appearance may resemble hives, with small red spots or bumps on the lower legs, buttocks, knees, and elbows. But these change to appear more like bruises. The rash usually affects both sides of the body equally and does not turn pale on pressing.

- **Arthritis.** Joint inflammation, involving pain and swelling, occurs in approximately three-quarters of cases, particularly affecting the knees and ankles. It usually lasts only a few days and does not cause any long-term, chronic joint problems.

- **Abdominal pain.** In more than half of people with HSP, inflammation of the gastrointestinal tract may cause pain or cramping; it may also lead to loss of appetite, vomiting, diarrhea, and occasionally blood in the stool. In some cases, patients may have abdominal pain before the rash appears. In rare cases, an abnormal folding of the bowel (intussusception) may cause a bowel blockage, which may require surgery to fix.

- **Kidney impairment.** HSP can cause kidney problems, indicated by such signs as protein or blood in the urine. This is usually only discovered on urine testing, since it does not generally cause any discomfort. In most patients, the kidney impairment is mild and goes away without any long-term damage. It's important to monitor the kidney problems closely and make sure they clear up, since about 5% of patients may develop progressive kidney disease. About 1% may go on to develop total kidney failure.

How to diagnose and treat HSP?

The diagnosis of HSP may be clear when the typical rash, arthritis, and abdominal pain are present. A doctor may order some tests to rule out other diagnoses, confirm the diagnosis, and assess its severity.

Occasionally, when the diagnosis is uncertain, particularly if the only symptom is the classic rash, your doctor may perform biopsies of the skin or kidney. Urine and blood tests will likely be done to detect signs of kidney involvement and may need to be repeated during follow-up to monitor any changes in kidney function.

Although there is no specific treatment for HSP, you can use over-the-counter pain medicines, such as acetaminophen or nonsteroidal anti-inflammatory drugs (NSAIDs), such as ibuprofen and naproxen for joint pain. In some cases, corticosteroid medication may be used.

The rash and joint pain will usually go away after four to six weeks without causing any permanent damage. Bouts of the rash may recur in approximately one-third of cases, but they are usually milder, do not involve joint and abdominal symptoms, and they clear up on their own.

Thrombocytopenic Purpura

What is thrombocytopenic purpura?

Thrombocytopenic purpura are purpura associated with a reduction in circulating blood platelets which can result from a variety of causes.

By tradition, the term idiopathic thrombocytopenic purpura is used when the cause is idiopathic. However, most cases are now considered to be immune-mediated.

Another form is thrombotic thrombocytopenic purpura.

Thrombotic thrombocytopenic purpura (TTP or *Moschcowitz syndrome*) is a rare disorder of the blood-coagulation system, causing extensive microscopic clots to form in the small blood vessels throughout the body. These small blood clots, calledthromboses, can damage many organs including the kidneys, heart and brain. In the era before effective treatment with plasma exchange, the fatality rate was about 90%. With plasma exchange, survival at six months is around 80%. Immunosuppressants, such asglucocorticoids, rituximab, cyclophosphamide, vincristine, orcyclosporine may also be used if there is relapse or recurrence following plasma exchange.

Most cases of TTP arise from inhibition of the enzyme ADAMTS13, a metalloprotease responsible for cleaving large multimers of von Willebrand factor (vWF) into smaller units. A rarer form of TTP, called Upshaw-Schülman syndrome, is genetically inherited as a dysfunction of ADAMTS13. If large vWF multimers persist there is tendency for increased coagulation.

Red blood cells passing the microscopic clots are subjected toshear stress which damages their membranes, leading to intravascular hemolysis and schistocyte formation. Reduced blood flow due to thrombosis and cellular injury results in end organ damage. Current therapy is based on support and plasmapheresis to reduce circulating antibodies against ADAMTS13 and replenish blood levels of the enzyme.

What are symptoms of TTP?

Classically, the following five features ("pentad") are indicative of TTP; in most cases, some of these are absent.

- Thrombocytopenia (low platelet count), leading to bruising or purpura
- Microangiopathic hemolytic anemia (anemia, jaundice and a blood film featuring evidence of mechanical fragmentation of red blood cells)
- Neurologic symptoms (fluctuating), such as hallucinations, bizarre behavior, altered mental status, stroke or headaches
- Kidney failure
- Fever

The symptoms of TTP may at first be subtle, starting with malaise, fever, headache and sometimes diarrhea. As the condition progresses clots (thrombi) form within blood vessels and platelets (clotting cells) are consumed. Bruising, and rarely bleeding, results and may be spontaneous. The bruising often takes the form of purpura while the most common site of bleeding, if it occurs, is from the nose or gums. Larger bruises (ecchymoses) may also develop.

Clots formed within the circulation can temporarily disrupt local blood supply. TTP preferentially affects the blood vessels of the brain and kidneys. Thus a patient may experience headache, confusion, difficulty speaking, transient paralysis, numbness or even fits whilst high blood pressure (hypertension) may be found on examination.

Differential diagnosis

TTP is characterized by thrombotic microangiopathy (TMA), the formation of blood clots in small blood vessels throughout the body, which can lead to microangiopathic hemolytic anemia and thrombocytopenia. This characteristic is shared by two related syndromes, hemolytic-uremic syndrome (HUS) and atypical hemolytic-uremic syndrome (aHUS). Consequently, differential diagnosis of these TMA-causing diseases is essential. In addition to TMA, one or more of the following symptoms may be present in each of these diseases: neurological symptoms (e.g. confusion, cerebral convulsionsseizures,); renal impairment (e.g. elevated creatinine, decreased estimated glomerular filtration rate (eGFR), abnormal urinalysis); and gastrointestinal (GI) symptoms (e.g. diarrhea nausea/vomiting, abdominal pain, gastroenteritis, Unlike HUS and aHUS, TTP is known to be caused by an acquired defect in the ADAMTS13 protein; a lab test showing ≤5% of normal ADAMTS13 levels is therefore indicative of TTP. ADAMTS13 levels above 5%, coupled with a positive test for Shiga-toxin/enterohemorrhagic E. coli (EHEC), are more likely indicative of HUS, whereas absence of Shiga-toxin/EHEC can confirm a diagnosis of aHUS.

TTP, as with other microangiopathic hemolytic anemias (MAHAs), is caused by spontaneous aggregation of platelets and activation of coagulation in the small blood vessels. Platelets are consumed in the coagulation process, and bind fibrin, the end product of the coagulation pathway. These platelet-fibrin complexes form microthrombi which circulate in the vasculature and cause shearing of red blood cells, resulting in hemolysis.

Roughly, there are two forms of TTP: *idiopathic* and *secondary* TTP. A special case is the inherited deficiency of ADAMTS13, known as the Upshaw-Schülman syndrome.

Idiopathic TTP

The *idiopathic* form of TTP was recently linked to the inhibition of the enzyme ADAMTS13 by antibodies, rendering TTP an autoimmune disease. ADAMTS13 is a metalloproteinase responsible for the breakdown of von Willebrand factor (vWF), a protein that links platelets, blood clots, and the blood vessel wall in the process of blood coagulation. Very large vWF multimers are more prone to lead to coagulation. Hence, without proper cleavage of vWF by ADAMTS13, coagulation occurs at a higher rate, especially in the microvasculature, part of the blood vessel system where vWF is most active due to high shear stress.

In idiopathic TTP, severely decreased (<5% of normal) ADAMTS13 activity can be detected in most (80%) patients, and inhibitors are often found in this subgroup (44-56%). The relationship of reduced ADAMTS13 to the pathogenesis of TTP is known as the Furlan-Tsai hypothesis, after the two independent groups of researchers who published their research in the same issue of the New England Journal of Medicine in 1998.

Secondary TTP

Secondary TTP is diagnosed when the patient's history mentions one of the known features associated with TTP. It comprises about 40% of all cases of TTP. Predisposing factors are:

- Cancer
- Bone marrow transplantation
- Pregnancy
- Medication use:
  - Quinine
  - Platelet aggregation inhibitors (ticlopidine, clopidogrel, and prasugrel)
  - Immunosuppressants (cyclosporine, mitomycin, tacrolimus/FK506, interferon-α)
- HIV-1 infection

The mechanism of secondary TTP is poorly understood, as ADAMTS13 activity is generally not as depressed as in idiopathic TTP, and inhibitors cannot be detected. Probable etiology may involve, at least in some cases, endothelial damage, although the formation of thrombi resulting in vessel occlusion may not be essential in the pathogenesis of secondary. These factors may also be considered a form of secondary aHUS; patients presenting with these features are therefore potential candidates for anti-complement therapy.

Upshaw-Schülman Syndrome

A hereditary form of TTP is called the Upshaw-Schülman syndrome; this is generally due to inherited deficiency of ADAMTS13 (frameshift and point mutations). Patients with this inherited ADAMTS13 deficiency have a surprisingly mild phenotype, but develop TTP in clinical situations with increased von Willebrand factor levels, e.g. infection. Reportedly, less than 1% of all TTP cases are due to Upshaw-Schülman syndrome. Patients with Upshaw-Schülman syndrome have 5-10% of normal ADAMTS13 activity.

How is it treated?

Due to the high mortality of untreated TTP, a presumptive diagnosis of TTP is made even when only microangiopathic hemolytic anemia and thrombocytopenia is seen, and therapy is started. Since the early 1990s, plasmapheresis has become the treatment of choice for TTP. This is an exchange transfusioninvolving removal of the patient's blood plasma through apheresis and replacement with donor plasma (fresh frozen plasma or cryosupernatant); the procedure must be repeated daily to eliminate the inhibitor and abate the symptoms. If apheresis is not available, fresh frozen plasma can be infused, but the volume that can be given safely is limited due to the danger of fluid overload. Lactate dehydrogenase (LDH) levels are generally used to monitor disease activity. Plasmapheresis may need to be continued for 1–8 weeks before patients with idiopathic TTP cease to consume platelets and begin to normalize their hemoglobin. No single laboratory test (platelet count, LDH, ADAMTS13 level, or inhibitory factor) is indicative of recovery; research protocols have used improvement or normalization of LDH as a measure for ending plasmapheresis. Although patients may be critically ill with failure of multiple organ systems during the acute illness, including renal failure, myocardial ischemia, and neurologic symptoms, recovery over several months may be complete in the absence of a frank myocardial infarct, stroke, or CNS hemorrhage.

Children with Upshaw-Schülman syndrome receive prophylactic plasma every two to three weeks; this maintains adequate levels of functioning ADAMTS13.

Measurements of LDH, platelets and schistocytes are used to monitor disease progression or remission.

中英文注释

关键词汇

anti-inflammatory [ˌæntiinfləˈmeitəri] adj. 抗炎的

cholera [ˈkɒlərə] n. 霍乱

ecchymosis [ˌeki'məʊsiːz] n. 瘀斑

endotoxin [ˈendəʊˌtɒksin] n. 内毒素

gastrointestinal [ˌgæstrɔinˈtɛstinl] adj. 胃肠的

immunosuppressant [imjənosə'prɛsənt] n. 免疫抑制剂

intussusception [intəsə'sepʃ(ə)n] n. 肠套叠

measles [ˈmiːzəlz] n. 麻疹；风疹

multimer [ˈmʌltimə(r)] n. 多聚体

neurologic [njuərə'lɒdʒikəl] adj. 神经病学的

paralysis [pə'ræləsis] n. 麻痹

plasmapheresis [ˌplæzmə'fɛrisis] n. 血浆除去法

plasmin [ˈplæzmin] n. 血纤维蛋白溶酶

purpura [ˈpɜːpjʊrə] n. 紫癜

scurvy [ˈskɜːvi] n. 坏血病

septicaemia [ˌsɛpti'simiə] n. 败血症；败血病

thrombocytopenia [ˌθrɑmbəˌsaitə'piniə] n. 血小板减少症

vaccinations [ˌvæksi'neiʃən] n. 接种疫苗

vasculitis [ˌvæskjʊ'laitis] n. 结节性脉管炎

主要短语

bone marrow transplantation 骨髓移植术

coagulation disorders 凝血功能障碍

disseminated intravascular coagulation (DIC) 弥散性血管内凝血

enterohemorrhagic E. coli (EHEC) 肠出血性大肠埃希菌

gastrointestinal tract 胃肠道

hageman factor 接触因子

hemolytic-uremic syndrome (HUS) 溶血性尿毒症综合征

Henoch-Schonlein purpura (HSP) 过敏性紫癜

hepatitis B 乙型肝炎

idiopathic thrombocytopenic purpura 特发性血小板减少性紫癜

lactate dehydrogenase (LDH) 乳酸脱氢酶

meningococcal meningitis 流行性脑脊髓膜炎

microangiopathic hemolytic anemias (MAHAs) 微血管病性溶血性贫血

platelet aggregation inhibitors 血小板聚集抑制因子

thrombocytopenic purpura 血小板减少性紫癜

thrombotic thrombocytopenic purpura 血栓形成性血小板减少性紫癜

von Willebrand factor 血管假性血友病因子

yellow fever 黄热病

土　锐　马志方

47 ——— Alzheimer's Disease
阿尔茨海默病

What is Alzheimer's disease?

Alzheimer's disease is a progressive neurologic disease of the brain leading to the irreversible loss of neurons and the loss of intellectual abilities, including memory and reasoning, which become severe enough to impede social or occupational functioning. Alzheimer's disease is also known as simply Alzheimer's, and Senile Dementia of the Alzheimer Type (SDAT). Once thought to be rare, Alzheimer's disease is the leading cause of dementia, accounting for about half of all cases.

During the course of the disease plaques and tangles develop within the structure of the brain. This causes brain cells to die. Patients with Alzheimer's also have a deficiency in the levels of some vital brain chemicals which are involved with the transmission of messages in the brain - neurotransmitters.

Alzheimer's disease is the most common form of dementia. The disease gets worse as it develops - it is a progressive disease. There is no current cure for Alzheimer's, although there are ways of slowing down its advance and helping patients with some of the symptoms. Alzheimer's is also a terminal disease - it is incurable and causes death.

According the National Institute on Aging, there are estimated to be between 2.4 million and 4.5 million Americans who have Alzheimer's. One third of all seniors in America die with Alzheimer's or some other dementia, according to the Alzheimer's Association. Deaths from Alzheimer's have risen by 68% from 2000 to 2010.

People who lead active lifestyles are more likely to slow down the progression of Alzheimer's disease, while active people who are Alzheimer's free have a lower risk of developing the disease or any kind of dementia, researchers from the University of California reported at the annual meeting of RSNA (the Radiological Society of North America) in November 2012.

Lifestyle factors that help ward off or slow down Alzheimer's include yard work, gardening, dancing, riding an exercise bike, and any type of aerobic exercise.

What are the causes of Alzheimer's disease?

Although a great deal of research has been done and is currently being done on the possible causes of Alzheimer's, experts are still not sure why the brain cells deteriorate. However, there are several factors which are known to be linked to a higher risk of developing the disease. These include:

- **Age.** After the age of 65 the risk of developing Alzheimer's doubles every five years. Although Alzheimer's is predominantly a disease that develops during old age, some younger people may also develop the condition. According to the Canadian Medical Association Journal the risk of developing Alzheimer's is as follows: Ages 65-74, 1 in 100; Ages 75-84, 1 in 14; Age over 85, 1 in 4.

- **Family history.** People who have a close family member who developed Alzheimer's have a slightly higher risk of developing it themselves - just a slightly higher risk, not a significantly higher risk. Only about 7% of all cases are associated with genes that cause the early onset inherited familial form of the disease. Among those who do inherit the condition, it may start at an earlier age.

- **Down's syndrome** People with Down's syndrome have an extra copy of chromosome 21, which contains a protein that exists in the brain of people with Alzheimer's. As people with Down's syndrome have a larger amount of this protein than others, their risk of developing the disease is greater.

- **Whiplash and head injuries.** Some studies have identified a link between whiplash and head injuries and a higher risk of developing Alzheimer's.

- **Aluminum (UK/Ireland/Australia: Aluminium)** The link here is a theory which most scientists have discarded. Aluminum exists in the plaques and tangles in the brains of Alzheimer's patients. Some have suggested that aluminum absorption by humans could increase the risk. However, studies have failed to find a link. Aluminum exists in some foods and plants. It is found in some cooking pans, medications and packaging. Scientists doubt there is a link because our bodies absorb minimum amounts and our bodies eliminate it through the urine.

- **Gender.** A higher percentage of women develop Alzheimer's than men. As women live longer than men, and Alzheimer's risk grows with age, this may partly explain the reason.

- **Mild cognitive impairment.** A person who has just mild cognitive impairment has memory problems but not Alzheimer's. His/her memory is worse than other healthy people's of the same age. A higher percentage of people with mild cognitive impairment develop Alzheimer's, compared to other people.

- **Atrial fibrillation.** A study of more than 37,000 patients showed a strong relationship between atrial fibrillation and the development of Alzheimer's disease.
- **Heart disease risk-factors.** People with the risk factors of heart disease - high blood pressure (hypertension), high cholesterol, and poorly controlled diabetes - also have a higher risk of developing Alzheimer's. If your high-blood pressure, high cholesterol, and or poorly controlled diabetes type 2 is a result of lifestyle, it is called a lifestyle factor. Eating a well balanced diet, doing plenty of exercise, aiming for your ideal bodyweight, and sleeping between 7 to 8 hours each night will probably eliminate these factors. If you cannot eliminate your diabetes 2, good diabetes control will help.
- **Academic level.** There is some data showing a higher risk of developing Alzheimer's among people with lower educational qualifications, compared to highly qualified individuals. However, nobody really knows why.
- **Processed foods and fertilizers (nitrates).** A study carried out by researchers at Rhode Island Hospital found a significant link between increased levels of nitrates in our environment and food, with increased deaths from diseases, including Alzheimer's, diabetes and Parkinson's. The study looked at progressive increases in human exposure to nitrates, nitrites and nitrosamines through processed and preserved foods as well as fertilizers.
- **Stress.** Sara Bengtsson and team from Umea University, Sweden found that stress can increase the likelihood of developing Alzheimer's. Dr. Riley said "Some research has already highlighted a possible link between chronic stress, cognitive decline and the development of Alzheimer's, and further study in people is needed to fully investigate these links. If we can better understand the risk factors for Alzheimer's we can also empower people to make lifestyle changes to reduce their risk."
- **Some other diseases and conditions.** The following diseases and conditions have been linked to a higher risk of developing Alzheimer's. Some chronic inflammatory conditions; A history of episodes of clinical depression; Strokes and/or ministrokes; Obesity.

What are the symptoms of Alzheimer's disease?

Most patients' symptoms of Alzheimer's disease progress slowly over a number of years. Symptoms may not be noticed early on. Sometimes, it is only when family members look back that they realize when the changes started to occur.

Common symptoms of Alzheimer's disease include:

- **Impaired memory and thinking.** The person has difficulty remembering things or learning new information. In the later stages of the disease, long-term memory loss occurs, which means that the person can't remember personal information, such as his or her place of birth or occupation, or names of close family members.

- **Disorientation and confusion.** People with Alzheimer's disease may get lost when out on their own and may not be able to remember where they are or how they got there. They may not recognize previously familiar places and situations. They also may not recognize familiar faces or know what time of the day it is, or even what year it is.

- **Misplacing things.** The person forgets where he or she put things used every day, such as glasses, a hearing aid, keys, etc. The person may also put things in strange places, such as leaving his or her glasses in the refrigerator.

- **Abstract thinking.** People with Alzheimer's disease may find certain tasks — such as balancing a checkbook — more difficult than usual. For example, they might forget what the numbers mean and what needs to be done with them.

- **Trouble performing familiar tasks.** The person begins to have difficulty performing daily tasks, such as eating, dressing, and grooming. Planning for normal day-to-day tasks is also impaired.

- **Changes in personality and behavior.** The person becomes unusually angry, irritable, restless, or quiet. At times, people with Alzheimer's disease can become confused, paranoid, or fearful.

- **Poor or decreased judgment.** People with Alzheimer's disease may leave the house on a cold day without a coat or shoes or could go to the store wearing pajamas.

- **Inability to follow directions.** The person has difficulty understanding simple commands or directions. The person may get lost easily and begin to wander.

- **Problems with language and communication.** The person can't recall words, name objects (even ones that are very familiar — like a pen), or understand the meaning of common words.

- **Impaired visual and spatial skills.** The person loses spatial abilities (the ability to judge shapes and sizes and the relationship of objects in space) and can't arrange items in a certain order or recognize shapes.

- **Loss of motivation or initiative.** The person may become very passive and require prompting to become involved and interact with others.

- **Loss of normal sleep patterns.** The person may sleep during the day and be wide-awake at night.

How is Alzheimer's disease diagnosed?

It is important to visit a doctor if you or a loved one experiences any of these symptoms of Alzheimer's disease so you can receive the proper evaluation and diagnosis. There are other conditions — such as depression, a head injury, stroke, certain chemical or vitamin imbalances, or the effects of some medications — that can produce symptoms that are similar to Alzheimer's disease. Many of these conditions are treatable.

Your doctor can only determine if the symptoms are probably due to Alzheimer's disease after a thorough medical, psychiatric, and neurological evaluation. Positron emission tomography, or a PET scan, of the brain may be useful if the person meets certain criteria. Because drugs exist that may lessen the symptoms of Alzheimer's disease, the doctor will evaluate other possible causes of dementia to rule out all other factors before settling on Alzheimer's disease as a diagnosis.

Currently, no definitive diagnostic test for Alzheimer's disease exists. A definite diagnosis of Alzheimer's disease is possible only after death when a pathologist can more closely examine a patient's brain for the telltale changes associated with the disease.

How is Alzheimer's disease treated?

The U.S. population is getting older, and as it ages, Alzheimer's disease is becoming an increasingly bigger concern. Within the next 50 years, the incidence of Alzheimer's is expected to quadruple, affecting one in 45 Americans.

Today, there is still no cure for Alzheimer's. People with the disease progressively lose memory and the ability to function. Researchers are still trying to fully understand how its brain plaques and tangles lead to memory loss and other cognitive, behavioral and psychiatric symptoms — and how to reverse those changes to prevent or stop the disease.

However, there are treatments available today that can help patients manage the symptoms of Alzheimer's disease, allowing them to function at a higher level for a longer period of time. Alzheimer's therapy involves a number of different treatments that address each of these problems. Because symptoms change over time, doctors need to adjust their Alzheimer's patients' therapies as new problems emerge.

Medications

Several different types of medications are used to treat the memory loss, behavior changes, sleep problems, and other symptoms of Alzheimer's disease. These medications won't stop the disease, but they can slow down the progression of symptoms for a few months or even years. All of these medications can have side effects, which can be even more pronounced in older people.

Four medications in two classes are FDA-approved specifically for Alzheimer's therapy.

Cholinesterase inhibitors help with the cognitive symptoms of Alzheimer's. They work by preventing the breakdown of a chemical messenger in the brain called acetylcholine, which is important for learning, memory, and attention.

Three cholinesterase inhibitors are approved for Alzheimer's disease therapy: Donepezil (Aricept) is approved to treat mild, moderate, and severe Alzheimer's. Rivastigmine (Exelon) and galantamine (Razadyne) are approved to treat mild to moderate Alzheimer's. Exelon is now also available in a skin patch, which is easier for some patients to use, because it is applied to the skin and the medication is slowly released throughout the day.

Side effects of the cholinesterase inhibitors include nausea, vomiting, diarrhea, weight loss, and dizziness.

Memantine (Namenda) works by regulating the amount of another chemical messenger in the brain, called glutamate. Namenda is approved for moderate to severe Alzheimer's disease. Side effects include dizziness, confusion, headache, constipation, nausea, and agitation. Because Namendadoes not work the same way as a cholinesterase inhibitor, it may be used in combination with one.

It's difficult to tell whether one drug is more effective than another for a given person. Alzheimer's patients (with the help of their doctors) should choose whichever drug works best for them.

A few Alzheimer's disease therapies treat the behavioral and psychiatric symptoms that may be related to the disease, including hallucinations, agitation, and sleep problems. However, none of these drugs is FDA-approved as an Alzheimer's therapy.

- Antidepressants, such as citalopram (Celexa), fluoxetine (Prozac), paroxetine (Paxil), and sertraline (Zoloft) treat irritability and mood.
- Anxiolytics, such as lorazepam (Ativan) and oxazepam (Serax) treat anxiety and restlessness.
- Antipsychotic medications, such as aripiprazole (Abilify), haloperidol (Haldol), and olanzapine (Zyprexa) treat hallucinations, delusions, agitation, and aggression. It's important to note that antipsychotic drugs have been linked to increased risk of death in patients with dementia, and currently carry the FDA's "black box" warning about their use in older patients with dementia. They can, however, still be necessary and helpful to many patients.

Other therapies

It has been suggested that some non-drug therapies also can help Alzheimer's patients cope with the symptoms of the condition.

Vitamin E. Vitamin E has been researched as a therapy for Alzheimer's disease, because it is an antioxidant that was thought to protect nerve cells from damage. However, many doctors no longer recommend vitamin E, because there is little scientific evidence that it is effective.

Hormone replacement therapy(HRT). Some studies have suggested that postmenopausal women who are taking hormone replacement therapy have a lower risk of developing Alzheimer's disease. The female hormone, estrogen, is thought to help nerve cells make connections, and interfere with the production of beta amyloid — a protein that is the main component in the plaques that lead to Alzheimer's disease. However, more recent research has found no improvement with HRT, and one study even suggested that estrogen use might actually increase the risk of developing Alzheimer's rather than protect against it. HRT also may increase the risk for heart attack, stroke, and breast cancer.

Sensory therapies. There is some evidence that sensory therapies such as music therapy and art therapy can improve Alzheimer's patients' mood, behavior, and day-to-day function. By stimulating the senses, these therapies may help trigger memory recall and enable Alzheimer's patients to reconnect with the world around them.

Alternative therapies. Some people have tried alternative remedies, including coenzyme Q10, coral calcium, huperzine A, and omega-3 fatty acids to prevent or treat Alzheimer's disease. However, there is not yet enough research on these treatments to recommend using any of them as an Alzheimer's therapy. The FDA does not regulate supplements as it does medications and there is not standard to prove efficacy. Supplements may cause dangerous side effects or interact with other medications patients are taking. Just because it is sold over the counter without a prescription does not guarantee that it will be safe for you.

Researchers are looking into several new treatment options for Alzheimer's. One of the most promising Alzheimer's therapies in development focuses on beta amyloid. Researchers are trying to develop new therapies that prevent beta amyloid from forming, or break it down before it leads to Alzheimer's.

What's the prognosis for Alzheimer's disease?

The course of Alzheimer's disease varies widely from person to person. The duration of the illness could be short (two to three years) or long (up to 20 years). Usually the parts of the brain that control memory and thinking are affected first, but overtime, cells die in other areas of the brain.

Eventually, a person with Alzheimer's will need complete care. If the person has no other serious illnesses, the loss of brain function itself will eventually cause death.

Can Alzheimer's disease be prevented?

Because the exact cause of Alzheimer's disease is not known, there is currently nothing that can be done to guarantee its prevention. Some interventions may be worth incorporating into your life as more research reveals some potentially controllable risk factors. Staying mentally and physically active, maintaining a normal blood pressure and avoiding head injury by wearing seat belts and helmets may decrease your chances of developing Alzheimer's dementia.

It is important to remember, however, that there are causes of dementia other than Alzheimer's disease that may be preventable such as eating properly, exercising, quitting smoking, and limiting how much alcohol you drink. Your doctor can advise you about other healthy lifestyle habits you can adopt that may help prevent dementia.

中英文注释

关键词汇

acetylcholine [ˌæsitail'kəʊliːn; -til-] n. 乙酰胆碱

agitation [ædʒi'teiʃ(ə)n] n. 激动；搅动；煽动；烦乱

aluminum [ə'ljuːminəm] n. 铝

antipsychotic [ˌæntisai'kɒtik] adj. 治疗精神病的，抗精神病的

cholinesterase [ˌkəʊli'nestəreiz] n. 胆碱酯酶

cognitive ['kɒgnitiv] adj. 认知的，认识的

confusion [kən'fjuːʒ(ə)n] n. 混淆，混乱；困惑

constipation [kɒnsti'peiʃ(ə)n] n. 便秘；受限制

delusion [di'luːʒən] n. 妄想；错觉

dementia [di'menʃə] n. 痴呆

deteriorate [di'tiəriəreit] vi. 恶化，变坏 vt. 恶化

disorientation [dis'ɔriɛnteʃən] n. 迷失方向；迷惑

dizziness ['dizinis] n. 头晕；头昏眼花

fertilizer ['fɜːtilaizə] n. 肥料

hallucination [həˌluːsi'neiʃ(ə)n] n. 幻觉，幻想；错觉

impede [im'piːd] vt. 阻碍；妨碍；阻止

irreversible [iri'vɜːsib(ə)l] adj. 不可逆的；不能取消的；不能翻转的

irritable ['iritəb(ə)l] adj. 过敏的，急躁的，易怒的

moderate ['mɒd(ə)rət] adj. 稳健的，温和的

neurological [ˌnjʊərə'lɒdʒikl] adj. 神经病学的，神经学上的

neuron ['njʊərɒn] n. 神经元，神经单位

neurotransmitter [ˌnjʊərəʊtrænz'mitə] n. 神经递质；神经传递素

nitrate ['naitreit] n. 硝酸盐

obesity [ə(ʊ)'biːsəti] n. 肥大，肥胖

paranoid ['pærənɒid] adj. 类似妄想狂的；属于偏执狂的；n. 患妄想狂的人；偏执狂患者

postmenopausal [pəʊst,menəʊ'pɔːzəl] adj.（妇女）绝经后的

psychiatric [,saiki'ætrik] adj. 精神病学的；精神病治疗的

sensory ['sens(ə)ri] adj. 感觉的；知觉的；传递感觉的

主要短语

Alzheimer's disease 阿尔茨海默病；阿兹海默症；老年痴呆症

Down's syndrome 唐氏综合征

FDA (Food and Drug Administration)（美）食品及药物管理局

high cholesterol 高胆固醇

hormone replacement therapy (HRT) 激素取代疗法

李 丹

48

Cerebral Infarction
脑 梗 死

What is cerebral infarction?

A cerebral infarction is an ischemicstroke resulting from a disturbance in the blood vessels supplying blood to the brain. It can be atherothrombotic or embolic. Stroke caused by cerebral infarction should be distinguished from two other kinds of stroke: cerebral hemorrhage and subarachnoid hemorrhage. A cerebral infarction occurs when a blood vesselthat supplies a part of the brain becomes blocked or leakage occurs outside the vessel walls. This loss of blood supply results in the death of that area of tissue. Cerebral infarctions vary in their severity with one third of the cases resulting in death.

There are various classification systems for a cerebral infarction.

The Oxford Community Stroke Project classification (OCSP, also known as the Bamford or Oxford classification) relies primarily on the initial symptoms. Based on the extent of the symptoms, the stroke episode is classified astotal anterior circulation infarct (TACI), partial anterior circulation infarct (PACI), lacunar infarct (LACI) or posterior circulation infarct (POCI). These four entities predict the extent of the stroke, the area of the brain affected, the underlying cause, and the prognosis.

- The TOAST (Trial of Org 10172 in Acute Stroke Treatment) classification is based on clinical symptoms as well as results of further investigations; on this basis, a stroke is classified as being due to (1) thrombosis or embolism due to atherosclerosis of a large artery, (2) embolism of cardiacorigin, (3) occlusion of a small blood vessel, (4) other determined cause, (5) undetermined cause (two possible causes, no cause identified, or incomplete investigation).

What causes cerebral infarction?

In thrombotic cerebral infarction a thrombus usually forms around atherosclerotic plaques. An embolic stroke refers to the blockage of an artery by an embolus, a traveling particle or debris in the arterial bloodstream originating elsewhere. An embolus is most frequently a thrombus, but it can also be a number of other substances including fat (e.g. from bone marrow in a broken bone), air, cancer cells or clumps of bacteria (usually from infectious endocarditis). The embolus may be of cardiac origin due to Atrial fibrillationor from atherosclerotic plaque of another (or the same) large artery.

What are the symptoms of cerebral infarction?

Symptoms of cerebral infarction are determined by topographical localisation of cerebral lesion. If the infarct is located in primary motor cortex- contralateral hemiparesis is said to occur. With brainstem localization, brainstem syndromes are typical: Wallenberg's syndrome, Weber's syndrome, Millard-Gubler syndrome, Benedikt syndrome or others. Infarctions will result in weakness and loss of sensation on the opposite side of the body. Physical examination of the head area will reveal abnormal pupil dilation, light reaction and lack of eye movement on opposite side. If the infarction occurs on the left side brain, speech will be slurred. Reflexes may be aggravated as well.

How is cerebral infarction diagnosed?

Computed tomography (CT) and MRI scanning will show damaged area in the brain, showing that the symptoms were not caused by a tumor, subdural hematoma or other brain disorder. The blockage will also appear on the angiogram.

What are the treatments for cerebral infarction?

In last decade, similar to myocardial infarction treatment, thrombolytic drugs were introduced in the therapy of cerebral infarction. The use of intravenous rtPA therapy can be advocated in patients who arrive to stroke unit and can be fully evaluated within 3 h of the onset.

Cut-away view of the Merci L5 retrieval system, used for clot removal in ischemic stroke patients.

If cerebral infarction is caused by a thrombus occluding blood flow to an artery supplying the brain, definitive therapy is aimed at removing the blockage by breaking the clot down (thrombolysis), or by removing it mechanically (thrombectomy). The more rapidly blood flow is restored to the brain, the fewer brain cells die. In increasing numbers of primary stroke centers, pharmacologic thrombolysis with the drug tissue plasminogen activator (TPA), is used to dissolve the clot and unblock the artery. Another intervention for acute cerebral ischaemia is removal of the offending thrombus directly. This is accomplished by inserting a catheter into the femoral artery, directing it into the cerebral circulation, and deploying a corkscrew-like device to ensnare the clot, which is then withdrawn from the body. Mechanical embolectomy devices have been demonstrated effective at restoring blood flow in patients who were unable to receive thrombolytic drugs or for whom the drugs were ineffective though no differences have been found between newer and older versions of the devices. The devices have only been tested on patients treated with mechanical clot embolectomy within eight hours of the onset of symptoms.

Angioplasty and stenting have begun to be looked at as possible viable options in treatment of acute cerebral ischaemia. In a systematic review of six uncontrolled, single-center trials, involving a total of 300 patients, of intra-cranial stenting in symptomatic intracranial arterial stenosis, the rate of technical success (reduction to stenosis of <50%) ranged from 90%~98%, and the rate of major peri-procedural complications ranged from 4%~10%. The rates of restenosis and/or stroke following the treatment were also favorable. This data suggests that a large, randomized controlled trial is needed to more completely evaluate the possible therapeutic advantage of this treatment.

If studies show carotid stenosis, and the patient has residual function in the affected side, carotid endarterectomy (surgical removal of the stenosis) may decrease the risk of recurrence if performed rapidly after cerebral infarction. Carotid endarterectomy is also indicated to decrease the risk of cerebral infarction for symptomatic carotid stenosis (>70 to 80 % reduction in diameter).

In tissue losses that are not immediately fatal, the best course of action is to make every effort to restore impairments through physical therapy, speech therapy and exercise.

中英文注释

关键词汇

catheter ['kæθitə] n. 导管，尿管

dilation [dai'leiʃən] n. 扩大

embolic [em'bɔlik] adj. 栓塞的

embolus ['embələs] n. 栓子

sensation [sen'seiʃ(ə)n] n. 感觉

slurred [slə:(r)əd] adj. 言语含糊的

stenosis [sti'nəʊsis] n. 狭窄

thrombus ['θrɒmbəs] n. 血栓

weakness ['wi:knis] n. 无力

主要短语

angioplasty and stenting 血管成形术和支架术

atherosclerotic plaques　动脉粥样硬化斑块

atrial fibrillation　房颤

carotid endarterectomy　颈动脉内膜切除术

cerebral hemorrhage　脑出血

embolism of cardiacorigin　心源性脑栓塞

femoral artery　股动脉

infectious endocarditis　感染性心内膜炎

occlusion of a small blood vessel　小动脉闭塞性（脑梗死）

pharmacologic thrombolysis　药物溶栓

reflexes aggravated　反射亢进

rtPA: recombinant plasminogen activator　重组组织型纤溶酶原激活剂

subarachnoid hemorrhage　蛛网膜下腔出血

subdural hematoma　硬膜下血肿

thrombosis or embolism due to atherosclerosis of a large artery　大动脉粥样硬化性脑梗死

undetermined cause　不明原因

闵国文　马志方

49 — Encephalitis

脑　炎

What is encephalitis?

Encephalitis, or inflammation of the brain tissue, is rare, affecting about one in 200,000 people each year in the U.S.

When it strikes, it can be very serious, causing personality changes, seizures, weakness, and other symptoms depending on the part of the brain affected.

Children, the elderly, and those with a weak immune system are most vulnerable. The disease is usually caused by one of several viral infections, so it's sometimes referred to as viral encephalitis.

Many people who have encephalitis fully recover. The most appropriate treatment and the patient's chance of recovery depend on the virus involved and the severity of the inflammation.

In acute encephalitis, the infection directly affects the brain cells. In para-infectious encephalitis, the brain and spinal cord become inflamed within one to two weeks of contracting a viral or bacterial infection.

What causes encephalitis?

Viral encephalitis may develop during or after infection with any of several viral illnesses including influenza, herpes simplex, measles, mumps, rubella, rabies, chickenpox, and arbovirus infection including West Nile virus.

Herpes simplex type 1 virus is one of the more common and serious causes of viral encephalitis. Herpes-related encephalitis can erupt rapidly, and may cause seizures or mental changes and even lead to coma or death. It occurs when the herpes simplex type 1 virus travels to the brain rather than moving through the body to the surface of the skin and producing its more common symptom, a cold sore. Early recognition and treatment of herpes encephalitis can be life-saving. You are not more likely to get encephalitis if you have cold sores.

Arbovirus encephalitis is another form of viral encephalitis. It is caused by various viruses that are carried by insects (such as mosquitoes and ticks). Unlike herpes, arboviral infections are seasonal, occurring primarily in summer and early fall, and are clustered in specific regions, such as in the case of St. Louis encephalitis.

In rare instances, bacterial, fungal, parasitic, or rickettsial infections cause encephalitis. Cancer or even exposure to certain drugs or toxins may also cause encephalitis,

What are the symptoms of encephalitis?

Symptoms in milder cases of encephalitis usually include:
- fever
- headache
- poor appetite
- loss of energy
- a general sick feeling

In more severe cases of encephalitis, a person is more likely to experience high fever and any of a number of symptoms that relate to the central nervous system, including:
- severe headache
- nausea and vomiting
- stiff neck
- confusion
- disorientation
- personality changes
- convulsions (seizures)
- problems with speech or hearing
- hallucinations
- memory loss
- drowsiness
- coma

It's harder to detect some of these symptoms in infants, but important signs to look for include:
- vomiting
- a full or bulging soft spot (fontanel)
- crying that doesn't stop or that seems worse when an infant is picked up or handled
- body stiffness

Because encephalitis can follow or accompany common viral illnesses, there sometimes are signs and symptoms of these illnesses beforehand. But often, the encephalitis appears without warning.

How is encephalitis diagnosed?

To diagnose encephalitis, the doctor will consider the patient's symptoms and ask about any recent illnesses and possible exposure to viruses — being near others who are ill or near mosquitoes or ticks, for example.

The doctor may also order a magnetic resonance imaging (MRI) scan, spinal tap, or an electroencephalogram (EEG).

Blood tests to check for the presence of bacteria or viruses and immune cells produced in response to them can also be helpful.

An analysis of a brain tissue sample (biopsy) may be necessary to confirm the diagnosis. It is very important to identify the type of encephalitis so that appropriate treatment can be given.

What are the treatments for encephalitis?

Some kids with very mild encephalitis can be monitored at home, but most will need care in a hospital, usually in an intensive care unit (ICU). Doctors will carefully monitor their blood pressure, heart rate, and breathing, as well as their body fluids, to prevent further swelling of the brain.

Because antibiotics aren't effective against viruses, they aren't used to treat most forms of encephalitis. However, antiviral drugs can be used to treat some forms of encephalitis, especially the type caused by the herpes simplex virus. Corticosteroids may also be used in some cases to reduce brain swelling. If a child is having seizures, anticonvulsants might be given. Over-the-counter (OTC) medications, like acetaminophen, can be used to treat fever and headaches.

Many people with encephalitis make a full recovery. In some cases, swelling of the brain can lead to permanent brain damage and lasting complications like learning disabilities, speech problems, memory loss, or lack of muscle control. Speech, physical, or occupational therapy may be needed in these cases. It's difficult to predict the outcome for each patient at the time the illness begins, but some types of encephalitis are known to cause more serious complications, such as Japanese encephalitis.

With proper care, many people recover from encephalitis. Infants and elderly people are at greater risk of sustaining permanent brain damage.

Rarely, if the brain damage is severe, encephalitis can lead to death. Infants (younger than 1 year old) and adults over 55 are at greatest risk of death from encephalitis.

中英文注释

关键词汇

acetaminophen [ə,si:tə'minəfen] n. 对乙酰氨基酚

arbovirus [ˌɑrbɔ'vairəs] n. 虫媒病毒

chickenpox ['tʃikənpɑks] n. 水痘

coma ['kəʊmə] n. 昏迷

disorientation [dis'ɔriɛntɛʃən] n. 定向障碍

drowsiness ['draʊzinis] n. 嗜睡

fontanel [ˌfɒntə'nel] n. 囟门

fungal ['fʌŋg(ə)l] adj. 真菌的

hallucinations [hɔ:lusineʃənz] n. 幻觉

influenza [ˌinflu'ɛnzə] n. 流行性感冒

measles ['mizəlz] n. 麻疹

mosquito [məs'ki:təu] n. 蚊子

mumps [mʌmps] n. 流行性腮腺炎

parasitic [pærə'sitik] adj. 寄生的

rabies ['rebiz] n. 狂犬病

rickettsial [ri'kɛtsiəl] adj. 立克次体属微生物的

rubella [rʊ'bɛləˈ] n. 风疹

ticks [tik] n. 扁虱

主要短语

antiviral drugs 抗病毒药物

herpes simplex 单纯疱疹

personality changes 人格改变

viral infections 病毒性感染

west nile virus 西尼罗河病毒

闵国文　马志方

50

Epilepsy
癫　病

What is epilepsy?

Seizures — abnormal movements or behavior due to unusual electrical activity in the brain — are a symptom of epilepsy. But not all people who appear to have seizures have epilepsy; epilepsy is a group of related disorders characterized by a tendency for recurrent seizures.

Non-epileptic seizures (called pseudoseizures) are not accompanied by abnormal electrical activity in the brain and may be caused by psychological issues or stress. However, non-epileptic seizures look like true seizures, which makes diagnosis more difficult. Normal EEG readings and lack of response to epileptic drugs are two clues they are not true epileptic seizures. These types of seizure may be treated with psychiatric medications.

Provoked seizures are single seizures that may occur as the result of trauma, low blood sugar (hypoglycemia), low blood sodium, high fever, or alcohol or drug abuse. Fever-related (or febrile) seizures may occur during infancy but are usually outgrown by age 6. After a careful evaluation to estimate the risk of recurrence, patients who suffer a single seizure may not need treatment.

Seizure disorder is a general term used to describe any condition in which seizures may be a symptom. Seizure disorder is a general term that it is often used in place of the term 'epilepsy'.

What causes epilepsy?

There are around 180,000 new cases of epilepsy each year. About 30% occur in children. Children and elderly adults are the ones most often affected.

There is a clear cause for epilepsy in only a minority of the cases. Typically, the known causes of seizure involve some injury to the brain. Some of the main causes of epilepsy include:

- low oxygen during birth
- head injuries that occur during birth or from accidents during youth or adulthood

- brain tumors
- genetic conditions that result in brain injury, such as tuberous sclerosis
- infections such as meningitis or encephalitis
- stroke or any other type of damage to the brain
- abnormal levels of substances such as sodium or blood sugar

In up to 70% of all case of epilepsy in adults and children, no cause can ever be discovered.

Causes of Seizures

Although the underlying causes of epilepsy are usually not known, certain factors are known to provoke seizures in people with epilepsy. Avoiding these triggers can help you avoid seizures and live better with epilepsy:

- missing medication doses
- heavy alcohol use
- cocaine or other drug use, such as ecstasy
- lack of sleep
- other drugs that interfere with seizure medications

For about one out of every two women with epilepsy, seizures tend to occur more around the time of menstrual periods. Changing or adding certain drugs before menstrual periods can help.

What are the symptoms of epilepsy?

While many types of repetitive behavior may represent a neurological problem, a doctor needs to establish whether or not they are seizures.

- **Generalized seizures:** All areas of the brain (the cortex) are involved in a generalized seizure. Sometimes these are referred to as grand mal seizures.
  - The person experiencing such a seizure may cry out or make some sound, stiffen for several seconds to a minute and then have rhythmic movements of the arms and legs. Often the rhythmic movements slow before stopping.
  - Eyes are generally open.
  - The person may appear to not be breathing and actually turn blue. This may be followed by a period of deep, noisy breathes.
  - The return to consciousness is gradual and the person may be confused for quite some time –minutes to hours.
  - Loss of urine is common.
  - The person will frequently be confused after a generalized seizure.
- **Partial or focal seizures:** Only part of the brain is involved, so only part of the body is affected. Depending on the part of the brain having abnormal electrical

activity, symptoms may vary.

- If the part of the brain controlling movement of the hand is involved, then only the hand may show rhythmic or jerky movements.
- If other areas of the brain are involved, symptoms might include strange sensations like a full feeling in the stomach or small repetitive movements such as picking at one's clothes or smacking of the lips.
- Sometimes the person with a partial seizure appears dazed or confused. This may represent a complex partial seizure. The term complex is used by doctors to describe a person who is between being fully alert and unconscious.
- **Absence or petit mal seizures:** These are most common in childhood.
  - Impairment of consciousness is present with the person often staring blankly.
  - Repetitive blinking or other small movements may be present.
  - Typically, these seizures are brief, lasting only seconds. Some people may have many of these in a day.

How is epilepsy diagnosed?

Evaluating patients with epilepsy is aimed at determining which type of seizures they are having (epileptic versus nonepileptic) and their cause. Various seizure types respond best to specific treatments. The diagnosis of epilepsy is based on: the patient's medical history, including any family history of seizures, associated medical conditions, and current medications. Also helpful to the doctor is the input of people who have witnessed a patient's seizures, especially if there is a loss of consciousness.

Some important questions a patient will be asked include:

- At what age did the seizures begin?
- What circumstances surrounded your first seizure?
- What factors seem to bring on the seizures?
- What do you feel before, during, and after the seizures?
- How long do the seizures last?
- Have you been treated for epilepsy before?
- What medications were prescribed and in what dosages?
- Was the treatment effective?

Tests that will be performed include:

- A complete physical and neurological exam of muscle strength, reflexes, eyesight, hearing, and ability to detect various sensations.
- An electroencephalogram (EEG) test, which measures electrical impulses in the brain*.

- Imaging studies of the brain, such as those provided by magnetic resonance imaging (MRI).
- Blood tests to measure red and white blood cell counts, blood sugar, blood calcium, and electrolyte levels; and to evaluate liver and kidney function; blood tests help rule out the presence of other illnesses.
- Other tests, as needed, including magnetic resonance spectroscopy (MRS), positron emission tomography (PET) and single photon emission computed tomography (SPECT).

An important part of the diagnostic process is the electroencephalogram (EEG), because it is the only test that directly detects electrical activity in the brain, and seizures are defined by abnormal electrical activity in the brain. During an EEG, electrodes (small metal disks) are attached to specific locations on your head. The electrodes are attached to a monitor to record the brain's electrical activity. The EEG is useful not only to confirm a diagnosis of epilepsy, but also to determine the type of epilepsy.

A routine EEG only records about 20-30 minutes of brain waves (however, the entire EEG procedure takes about 90 minutes). Because 30 minutes is such a short amount of time, the results of routine EEG studies are often normal, even in people known to have epilepsy. Therefore, prolonged EEG monitoring may be necessary. Some monitors allow the patient to stay at home and continue his or her normal activities.

Prolonged EEG-video monitoring is another diagnostic method. During this type of monitoring, an EEG monitors the brain's activity and cameras videotape body movements and behavior during a seizure. Prolonged monitoring often requires the patient to spend time in a special hospital facility for several days. Prolonged EEG-video monitoring is the only definitive way to diagnose epilepsy.

What are the treatments for epilepsy?

The majority of epileptic seizures are controlled by medication, particularly anticonvulsant drugs. The type of treatment prescribed will depend on several factors, including the frequency and severity of the seizures and the person's age, overall health, and medical history. An accurate diagnosis of the type of epilepsy is also critical to choosing the best treatment.

Drug therapy

Many drugs are available to treat epilepsy, several of which have only recently been released. Although generic drugs are safely used for most medications, anticonvulsants are one category where doctors proceed with caution. Most doctors prefer to use brand name anticonvulsants, but realize that many insurance companies will not cover the cost. As a result, it is acceptable to start taking a generic anticonvulsant medication, but if the desired control is not achieved, the patient should be switched to the brand name drug.

Classic medications used to treat epilepsy include:

- Dilantin or Phenytek
- Phenobarbital
- Tegretol or Carbatrol
- Mysoline
- Zarontin
- Depakene
- Depakote, Depakote ER
- Valium and similar tranquilizers, such as Tranxene and Klonopin

Newer drugs to treat epilepsy include:

- Felbatol
- Fycompa
- Gabitril
- Keppra
- Lamictal
- Lyrica
- Neurontin
- Oxteller XR
- Topamax
- Trileptal
- Zonegran

The choice of drug is most often based on factors like the patient's tolerance of side effects, other illnesses he or she might have, and the medication's delivery method.

Although the different types of epilepsy vary greatly, in general, medications can control seizures in about 70% of patients.

Side effects of epilepsy drugs

Before any epilepsy drug is prescribed, your health care provider will discuss with you the potential benefits, side effects, and risks.

As is true of all drugs, the drugs used to treat epilepsy have side effects. The occurrence of side effects depends on the dose, type of medication, and length of treatment. The side effects are usually more common with higher doses, but tend to be less severe with time as the body adjusts to the medication. Anti-epileptic drugs are usually started at lower doses and increased gradually to make this adjustment easier. One of the best rules in medicine is to "go low and go slow".

There are three types of side effects:

- **Common or predictable side effects.** These are common, nonspecific, and dose-related side effects which occur with any epilepsy drug, because it affects the central nervous system. These side effects include blurry or double vision, fatigue, sleepiness, unsteadiness, and stomach upset.

- **Idiosyncratic side effects.** These are rare and unpredictable reactions which are not dose-related. Most often, these side effects are skin rashes, low blood cell counts, and liver problems.

- **Unique side effects.** These are those that are not shared by other drugs in the same class. For example, Dilantin and Phenytek (phenytoin) can cause the gums to swell and Depakene (valproic acid) can cause hair loss and weight gain. Your doctor will discuss any unique side effects before prescribing the medication.

How long epilepsy treatment lasts

In some types of epilepsy, patients can be taken off treatment after a few years, while other types of epilepsy require lifelong treatment. With few exceptions, patients who are seizure-free for a certain period should be re-evaluated to determine whether the drug can be discontinued. How long the seizure-free period should be varies among the types of epilepsy and is controversial even for a given type. The decision to discontinue a medication also depends on more than the length of the seizure-free period.

What is clear, however, is that epilepsy drugs should at least be considered for discontinuation in patients who are seizure-free for 10 years. If a medication is going to be discontinued, it should be weaned gradually to avoid triggering a seizure.

Surgery for epilepsy

Most patients with epilepsy do not require surgery. However, if seizures are not controlled after a trial of two or three medications (usually accomplished within two years) then re-evaluation is suggested. This information is critical in deciding if epilepsy surgery is an option. Of the 30% of patients whose seizures cannot be controlled with drugs, approximately one third (more than 100,000 in the U.S.) may be candidates for epilepsy surgery. However, only about 3,000 epilepsy surgeries are performed annually.

Before surgery is considered, a comprehensive presurgical exam is performed. This evaluation is performed to ensure that the operation will likely improve the seizures and will not cause damage to essential functions such as speech and memory. The evaluation requires prolonged EEG-video monitoring and other tests to pinpoint the exact location of the injured brain cells causing the seizures. The location of the damaged cells determines whether the surgery can be performed and what technique should be used. The multidisciplinary evaluation is directed by a neurologist specializing in epilepsy (an epileptologist). A patient's eligibility for surgery is determined jointly by the neurosurgeon, neuroradiologist, neuropsychologist, social worker, and epileptologist. The decision to have the surgery is made jointly by the patient and the epileptologist after carefully reviewing the risks and benefits of the procedure.

Surgery is most commonly performed to treat partial epilepsy, since only one area of the brain is involved. During surgery, the area of the brain that triggers the seizures (usually a portion of the anterior temporal lobe) is removed. After surgery, some patients will be completely free of seizures; in others, the seizures will be better controlled. A few patients may need additional surgery.

Other surgical approaches are reserved for specific types of epilepsy and are most often performed in young children. One approach is to remove a large part of one side of the brain (a hemispherectomy); another is to cut the nerve fibers connecting the two sides of the brain (a corpus callosotomy).

Other epilepsy treatment options

The ketogenic diet — a high-fat, low-carb plan — has received much attention lately and is effective for treating certain types of epilepsy. Specifically, it is used most frequently in children with seizures that have not responded to medical therapy. However, the diet requires careful planning and may be difficult to follow, so it is usually not recommended in older children or adults. The diet is usually started in the hospital, and when successful, it is most often maintained for two to three years.

A relatively new treatment involves electrical stimulation of the vagus nerve. This treatment requires minor surgery to implant a stimulator, which is about the size of a silver dollar. The stimulator is placed under the skin in the upper chest, like a pacemaker. The treatment appears to be effective for seizures that do not respond well to medications alone. The degree of effectiveness of the vagus nerve stimulator is approximately the same as medication. Vagus nerve stimulation decreases seizure numbers by half or more in 40% to 50% of patients, but rarely eliminates all seizures. Almost all patients need to continue taking medications after the stimulator has been placed, although many people can take fewer drugs.

中英文注释

关键词汇
anticonvulsant [ˌæntikən'vʌlsənt] adj. 抗惊厥的
electrode [i'lɛktrod] n. 电极片

electroencephalogram (EEG) [i,lektrəʊin'sef(ə)ləgræm] n. 脑电图

encephalitis [ɛn,sɛfə'laitəs] n. 脑炎

epilepsy ['ɛpə'lɛpsi] n. 癫痫

gums [gʌmz] n. 牙龈

hemispherectomy [,hemisfi'rɛktəmi] n. 大脑半球切除术

hypoglycemia [,haipoglai'simiə] n. 低血糖

idiosyncratic [,idiəsiŋ'krætik] adj. 特质的, 特殊的

meningitis [,menin'dʒaitis] n. 脑膜炎

pinpoint ['pinpɔint] n. 精确定位

pseudoseizures [sju:dəʊ'si:ʒəz] n. 假性发作

rhythmic ['riðmik] adj. 有节律的

seizure ['siʒɚ] n. 痫性发作

stiffen ['stifn] vt. vi. 僵硬

witness ['witnəs] n. 目击、见证

keppra 开浦兰（药名）

lamictal 拉莫三嗪（药名）

lyrica 普瑞巴林（药名）

neurontin 加巴喷丁（药名）

topamax 妥泰（药名）

主要短语

absence or petit mal seizures 癫痫小发作或失神发作

complex partial seizure 复杂部分性发作

generalized seizures 全身性大发作

ketogenic diet 生酮饮食

prolonged EEG-video monitoring 长时程视频脑电监测

tuberous sclerosis 结节性硬化症

vagus nerve 迷走神经

闵国文　马志方

51 — Guillain-Barre Syndrome (GBS)
格林巴利综合征

What is GBS?

GBS is a problem with your nervous system. It causes muscle weakness, loss of reflexes, and numbness or tingling in your arms, legs, face, and other parts of your body.

GBS can cause paralysis and lead to death. But most people get better and have few lasting problems.

GBS is rare.

What causes GBS?

Experts don't know what causes GBS. They think that the nerves are attacked by your body's own defense system (the immune system). This is called an autoimmune disease.

In GBS, the immune system attacks the covering (myelin sheath) of certain nerves. This causes nerve damage.

Infections that may trigger GBS

GBS usually begins to affect the nerves after you've had a viral or bacterial infection. Often it is after an infection of the lungs or stomach and intestines.

Infections that may trigger GBS include:

- Campylobacter jejuni, which can cause a type of food poisoning.
- Mycoplasma, which can cause pneumonia.
- Cytomegalovirus (CMV), which can cause fever, chills, sore throat, swollen glands, body aches, and fatigue.
- Epstein-Barr virus (EBV), which can cause mononucleosis (mono).
- Varicella-zoster virus, which can cause chickenpox and shingles.

What are the symptoms of GBS?

Symptoms of GBS include:

- Numbness or tingling in the hands and feet and sometimes around the mouth and lips.

- Muscle weakness on both sides of the body in the legs, arms, and face.
- Difficulty speaking, chewing, and swallowing.
- Inability to move the eyes.
- Back pain.

The first symptoms of GBS include tingling in the fingers and toes and weakness in the arms and legs that may appear several days or weeks after a respiratory or gastrointestinal infection. Tingling is a very common symptom that may be caused by a wide variety of medical problems. But after muscle weakness develops in addition to tingling, GBS becomes a more likely cause of these symptoms. Tingling and weakness may spread to the arms and upper body. GBS can become life-threatening if weakness spreads to muscles that control breathing, heart rate, and blood pressure.

Muscle weakness caused by GBS often gets worse over 1 to 4 weeks before it stabilizes and then gradually improves. In some people, symptoms continue to get worse for up to 3 months.

There are different forms of GBS, but symptoms are often a lot alike. Most GBS symptoms are caused by damage to nerve coverings (demyelination). This causes problems with how messages travel between the brain and the rest of the body.

How is GBS diagnosed?

There are six different subtypes of GBS exist:

Acute inflammatory demyelinating polyneuropathy (AIDP) is the most common form of GBS, and the term is often used synonymously with GBS. It is caused by an auto-immune response directed against Schwann cell membranes.

Miller Fisher syndrome (MFS) is a rare variant of GBS. Accounting for approximately 5% of GBS cases, it manifests as a descending paralysis, proceeding in the reverse order of the more common form of GBS. It usually affects the eye muscles first and presents with the triad of ophthalmoplegia, ataxia, and areflexia. The ataxia predominantly affects the gait and trunk, with the limbs relatively spared. Anti-GQ1b antibodies are present in 90% of cases.

Acute motor axonal neuropathy (AMAN), also known as **Chinese paralytic syndrome**, attacks motor nodes of Ranvier and is prevalent in China and Mexico. It is probably due to an auto-immune response directed against the axoplasm of peripheral nerves. The disease may be seasonal and recovery can be rapid. Anti-GD1a antibodies are present. Anti-GD3 antibodies are found more frequently in AMAN.

Acute motor sensory axonal neuropathy (AMSAN) is similar to AMAN but also affects sensory nerves with severe axonal damage. Like AMAN, it is probably due to an auto-immune response directed against the axoplasm of peripheral nerves. Recovery is slow and often incomplete.

Acute panautonomic neuropathy is the most rare variant of GBS, sometimes accompanied by encephalopathy. It is associated with a high mortality rate, owing to cardiovascular involvement, and associated dysrhythmias. Frequently occurring symptoms include impaired sweating, lack of tear formation, photophobia, dryness of nasal and oral mucosa, itching and peeling of skin, nausea, dysphagia, and constipation unrelieved by laxatives or alternating with diarrhea. Initial nonspecific symptoms of lethargy, fatigue, headache, and decreased initiative are followed by autonomic symptoms including orthostatic lightheadedness, blurring of vision, abdominal pain, diarrhea, dryness of eyes, and disturbed micturition. The most common symptoms at onset are related to orthostatic intolerance, as well as gastrointestinal and sudomotor dysfunction (Suarez et al. 1994). Parasympathetic impairment (abdominal pain, vomiting, constipation, ileus, urinary retention, dilated unreactive pupils; loss of accommodation) may also be observed.

Bickerstaff's brainstem encephalitis (BBE) is a further variant of GBS. It is characterized by acute onset of ophthalmoplegia, ataxia, disturbance of consciousness, hyperreflexia or Babinski's sign. The course of the disease can be monophasic or remitting-relapsing. Large, irregular hyperintense lesions located mainly in the brainstem, especially in the pons, midbrain and medulla, are described in the literature. Despite severe initial presentation, BBE usually has a good prognosis. Magnetic resonance imaging (MRI) plays a critical role in the diagnosis of BBE. A considerable number of BBE patients have associated axonal GBS, indicative that the two disorders are closely related and form a continuous spectrum.

The diagnosis of GBS usually depends on findings such as rapid development of muscle paralysis, areflexia, absence of fever, and a likely inciting event. Cerebrospinal fluid analysis (through a lumbar spinal puncture) and electrodiagnostic tests of nerves and muscles (such as nerve conduction studies) are common tests ordered in the diagnosis of GBS.

Testing

In cerebrospinal fluid, characteristic findings include albumino-cytological dissociation. As opposed to infectious causes, this is an elevated protein level (100–1000 mg/dL), without an accompanying increased cell count (absence of pleocytosis). A sustained increased white blood cell count may indicate an alternative diagnosis such as infection.

Electromyography (EMG) and nerve conduction studies (NCS) may show prolonged distal latencies, conduction slowing, conduction block, and temporal dispersion of compound action potential in demyelinating cases. F waves and

H-reflexes may be prolonged or absent. Needle EMG is frequently normal in acute cases. Reduced, neuropathic recruitment in weak muscles can be seen. Fibrillations will be seen on needle EMG if there is some axonal injury after 3 to 4 weeks. In primary axonal damage, the findings include reduced amplitude of the action potentials without conduction slowing.

Criteria

Features required for diagnosis are progressive weakness in legs and often arms and are flexia (the absence of deep tendon reflexes).

Features that strongly support diagnosis are progression of symptoms over days to 4 weeks, relative symmetry of symptoms, mild sensory symptoms or signs, cranial nerve involvement (especially bilateral weakness of facial muscles), autonomic dysfunction, pain (often present), high concentration of protein in CSF, and typical electrodiagnostic features.

Features that should raise doubt about the diagnosis include severe pulmonary dysfunction with limited limb weakness at onset, severe sensory signs with limited weakness at onset, bladder or bowel dysfunction at onset, fever at onset, sharp sensory level, slow progression with limited weakness without respiratory involvement (subacute inflammatory demyelinating polyneuropathy or CIDP is more likely), marked persistent asymmetry of weakness, persistent bladder or bowel dysfunction, increased number of mononuclear cells in CSF ($>50\times106/L$), and polymorphonuclear cells in CSF.

How is it treated?

Supportive care is the cornerstone of successful management in the acute patient. Of greatest concern is respiratory failure due to paralysis of the diaphragm, the muscle most important for breathing. Intubation may be needed when there is evidence of impending failure of the muscles of breathing – when the vital capacity (VC) is less than 20 ml/kg, the negative inspiratory force (NIF) is less negative (i.e., closer to zero) than -25 cmH_2O, more than 30% decrease in either VC or NIF within 24 hours, rapid progression of disorder, or autonomic instability.

Subsequent treatment consists of attempting to reduce the body's attack on the nervous system, either by plasmapheresis, filtering antibodies out of the blood stream, or by administering intravenous immunoglobulins (IVIg), to neutralize harmful antibodies and inflammation causing disease. These two treatments are equally effective and a combination of the two is not significantly better than either alone. Glucocorticoids have not been found to be effective in GBS. Treatment is usually begun as soon as the diagnosis is made. Plasmapheresis hastens recovery when used within 4 weeks of the onset of symptoms. IVIg has equivalent efficacy to plasmapheresis when started within 2 weeks of the onset of symptoms, and has fewer complications. IVIg is usually used first because of its ease of administration and safety profile. The use of intravenous immunoglobulins is not without risk, occasionally causing hepatitis, or in rare cases, renal failure if used for longer than five days.

Following the acute phase, treatment often consists of rehabilitation with the help of a multidisciplinary team to focus on improving activities of daily living (ADLs). Occupational therapists may offer equipment (such as wheelchair and special cutlery) to help the patient achieve ADL independence. Physiotherapists assist to correct functional movement, avoiding harmful compensations that might have a negative effect in the long run. There is also some evidence supporting physiotherapy in helping patients with GBS regain strength, endurance, and gait quality, as well as helping them prevent contractures, bedsores, and cardiopulmonary difficulties. Speech and language therapists help regain speaking and swallowing ability, especially if the patient was intubated or received a tracheostomy.

How long will it take to recover?

You may need 3 to 6 months or longer to recover from GBS. And you may have to wait several months before you can return to your regular activities.

Many people have long-term effects from GBS, such as numbness in the toes and fingers. In most cases, these problems won't get in the way of your daily life. Some people have more serious problems, such as long-term weakness or balance problems..

Support at home is important during this time. You may need some help with some of your activities and chores until you're stronger.

Regular exercise can help you strengthen your weakened muscles. Talk to your doctor about exercising during your recovery. If you have severe muscle weakness, you may need physical or occupational therapy.

中英文注释

关键词汇

areflexia [ˌeiriˈfleksiə] n. 无反射

ataxia [əˈtæksiə] n. 共济失调

bedsore [ˈbɛdsɔː] n. 褥疮

contractures [ˈkɒntræktʃəz] n. 挛缩

cytomegalovirus [ˌsaitə(ʊ)ˈmeg(ə)lə(ʊ)ˌvairəs] n. 巨细胞病毒（CMV）

electromyography [iˌlɛktromaiˈagrəfi] n. 肌电图（EMG）

encephalopathy [ɛnˌsɛfəˈlapəθi] n. 脑病

hyperreflexia [ˌhaipəriˈfleksiə] n. 反射亢进

micturition [ˌmiktjʊəˈriʃən] n. 尿频

mononucleosis (mono) [ˌmɒnə(ʊ)njuːkliˈəʊsis] n. 单核细胞增多症

monophasic [ˌmɔnəuˈfeizik] adj. 单相的

mycoplasma [ˌmɑikə(ʊ)ˈplæzmə] n. 支原体

neutralize [ˈnʊtrəˈlaiz] vt. vi. 中和

numbness [ˈnʌmnəs] n. 麻木

ophthalmoplegia [ɔfˌθælməˈpliːdʒiə] n. 眼外肌麻痹

plasmapheresis [ˌplæzməˈfɛrisis] n. 血浆置换

polymorphonuclear [ˌpɒliˌmɔːfə(ʊ)ˈnjuːkliə] n. 多形核细胞

tingling [ˈtiŋgliŋ] n. 刺痛，麻刺感

主要短语

acute inflammatory demyelinating polyneuropathy (AIDP) 急性炎症性脱髓鞘性多发性神经病

acute motor axonal neuropathy (AMAN) 急性运动轴索性神经病

acute motor sensory axonal neuropathy (AMSAN) 急性感觉轴索性神经病

acute panautonomic neuropathy 急性自主神经系统性神经病

Bickerstaff's brainstem encephalitis (BBE) 脑干脑炎

campylobacter jejuni 空肠弯曲杆菌

cerebrospinal fluid 脑脊液

food poisoning 食物中毒

intravenous immunoglobulins (IVIg) 静脉注射用丙种球蛋白

Miller Fisher syndrome (MFS) 米勒费雪综合征

muscle weakness 肌无力

myelin sheath 髓鞘

varicella-zoster virus 水痘-带状疱疹病毒

闵国文　马志方

52. Myasthenia Gravis
重症肌无力

What is myasthenia gravis?

Myasthenia gravis is a chronic condition that causes muscles to tire and weaken easily. For example, if you have myasthenia gravis, you may notice that during a meal, your jaw muscles become tired and weak, interfering with your ability to chew food. After you have rested for a little while, the muscles may become strong again, allowing you to resume eating.

This waxing-and-waning weakness of muscles, worsening with use and improving with rest, is a hallmark of this particular disease. There typically are periods when you may notice more symptoms (called an exacerbation), interspersed with periods when your symptoms decrease or disappear (remission).

The disease most commonly affects muscles that control eye and eyelid movement, so the first symptoms you notice may be eyelid drooping and/or blurred or doubled vision. Many myasthenia gravis patients start out with this "ocular myasthenia". The majority will go on to develop weakness in other muscle groups within one or two years.

Myasthenia gravis affecting multiple muscle groups throughout the body is called generalized myasthenia gravis. Other common muscle groups that are affected may make it difficult for you to chew, swallow, smile, shrug, lift your arm up, grip, rise to a stand, or walk up stairs. When the muscles necessary for breathing are affected, a patient is said to be in myasthenic crisis. This is a life-threatening situation.

Though anyone can develop myasthenia gravis, those most likely to do so are women between age 20 and 40 or men between 50 and 70. If a woman with myasthenia gravis gives birth, the baby may have some temporary, but potentially life threatening, muscle weakness (neonatal myasthenia) because of antibodies that have transferred from the mother's bloodstream. Typically, during the baby's first weeks of life, the antibodies are cleared from the baby's circulation and the baby develops normal muscle tone and strength.

What causes myasthenia gravis?

Under normal conditions, your nerves direct your muscles to work by sending a message through an area called a receptor. The chemical that delivers the message is called acetylcholine. When acetylcholine binds to a nerve receptor, your muscle knows to contract. In myasthenia gravis, you have fewer acetylcholine receptors than you need.

Myasthenia gravis is considered to be an autoimmune disorder. In an autoimmune disease, some of your body's antibodies (cells in your body that are supposed to be programmed to fight foreign invaders such as bacteria, viruses, or fungi) mistake a part of your own body as foreign, resulting in its destruction. In the case of myasthenia gravis, your antibodies attack and destroy the acetylcholine receptors needed for muscle contraction.

No one knows exactly what causes your body to begin producing the antibodies that destroy acetylcholine receptors. In some cases, the process seems to be related to the thymus gland, which helps produce antibodies.

About 15% of all myasthenia gravis patients are found to have a thymoma, a tumor of the thymus. Although most thymomas are benign, the thymus is usually removed (thymectomy) to prevent the potential spread of cancer. In fact, thymectomy seems to improve symptoms of myasthenia gravis in some patients, even if no tumor is present.

What are the symptoms of myasthenia gravis?

The symptoms of myasthenia gravis include:
- Droopy eyelids (ptosis)
- Double vision (diplopia)
- Difficulty swallowing (dysphagia) with an increased risk of gagging and choking
- Change in the quality of one's voice
- Increasing weakness of a particular muscle group during continuous use of those muscles
- Improved strength of muscles after resting those muscle groups
- Weak cough
- Difficulty breathing, leading to respiratory failure (myasthenic crisis)

How is myasthenia gravis diagnosed?

During a physical exam to diagnose myasthenia gravis, your health care provider may observe signs such as a droopy eyelid, difficulty holding your arms out at shoulder length for a reasonable length of time, or a weak grasp. Blood tests may reveal the presence of acetylcholine-receptor or muscle-specific tyrosine kinase-seropositive (MuSK) antibodies. Specialized tests use electricity to stimulate muscles, and at the same time, measure the strength of muscle contraction.

If you have myasthenia gravis, muscle strength will decrease predictably over the course of testing. You may be given certain medications — edrophonium or neostigmine — as part of a diagnostic exam. In a patient with myasthenia gravis, these drugs will significantly and noticeably improve muscle strength for a short time. This helps to further confirm the diagnosis.

Because other conditions sometimes occur along with myasthenia gravis and can interfere with treatment, your health care provider may order other tests. You may need a CT scan or an MRI to check for a thymoma. You'll be checked for high blood pressure and glaucoma, and you'll probably have your blood tested to see if you have thyroid disease, other autoimmune diseases (such as rheumatoid arthritis or systemic lupus erythematosus), diabetes, kidney problems, or any infections.

What are the treatments for myasthenia gravis?

There is no cure for myasthenia gravis, but it is treated with medications and sometimes surgery. You may be put on a drug called pyridostigmine, that increases the amount of acetylcholine available to stimulate the receptors. Prednisone and other immunosuppressant drugs, like azathioprine, cyclosporine, or cyclophosphamide, may be given to slow down the production of anti-acetylcholine antibodies.

Research is under way to determine if another immunosuppressant, mycophenola-temofetil (CellCept), is as effective. Promising initial results show the drug produces fewer side effects than azathioprine and cyclosporine.

In severe cases, you may need to have your blood sent through a special machine that removes the antibody-containing plasma and replaces it with antibody-free plasma. This is called plasmapheresis. You may also be given a preparation called immunoglobulin through a needle in a vein.

If you have a thymoma, you will need surgery to remove your thymus (thymectomy). In fact, your doctor may recommend that you undergo this surgery even if no tumor is present, because removal of the thymus seems to improve symptoms in many patients.

If you begin to have difficulty breathing due to weakness of the respiratory muscles, you may need to be admitted to the hospital intensive care unit and placed temporarily on a respirator. Myasthenic crisis often occurs when you develop a severe infection, so you'll probably need to be treated with antibiotics as well.

Situations that affect myasthenia gravis include:

- Changes in thyroid function
- Surgery
- Radiation therapy
- Infection

Certain medications can exacerbate symptoms of myasthenia gravis, including:

- Antibiotics (particularly those called aminoglycosides)
- Narcotic drugs
- Penicillamine
- Magnesium
- Anesthetic drugs
- Muscle relaxants
- Some drugs used to treat heart arrhythmias

Some women notice that their symptoms worsen around the time of their menstrual period. Pregnancy's effect on myasthenia gravis is unpredictable. About one-third of all women have an improvement in their symptoms, one-third have no change, and one-third get worse.

中英文注释

关键词汇

acetylcholine [ˌæsətil'kolin] n. 乙酰胆碱

azathioprine [ˌæzə'θaiəˌprin] n. 硫唑嘌呤

benign [bi'nain] adj. 良性的

diplopia [di'pləʊpiə] n. 复视

dysphagia [dis'feidʒiə] n. 吞咽困难

edrophonium [ˌedrə'fəʊniəm] n. 滕喜龙（药名）

glaucoma [glɔː'kəʊmə] n. 青光眼

neostigmine [ˌniə'stigmin] n. 新斯的明（药名）

ptosis ['təʊsis] n. 上睑下垂

pyridostigmine [ˌpiridə(ʊ)'stigmiːn] n. 溴吡斯的明（药名）

thymoma [θai'məmə] n. 胸腺瘤

aminoglycoside 氨基糖苷类抗生素

主要短语

muscle relaxants 肌松剂

myasthenic crisis 重症肌无力危象

narcotic drugs 毒品

rheumatoid arthritis 类风湿关节炎
systemic lupus erythematosus (SLE) 系统性红斑狼疮
thymus gland 胸腺
thyroid disease 甲状腺疾病

闵国文　马志方

53

Parkinson's Disease
帕 金 森 病

What is Parkinson's disease?

Parkinson's disease, which mostly affects older people but can occur at any age, results from the gradual degeneration of nerve cells in the portion of the midbrain that controls body movements. The first signs are likely to be barely noticeable — a feeling of weakness or stiffness in one limb, perhaps, or a fine trembling of one hand when it is at rest. Eventually, the shaking worsens and spreads, muscles tend to stiffen, and balance and coordination deteriorate. Depression, cognitive issues, and other mental or emotional problems are common as well.

Stages of Parkinson's disease

It may be helpful for people with Parkinson's disease and their families to be familiar with some of the ways the disease is described. Experts describe symptoms and stages of the disease differently.

Parkinson's disease sometimes is described as early, moderate, or advanced.

Early disease describes the stage when a person has a mild tremor or stiffness but is able to continue work or other normal daily activities. This often refers to a person who has been newly diagnosed with Parkinson's disease.

Moderate disease describes the stage when a person begins to experience limited movement. A person with moderate Parkinson's disease may have a mild to moderate tremor with slow movement.

Advanced disease describes the stage when a person is significantly limited in his or her activity, despite treatment. Daily changes in symptoms, medicine side effects that limit treatment, and loss of independence in activities of daily living are common. A person with advanced Parkinson's disease may have significant changes in posture and movement, speech problems, and frequent changes in movement.

Parkinson's disease may also be described by five stages:

Stage I: Symptoms affect only one side of the body.

Stage II: Both sides of the body are affected, but posture remains normal.

Stage III: Both sides of the body are affected, and there is mild imbalance during standing or walking. But the person remains independent.

Stage IV: Both sides of the body are affected, and there is disabling instability while standing or walking. The person in this stage requires substantial help.

Stage V: Severe, fully developed disease is present. The person is restricted to a bed or chair.

Medical professionals may refer to this scale when discussing the disease. Parkinson's disease usually begins between the ages of 50 and 65, striking about 1% of the population in that age group; it is slightly more common in men than in women. Medication can treat its symptoms, and the disorder is not directly life-threatening.

What causes Parkinson's disease?

Parkinson's disease affects the way you move. It happens when there is a problem with certain nerve cells in the brain. Normally, these nerve cells make an important chemical called dopamine. Dopamine sends signals to the part of your brain that controls movement. It lets your muscles move smoothly and do what you want them to do. When you have Parkinson's, these nerve cells break down. Then you no longer have enough dopamine, and you have trouble moving the way you want to. Researchers believe that genetics sometimes plays a role in this cellular breakdown. In rare instances, Parkinson's disease may be caused by a viral infection or by exposure to environmental toxins such as pesticides, carbon monoxide, or the metal manganese. But in the great majority of Parkinson's cases, the cause is unknown.

Parkinson's is progressive, which means it gets worse over time. But usually this happens slowly, over a period of many years. And there are good treatments that can help you live a full life.

Parkinson's disease is a form of parkinsonism. This is a more general term used to refer to the set of symptoms that is commonly associated with Parkinson's disease but sometimes stems from other causes. The distinction is important because these other causes of parkinsonism may be treatable, while others do not respond to treatment or medication. Other causes of parkinsonism include:

- An adverse reaction to prescription drugs.
- Use of illegal drugs.
- Exposure to environmental toxins.
- Stroke.
- Thyroid and parathyroid disorders.
- Repeated head trauma (for example, the trauma associated with boxing).
- Brain tumor.
- An excess of fluid around the brain (called hydrocephalus).

- Brain inflammation (encephalitis) resulting from infection.

Parkinsonism may also be present in persons with other neurological conditions, including Alzheimer's disease, amyotrophic lateral sclerosis (ALS, or Lou Gehrig's disease), Creutzfeldt-Jakob disease, Wilson's disease, and Huntington's disease.

Who gets Parkinson's disease?

Approximately one million Americans have Parkinson's disease, including three out of every 100 people over the age of 60. Over 50,000 Americans are diagnosed with Parkinson's disease each year. There is increasing evidence that Parkinson's disease may be inherited (genetically passed on between family members). Men are slightly more likely to develop the disease than women.

The average age at which it is diagnosed is 60. However, about 10%~20% of those diagnosed with Parkinson's disease are under age 50, and about half of those are diagnosed before age 40. When the diagnosis is made early, it is referred to as "young-onset" Parkinson's disease.

What are the symptoms of Parkinson's disease?

Parkinson's disease is a movement disorder that progresses slowly. Some people will first notice a sense of weakness, difficulty walking, and stiff muscles. Others may notice a tremor of the head or hands. Parkinson's is a progressive disorder and the symptoms gradually worsen. The general symptoms of Parkinson's disease include:

- Slowness of voluntary movements, especially in the initiation of such movements as walking or rolling over in bed.
- Decreased facial expression, monotonous speech, and decreased eye blinking.
- A shuffling gait with poor arm swing and stooped posture.
- Unsteady balance; difficulty rising from a sitting position.
- Continuous "pill-rolling" motion of the thumb and forefinger.
- Abnormal tone or stiffness in the trunk and extremities.
- Swallowing problems in later stages.

How is Parkinson's disease diagnosed?

Diagnosing Parkinson's disease is often difficult, especially in its early stages. It has been estimated that nearly 40% of people with the disease may not be diagnosed, and as many as 25% are misdiagnosed. Even as the disease progresses, symptoms may be difficult to assess and may mirror other disorders. For example, tremor may not be apparent while a person is sitting or posture changes may be written off as osteoporosis or simply a sign of aging. Some doctors, who think that tremor is a requirement for diagnosis, may not realize that as many as a third of people with Parkinson's disease may not have tremor.

Furthermore, making the diagnosis is even more difficult since there are currently no sophisticated blood or lab tests available to diagnose the disease. Some tests, such as a CT Scan (computed tomography) or MRI (magnetic resonance imaging), may be used to rule out other disorders that cause similar symptoms. Given these circumstances, a doctor may need to observe the patient over time to recognize signs of tremor and rigidity, and pair them with other characteristic symptoms. The doctor will also compile a comprehensive history of the patient's symptoms, activity, medications, other medical problems, and exposures to toxic chemicals. This will likely be followed up with a rigorous physical exam with concentration on the functions of the brain and nervous system. Tests are conducted on the patient's reflexes, coordination, muscle strength, and mental function. Making a precise diagnosis is essential for prescribing the correct treatment regimen. The treatment decisions made early in the illness can have profound implications on the long-term success of treatment.

Because the diagnosis is based on the doctor's exam of the patient, it is very important that the doctor be experienced in evaluating and diagnosing patients with Parkinson's disease. If Parkinson's disease is suspected, you should see a specialist, preferably a movement disorders trained neurologist.

What are the treatments for Parkinson's disease?

Most Parkinson's disease treatments aim to restore the proper balance of the neurotransmitters acetylcholine and dopamine by increasing dopamine levels. Drugs are the standard way of doing this, but many patients, as their disease worsens, may be candidates for having a brain stimulator surgically implanted.

Conventional medicine for parkinson's disease

Symptoms of Parkinson's disease can often be effectively controlled for years with medication.

Levodopa — also called L-dopa — is the drug most often prescribed. The body metabolizes it to produce dopamine. Giving dopamine directly is ineffective, though; the brain's natural defense blocks it from being used by the body. To suppress nausea and other possible side effects, levodopa is often used in conjunction with a related drug called carbidopa.

But some patients cannot tolerate carbidopa and take levodopa alone. If you take only levodopa, it's important not to take it at the same time as food or vitamins containing vitamin B-6, which interferes with its effectiveness.

Most doctors try to postpone starting patients on levodopa as long as possible, because the drug tends to lose effectiveness over time. However, there is some controversy about waiting to begin treatment with levodopa because it can be so beneficial. Researchers have thus investigated ways to offset the loss of effectiveness.

COMT inhibitors such as tolcapone (Tasmar) and entacapone (Comtan) are drugs that are taken with levodopa. They prolong the duration of symptom relief by blocking the action of an enzyme that breaks down levodopa.

Stalevo is a combination tablet that combines carbidopa/levodopa with entacapone. While carbidopa reduces the side effects of levodopa, entacapone extends the time levodopa is active in the brain.

Dopamine agonists are dopamine-like drugs that directly imitate dopamine's activity in the brain. Pramipexole, rotigotine, and ropinirole used alone or in combination with L-dopa treat the motor symptoms of Parkinson's disease.

Other medications prescribed for Parkinson's disease include apomorphine, benztropine, amantadine, selegiline, and anticholinergic drugs; all can help control various symptoms — in some cases by releasing dopamine from nerve cells, in others by reducing the effects of acetylcholine, a neurotransmitter that can cause a drop in dopamine.

Other types of treatment for Parkinson's disease

Neurologists and neurosurgeons have explored various ways of grafting dopamine-producing cells in the brain of those with Parkinson's disease, rather than trying to correct the neurotransmitter imbalance with drugs. There is research using stem cells for this purpose.

Another surgical technique creates lesions in the globus pallidus or thalamus. These are the parts of the brain involved in Parkinson's disease. This was successful for many years but has mostly been replaced by deep brain stimulation (DBS). In this procedure, a wire is placed deep inside the brain in a specific location depending on the symptoms that need to be treated. DBS can provide dramatic improvements in many people.

Scientists are also investigating the use of glial cell-derived nerve growth factor to treat Parkinson's and other neurodegenerative diseases. This substance is produced naturally by tissues throughout the body. Some experiments indicate that injections of this nerve growth factor may help preserve and even restore nerve cells in the brain and spinal cord — specifically those that produce dopamine and that help initiate muscle movement. Time will tell if this and other research will be beneficial.

Some treatments focus on the effects of the disorder, rather than the causes. Your doctor might refer you to a physical therapist to restore normal body alignment, enhance balance and motor responses, and improve the ability to initiate motion. A physical therapist may also teach muscle-strengthening exercises to help with speaking or swallowing.

In many Parkinson's patients, a weakening of social ties because of physical difficulties can lead to depression. Antidepressants can help. In addition, the American Parkinson Disease Association can provide information about support groups and exercise classes in your area — valuable sources of companionship.

How can Parkinson's disease be prevented?

The prevention of Parkinson's disease is difficult. As researchers have not been able to pinpoint the exact causes for the disease it is difficult to prevent Parkinson's. They are currently researching how genetics and environment affect the likelihood an individual will get Parkinson's disease. Researchers are looking for a biomarker (a biochemical abnormality that all individuals with Parkinson's disease might share) that could be seen through screening techniques or chemical testing. They believe that by taking the following precautions an individual may be able to lower their risk of getting Parkinson's:

Reducing exposure to pesticides and herbicides: Direct contact with pesticides and herbicides has been linked to Parkinson's disease. Studies have shown individuals from rural areas that are exposed to pesticides and herbicides for prolonged amounts of times are at a higher risk of getting Parkinson's.

Increasing/Reducing caffeine levels: New research shows that caffeine may actually help in the prevention of Parkinson's. Researchers studied over 8,000 American men over a 30 year period and found that the men who drank three or more cups of coffee each day were five times less likely to develop Parkinson's. One theory is that caffeine reduces the number of neurotransmitters that damage the brain. On the other hand, a study by the Harvard School of Medical Health found that woman who drank more than five cups of coffee a day were at a higher risk of developing Parkinson's.

Starting/Stopping smoking: Smoking may reduce the risk of some individuals getting Parkinson's disease. An American study found that for individuals with certain genetic profiles, smoking acts as protection against the disease. People without the genetic susceptibility may actually increase their chances of getting Parkinson's if they do smoke however.

Maintaining estrogen levels for women: Researchers now believe that reduced estrogen levels may put some women at a higher risk of getting Parkinson disease. This may explain why menopausal woman who do not take hormone replacement therapy are more likely to develop Parkinson.

Maintaining folate levels: Research found that mice with low vitamin B folate levels developed severe Parkinson's disease symptoms while mice with normal levels remained healthy. Researchers now believe that consuming adequate amounts of folate or folic acid may reduce an individual's risk of developing Parkinson's.

Reducing Exposure to Toxins: Exposure to toxins like manganese dust and MPTP may cause Parkinson's disease. Scientists first became aware of this in the 1980's when heroine addicts using a street drug contaminated with MPTP developed severe symptoms of Parkinson's.

It is hard to prevent Parkinson's disease as researchers have not yet been able to determine what the exact causes of the disease are. They have, however, been able to speculate on ways to prevent the disease based on research. The nature of the disease makes it difficult for researchers to determine exact ways to prevent the disease.

中英文注释

关键词汇

blinking ['bliŋkiŋ] adj. 眨眼的；闪光的

cognitive ['kɒgnitiv] adj. 认知的，认识的

deteriorate [di'tiəriəreit] vi. 恶化，变坏

dopamine ['dəupəmi:n] n. [生化]多巴胺（一种治脑神经病的药物）

encephalitis [en,sefə'laitis; –,kefə–] n. [内科]脑炎

extremities [iks'tremitis] n. 四肢，骨端；末端，极限（extremity 复数形式）；手足

facial ['feiʃ(ə)l] adj. 面部的，表面的；脸的，面部用的 n. 美容，美颜；脸部按摩

herbicide ['hə:bisaid; 'ə:–] n. 灭草剂，除莠剂

hydrocephalus [,haidrə'sef(ə)ləs; –'kef–] n. 脑积水

inherited [in'heritid] adj. 遗传的；继承权的；通过继承得到的

lesion ['li:ʒ(ə)n] n. 损害；身体上的伤害；功能障碍

levodopa [,livə'dopə] n. [药]左旋多巴（等于 L-dopa）

midbrain ['midbrein] n. 中脑

moderate ['mɒd(ə)rət] adj. 稳健的，温和的；适度的，中等的；有节制的

monotonous [mə'nɒt(ə)nəs] adj. 单调的，无抑扬顿挫的；无变化的

neurologist [,njʊə'rɒlədʒist] n. 神经病学家；神经科专门医师

neurosurgeons [,njuərəu'sə:dʒən] n. 神经外科医师

neurotransmitter [,njuərəutrænz'mitə] n. [生理]神经递质；[生理]神经传递素

osteoporosis [,ɒstiəupə'rəusis] n. 骨质疏松症

parathyroid [pærə'θairɒid] adj. 副甲状腺的；n. 甲状旁腺

pesticide ['pestisaid] n. 杀虫剂

regimen ['redʒimən] n. [医]养生法；生活规则；政体；支配

rigorous ['rɪg(ə)rəs] adj. 严格的，严厉的；严密的；严酷的

stiffness ['stɪfnɪs] n. 僵硬；坚硬；不自然；顽固

thalamus ['θæləməs] n.［解剖］丘脑

thyroid ['θaɪrɒɪd] n. 甲状腺；甲状软骨；甲状腺

toxin ['tɒksɪn] n. 毒素

tremor ['tremə] n.［医］震颤；颤动

主要短语

amyotrophic lateral sclerosis (ALS) 肌萎缩性脊髓侧索硬化症

deep brain stimulation (DBS) 深部脑刺激

globus pallidus［解剖］苍白球

Parkinson's disease 帕金森氏病；震颤性麻痹

李 丹

Acquired Immunodeficiency Syndrome (AIDS)

54

获得性免疫缺陷综合征

What is AIDS?

AIDS stands for the acquired immunodeficiency syndrome. It is caused by HIV (Human Immunodeficiency Virus). The virus is passed from one person to another through blood-to-blood and sexual contact. After getting into the body, the virus kills or damages cells of the body's immune system, and occurs when the virus has destroyed so much of the body's defenses that immune-cell counts fall to critical levels or certain life-threatening infections or cancers develop.

How about the HIV virology?

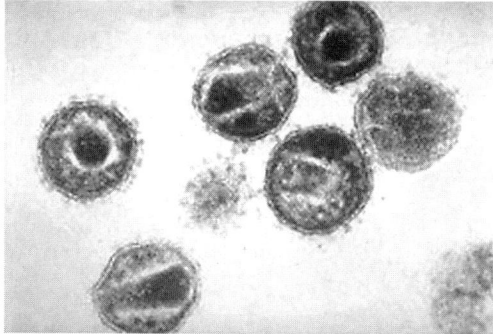

HIV is a member of the genusLentivirus. Upon entry into the target cell, the viral RNA genome is converted (reverse transcribed) into double-stranded DNA by a virally encoded reverse transcriptase that is transported along with the viral genome in the virus particle. The resulting viral DNA is then imported into the cell nucleus and integrated into the cellular DNA by a virally encoded integrase and host co-factors. Once integrated, the virus may become latent, allowing the virus and its host cell to avoid detection by the immune system. Alternatively, the virus may be transcribed, producing new RNA genomes and viral proteins that are packaged and released from the cell as new virus particles that begin the replication cycle anew.

Two types of HIV have been characterized: HIV-1 and HIV-2. HIV-1 is the virus that was originally discovered. It is more virulent, more infective, and is the cause of the majority of HIV infections globally. The lower infectivity of HIV-2 as compared with HIV-1 implies that fewer people exposed to HIV-2 will be infected per exposure. Because of its relatively poor capacity for transmission, HIV-2 is largely confined to West Africa.

What is the epidemiology of AIDS?

HIV disease continues to be a serious health issue for parts of the world. Worldwide, there were about 2.5 million new cases of HIV in 2011. About 34.2 million people are living with HIV around the world. In 2010, there were about 1.8 million deaths in persons with AIDS, and nearly 30 million people with AIDS have died worldwide since the epidemic began. Even though Sub-Saharan Africa bears the biggest burden of HIV/AIDS, countries in South and Southeast Asia, Eastern Europe and Central Asia, and those in Latin America are significantly affected by HIV and AIDS.

There are currently an estimated 780,000 people living with HIV in China. During 2011 around 28,000 people died from AIDS. These numbers must be considered in the context of China's extremely large population which is estimated at around 1.3 billion. Although China's HIV epidemic remains one of low prevalence overall, there are pockets of high infection among specific sub-populations and the danger of the epidemic spreading further into the general population persists. This became particularly evident in 2009 when China reported that AIDS had become the country's leading cause of death among infectious diseases for the first time ever, surpassing both tuberculosis and rabies.

Sources of Infection

AIDS patients and asymptomatic carriers are source of infection, especially the latter. Virus is mainly present in the blood, semen, vaginal secretions and in the uterus. Other body fluids such as saliva, tears and milk also contain virus.

Route of transmission

HIV can be spread in a number of ways, however, only certain fluids-blood, semen (cum), pre-seminal fluid (pre-cum), rectal fluids, vaginal fluids, and breast milkfroman HIV-infected person can transmit HIV.

- Unprotected penetrative sex: HIV is spread most commonly by having unprotected sex with an infected partner. The virus can enter the body through the lining of the vagina, vulva, penis, rectum, or mouth during sex. HIV can infect anyone who practices risky behaviors, such as: Having sexual contact, including oral sex, with an infected person without using a condom. Having sexual contact with someone whose HIV status is unknown.

- Infected Blood: Injection or transfusion of contaminated blood or blood products, donations of semen (artificial insemination), skin grafts or organ transplants taken from someone who is infected.

- Contaminated Needles: Sharing unsterilizedinjection equipment that has previously been used by someone who is infected.

- Mother to Child: Women can transmit HIV to their babies during pregnancy or child birth. Approximately one-quarter to one-third of all untreated pregnant women infected with HIV will pass the infection to their babies. HIV transmission to babies can also occur through the breast milk of mothers infected with the virus. If the mother takes certain drugs during pregnancy, she can significantly reduce the chances that her baby will get infected. If healthcare providers treat HIV-infected pregnant women and deliver their babies by cesarean section, the chances of the baby being infected can be reduced to a rate of 1 percent.

How about the pathogenesis and pathology of AIDS?

After the virus enters the body there is a period of rapid viral replication, leading to an abundance of virus in the peripheral blood. During primary infection, the level of HIV may reach several million virus particles per milliliter of blood. This response is accompanied by a marked drop in the number of circulating CD4+ T cells. The acute viremia is almost invariably associated with activation of CD8+ T cells, which kill HIV-infected cells, and subsequently with antibody production, or seroconversion. The CD8+ T cell response is thought to be important in controlling virus levels, which peak and then decline, as the CD4+ T cell counts recover. A good CD8+ T cell response has been linked to slower disease progression and a better prognosis, though it does not eliminate the virus.

The pathophysiology of AIDS is complex. Ultimately, HIV causes AIDS by depleting CD4+ T cells. This weakens the immune system and allowsopportunistic infections. T cells are essential to the immune response and without them, the body cannot fight infections or kill cancerous cells. The mechanism of CD4+ T cell depletion differs in the acute and chronic phases. During the acute phase, HIV-induced cell lysis and killing of infected cells by cytotoxic T cells accounts for CD4+ T cell depletion, although apoptosis may also be a factor. During the chronic phase, the consequences of generalized immune activation coupled with the gradual loss of the ability of the immune system to generate new T cells appear to account for the slow decline in CD4+ T cell numbers.

Although the symptoms of immune deficiency characteristic of AIDS do not appear for years after a person is infected, the bulk of CD4+ T cell loss occurs during the first weeks of infection, especially in the intestinal mucosa, which harbors the majority of the lymphocytes found in the body. The reason for the preferential loss of mucosal CD4+ T cells is that the majority of mucosal CD4+ T cells express the CCR5 protein which HIV uses as aco-receptor to gain access to the cells, whereas only a small fraction of CD4+ T cells in the bloodstream do so.

What are the symptoms of AIDS?

Acute infection

The initial period following the contraction of HIV is called acute HIV, primary HIV or acute retroviral syndrome. Many individuals develop an influenza-like illness a mononucleosis-like illness 2~4 weeks post exposure while others have no significant symptoms. Symptoms occur in 40%~90% of cases and most commonly include fever, large tender lymph nodes, throat inflammation, a rash, headache, and/or sores of the mouth and genitals. The rash, which occurs in 20%~50% of cases, presents itself on the trunk and is maculopapular, classically. Some people also develop opportunistic infections at this stage. Gastrointestinal symptoms such as nausea, vomiting or diarrhea may occur, as may neurological symptoms of peripheral neuropathy or Guillain-Barre syndrome. The duration of the symptoms varies, but is usually one or two weeks.

Due to their nonspecific character, these symptoms are not often recognized as signs of HIV infection. Even cases that do get seen by a family doctor or a hospital are often misdiagnosed as one of the many common infectious diseases with overlapping symptoms. Thus, it is recommended that HIV be considered in patients presenting an unexplained fever who may have risk factors for the infection.

Clinical latency

The initial symptoms are followed by a stage called clinical latency, asymptomatic HIV, or chronic HIV. Without treatment, this second stage of the natural history of HIV infection can last from about three years to over 20 years (on average, about eight years). While typically there are few or no symptoms at first, near the end of this stage many people experience fever, weight loss, gastrointestinal problems and muscle pains. Between 50% and 70% of people also develop persistent generalized lymphadenopathy, characterized by unexplained, non painful enlargement of more than one group of lymph nodes (other than in the groin) for over three to six months.

Although most HIV-1 infected individuals have a detectable viral load and in the absence of treatment will eventually progress to AIDS, a small proportion (about 5%) retain high levels of CD4+ T cells (T helper cells) without antiretroviral therapy for more than 5 years. These individuals are classified as HIV controllers or long-term nonprogressors (LTNP). Another group is those who also maintain a low or undetectable viral load without anti-retroviral treatment who are known as "elite controllers" or "elite suppressors". They represent approximately 1 in 300 infected persons.

Acquired immunodeficiency syndrome

Acquired immunodeficiency syndrome (AIDS) is defined in terms of either a CD4+ T cell count below 200 cells per μl or the occurrence of specific diseases in association with an HIV infection. In the absence of specific treatment, around half of people infected with HIV develop AIDS within ten years. The most common initial conditions that alert to the presence of AIDS are pneumocystis pneumonia (40%), cachexia in the form of HIV wasting syndrome (20%) and esophageal candidiasis. Other common signs include recurring respiratory tract infections.

Opportunistic infections may be caused by bacteria, viruses, fungi and parasites that are normally controlled by the immune system. Which infections occur partly depends on what organisms are common in the person's environment. These infections may affect nearly every organ system.

People with AIDS have an increased risk of developing various viral induced cancers including: Kaposi's sarcoma, Burkitt's lymphoma, primary central nervous system lymphoma, and cervical cancer. Kaposi's sarcoma is the most common cancer occurring in 10% to 20% of people with HIV. The second most common cancer is lymphoma which is the cause of death of nearly 16% of people with AIDS and is the initial sign of AIDS in 3% to 4%. Both these cancers are associated with human herpesvirus. Cervical cancer occurs more frequently in those with AIDS due to its association withhuman papillomavirus (HPV).

Additionally, people with AIDS frequently have systemic symptoms such as prolonged fevers, sweats (particularly at night), swollen lymph nodes, chills, weakness, and weight loss. Diarrhea is another common symptom present in about 90% of people with AIDS. They can also be affected by diverse psychiatric and neurological symptoms independent of opportunistic infections and cancers.

How to diagnose AIDS?

Infection with HIV is a multisystem disease. Making a diagnosis of HIV requires a synopsis of clinical information and the results of laboratory tests.

Typical clinical manifestation

Clinical AIDS in an adult is defined as an individual who has been identified as meeting the two criteria below: Positive test for HIV infection by two tests based on preferably two different antigens. Any one of the following criteria:

- Weight loss of 10% body weight or cachexia, not known to be due to a condition unrelated to HIV infection. Chronic diarrhea of one month duration, intermittent or constant.
- Disseminated, miliary or extrapulmonary tuberculosis.
- Candidiasis of the oesophagus diagnosable as dysphagia odynophagia and oral candidiasis.
- Neurological impairment restricting daily activities, not known to be duo to a condition unrelated to HIV.
- Kaposis sarcoma.

Although symptomatic HIV infection can be recognized without laboratory testing, wherever HIV testing is available and affordable it can be used to substantiate the clinical suspicion.

Laboratory Diagnosis

- Antibody Tests: The most common HIV tests look for HIV antibodies in your body, rather than looking for HIV itself:

  Enzyme immunoassay (EIA) tests use blood, oral fluid, or urine to detect HIV antibodies. Results for these tests can take up to two weeks.

  Rapid HIV antibody tests also use blood, oral fluid, or urine to detect HIV antibodies. Results for these tests can take 10–20 minutes.

  If you get a positive result from either of these tests, you will need to take another test, called a Western blot test, to confirm that result. It can take up to two weeks to confirm a positive result.
- Antigen Tests: These tests are not as common as antibody tests, but they can be used to diagnose HIV infection earlier—from 1-3 weeks after you are first infected with HIV. Antigen tests require a blood sample.
- PCR Test (Polymerase chain reaction test): This test detects the genetic material of HIV itself, and can identify HIV in the blood within 2-3 weeks of infection.

What is the treatment for AIDS?

There is currently no cure or effective HIV vaccine. Treatment consists of high active antiretroviral therapy (HAART) which slows progression of the disease and as of 2010 more than 6.6 million people were taking them in low and middle income countries. Treatment also includes preventive and active treatment of opportunistic infections.

Antiviral therapy

- Nucleoside Reverse Transcriptase Inhibitors (NRTI)

  These drugs interrupt the virus from duplicating, which may slow the spread of

HIV in the body. They include:

Abacavir (Ziagen, ABC)

Didanosine (Videx, dideoxyinosine, ddI)

Emtricitabine (Emtriva, FTC)

Lamivudine (Epivir, 3TC)

Stavudine (Zerit, d4T)

Tenofovir (Viread, TDF)

Zalcitabine (Hivid, ddC)

Zidovudine (Retrovir, ZDV or AZT)

Combinations of NRTIs make it possible to take lower doses and maintain effectivenss. These drugs include Combivir (Zidovudine and Lamivudine), Trizivir (Zidovudine, Lamivudine and Abacavir), Epzicom (Abacavir and Lamivudine) and Truvada (Tenofovir and Lamivudine). We expect more combination drugs to be available in the future.

- Non-Nucleoside Reverse Transcriptase Inhibitors (NNRTI)

  Non-nucleoside reverse transcriptase inhibitors (NNRTIs) block the infection of new cells by HIV. These drugs may be prescribed in combination with other anti-retroviral drugs. NNRTs include:

  Delvaridine (Rescriptor, DLV)

  Efravirenz (Sustiva, EFV)

  Nevirapine (Viramune, NVP)

- Protease Inhibitors (PI)

  These FDA-approved drugs interrupt virus replication at a later step in the virus life cycle. Protease inhibitors include:

  Amprenavir (Agenerase, APV)

  Atazanavir (Reyataz, ATV)

  Fosamprenavir (Lexiva, FOS)

  Indinavir (Crixivan, IDV)

  Lopinavir (Kaletra, LPV/r)

  Ritonavir (Norvir, RIT)

  Saquinavir (Fortovase, Invirase, SQV)

- Other AIDS Medications

  Fusion Inhibitors: Fusion inhibitors are a new class of drugs that act against HIV by preventing the virus from fusing with the inside of a cell, preventing it from replicating. The group of drugs includes Enfuvirtide, also known as Fuzeon or T-20.

  Highly Active Antiretroviral Therapy (HAART): In 1996, highly active antiretroviral therapy (HAART) was introduced for people with HIV and AIDS. HAART — often referred to as the anti-HIV "cocktail" — is a combination of three or more drugs, such as protease inhibitors and other anti-retroviral medications. The treatment is highly effective in slowing the rate at which the HIV virus replicates itself, which may slow the spread of HIV in the body. The goal of HAART is to reduce the amount of virus in your body, or the viral load, to a level that can no longer be detected with blood tests.

Treatment of Complications

- Pneumocystis Carinii Pneumonia (PCP)

  The most effective treatment for PCP is a combination of the drugs trimethoprim and sulfamethoxazole (TMP-SMX). Unfortunately, many people are allergic to the sulfur in sulfamethoxazole. Alternative treatments for PCP include pentamidine, clindamycin-primaquine, trimethoprim (TMP)-dapsone, Trimetrexate-leucovorin, aerosolized pentamidine (NebuPent) and prednisone, which can be taken to control the symptoms of PCP.

- Tuberculosis (TB)

  The treatment for tuberculosis depends on whether the infection is latent or active. Latent tuberculosis is treated with isoniazid (which is usually taken with pyridoxine to help prevent peripheral neuropathy) or the combination of rifampin and pyrazinamide. Active tuberculosis is usually treated with a combination of four drugs: isoniazid, rifampin, pyrazinamide and ethambutol. Pyridoxine is also taken to prevent peripheral neuropathy. Rifabutin has fewer drug-drug interactions with protease inhibitors. Patients on protease inhibitor regimens should receive rifabutin instead of rifampin for TB treatme. Pyridoxine is also taken as an adjunct to isoniazid to prevent peripheral neuropathy.

- Herpes Simplex Virus (HSV)

  Herpes cannot be cured but it can be treated. There are three treatments available: acyclovir, valacyclovir and famciclovir. Therapy should be started within 48 to 72 hours of onset of symptoms and continued until lesions are healed, particularly in the immunocompromised, HIV population. In some rare cases herpes does not respond to these drugs, probably due to the emergence of resistant strains. The most common treatment for acyclovir-resistant herpes is foscarnet. Foscarnet is available in an intravenous form only and should be reserved for patients who have failed initial treatments of choice.

  Therapy should be continued until all lesions are healed, particularly in the immunocompromised, HIV population. Treatment of genital herpes with topical antiviral creams is not recommended.

- Candidiasis

  The three most common types of candidiasis are oral, vaginal and esophageal candidiasis. Oral candidiasis (thrush) is treated with liquids or lozenges containing clotrimazole, nystatin ormiconazole.

  If these drugs are unsuccessful in the HIV-patient, more potent systemic drugs such asitraconazole or fluconaozle oral suspension can be used. Ketoconazole and itraconazole capsules may be used as second-line therapy. Increasingly, azole resistance has been seen, and treatment with higher fluconazole doses (i.e., 800 mg/day) may be needed.

  Uncomplicated vaginal candidiasis can treated with a short course (1 to 3 days) of vaginal cream or vaginal suppository containing clotrimazole or other topical azole. If unsuccessful, more potent drugs such as oral fluconazole can be used.

- Human Papillomavirus (HPV) - Genital Warts

  Immunocompromised patients can be resistant to standard HPV treatment and recurrence is possible. It is important to treat HPV in HIV+ patients to lessen the likelihood of development of squamous cell carcinoma. Treatment depends upon extent of lesions and location (internal or external). Extended treatment periods, a combination of drugs, cryotherapy, or surgical removal may be required in this patient population.

  Topical medications such as podophyllotoxin, trichloroacetic acid, and imiquimod are used only for the treatment of genital warts. Podophyllum is not recommended for use anymore due to mutagenic potential. The quadrivalent HPV vaccine Gardasil is currently being investigated for use in HIV+ women.

  Other treatments available for refractory HPV in HIV+ patients are procedures to remove or destroy irregular cells such as those that make up genital warts or cervical cancer. Treatment depends on the location and the severity of the disease and can include cryotherapy, laser treatment, LEEP (loop electrical excision procedure), surgery/cold-knife cone biopsy or radical surgery/radiation/chemotherapy.

- Kaposi's Sarcoma (KS)

  KS cutaneous lesions of the skin do not necessarily need to be treated.

  There are localized therapies available such as alitretinoin (Panretin Gel) or locally injected vinblastine, which treat the lesions, but are generally not effective in prevention. Systemic therapy can treat and prevent the lesions but has serious side effects. KS lesions in the digestive tract and in the lungs require systemic therapy such as antiretroviral therapy (HAART), Interferon alfa (Roferon-A, Intron A), liposomal chemotherapy (Doxil or DaunoXome) or standard chemotherapy (doxorubicin, vincristine, bleomycin, etoposide, paclitaxel).

- Cryptococcal Meningitis

  Drugs used in the treatment of Cryptococcal meningitis include amphotericin B, flucytosine and fluconazole.

- Toxoplasmosis

  Toxoplasmosis is treated with pyrimethamine and sulfadiazine.

- Salmonellosis

  Salmonellosis (food poisoning) is an infection caused by the salmonella bacterium, which is contracted from contaminated food or water. Symptoms include severe diarrhea, fever, chills, abdominal pain and sometimes vomiting. Salmonellosis is treated with antibiotics such as ciprofloxacin, ampicillin, ceftiraxone and sulfamethoxazole/trimethoprim. Resistance may occur in some strains, so susceptibility should be checked.

How to prevent AIDS?

Sexual contact

Consistent condom use reduces the risk of HIV transmission by approximately 80% over the long term. When condoms are used consistently by a couple in which one person is infected, the rate of HIV infection is less than 1% per year. There is some evidence to suggest thatfemale condoms may provide an equivalent level of protection. Application of a vaginal gel containing tenofovir (a reverse transcriptase inhibitor) immediately before sex seems to reduce infection ratesby approximately 40% among African women. By contrast, use of thespermicidenonoxynol-9 may increase the risk of transmission due to its tendency to cause vaginal and rectal irritation. Circumcision in Sub-Saharan Africa "reduces the acquisition of HIV by heterosexual men by between 38% and 66% over 24 months". Based on these studies, the World Health Organization and UNAIDS both recommended male circumcision as a method of preventing female-to-male HIV transmission in 2007. Whether it protects against male-to-female transmission is disputed and whether it is of benefit in developed countries and among men who have sex with men is undetermined. Some experts fear that a lower perception of vulnerability among circumcised men may cause more sexual risk-taking behavior, thus negating its preventive effects.

Pre-exposure

Treating people with HIV whose CD4 count $\geqslant$ 350cells/μl with antiretrovirals protects 96% of their partners from infection. This is about a 10 to 20 fold reduction in transmission risk. Pre-exposure prophylaxis with a daily dose of the medicationstenofovir, with or without emtricitabine, is effective in a number of groups including men who have sex with men, couples where one is HIV positive, and young heterosexuals in Africa.

Universal precautions within the health care environment are believed to be effective in decreasing the risk of HIV. Intravenous drug use is an important risk factor and harm reduction strategies such as needle-exchange programmes and opioid substitution therapy appear effective in decreasing this risk.

Post-exposure

A course of antiretrovirals administered within 48 to 72 hours after exposure to HIV positive blood or genital secretions is referred to as post-exposure prophylaxis. The use of the single agent zidovudine reduces the risk of subsequent HIV infection fivefold following a needle stick injury. Treatment is recommended after sexual assault when the perpetrator is known to be HIV positive but is controversial when their HIV status is unknown. Current treatment regimes typically uselopinavir/ritonavir and lamivudine/zidovudine or emtricitabine/tenofovir and may decrease the risk further. The duration of treatment is usually four weeks and is frequently associated with adverse effects (with zidovudine in about 70% of cases, including nausea in 24%, fatigue in 22%, emotional distress in 13%, and headaches in 9%).

Mother-to-child

Programs to prevent the vertical transmission of HIV (from mothers to children) can reduce rates of transmission by 92%~99%. This primarily involves the use of a combination of antiviral medications during pregnancy and after birth in the infant and potentially includes bottle feeding rather than breastfeeding. If replacement feeding is acceptable, feasible, affordable, sustainable, and safe, mothers should avoid breastfeeding their infants; however exclusive breastfeeding is recommended during the first months of life if this is not the case. If exclusive breastfeeding is carried out, the provision of extended antiretroviral prophylaxis to the infant decreases the risk of transmission.

Vaccination

As of 2013 there is no effective vaccine for HIV or AIDS. A single trial of the vaccine RV 144 published in 2009 found a partial reduction in the risk of transmission of roughly 30%, stimulating some hope in the research community of developing a truly effective vaccine.

中英文注释

关键词汇

abacavir [æbækæ'viə] n. 阿巴卡韦（药名）

cachexia [kə'keksiə] n. 恶病质

cryotherapy ['kraiəʊθerəpi] n. 冷冻疗法

dysphagia [dis'feidʒiə] n. 吞咽困难

emtricitabine [emt'risaitæbin] n. 恩曲他滨（药名）

epidemiology [ˌɛpiˌdimi'ɑlədʒi, -ˌdɛmi-] n. 流行病学

immunodeficiency [iˌmjuːnəʊdi'fiʃnsi] n. 免疫缺陷

maculopapule [mækjʊlə'pæpjuːl] n. 斑丘疹

misdiagnose [mis'daiəgnəuz] vt. 误诊

nonprogressors [nɒnp'rəgresəz] n. 无进展者

odynophagia [ədinɒ'feigə] n. 吞咽痛

oesophagus [ai'sɔfəgəs] n. 食道

papillomavirus [pæpiləʊ'mævairəs] n. 乳头瘤病毒

prevalence ['prevələns] n. 流行

quadrivalent [ˌkwɒdri'veilənt] adj. 四价的

seroconversion [ˌsiərəukən'vəːʒən] n. 血清学转换

virology [vai'rɔlədʒiː] n. 病毒学

主要短语

antiretroviral therapy 抗逆转录病毒治疗

acquired immunodeficiency syndrome (AIDS) 获得性免疫缺陷综合征

Burkitt's lymphoma 伯基特氏淋巴瘤

cervical cancer 子宫颈癌

clinical latency 临床潜伏期

cryptococcal Meningitis 隐球菌性脑膜炎

cytotoxic T cells 细胞毒性 T 细胞

enzyme immunoassay tests 酶免疫试验

high active antiretroviral therapy (HAART) 高活性抗逆转录病毒疗法

immune activation 免疫激活

infectious diseases 传染性疾病

initial period 初始期

intestinal mucosa 肠黏膜

Kaposi's sarcoma 卡波西肉瘤

miliary tuberculosis 粟粒性肺结核

Non-Nucleoside Reverse Transcriptase Inhibitors (NNRTI) 非核苷类逆转录酶抑制剂

opportunistic infection 机会性感染

oral candidiasis 口腔念珠菌病

peripheral blood [pə'rifərəl blʌd] 外周血

persistent generalized lymphadenopathy 持续性全身淋巴结肿大
pneumocystis Carinii Pneumonia (PCP) 卡氏肺囊虫肺炎
protease Inhibitors 蛋白酶抑制剂
replication cycle 复制周期
route of transmission 传播途径
sources of Infection 传染源
trichloroacetic acid 三氯乙酸
unexplained fever 原因不明发热

杨 慧

55

Brucellosis

布 氏 菌 病

What is brucellosis?

Brucellosis, also called abortus fever, is an infectious disease caused by the bacteria of the genus Brucella. In humans brucellosis can cause a range of symptoms including fever, sweats, headaches, physical weakness and so forth. Brucellosis can also cause long-lasting or chronic symptoms such as recurrent fevers, joint pain, and splenohepatomegalia. Human brucellosis has a serious medical impact worldwide, and its eradication poses major difficulties.

How about the aetiology?

Brucella are aerobic Gram-negative bacteria shaped of globular and rhabditiform. There are 6 main different species of Brucella were identified and named primarily for the source animal or different biochemical event. They are Br. Melitensis (from sheep), Br. Abortus (from cattle), Br. Suis (from pigs), Br. canis (from dogs), Br. ovis and Br. neotomae. Among of them, Br. melitensis has the highest pathogenicity that can cause more serious clinical symptom. Br. Suis' pathogenicity takes second place.

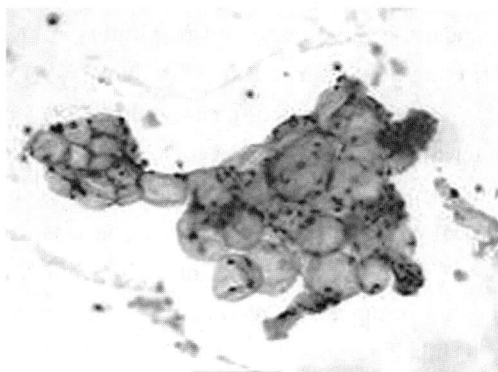

Brucella needs various kinds of amino acids and vitamin in its proliferation, few species need 5%~10% carbon dioxide in culture. Because they grow slowly, the time of isolating these bacteria from the infected individual needs more than one week or even one month.

Brucella has more than 20 kinds of antigens and lipopolysaccharide (endotoxin) which play an important role on the pathopoiesis. All species of the bacterium have the common antigen, therefore we can make living bacteria vaccine by using the strains that have lower toxicity.

Brucella is sensitive to ultraviolet ray, heat and disinfectant commonly used, and can be killed by 3% bleaching powder and lysol in a few minutes. But it has strong vitality in natural environment and can survive for a long time in milk, milk products, fur, frozen meat and so on.

What is the epidemiology ofbrucellosis?

Brucellosis is a global infectious disease. In China, it is mainly epidemic in Neimeng, Jilin, Heilongjiang, Xinjiang and Tibet's pastoral area. The other provinces all have the case of this disease reported. The main epidemic species of Brucella in our country is Br. melitensis, and then Br. Abortus. Br. suis is only found in partly area of Guangxi and Guangdong. Researcher's study showed a prevalence of 5.33% in animal handlers working in an urban city. The prevalence would definitely be higher in a population from a rural area than that from urban city.

Sources of Infection

The mainly sources of infection is sick livestock, including sheep, goat, scalper, carabao, cow and pig. Other animals such as dog, deer, horse, camel also have been reported to be infected with this bacteria.

Routes of transmission

Humans become infected generally through follow routes: The bacteria enter the body through skin wounds; digestive route and respiratory route. The most common way is by eating or drinking contaminated milk products. When sheep, goats, cows, or camels are infected, their milk is contaminated with the bacteria. If the milk is not pasteurized, these bacteria can be transmitted to persons who drink the milk or eat cheeses made of it. Contamination of skin wounds may be a problem for persons working in slaughterhouses or meat packing plants or for veterinarians. Inhalation of Brucella organisms' aerosol is not a common route of infection, but it can be a significant hazard for people in certain occupations, such as those working in laboratories where the organism is cultured. Inhalation is often responsible for a significant percentage of cases in abattoir employees.

Susceptibility

People are generally susceptible to this bacteria. Patients recovered from brucella infection can obtain certainimmunity.

How about the pathology ofbrucellosis?

The pathogenesis of this disease is very complicated. Bacterium, toxin and allergy all have effects on the development of the disease in different degree.

Pathogen which enter human body move through lymphatic vessel into local lymph node, multiply and cause primary focus, and then a lot of pathogens break through lymph barrier and enter into blood causing bacteriemia. The multiplication of brucella in blood is effected by many immune factories of human body, which can lead to brucella lysis and releasing endotoxin or other matters, and induce toxemia. A few pathogens can multiply in mononuclear macrophage after phagocytized by these cells, and spread to all parts of the body in the bloodstream. It propagates mainly in liver, spleen, marrow and kidney, which lead to the injury of tissues including degeneration, necrosis and so on. Pathogen can enter into the blood repetitively, and aggravate the clinical symptom repeatedly. When T-cells in the focus of infection is allergized by bacterium and recontact with antigen, they can release cytokine, chemotaxis and activate macrophage which get together around Brucella, kill Brucella and form granuloma which can package the focus. Brucella that can't be killed by macrophage can still parasitize and multiple in macrophage, which can lead to the parasitical cells breaking and the disease relapse.

Brucellosis is a systemic disease that can affect many organs, but the most commonly affected systems are mononuclear macrophage system, bone and joint system, nervous system and so on. The exudation of inflammation cells, degeneration and necrosis of histiocytes can be seen in the initial stage of this disease. In subacute stage and chronic stage, we can see proliferation of histiocytes. There are some proligerous nodi and granulomas can be seen in liver, spleen, lymph node and so on. In chronic stage, granulation tissues in some patients trend to fibrosclerosis that arise sequela in clinic.

What are the symptoms of brucellosis?

Incubation period is 1-3 weeks (3 days to several months) in common. It can be divided into acute stage and chronic stage.

Acute stage

The onset of brucellosis is often slow, occassionally is sudden. The mainly manifestations are:

● Fever. The types of fever are variety, most are irregular fever, the typical undulant fever is not in common. Different strain infection has different fever type. Fever is obvious in Br. melitensis infection, mild fever is common in Br. abortus.

Patients who have hyperpyretic have no obviously discomfort, but the symptoms will increase after temperature dropping, which is of the characteristic of brucellosis. It is very important for diagnose. In addition, arterial pulse seperated with the temperature, which is called relative infrequent pulse.

- Sweats. Sweats is one of the main symptoms of this disease whether patients have fever or not. Sweating sometimes can induce collapse.
- Arthralgia. It occurs at the beginning of the disease caused by osteoarthritis, sometimes this symptom emerges after a month. It is common in big joint such as knee, waist, shoulder and sacroiliac joint and so forth. Beside osteoarthritis, it also has synovitis, tenosynovitis and the inflammation in the tissues around joint.
- A study of 197 patients with brucellosis showed that the sites most commonly affected were the sacroiliac joints (53%) and spine (19%), followed by the shoulders (16%). Osteoarticular involvement was more common in females (72%) than in males (28%), and the acute stage (62%) was observed more than the chronic stage (38%). Bone and joint involvement occurred at any age, but the most common age group was 40-60 years.
- Symptom of nervous system. It is common for neuralgia, most of patients have sciatica and lumbago. Only a few have meningoencephalitis, myelitis and so on.
- Symptom of urogenital system. Brucella can cause orchitis, epididymitis, prostatitis, oaritis, salpingitis and endometritis. Specific mastitis, which appears mammary gland engorgement with exudation but no tenderness, can also be seen in some patients. In addition a few patients have nephritis and cystitis.
- Splenohepatomegalia and lymphadenectasis. About 50% patients have hepatomegaly and liverache. People infected with Br. abortus can occur non-specific hepatitis or granuloma, which can develop into hepatic cirrhosis without treatment. People infected with Br. suis always have liver fester and splenomegaly. Lymphadenectasisis related to the routes of infection. Those who infected through mouth may have lymphadenectasis in neck, the post-wall of pharynx and jaw. People who infected through skin may have armpit or groin lymphadenectasis. Sometimes lymphadenectasis in abdominal cavity or thoracic cavity can also be seen. The intumescentedlymph nodes generally have no obviously pain and can disappear by itself. It can also lead to suppuration, break and form the fist in some patients.

More than 10% patients who have brucellosis in acute stage will relapse after antibiosis treatment. It usually happens after several months of acute infection or after 2 years of treatment. This is probably caused by bacterium which parasitize in cells and escape from the clearing of antibiotic and the immune function of host. Sometimes it is difficult to distinguish relapse and reinfection in epidemic area.

Chronic phase

Chronic phase is that the course of disease persist for more than one year. It may be caused by inadequate treatment in acute stage or undiscovered symptoms in time. Symptoms may include fixed and reparoxysmal arthralgia and muscle pain, sometimes the organic damage of bone and joint may occurs. In addition, mental symptoms such as ademosyne, insomnia, and impaired concentration can also be seen.

Chronic phase can be divided in two types:

- Chronic active stage: With normal temperature or low fever, recurrent of symptom and physical sign which can repeat and aggravates gradually. Serologic examination positive.
- Chronic relative stable type: With normal temperature, symptom and physical sign reappear only when climate change or tired.

How about the laboratory examination of brucellosis?

Hemogram

Leucocytes count is normal or decline, lymphocyte or mononuclear cell is increased. The platelet is decline in some patients.

Pathogen cultivation

Isolation and cultivation of a Brucella sp. is the most certain means of reaching a diagnosis. Blood or bone narrow are the main sample used for cultivation, positive rates of the latter is higher than former. We can also get the positive results from lymph gland tissue, diapyetic matter or cerebrospinal fluid of meningitis patients. Cultivating the bacterium needs special medium and 10 days longer to get the result because the bacterium grows very slowly.

At present, the lysis centrifugation blood cultivationtechnique has been found to be more sensitive in both acute (20% higher sensitivity) and chronic (40% higher sensitivity) forms of brucellosis. The major advantage of this methodis that it needs shorter time to get positive results, which is only 2.4 days in acute and 2.7 days in chronic cases.

Serology detection

- Agglutination test. The serum agglutination test (SAT) including test tube method and glass slide method has been the principal serological test used to detect brucellosis antibodies which include specific IgG, IgA, and IgM. The latter way is easy to operate and always used for epidemic surveillance. The former way is significant in diagnose when the title of double serum increased at least 4 times.

- ELISA. The ELISA has proven to be specific and as sensitive as the MRT and SAT in detecting Brucella antibodies in milk and serum.
- Other immunology test. It includes immunofluorescence test, Coomb's test, α-mercaptoethanol test, RIA and so on.

The serology tests all above have cross-reaction with other bacterium infection such as comma bacillus, tubercle bacillus and yersinia on different degrees. Accordingly, we should make diagnosis of the disease by combining clinical manifestation with epidemic history.

PCR Technology

Polymerase chain reaction (PCR) assays can be used to examine the DNA of Brucella recently which is a rapid and sensitive laboratory diagnosis means.

Some research prove that PCR assay can be applied with serology for the diagnosis of brucellosis suspected cases and relapses regardless of the duration or type of the disease without relying on the blood cultures, especially in chronic cases. Research show that real time PCR (RT-PCR) assay in cerebrospinal fluid (CSF) samples is more rapid and sensitive than conventional microbiological tests such as sheep, pig, cow or there furs in epidemic areas, eaF cultures and seroagglutination tests. In addition, a simple PCR-enzyme-linked immunosorbent assay (PCR-ELISA) was developed, it seems to be a practical and reliable tool for the diagnosis of human brucellosis.

Intracutaneous test (Burnet reaction)

Brucella antigen is used to do intradermal injection, and then observe the injected skin reaction 48 hours latter, it is positive if the injected skin become red swelling and the rage of infiltration is larger than 2.5cm×2.5cm. This reaction is called delayed anaphylaxis, the positive results demonstrate that infection exist now or before. The negative result is helpful to exclude this disease.

How to diagnose brucellosis?

Epidemic history

The history includes contacting with or drinking contaminated milk products, all these are significantfor reference.

Clinical manifestation

The typical acute case is easy to diagnose, chronic patient is difficult to diagnose. Fever, sweats, malaise, anorexia, headache, myalgia, joint and nerve pain, splenohepatomegalia and lymphadenectasis. In the chronic phase, neurologic and psychiatric symptoms may occur, and the damage of bones, joints system can also be seen.

Laboratory examination

Brucellosis is diagnosed in laboratory by finding Brucella organisms in samples of blood, bone marrow or other humeral substance. We can also make a definite diagnosis on the basis of positive results of serology examination in combination with medical history and physical signs.

Brucella-specific IgM and IgG detection kit are available for rapid diagnosis of human brucellosis, which perform equally well in diagnosing patients at different stages of illness including patients with acute, subacute, or chronic disease and with relapse, and can be used to monitor the efficiency of treatment.

Acute brucellosis should be differentiatedfrom rheumatic fever, typhoid, dysentery, septicemia and tuberculosis. Brucellosis in chronic phase should be differentiated from the damage of bone, joint and neurosis caused by other disease.

How about the prognosis of brucellosis?

The prognosis of this disease is satisfactory in common. Most patients have the trend of autotherapy without management, and can rehabilitate within 1-3 months without using antibiotic, but these patients are easy to relapse. The course of the disease can be shorten by treatment in time. The death of the patients is mainly caused by endocarditis, severe complication of nervous system and so on. A few cases can have joint and muscle tendon spasm, which affect the action of body.

How to treat brucellosis?

Acute stage

- General treatment and symptomatic treatment. Having bed rest, liberal supplement of vitamin and water. Patients with hyperpyrexia should use physical way to reduce the temperature. Calmative can be used for patients with severe headache and jointache. Adrenal cortical hormone should be used for somebody who has obviously toxic symptom and orchitis.
- Pathogen treatment. As Brucellae are facultative intracellular bacteria, relapses after treatment usually occur. Therefore, efforts are made to prevent or eradicate brucellosis. So we should select antibiotics such as tetracyclines, aminoglycosides and rifadin that can easily enter into the cells and kill the bacteria in the cells. Generally, combining the antibiotic and multi-course of treatment are used to enhance curative effect, reduce relapse and prevent the generation of drug resistant strain.

Nowadays, rifadin is considered to have the best curative effect, its common dose is 600-1200mg/d, children is 15mg/d, use 6 weeks continuously. Rifadin can enhance the bactericidal action of streptomycin and have synergism to kill Brucella with doxycycline. The dose of streptomycin is usually 1g/d, 1-2 times im, for 2-4 weeks. Doxycycline 200mg, 2 times, for 6 weeks, take orally. It has been reported that rifadin combining with streptomycin is better than rifadin combining with doxycycline.

Trimethoprim Sulfamethoxazole (TMP SMZ) can permeate into the cells and can be used to reduce the temperature in acute stage. Its common dose is 4-6 tablets per day (every tablet contains TMP 80mg, SMZ 400mg), take orally 2 times per day for 4-6 weeks.

Chronic phase

The treatment is complex, it includes pathogen treatment, desensitization treatment and symptomatic treatment.

- Antibacteriatreatment. Chronic patients with acute episode type, chronic active type, local lesion or positive result for bacterial culture all should be treated with antibiotic. The method of treatment is as same as acute stage.
- Desensitizing therapy. T lymphocyte which sensitized by Brucella is now considered to be the basis of body damage. Injecting small amounts of brucella antigen repeatedly can cause sensitized T lymphocyte releasing cytokine for small amounts but many times, it can avoid intense tissue damage as well as consume sensitized T lymphocyte.

  Brucella thallus vaccine, bacteriolysin and hydrolysable matters usually be used for subcutaneous injection, intramuscular injection or intravenous injection. The reaction for intravenous injection is more intensive. It mustn't be used for patients with damage of nerve, cardiac muscle, liver and kidney.
- Symptomatic treatment. It includes physiatrics and so on.

How to prevent the disease of brucellosis?

Prevention measures include isolating the patients and curing the sick livestocks, enhancing the health supervision of livestock products, making individual protection and professional people's protection. Vaccine can be used to do prophylactic immunization for people probably infected this bacterium. Livestocks can also be inoculated with vaccine which can prevent the animal infect with brucellosis in areas with endemic brucellosis, or reduces the number of infected animals and eventually permits disease control.

中英文注释

关键词汇

aetiology [ˌiːtiˈɔlədʒi] n. 病原学

aminoglycosides [æminəgli'kəʊsaidz] n. 氨基糖苷类

arthralgia [ɑːˈθrældʒiə] n. 关节痛

bacteriemia [bæktəˈriəmjə] n. 菌血症

disinfectant [ˌdisinˈfektənt] n. 消毒剂

endocarditis [ˌendəʊkɑːˈdaitis] n. 心内膜炎

engorgement [inˈgɔːdʒmənt] n. 暴饮暴食

eradication [iˌrædiˈkeiʃn] n. 根除

granuloma [ˌgrænjuˈləumə] n. 肉芽肿

hyperpyretic [ˌhaipəpaiˈretik] adj. 体温过高

lipopolysaccharide [ˈlipəuˌpɔliˈsækəraid] n. 脂多糖

inhalation [ˌinhəˈleiʃən] n. 吸入

macrophage [ˈmækrəˌfeidʒ] n. 巨噬细胞

nephritis [neˈfraitis] n. 肾炎

osteoarthritis [ɔstiːˌəuɑːˈθraitis] n. 骨关节炎

splenohepatomegalia [spliːnəʊhpɑːtəmeˈgeiliə] n. 肝脾大

tetracyclines [tetrəsikˈlainz] n. 四环素类

toxemia [tɒksˈiːmiə] n. 毒血症

主要短语

abortus fever 波浪热

a significant percentage 显著比例

be contaminated with 被污染

desensitization treatment 脱敏治疗

digestive route 消化途径

infectious diease 感染性疾病

local lymph node 局部淋巴结

lower toxicity 较低毒性

lymphatic vessel 淋巴管

mononuclear macrophage 单核巨噬细胞

pastoral area 牧区

physical weakness 身体虚弱

respiratory route 呼吸途径

rural area 农村地区

sick livestock 病畜

skin wounds 皮肤破损处

subcutaneous injection 皮下注射

symptomatic treatment 对症治疗

the common antigen 共同抗原
the highest pathogenicity 最高的致病性
trimethoprim sulfamethoxazole 甲氧苄啶磺胺甲噁唑
ultraviolet ray 紫外线
urogenital system 泌尿生殖系统

杨 慧

56 — Epidemic Typhus
流行性斑疹伤寒

What is Rickettsiae infection?

Rickettsiosis is an acute infectious disease caused by several rickettsiae. Rickettsiosis of human can be divided into 5 groups:

- Typhus fever (it includes epidemic typhus and endemic typhus)
- Spotted fever (it includes spotted fever, Marseilles fever, Australia tick typhus fever and rickett's organism pox disease)
- Scrub typhus (it includes tsutsugamushi disease)
- Q fever (includes Q fever)
- Paroxysmal rickettsiosis (includes trench fever). Epidemic typhus, endemic typhus, Scrub typhus and Q fever have been found in China.

Rickettsiae is a microorganism between bacterium and virus, it has follow characteristics:

- Intracellular parasites. We cannot use the lifeless culture medium to isolate it.
- Having cell wall, DNA and RNA. These organisms are small, pleomorphic coccobacilli that can be seen by light microscope after dyeing.
- Having the common antigen with certain bacillus proteus (OX19, OX2 or OXκ) except Q fever, trench fever and rickettsiae pox disease. We can carry on Weil-Felix reaction to diagnose this disease.
- Sensitive to broad-antibiotic such as tetracyclines and chloromycetin.
- Having weak resistance to hot and the common disinfectant except Q fever rickettsiae, but has better resistance to low temperature and drying.

The common characteristics of rickettsiosis are: The proliferation of pathogen in nature is mainly in reservior host such as rodent animal (mice) and domestic animal (dog, cow, sheep). The anthropodinhausting blood like louse, flea, tick and acari are the main vector. The pathological change is mainly polyangitis and perivasculitis. Clinical manifestation: Incubation period is ususlly 10-14 days, the cardinal symptom are febrilis, headache and rash (except for Q fever), antibiotic has satisfactory effect for it.

What is epidemic typhus?

Epidemic typhus, also called louse-borne typhus or classic typhus, is an acute infectious disease that is caused by the organism Rickettsia prowazekii and transmitted by the human body louse. Symptoms are headache, fever, chills, exhaustion, and rash. The course of this disease is about 2-3 weeks.

Epidemic typhus has been found throughout the world. Prominent outbreaks occurred during World War I and II. In our country, there was a high morbidity of this disease before liberation, but it has been controlled largely at present. As a reappeared disease, it is epidemic partly in Russia, Peru, Algeria and Middle African. During the period of epidemic, the case-fatality rate is between 6% and 30%.

How about the aetiology?

Rickettsia is small, pleomorphic coccobacilli about 1μm. Their structure is typical of Gram-negative, obligate intracellular bacteria, lavender in Giemsa stain. Rickettsia has two kinds of antigens:

- Soluble antigen. It is a group-specific antigen, and can be differentiated from other Rickettsia.
- Thermolabile particulate antigen. It contains species-specific antigen, which can be used to distinguish epidemic typhus from endemic typhus. Rickettsia possess antigens that cross-react with the antigens of Proteus vulgaris OX19, so the antirickettsial antibodies in patient's serum can cause the agglutination of the Proteus organisms which help diagnosing epidemic typhus, this reaction is so called Weil-Felix test.

Rickettsia is sensitive to ultraviolet ray, heat and common disinfectant. It will lose its vitality at 56℃ for 30 minutes or 37℃ for 5 to 7 hours. Rickettsia is able to endure low temperature and dry, so it can be saved for long times below 20℃ and survive in louse dry fecula for many months.

What is the epidemiology of epidemic typhus?

Sources of infection

Patients are the major source of infection at the end of incubation period. The infectivity is the strongest in the first week and will not lasting for 3 weeks.

Rickettsiae prowazeki still has nonhuman nature host. In East American, Rickettsiae prowazeki has been isolated from petaurist, its characteristics of biology and biochemy are similar to the Rickettsiae prowazeki from patients. There are some reports about scattered case that was caused by contacting with petaurist.

Routes of transmission

The body louse is the main vector, and then the head louse, the pubic louse doesn't transmit. The life history of Rickettsiae prowazeki is very special which can be finished between human and the human body louse. Lice become infected when they feed on the blood of rickettsiae infected patients. Whenever lice bite people, they will defecate at the same time and the bacteria are found in the feces. Transmission occurs when organisms in the louse feces or crushed lice are rubbed into the bite wound or other breaks in the skin. Lice like to live at 29℃, so they can leave hyperpyretic patient or dead people to find new host that improve the transmission of the disease among people. Transmission is also possible when dry louse faeces are inhaled via aerosol.

Susceptibility

Susceptibility is general. One time infection usually confers long-lasting immunity, but a few patients will reinfect because of the deficiency of immunity or relapse because of the re-proliferation of rickettsia that incubate in the body.

Epidemic characteristics

Epidemic of this disease is closely related with louse. Human conditions that foster the proliferation of lice are especially common during winter and during war or natural disasters-wherein clothing is not changed, crowding occurs, and bathing is very infrequent.

It seems that major epidemics, which occurred in Middle African, Russia, Peru and Algeria, derive from the Civil War of Burundi since 1995.

How about the pathology ofepidemic typhus?

Pathogenesis

Rickettsia prowazekii produces a vasculitis by intracellular proliferating in the endothelium of small blood vessels. Endothelial damage results in focal occlusive endangiitis in small venules and arterioles. In this way, ageneralised, multifocal, multi-organ vasculitis occurs, these can lead to thrombosis and vascular occlusion, possibly with edema and local necrosis.

Rickettsia can cause latent infection and present in lymph tissues persistently which are the causes of Brill-Zinsser.

Pathology

Rickettsiae enter via the skin and spread through the bloodstream to infect vascular endothelium in the skin, brain, lungs, heart, kidneys, liver, gastrointestinal tract, and other organs. If local thrombosis is extensive, gangrene of skin or distal portions of the extremities, or both, occurs. There are some alteration such as bronchial pneumonia, interstitial nephritis, interstitial myocarditis, interstitial hepatitis and haemorrhage, oedema in paranephros. The central nervous system pathology is broadly. Acute swell happens in spleen because of the monocyte, macrophage proliferation.

What are the symptoms of epidemic typhus?

Incubation period is 10-14 days (5-23 days).

Typical epidemic typhus

- Fever. The onset of epidemic typhus is often sudden. The temperature reaches 39℃ rapidly in 1 to 2 days, continues for one week and then tend to become remittent in the second week. The fever lasts approximately 2 to 3 weeks and drops to normal in 3 to 4 days if no complications occur and without any treatment. The symptoms also include chills, weakness, keen headaches, blood shot in face and conjunctiva and so forth.

- Rash. Rash is an important symptom of this disease at 4 to 5 days of the course in approximately 90% cases. Small pink macules usually appear first on the upper trunk then spread to the entire body in 1 or 2 days with the exception of the face. As the disease progresses, the rash usually becomes dark and maculopapular or, in severe cases, petechial and hemorrhagic. The rashes are isolated from each other and disappear in one weak, but the petechial rash will last for 2 weeks.

- Symptom of central nervous system. It appears early and apparently, such as keen headache, accompanied with dizziness, tinnitus and descent hearing. It also causes slow response or alarm, deliriant, accidentally result in meningeal excitation and hands or tongue shakes, even encopresis, aconuresis and comatose.

- Splenomegaly and hepatomegaly. Some studies showed splenomegaly occurs in approximately 90% of cases, slight hepatomegaly can be seen in few patients.

- Symptom of cardiovascular system. Some patients have rapid pulse, some have low and blunt cardiac sounds, arrhythmia, gallop rhythm, falling blood pressure and even circulation failure.

- Others. Symptom of respiratory tract, alimentary tract and acute renal failure.

Mild epidemic typhus

Mild typhus usually occurs in recent years in China. The fever lasts for 8 to 9 days and the temperature is lower than 39℃, the symptoms of toxication of whole body is mild, the headache and the body pain are obvious, but few patient has conscience trouble and other symptoms of central nervous system. Rash is congestive and often barely visible or absent, and always disappears 1 to 2 days later. Hepatomegaly and splenomegaly are seldom seen.

Brill-Zinsser disease

It is the relapse epidemic typhus. After primary infection, Rickettsia prowazekii stays in the lymph node of human body for many years without any clinical manifestation and multiply once the immunity decline, which induce the relapse of epidemic typhus. Brill-Zinsser happens either in the crowds of areas where the epidemic typhus is prevalent, or in the crowds that moves from epidemic areas. At present, the dispersed cases mainly appear in Eastern Europe and emigration settled in America and Canada from Eastern Europe, there are a few reports in our country. The clinical course of the disease is similar to epidemic typhus but is milder and recovery is faster, the case-fatality rate is low. The differential diagnosis can be carried out by immunology checking between this and primary infection. Patients with Brill-Zinsser disease initially have an IgG response not IgM response, which reach the peak after 10 days of the disease. All of these suggest that there are still some immunity in the body.

How about the laboratory examination of epidemic typhus?

Blood and urine routine examination

Leucocyte count is normal in majority, neutrophil always increase, eosinophil decrease or disappear phenomenally, platelet always decline. Albumen in the urine is usually positive.

Cerebrospinal fluid examination

The leucocyte and albumen increases in the Cerebrospinal fluid of Patients who have meningeal excitation, but the sugar is normal.

Serology examination

● Weil-Felix reaction (Agglutination reaction of Proteus vulgaris OX19). Epidemic typhus is usually diagnosed by serology. Titers usually become detectable during the first week, and the peak is in 2 to 3 weeks, and persists many weeks to 3 months. It is valuable for diagnoses that titers beyond 1:160 or fourfold raise during the course of disease. The positive-rate is 70% to 80%. It is easy for operation but poor for specialization. This test cannot be used to distinguish from endemic typhus and emerge false positive caused by cross agglutination with relapsing fever Borrelia, brucellosis and tubercle bacillus.

● Antibody examination. Indirect immunofluorescence (IFA) is the most frequently used laboratory examination method. Enzyme-Linked Immunosorbent Assay (ELISA) is the most sensitive essay, especially to detect the specific antibody IgM. Complement fixation (CF) and Latex agglutination (LG) are also used in serologic tests for rickettsia. Reports showed that combination of western blotting and IFA methods can differentiate R. prowazekii from R. typhi infection.

Pathogen isolation

Isolation and identification of R. prowazekii is not widely available, as rickettsia are both fastidious and dangerous to laboratory personnel or animals. Embryonated hen's eggs widely used before have some limitation because it is difficult to get in time and simply. However, a centrifugation-enhanced microcell culture system, the shell vial assay used for cytomegalovirus isolation, has been successfully applied to rickettsial isolation because of its rapidity and convenience.

Nucleic acid detection

Molecular hybridization is specific to detect rickettsia which is better for early diagnosis. Polymerase chain reaction (PCR) assays may be available in some laboratories that can increase sensitivity.

What are the complications of epidemic typhus?

Bronchial pneumonia, Myocarditis, Otitis media and Parotitis. However, occasional patients complicate with infectious psychopathy, digits, tootsy and tip of nose gangrene.

How to diagnose epidemic typhus?

The special clinical manifestations are absent in patients with epidemic typhus:

- Epidemiology. The materials for epidemiology are valuable for reference. There is no epidemic typhus if there is no louse, so it is very important to ask the details about the contact history with louse.
- Clinical manifestation. We should pay special attention to patient's ardent fever, the rash appear at about the 4-5 days of illness and spreads centrifugally. Patients will have severe headache and other nervous symptom.
- Laboratory examinations. Laboratory examinations are necessary for diagnosis. The Weil-Felix reaction that titers beyond 1:160 or fourfold rise during the course of disease can be used to diagnose. Others special serologic methods are significant.

Differential diagnosis

- Others Rickettsia disease. The differential diagnosis with endemic typhus see table 1. A careful examination reveals an eschar at the site of the chigger bite and swollen lymph nodes, positive agglutinate reaction of Proteus vulgaris OXK, in Patients with tsutsugamushi disease. The main clinical manifestations in Q fever patients with no rash include interstitial pneumonia, negative Weil-Felix reaction and positive serology test.

Table 1 Differentiate between epidemic typhus and endemic typhus

	Epidemic typhus	Endemic typhus
Character of disease	Medium to heaviness	Light to medium
Difference of epidemic	Epidemic, most in winter and spring	Endemic distribution, at all seasons, more in summer
Rash	Macularpopular, often see petechial/macular, all over the body	Macularpopular, rarely seen
Thrombocytopenia	often see	rarely seen
Weil-Felix reaction	Strong positive, 1:320 to 1:5120	1:160 to 1:640
Vaccination test	Pathogen can not induce guineapig cobblers swell, seldom and slightly	Pathogen causes guineapig cobblers swell seriously.
The case-fatality rate	6% to 30%	< 1%

- Typhoid fever. The onset of typhoid fever is often slow and the symptom of toxaemia is slight. It is seldom to see special manifestations such as rose exanthema, relative slow pulsus. The diagnose depends on typhoid bacillus culture in blood (or cholera, medulla) and/or positive Widal reaction.
- Relapsing fever. The onset is sudden, patients have fever and refever after defervescence for days. Borrelia can be detected by blood or medulla smear. Because relapsing fever is transmitted by the body louse too, it can infect the patient who get epidemic typhus at the same time.
- Epidemic hemorrhagic fever. An acute viral hemorrhagic fever characterized by high fever, haemorrhage, shock and kidney failure. Typical clinical manifestation consists of five stages: Febrile (toxic), hypotensive, oliguric, polyuric and convalescent period. Specific IgM antibody in acute phase sera or an increase specific IgG antibody titer are useful for diagnose this disease.

What is the treatment for epidemic typhus?

General treatment

Having bed rest, eating foods which contain rich vitamins and drinking more water. Taking intensive nursing care and preventing complications.

Pathogen treatment

Early treatment with tetracyclines and doxycycline are highly effective. The recommended dose for tetracycline is 2g per day for adult, 25 mg/kg of body weight per day for children, in four equally divided oral doses. A single dose of doxycycline, 200 to 300 mg orally for adult, is curative. Therapy should be continued for 3 to 4 days after defervescence. If the patient is too ill to take drugs orally, an intravenous injection is recommended for use. Chloramphenicol is also effective, but cannot be chosen first because of its side effect of medulla inhibition. Sulfa drug is forbidden to use that can lead the patient's condition to worse.

Symptom treatment

Anodyne and sedative can be applied to patients who have keen headache. The symptom of toxaemia can be alleviated by using glucocorticoid carefully. Antibiotics can inhibit the growth of Rickettsia, but can not eradicate it, the recovery partly depends on patients' immunity.

How to prevent the disease of epidemic typhus?

Practicing personal hygiene and wiping off the louse are the key measures in preventing epidemic typhus.

Manage Sources of infection

Control of the human body louse and the conditions that foster its proliferation is the key measure in preventing louse-borne typhus. The patient should be isolated earlier and handled with delousing. Somebody who contact with patient closely should be given medical observation for 21 days.

Cut off routes of transmission

We should enforce hygienic concept, have bath and change dress usually, delouse the clothes and beddings that hiding lice. Physical method is the most effective such as cooking, steaming, scalding, burning and so forth. Delousing also should be done with an insecticide shown to be lousicidal for the infecting lice, usually, malathion or dichlorvos is effective.

Protect susceptibility

A inactivated typhus vaccine derived from murine lung is available and is recommended for use in high-risk populations, such as scientific investigators; Some government workers who live in or visit foreign countries where typhus actually occur and who will be in close contact with the local people; medical worker, including nurses and attendants, who provide care for patients in the areas where louse-borne typhus epidemic; and laboratory personnel who work with R. prowazekii. The usage of vaccine is 3 times injection in the first year, then intensive injection every year. After 6 times' inoculation, the body can get long-lasting immunity. But vaccination against epidemic typhus can only alleviate the condition of patient, cannot reduce the morbidity apparently.

中英文注释

关键词汇

agglutination [ə,gluːtin'eiʃən] n. 聚集

coccobacilli [ˌkɔkəubəˈsilai,–ˈsiliː] n. 球杆菌

defervescence [ˌdifəˈvesəns] n. 退热

generalised [ˈdʒenrəlaizd] adj. 广泛的，普遍的

multifocal [ˈmʌltifəʊkl] adj. 多病灶的

paranephros [ˌpærəˈnefrɒs] n. 肾上腺

parasites [ˈpærəsaits] n. 寄生虫

pleomorphic [ˌpliːəˈmɔːfik] adj. 多形态的

polyangitis [pɒljændˈʒitis] n. 小血管炎

prowazeki [prəʊtəˈzəʊik] adj. 原生的

reservoir [ˈrezəvwɑː(r)] n. 储存

rickettsiosis [riketsiˈəʊsis] n. 立克次体病

sporadic [spəˈrædik] adj. 间断发生的，散发的

主要短语

acute infectious disease 急性传染病

anthropodinhausting blood 吸血性节肢动物

hyperpyretic patient 高热患者

infectious psychopathy 感染性精神疾患

louse-borne typhus 虱传斑疹伤寒

paroxysmal rickettsiosis 阵发性立克次体病

pleomorphic coccobacilli 多形性球杆菌

rickettsia agglutination examination 立克次体凝集实验

scrub typhus 恙虫病

spotted fever 斑点热

thermolabile particulate antigen 不耐热颗粒性抗原

typhus fever 斑疹伤寒

ultraviolet ray 紫外线

Weil-Felix reaction 外斐氏反应

杨　慧

57 — Endemic Typhus
地方性斑疹伤寒

What is endemic typhus?

Endemic typhus, also called flea-borne typhus or murine typhus, is an acute infectious disease which is caused by the organism Rickettsia mooseri (Rickettsia Typhi) and transmitted by the murine flea. The clinical course of the disease is similar to epidemic typhus, but the condition is milder and recovery is faster, few are lethal except old patients.

What causes endemic typhus?

The feature, physics and chemistry property in Rickettsia mooseri are similar to Rickettsia prowazekii. But there are some differences below:

- The feature is short and filiform not visibly pleomorphic.
- They have same soluble and heat-resistant antigens which can cause cross reaction. But they have different heat-sensitive granule antigen that can be discriminated by complement fixation and Rickettsia agglutination test.
- It can cause scrotum and cobblers swollen of male-guineapigs.
- Mouse and rat can be infected by endemic typhus, and thus can be used to isolate and conserve pathogen.

What is the epidemiology of endemic typhus?

Sources of infection

The common house mouse is the primary source of infection, Rickettsia mooseri is transmitted from mouse to mouse by the rat flea vector. The normal cycle is rat to flea to rat, and humans are accidentally infected by the bite of fleas after the rat death. Furthermore, patient, cow, sheep, pig, horse, mule and so forth also can become the source of infection.

Routes of transmission

Rickettsia mooseri is transmitted by rat flea. When a flea parasited on person, it may defecate as it feeds. When the person scratches the itchy spot where the flea was feeding, the bacteria-laden feces are scratched into the skin, and thus cause infection. Sometimes person become illness by eating foods contaminated with excretion of sick rat. People can also be infected by inhale flea feces melting in the air through the mucous membranes of respiratory tract and conjunctiva. Louse infesting human body can also be transmission media.

Susceptibility

Susceptibility is general. One time of infection usually confers long-lasting immunity. It has cross-reaction with epidemic typhus.

Epidemic characteristics

This disease distributes worldwidely, mostly in Torrid Zone and Subtropics. In China, Henan, Hebei, Yunnan, Shandong, Liaoning and Beijing have large number of cases reported. Endemic typhus occurs more commonly in late summer and autumn, and present in the same region with epidemic typhus at the same time.

How about the pathogenesis and morbid anatomy?

The pathogenesis and morbid anatomy is parallel with epidemic typhus, but it is milder. It is seldom to see the thrombosis in small vessels.

What are the symptoms of endemic typhus?

Incubation period is 1 to 2 weeks. The course of the illness is the same as epidemic typhus, but it is milder and shorter.

Fever

The highest temperature is between 38℃ and 40℃, most common type is remittent fever. Patient may have general toxic symptoms, such as limpsy, headache and backache. The conjunctiva always has hyperaemia, but all above are more slight than epidemic typhus. The general course of fever are 9-14 days (4-25 days).

Rash

Rash occurs at about 30-80% cases of this disease, it usually appears on the 5th day (the 2 -8th day) of this disease. The distribution of rash is similar to epidemic typhus. The rash can be seen on chest and abdomen at the beginning and spread to back, shoulder, upper limb and lower limb within 24h, but the amount of rash is small than epidemic typhus. There is no rash on face, neck, hands and sole of foot. The diameter of rash is about 1-4mm. Initially, the rash consists of pink macules, then becomes maculopapular and darker. It always lasts for 7-10 days. The hemorrhagic rash are rarely to see.

Others

The nervous symptoms are always slightly, most patients only have headache and some have conscious disturbance. There are no obvious changes in circulatory system, just tachycardia or hypotension appears. About 30% patients may have slight splenomegaly.

Reports coming from 97 child cases of American and 104 cases of Spain showed that the proportion of fever, headache and rash is 100%, 75% and 63%, fever accompanied with headache or rash is 90%, the presence of three symptoms at same times only 49% which will increase as the age of patients increasing. More than half child patients occurs gastrointestinal symptom that occurs only in one fourth of adult patients. About 78% adult patients have pain of arthrosis and muscle that present in 35% child patients. Most rash are macularpopular (80%), seldom erythema (10%) or hemostasis (10%). Lymph node swollen is more often seen in child more than adult patients (16% to 2%). The presence of splenomegaly is in about 24% adult patients and no reports in child. 12% child patients have pneumonia without meningitis and other complications. Complications occur in 9% adult patients, 6 cases pneumonia, 1 case cerebellitis, 2 cases multi-organ function failure. No one die.

How to diagnose endemic typhus?

The clinical manifestation of this disease is often nonspecific and milder, so it is easy to neglect and misdiagnosis. Epidemic materials are helpful to the diagnosis. We should be alert to the fever patient in epidemic region or the patient who has been to the epidemic region one month before. Report coming from Spanish recently showed that there are 104 cases (6.7%) infected with endemictyphus in 926 cases who have medium-term fever. Only 3.8% patients acknowledged that they had been bitten by flea. Antibiotic is highly effective, some patients have been cured before diagnosis because the condition of disease is milder. Weil-Felix reaction are valuable for diagnosis, the further laboratory diagnosis methods depends on complement fixation and Rickettsia agglutination examination.

How about the laboratory examination of endemic typhus?

Hemogram

Leucocyte count and sorting is normal, a few patients' platelet decline early in the course of disease.

Biochemy examination

Serum AST, ALT, ALP and LDH increase slightly in approximately 90% patients.

Immunology examination

Weil-Felix reaction is positive, but the titer is low. Complement fixation (CF) and Latex agglutination (LG) are also developed for discrimination by using rickettsia mooseri special antigen.

Pathogen isolation

Guineapig scrotum reaction experiment is not widely available in normal laboratory because rickettsia are both fastidious and dangerous to laboratory personnel or animals.

How to treat endemic typhus?

The treatment is the same as epidemic typhus, some reports in our country suggest that doxycycline is more effective than tetracycline. Recently, quinolones have been used such as ciprofloxacin, ofloxacin and perfloxacinum which are also effective in treatment. The temperature can be normal in 1 to 3 days after treatment. Therapy should be continued for 3 to 4 days after defervescence.

How to prevent endemic typhus?

- Prevention is mainly toward the control of flea and potential flea hosts. The patient should be isolated earlier.
- Endemic typhus is a sporadic infectious disease, so there is no necessary to inject vaccine to prevent this disease.

中英文注释

关键词汇

arthrosis [ar'θrosis] n.[解剖]关节；[外科]关节病
defervescence [ˌdifə'vesəns] n. 退热
hyperaemia [ˌhaipə'ri:miə] n. 充血
maculopapular [ˌmækjulə'pæpju:lə] adj. 斑丘疹的
rash [ræʃ] n.[皮肤]皮疹

主要短语

complement fixation examination 补体结合实验
cross reaction 交叉反应
endemic typhus 地方性斑疹伤寒
epidemic region 疫区
flea-borne typhus or murine typhus 蚤传性斑疹伤寒或鼠型斑疹伤寒
house mouse 家鼠
rat/murine flea 鼠蚤
Rickettsia mooseri 莫氏立克次体
source of infection 传染源,感染源

杨　慧

58

Rabies

狂 犬 病

What is rabies?

Rabies, also named as hydrophobia, is an acute zoonotic disease that is caused by a virus which mainly to invade central nervous system (CNS) of body. Rabies is spread to people through close contact with infected animal via bites or scratches. The main route of rabies transmission to humans is the bite of rabid dogs. The clinical manifestation is specific hydrophobia, photophobia, aerophobia, intense anxiety, pharyngismus, progressive paralysis and so on.

Rabies is present on all continents with the exception of Antartica, but more than 95% of human deaths occur in Asia and Africa. Once symptoms of the disease develop, the case fatality rate almost 100%.

How about the rabies virus?

The rabies virus is the type species of the Lyssavirusgenus, in the family Rhabdoviridae, order Mononegavirales. Lyssaviruses have helical symmetry, with a length of about 180 nm and a cross-section of about 75 nm. These viruses are enveloped and have a single-stranded RNA genome with negative sense. The genetic information is packed as a ribonucleoprotein complex in which RNA is tightly bound by the viral nucleoprotein. The RNA genome of the virus encodes five genes whose order is highly conserved: nucleoprotein (N), phosphoprotein (P), matrix protein (M), glycoprotein (G), and the viral RNA polymerase (L).

Once within a muscle or nerve cell, the virus undergoes the replication. The trimeric spikes on the exterior of the membrane of the virus interact with a specific cell receptor, the most likely one being the acetylcholine receptor. The cellular membrane pinches in a procession known as pinocytosis and allows entry of the virus into the cell by way of an endosome.

From the point of entry, the virus is neurotropic, traveling quickly along the neural pathways into the central nervous system, and then to other organs. The salivary glandsreceive high concentrations of the virus, thus allowing further transmission.

What is the epidemiology of rabies?

Rabies has been known since circa 2000 B.C. because of its potentially violent nature. Rabies is widely distributed across the globe. Although it is a vaccine-preventable disease, rabies still poses a significant public health problem in many countries in Asia and Africa where 95% of human deaths occur even though safe, effective vaccines for both human and veterinary use exist.

Sources of Infection

Dogs are still the main rabies carriers in Africa and Asia and are responsible for human infections and subsequent deaths worldwide. Many animal species are involved in the maintenance and transmission of the disease in nature. Fox rabies has been brought under control in Western Europe, but skunk, raccoon and fox rabies remain prevalent in parts of Canada and the United States. Bat rabies has been emerging as a problem in Europe and the Americas over the last decade which have overtaken dogs as the main source of human infection in South America.

The World Health Organization says that "Human rabies deaths following exposure to wild foxes, raccoons, skunks, jackals and wolves are very rare. Livestock, horses and deer can become infected with rabies, but although they could transmit the virus to other animals or people, this rarely occurs." The Centers for Disease Control and Prevention (CDC), USA, says that beavers, coyotes, monkeys, and woodchucks may also become infected and transmit to humans.

Pets and farm animals, such as dogs, cats, cows, ferrets, goats, horses and rabbits can become sources of infection and there is a risk of transmission to humans. The virus carrying rate up to 22.4% in our country. In most developed nations this risk is extremely small due to effective vaccination programs.

Route of Transmission

Rabies transmission can be made through lots of paths. The virus is usually present in the nerves and saliva of a rabid animal. The most common rabies transmission is through bites, scratches from an infected animal. Transmission can also occur when infectious material, usually alive, comes into direct contact with human mucosa or fresh skin wounds. Human-to-human transmission by bite is theoretically possible but has never been confirmed although it can happen through transplant surgery, or, even more rarely, through bites, kisses or sexual relations. Rarely, rabies may be contracted by inhalation of virus-containing aerosol in caves containing bats. Ingestion of raw meat or other tissues from animals infected with rabies is not a source of human infection.

Susceptible Population

People are generally susceptible to rabies virus. People most at risk live in rural areas where human vaccines and immunoglobulin are not readily available or accessible. Poor people are at a higher risk, as the average cost of rabies post-exposure prophylaxis after contact with a suspected rabid animal is higher than the average daily income in Africa and Asia.

Although all age groups are susceptible, rabies is most common in children aged under 15. On average 40 % of post-exposure prophylaxis regimens are given to children aged 5-14 years, and the majority are male.

Anyone in continual, frequent or increased danger of exposure to rabies virus is also at risk either by nature of their residence or occupation. Travelers with extensive outdoor exposure in rural, high-risk areas where immediate access to appropriate medical care may be limited should be considered at risk regardless of the duration of their stay. Children living in or visiting rabies-affected areas are at particular risk.

The morbidity of rabies is 15%~30% by rabid dog, and 50%~60% by rabid wolf.

What are the factors related to rabies occurrence?

Whether people bitted by sick animal will suffer rabies or not is associated with the following factors:

- The location of the bite. Head, face, neck, fingers were bitten by rabies animal are more likely to suffer from the disease.
- The severity of the bite. The profound and large wound will increase the incidence of overt infection.
- The treatment of local wound. Cleaning the wound quickly and thoroughly as much as possible will decrease the incidence of rabies greatly.
- Dressing thick or not. People dressing more thick will have less chance to be infected after being bitten.
- Vaccination. Immediately, sufficiently and full range vaccination after being bitten will decrease the morbidity.
- Immunologic function. People with immune dysfunction or deficiency have more susceptible to rabies after being bitten.

What are the symptoms of rabies?

The incubation period of rabies varies from 2 weeks to 6 years and beyond (but usually develops between 2 and 3 months after exposure), depending on the location and severity of the inoculating wound and the amount of virus introduced.

- Prodromal period. The first symptoms of rabies may be very similar to those of the flu including general weakness or discomfort, fever, or headache. These symptoms usually last from 2 to 4 days. The place that was bitten is also generally sore, itchy, and may have a prickly feeling. After a few days more serious signs will likely start to occur.

● Furious period. In this period, an infected person will become confused, agitated, or extremely anxious, which are all signs of central nervous system dysfunction lasting about 1 to 3 days. The hyperactivity may predominate. The fever of patients always rises 38-40℃, paresthesia, nuchal rigidity, hyperventilation, and hypersalivation may occur. Hydrophobia is the characteristic of this disease, but not all cases have. The typical patients feel extremely thirsty but afraid to drink, because their throat muscle will spasm severely when seeing water, hearing the sound of running water, drinking water or just talking about the water. A variety of external stimuli in surrounding condition such as light, sound, wind or voice can also cause pharyngeal muscle spasm. Patients often showed hoarseness due to vocal cord spasms and even spit the word unclearly. In severe cases, it can develop to paroxysmal muscle fasciculation, focal and generalized convulsions, and then lead to dyspnea and cyanosis. The sympathetic nerve function in patients is always hyperthyroidism in accentuation with symptoms of hypersalivation, hyperventilation, sweating, tachycardia and hypertension. The patient was more clear without losing the consciousness, but can appear disorders in mental, visual hallucination and auditory hallucination.

● Paralytic period. Patients in this stage enter the systemic flaccid paralysis with muscle cramps stop and go into a coma from quiet. This period lasts only 6 to 18 hours. Finally, patients with this infection typically die of respiratory and circulatory failure.

Generally, death almost invariably results 2 to 10 days after first symptoms. Once symptoms have presented, survival is rare, even with the administration of proper and intensive care. To date less than 10 documented cases of human survival from clinical rabies have been reported and only two have not had a history of pre- or postexposure prophylaxis.

How to diagnose rabies?

Usually, the diagnosis of human rabies includes three parts: epidemiological history of an animal bite or saliva exposure, typical clinical manifestation and confirmed laboratory examination.

Epidemiological history

People bite by animal species that is susceptible to rabies such as rats, mice, hamsters, and gerbils are rarely infected with rabies. Wild animal bites, especially from skunks or raccoons, are always suspected to have rabies.

Typical clinical manifestation

The symptoms and signs of rabies in humans may consist of some or many of the following according to the CDC and NIH:

- Anxiety, stress, and tension
- Delirium
- Drooling
- Convulsions
- Exaggerated sensation at the bite site
- Excitability or combativeness
- Hallucinations
- Loss of feeling in an area of the body
- Loss of muscle function
- Low-grade fever
- Muscle spasms
- Numbness and tingling
- Pain at the site of the bite
- Restlessness, insomnia
- Swallowing difficulty (drinking causes throat spasms and the person may become hydrophobic)

When these symptoms develop, the person will likely die from the disease. Less than 10 people have survived after developing such clinical rabies symptoms, and most of the few survivors had some previous level of treatment. When people develop clinical rabies, the best treatment is supportive care.

Laboratory examination

Rapid and accurate laboratory diagnosis of rabies in humans is essential for timely administration of postexposure prophylaxis. The laboratory results may save a patient from unnecessary physical and psychological trauma, and financial burdens, if the animal is not rabid. In addition, laboratory identification of positive rabies cases may aid in defining current epidemiologic patterns of disease and provide appropriate information for the development of rabies control programs. Several tests are necessary to diagnose rabies ante-mortem (before death) in humans; no single test is sufficient. Saliva can be tested by virus isolation or reverse transcription followed by polymerase chain reaction (RT-PCR). Serum and spinal fluid are tested for antibodies to rabies virus.

- The peripheral blood and cerebrospinal fluid

  Mild to moderate increase in white blood cell count, neutrophils accounted for more than 80%. The number of cells and protein in cerebrospinal fluid can be increased slightly, sugar and chloride are normal.

● Etiological examination

The patient's saliva, cerebrospinal fluid, tear or brain tissue was inoculated into the rat brain for virus separating.

Negri bodies are found most frequently in the pyramidal cells of Ammon's horn, and the Purkinje cells of the cerebellum. They are also found in the cells of the medulla and various other ganglia. Negri bodies can also be found in the neurons of the salivary glands, tongue, or other organs. Staining with Mann's, giemsa, or Sellers stains can permit differentiation of rabies inclusions from other intracellular inclusions. With these stains, Negri bodies appear magenta in color and have small (0.2 μm to 0.5 μm), dark-blue interior basophilic granules. RT-PCR were used for the detection of rabies virus nucleic acid.

The corneal imprint, hairy skin tissue or brain tissue can be used to detect the virus antigen by immunofluorescence antibody technique, the positive rate up to 98%.

● Virus antibody detection

Rapid fluorescent focus inhibition test (RFFIT) can be used to detect the neutralizing antibody of serum or cerebrospinal fluid (CSF) which were recommended by WHO and the United States of America CDC. In our country, ELISA can be used to detect the specific antibody in serum, mainly used for epidemiological investigation, also used to confirm the diagnosis of rabies.

What is the treatment for rabies in humans?

Anybody who is bitten by an animal that might have rabies needs to see a doctor immediately and receive treatment. If left untreated and symptoms eventually develop, the individual will die. Treatment for rabies consists of giving a person an injection of rabies immune globulin and another injection of rabies vaccine as soon as possible after the bite or exposure to saliva from an infected animal. Most researchers and clinicians suggest that the treatment begin as soon as possible after exposure. The reason about using human rabies immune globulin is that it immediately attacks the virus and slows or stops viral progression through the nerves. Vaccine is used to stimulate the body's immune response enough to make the body develop enough of an immune response to eventually kill all of the virus population in the body. Timing and the ability of the patient to respond by making a good immune response is a key to patient survival.

Guide for pre-exposure prophylaxis (PrEP)

PrEP may be performed with any of the modern cell-derived vaccines and is recommended for anyone at increased risk of exposure to rabies virus. Traditionally,

PrEP is recommended for anyone who is at continual, frequent or increased risk of exposure to the rabies virus either as a result of their residence or occupation (for example laboratory workers dealing with rabies virus and other lyssaviruses, veterinarians and animal handlers). Travelers with extensive outdoor exposure and children living in rural high-risk areas are at particular risk. PrEP schedule requires intramuscular doses of 2 ml given on days 0, 7 and 21. Strengthen injection every 1 to 3 years.

Guide for post-exposure prophylaxis (PEP)

PEP which consists of local treatment of the wound, followed by vaccine therapy (with or without rabies immunoglobulin) should be initiated immediately following a transdermal bite or scratch by an animal suspected of being rabid or when possibly infectious material, usually saliva comes into direct contact with the victim's mucosa or with fresh skin wounds.

- After being bitten place the wound should be cleaned thoroughly as soon as possible by using 20% soapy water or 0.1% Bromogeramine (quaternary ammonium disinfectant) repeated washing at least half an hour (quaternary amines with soap and water can not be used), to remove the dog saliva, extrusion dirty blood. the wound should be scrubbed by using 70% alcohol scrub and concentrated iodine repeatedly. If there is not profuse bleeding, do not try to close up or stitch the wound.
- If the patient was not vaccinated before being bitten the doctor will inject HRIG (human rabies immunoglobulin), mostly around the site of the wound and partly by deep intramuscular injection.
- The initial rabies vaccine should be given immediately, with the other doses on days 3, 7, 14 and 30 after the first. If the bites are serious, full 10 injections of the rabies vaccine should be given, from the first day to the sixth day daily one, then on days 10, 14, 30, 90 days of the injection.
- If a patient has already received pre-exposure vaccination, they should only receive the post-exposure vaccinations on days 0 and 2, and not be given the HRIG injections.

How is rabies prevented?

Travelling

Anybody travelling abroad into an area with rabies and know they will be in contact with possibly infected animals - for example, exploring bat caves - should have a pre-exposure anti-rabies vaccination. The vaccination gives the individual more time to get medical help; it does not offer full protection, but slows the virus down.

Contacting with animals

Do not touch unknown animals, no matter how friendly, furry, pretty and cute they seem. This is especially the case in areas that are not rabies-free. The National Health Service, UK informs that an early sign of rabies in an animal is unusual tameness.

Vaccinating animals

If you do not live in a rabies-free country or area, make sure your pets and farm animals' vaccinations are up-to-date. If you are not sure, talk to a veterinarian (animal doctor).

中英文注释

关键词汇

acetylcholine [ˌæsitilˈkɒliːn] n. 乙酰胆碱

aerophobia [ˌeərəˈfəubiə] n. 恐风症，恐高症

aerosol [ˈeərəˌsɔːl, -ˌsɔl] n. 气溶胶

convulsion [kənˈvʌlʃən] n. 抽搐

hallucination [həˌluːsiˈneiʃn] n. 幻觉

hoarseness [ˈhɔːsnəs] n. 嘶哑

hydrophobia [ˌhaidrəˈfəubiə] n. 恐水症

hyperthyroidism [ˌhaipəˈθairɔidizəm] n. 甲状腺功能亢进

hyperventilation [ˌhaipəˌventiˈleiʃn] n. 过度通气

inhalation [ˌinhəˈleiʃn] n. 吸入物

neurotropic [ˌnjuərəuˈtrɔpik] adj. 嗜神经的

paresthcsia [ˌpærisˈθiːʒiə] n. 感觉异常

pharyngeal [fəˈrindʒiəl] n. 咽部

pharyngismus [færiɒpəngizˈmʌs] n. 咽肌痉挛

photophobia [ˌfəutəuˈfəubiə] n. 恐光症

pinocytosis [painəusaiˈtəusis] n. 胞饮作用

ribonucleoprotein [raibəunjukliːəuˈprəutiːn] n. 核蛋白

salivary [ˈsæləˌveriː] adj. 唾液的

veterinary [ˈvetnri] n. 兽医

主要短语

acute zoonotic disease 急性传染病

central nervous system 中枢神经系统

cerebrospinal fluid 脑脊液

dyspnea and cyanosis 呼吸困难、发绀

fatality rate 病死率

furious period　兴奋期

helical symmetry　螺旋状对称

paralytic period　麻痹期

paroxysmal muscle fasciculation　阵发性肌颤

peripheral blood　外周血

post-exposure prophylaxis　暴露后预防

pre-exposure prophylaxis　暴露前预防

prodromal period　前驱期

progressive paralysis　进行性麻痹

psychological trauma　心理创伤

pyramidal cells　锥体细胞

杨　慧

Section Three: Obstetrical and Gynecological Disease

第三部分　妇产科疾病

59 Dysfunctional Uterine Bleeding
功能失调性子宫出血

What is dysfunctional uterine bleeding?

Dysfunctional uterine bleeding is irregular bleeding from the uterus. For example, you may get your period more often than every 21 days or farther apart than 35 days. Your period may last longer than 7 days. It is not serious, but it can be annoying and disrupt your life.

In most cases, this problem is related to changes in hormone levels. It is not caused by other medical conditions, such as miscarriage, fibroids, cancer, or blood clotting problems. Your doctor will rule out these and other causes of vaginal bleeding to confirm that you have dysfunctional uterine bleeding.

What causes dysfunctional uterine bleeding?

Dysfunctional uterine bleeding is usually caused by changes in hormone levels. In some cases the cause of the bleeding isn't known.

Normally one of your ovaries releases an egg during your menstrual cycle. This is called ovulation. Dysfunctional uterine bleeding is often triggered when women don't ovulate. This causes changes in hormone levels and in some cases can lead to unexpected vaginal bleeding.

Women can also get this condition even though they ovulate, although this is less common. Experts don't fully understand this type of vaginal bleeding. It may be caused by changes in certain body chemicals.

What are the symptoms of dysfunctional uterine bleeding?

You may have dysfunctional uterine bleeding if you have one or more of the following symptoms:

- You get your period more often than every 21 days or farther apart than 35 days. A normal adult menstrual cycle is 21 to 35 days long. A normal teen cycle is 21 to 45 days.
- Your period lasts longer than 7 days (normally 4 to 6 days).

413

- Your bleeding is heavier than normal. If you are passing blood clots and soaking through your usual pads or tampons each hour for 2 or more hours, your bleeding is considered severe and you should call your doctor.

Talk to your doctor if you have had irregular vaginal bleeding for three or more menstrual cycles or if your symptoms are affecting your daily life.

How is dysfunctional uterine bleeding diagnosed?

The doctor must first rule out all other causes of vaginal bleeding before diagnosing dysfunctional uterine bleeding. These causes include miscarriage and problems with pregnancy. Vaginal bleeding may also be caused by common conditions, such as uterine fibroids.

The doctor will ask how often, how long, and how much you have been bleeding. The patients may also have a pelvic exam, urine test, blood tests, and possibly an ultrasound. These tests will help your doctor check for other causes of your symptoms. He or she may also take a tiny sample (biopsy) of tissue from your uterus for testing.

You have dysfunctional uterine bleeding if, after testing, your doctor finds no other diseases or conditions that are causing your symptoms.

How is it treated?

There are many things you can do to treat dysfunctional uterine bleeding. Some are meant to return the menstrual cycle to normal. Others are used to reduce bleeding or to stop monthly periods. Each treatment works for some women but not others. Treatments include:

- Hormones, such as a progestin pill or daily birth control pill (progestin and estrogen). These hormones help control the menstrual cycle and reduce bleeding and cramping.
- A short course of high-dose estrogen. Estrogen is a hormone that is often used to stop dangerously heavy bleeding.
- Use of the levonorgestrel IUD, which releases a progesterone-like hormone into the uterus. This reduces bleeding while preventing pregnancy.
- Rarely used medicines that stop estrogen production and menstruation, such as gonadotropin-releasing hormones. These drugs can cause severe side effects but are used in special cases.
- Surgery, such as endometrial ablation or hysterectomy, when other treatments do not work.

If you also have menstrual pain or heavy bleeding, you can take regular doses of a nonsteroidal anti-inflammatory drug (NSAID), such as ibuprofen.

In some cases, doctors use watchful waiting, or a wait-and-see approach. It may be okay for a teen or for a woman nearing menopause. Some teens have times of irregular vaginal bleeding. This usually gets better over time as hormone levels even out. Women in menopause can expect their periods to stop. They may choose to wait and see if this happens before they try other treatments.

中英文注释

关键词汇

estrogen ['estrədʒən] n. 雌性激素

fibroid ['faibrɒid] n. 子宫肌瘤

menopause ['menəpɔːz] n. 更年期

miscarriage [mis'kæridʒ; 'miskæridʒ] n. 流产

ultrasound ['ʌltrəsaʊnd] n. 超声

主要短语

dysfunctional uterine bleeding 功能失调性子宫出血

endometrial ablation 子宫内膜切除

gonadotropin-releasing hormones 促性腺激素释放激素

irregular vaginal bleeding 阴道不规则流血

menstrual cycle 月经周期

rule out 排除

付永良 马志方

60

Ectopic Pregnancy
异 位 妊 娠

What is ectopic pregnancy?

In a normal pregnancy, your ovary releases an egg into your fallopian tube. If the egg meets with a sperm, the fertilized egg moves into your uterus to attach to its lining and continues to grow for the next 9 months.

But in up to 1 of every 50 pregnancies, the fertilized egg stays in your fallopian tube. In that case, it's called an ectopic pregnancy or a tubal pregnancy. In rare cases, the fertilized egg attaches to one of your ovaries or another organ in your abdomen. In either case, instead of celebrating your pregnancy, you find your life is in danger. Ectopic pregnancies require emergency treatment.

Most often, ectopic pregnancy happens within the first few weeks of pregnancy. You might not even know you're pregnant yet, so it can be a big shock. Doctors usually discover it by the 8th week of pregnancy.

Ectopic pregnancies can be scary and sad. The baby cannot survive, so it's a loss that may take some time to get over. It may comfort you to know that if you have an ectopic pregnancy, you'll likely be able to have a healthy pregnancy in the future.

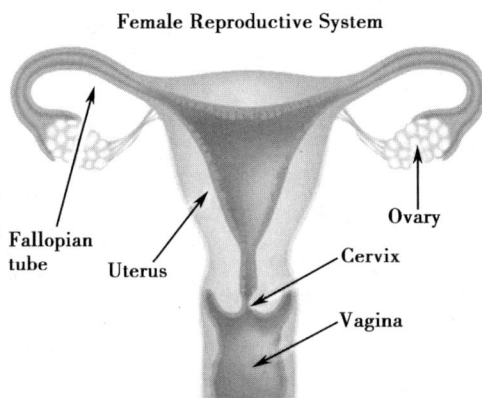

Female Reproductive System

Fallopian tube
Uterus
Ovary
Cervix
Vagina

What are causes of ectopic pregnancy?

One cause of an ectopic pregnancy is a damaged fallopian tube that doesn't let a fertilized egg into your uterus, so it implants in the fallopian tube or somewhere else.

You might not ever know what caused an ectopic pregnancy. But you are higher risk if you have:

- Use of an intrauterine device (IUD), a form of birth control, that is inserted at the time of conception
- History of pelvic inflammatory disease (PID)
- Sexually-transmitted diseases such as chlamydia and gonorrhea
- Congenital abnormality (problem present at birth) of the fallopian tube
- History of pelvic surgery (because scarring may block the fertilized egg from leaving the fallopian tube)
- History of ectopic pregnancy
- Unsuccessful tubal ligation (surgical sterilization) or tubal ligation reversal
- Use of fertility drugs
- Infertility treatments such as in vitro fertilization (IVF)

What are symptoms of an ectopic pregnancy?

- Light vaginal bleeding
- Nausea and vomiting
- Lower abdominal pain
- Sharp abdominal cramps
- Pain on one side of your body
- Dizziness or weakness
- Pain in your shoulder, neck, or rectum

If the fallopian tube ruptures, the pain and bleeding could be severe enough to cause fainting.

If you are experiencing the symptoms listed above, contact your health care provider immediately and go to the emergency room. Getting to the hospital quickly is important to reduce the risk of hemorrhaging (severe bleeding) and to preserve your fertility.

How to diagnose ectopic pregnancy?

Once you arrive at the hospital, a pregnancy test, a pelvic exam, and an ultrasound test may be performed to view the uterus' condition and fallopian tubes.

If an ectopic pregnancy has been confirmed, the health care provider will decide on the best treatment based on your medical condition and your future plans for pregnancy.

How is it treated?

If the doctor suspects that the fallopian tube has ruptured, emergency surgery is necessary to stop the bleeding. In some cases, the fallopian tube and ovary may be damaged and will have to be removed.

If the fallopian tube has not ruptured and the pregnancy has not progressed very far, laparoscopic surgery may be all that is needed to remove the embryo and repair the damage. A laparoscope is a thin, flexible instrument inserted through small incisions in the abdomen. During this surgery, a tiny incision is made in the fallopian tube and the embryo is removed, preserving the fallopian tube's integrity.

In some cases, medication may be used to stop the growth of pregnancy tissue. This treatment option may be appropriate if the tube is not ruptured and the pregnancy has not progressed very far.

After treatment for an ectopic pregnancy, you will usually have to have additional blood tests to make sure that the entire tubal pregnancy was removed. The blood tests detect the hCG level, the hormone that is produced during pregnancy.

Getting Pregnant After an Ectopic Pregnancy

Most women who have an ectopic pregnancy have normal pregnancies and births in the future, even if a fallopian tube was removed. As long as you have one normally working fallopian tube, you can get pregnant. If the ectopic pregnancy was caused by a treatable illness, such as a sexually transmitted disease, getting treated for it can improve your chances of a successful pregnancy.

Talk with your doctor about how long to wait after an ectopic pregnancy before trying to conceive again. Some doctors suggest waiting 3 to 6 months.

After an ectopic pregnancy, take the time you need to heal your body and mind. Above all, don't blame yourself. Counseling or pregnancy loss support groups can help you and your partner cope. Ask your doctor about groups near you.

中英文注释

关键词汇

chlamydia [klə'midiə] n. 衣原体

dizziness ['dizinis] n. 头晕

embryo ['embriəʊ] n. 胚胎

fainting ['feintiŋ] n. 昏厥

fertility [fə'tiliti; fɜː'tiliti] n. 生育能力

gonorrhea [ˌɡɒnəˈriə] n. 淋病
ovary [ˈəʊv(ə)ri] n. 卵巢
pregnancy [ˈpreɡnənsi] n. 怀孕
rectum [ˈrektəm] n. 直肠
sperm [spɜːm] n. 精子

主要短语

ectopic pregnancy 异位妊娠
fallopian tube 输卵管
intrauterine device (IUD) 宫内节育器
in vitro fertilization (IVF) 体外受精
laparoscopic surgery 腹腔镜手术
pelvic inflammatory disease (PID) 盆腔炎
sexually transmitted disease 性病

付永良　马志方

Section Four: Pediatric Disease

第四部分 儿科疾病

61 Childhood Leukemia
小儿白血病

What is childhood leukemia?

Childhood leukemia, the most common type of cancer in children and teens, is a cancer of the white blood cells. Abnormal white blood cells form in the bone marrow. They quickly travel through the bloodstream and crowd out healthy cells. This increases the body's chances of infection and other problems.

As tough as it is for a child to have cancer, it's good to know that most children and teens with childhood leukemia can be successfully treated.

Risk Factors for Childhood Leukemia

Doctors don't know exactly what causes most cases of childhood leukemia. But certain factors may increase the chances of getting it. Keep in mind, though, that having a risk factor does not necessarily mean a child will get leukemia. In fact, most children with leukemia don't have any known risk factors.

The risk for childhood leukemia increases if your child has:

- An inherited disorder such as Li-Fraumeni syndrome, Down syndrome, or Klinefelter syndrome
- An inherited immune system problem such as ataxia telangiectasia
- A brother or sister with leukemia, especially an identical twin
- A history of being exposed to high levels of radiation, chemotherapy, or chemicals such as benzene (a solvent)
- A history of immune system suppression, such as for an organ transplant

Although the risk is small, doctors advise that children with known risk factors have regular checkups to spot any problems early.

Types of childhood leukemia

Almost all cases of childhood leukemia are acute, which means they develop rapidly. A tiny number are chronic and develop slowly.

Types of childhood leukemia include:

- Acute lymphoblastic leukemia (ALL), also called acute lymphocytic leukemia.

ALL accounts for three out of every four cases of childhood leukemia.

- Acute myelogenous leukemia (AML). AML is the next most common type of childhood leukemia.
- Hybrid or mixed lineage leukemia. This is a rare leukemia with features of both ALL and AML.
- Chronic myelogenous leukemia (CML). CML is rare in children.
- Chronic lymphocytic leukemia (CLL). CLL is very rare in children.
- Juvenile myelomonocytic leukemia (JMML). This is a rare type that is neither chronic nor acute and occurs most often in children under age 4.

What are symptoms of childhood leukemia?

Symptoms of leukemia often prompt a visit to the doctor. This is a good thing because it means the disease may be found earlier than it otherwise would. Early diagnosis can lead to more successful treatment.

Many signs and symptoms of childhood leukemia occur when leukemia cells crowd out normal cells.

Common symptoms include:

- Fatigue or pale skin
- Infections and fever
- Easy bleeding or bruising
- Extreme fatigue or weakness
- Shortness of breath
- Coughing

Other symptoms may include:

- Bone or joint pain
- Swelling in the abdomen, face, arms, underarms, sides of neck, or groin
- Swelling above the collarbone
- Loss of appetite or weight loss
- Headaches, seizures, balance problems, or abnormal vision
- Vomiting
- Rashes
- Gum problems

How is childhood leukemia diagnosed?

To diagnose childhood leukemia, the doctor will take a thorough medical history and perform a physical exam. Tests are used to diagnose childhood leukemia as well as classify its type.

Initial tests may include:

- Blood tests to measure the number of blood cells and see how they appear.
- Bone marrow aspiration and biopsy, usually taken from the pelvic bone, to confirm a diagnosis of leukemia.
- Lumbar puncture, or spinal tap, to check for spread of leukemia cells in the fluid that bathes the brain and spinal cord.

A pathologist examines cells from the blood tests under a microscope. This specialist also checks bone marrow samples for the number of blood-forming cells and fat cells.

Other tests may be done to help determine which type of leukemia your child may have. These tests also help the doctors know how likely the leukemia is to respond to treatment.

Certain tests may be repeated later to see how your child responds to treatment.

How is it treated?

Have a "heart-to-heart" talk with your child's doctor and other members of the cancer care team about the best options for your child. Treatment depends mainly upon the type of leukemia as well as other factors.

The good news is the survival rates for most types of childhood leukemia have increased over time. And treatment at special centers for children and teens provides the advantages of specialized care. In addition, childhood cancers tend to respond to treatment better than adult cancers do, and children's bodies often tolerate treatment better.

Before cancer treatment begins, sometimes a child needs treatment to address illness complications. For example, changes in blood cells can lead to infections or severe bleeding and may affect the amount of oxygen reaching the body's tissues. Treatment may involve antibiotics, blood transfusions, or other measures to fight infection.

Chemotherapy is the main treatment for childhood leukemia. Your child will receive anticancer drugs by mouth, or into a vein, a muscle, or the spinal fluid. To keep leukemia from returning, maintenance therapy occurs in cycles over a period of two or three years.

Targeted therapy is also sometimes used for leukemia. This therapy targets specific parts of cancer cells, working differently than standard chemotherapy. Effective for certain types of childhood leukemia, targeted therapy often has less severe side effects.

Other types of treatment may include radiation therapy, which uses high-energy radiation to kill cancer cells and shrink tumors. It may be used to help prevent or treat the spread of leukemia to other parts of the body. Surgery is rarely used to treat childhood leukemia.

If standard treatment is likely to be less effective, a stem cell transplant may be the best option. It involves a transplant of blood-forming stem cells after whole body radiation combined with high-dose chemotherapy to first destroy the child's bone marrow.

中英文注释

关键词汇

chemotherapy [kiːmə(ʊ)ˈθerəpi] n. 化疗

complication [kɒmpliˈkeiʃ(ə)n] n. 并发症

leukemia [ljuˈkiːmiə] n. 白血病

marrow [ˈmærəʊ] n. 骨髓

rash [ræʃ] n. 皮疹

主要短语

blood-forming stem cells 造血干细胞

blood transfusions 输血

bone marrow aspiration and biopsy 骨髓穿刺活检

childhood leukemia 儿童白血病

easy bleeding or bruising 容易出血或挫伤

extreme fatigue or weakness 极度疲乏或虚弱

fatigue or pale skin 疲乏或皮肤苍白

infections and fever 感染和发烧

inherited disorder 遗传病

loss of appetite 食欲缺乏

lumbar puncture 腰椎穿刺

maintenance therapy 维持治疗

spinal cord 脊髓

魏　亮　马志方

62 ——————— Pneumonia In Children
小 儿 肺 炎

What is pneumonia in children?

Pneumonia is an infection in one or both lungs. Often, pneumonia begins after an infection of the upper respiratory tract (nose and throat). This causes fluid to collect in the lungs, making it hard to breathe.

What causes pneumonia in children?

Pneumonia can be caused by different types of germs, including bacteria, viruses, fungi, and parasites. Viruses are usually the cause of pneumonia in children. Children with viral pneumonia can also develop bacterial pneumonia. Pneumonia can also occur if foreign material, such as food or stomach acid, is inhaled into the lungs.

What may increase the risk for pneumonia in children?
- Premature birth
- Breathing secondhand smoke
- Asthma or certain genetic disorders, such as sicklecell anemia
- Heart defects, such as ventricular septal defect (VSD), atrial septal defect (ASD), or patent ductus arteriosus (PDA)
- Poor nutrition
- A weak immune system
- Spending time in a crowded place, such as a daycare center

What are symptoms of pneumonia in children?

The signs and symptoms depend on what caused the pneumonia and the age of the child. The signs and symptoms of pneumonia caused by bacteria usually begin more quickly than a viral infection. Your child may have one or more of the following:
- Cough, usually with yellow or green mucus
- Fever
- Crying more than usual, or more irritable or fussy than normal
- Poor appetite

427

- Loose bowel movements
- Shortness of breath or difficulty breathing
- Pale or bluish lips, fingernails, or toenails

How do I know if my child is having trouble breathing?

Your child's nostrils open wider when he breathes in.

Your child's skin between his ribs and around his neck pulls in with each breath.

Your child is wheezing, which means you hear a high-pitched noise when he breathes out.

Your child is breathing fast:

- More than 60 breaths in one minute for newborn babies up to 2 months old
- More than 50 breaths in one minute for a baby 2 months to 12 months old
- More than 40 breaths in one minute for a child older than 1 year

How is pneumonia in children diagnosed?

- Blood tests: You may need blood taken to give caregivers information about how your body is working. The blood may be taken from your hand, arm, or IV.
- Chest X-ray: This is a picture of your child's lungs and heart. Caregivers may use this to look for signs of infection (such as pneumonia) or other problems.
- Sputum culture: These tests are used to look for germs in your child's spit or in the mucus your child coughs up.

How is pneumonia in children treated?

Many children can be treated at a doctor's office and at home. If the pneumonia is severe, a caregiver may want your child to stay in the hospital for treatment. Trouble breathing, dehydration, high fever, and the need for oxygen or medicines are reasons to stay in the hospital.

- Medicines: Your child will usually need to take antibiotics if he has bacterial pneumonia. Viral pneumonia will usually go away without antibiotics.
- Oxygen: Your child may need oxygen if his blood oxygen level is lower than it should be. Oxygen will help your child breathe easier. Your child may get oxygen through small tubes placed in his nostrils, or through a mask. He may instead be placed in an oxygen tent. Nevertake off your child's oxygen tubes or mask or remove him from the tent without asking his caregiver first.

How can pneumonia in children be prevented?

- Your child may be able to take preventative antibiotics if he has been exposed to pneumonia or if he has weak immune system. Ask your child's caregiver for information.

● Do not let anyone smoke around your child. Smoke can make your child's coughing or breathing worse.

● Get your child vaccinated against viruses or bacteria that cause infections such as pneumonia.

● Keep your child away from people with a cold.

● Wash your hands and your child's hands often with soap to prevent the spread of germs.

● Do not let your child share food, drinks, or utensils with others.

What are the risks of pneumonia in children?

The risks of serious illness or death are small if you follow your child's caregiver's advice. If left untreated, pneumonia can be life-threatening.

中英文注释

关键词汇

asthma ['æsmə] n. 哮喘

bacteria [bæk'tiəriə] n. 细菌

fungus ['fʌŋgəs] n. 真菌

life-threatening ['laif'θretəniŋ] adj. 威胁生命的

mucus ['mju:kəs] n. 黏液

nostril ['nɔstril] n. 鼻孔

parasite ['pærəsait] n. 寄生虫

pneumonia [nju:'məunjə] n. 肺炎

sign [sain] n. 症状

symptom ['simptəm] n. 症状

vaccinate ['væksineit] vt. 给…接种疫苗

wheeze [hwi:z] vi. 喘息

主要短语

atrial septal defect (ASD) 房间隔缺损

breathing secondhand smoke 吸二手烟

chest X-ray 胸部 X 光片

foreign material 异物

newborn baby 新生儿

patent ductus arteriosus (PDA) 动脉导管未闭

poor appetite 食欲缺乏
poor nutrition 营养不良
premature birth 早产
sicklecell anemia 镰状细胞贫血
sputum culture 痰培养
stomach acid 胃酸
upper respiratory tract 上呼吸道
ventricular septal defect (VSD) 室间隔缺损
weak immune system 免疫力低下

高宏飞　马志方

63 • Congenital Heart Disease (CHD)
先天性心脏病

What is congenital heart disease?

Congenital heart disease is a category of heart disease that includes abnormalities in cardiovascular structures that occur before birth.

These defects occur while the fetus is developing in the uterus and may affect approximately 1 in 100 children.

Congenital heart defects may produce symptoms at birth, during childhood, or not until adulthood. Other congenital defects may cause no symptoms.

About 500,000 adults in the U.S. have congenital heart disease.

What causes congenital heart disease?

In the majority of people, the cause of congenital heart disease is unknown. However, there are some factors that are associated with an increased chance of having congenital heart disease. These risk factors include:

- Genetic or chromosomal abnormalities in the child, such as Down syndrome
- Taking certain medications or alcohol or drug abuse during pregnancy
- Maternal viral infection, such as rubella (German measles) in the first trimester of pregnancy

The risk of having a child with congenital heart disease may double if a parent or a sibling has a congenital heart defect.

What types of congenital heart problems are there?

The most common congenital heart problems include:

- **Heart valve defects.** These can result in a narrowing or stenosis of the valves, or a complete closure that impedes or obstructs forward blood flow. Other valve defects include leaky valves that don't close properly, thereby allowing blood to leak backwards.
- **Defects in the walls between the atria and ventricles of the heart (atrial and ventricular septal defects).** Holes or passageways between the heart's different

chambers may allow abnormal mixing of oxygenated and unoxygenated blood between the right and left sides of the heart.

- **Heart muscle abnormalities that can lead to heart failure.**

What are the symptoms of congenital heart disease in adults?

Congenital heart disease may be diagnosed before birth, right after birth, during childhood, or not until adulthood. It is possible to have a defect and no symptoms at all. In adults, if symptoms are present, they may include:

- Shortness of breath
- Limited ability to exercise

How is congenital heart disease diagnosed?

Congenital heart disease is often first detected when your doctor hears an abnormal heart sound or heart murmur when listening to the heart.

Depending on the type of murmur your doctor hears, he or she may order further testing such as:

- **The Basics of EKG.** Whether you spell it EKG or ECG, it's an electrocardiogram.
- **Chest X-Ray.**
- **Stress Test.**
- **Tilt Table Test.** The head-up tilt table test is used to help find the cause of fainting spells.
- **Echocardiogram.** There are several variations on the echocardiogram, or "echo", as doctors call it.
- **Cardiac Catheterization.** Cardiac catheterization — also called a coronary angiogram — means running a catheter into your heart. It's done to help doctors see what's going on in there, and whether they need to operate.
- **Electrophysiology Test.** Electrophysiology — the EP test — takes measurements of your heart rhythm — recording the electrical activity and pathways of your heart.
- **CT Heart Scan.** Computed tomography (CT scan) of the heart can visualize your heart's anatomy. Calcium-score heart scan and coronary CT angiography are just a few types used to diagnose heart disease.
- **Myocardial Biopsy.** A myocardial biopsy is when a doctor uses a special catheter to remove a piece of your heart tissue for examination.
- **Heart MRI.** A heart MRI is a great way for doctors to get a look — from the outside — at how your heart is working.

- **Pericardiocentesis.** Pericardiocentesis — also called a pericardial tap — means using a needle to get a sample of the fluid in the sac surrounding the heart.

How is congenital heart disease treated?

Treatment is based on the severity of the congenital heart disease. Some mild heart defects do not require any treatment. Others can be treated with medications, procedures, or surgery. Most adults with congenital heart disease should be monitored by a heart specialist throughout their lifetime.

Some people with congenital heart disease are at risk for getting endocarditis, especially if the heart was repaired or replaced through surgery. To protect yourself:

- Tell all doctors and dentists you have congenital heart disease. You may want to carry a card with this information.
- Call your doctor if you have symptoms of an infection (sore throat, general body aches, fever).
- Take good care of your teeth and gums to prevent infections. See your dentist for regular visits.
- Take antibiotics according to the American Heart Association guidelines before you undergo a procedure that may cause bleeding, such as: dental work, invasive tests (any test that may involve blood or bleeding), and most major or minor surgeries. Check with your doctor about the type and amount of antibiotics that you should take.

Congenital heart defects in children

There are several congenital heart defects that are detected and treated early in infancy. Most of them are abnormal connections among the veins, as well as other arteries of the heart (aortic and pulmonary). These abnormal connections can allow unoxygenated blood to flow to the body instead of to the lungs, or allow oxygenated blood to flow to the lungs instead of to the body. They may also cause heart failure. Some examples of congenital heart disease in infants and children include:

- Patent ductus arteriosus (when blood bypasses the lungs, preventing oxygen from circulating throughout the body)
- Tetralogy of Fallot (four different heart defects that occur together)
- Transposition of the great vessels (blood from the left side of the heart and right side of the heart intermix because the large artery connections are incorrect)
- Coarctation of the aorta (a pinched aorta)
- Heart valve problems

What are the symptoms of congenital heart disease in infants and children?

The symptoms of congenital heart disease in infants and children include:
- Cyanosis (a bluish tint to the skin, fingernails, and lips)
- Fast breathing and poor feeding
- Poor weight gain
- Recurrent lung infections
- Inability to exercise

How are congenital heart defects in children treated?

Some congenital heart defects will require surgery or an interventional procedure to repair the problem. Children with congenital heart disease may also need treatment with medication to improve heart function.

Children and adults with congenital heart disease should be treated by a cardiologist who specializes in congenital heart disease. Some types of disease may require a team approach as the child grows into an adult.

It is important to continue to see a cardiologist as an adult.

中英文注释

关键词汇

cardiovascular [kɑrdio'væskjələ˞] adj. 心血管的

echocardiogram [ˌɛko'kardiəˌgræm] n. 超声心动图

electrocardiogram [iˌlɛktro'kardiogræm] n. 心电图

electrophysiology [iˌlektrəʊfizi'ɒlədʒi] n. 电生理学

endocarditis [ˌɛndokar'daitis] n. 心内膜炎

fetus ['fitəs] n. 胎儿

pericardia [pɛri'kardiəl] n. 心包

pericardiocentesis ['periˌka:diəusenti:sis] n. 心包穿刺术

rubella [rʊ'bɛlə˞] n. 风疹

主要短语

atrial and ventricular septal defects　室间隔缺损

cardiac catheterization　心导管置入术

coarctation of the aorta　主动脉狭窄

congenital heart disease　先天性心脏病

coronary angiogram　冠状动脉造影

heart murmur 心杂音
heart rhythm 心脏节律
heart valve defects 心脏瓣膜缺陷
myocardial biopsy 心肌组织活检
patent ductus arteriosus 动脉导管未闭
shortness of breath 呼吸急促
tetralogy of Fallot 法洛四联症
unoxygenated blood 缺氧血

阎小挺　马志方

64

Newborn Jaundice
新生儿黄疸

What is newborn jaundice?

Many newborn babies develop jaundice, a condition in which the skin and whites of the eyes are yellowish in color, within a few days after birth. In fact, about half of all newborns develop mild jaundice in the first few days. In premature babies, jaundice may start early and last longer than in full-term babies.

If bilirubin levels become extremely high, complications such as brain damage (kernicterus), cerebral palsy, and deafness can occur.

What causes newborn jaundice?

Jaundice typically occurs because newborns normally produce increased levels of bilirubin which is referred to as "physiologic jaundice". Bilirubin, which is yellowish in color, is produced when red blood cells are broken down. Bilirubin is removed from the bloodstream by the liver. In newborns, the body may produce more bilirubin than the liver can process.

Physiologic jaundice usually appears within a few days after birth and resolves within two weeks. Other types of newborn jaundice can be due to prematurity, problems related to breastfeeding, infection, and blood or liver problems.

Since many mothers and babies leave the hospital soon after delivery, jaundice may not appear until babies are at home.

It is important to contact your doctor if you notice signs of jaundice in your baby and you may need to see the doctor that same day. While jaundice is usually very treatable, in the most extreme cases it can cause brain damage.

What are the symptoms of newborn jaundice?

The most common symptom of jaundice in newborns is a yellowish tinge to the skin, the white part of the eyes, or the inside of the mouth. This yellow tint usually appears first in the infant's face and chest between 1 and 5 days after birth, although the exact timing may vary by child and by the type of jaundice.

- Physiologic jaundice develops in all babies (although it may be very slight and not noticeable) sometime after the first day of life. It occurs because babies' organs are not yet able to get rid of excess bilirubin effectively. If noticeable, the yellowing of the skin and eyes usually appears about 24 hours after birth and increases until about the third or fourth day. Most often, the blood bilirubin level then gradually lowers, and the yellowing fades or disappears in about a week without causing problems.
- Breast-feeding jaundice is caused by mild dehydration, which prolongs and intensifies physiologic jaundice. Dehydration contributes to jaundice because it makes removing bilirubin from the body even harder for babies' immature systems. Breast-feeding jaundice can occur when a baby does not get enough fluids, most often because feedings are spaced too far apart. Typically, if feedings become more frequent, this type of jaundice decreases or resolves sometime between 5 and 7 days after birth.
- Breast milk jaundice is a rise in bilirubin levels that occurs about 10 to 14 days after birth. It is likely related to how certain components of breast milk affect bilirubin elimination in the infant. Breast milk jaundice usually begins to fade by the second month, although a slight yellow tint may be visible throughout the duration of breast-feeding.

In rare cases, jaundice in a newborn may be caused by an underlying condition. Symptoms that begin to appear less than 24 hours after birth are unlikely to be jaundice and need to be evaluated carefully for other possible causes.

In general, call your health professional if the yellowing appears to increase after your baby's third day of life or has not decreased by the fifth day. Remember, however, that if you are breast-feeding, increasing the frequency of feedings may help to lower your baby's bilirubin levels and decrease jaundice.

Brain damage (kernicterus) can develop if a baby with a high bilirubin blood level is not treated. See your health professional right away if your baby develops signs of a high bilirubin level, which include:

- Sluggishness and poor sucking ability.
- Irritability, jitteriness, and crying.
- Arching of the baby's back.
- A shrill, high-pitched cry.

Signs of a very high level of bilirubin may include:

- Periods of not breathing (apnea) or difficulty breathing (dyspnea).
- Seizures.

How is newborn jaundice diagnosed?

Your baby's doctor will do a physical exam and take a medical history to diagnose jaundice. As part of the medical history, the doctor may ask questions about:

- Your general health, particularly during the pregnancy.
- Whether your baby was born prematurely or at full term.
- Whether your baby had any difficulties during delivery.
- Your baby's birth weight and whether there has been any weight gain or loss since birth.
- Your baby's feeding and elimination habits since birth.
- Whether the baby and you have incompatible blood types (ABO or Rh incompatibility).
- Your family history of health conditions that could cause jaundice.

During the exam, the doctor will check your baby's skin color. This may include pressing a finger lightly on your baby's skin. The doctor will note whether yellowing related to jaundice is visible only in the eyes, face, and head or if it is also noticed on the chest and lower body. He or she may also look for signs of underlying conditions that can cause jaundice.

A transcutaneous jaundice meter may be used to measure your baby's bilirubin level. If the results are concerning, a bilirubin test may be done to more precisely measure the bilirubin level in your baby's blood. The results will help your baby's doctor decide whether treatment is needed.

If the doctor thinks that another condition is causing your baby to have too much bilirubin in the blood (hyperbilirubinemia), more tests may be done. For example, the doctor may do blood type tests if the cause of hyperbilirubinemia could be that you and your baby have different blood types (ABO or Rh incompatibility).

Many mothers and their newborns leave the hospital within 48 hours of the baby's birth, often before signs of jaundice start. Your baby needs a follow-up exam within the first 5 days after birth. Call your baby's doctor if at any time you notice a yellow tinge to your baby's skin and eyes.

How is newborn jaundice treated?

Most of the time no medical treatment is needed for jaundice in a newborn (hyperbilirubinemia). But watch for increasing intensity of the yellow tint in the skin and eyes or any change in your baby's behavior.

Babies who have bilirubin in their blood at a level that could be harmful need treatment. Whatever the cause, if the condition is not treated, excessive amounts of bilirubin in the blood may lead to brain damage (kernicterus), which could result in hearing loss, intellectual disability, and behavior problems.

The most common treatment for hyperbilirubinemia is phototherapy, which uses fluorescent light to help transform bilirubin into a form the body can more quickly eliminate. Standard phototherapy is usually done in a hospital. But babies with jaundice who are otherwise healthy may be treated at home with a type of phototherapy that uses a fiber-optic wrap, usually a blanket or a band. These wraps usually reduce blood bilirubin levels more slowly than standard phototherapy, so generally they are used only for mild jaundice. Sometimes standard therapy and fiber-optic wrap therapy are used together.

If your newborn is receiving phototherapy for jaundice in the hospital, you can help by:

- Asking whether you can stay in the hospital overnight so you can continue to care for your baby. If you are not able to stay, visit frequently.
- Touching your baby often during phototherapy sessions in the enclosed plastic crib (incubator). You can reach into the incubator through specially made armholes on both sides of the incubator.
- Talking or singing to your baby, because babies can hear through the incubator.
- Holding your baby during the short periods when he or she is taken out from under the light.

The fluorescent lights used in phototherapy for babies with jaundice are not harmful if precautions are taken. Eye shields are placed over the baby's eyes to protect them while under the light. The shields are removed during feedings. Babies are accustomed to being in the dark after months in the womb, so the shields should not bother your baby.

If your baby is being treated at home for jaundice, be sure you understand how to use all of the equipment. Ask your baby's doctor for help if you have questions or concerns. You may need to take your baby to a lab each day to get his or her bilirubin checked. A home health nurse may visit to make sure all is going well.

If the baby's jaundice is being caused by an underlying condition, other treatments may be needed. For example, if severe jaundice is caused by the baby's body destroying red blood cells (blood type incompatibility), the baby may need immunoglobulin (IG). If that doesn't help, the baby may need to be admitted to a hospital and given a blood transfusion.

中英文注释

关键词汇

apnea [æp'niə] n. 呼吸暂停

bilirubin [ˌbiliˈrubin] n. 胆红素

hyperbilirubinemia [ˌhaipəˌbiləˌruːbəˈniːmiə] n. 高胆红素血症

immunoglobulin [ˌimjənoˈglabjələn] n. 免疫球蛋白

incubator [ˈiŋkjubetɚ] n. 保温箱

irritability [ˌirətəˈbilətl] adj. 易怒的

jaundice [ˈdʒɔndis] n. 黄疸

kernicterus [kəˈniktərəs] n. 核性黄疸, 胆红素脑病

phototherapy [ˌfotəˈθɛrəpi] n. 光线疗法

seizures [ˈsiʒɚ] n. 癫痫

主要短语

blood type 血型

blood transfusion 输血

cerebral palsy 脑瘫

full-term baby 足月儿

mild dehydration 轻度脱水

physiologic jaundice 生理性黄疸

premature baby 早产儿

阎小挺　马志方

65 Undescended Testicle
隐　　睾

What is undescended testicle?

As a baby boy grows inside his mother, he develops testicles. Early in his development, his testicles are in his belly. Normally, before he is born, his testicles move down into his scrotum, the sac that hangs below the penis. When one testicle does not move into the scrotum as it should, the baby has an undescended testicle. In rare cases, both testicles are undescended.

About 5 out of 100 baby boys are born with an undescended testicle. It is most common in babies who were born before their due date or who were very small at birth.

Doctors don't really know what causes an undescended testicle. This common condition runs in some families (can be inherited).

Most of the time, the testicle descends (drops) on its own by the time the baby is 3 months old. If your baby's testicle hasn't dropped by the time he is 6 months of age, your doctor may suggest treatment.

What are the symptoms of undescended testicle?

An undescended testicle doesn't cause pain or other symptoms. The scrotum may look a little smoother or less developed on one side, or the side without a testicle may look smaller and flatter. You can't feel the testicle in the scrotum on the side where it hasn't descended.

How is undescended testicle diagnosed?

At newborn and well-baby visits, your doctor will check your baby's scrotum.
- If the testicle can be felt but it is not in the scrotum, the doctor will probably want to check your baby again at 3 to 6 months of age. By this time, the testicle may have moved into place on its own.
- Sometimes the doctor can't feel the testicle at all. It could still be in the baby's belly, it could be too small to feel, or it could be absent. The doctor may recommend a type of surgery called laparoscopy to see if he or she can find the

testicle. Laparoscopy requires only a small cut below the belly button, which heals quickly.

● If both testicles are undescended and can't be felt in the groin, the doctor will do a blood hormone test to find out if the testicles are absent. This means having no testicles at all. It is very rare to have two absent testicles.

Some other conditions are closely related to undescended testicles, such as an ectopic or retractile testicle. In both of these conditions, the testicle is in an abnormal position in the groin or scrotum. Your doctor will take care to make the correct diagnosis so your child can get the right treatment.

How is it treated?

Usually doctors recommend a wait-and-see approach for newborns. If the testicle hasn't dropped on its own within 6 months, your doctor may recommend surgery (orchiopexy or orchidopexy). Surgery is done when the baby is 9 to 15 months old. It is safe and effective and has few risks. Most babies recover quickly.

When babies have a testicle that can't be felt, doctors may do a different surgery that needs only a small cut (laparoscopy).

Another treatment is hormone therapy. It may cause the testicle to drop down into the scrotum. If it works, surgery isn't needed. But it doesn't always work, and it may cause side effects.

Why is it important to treat undescended testicle?

Treatment is important, because having an undescended testicle increases the risk of:

● Infertility. Damage to a testicle's sperm-making ability can begin as early as 12 months of age. That's why many doctors advise treating an undescended testicle by the time a baby is 1 year old and no later than age 2.

● Cancer of the testicles. Men who have undescended testicles have a higher rate of testicular cancer than other men. But this cancer is rare. It can be cured if found early. If you are a young man who has an undescended testicle, talk to your doctor about what you should do.

中英文注释

关键词汇

belly ['bɛli] n. 腹部

cryptorchidism [krip'tɔrkidizəm] n. 隐睾

groin [grɔin] n. 腹股沟

inherit [inˈhɛrit] v. 继承，遗传
laparoscopy [ˌlæpəˈrɑskəpi] n. 腹腔镜
orchidopexy [ˈɔːkidəuˌpeksi] n. 睾丸固定术
scrotum [ˈskrotəm] n. 阴囊
testicle [ˈtɛstikl] n. 睾丸

主要短语
belly button　肚脐
hormone therapy　激素治疗
testicular cancer　睾丸癌

阎小挺　王东文

Section Five: Cancer

第五部分 恶性肿瘤

66 Breast Cancer
乳　腺　癌

What is breast cancer?

Before discussing breast cancer, it's important to be familiar with the anatomy of the breast. The normal breast consists of milk-producing glands that are connected to the surface of the skin at the nipple by narrow ducts. The glands and ducts are supported by connective tissue made up of fat and fibrous material. Blood vessels, nerves, and lymphatic channels to the lymph nodes make up most of the rest of the breast tissue. This breast anatomy sits under the skin and on top of the chest muscles.

As in all forms of cancer, the abnormal tissue that makes up breast cancer is the patient's own cells that have multiplied uncontrollably. Those cells may also travel to locations in the body where they are not normally needed, which means the cancer is metastatic.

Breast cancer develops in the breast tissue, primarily in the milk ducts (ductal carcinoma) or glands (lobular carcinoma). The cancer is still called and treated as breast cancer even if it is first discovered after traveling to other areas of the body. In those cases, the cancer is referred to as metastatic or advanced breast cancer.

Breast cancer usually begins with the formation of a small, confined tumor (lump), or as calcium deposits (microcalcifications) and then spreads through channels within the breast to the lymph nodes or through the blood stream to other organs. The tumor may grow and invade tissue around the breast, such as the skin or chest wall. Different types of breast cancer grow and spread at different rates — some take years to spread beyond the breast while others grow and spread quickly.

Some lumps are benign (not cancerous), however these can be premalignant. The only safe way to distinguish between a benign lump and cancer is to have the tissue examined by a doctor through a biopsy.

Men can get breast cancer, too, but they account for one percent of all breast cancer cases. Among women, breast cancer is the most common cancer and the second leading cause of cancer deaths after lung cancer.

If eight women were to live to be at least 85, one of them would be expected to develop the disease at some point during her life. Two-thirds of women with breast cancer are over 50, and most of the rest are between 39 and 49.

Fortunately, breast cancer is very treatable if detected early. Localized tumors can usually be treated successfully before the cancer spreads; and in nine in 10 cases, the woman will live at least another five years. However, late recurrences of breast cancer are common.

Once the cancer begins to spread, treatment becomes difficult, although treatment can often control the disease for years. Improved screening procedures and treatment options mean that at least seven out of 10 women with breast cancer will survive more than five years, after initial diagnosis, and half will survive more than 10 years.

What causes breast cancer?

Although the precise causes of breast cancer are unclear, we know what the main risk factors are. Still, most women considered at high risk for breast cancer do not get it. On the other hand, 75% of women who develop breast cancer have no known risk factors. Among the most significant factors are advancing age and family history. Risk increases slightly for a woman who has had a benign breast lump and increases significantly for a woman who has previously had breast cancer or endometrial, ovarian, or colon cancer.

A woman whose mother, sister, or daughter has had breast cancer is two to three times more likely to develop the disease, particularly if more than one first-degree relative has been affected. This is especially true if the cancer developed in the woman while she was premenopausal, or if the cancer developed in both breasts. Researchers have now identified two genes responsible for some instances of familial breast cancer — *BRCA1* and *BRCA2*. About one woman in 200 carries one of these genes. Having a BRCA 1 or BRCA 2 gene predisposes a woman to breast cancer and — while it does not ensure that she will get breast cancer — her lifetime risk is 56%~85%. These genes also predispose to ovarian cancer and are associated with pancreas cancer, melanoma, and male breast cancer (BRCA2).

Because of these risks prevention strategies and screening guidelines for those with the BRCA genes are more aggressive. There are other genes that have been identified as increasing the risk of breast cancer, including the PTEN gene, the ATM gene, the TP53 gene, and the CHEK2 gene. However, these genes carry a lower risk for breast cancer development than the BRCA genes.

Generally, women over 50 are more likely to get breast cancer than younger women, and African-American women are more likely than Caucasians to get breast cancer before menopause.

A link between breast cancer and hormones is gradually becoming clearer. Researchers think that the greater a woman's exposure to the hormone estrogen, the more susceptible she is to breast cancer. Estrogen tells cells to divide; the more the cells divide, the more likely they are to be abnormal in some way, potentially becoming cancerous.

A woman's exposure to estrogen and progesterone rises and falls during her lifetime. This is influenced by the age she starts menstruating (menarche) and stops menstruating (menopause), the average length of her menstrual cycle, and her age at first childbirth. A woman's risk for breast cancer is increased if she starts menstruating before age 12 (less than 2 times the risk), has her first child after 30, stops menstruating after 55, or does not breast feed. Current information about the effect of birth control pills and breast cancer risk is mixed. Some studies have found that the hormones in birth control pills probably do not increase breast cancer risk or protect against breast cancer. However other studies suggest that the risk of breast cancer is increased in women who have taken birth control pills recently, regardless of how long she has taken them.

Some studies suggest that the use of hormone replacement therapy with estrogen and progesterone containing compounds increases the risk of developing breast cancers. They also show, after a 7 year follow up, that the use of estrogens alone does not increase or decrease the risk of breast cancer development.

High doses of radiation, such as with nuclear exposure, or therapeutic radiation, such as used for Hodgkin lymphoma. are a factor, for breast cancer development, after 15~20 years. Mammography poses almost no risk of breast cancer development.

The link between diet and breast cancer has been debated. Obesity is a noteworthy risk factor, predominately in postmenopausal women, because obesity alters a woman's estrogen metabolism. Drinking alcohol regularly — more than two drinks a day — also increases the risk of breast cancer. Many studies have shown that women whose diets are high in fat, either from red meat or high-fat dairy products, are more likely to get the disease. Researchers suspect that if a woman lowers her daily calories from fat — to less than 20~30 percent — her diet may help protect her from developing breast cancer.

What are the risk factors of breast cancer?

Nearly one in eight U.S. women develops breast cancer some time in her life. Doctors don't always know why breast cancer starts, but some risk factors stand out.

● Genetic Breast Cancer Risk Factors

Testing for Breast Cancer Genes

Checking for the BRCA1 or BRCA2 gene mutations may help screen for breast cancer. But the results don't mean breast cancer is certain or impossible. Get the facts.

- Race, Ethnicity and Breast Cancer Risk

Breast cancer affects all women. But it may differ by racial and ethnic group. For instance, breast cancer is found more often in white women but kills more black women.

- Hormone Replacement Therapy and Breast Cancer Risk

Hormone replacement therapy (HRT) has been linked to a higher breast cancer risk. Get the facts on hormone replacement therapy and breast cancer.

- Birth Control Pills and Breast Cancer Risk

Birth control pills may play in breast cancer risk.

- Alcohol and Breast Cancer Risk

Drinking alcohol regularly may raise a woman's risk of breast cancer.

Breast Cancer Prevention

Doctors can't make any promises, but some habits — like exercise and a healthy diet — may cut your risk of breast cancer.

Tamoxifen for Breast Cancer Prevention

The drug tamoxifen may be used to help prevent breast cancer in women at high risk of breast cancer.

Preventive Mastectomy

Preventive mastectomy is the surgical removal of the breasts to avoid breast cancer in high-risk women. Learn about it here.

What are symptoms of breast cancer?

In its early stages, breast cancer usually has no symptoms. As a tumor develops, you may note the following signs:

- A lump in the breast or underarm that persists after your menstrual cycle. This is often the first apparent symptom of breast cancer. Lumps associated with breast cancer are usually painless, although some may cause a prickly sensation. Lumps are usually visible on a mammogram long before they can be seen or felt.
- Swelling in the armpit.
- Pain or tenderness in the breast. Although lumps are usually painless, pain or tenderness can be a sign of breast cancer.
- A noticeable flattening or indentation on the breast, which may indicate a tumor that cannot be seen or felt.
- Any change in the size, contour, texture, or temperature of the breast. A reddish, pitted surface like the skin of an orange could be a sign of advanced breast cancer.

- A change in the nipple, such as a nipple retraction, dimpling, itching, a burning sensation, or ulceration. A scaly rash of the nipple is symptomatic of Paget's disease, which may be associated with an underlying breast cancer.
- Unusual discharge from the nipple that may be clear, bloody, or another color. It's usually caused by benign conditions but could be due to cancer in some cases.
- A marble-like area under the skin.
- An area that is distinctly different from any other area on either breast.

Types

Invasive Breast Cancer

Invasive breast cancers have spread beyond the milk ducts and milk-making glands to other breast tissue.

Breast Cancer Recurrence

Breast cancer recurrence (return) is possible after treatment, and it doesn't always come back to the breast.

Breast Cancer in Young Women

Breast cancer is generally seen in women after menopause. But it can strike much earlier.

Breast Cancer in Pregnancy

Breast cancer in pregnancy is very rare. But it can happen.

Male Breast Cancer

The vast majority of breast cancer patients are women. But every year, about 1,700 U.S. men get breast cancer.

Inflammatory Breast Cancer

Inflammatory breast cancer is a rare type of breast cancer in which the breast appears swollen and inflamed. It doesn't always involve a lump.

Complications

Breast cancer treatments are powerful medicine and can have side effects.

Lymphedema and Breast Cancer

Lymphedema is abnormal fluid build-up, usually in the arms or legs, and it needs prompt treatment. Breast cancer treatments may affect young women's ability to bear children.

How to diagnose breast cancer?

The earlier breast cancer is detected, the better it may be for the patient's long-term health. Get a brief overview of the tests that can help detect breast cancer.

For women at normal risk of breast cancer, self-exams, clinical exams, and mammography starting at 40 may screen for breast cancer. Abnormal results or high-risk women may need earlier screening or additional tests.

Tests

- Breast Self-Exam

Do you do regular breast self-exams? While some cancers are too tiny to feel, and most lumps aren't cancer, self-exams are a proactive way to help take care of yourself.

- Clinical Breast Exam

A clinical breast exam is a breast exam performed by a health care professional. It's a basic part of women's check-ups, starting at age 20.

- Mammogram

A mammogram is a special type of X-ray taken to look for abnormal growths or changes in breast tissue. It's a key tool in breast cancer detection, though no test is perfect.

Understanding the Mammogram Results

Most abnormal mammogram results aren't breast cancer. But more testing is needed to make sure. The bottom line: Don't panic, but do get the follow-up tests.

Video: Surviving Mammography

Do you find mammograms uncomfortable? Don't skip the test; just learn how to handle it better.

- Breast Ultrasound

Doctors sometimes use ultrasound images to check whether a breast lump is a cyst (a fluid-filled sac that is not cancer) or a solid mass.

- Breast MRI

MRI stands for magnetic resonance imaging. L

- Breast Biopsy

When doctors perform a biopsy, they remove cells from a suspicious mass to see if it's cancer.

Minimally Invasive Breast Biopsy

This type of breast biopsy generally uses a needle, not surgery.

Sentinel Node Biopsy

In a sentinelnode biopsy, doctors check a few lymph nodes under the arm to see if cancer has spread into the lymph system. Learn what's involved in a sentinel node biopsy.

- Ductal Lavage

Ductal lavage checks cells from the milk ducts for precancerous cells.

What are treatments for breast cancer?

Breast cancer treatments have come a long way in the past few generations. Get a general overview of treatment options for today's breast cancer patients.

There are two major goals of breast cancer treatment:

- To rid the body of the cancer as completely as possible.
- To prevent cancer from returning.

How is the type of breast cancer treatment determined?

The type of breast cancer treatment recommended for you will depend on the size of your tumor, the extent of disease in your lymph nodes and/or throughout your body (the stage), and the presence of the HER2 oncogene and endocrine receptors (estrogen and progesterone receptors). Age, menstrual status, underlying health issues, and personal preferences play a role in this decision making process as well.

What are the types of breast cancer treatment?

Breast cancer treatments are local or systemic.

Local treatments are used to remove or destroy the disease within the breast and surrounding regions, such as lymph nodes. These include:

- **Surgery** either mastectomy or lumpectomy — also called breast-conserving therapy. There are different types of mastectomies and lumpectomies.
- **Radiation therapy**

Systemic treatments are used to destroy or control cancer cells all over the body and include:

- **Chemotherapy** uses drugs to kill cancer cells. Side effects can include nausea, hair loss, early menopause, hot flashes, fatigue, and temporarily lowered blood counts.
- **Hormone therapy** (endocrine therapy) such as tamoxifen in premenopausal and postmenopausal women and the aromatase inhibitors Arimidex, Aromasin, and Femara in postmenopausal women. Hormone therapy uses drugs to prevent hormones, especially estrogen, from promoting the growth of breast cancer cells that may remain after breast cancer surgery. Side effects can include hot flashes and vaginal dryness.
- **Biological Therapy** such as Herceptin, Perjeta, or Tykerb, which work by using the body's immune system to destroy cancer cells. These drugs target breast cancer cells that have high levels of a protein called HER2.

Systemic therapy may be given after local treatment (adjuvant therapy) or before (neoadjuvant therapy). Adjuvant therapy is used after local treatments to kill any cancer cells that may remain in the body, but are undetectable.

You may have just one form of breast cancer treatment or a combination of treatments, depending on your needs.

Choosing your best breast cancer treatment

Patients' preferences are part of the decision-making process in choosing breast cancer treatments.

After breast cancer treatment: Follow-Up Care

After breast cancer treatment, follow-up care is a must.

中英文注释

关键词汇

anatomy [ə'nætəmi] n. 解剖

armpit ['aːmpit] n. 腋窝

colon ['kəʊlən] n. 结肠

endometrial [ˌendəu'miːtriəl] adj. 子宫内膜的

fertility [fə'tiliti] n. 生育能力

lymphedema [limfi'diːmə] n. 淋巴水肿

mammography [mæ'mɒgrəfi] n. 乳房 X 线

mastectomy [mæ'stektəmi] n. 乳房切除术

melanoma [melə'nəʊmə] n. 黑色素瘤

nipple ['nip(ə)l] n. 乳头

osteoporosis [ɒstiəʊpə'rəʊsis] n. 骨质疏松症

pancreas ['pæŋkriəs] n. 胰腺

recurrence [ri'kʌrəns] n. 复发

tamoxifen [tə'mɔksifen] n. 三苯氧胺，他莫昔芬

ulceration [ʌlsə'reiʃən] n. 溃疡

主要短语

breast biopsy 乳腺活组织检查

breast cancer 乳腺癌

breast ultrasound 乳腺超声检查

ductal carcinoma 导管癌

ductal lavage 导管灌洗

inflammatory breast cancer 炎性乳腺癌

initial diagnosis 初次诊断

invasive breast cancer 乳腺浸润性癌

lobular carcinoma　小叶癌
lymph node　淋巴结
milk ducts　乳导管
milk-producing gland　泌乳腺
Paget's disease　佩吉特病
pancreas cancer　胰腺癌
preventive mastectomy　预防性乳房切除术
starts menstruating　月经来潮
stops menstruating　月经停止

魏　亮　晋建华

67

Esophagus Cancer

食 管 癌

What is esophagus cancer?

Esophageal cancer occurs when cancer cells develop in the esophagus, a tube-like structure that runs from your throat to your stomach. Food goes from the mouth to the stomach through the esophagus. The cancer starts at the inner layer of the esophagus and can spread throughout the other layers of the esophagus and to other parts of the body (metastasis).

There are two main types of esophageal cancer. One type is squamous cell carcinoma. Squamous cells line the inner esophagus, and cancer developing from squamous cells can occur along the entire esophagus. The other type is called adenocarcinoma. This is cancer that develops from gland cells. To develop adenocarcinoma of the esophagus, squamous cells that normally line the esophagus are replaced by gland cells. This typically occurs in the lower esophagus near the stomach and is believed to be related to acid exposure to the lower esophagus.

What causes esophageal cancer?

There are a number of factors which increase a person's risk of developing esophageal cancer. They include:
- Smoking or other use of tobacco.
- Heavy alcohol use.
- Gastroesophageal reflux disease (GERD), in which contents and acid from the stomach back up into the esophagus, can increase the risk of adenocarcinoma of the esophagus by 2 to 16 times normal. It is estimated that about 30% of esophageal cancers are related to GERD.
- Barrett's esophagus, a condition that affects the lower part of the esophagus and can lead to esophageal cancer. Barrett's esophagus may be caused by GERD. Over time, it can cause changes in the cells of the esophagus that increase risk for adenocarcinoma.

In addition, certain groups — men, the elderly, and African-Americans — are at greater risk for esophageal cancer.

What are the symptoms of esophageal cancer?

Symptoms of esophageal cancer include:
- Difficulty or pain when swallowing
- Weight loss
- Pain in the chest, behind the breastbone
- Coughing
- Hoarseness
- Indigestion and heartburn

How is esophageal cancer diagnosed?

To diagnose esophageal cancer, your doctor will review your symptoms, medical history, and examine you. In addition, he or she may order certain blood tests and X-ray exams.

Tests for esophageal cancer may include:
- Barium swallow X-ray, in which you drink a liquid that coats your esophagus. This makes the esophagus stand out on the X-ray so that your doctor can identify certain problems.
- Endoscopy: the doctor passes an endoscope, a thin, lighted tube, down your throat into your esophagus to examine it. Endoscopic ultrasound uses sound waves to provide more information about the extent of tumor involvement in nearby tissues.
- Biopsy: during an endoscopy, the doctor can take cells or tissue from your esophagus. The cells are examined under a microscope for the presence of cancer.

Other tests, including computed tomography (CT) scans, positron emission tomography (PET) scan, thoracoscopy, and laparoscopy, may be performed to determine if the cancer has spread, or metastasized, outside of the esophagus. This process is called "staging." The doctor needs this information in order to plan your treatment.

What are the stages of esophageal cancer?

The stages of esophageal cancer are given a number (I through IV); the higher the number, the more advanced the cancer. The stages are:
- **Stage 0.** The cancer cells are only found in the layer of cells that line the esophagus.

- **Stage I.** The cancer has grown into the next layer or two of cells in the esophagus.
- **Stage II.** The cancer has reached the muscle layer or the outer wall of the esophagus. In addition, the cancer may have spread to 1 to 2 nearby lymph nodes (small glands that are part of the immune system).
- **Stage III.** The cancer has reached the muscle layer or the outer wall or has spread beyond the esophagus and/or has spread to more lymph nodes near the esophagus.
- **Stage IV.** This is the most advanced stage. The cancer has spread to other organs in the body and/or to lymph nodes far from the esophagus.

There are several tests to determine the stage of esophageal cancer, including:

- **Chest X-ray.**
- **Bronchoscopy.** The trachea (windpipe) and airways are examined with a bronchoscope, a thin, lighted tube that is inserted through the nose or mouth. This test is used to check for cancer involvement in the trachea or branching airways.
- **CT scan.** A procedure that creates sharp pictures of the inside of the body.
- **Endoscopic.** ultrasound, or endosonography. Used during endoscopy, sound waves bounce off organs in the body to create pictures called sonograms. This test can provide more information on the size and extent of the tumor.
- **Thoracoscopy.** An endoscope is placed into the chest through an incision to examine the inside of the chest to look for lymph nodes and other chest organs that may have cancer spread. Biopsies can be done during this procedure.
- **Laryngoscopy.** A procedure where a doctor uses a mirror or a laryngoscope to examine the larynx (voice box).
- **Laparoscopy.** The lighted tube is inserted through an incision in the abdomen to examine the abdominal organs and take tissue samples to check for cancer spread.

How is esophageal cancer treated?

As with many cancers, esophageal cancer treatment has a greater chance of success if the cancer is caught early. Unfortunately, by the time esophageal cancer is diagnosed for many people, it is often already in an advanced state (has spread throughout the esophagus and beyond).

Treatment of esophageal cancer depends on many factors, including the stage of the cancer and the overall health of the patient.

- Surgery. Part or all of the esophagus may be removed.
- Radiation therapy. Kills cancer cells with radiation.

- Chemotherapy. Powerful drugs that target cancer cells throughout the body. Typically used in combination with radiation therapy and/or surgery.
- Photodynamic therapy. Targets cancer cells with a special laser light.
- Electrocoagulation. Uses electric current to destroy cancer cells.

Endoscopic mucosal resection may be done to treat precancers or very small early cancers by removing the inner lining of the esophagus. Radiofrequency ablation treatment using a device that targets cancer cells with radiofrequency energy is sometimes used for early cancers.

In addition, your doctor may recommend that you take part in a clinical trial, in which new drugs or treatments are tested in patients. The success of these tests helps determine if the drugs or treatments will be approved by the Food and Drug Administration.

How are the stages of esophageal cancer treated?

Treatment options for esophageal cancer by stage involve the following:

- **Stage 0.** Usually surgery. Other options include photodynamic therapy, radiofrequency ablation, or endoscopic mucosal resection.
- **Stage I, II, and III.** Surgery, clinical trials of chemotherapy and radiation, or clinical trials of new therapies.
- **Stage IV.** Chemotherapy, radiation, laser therapy, electrocoagulation therapy, or clinical trials. Treatment for this stage focuses on "palliative" therapy. Palliative therapy is meant to relieve the pain and difficulty swallowing caused by cancer, and is often given to patients who are in an advanced stage of cancer, or who are near the end of their lives.

According to the American Cancer Society, the percentages of people who live for at least five years after being diagnosed with esophageal cancer (taking into account that some people with esophageal cancer will have other causes of death) is 37% for localized cancer to the esophagus, 18% for cancer that has spread regionally, and 3% with distant cancer spread.

中英文注释

关键词汇

acid ['æsid] n. 酸

alcohol ['ælkəhɔl] n. 酒精

coat [kəut] vt. 覆盖

endoscopy [en'dɔskəpi] n. 内窥镜检查

entire [in'taiə] adj. 全部的

estimated ['estimetid] adj. 估计的
identify [ai'dentifai] vt. 识别
recommend [ˌrekə'mend] v. 推荐
stage [steidʒ] n. 阶段
swallow ['swɔləu] v. 吞咽

主要短语
clinical trial 临床试验
gastroesophageal reflux disease (GERD) 胃食管反流病
over time 时间推移
palliative therapy 姑息治疗
squamous cell carcinoma 鳞状细胞癌
stand out 脱颖而出

郝　斌　马志方

68 ━━━━━━━━━━━━━━━━ Liver Cancer
肝　　癌

What is liver cancer?

The liver continuously filters blood that circulates through the body, converting nutrients and drugs absorbed from the digestive tract into ready-to-use chemicals. The liver performs many other important functions, such as removing toxins and other chemical waste products from the blood and readying them for excretion. Because all the blood in the body must pass through it, the liver is unusually accessible to cancer cells traveling in the bloodstream.

The liver can be affected by primary liver cancer, which arises in the liver, or by cancer which forms in other sites and then spreads to the liver. Most liver cancer is secondary or metastatic, meaning it started elsewhere in the body. Primary liver cancer, which starts in the liver, accounts for about 2% of cancers in the U.S., but up to half of all cancers in some undeveloped countries. This is mainly because of the prevalence of hepatitis, caused by contagious viruses, that predisposes a person to liver cancer. Worldwide, primary liver cancer strikes twice as many men as women, making it the most common type of cancer in males, with it mostly affecting people over 50.

Because the liver is made up of several different types of cells, several types of tumors can form in the liver. Some of these are benign (noncancerous), and some are cancerous and can spread to other parts of the body (metastasize). These tumors have different causes and are treated differently. The outlook for your health or recovery depends on what type of tumor you have.

What causes liver cancer?

Primary liver cancer (hepatocellular carcinoma) tends to occur in livers damaged by birth defects, alcohol abuse, or chronic infection with diseases such as hepatitis B and C, hemochromatosis (a hereditary disease associated with too much iron in the liver), and cirrhosis. More than half of all people diagnosed with primary liver cancer have cirrhosis — a scarring condition of the liver commonly caused by alcohol abuse. Hepatitis B and C and hemochromatosis can cause permanent damage and liver failure.

Liver cancer may also be linked to obesity and fatty liver disease.

Various cancer-causing substances are associated with primary liver cancer, including certain herbicides and chemicals such as vinyl chloride and arsenic. Smoking, especially if you abuse alcohol as well, also increases risk. Aflatoxins, cancer-causing substances made by a type of plant mold, have also been implicated. Aflatoxins can contaminate wheat, peanuts, rice, corn, and soybeans. These are rare problems in most developed countries like the U.S. Other causes include the hormones androgen and estrogen and a dye formerly used in medical tests called thorotrast.

What are the symptoms of liver cancer?

The initial symptoms (the clinical presentations) of liver cancer are variable. It is becoming much more common for patients to be identified by screening people at high risk for the cancer and finding the cancer before there are any symptoms at all. In countries where liver cancer is very common, the cancer generally is discovered at a very advanced stage of disease for several reasons. For one thing, areas where there is a high frequency of liver cancer are generally developing countries where access to health care is limited. For another, screening examinations for patients at risk for developing liver cancer are not available in these areas. In addition, patients from these regions may actually have more aggressive liver cancer disease. In other words, the tumor usually reaches an advanced stage and causes symptoms more rapidly. In contrast, patients in areas of low liver cancer frequency tend to have liver cancer tumors that progress more slowly and, therefore, remain without symptoms longer.

There are no specific symptoms of liver cancer, and in fact, the earliest signs are usually subtle and can be mistaken for simple worsening of cirrhosis and liver function. Abdominal pain is uncommon with liver cancer and usually signifies a very large tumor or widespread involvement of the liver. Additionally, unexplained weight loss or unexplained fevers are warning signs of liver cancer in patients with cirrhosis. These symptoms are less common in individuals with liver cancer in the U.S. because these patients are usually diagnosed at an earlier stage. However, whenever the overall health of a patient with cirrhosis deteriorates, every effort should be made to look for liver cancer.

A common initial presentation of liver cancer in a patient with compensated cirrhosis (meaning that there are no complications of liver disease) is the sudden onset of a complication. For example, the sudden appearance of ascites (abdominal fluid and swelling), jaundice (yellow color of the skin), or muscle wasting without causative (precipitating) factors (for example, alcohol consumption) suggests the possibility of liver cancer. What's more, the cancer can invade and block the portal vein (a large vein that brings blood to the liver from the intestine and spleen). When this happens, the blood will travel paths of less resistance, such as through esophageal veins. This causes increased pressure in these veins, which results in dilated (widened) veins called esophageal varices. The patient then is at risk for hemorrhage from the rupture of the varices into the gastrointestinal tract. Rarely, the cancer itself can rupture and bleed into the abdominal cavity, resulting in bloody ascites.

On physical examination, an enlarged, sometimes tender, liver is the most common finding. Liver cancers are very vascular (containing many blood vessels) tumors. Thus, increased amounts of blood feed into the hepatic artery (artery to the liver) and cause turbulent blood flow in the artery. The turbulence results in a distinct sound in the liver (hepatic bruit) that can be heard with a stethoscope in about one-quarter to one-half of patients with liver cancer. Any sign of advanced liver disease (for example, ascites, jaundice, or muscle wasting) means a poor prognosis. Rarely, a patient with liver cancer can become suddenly jaundiced when the tumor erodes into the bile duct. The jaundice occurs in this situation because both sloughing of the tumor into the duct and bleeding that clots in the duct can block the duct.

In advanced liver cancer, the tumor can spread locally to neighboring tissues or, through the blood vessels, elsewhere in the body (distant metastasis). Locally, liver cancer can invade the veins that drain the liver (hepatic veins). The tumor can then block these veins, which results in congestion of the liver. The congestion occurs because the blocked veins cannot drain the blood out of the liver. (Normally, the blood in the hepatic veins leaving the liver flows through the inferior vena cava, which is the largest vein that drains into the heart.) In African patients, the tumor frequently blocks the inferior vena cava. Blockage of either the hepatic veins or the inferior vena cava results in a very swollen liver and massive formation of ascites. In some patients, as previously mentioned, the tumor can invade the portal vein and lead to the rupture of esophageal varices.

Regarding distant metastases, liver cancer frequently spreads to the lungs, presumably by way of the bloodstream. Usually, patients do not have symptoms from the lung metastases, which are diagnosed by radiologic (X-ray) studies. Rarely, in very advanced cases, liver cancer can spread to the bone or brain. These are an infrequent problem in many patients who do not live long enough to develop these complications.

How is it diagnosed?

Screening for early detection of primary liver cancer is not performed routinely, but it may be considered for people at high risk for the disease. However, studies haven't determined if screening is beneficial for anyone. To diagnose liver cancer, a doctor must rule out other causes of liver dysfunction.

Patients at high risk include patients with a condition called hemochromatosis, chronic hepatitis, and alcoholics.

Additional tests include:

- Blood tests that measure tumor markers — the levels of these substances rise in the blood if someone has a particular cancer — can aid diagnosis. Liver cancers secrete a substance called alpha fetoprotein (AFP) that is normally present in fetuses but goes away at birth. An elevated AFP in adults may indicate liver cancer as it is produced in 70% of liver cancers. Elevated levels of iron may also be a tumor marker.

- Imaging with ultrasound is the initial diagnostic test as it can detect tumors as small as one centimeter. High resolution CT scans and contrast MRI scans are used to diagnose and stage these tumors.

- A liver biopsy will distinguish a benign tumor from a malignant one. However, depending on the results of other tests, a biopsy might not be required to diagnose cancer.

- Laparoscopy is useful for detecting small tumors, determining the extent of cirrhosis, or obtaining a biopsy, and confirm previous tests, among other things.

What are the treatments for liver cancer?

Any liver cancer is difficult to cure. Primary liver cancer is rarely detectable early, when it is most treatable. Secondary or metastatic liver cancer is hard to treat because it has already spread. The liver's complex network of blood vessels and bile ducts makes surgery difficult. Most treatment concentrates on making patients feel better and perhaps live longer.

Patients with early-stage tumors that can be removed surgically have the best chance of long-term survival. Unfortunately, most liver cancers are inoperable at the time it's diagnosed, either because the cancer is too advanced or the liver is too diseased to permit surgery. In some patients, chemotherapy is given directly into the liver (chemoembolization) to reduce tumors to a size that may make surgery possible. This may also be done without chemotherapy (bland embolization) in some cases, using ethanol instead. After surgery, radiation and chemotherapy have shown no advantage in improving survival. Patients in remission must be monitored closely for potential recurrence.

Cryotherapy, or freezing the tumor, and radiofrequency ablation (RFA), using radio waves to destroy the tumor, may be used to treat some cases of liver cancer. Radiation therapy can be given in various ways, but has its limitations due to the liver's low tolerance to radiation. When used, the role of radiation is to alleviate symptoms outside of the liver or to relieve pain within the liver by shrinking the tumor. Radioembolization therapy uses substances to cut off the blood supply to the tumor.

A liver transplant may be an option for those with both liver cancer and cirrhosis. Although this procedure is risky, it offers some chance of long-term survival.

Advanced liver cancer has no standard curative treatment. Chemotherapy and low-dose radiation may control the cancer's spread and ease pain, however these are of modest benefit in this type of cancer. Most patients receive strong painkilling medication along with drugs to relieve nausea, improve appetite, and reduce abdominal or lower body swelling. The drug sorafenib (Nexavar) is the first drug to significantly improve the overall survival with advanced liver cancer and is considered the drug of choice for such patients.

People with advanced liver cancer may choose to join clinical trials testing new approaches to treatment.

中英文注释

关键词汇

absorbed [əb'sɔːb, -'zɔːb] adj. 被吸收的

cirrhosis [si'rəʊsis] n. 肝硬化

contaminate [kən'tæmi,neit] vt. 污染

implicate ['implikeit] vt. 使牵连

jaundice ['dʒɔːndis] vt. 使有偏见，使患黄疸

metastatic [,metə'stætik] adj. 转移的

primary ['praiməri] adj. 原发的，主要的

significantly [sig'nifəkəntli] adv. 显著地

transplant [træns'plɑːnt] vt. 移植

主要短语

access to 接近，获得

in contrast 相比之下

monitorcolsely 密切观察

plant mold 植物模具

poor prognosis 不良预后

spread to 蔓延到

tend to 往往

tumor marker 肿瘤标志物

郝　斌　马志方

Stomach Cancer
胃　　癌

What is stomach cancer?

Stomach cancer, also called gastric cancer, is a malignant tumor arising from the lining of the stomach. There has been a significant decrease in the number of people diagnosed with stomach cancer in the past 60 years. According to the American Cancer Society, the estimated numbers of new cases (people diagnosed with the condition) will be 21,320, and deaths from gastric cancer in the United States in 2012 will be 15,070.

Stomach cancers are classified according to the type of tissue where they originate. The most common type of stomach cancer is adenocarcinoma, which starts in the glandular tissue of the stomach and accounts for 90% to 95% of all stomach cancers. Other forms of stomach cancer include lymphomas, which involve the lymphatic system and sarcomas, which involve the connective tissue (such as muscle, fat, or blood vessels).

Stomach cancer may often be cured if it is found and treated at an early stage. Unfortunately, the outlook is poor if the cancer is already at an advanced stage when discovered. In most cases, stomach cancer is found at later stages.

What causes stomach cancer?

The exact cause of stomach cancer is unknown, but a number of factors can increase the risk of the disease, including:

- Gender — men have more than double the risk of getting stomach cancer than women.
- Race — being African-American or Asian may increase your risk.
- Genetics — genetic abnormalities and some inherited cancer syndromes may increase your risk.
- Geography — stomach cancer is more common in Japan, the former Soviet Union, and parts of Central America and South America.
- Blood type — individuals with blood group A may be at increased risk.
- Advanced age — stomach cancer occurs more often around ages 70 and 74 in

men and women, respectively.

- Family history of gastric cancer can double or triple the risk of stomach cancer.
- Lifestyle factors such as smoking, drinking alcohol, and eating a diet low in fruits and vegetables or high in salted, smoked, or nitrate-preserved foods may increase your risk.
- Helicobacter pylori (H. pylori) infection of the stomach. H. pylori is a bacterium that infects the lining of the stomach and causes chronic inflammation and ulcers.
- Certain health conditions including chronic gastritis, pernicious anemia, gastric polyps.
- Work-related exposure due to coal mining, nickel refining, and rubber and timber processing and asbestos exposure.

What are the symptoms of stomach cancer?

In the early stages of stomach cancer, you may have very few symptoms. These may include:

- Indigestion and stomach discomfort
- A bloated feeling after eating
- Mild nausea
- Loss of appetite
- Heartburn

These symptoms are similar to those caused by a peptic ulcer. If you are experiencing any of these symptoms you should see your health care provider so that a proper diagnosis can be made and timely treatment given. A stomach cancer can grow very large before it causes other symptoms.

In more advanced cancer, you may have:

- Discomfort in the upper or middle part of the abdomen.
- Blood in the stool (which appears as black, tarry stools).
- Vomiting or vomiting blood.
- Weight loss.
- Pain or bloating in the stomach after eating.
- Weakness or fatigue associated with mild anemia (a deficiency in red blood cells).

How is stomach cancer diagnosed?

Your health care provider can often detect advanced stomach cancer by performing a physical exam. He or she may find enlarged lymph nodes, an enlarged liver, increased fluid in the abdomen (ascites), or abdominal lumps felt during a rectal exam.

However, if you are having vague symptoms, such as indigestion, weight loss, nausea, and loss of appetite, screening tests may be recommended. These tests may include:

- Upper GI series. These are X-rays of the esophagus, stomach, and first part of the intestine taken after you drink a barium solution. The barium outlines the stomach on the X-ray, which helps the doctor, using special imaging equipment, to find tumors or other abnormal areas.

- Gastroscopy and biopsy. This test examines the esophagus and stomach using a thin, lighted tube called a gastroscope, which is passed through the mouth to the stomach. Through the gastroscope, the doctor can look directly at the inside of the stomach. If an abnormal area is found, the doctor will remove some tissue (biopsy) to be examined under a microscope. A biopsy is the only sure way to diagnose cancer. Gastroscopy and biopsy are the best methods of identifying stomach cancer.

Once stomach cancer is diagnosed, more tests may be done to determine if the cancer has spread. These tests may include CT scans, PET scans, bone scans, laparoscopy and endoscopic ultrasound.

How is stomach cancer treated?

Treatments for stomach cancer may include one or more of the following:

- Surgery, called gastrectomy, removes all or part of the stomach, as well as some of the tissue surrounding the stomach. Lymph nodes near the stomach are also removed andbiopsied to check for cancer cells. Only about one-third of stomach cancer cases can be treated surgically.

- Chemotherapy is the use of anticancer drugs. This may be used before and after surgery or for cancers that have spread to other organs. Prior to surgery, chemotherapy — with or without radiation — is sometimes used to shrink the tumor or to make an inoperable tumor suitable for surgery (known as neo-adjuvant therapy).

- Radiation therapy is the use of ionizing X-rays to kill cancer cells and shrink tumors. This is used with chemotherapy before or after surgery and sometimes both. It can also be used to relieve symptoms in those with localized cancer (cancer that hasn't spread to other parts of the body) or to relieve localized symptoms in persons whose cancer has metastasized.

If treated at an early stage before it spreads, stomach cancer may be associated with a long survival. A patient whose tumor is removed completely has a good chance of surviving at least five years. Unfortunately, by the time most cases of stomach cancer are diagnosed, the cancer has spread to local lymph nodes or other organs. Fewer than one in five patients diagnosed with stomach cancer that has spread to other organs or lymph nodes will survive five years.

中英文注释

关键词汇

adenocarcinoma [ˌædinəʊˌkɑːsiˈnəʊmə] n. 腺癌
esophagus [iːˈsəfəgəs] n. 食管
gastrectomy [gæˈstrektəmi] n. 胃切除术
indigestion [ˌindiˈdʒestʃ(ə)n] n. 消化不良
laparoscopy [ˌlæpəˈrɒskəpi] n. 腹腔镜检查
lymphoma [limˈfəʊmə] n. 淋巴瘤
sarcoma [sɑːˈkəʊmə] n. 肉瘤

主要短语

blood in the stool 便血
chronic gastritis 慢性胃炎
gastric polyps 胃息肉
gastroscopy and biopsy 胃镜检查活检
helicobacter pylori 幽门螺杆菌
intestinal metaplasia 肠上皮化生
peptic ulcer 消化性溃疡
pernicious anemia 恶性贫血
upper GI series 上消化道系列

魏　亮　马志方

70

Colorectal Cancer

结 直 肠 癌

What is colorectal cancer?

Inside your abdominal cavity is the long, tubular digestive tract. The second part of this tube — the large intestine — is composed of the colon, which stretches 4 feet to 6 feet, and the rectum, which is only 4 inches to 6 inches long.

The inner lining of this "colorectal tube" can be a fertile breeding ground for small tumors, called polyps. About a quarter of all adults in the U.S. older than age 50 will have at least one colorectal polyp. Most colorectal cancers develop from polyps in glandular tissue of the intestinal lining.

Most polyps are benign, but at least one type is known to be precancerous. These are called adenomatous polyps.

The size of the polyp correlates with the development of cancer. Polyps less than 1 centimeter in size have a slightly greater than a 1% chance of becoming cancer, but those 2 centimeters or greater have a 40% chance of transforming into cancer. Overall, the incidence is about 5%. Most colorectal cancers develop from polyps in glandular tissue of the intestinal lining.

If colorectal cancer is diagnosed and treated early while the tumor is still localized, the disease is highly curable, with five-year survival rates of about 90%. If the tumor continues to grow, cancer can spread directly through the bowel wall to surrounding lymph nodes, tissues, and organs, as well as into the bloodstream.

Once the cancer spreads to lymph nodes or other organs, successful treatment becomes more difficult. Depending on how advanced the disease is, five-year survival rates range from 9% to 93%. Cancers of the colon and rectum are the third most common cancer in the U.S., with approximately 150,000 cases diagnosed each year. Like many cancers, colorectal cancer is of particular concern for people older than age 50.

Although diagnosis is often possible at an early stage, many people delay seeking medical care because they are embarrassed or fearful of symptoms related to their bowels. Risk increases significantly after age 50 and continues to increase with age.

What causes colorectal cancer?

The exact cause of colorectal cancer is not known. But there are several risk factors for the disease.

- **Other diseases.** Colorectal cancer is strongly associated with certain other diseases. Those people considered at high risk include anyone with a personal or family history of colon polyps or colon cancer, inflammatory disease of the colon such as ulcerative colitis or Crohn's disease, and cancers of the pancreas, breast, ovaries, or uterus.

- **Heredity.** As with any cancer, susceptibility to colorectal cancer is at least partly determined by genetic makeup. A few people inherit medical conditions, such as familial adenomatous polyposis (FAP), MYH-associated polyposis (MAP), Gardner's syndrome, Turcot's syndrome, Peutz-Jagher's syndrome, juvenile polyposis, and Cowden's disease. In all of these disorders, colon polyps develop at an early age and unless treated, these people are almost certain to develop colorectal cancer.

- **Hereditary nonpolyposis colon cancer.** The disease extends from generation to generation and causes a person to develop colon cancer at a young age with up to 100 colon polyps (which is why it's called "non-polyposis"). This disease is associated with other cancers including endometrial, small bowel, upper urinary tract, bladder, ovary, stomach, bile duct, skin, and some pancreatic cancers. This is known as the Lynch Syndrome.

- **Diet.** Diet also contributes to the risk of colorectal cancer, although the cause-and-effect relationship is still unclear. People whose diets are high in fruits and vegetables seem to have a reduced risk. Many studies implicate animal fat and protein as promoters of colorectal cancer, although researchers are cautious about drawing any definite conclusions. Some studies show that regularly eating red meat, which is rich in saturated fat and protein, increases risk, while others find no connection. Some scientists note that fat is the main culprit, while others suspect protein. Others contend that it's not the fat and protein themselves, but the way they are cooked. They note that fats and protein cooked at high temperatures — especially when broiled and barbecued — can produce a host of potentially carcinogenic substances linked to colorectal cancer.

- **Chemical exposure.** Heavy exposure to certain chemicals, including chlorine — which in small amounts is commonly used to purify drinking water — may increase the risk of colorectal cancer. Exposure to asbestos is thought to be potentially harmful because it has been implicated in causing formation of polyps in the colon.

- **History of certain types of surgery.** Surgeries such as ureterosigmoidostomy, which is performed in the treatment of bladder cancer, and a cholecystectomy (the removal of the gallbladder). The bladder has been implicated as a risk for colon cancer development in some studies, but not in others.
- **History of colon cancer.** A prior case of colon cancer increases the risk of a second colon cancer, especially if the first cancer was diagnosed before the age of 60.
- **Lifestyle.** Smoking and alcohol intake of more than 4 drinks per week increases the risk of developing colon cancer.
- **Family history.** Those with a first-degree relative with colorectal cancer have an increased risk of the disease. The risk increases if more than one first-degree relative has colon cancer.
- **Radiation.** Prior radiation increases the risk of cancer to the radiated tissue only.

What are the symptoms of colorectal cancer?

In its early stage, colorectal cancer usually produces no symptoms. The most likely warning signs include:

- Changes in bowel movements, including persistent constipation or diarrhea, a feeling of not being able to empty the bowel completely, an urgency to move the bowels, rectal cramping, or rectal bleeding
- Dark patches of blood in or on stool; or long, thin, "pencil stools"
- Abdominal discomfort or bloating
- Unexplained fatigue, loss of appetite, and/or weight loss
- Pelvic pain, which occurs at later stages of the disease

How is colorectal cancer diagnosed?

Beginning at the age of 50, everyone should be screened regularly for colorectal cancer (earlier screening is recommended for some high-risk groups). There are several options.

The traditional screening routine was for the doctor to perform a digital rectal exam once a year and for you to collect three stool samples to be tested for traces of blood. Also, every three to five years you would receive a sigmoidoscopy and a double-contrast barium enema to look at the lower part of the bowel. If anything were abnormal then you would be referred for a colonoscopy. The colonoscopy is a complete evaluation of the colon and rectum with a scope or long, flexible tube similar to the sigmoidoscope but longer.

Biopsies or tissue samples of any suspicious-looking areas can be obtained during a colonoscopy for laboratory analysis.

Now, most doctors advocate going right to colonoscopy every 10 years. However, other studies are sometimes recommended when a patient is unable or unwilling to undergo colonoscopy.

A noninvasive screening procedure called virtual colonoscopy is becoming available. It does away with the tube and instead uses spiral computed tomography, which produces a three-dimensional image of the colon after it has been emptied and partially inflated with air.

The current American Cancer screening guidelines for colon cancer in an average risk patient begin at the age of 50 and include: testing of stool samples for traces of blood yearly, a flexible sigmoidoscopy every five years, a double contrast barium enema every five years, virtual colonoscopy every five years, and a colonoscopy every 10 years. However, if you are at high risk of colon cancer due to a family history of colon cancer or polyps, or if you are African-American, screening intervals should begin earlier and be more frequent.

Any suspicious symptoms or abnormalities will alert your doctor to perform a colonoscopy to get a biopsy.

Should a biopsy confirm cancer, imaging tests using chest X-rays and CT scans of the abdomen, pelvis, and possibly chest are performed to find out whether the cancer has spread to other sites. Positron Emission Tomography (PET) scanning is a highly sensitive study for detecting colon cancer metastasis. Usually this test is more helpful in detecting recurrences than when used for the initial staging of early disease.

Blood tests will also be ordered to find out how well the liver and kidneys are functioning, to determine if you are anemic, and to measure the blood level of a substance called carcinoembryonic antigen (CEA), often found in higher-than-normal concentration in the presence of colorectal cancer, especially if it has spread.

What are the treatments for colorectal cancer?

Colorectal cancer treatment involves not only specific therapies for curing or controlling the disease, but also strategies for meeting a patient's emotional and physical needs. Restoring and maintaining quality of life is a central issue for doctors, as it should be for family members and friends as well. Many complementary cancer therapies can be valuable adjuncts when pursued along with standard medical treatment to help make the stresses of cancer and its treatment more tolerable. However, complementary therapies should never replace standard care.

The main types of treatment for colorectal cancer are surgery, radiation therapy, and chemotherapy. Depending on the stage of the cancer, these treatments may be combined.

Surgery is the most effective treatment for local colorectal tumors. Very small tumors can be removed through a colonoscope, but even with small tumors, removing the portion of the colon containing the tumor, the surrounding fat, and nearby lymph nodes is often the best treatment. Surgery may be performed either laparoscopically or by the open method, which uses larger incisions.

Usually, the surgeon can reconnect the healthy sections of the colon and rectum. When this is not possible, the surgeon forms an opening — known as a stoma — in the abdomen and reroutes the severed colon to it. Waste is collected in a bag worn over the stoma. This procedure, known as a colostomy, often is only temporary. Once the bowel has had time to heal, a second operation reconnects the colon and rectum. The need for permanent colostomy is more common with rectal cancer, since retaining the rectum may be difficult.

In the immediate period after surgery, the patient can expect to receive painkillers and other medication to ease temporary diarrhea or constipation. After surgery, patients are encouraged to eat nutritious foods, rich in calories and proteins, in order to gain strength and heal properly.

Radiation therapy is treatment with high-energy rays that destroy the cancer cells. For rectal cancer, radiation is usually given after surgery, along with chemotherapy (known as adjuvant therapy), in order to destroy any cancer cells left behind. In addition, it can be used along with chemotherapy before surgery (known as neoadjuvant therapy) in order to shrink a large tumor, making the surgery easier. In advanced rectal cancer, radiation can be used to shrink tumors that cause symptoms of bowel obstruction, bleeding, or pain.

Radiation therapy can be used in people with colon cancer when the tumor has attached to another organ in the abdomen, or if a tumor is found near the margins of the cancer that was removed.

Chemotherapy drugs are used to treat various stages of colorectal cancer. They include 5-flurouracil, Xeloda, Camptosar, and Eloxatin. These drugs are commonly used in combination with one another. Chemotherapy can also be administered directly into the liver if the colon cancer has metastasized there.

The FDA has approved five drugs for treating colon cancer that work an entirely different way. The drugs, Erbitux, Avastin, Stivarga, Zaltrap, and Vectibix are a form of cancer therapy called immunotherapy or biologic therapy. These drugs work by blocking the cancer's blood supply or blocking a protein made by the cancer to enhance its growth. They can be used to treat advanced colorectal cancer that has spread (metastasized) to other parts of the body.

Once cancer of either the colon or rectum is in remission, follow-up exams to check for recurrence are essential indefinitely. But hundreds of thousands of people are living comfortable, normal lives even after colorectal surgery and a colostomy. Although adjusting to life after a colostomy requires time, support, and understanding, people with stomata have discovered for the most part they can eat, play, and work as well as they did before.

中英文注释

关键词汇

advocate ['ædvəkeit] vt. 提倡

associate [ə'səuʃieit] vt. 交往，结交

bloating ['bləutiŋ] adj. 鼓胀的

colonoscopy [ˌkəulə'nɒskəpi] n. 结肠镜检查

compose [kəm'pəuz] vt. 组成

correlates ['kɒrəleit] vt. 关联

embarrass [im'bærəs] vt. 使局促不安

inherit [in'herit] vt. 继承

intestine [in'testin] n. 肠

margin ['mɑːdʒin] n. 边缘

precancerous [priː'kæns(ə)rəs] adj. 癌症前期的

promoters [prəu'məutə] n. 发起人，倡导者

restore [ri'stɔː] v. 恢复

suspect [sə'spekt] vt. 怀疑

主要短语

abdominal cavity 腹腔

adenomatous polyps 腺瘤性息肉

complementary therapies 互补疗法

fertile breading ground 肥沃的滋生地

generation to generation 代代相传

glandular tissue 腺组织

Lynch Syndrome 林奇综合征

noninvasive procedure 无创过程

potentially carcinogenic substances 潜在的致癌物质

screened regularly 定期筛查

tubular digestive tract 消化管道

郝　斌　马志方

71 Lung Cancer
肺 癌

What is lung cancer?

Although lung cancer is the leading cause of cancer death in the U.S. in both men and women, it is also one of the most preventable kinds of cancer. At least four out of five cases are associated with cigarette smoking, and the cause-and-effect relationship has been extensively documented. During the 1920s, large numbers of men began to smoke cigarettes, presumably in response to increased advertising. Twenty years later, the frequency of lung cancer in men climbed sharply. In 1940s, significantly more women became smokers. Twenty years later, there was a similar dramatic increase in lung cancer among women.

Lung tumors almost always start in the spongy, pinkish gray walls of the bronchi — the tubular, branching airways of the lungs. More than 20 types of cancerous tumors that originate in the lung itself — primary lung cancer — have been identified. The major types of lung cancer are small-cell lung cancer and non-small cell lung cancer. The more common non-small cell variety is further divided into squamous cell carcinoma, adenocarcinoma, large-cell carcinoma, and more. Mixed tumors may also occur.

Non-Small Cell Lung Cancer

Squamous cell carcinoma usually starts in cells of the central bronchi, the largest branches of the bronchial tree. It accounts for 30% of lung cancers, and occurs more commonly in men and in smokers. It's the easiest to detect early, since its distinctive cells are likely to show up in tests of mucus samples. It also tends to be most curable if found early because it spreads relatively slowly and often does not spread outside of the lung.

Adenocarcinoma is the most common type of lung cancer accounting for 40% of all cases with its incidence increasing. It is most commonly seen in women and nonsmokers. It tends to originate along the outer edges of the lungs in the smaller airways. Adenocarcinoma tends to spread to the lymph nodes and distant organs. It's commonly a mixed type of tumor and may cause no symptoms initially.

Large-cell carcinomas are a group of cancers with large, abnormal-looking cells that tend to originate along the outer edges of the lungs. They are the least common of the non-small cell lung cancers accounting for 10%~15% of all cases. However, this type of tumor has a high tendency to spread to nearby lymph nodes and distant sites.

Small Cell Lung Cancer

Small-cell lung cancer is the most aggressive form of lung cancer. This cancer usually originates in the large, central bronchi. It spreads quickly, usually within 90 days, often before symptoms appear, making it particularly threatening. In fact, in up to 75% of patients with this type of cancer, the disease has spread by the time it's diagnosed. It frequently spreads (metastasizes) to the liver, bone, and brain. Although responsive to chemotherapy, small-cell lung cancer is rarely associated with long-term survival.

About 226,000 people in the U.S. will be diagnosed with lung cancer in 2012. It is the second most common cancer in both men and women. However, it is the leading cause of cancer deaths in both sexes — killing over 160,000 people each year.

An individual cancer sufferer's prognosis will vary according to the type of lung cancer involved, the person's overall health, and the stage of the cancer at the time of initial diagnosis.

What causes lung cancer?

About 85% of lung cancer is caused by smoking and, as with any cancer, each person's genetics. The fact that lung cancer runs in some families suggests that a predisposition can be inherited. Additionally, certain genetic traits have been identified that make some people more susceptible than others to cancer-causing substances like those found in tobacco smoke.

Nonetheless, anyone who smokes one pack of cigarettes daily is 20 times more likely than a nonsmoker to develop lung cancer. For people who smoke more than two packs a day, the risk more than triples. Breaking the smoking habit reduces risk significantly, yet former smokers are always slightly more susceptible than nonsmokers. Secondhand tobacco smoke can also cause lung cancer, giving nonsmokers who live or work with smokers a somewhat higher lung cancer risk than those in smoke-free environments. In fact, approximately 3,000 people die each year of lung cancer associated with second hand smoke exposure. And those living in a home with a smoker have a 30% higher risk of developing lung cancer than in a smoke-free home.

Cancer-causing substances other than those found in tobacco or tobacco smoke can also cause lung cancer if inhaled over time. However, experts disagree about how much exposure to specific cancer-causing substances is dangerous. Workers who are exposed on a daily basis to asbestos have a 90-fold increase of getting lung cancer when compared to non-exposed persons. Workers exposed to uranium dust or the radioactive gas radon are also much more likely than the average person to develop lung cancer, especially if they are smokers.

Lung tissue that has been scarred by disease or infection, such as scleroderma or tuberculosis, is more susceptible to tumor growth within the scar tissue (called a scar carcinoma). Because of a high frequency of lung cancer among people who eat large amounts of fat and cholesterol, some researchers speculate that diet may also influence lung cancer risk.

What are the symptoms of lung cancer?

In its early stages, lung cancer normally has no symptoms. When symptoms start to appear, they are usually caused by blocked breathing passages or the spread of cancer further into the lung, surrounding structures, other parts of the body.

Lung cancer symptoms may include:
- Chronic, hacking, raspy coughing, sometimes with blood-streaked mucus
- Recurring respiratory infections, including bronchitis or pneumonia
- Increasing shortness of breath, wheezing, persistent chest pain
- Hoarseness
- Swelling of the neck and face
- Pain and weakness in the shoulder, arm, or hand
- Fatigue, weakness, loss of weight and appetite, intermittent fever, severeheadaches, and body pain
- Difficulty swallowing

How is lung cancer diagnosed?

The doctor may suspect lung cancer if a routine physical exam reveals:
- Swollen lymph nodes above the collarbone
- A mass in the abdomen
- Weak breathing
- Abnormal sounds in the lungs
- Dullness when the chest is tapped
- Rounding of the fingernails
- Unequal pupils
- Droopy eyelids
- Weakness in one arm
- Expanded veins in the arms, chest, or neck
- Swelling of the face

Some lung cancers produce abnormally high blood levels of certain hormones or substances such as calcium. If a person shows such evidence and no other cause is apparent, a doctor should consider lung cancer.

Lung cancer, which originates in the lungs, can also spread to other parts of the body, such as distant bones, the liver, adrenal glands, or the brain. It may be first discovered in a distant location, but is still called lung cancer if there is evidence it started there.

Once lung cancer begins to cause symptoms, it is usually visible on an X-ray. Occasionally, lung cancer that has not yet begun to cause symptoms is spotted on a chest X-ray taken for another purpose. A CT scan of the chest may be ordered for a more detailed exam.

Though exams of mucus or lung fluid may reveal fully developed cancer cells, diagnosis of lung cancer is usually confirmed through a lung biopsy. With the patient lightly anesthetized, the doctor guides a thin, lighted tube through the nose and down the air passages to the site of the tumor, where a tiny tissue sample can be removed. This is called a bronchoscopy and the scope is called a bronchoscope. This is useful for tumors near the center of the lung.

If the biopsy confirms lung cancer, other tests will determine the type of cancer and how far it has spread. Nearby lymph nodes can be tested for cancer cells with a procedure called a mediastinoscopy, while imaging techniques such as CT scans, PET scans, bone scans, and either an MRI or a CT scan of the brain can detect cancer elsewhere in the body.

If fluid is present in the lining of the lung, removal of the fluid with a needle (called a thoracentesis) may help diagnose cancer as well as improve breathing symptoms. If the fluid tests negative for cancer cells — which occurs about 60% of the time — then a procedure known as a video-assisted thoracoscopic surgery (or VATS) may be performed to examine the lining of the lung for tumors and to perform a biopsy.

Because saliva, mucus, and chest X-rays have not proved particularly effective in detecting small tumors characteristic of early lung cancer, annual chest X-rays for lung cancer screening are not recommended by the American Cancer Society, the National Cancer Institute, or the American College of Radiology.

Screening CT scan clinical trials have been performed and some are completed. In one study, over 31,000 people were screened with CT scans and 484 — or 1.5% — were found to have lung cancer. Other studies, however, have shown no reduction in lung cancer deaths with CT scanning.

One of the problems with CT scan screening is the increased risk of radiation exposure and subsequent development of radiation related cancers. Another problem is a high incidence of false positive results.

How is it treated?

Six types of standard treatment are used:

Surgery

Four types of surgery are used:

- Wedge resection: Surgery to remove a triangle-shaped slice of tissue. Wedge resection is used to remove a tumor and a small amount of normal tissue around it. When a slightly larger amount of tissue is taken, it is called a segmental resection.
- Lobectomy: Surgery to remove a whole lobe (section) of the lung.
- Pneumonectomy: Surgery to remove one whole lung.
- Sleeve resection: Surgery to remove part of the bronchus.

Radiation therapy

Radiation therapy is a cancer treatment that uses high-energy X-rays or other types of radiation to kill cancer cells. There are two types of radiation therapy. External radiation therapy uses a machine outside the body to send radiation toward the cancer. Internal radiation therapy uses a radioactive substance sealed in needles, seeds, wires, or catheters that are placed directly into or near the cancer.

Radiosurgery is a method of delivering radiation directly to the tumor with little damage to healthy tissue. It does not involve surgery and may be used to treat certain tumors in patients who cannot have surgery.

The way the radiation therapy is given depends on the type and stage of the cancer being treated.

Chemotherapy

Chemotherapy is a cancer treatment that uses drugs to stop the growth of cancer cells, either by killing the cells or by stopping the cells from dividing. When chemotherapy is taken by mouth or injected into a vein or muscle, the drugs enter the bloodstream and can reach cancer cells throughout the body (systemic chemotherapy). When chemotherapy is placed directly into the spinal column, an organ, or a body cavity such as the abdomen, the drugs mainly affect cancer cells in those areas (regional chemotherapy). The way the chemotherapy is given depends on the type and stage of the cancer being treated.

Extensive research and clinical trials have studied the different chemotherapy medicines used to treat lung cancer. Your oncologist will discuss and recommend chemotherapy treatment specific to your condition. Some of the more common chemotherapy medicines include the following:

- Carboplatin

- Cisplatin
- Docetaxel
- Erlotinib
- Etoposide
- Gemcitabine
- Irinotecan
- Paclitaxel
- Pemetrexed
- Vinorelbine

Bevacizumab is an intravenous (IV) drug that helps prevent formation of blood vessels that supply the tumor with nutrients and help the cancer grow and multiply. Bevacizumab may be used with other chemotherapy drugs, such as carboplatin and paclitaxel, for treating non-small cell lung cancer.

Laser therapy

Laser therapy is a cancer treatment that uses a laser beam (a narrow beam of intense light) to kill cancer cells.

Photodynamic therapy (PDT)

Photodynamic therapy (PDT) is a cancer treatment that uses a drug and a certain type of laser light to kill cancer cells. A drug that is not active until it is exposed to light is injected into a vein. The drug collects more in cancer cells than in normal cells. Fiberoptic tubes are then used to deliver the laser light to the cancer cells, where the drug becomes active and kills the cells. Photodynamic therapy causes little damage to healthy tissue. It is used mainly to treat tumors on or just under the skin or in the lining of internal organs.

Watchful waiting

Watchful waiting is closely monitoring a patient's condition without giving any treatment until symptoms appear or change. This may be done in certain rare cases of non-small cell lung cancer.

Small-Cell Lung Cancer Treatment Overview:

There are different types of treatment for patients with small cell lung cancer.

Different types of treatment are available for patients with small cell lung cancer. Some treatments are standard (the currently used treatment), and some are being tested in clinical trials. Before starting treatment, patients may want to think about taking part in a clinical trial. A treatment clinical trial is a research study meant to help improve current treatments or obtain information on new treatments for patients with cancer. When clinical trials show that a new treatment is better than the standard treatment, the new treatment may become the standard treatment.

Clinical trials are taking place in many parts of the country. Information about ongoing clinical trials is available from NCI Web site. Choosing the most appropriate cancer treatment is a decision that ideally involves the patient, family, and health care team.

Three types of standard treatment are used:

Surgery

Surgery may be used if the cancer is found in one lung and in nearby lymph nodes only. Because this type of lung cancer is usually found in both lungs, surgery alone is not often used. Occasionally, surgery may be used to help determine the patient's exact type of lung cancer. During surgery, the doctor will also remove lymph nodes to see if they contain cancer. Laser therapy (the use of an intensely powerful beam of light to kill cancer cells) may be used.

Even if the doctor removes all the cancer that can be seen at the time of the operation, some patients may be given chemotherapy or radiation therapy after surgery to kill any cancer cells that are left. Treatment given after the surgery, to increase the chances of a cure, is called adjuvant therapy.

Chemotherapy

Chemotherapy is a cancer treatment that uses drugs to stop the growth of cancer cells, either by killing the cells or by stopping the cells from dividing. When chemotherapy is taken by mouth or injected into a vein or muscle, the drugs enter the bloodstream and can reach cancer cells throughout the body (systemic chemotherapy). When chemotherapy is placed directly into the spinal column, an organ, or a body cavity such as the abdomen, the drugs mainly affect cancer cells in those areas (regional chemotherapy). The way the chemotherapy is given depends on the type and stage of the cancer being treated.

Radiation therapy

Radiation therapy is a cancer treatment that uses high-energy X-rays or other types of radiation to kill cancer cells. There are two types of radiation therapy. External radiation therapy uses a machine outside the body to send radiation toward the cancer. Internal radiation therapy uses a radioactive substance sealed in needles, seeds, wires, or catheters that are placed directly into or near the cancer. Prophylactic cranial irradiation (radiation therapy to the brain to reduce the risk that cancer will spread to the brain) may also be given. The way the radiation therapy is given depends on the type and stage of the cancer being treated.

Other types of treatment are being tested in clinical trials.

中英文注释

关键词汇

aggressive [ə'gresiv] adj. 激进的

distinctive [dis'tiŋktiv] adj. 独特的

documented ['dɔkjuməntid] adj. 有记载的

mediastinoscopy 纵隔镜检查

preventable [pri'ventəbl] adj. 可预防的

speculate ['spekjuleit] v. 推断

spongy ['spʌndʒi] adj. 海绵状的

survival [sə'vaivəl] n. 生存

susceptible [sə'septəbl] adj. 易受影响的

tendency ['tendənsi] n. 趋势

主要短语

adjuvant therapy 辅助疗法

close up 关闭

range from 范围从

result from 起源于

systemic treatment 系统治疗

郝　斌　马志方

72

Cervical Cancer
宫 颈 癌

What is cervical cancer?

Cervical cancer occurs when abnormal cells on the cervix grow out of control. The cervix is the lower part of the uterus that opens into the vagina. Cervical cancer can often be successfully treated when it's found early. It is usually found at a very early stage through a Pap test.

What causes cervical cancer?

Most cervical cancer is caused by a virus called human papillomavirus, or HPV. You can get HPV by having sexual contact with someone who has it. There are many types of the HPV virus. Not all types of HPV cause cervical cancer. Some of them cause genital warts, but other types may not cause any symptoms.

You can have HPV for years and not know it. It stays in your body and can lead to cervical cancer years after you were infected. This is why it is important for you to have regular Pap tests. A Pap test can find changes in cervical cells before they turn into cancer. If you treat these cell changes, you may prevent cervical cancer.

What are the symptoms of cervical cancer?

Abnormal cervical cell changes rarely cause symptoms. If cervical cell changes progress to cancer, symptoms may include:

- Abnormal vaginal bleeding or discharge that may have mucus and be tinged with blood.
- A significant unexplained change in your menstrual cycle.
- Bleeding when something comes in contact with the cervix, such as during sex or when you insert a diaphragm.
- Pain during sex.

The symptoms of advanced cervical cancer may include:

- Anemia because of abnormal vaginal bleeding.
- Ongoing pelvic, leg, or back pain.

- Urinary problems because of blockage of a kidney or ureter.
- Leakage of urine or stool into the vagina. This can happen when an abnormal opening (fistula) has developed between the vaginaand the bladder or rectum.
- Weight loss.

How is cervical cancer diagnosed?

Early detection

The Pap test is a routine screening test used to find abnormal cell changes of the cervix and to screen for cervical cancer. Regular Pap test screening is the most important tool in finding and treating cervical cell changes before they progress to cervical cancer.

The recommended Pap test schedule is based on your age and things that increase your risk. For most women, it is best to have a Pap test every 1 to 3 years. Talk to your doctor about when to have your first Pap test and how often to have this test.

Diagnostic tests

If cervical cancer is suspected, your doctor will ask about your medical history and perform a physical exam, including a pelvic exam and a Pap test.

Tests to confirm a diagnosis of cervical cancer include:

- A colposcopy and cervical biopsy. This test can find out whether and where cancer cells are on the surface of the cervix.
- An endocervical biopsy (or curettage). This test is to find out whether cancer cells are in the cervical canal.
- A cone biopsy or loop electrosurgical excision procedure (LEEP). These tests are sometimes recommended to remove cervical tissue for examination under a microscope.

Tests to find out the stage and treatment

Tests to find the extent (stage) of cervical cancer include:

- A cone biopsy or loop electrosurgical excision procedure (LEEP). These tests are sometimes recommended to look for the spread of cancer in cervical tissue.
- A cystoscopy, to look at the interior lining of the bladder and the urethra to see if the cancer has spread to the urinary system.
- A proctoscopy, to look at the lower part of the large intestine (colon) to see if the cancer has spread to the rectum.
- An intravenous pyelogram, to see if there is any blockage of a kidney.

A surgery or procedure may be done to find out the extent of cervical cancer and treat it at the same time. For more information, see Surgery.

Other tests may be done to help guide treatment decisions. For example, you may have:

- Blood tests, such as a complete blood count (CBC) to check for anemia or a chemistry screen to find out how the liver and kidneys are working.
- Imaging tests, such as a chest X-ray, a CT scan, an MRI, or a position emission tomography (PET). These tests are done to see if the cancer has spread beyond the cervix.

How is it treated?

Cervical cancer found in its early stages can be successfully treated. The choice of treatment and the long-term outcome (prognosis) of cervical cancer depend on the type and stage of cancer. The patient's age, overall health, quality of life, and desire to be able to have children must also be considered.

Types of treatment

Treatment choices for cervical cancer may be a single therapy or a combination of therapies, such as:

- **Surgery** to remove the cancer. The type of surgery needed depends on the location and extent of cervical cancer and whether you want to have children.
- **Chemotherapy** which uses medicines to kills cancer cells. It is usually used as the main treatment or after a hysterectomy. It may also be used along with radiationtherapy.
- **Radiation therapy** which uses high-dose X-rays or implants in the vaginal cavity to kill cancer cells. It is used for certain stages of cervical cancer. It is often used in combination with surgery.

Side effects

Most treatments for cervical cancer cause side effects. Your doctor can talk to you about your treatment choices and the side effects from each treatment.

- Side effects of surgery depend on the surgery used to treat the stage of your cancer.
- Side effects of chemotherapy may include loss of appetite, nausea, vomiting, diarrhea, mouth sores, or hair loss.
- Side effects of radiation therapy may include fatigue, skin irritation, or changes in your bowel or urinary habits.

Coping with emotions during treatment

When you first find out that you have cancer, you may feel scared or angry. Or you may feel very calm. It's normal to have a wide range of feelings and for those feelings to change quickly. Some people find that it helps to talk about their feelings with family and friends.

If your emotional reactions to cancer get in the way of your ability to make decisions about your health, it's important to talk with your doctor. Your cancer treatment center may offer psychological or financial services.

Body image and sexual problems

Your feelings about your body and your sexuality may change following treatment for cancer. Managing body image issues may involve talking openly with your partner about your feelings and discussing your concerns with your doctor. Your doctor may be able to refer you to organizations that can offer additional support and information.

Treatment during pregnancy

Cancer treatment during pregnancy is the same as for nonpregnant women. But when you'll get treatment may depend on the stage of your cancer and what trimester you are in. For example, if you have early-stage cervical cancer and you are in your third trimester, your treatment may be delayed until after you deliver your baby. Treatment may cause problems such as an early delivery or even the loss of the baby.

Follow-up care

After treatment for cervical cancer, it is important to receive follow-up care. Your oncologist or gynecologic oncologist will schedule regular checkups that will include:

- A pelvic exam and Pap test every 3 to 6 months for the first 2 years.
- After the first 2 years, a pelvic exam and Pap test every 6 months for another 3 to 5 years.
- After 5 years, a pelvic exam and Pap test every year.

Follow-up tests that may be recommended by your oncologist include an abdominal and pelvic computed tomography (CT) scan. This test is to see if cancer has spread to other organs in the belly or pelvis.

Cervical cancer that comes back

Cervical cancer can return, or recur, after treatment. About 35 out of 100 women with cervical cancer will have persistent or recurrent disease. That means that the cancer doesn't come back in 65 out of 100 cases. The chance that your cancer will return depends on the stage of the initial cancer. Cancer found early is less likely to come back than cancer found at a later stage.

Your long-term outcome (prognosis) for recurrent cervical cancer depends greatly on how much the cancer has spread when the recurrence is diagnosed.

Palliative care

Cancer treatment has two main goals: curing cancer and making your quality of life as good as possible. Palliative care can improve your quality of life by helping you manage your symptoms. It can also help you with other concerns that you may have when you are living with a serious illness.

For some people who have advanced cancer, a time comes when treatment to cure cancer no longer seems like a good choice. This can be because the side effects, time, and costs of treatment are greater than the promise of cure or relief. But this isn't the end of treatment. You and your doctor can decide when you may be ready for hospice care.

中英文注释

关键词汇

cervix ['sɜːviks] n. 子宫颈

cystoscopy [sis'tɒskəpi] n. 膀胱镜检查

diarrhea [daiə'riə] n. 腹泻

fistula ['fistjʊlə] n. 瘘管

hysterectomy [histə'rektəmi] n. 子宫切除术

pelvic ['pelvik] n. 骨盆的

proctoscopy [prɒk'tɒskəpi] n. 直肠镜检查

recurrence [ri'kʌrəns] n. 复发

uterus ['juːt(ə)rəs] n. 子宫

vagina [və'dʒainə] n. 阴道

主要短语

abnormal vaginal bleeding 不正常的阴道出血

cervical cancer 宫颈癌

cone biopsy or loop electrosurgical excision procedure (LEEP) 宫颈锥形切除活检或环形电切术

genital wart 生殖器疣

gynecologic oncologist 妇产肿瘤医师

human papillomavirus(HPV) 人乳头瘤病毒

intravenous pyelogram 静脉肾盂造影

leakage of urine or stool into the vagina 尿液或粪便泄漏进阴道

menstrual cycle 月经周期

mouth sores 口疮

pain during sex 性交痛

palliative care 姑息治疗

skin irritation 皮肤刺激

the Pap test 巴氏涂片检查

weight loss. 体重下降

魏 亮 马志方

73 ————————————— Ovarian Cancer
卵 巢 癌

What is ovarian cancer?

Ovarian cancer happens when cells that are not normal grow in one or both of your ovaries. The ovaries are two small glands, located on either side of your uterus. They produce female sex hormones and store and release eggs (ova).

Treatments for ovarian cancer are more successful when the cancer is found early. But most of the time, cancer has already spread by the time it is found.

This topic is about epithelial ovarian cancer. This is cancer that grows in the tissue covering the ovaries. It is the most common type of ovarian cancer and usually occurs in women who are past menopause.

What causes ovarian cancer?

Experts don't know exactly what causes ovarian cancer. Genetics, such as DNA changes, are a risk factor for some women.

In general, about 1 out of 100 women will get ovarian cancer. That risk goes up to 5 out of 100 if one family member has had ovarian cancer, and 7 out of 100 if two or three relatives have had it.

About 10 out of 100 ovarian cancers are thought to be caused by gene mutations in the BRCA1 or BRCA2 genes. The risk for women who have these gene changes is much higher than for women without them.

What are the symptoms of ovarian cancer?

In some cases, ovarian cancer may cause early symptoms. The most common symptoms of ovarian cancer include:

- Frequent bloating.
- Pain in your belly or pelvis.
- Trouble eating, or feeling full quickly.
- Urinary problems, such as an urgent need to urinate or urinating more often than usual.

489

If you have one or more of these symptoms, and it occurs almost daily for more than 2 or 3 weeks, talk with your doctor.

These symptoms are common for some women. They may not mean that you have ovarian cancer. But the early symptoms of ovarian cancer follow a pattern:

- They start suddenly
- They feel different than your normal digestive or menstrual problems.
- They happen almost every day and don't go away.

Other symptoms that affect some women with ovarian cancer include:

- Fatigue.
- Indigestion.
- Back pain.
- Pain with intercourse.
- Menstrual cycle changes.

But these symptoms are also common in some women who don't have ovarian cancer.

How is ovarian cancer diagnosed?

Some exams and tests that are done to look for or diagnose ovarian cancer include:

- A biopsy, which is the only way to know for sure if a woman has ovarian cancer. This usually is done with a laparotomy, through a cut (incision) in the belly.
- A physical exam, including a pelvic exam and Pap test. An ovarian lump may be felt during a pelvic exam. A rectovaginal exam may also be done to feel the pelvic organs.
- A cancer antigen 125 (CA-125) level, to measure a protein found on the surface of many ovarian cancer cells.
- A pelvic and transvaginal ultrasound, to look for an ovarian lump.
- A pelvic or abdominal CT scan or MRI, to check for the spread of cancer.

Early detection

The United States Preventive Services Task Force (USPSTF) doesn't recommend routine screening for ovarian cancer. There is no proof that having regular tests helps women live longer by finding ovarian cancer early.

Still, some experts recommend that women who have inherited a BRCA gene change and have not had their ovaries removed have a transvaginal ultrasound and a CA-125 blood test at least once a year, starting at age 35. Women who have inherited a BRCA1 gene change (not a BRCA2 gene change) may want to start having these tests as early as age 25.

How is it treated?

The choice of treatment and the long-term outcome (prognosis) for women who have ovarian cancer depends on the type and stage of cancer. Your age, overall health, quality of life, and desire to have children must also be considered.

The main treatment choices are:

- Surgery to find out if you have cancer and to treat it. This may include taking biopsies to check for the spread of cancer.
- Chemotherapy, which uses medicines to kill cancer cells. It is recommended after surgery for most stages of ovarian cancer.

Women with more advanced ovarian cancer may have part of their chemotherapy before surgery and the rest of it after surgery. This can make the surgery safer for these women.

Radiation therapy may be used to destroy cancer cells using high-dose X-rays or other high-energy rays.

Side effects of treatment

Most treatments for ovarian cancer cause side effects. They may differ, depending on the type of treatment and your age and overall health.

- Side effects of surgery depend on the extent of your surgery. If the doctor removes your ovaries, you will no longer be able to bear children. And if you were still menstruating before your surgery, you will start menopause.
- Side effects of chemotherapy may include loss of appetite, nausea, vomiting, fatigue, and hair loss. There is also an increased chance of getting a serious infection.

Radiation treatment also can cause side effects. For more information, see Other Treatment.

Home treatment may help you manage the side effects.

Advanced-stage ovarian cancer

Surgery in advanced-stage ovarian cancer involves removing as much of the cancer as possible. The uterus, the tissue lining the abdominal wall (omentum), and any areas of visible cancer are removed. This may include surgery on the intestines, urinary system, or spleen, or scraping of the diaphragm to remove all the cancer. The long-term outcome is better if no cancer cells remain.

Clinical trials

Your doctor may talk to you about being in a clinical trial of a treatment such as immunotherapy or targeted therapy.

Coping with emotions

When you first find out that you have cancer, you may feel scared or angry. Or you may feel very calm. It's normal to have a wide range of feelings and for those feelings to change quickly. Some people find that it helps to talk about their feelings with family and friends.

If your emotional reaction to cancer gets in the way of your ability to make decisions about your health, it's important to talk with your doctor. Your cancer treatment center may offer psychological or financial services.

Body image and sexual problems

Your feelings about your body may change after treatment for cancer. Managing body image issues may involve talking about your concerns with your partner and discussing your feelings with your doctor. Your doctor may also be able to refer you to groups that can offer support and information.

Sexual problems can be caused by the physical or emotional effects of cancer or its treatment. Some women may feel less sexual pleasure or lose their desire to be intimate.

Follow-up care

After treatment for ovarian cancer, it's important to receive follow-up care, because ovarian cancer may come back (recur). Your doctor will set up a schedule of checkups and tests.

If the cancer recurs or spreads (metastasizes), it's usually treated with chemotherapy. Surgery may also be done. Or your doctor may recommend that you join a clinical trial for treatment with surgery or immunotherapy.

The long-term outcome for recurrent ovarian cancer depends on whether the cancer has spread. Even with no sign of cancer after treatment, 3 to 5 out of 10 women who are treated for ovarian cancer have cancer return within 5 years. This also means that cancer doesn't recur within 5 years in 5 to 7 out of 10 women.

Palliative care

Cancer treatment has two main goals: curing cancer and making your quality of life as good as possible. Palliative care can improve your quality of life by helping you manage your symptoms. It also can help you with other concerns that you may have when you are living with a serious illness.

For some people who have advanced cancer, a time comes when treatment to cure cancer no longer seems like a good choice. This can be because the side effects, time, and costs of treatment are greater than the promise of cure or relief. But this isn't the end of treatment. You and your doctor can decide when you may be ready for hospice care.

It can be hard to decide when to stop treatment to prolong your life and shift the focus to end-of-life care.

中英文注释

关键词汇

belly ['beli] n. 腹部；胃

menopause ['menəupɔːz] n. 更年期

omentum [əʊ'mentəm] n. [解剖] 网膜

pattern ['pætən] n. 模式

pelvis ['pelvis] n. 骨盆

prolong [prə'lɒŋ] vt. 延长

scared [skɛə] adj. 受惊的，害怕的

urinate ['jʊərineit] vi. 小便，撒尿

主要短语

epithelial ovarian cancer 卵巢上皮癌

pain with intercourse 性交痛

palliative care 姑息治疗

quality of life 生活质量

recurs or spreads 复发或转移

removing as much of the cancer as possible 尽量切除肿物

sex hormones 性激素

transvaginal ultrasound 经阴道超声

郝　斌　马志方

74 Bladder Cancer
膀 胱 癌

What is bladder cancer?

Cancer is the growth of abnormal cells in the body. These extra cells grow together and form masses, called tumors. In bladder cancer, these growths happen in the bladder.

The bladder is the part of your urinary tract that stores your urine until you are ready to let it out.

Bladder cancer can usually be successfully treated if it is found and treated early. And most bladder cancer is found early.

What causes bladder cancer?

The cause of bladder cancer is not known. Changes in the genetic material (DNA) of bladder cells may play a role. Chemicals in the environment and cigarette smoking also may play a role. And when the lining of the bladder is irritated for a long time, cell changes that lead to cancer may occur. Some things that cause this are radiation treatment, having catheters in place for a long time, or having the parasite that causes schistosomiasis.

Bladder cancer is twice as likely to develop in smokers than in nonsmokers. Experts believe that smoking causes about half of bladder cancer in men and more than one-fourth of bladder cancer in women.

Exposure to chemicals and other substances at work-including dyes, paints, leather dust, and others-may also cause bladder cancer.

What are the symptoms of bladder cancer?

The most common symptoms of bladder cancer include:
- Blood or blood clots in the urine (hematuria). Hematuria occurs in 8 or 9 out of 10 people who have bladder cancer and is the most common symptom. Usually it is not painful.
- Pain during urination (dysuria).
- Urinating small amounts frequently.

- Frequent urinary tract infections (UTIs).

Symptoms that may indicate more advanced bladder cancer include:

- Pain in the lower back around the kidneys (flank pain).
- Swelling in the lower legs.
- A growth in the pelvis near the bladder (pelvic mass).

Other symptoms that may develop when bladder cancer has spread include:

- Weight loss.
- Bone pain or pain in the rectal, anal, or pelvic area.
- Anemia.

The symptoms of bladder cancer may be similar to symptoms of other bladder conditions.

How is bladder cancer diagnosed?

To find out whether bladder cancer may be the cause of your urinary symptoms, your doctor will:

- Do a physical exam. This may include a rectal exam, a prostate exam for men, or a pelvic exam for women.
- Ask questions about your medical history, including:
  - Your smoking history.
  - Your possible exposure to cancer-causing chemicals.
  - Your family history of cancer.
- Order a urine test and urine culture to check for the presence of blood, infection, and other abnormal cells.

Cystoscopy

You will have a cystoscopy, a test that allows your doctor to look at your bladderwith a thin, lighted tube. The doctor can use the same tube to take small tissue samples (biopsies) of any abnormal areas. The samples will be looked at under a microscope to find out whether cancer cells are present and what the cells look like.

Tests to determine stage and grade

Bladder cancer is classified by stage and grade. The stage is determined by the cancer growth in the bladder wall and how far it has spread to nearby tissues and other organs, such as the lungs, the liver, or the bones. The grade of bladder cancer is determined by how the cancer cells look in comparison with normal bladder cells.

Your doctor finds out the stage and grade of your bladder cancer by gathering information from several tests, including:

- Biopsies from the cystoscopy.
- CT scan or MRI. These help find out if the cancer has spread to lymph nodes,

the lungs, the liver, or other abdominal organs.

- Chest X-ray. This finds out if the cancer has spread to the lungs.
- Bone scan. This finds out if the cancer has spread to the bones.

The stage and grade of your cancer are important in choosing the right treatments.

Other tests

Other diagnostic tests that may be done include:

- A complete blood count (CBC) to find out if you have anemia.
- A chemistry screen to evaluate kidney, liver, and bone functions.
- An intravenous pyelogram or computed tomography (CT urogram) to look for a mass near the kidneys, ureters, or bladder.

Early detection of returning cancer

Bladder cancer often comes back, so it's important to have regular checkups. Then, if the cancer does come back, you have a better chance of finding it early enough for successful treatment.

How is it treated?

The choice of treatment and the long-term outcome (prognosis) for people who have bladder cancer depend on the stage and grade of cancer. When deciding about your treatment, your doctor also considers your age, overall health, and quality of life.

Bladder cancer has a better chance of being treated successfully if it is found early.

Treatment choices for bladder cancer may include:

- **Surgery**

Surgery is used to treat most stages of bladder cancer.

- Transurethral resection (TUR) is surgery done through the urethra. A thin, lighted tube called a cystoscope is used to remove or destroy tumors in the bladder.
- Cystectomy is surgery to remove the bladder.
- Partial cystectomy removes only part of the bladder. It is used to treat cancer that has invaded the bladder wall in just one area.
- Simple cystectomy removes all of the bladder.
- Radical cystectomy removes all of the bladder as well as nearby lymph nodes, part of the urethra, and nearby organs that may contain cancer.
- Urinary diversion is surgery that makes a new way for your body to store urine. This can be done with a pouch created inside your body from part of your intestines, called a continent reservoir. Or the surgeon may make an artificial opening, called an ileal conduit, and you will wear a flat bag to store urine outside your body.

● **Chemotherapy**

Medicines may be used to control the growth of bladder cancer cells and to relieve symptoms. These medicines may be taken by mouth, injected into a vein (intravenous, or IV), or delivered directly into the bladder using a catheter.

- **Chemotherapy** uses medicines to destroy cancer cells.
- **Immunotherapy** also called biological therapy, uses medicines that cause your body's immune system to attack cancer cells in your bladder. It is most often used for early-stage bladder cancer. It may also be used after a transurethral resection (TUR) to help keep cancer from coming back.

  Most chemotherapy causes some side effects. Home treatment may be all that is needed to manage your symptoms. But some people may need medicines to control nausea and vomiting.

Medication choices

Chemotherapy medicines

- Gemcitabine and cisplatin.
- MVAC, a combination of methotrexate, vinblastine, doxorubicin, and cisplatin.
- Mitomycin. This medicine may be used to help keep cancer from coming back.

Immunotherapy medicines

- Bacillus Calmette-Guerin (BCG).
- Interferon.

● **Radiation therapy**

Radiation treatment for bladder cancer uses high-energy X-rays to kill cancer cells and shrink tumors. It may be given after surgery. It may be used along with chemotherapy. Sometimes it is used instead of surgery or chemotherapy.

- External beam radiation comes from a machine outside the body. The machine aims radiation at the area where the cancer cells are found.
- Internal radiation uses needles, seeds, wires, or catheters that contain radioactive materials placed close to or directly into the bladder.

Which treatment you receive will depend on the type and stage of your cancer.

● **Immunotherapy**

This treatment causes your body's natural defenses, known as your immune system, to attack bladder cancer cells.

Side effects of treatment

- Most treatments for bladder cancer cause side effects. Side effects may differ, depending on the type of treatment used and your age and overall health.

- Side effects of chemotherapy may include loss of appetite, nausea, vomiting, diarrhea, mouth sores, or hair loss. There is also an increased chance of getting a serious infection during chemotherapy treatment.
- Side effects of surgery depend on how extensive your surgery was to treat the stage of your cancer. Men may have erection problems after surgery if the bladder is removed (cystectomy). If you choose a surgeon who does many of these procedures, you will have fewer side effects and you will recover faster.
- Side effects of radiation may include nausea, vomiting, diarrhea, pain or discomfort when urinating, and bladder inflammation and scarring (radiation cystitis). You may also have an increased risk of infection.
- Side effects of immunotherapy vary depending on the medicine. Bacillus Calmette-Guerin (BCG) is a tuberculosis vaccine used in countries outside the United States. With BCG, the side effects may include fever, joint pain, inflammation of the prostate, or disseminated tuberculosis.

Body image and sexual problems

Sexual problems can be caused by physical or psychological factors related to the cancer or its treatment. You may experience less sexual pleasure or lose your desire to be sexually intimate.

Women who have the bladder removed (radical cystectomy) will also have the ovaries and uterus removed. They cannot become pregnant and may experience menopause soon after having the cystectomy.

Men who have their prostate glands and seminal vesicles removed may have erection problems and will no longer produce semen.

Your feelings about your body may change following treatment for cancer. Managing body image issues may involve talking openly about your concerns with your partner and discussing your feelings with your doctor. Your doctor may also be able to refer you to groups that can offer support and information.

Bladder cancer that comes back

After initial treatment for bladder cancer, it is important to receive follow-up care, because bladder cancer often comes back (recurs). Your doctor will set up a regular schedule of checkups and tests.

Bladder cancer may recur in the bladder, or it may spread (metastasize) to other parts of the body. Recurrent bladder cancer may be treated with surgery or chemotherapy to slow cancer growth and relieve symptoms.

Participation in a clinical trial may be recommended if you have been diagnosed with recurrent bladder cancer.

Palliative care

Cancer treatment has two main goals: curing cancer and making your quality of life as good as possible. Palliative care can improve your quality of life by helping you manage your symptoms. It can also help you with other concerns that you may have when you are living with a serious illness.

For some people who have advanced cancer, a time comes when treatment to cure cancer no longer seems like a good choice. This can be because the side effects, time, and costs of treatment are greater than the promise of cure or relief. But this isn't the end of treatment. You and your doctor can decide when you may be ready for hospice care.

中英文注释

关键词汇

bladder ['blædə] n. 膀胱

biopsy ['baiɒpsi] n. 活组织检查；活组织切片检查；切片检查法

cystectomy [sis'tektəmi] n. 膀胱切除术；胆囊切除术

cystoscopy [sis'tɒskəpi] n. 膀胱镜检查

dysuria [dis'juəriə] n. 排尿困难

hematuria [ˌhiːmə'tjuəriə] n. 血尿；血尿症

immunotherapy [i'mjənoˈθɛrəpi] n. 免疫疗法

kidney ['kidni] n. 肾脏

schistosomiasis [ˌʃistə(ʊ)sə'maiəsis] n. 血吸虫病

urethra [jʊ'riːθrə] n. 尿道

ureter [jʊ'ritɚ] n. 输尿管

主要短语

abdominal organ 腹部器官

bacillus Calmette-Guerin (BCG) 卡介菌

bladder cancer 膀胱癌

blood clot 血凝块，血块

bone scan 骨扫描

comes back (recurs) 复发

CT urogram CT 尿路成像

external beam radiation 外放疗

gemcitabine and cisplatin 吉西他滨和顺铂

hospice care 临终关怀

internal radiation 内放疗

intravenous pyelogram 静脉肾盂造影

lymph node 淋巴结

pelvic mass 盆腔肿块

radiation treatment 放射疗法

radical cystectomy remove 根治性膀胱切除术

rectal exam 肛诊

transurethral resection (TUR) 经尿道切除（手术）

urinary diversion 尿流改道术

urinary tract 尿路

urinary tract infection 尿路感染

茹 峰 王东文

75

Kidney Cancer

肾　　癌

What is kidney cancer?

Kidney cancer — also called renal cancer — is a disease in which kidney cells become malignant (cancerous) and grow out of control, forming a tumor. Almost all kidney cancers first appear in the lining of tiny tubes (tubules) in the kidney. This type of kidney cancer is called renal cell carcinoma. The good news is that most of kidney cancers are found before they spread (metastasize) to distant organs. And cancers caught early are easier to treat successfully. However, these tumors can grow to be quite large before they are detected.

What causes kidney cancer?

The kidneys are two bean-shaped organs, each about the size of a fist. They lie in your lower abdomen on each side of your spine. Their main job is to clean your blood, removing waste products and making urine.

Doctors don't know the causes of kidney cancer. But certain factors appear to increase the risk of getting kidney cancer. For example, kidney cancer occurs most often in people older than age 40. These are some other risk factors for kidney cancer:

- **Smoking.** If you smoke cigarettes, your risk for kidney cancer is twice that of nonsmokers. Smoking cigars may also increase your risk.
- **Being male.** Men are about twice as likely as women to get kidney cancer.
- **Being obese.** Extra weight may cause changes to hormones that increase your risk.
- **Using certain pain medications for a long time.** This includes over-the-counter drugs in addition to prescription drugs.
- **Having advanced kidney disease** or being on long-term dialysis, a treatment for people with kidneys that have stopped working.
- **Having certain genetic conditions,** such as von Hippel-Lindau (VHL) disease or inherited papillary renal cell carcinoma.
- **Having a family history of kidney cancer.** The risk is especially high in siblings.

- **Being exposed to certain chemicals.** such as asbestos, cadmium, benzene, organic solvents, or certain herbicides.
- **Having high blood pressure.** Doctors don't know whether high blood pressure or medication used to treat it is the source of the increased risk.
- **Being black.** The risk in blacks is slightly higher than in whites. No one knows why.
- **Having lymphoma.** For an unknown reason, there is an increased risk of kidney cancer in patients with lymphoma.

Having these risk factors does not mean you will get kidney cancer. And it's also true that you can have none of them and still get the disease.

What are the symptoms of kidney cancer?

In many cases, people may have no early symptoms of kidney cancer. As the tumor grows larger, symptoms may appear. You may have one or more of these kidney cancer symptoms:

- Blood in your urine
- A lump in your side or abdomen
- A loss of appetite
- A pain in your side that doesn't go away
- Weight loss that occurs for no known reason
- Fever that lasts for weeks and isn't caused by a cold or other infection
- Extreme fatigue
- Anemia
- Swelling in your ankles or legs

Kidney cancer that spreads to other parts of your body may cause other symptoms, such as:

- Shortness of breath
- Coughing up blood
- Bone pain

Maybe you've had kidney cancer symptoms such as pain in your side, weight loss, or extreme fatigue. Or maybe your doctor has found a lump in your side during a routine exam or a sign of kidney cancer during a test for another disease. Regardless, to confirm a diagnosis of kidney cancer, you will need a thorough physical exam, health history, and tests.

Your doctor will feel your abdomen and side for lumps and check for fever and high blood pressure, among other things. You will also answer questions about your health habits, any past illnesses, and types of treatment. To make a diagnosis of kidney cancer, your doctor will also order one or more tests like these:

- **Urine tests** check for blood in your urine or other signs of problems.
- **Blood tests** show how well your kidneys are working.
- **Intravenous pyelogram (IVP)** involves X-raying your kidneys after the doctor injects a dye that travels to your urinary tract, highlighting any tumors.
- **Ultrasound** uses sound waves to create a picture of your kidneys. It can help tell if a tumor is solid or fluid-filled.
- **A CT scan** uses X-rays and a computer to create a series of detailed pictures of your kidneys. This may also require an injection of dye. CT scans have virtually replaced pyelogram and ultrasound as a tool for diagnosing kidney cancer.
- **Magnetic resonance imaging (MRI)** uses strong magnets and radio waves to create detailed images of soft tissues in your body. You may need an injection of a contrast agent to create better pictures.
- **Renal arteriogram.** This test is used to evaluate the blood supply to the tumor. It is not given often but may help diagnose small tumors and has other uses as well.

Unlike with many other cancers, your doctor may be pretty certain about a diagnosis of kidney cancer without a biopsy. Sometimes, a biopsy will be done to confirm the diagnosis. A doctor may use a needle biopsy to remove a sample of tissue, which is then examined under a microscope for cancer cells. The biopsy may also tell the grade of the cancer, how aggressive the cancer is likely to be. Often the surgeon will simply remove the entire tumor and then have a sample of tissue examined.

Once your doctor makes a diagnosis of kidney cancer, you may need other tests to tell if the cancer has spread within your kidney, to the other kidney, or to other parts of your body. When cancer spreads from the place where it first started, it has metastasized. You might need a CT scan or MRI. A chest X-ray can show whether the cancer has spread to your lungs. A bone scan can see if it is in your bones. These tests will help your doctor determine the stage of kidney cancer.

What are the stages of kidney cancer?

Your prognosis depends on your general health, as well as the grade and stage of your kidney cancer.

These are the stages of kidney cancer. The higher the stage, the more advanced the cancer.

Stage I

- A tumor 7 centimeters or smaller that is only in the kidney

Stage II

● A tumor larger than 7 centimeters that is only in the kidney

Stage III

● A tumor that is in the kidney and in at least one nearby lymph node

● A tumor that is in the kidney's main blood vessel and may also be in nearby lymph node

● A tumor that is in the fatty tissue around the kidney and may also involve nearby lymph nodes

● A tumor that extends into major veins or perinephric tissues, but not into the ipsilateral adrenal gland and not beyond Gerota's fascia

Stage IV

● Cancer has spread beyond the fatty layer of tissue around the kidney, and it may also be in nearby lymph nodes

● Cancer may have spread to other organs, such as the bowel, pancreas, or lungs

● Cancer has spread beyond Gerota's fascia (including contiguous extension into the ipsilateral adrenal gland)

What are the treatments for kidney cancer?

Once you have a diagnosis and know your stage of kidney cancer, you and your doctor can plan treatment. You may want to gather information to help you feel more informed about your decision. Your doctor may refer you to a specialist for treatment. This could include an urologist, a medical or radiation oncologist, or a surgeon. Before beginning treatment, many people find it helpful to get a second opinion about the diagnosis of kidney cancer and the treatment plan.

Kidney cancer is one of the more common cancers to undergo spontaneous remission. However, the incidence is quite low (approximately 0.5%).

There are several standard types of treatment for kidney cancer. In most cases, surgery is the first step. Even if surgery removes the entire tumor, though, your doctor may suggest an extra treatment to kill any remaining cancer cells that can't be seen.

Surgery for kidney cancer

These are the main types of surgery for kidney cancer. Which type you have depends on how advanced your cancer is.

● Radical nephrectomy removes the kidney, adrenal gland, and surrounding tissue. It also often removes nearby lymph nodes. It is the most common surgery for kidney cancer and can now be done through a small incision with a laparoscope.

● Simple nephrectomy removes the kidney only.

- Partial nephrectomy removes the cancer in the kidney along with some tissue around it. This procedure is used for patients with smaller tumors (less than 4 cm) or in those patients in which a radical nephrectomy might hurt the other kidney.

You can survive with just a part of one kidney as long as it is still working. If the surgeon removes both kidneys or if both kidneys are not working, you will need a machine to clean your blood (dialysis) or a new kidney (kidney transplant). A transplant is possible if your cancer was found only in your kidney and a donated kidney is available.

If surgery can't remove your kidney cancer, your doctor may suggest another option to help destroy the tumor.

- Cryotherapy uses extreme cold to kill the tumor.
- Radiofrequency ablation uses high-energy radio waves to "cook" the tumor.
- Arterial embolization involves inserting material into an artery that leads to the kidney. This blocks blood flow to the tumor. This procedure may be done to help shrink the tumor before surgery.

Biologic therapy for kidney cancer

This therapy uses your immune system to fight cancer by boosting, directing, or restoring your body's natural defenses. Substances for biologic therapy are made by your body or in a lab. Examples of biologic therapy for metastatic kidney cancer include interferon alpha or interleukin-2.

Targeted therapy for kidney cancer

This therapy uses drugs or other substances to find and target cancer cells without harming normal cells. One type of targeted therapy is anti-angiogenic agents. These keep blood vessels from feeding a tumor, causing it to shrink or stop growing. Another type of targeted agent is known as multikinaseinhibitors or tyrosine kinase inhibitors. These oral drugs block an enzyme pathway that allows cancer cells to grow. A third type of targeted therapy is known as m-TOR inhibitors. There are two of these drugs available, one oral and one by IV. They block a pathway that allows blood vessels to help tumor cells grow. Each of these drugs has a unique place in the management of advanced kidney cancer.

Radiation therapy for kidney cancer

Often used to help with symptoms of kidney cancer or in patients who cannot have surgery, this treatment uses high-energy X-rays or other types of radiation to kill cancer cells or halt their growth. External radiation therapy sends radiation to the cancer from a machine outside the body.

Chemotherapy for kidney cancer

This therapy uses drugs to kill cancer cells or stop them from multiplying. Less effective for kidney cancer than for other types of cancer, chemotherapy is used when other types of treatment do not work well.

If surgery can't remove your kidney cancer, your doctor may suggest another option to help destroy the tumor.

中英文注释

关键词汇

abdomen ['æbdəmən] n. 腹部；下腹；腹腔

cancerous ['kænsɚrəs] adj. 癌的；生癌的；像癌的

cryotherapy [ˌkraio'θɛrəpi] n. 冷冻疗法

incision [in'siʒən] n. 切口；切割；切开

lymphoma [lim'fomə] n. 淋巴瘤

metastasize [mə'tæstəsaiz] vi. 转移

sibling ['sibliŋ] n. 兄弟姊妹

spine [spain] n. 脊柱，脊椎

swelling ['swɛliŋ] n. 肿胀；膨胀；adj. 膨胀的；肿大的；突起的；v. 肿胀；膨胀

主要短语

adrenal gland　肾上腺

anti-angiogenic agent　抗血管生成剂

arterial embolization　肾动脉栓塞

bone pain　骨痛

Gerota's fascia　吉氏筋膜，肾周筋膜

interferon alpha　干扰素 α

interleukin-2　白细胞介素 -2

intravenous pyelogram (IVP)　静脉肾盂造影

kidney cancer　肾癌

multikinase inhibitor　多激酶抑制剂

prescription drug　处方药

radiation oncologist　放射肿瘤医师放射肿瘤学家

radical nephrectomy　根治性肾切除术

radiofrequency ablation　射频消融

shortness of breath　气促；呼吸浅短

simple nephrectomy　单纯性肾切除

targeted therapy　靶向治疗

tyrosine kinase inhibitor　酪氨酸激酶抑制剂

茹　峰　王东文

76 Prostate Cancer
前 列 腺 癌

What is prostate cancer?

Prostate cancer is the most common cancer in American men, and in most men it grows very slowly. Get an overview of the disease.

The prostate is a gland in the male reproductive system that produces the majority of seminal fluid that carries sperm. The walnut-sized gland is located beneath a man's bladder and surrounds the upper part of the urethra, the tube that carries urine from the bladder. Prostate function is regulated by testosterone, a male sex hormone produced mainly in the testicles.

Prostate cancer is a major health concern for American men. Although the disease is rare before age 50, experts believe that most elderly men have at least traces of it.

More than 241,000 new cases will be diagnosed, and about 28,000 deaths will be attributed to prostate cancer, in 2012 in the U.S. For reasons not fully understood, African-American men have the highest frequency of prostate cancer in the world and the highest death rate from the disease. In other parts of the world — notably Asia, Africa, and Latin America — prostate cancer is rare.

Prostate cancer is typically a very slow growing tumor, often causing no symptoms until it is in an advanced stage. Most men with prostate cancer die of other causes — many without ever realizing that they have the disease. But once prostate cancer begins to grow more rapidly or spreads outside the prostate, it is dangerous. This aggressive type of prostate cancer can occur at any age. Although the disease tends to progress slowly, it is generally fatal if it spreads beyond the prostate gland itself.

Prostate cancer in its early stages (confined to the prostate gland) can be effectively treated, with very good outcomes for survival. Fortunately, about 85% of American men with prostate cancer are diagnosed in an early stage of the disease.

Cancer that has spread beyond the prostate to distant tissues (such as the bones, lymph nodes, and lungs) is not curable, but it may be controlled for many years. Because of the many advances in available treatments, the majority of men whose prostate cancer becomes widespread can expect to live five years or more.

What causes prostate cancer?

Diet and genetics may be factors in prostate cancer development, but they are not the only ones. Find out what the research shows.

Prostate cancer affects mainly older men. Four out of five cases are diagnosed in men over 65, but less than 1% in men under 50. Though rare, prostate cancer can be seen in men in their 30's and 40's. Men with a family history of prostate cancer are more likely to develop the disease than the general population. On a case-by-case basis, doctors cannot say with certainty what causes prostate cancer, but experts generally agree that diet contributes to the risk. Men who consume large amounts of fat — particularly from red meat and other sources of animal fat — are most likely to develop prostate cancer. The disease is much more common in countries where meat and dairy products are dietary staples than in countries where the basic diet consists of rice, soybean products, and vegetables.

Risk Factors

Age, race, diet, family history — even a sedentary lifestyle — may all play a part in contributing to your prostate cancer risks.

What are the symptoms of prostate cancer?

There are no warning signs or symptoms of early prostate cancer. Once a malignant tumor causes the prostate gland to swell significantly, or once cancer spreads beyond the prostate, the following symptoms may be present:

- A frequent need to urinate, especially at night
- Difficulty starting or stopping a stream of urine
- A weak or interrupted urinary stream
- Leaking of urine when laughing or coughing
- Inability to urinate standing up
- A painful or burning sensation during urination or ejaculation
- Blood in urine or semen

These are not symptoms of the cancer itself; instead, they are caused by the blockage from the cancer growth within the prostate and surrounding tissues.

Symptoms of advanced prostate cancer include:

- Dull, incessant deep pain or stiffness in the pelvis, lower back, ribs, or upper thighs; pain in the bones of those areas
- Loss of weight and appetite, fatigue, nausea, or vomiting
- Swelling of the lower extremities
- Weakness or paralysis in the lower limbs, often associated with constipation

How is prostate cancer diagnosed?

Two initial tests are commonly used to look for prostate cancer in the absence of any symptoms. One is the digital rectal exam, in which a doctor feels the prostate through the rectum to find hard or lumpy areas known as nodules. The other is a blood test used to detect a substance made by the prostate called "prostate-specific antigen" (PSA). When used together, these tests can detect abnormalities that might suggest prostate cancer.

Neither of these initial tests for prostate cancer is perfect. Many men with a mildly elevated PSA do not have prostate cancer, and men with prostate cancer may have normal levels of PSA. Also, the digital rectal exam does not detect all prostate cancers.

The diagnosis can only be confirmed by examining prostate cells under a microscope. This is done by performing a biopsy in an urologist's office. A small sample of tissue is taken from the prostate for testing and evaluation under a microscope.

Digital Rectal Examination for Prostate Problems

A digital rectal exam is an early, simple test to screen for prostate cancer. It can catch the disease early, when it's most treatable.

Prostate-Specific Antigen Blood Test: Diagnosing Prostate Cancer

Prostate-specific antigen (PSA) is a substance produced by the prostate gland. Elevated PSA levels may indicate prostate cancer, a noncancerous condition such as prostatitis, or an enlarged prostate.

Most men have PSA levels under four (ng/mL) and this has traditionally been used as the cutoff for concern about the risk of prostate cancer. Men with prostate cancer often have PSA levels higher than four, although cancer is a possibility at any PSA level. According to published reports, men who have a prostate gland that feels normal on examination and a PSA less than four have a 15% chance of having prostate cancer. Those with a PSA between four and 10 have a 25% chance of having prostate cancer and if the PSA is higher than 10, the risk increases to 67%.

In the past, most experts viewed PSA levels less than 4 ng/mL as normal. Due to the findings from more recent studies, some recommend lowering the cutoff levels that determine if a PSA value is normal or elevated. Some researchers encourage using less than 2.5 or 3 ng/mL as a cutoff for normal values, particularly in younger patients. Younger patients tend to have smaller prostates and lower PSA values, so any elevation of the PSA in younger men above 2.5 ng/mL is a cause for concern.

Just as important as the PSA number is the trend of that number (whether it is going up, how quickly, and over what period of time). It is important to understand that the PSA test is not perfect. Most men with elevated PSA levels have noncancerous prostate enlargement, which is a normal part of aging. Conversely, low levels of PSA in the bloodstream do not rule out the possibility of prostate cancer. However, most cases of early prostate cancer are found by a PSA blood test.

Prostate Ultrasound and Biopsy to Diagnose Prostate Cancer

Prostate ultrasound and biopsy both evaluate the abnormal results of a digital rectal exam or an elevated prostate-specific antigen (PSA) blood test.

Prostate ultrasound involves a probe about the size of a finger that is inserted a short distance into the rectum. This probe produces harmless high-frequency sound waves, inaudible to the human ear, that bounce off the surface of the prostate. The sound waves are recorded and transformed into video or photographic images of the prostate gland.

The probe can provide images at different angles to help your doctor estimate the size of your prostate and detect any abnormal growths.

A prostate biopsy uses transrectal ultrasound imaging to guide several small needles through the rectum wall into areas of the prostate where abnormalities are detected. The needles remove a tiny amount of tissue. Usually six or more biopsies are taken to test various areas of the prostate. The tissue samples are then analyzed in a laboratory. The results will help doctors diagnose disorders and diseases in the prostate. If cancer is identified, the doctor will be able to grade the cancer and determine its aggressiveness or likelihood of spreading.

Cystoscopy or Bladder Scope Test to Diagnose Prostate Cancer

Cystoscopy, also called a cystourethroscopy or a bladder scope, measures the health of the urethra and bladder.

CT Scans and Prostate Cancer Diagnosis

A CT scan uses X-rays and computers to produce an image of a cross-section of the body. This image allows your doctor to check for swollen or enlarged lymph nodes, which might mean that cancer has spread.

Generally, a CT scan is only used if the cancer is large, looks aggressive, or is associated with a very high PSA level.

MRI to Diagnose Prostate Cancer

MRI use a large magnet, radio waves, and a computer to examine the prostate and nearby lymph nodes, distinguishing between noncancerous and cancerous areas.

How is it treated?

Treatment for prostate cancer may include everything from "watchful waiting" to removal of the entire prostate gland.

Prostate Cancer Staging

One of the most important factors in deciding how to treat prostate cancer is staging. The size, location, and whether your cancer has spread will help your medical team plan the right treatment.

Prostate Cancer Surgery

● **Radical Prostatectomy for Prostate Cancer**

Radical prostatectomy involves surgically removing the entire prostate gland and some surrounding tissue. This treatment is recommended to treat early stages of the disease.

● **Minimally Invasive Surgery for Prostate Cancer**

Laparoscopic prostate surgery is a type of minimally invasive surgery performed with the aid of a small camera.

Radiation Treatment for Prostate Cancer

Radiation therapy, also called X-ray therapy, is used to treat cancer cells only in the treated area. Various techniques are used to deliver this type of treatment.

Radioactive seed implants, also called brachytherapy or internal radiation therapy, are forms of therapy for prostate cancer.

Hormone Therapy for Prostate Cancer

Hormone treatment means removing, blocking, or adding hormones to fight prostate cancer.

Why Is Hormone Treatment Used for Prostate Cancer?

Prostate cancer grows when exposed to the male hormone testosterone and its related hormones, called androgens. Hormone treatment for prostate cancer is used to stop the production of testosterone and all androgens either temporarily or permanently.

Hormone treatments can be given in many ways such as by injection or as pills. Drugs can stop the testicles from producing testosterone and protect cells from any other androgens that remain in the body. Hormone medications may include:

- The use of various hormones such as estrogen to counter the effects of testosterone.
- The use of drugs that lower testosterone levels or block the activity of male hormones in the body. These include antiandrogen agents, lutenizing hormone-releasing hormone (LHRH) analogs, or agonists.
- The use of combined hormone therapy that decreases testosterone production from the testicles as well as from glands located on the kidneys, called adrenal glands, that produce hormones.

Hormone treatment may also include surgical removal of the testicles (called orchiectomy) where testosterone is produced. This prevents male hormones from further stimulating the growth of the prostate cancer.

When Is Hormone Treatment Used for Prostate Cancer?

Hormone treatment is primarily used if prostate cancer has spread outside the prostate. It does not cure cancer. The purpose of hormone therapy is first to delay the progression of the cancer and second to increase survival while maximizing quality of life.

If a patient doesn't respond to initial hormone treatment, a doctor may try other hormonal methods before recommending chemotherapy.

Who Is a Candidate for Hormone Treatment?

Hormone treatment can be used in men with various degrees of prostate cancer. For example, it is often used in men after surgery for better results, as well as in men who don't want to have any other type of treatment. Factors to consider are quality of life, cost of the treatment, and how effective and safe hormone treatment may be in a particular case.

Prostate Cancer Chemotherapy

The use of any one or combination of cancer-killing drugs, chemotherapy is prescribed in cases of recurrent or advanced prostate cancer that has not responded to hormone treatment.

How Is Chemotherapy Given?

Generally, chemotherapy drugs are given intravenously (directly into the vein) or rarely, by mouth. Once the drugs enter the bloodstream, they travel to all parts of the body to reach cancer cells that may have spread beyond the prostate.

When Is Chemotherapy Given?

Chemotherapy may be ordered for advanced prostate cancer that has not responded to hormone treatment. It may also be given for metastatic disease (disease that has spread). Metastatic disease may be present at diagnosis or, in some cases, the cancer can return in a distant location months or years after initial treatment.

Chemotherapy is given to cause the cancer to shrink and, hopefully, disappear. Even if the cancer does not disappear, symptoms may be relieved.

What Are the Side Effects?

Because chemotherapy acts to kill rapidly dividing cancer cells, it also kills other rapidly dividing healthy cells in the bodies, such as the membranes lining the mouth, the lining of the gastrointestinal tract, hair follicles, and bone marrow. As a result, the side effects of chemotherapy relate to these areas of damaged cells. The good news is that the damaged non-cancerous cells will be replaced with healthy cells, so the side effects are only temporary.

The specific side effects you have depend on the type and amount of medicines you are given and how long you are taking them. The most common, temporary side effects of chemotherapy include:

- Nausea and vomiting
- Loss of appetite
- Hair loss
- Mouth sores
- Diarrhea
- Infertility (a potential permanent side effect of chemotherapy)

Other side effects associated with chemotherapy's effects on bone marrow include an increased risk of infection (due to low white blood cell counts), bleeding or bruising from minor injuries (due to low blood platelet counts), and anemia-related fatigue (due to low red blood cell counts).

Some medications help control certain side effects, such as nausea and vomiting or diarrhea. Although it may take some time, side effects related to chemotherapy will go away when the treatments stop.

A Newer Treatment for Prostate Cancer: Cryotherapy

Cryotherapy involves freezing areas of the prostate. However its long-term effectiveness is unknown.

中英文注释

关键词汇

agonist ['ægənist] n. 兴奋剂

androgen ['ændrədʒ(ə)n] n. 雄性激素

chemotherapy [ki:mə(ʊ)'θerəpi] n. 化学治疗

combination [kɒmbi'neiʃ(ə)n] n. 联合（治疗，用药等）

cryotherapy [kraiə(ʊ)'θerəpi] n. 冷冻疗法

cystoscopy [sis'tɒskəpi] n. 膀胱镜检查

diarrhea [daiə'riə] n. 腹泻，痢疾

infertility [infə'tiliti] n. 不孕症，不育症

orchiectomy [ɔ:ki'ektəmi] n. 睾丸切除术

prostate ['prɒsteit] n. 前列腺

testicle ['testik(ə)l] n. 睾丸

testosterone [te'stɒstərəʊn] n. 睾酮

主要短语

adrenal gland 肾上腺

a frequent need to urinate 尿频

cost of the treatment　治疗成本
digital rectal exam (DRE)　直肠指诊
family history　家族史
hormone treatment　内分泌治疗
loss of weight　体重减轻
lymph node　淋巴结
prostate cancer　前列腺癌
prostate-specific antigen (PSA)　前列腺特异抗原
radiation therapy　放射治疗
radical prostatectomy　根治性前列腺切除术
radioactive seed implants　放射性粒子植入
risk factors　危险因素
tissue sample　组织标本
transrectal ultrasound (TRUS)　经直肠超声
watchful waiting　观察等待

马志方

77 Bone Tumors Overview
骨肿瘤概述

What are bone tumors?

Bone tumors develop when cells in the bone divide without control, forming a mass of tissue. Most bone tumors are benign, which means they are not cancer and cannot spread. However, they may still weaken bone and lead to fractures or cause other problems. Bone cancer destroys normal bone tissue and may spread to other parts of the body (called metastasis).

Benign bone tumors

Benign tumors are more common than malignant tumors of the bones. These are a few common types of benign bone tumors:

- Osteochondroma is the most common benign bone tumor. It is more common in people under age 20.
- Giant cell tumor is a benign tumor, typically affecting the leg (malignant types of this tumor are uncommon).
- Osteoid osteoma is a bone tumor, often occurring in long bones, that occurs commonly in the early 20s.
- Osteoblastoma is a single tumor that occurs in the spine and long bones, mostly in young adults.
- Enchondroma usually appears in bones of the hand and feet. It often has no symptoms. It is the most common type of hand tumor.

Metastatic cancer

When people have cancer in bones, often it is cancer that has spread there from elsewhere in the body. This is metastatic cancer. Even though it spreads to bone, it is not considered bone cancer because the tumor cells are from the primary cancer. For example, a person with lung cancer that has spread to the bone is considered to have lung cancer with metastasis to the bone—not lung cancer and bone cancer.

Cancers that commonly spread to bone include:

- Breast cancer
- Prostate cancer
- Lung cancer

Primary bone sarcoma

Primary bone sarcoma is a tumor that forms first in bone. It is less common than metastatic cancer. The cause of bone sarcoma is not certain, but heredity may play a role. High-dose radiation therapy or cancer drugs may increase the risk of this type of cancer. These are some of the most common types of bone cancer:

- Osteosarcoma begins in bone cells and is most common around the knee and upper arm. Most of the time, it is found in teens and young adults. There is an adult form of this tumor that is usually seen in persons with pre-existing Paget's disease of bone.
- Ewing's sarcoma also is seen in younger people between the ages of 5 and 20. The ribs, pelvis, leg, and upper arm are the most common sites. It usually shows up in bone, but it can also start in soft tissue around bones.
- Chondrosarcoma occurs most often in people between 40 and 70. The hip, pelvis, leg, arm, and shoulder are common sites of this cancer, which begins in cartilage cells.
- Although almost always found in bone, multiple myeloma is not a primary bone cancer. It is a bone marrow cancer. Bone marrow is the soft tissue inside bones.

What are the symptoms of bone tumors?

The patient may has no symptoms of a bone tumor. This is common. The doctor may find a tumor when looking at an X-ray of another problem, such as a sprain. But symptoms of a bone tumor may include pain that:

- Is in the area of the tumor
- Is often felt as dull or achy
- May get worse with activity
- Often awakens people at night

Trauma does not cause a bone tumor, but it may break a bone that is weakened by a tumor. This may then cause severe pain.

Other symptoms related to bone tumors may include:

- Fevers
- Night sweats
- Unusual swelling around a bone
- Limping

If you think you might have a bone tumor, see your doctor right way. Your doctor will ask you questions about your symptoms and medical history and conduct aphysical exam. You may need blood and imaging tests. To confirm a diagnosis, your doctor may remove tissue through a needle or incision and have it examined under a microscope for signs of cancer. This is called a biopsy.

How to treat bone tumors?

Cancerous bone tumors require more aggressive treatment to enhance survival.

Benign tumors are watched or may be treated with medication. The doctor may remove benign tumors that are more likely to spread or become cancer. In some cases, tumors come back, even after treatment.

Malignant tumors may require the attention of several cancer specialists. Treatment depends on the stage of cancer—how far it has spread. Cancer cells confined to the bone tumor and surrounding area are at a localized stage. Bone cancers that spread to other areas of the body are at a metastatic stage. These are more serious and a cure is more difficult. Cancers of the bone are most often removed with surgery.

These are common types of treatment for bone cancer:

- Limb salvage surgery removes the part of the bone with cancer. Nearby muscles, tendons, and other tissues are not removed. A metallic implant (prosthesis) replaces the portion of bone that was removed.
- Amputation may be needed if a tumor is large or extends to nerves and blood vessels. A prosthetic limb can aid function after amputation.
- Radiation therapy kills cancer cells and shrinks tumors with high-dose X-rays. It is often used in combination with surgery and may be used before or after surgery.
- Systemic chemotherapy kills tumor cells that have spread through the bloodstream with cancer drugs. Chemotherapy may be given before surgery, after surgery, or for metastatic disease.

The doctor may recommend that onepatient participates in a clinical trial, which tests new therapies. Regardless of his type of treatment, he will need regular follow-up with the doctor.

中英文注释

关键词汇

amputation [ˌæmpjuˈteiʃən] n. 截肢（术）

chondrosarcoma [ˌkɔndrəusɑːˈkəumə] n. 软骨肉瘤

enchondroma [ˌenkɔnˈdrəumə] n. 内生软骨瘤

heredity [hiˈrediti] n. 遗传

metastasis [məˈtæstəsis] n. 转移灶

osteoblastoma [ˌɔstiəublæsˈtəumə] n. 成骨细胞瘤

osteochondroma [ˌɔstiəkɔnˈdrəumə] n. 骨软骨瘤

osteosarcoma [ˌɔstiəusɑːˈkəumə] n. 骨肉瘤

prosthesis [ˈprɔsθisis] n. 假体

sprain [sprein] n. 扭伤

tendon [ˈtendən] n. 肌腱

trauma [ˈtrɔːmə] n. 创伤

主要短语

aggressive treatment 积极治疗

benign bone tumors 良性骨肿瘤

bone cancer 骨癌

bone marrow 骨髓

bone tumor 骨肿瘤

cancer drugs 抗癌药物

cartilage cells 软骨细胞

clinical trial 临床试验

common sites 好发部位

enhance survival 提高生存

Ewing's sarcoma 尤因肉瘤

giant cell tumor 骨巨细胞瘤

limb salvage surgery 保肢手术

malignant tumors 恶性肿瘤

metallic implant 金属植入物

metastatic cancer 转移癌

multiple myeloma 多发骨髓瘤

night sweats 盗汗

osteoid osteoma 骨样骨瘤

Paget's disease of bone 畸形性骨炎，骨 Paget 病

primary bone sarcoma 原发骨肉瘤

primary cancer 原发癌

prosthetic limb 假肢

regular follow-up 定期随访

severe pain 剧痛

systemic chemotherapy 全身化疗

upper arm 上臂

高宏飞　马志方

78

Osteosarcoma
骨　肉　瘤

What is osteosarcoma?

Osteosarcoma is an aggressive malignant neoplasm arising from primitive transformed cells of mesenchymal originthat exhibit osteoblastic differentiation and producemalignant osteoid. It is the most common histological form of primary bone cancer.

What causes osteosarcoma?

The causes of osteosarcoma are not known. Several research groups are investigating cancer stem cells and their potential to cause tumors. The connection between osteosarcoma and fluoride has been investigated; there is some association betweenwater fluoridation and deaths due to osteosarcoma. One study showed 6.9 times the occurrence of osteosarcoma in fluoridated communities compared to non-fluoridated areas. Radiotherapy for unrelated conditions may be a rare cause.

What are the symptoms of osteosarcoma?

- Many patients first complain of pain that may be worse at night, and may have been occurring for some time.
- If the tumor is large, it can appear as a swelling.
- The affected bone is not as strong as normal bones and may fracture with minor trauma (a pathological fracture).

According to The Bone Cancer Research Trust (BCRT) the pain may come and go and vary in intensity. The swelling will not be visible if it is not near the surface of the body such as on the pelvis.

How is osteosarcoma diagnosed?

Family physicians and orthopedists rarely see a malignant bone tumor (most bone tumors are benign). Thus, many patients are initially misdiagnosed with cysts or muscle problems, and some are sent straight tophysical therapy without an X-ray.

The route to osteosarcoma diagnosis usually begins with an X-ray, continues with a combination of scans (CT scan, PET scan, bone scan, MRI) and ends with a surgical biopsy. A characteristic often seen in an X-ray is the 'Codman's Triangle' which is basically a subperiosteal lesion formed when the periosteum is raised due to the tumor. Films are suggestive, but bone biopsy is the only definitive method to determine whether a tumor is malignant or benign.

The biopsy of suspected osteosarcoma should be performed by a qualified orthopedic oncologist. The American Cancer Society states: "Probably in no other cancer is it as important to perform this procedure properly. An improperly performed biopsy may make it difficult to save the affected limb from amputation".

How is osteosarcoma treated?

Complete radical surgical en bloc resection is the treatment of choice in osteosarcoma.

Although about 90% of patients are able to have limb-salvage surgery, complications particularly infection, prosthetic loosening and non-union or local tumor recurrence may cause the need for further surgery or amputation. Mifamurtide is used after a patient has had surgery to remove the tumor and together with chemotherapy to kill remaining cancer cells to reduce the risk of cancer recurrence.

Patients with osteosarcoma are best managed by a medical oncologist and an orthopedic oncologistexperienced in managing sarcomas. Current standard treatment is to use neoadjuvant chemotherapy (chemotherapy given before surgery) followed by surgical resection. The percentage of tumor cell necrosis (cell death) seen in the tumor after surgery gives an idea of the prognosis and also lets the oncologist know if the chemotherapy regime should be altered after surgery.

Rotationplasty is also another surgical technique that may be used. Ifosfamide can be used as an adjuvant treatment if the necrosis rate is low.

Despite the success of chemotherapy for osteosarcoma, it has one of the lowest survival rates for pediatric cancer. The best reported 10-year survival rate is 92%; the protocol used is an aggressive intra-arterial regimen that individualizes therapy based on arteriographic responce. Three-year event-free survival ranges from 50% to 75%, and five-year survival ranges from 60% to 85+% in some studies. Overall, 65%~70% patients treated five years ago will be alive today. These survival rates are overall averages and vary greatly depending on the individual necrosis rate.

Fluids are given for hydration, while drugs like Kytril and Zofran help with nausea and vomiting. Neupogen and Neulasta help with white blood cell counts and neutrophil counts. Blood transfusions and epogen help with anemia.

Prognosis

Prognosis is separated into three groups.

Stage I osteosarcoma is rare and includes parosteal osteosarcoma or low-grade central osteosarcoma. It has an excellent prognosis (>90%) with wide resection.

Stage II prognosis depends on the site of the tumor (proximal tibia, femur, pelvis, etc.), size of the tumor mass (in cm.), and the degree of necrosis from neoadjuvant chemotherapy (chemotherapy prior to surgery). Other pathological factors such as the degree of p-glycoprotein, whether the tumor is CXCR4-positive, or Her2-positive are also important, as these are associated with distant metastases to the lung. The prognosis for patients with metastatic osteosarcoma improves with longer times to metastases, (more than 12 months-24 months), a smaller number of metastases, and their resectability. It is better to have fewer metastases than longer time to metastases. Those with a longer length of time (>24months) and few nodules (two or fewer) have the best prognosis with a 2-year survival after the metastases of 50%, 5-year of 40% and 10 year of 20%. If metastases are both local and regional, the prognosis is worse.

Initial presentation of **stage III** osteosarcoma with lung metastases depends on the resectability of the primary tumor and lung nodules, degree of necrosis of the primary tumor, and maybe the number of metastases. Overall survival prognosis is about 30%.

中英文注释

关键词汇

adriamycin [ˌeidriə'maisin] n. 阿霉素

bleomycin [ˌbli:əu'maisin] n. 博来霉素

cisplatin [sis'plætən] n. 顺铂

cyclophosphamide [ˌsaikləu'fɔsfəmaid] n. 环磷酰胺

dactinomycin [ˌdæktinəu'maisin] n. 更生霉素

fluoride ['fluəraid] n. 氟化物

histological [ˌhistə'lɑdʒikl] adj. 组织学的

hydration [hai'dreiʃən] n. 水化

ifosfamide [ifəusfæ'maid] n. 异环磷酰胺

intra-arterial [ˌintrɑa'tiəriəl] adj. 动脉注射的

leucovorin [lju:'kɔvərin] n. 甲酰四氢叶酸

mesna ['mesnə] n. 巯乙磺酸钠

methotrexate [ˌmeθə'trekseit] n. 甲氨蝶呤

misdiagnose [ˌmis'daiəgnəuz] vt./vi. 误诊

neutrophil ['nju:trəfil] n. 嗜中性粒细胞

orthopedist [ˌɔ:θəu'pi:dist] n. 骨科医生

osteoid ['ɔstiɔid] n. 类骨质

osteosarcoma [ˌɔstiəusɑ:'kəumə] n. 骨肉瘤

pediatric [ˌpiːdiˈætrik] adj. 小儿科的

prognosis [prɔgˈnəusis] n. 预后

sarcoma [saːˈkəumə] n. 肉瘤

主要短语

blood transfusions 输血

cancer recurrence 癌症复发

Codman's Triangle 科德曼三角

distant metastases 远处转移

family physicians 家庭医生

medical oncologist 肿瘤内科专家

mesenchymal origin 间充质来源

muramyl tri-peptite (MTP) 胞壁酰三肽

neoadjuvant chemotherapy 新辅助化疗

non-union 骨不连

orthopedic oncologist 骨科肿瘤专家

osteoblastic differentiation 成骨细胞分化

parosteal osteosarcoma 骨旁骨肉瘤

pathological fracture 病理性骨折

physical therapy 理疗

prosthetic loosening 假体松动

rotation plasty 旋转成形术

standard treatment 标准治疗

survival rates 存活率

高宏飞　马志方

79

Glioma
神经胶质瘤

What is glioma?

"Glioma" is a general term used to describe any tumor that arises from the supportive ("gluey") tissue of the brain. This tissue, called "glia," helps to keep the neurons in place and functioning well.

There are three types of normal glial cells that can produce tumors. An astrocyte will produce astrocytomas (including glioblastomas), an oligodendrocyte will produce oligodendrogliomas, and ependymomas come from ependymal cells. Tumors that display a mixture of these different cells are called mixed gliomas.

Tumors such as "optic nerve glioma" and "brain stem glioma" are named for their locations, not the tissue type from which they originate.

Three types of normal glial cells can produce tumors—astrocytes, oligodendrocytes, and ependymal cells. Tumors that display a mixture of these cells are called mixed gliomas.

Astrocytoma

Astrocytomas are tumors that arise from astrocytes—star-shaped cells that make up the "glue-like" or supportive tissue of the brain. These tumors are "graded" on a scale from I to IV based on how normal or abnormal the cells look. There are low-grade astrocytomas and high-grade astrocytomas. Low-grade astrocytomas are usually localized and grow slowly. High-grade astrocytomas grow at a rapid pace and require a different course of treatment. Most astrocytoma tumors in children are low grade. In adults, the majority are high grade.

Below are descriptions of the various grades of these tumors:

- Pilocytic Astrocytoma (also called Juvenile Pilocytic Astrocytoma)—These grade I astrocytomas typically stay in the area where they started and do not spread. They are considered the "most benign" (noncancerous) of all the astrocytomas. Two other, less well known grade I astrocytomas are cerebellar astrocytoma and desmoplastic infantile astrocytoma.

523

- Diffuse Astrocytoma (also called Low-Grade or Astrocytoma Grade II) Types: Fibrillary, Gemistocytic, Protoplasmic Astrocytoma—These grade II astrocytomas tend to invade surrounding tissue and grow at a relatively slow pace.
- Anaplastic Astrocytoma—An anaplastic astrocytoma is a grade III tumor. These rare tumors require more aggressive treatment than benign pilocytic astrocytoma.
- Astrocytoma Grade IV (also called Glioblastoma, previously named "Glioblastoma Multiforme," "Grade IV Glioblastoma," and "GBM")— There are two types of astrocytoma grade IV—primary, or de novo, and secondary. Primary tumors are very aggressive and the most common form of astrocytoma grade IV. The secondary tumors are those which originate as a lower-grade tumor and evolve into a grade IV tumor.
- Subependymal Giant Cell Astrocytoma—Subependymal giant cell astrocytomas are ventricular tumors associated with tuberculous sclerosis.

Location

Astrocytomas can appear in various parts of the brain and nervous system, including the cerebellum, the cerebrum, the central areas of the brain, the brainstem, and the spinal cord.

Description

Pilocytic Astrocytomas generally form sacs of fluid (cysts), or may be enclosed within a cyst. Although they are usually slow-growing, these tumors can become very large.

Diffuse Astrocytomas tend to contain microcysts and mucous-like fluid. They are grouped by the appearance and behavior of the cells for which they are named.

Anaplastic Astrocytomas tend to have tentacle-like projections that grow into surrounding tissue, making them difficult to completely remove during surgery.

Astrocytoma Grade IV (glioblastoma) may contain cystic material, calcium deposits, blood vessels, and/or a mixed grade of cells.

Ependymoma

Ependymomas arise from the ependymal cells that line the ventricles of the brain and the center of the spinal cord. These tumors are divided into four major types:

- Subependymomas (grade I): Typically slow-growing tumors.
- Myxopapillary ependymomas (grade I): Typically slow-growing tumors.
- Ependymomas (grade II): The most common of the ependymal tumors. This type can be further divided into the following subtypes, including cellular ependymomas, papillary ependymomas, clear cell ependymomas, and tancytic ependymomas.

● Anaplastic ependymomas (grade III): Typically faster-growing tumors.

Location

The various types of ependymomas appear in different locations within the brain and spinal column. Subependymomas usually appear near a ventricle. Myxopapillary ependymomas tend to occur in the lower part of the spinal column. Ependymomas are usually located along, within, or next to the ventricular system. Anaplastic ependymomas are most commonly found in the brain in adults and in the lower back part of the skull (posterior fossa) in children. They are rarely found in the spinal cord.

Description

Ependymomas are soft, grayish, or red tumors which may contain cysts or mineral calcifications.

Mixed Glioma (also called Oligoastrocytoma):

These tumors usually contain a high proportion of more than one type of cell, most often astrocytes and oligodendrocytes. Occasionally, ependymal cells are also found. The behavior of a mixed glioma appears to depend on the grade of the tumor. It is less clear whether their behavior is based on that of the most abundant cell type.

Oligodendroglioma:

Oligodendrogliomas come from oligodendrocytes, one of the types of cells that make up the supportive, or glial, tissue of the brain. They can be low-grade (grade II) or high-grade (grade III, or anaplastic).

Location

These tumors can be found anywhere within the cerebral hemisphere of the brain, although the frontal and temporal lobes are the most common locations.

Description

Oligodendrogliomas are generally soft, grayish-pink tumors. They often contain mineral deposits (called calcifications), areas of hemorrhage, and/or cysts. Under the microscope, these tumor cells appear to have "short arms," or a fried-egg shape.

Sometimes oligodendrogliomas are mixed with other cell types. These tumors may be graded using an "A to D" system, which is based on microscopic features of the individual tumor cells. The grade indicates how quickly the tumor cells reproduce and how aggressive the tumor is.

Optic Glioma

These tumors may involve any part of the optic pathway, and they have the potential to spread along these pathways. Most of these tumors occur in children under the age of 10. Grade I pilocytic astrocytoma and grade II fibrillary astrocytoma are the most common tumors affecting these structures. Higher-grade tumors may also arise in this location. Twenty percent of children with neurofibromatosis (NF-1) will develop an optic glioma.

Gliomatosis Cerebri

This is an uncommon brain tumor that features widespread glial tumor cells in the brain. This tumor is different from other gliomas because it is scattered and widespread, typically involving two or more lobes of the brain. It could be considered a "widespread low-grade glioma" because it does not have the malignant features seen in high-grade tumors.

The widespread nature of gliomatosis cerebri causes enlargement of any part of the brain it involves. This may include the cerebral hemispheres, or less often, the cerebellum or brain stem.

What causes glioma?

Like many tumor types, the exact cause of glioma is not known. Hereditary genetic disorders such as neurofibromatoses (type 1 and type 2) and tuberous sclerosis complex are known to predispose to their development.

Gliomas have been correlated to the electromagnetic radiation from cell phones, and a link between the cancer and cell phone usage is considered plausible, though there is no conclusive evidence. Most glioblastomas are infected with cytomegalovirus, however the significance of this is not known.

What are the symptoms of glioma?

Symptoms vary based on tumor type:

Astrocytoma

Headaches, seizures, memory loss, and changes in behavior are the most common early symptoms of astrocytoma. Other symptoms may occur depending on the size and location of the tumor.

Ependymoma:

Symptoms of an ependymoma are related to the location and size of the tumor. In babies, increased head size may be one of the first symptoms. Irritability, sleeplessness, and vomiting may develop as the tumor grows. In older children and adults, nausea, vomiting, and headache are the most common symptoms.

Mixed Glioma (also called Oligoastrocytoma)

The initial symptoms, including headache and nausea, usually are the result of increased pressure inside the brain. Vision problems, as well as changes in behavior and personality, are also fairly common in mixed glioma patients.

Oligodendroglioma

Because of their generally slow growth, oligodendrogliomas are often present for years before they are diagnosed. The most common symptoms are seizures, headaches, and personality changes. Other symptoms vary by location and size of the tumor. Tumors of the frontal lobe may cause weakness on one side of the body, personality or behavior changes, and difficulty with short-term memory. Temporal lobe tumors are usually "silent," causing few symptoms other than perhaps seizures or language problems.

Optic Glioma

These tumors may cause few or no symptoms. Their placement along the optic nerve, however, can cause vision loss (depending on the location of the tumor) or strabismus ("crossed eyes"). Hormonal disturbance might also occur, causing developmental delay (s), early puberty, and other symptoms.

Gliomatosis Cerebri

Symptoms are often nonspecific and can include personality and behavioral changes, memory disturbance, increased intracranial pressure with headache and sometimes seizures.

How is glioma diagnosed?

It is very important to remain aware of the clinical and radiographic mimics of brain tumor as well of those times when patients who harbor brain tumors have clinical presentations that mimic other diseases. Acute stroke in the luxury perfusion stage is probably the most common mimic of a brain tumor. More importantly, of course, a brain tumor patient who has had several seizures can often be quite clinically similar to a patient who has had a subacute stroke, though diffusion MRI sequences are making differentiating between those 2 possibilities somewhat less of a problem. Perfusion CT scan can also be quite helpful in differentiating stroke from tumor by showing hypoperfusion as would be expected, rather than hyperperfusion seen in tumors. It is known that tumefactive MS needs to be considered in the differential diagnosis of a brain tumor but less well known is that, radiographically, demyelinating disease can also mimic a high-grade butterfly glioma. This case report was of a 58-year-old woman who presented with personality change and was found to have a contrast-enhancing lesion, which crossed the corpus callosum and lacked the usual partial ring enhancement often seen in cases of MS. On the more esoteric end of the spectrum, in children, mitochondrial disorders can mimic brainstem tectal gliomas.

How is it treated?

Treatment is based on tumor type:

Astrocytoma

Treatment options depend on the type, size, and location of the tumor, if and how far it has spread, previous treatment received, and the patient's overall health. Treatment methods for the various types of astrocytomas are briefly explained below.

- Pilocytic Astrocytoma: These tumors are often removed by surgery alone. In adults and older children, radiation may follow surgery if the tumor cannot be completely removed. Or, the patient may be watched carefully for signs that the tumor has returned.
- Diffuse Astrocytoma: If the tumor is accessible and can be completely removed, the only additional care required is follow-up scans. In adults and older children, radiation may be suggested in addition to surgery. Radiation may also be used to treat an unremovable low-grade astrocytoma. The role of chemotherapy in treating these tumors is being investigated.
- Anaplastic Astrocytoma: The first step in treatment of anaplastic astrocytoma is surgery. Radiation is then used to treat the remaining tumor. Chemotherapy may be recommended immediately after radiation or when and if the tumor recurs.
- Astrocytoma Grade IV: The first treatment step is surgery to remove as much tumor as possible. Surgery is almost always followed by radiation. Chemotherapy is often given at the same time as radiation and may be used to delay radiation in young children.

Ependymoma

The first step of ependymoma treatment is to remove as much of the tumor as possible. Radiation is usually recommended for older children and adults following surgery, in some cases even if the tumor was completely removed. The role of chemotherapy in treating newly diagnosed ependymoma is not clear. However, it may be used to treat tumors that have grown back after radiation therapy, or to delay radiation in infants and very young children.

Mixed Glioma (also called Oligoastrocytoma)

Treatment may include surgery followed by radiation therapy, particularly if the tumor is high-grade. Chemotherapy will also generally be used in high-grade tumors.

Oligodendroglioma

If the tumor is accessible, standard treatment for oligodendroglioma is surgical removal of as much of the tumor tissue as possible. Biopsy is typically performed on tumors that are not accessible to confirm the diagnosis and determine the grade of tumor. Recurrent low-grade oligodendrogliomas can be treated with surgery, radiation therapy (if not given initially), and chemotherapy.

- Grade II Oligodendrogliomas: Close follow-up with regular MRI scans is recommended following the successful removal of low-grade oligodendrogliomas. If some of the tumor remains (also called "residual" tumor), radiation treatment is recommended following surgery. The best timing for radiation therapy (ie, immediately or when the tumor appears to be growing again), is currently being studied in clinical trials.
- Grade III Oligodendrogliomas: Anaplastic oligodendroglioma is typically treated with a combination of radiation therapy and chemotherapy. Recurrent anaplastic oligodendroglioma may be treated with surgery and/or chemotherapy.

Optic Glioma

Careful observation may be an option for patients with stable or slow-growing tumors. Surgery might be recommended for a growing tumor which involves only the optic nerve. Radiation might be used for a tumor of the chiasm or other pathways. Local radiation and chemotherapy with radiation therapy are used for recurrent tumors. Patients with primary and/or recurrent tumors may wish to take part in a clinical trial.

Gliomatosis Cerebri

Treatment is less well defined because this tumor is so rare. Surgical removal is generally not attempted, because it is so widespread. Radiation and chemotherapy may be considered.

中英文注释

关键词汇

astrocyte ['æstrə,saɪt] n.（脑和骨髓的）星细胞，星形胶质细胞

astrocytoma [,æstrosaɪ'tomə] n. 星形细胞瘤

demyelinate [di'maɪələ,net] vt. 使（神经）脱髓鞘

ependymoma [e,pendɪ'məumə] n. 室管膜（细胞）瘤；脑室膜瘤

glioma [gli'omə, glaɪ-] n.（神经）胶质瘤

noncancerous ['nɔn'kænsərəs] adj. 非癌的

oligodendrocyte [ˌɑligoˈdɛndrəsait] n. 少突细胞

主要短语

anaplastic astrocytoma　间变性星形细胞瘤

diffuse astrocytoma　弥漫性星形细胞瘤

fluid-attenuated inversion recovery(flair)　液体衰减反转恢复

glioblastoma multiforme　多形性成胶质细胞瘤

gliomatosis cerebri　大脑神经胶质瘤病

mixed glioma　混合性胶质瘤

optic glioma　视神经胶质瘤

pilocytic astrocytoma　毛细胞性星形细胞瘤

subependymal giant cell astrocytoma　室管膜下巨细胞性星形细胞瘤

vascular endothelial growth factor　血管内皮生长因子

刘晓东

80 Meningioma
脑 膜 瘤

What is meningioma?

Meningioma is the most common type of primary brain tumor, accounting for more than 35% of primary brain tumors (tumors that start in the brain) in the United States and occurs in approximately seven of every 100,000 people. These are a diverse set of tumors arising from the meninges, the membranous layers surrounding the central nervous system. Get an overview of the disease.

The membranes which surround and protect the brain are called the meninges, The nerves of the spinal cord form a tube that begins at brain and extends the entire length of the vertebral column. This cord and the brain comprise the central nervous system, a complex and delicate structure that requires many layers of protection. The meninges help provide this protection. In the form of a set of membranes that surround and support the spinal cord and brain. They are composed of three membranes, called the pia mater, the arachnoid mater and the dura mater.

Meningiomas are the most common type of tumor that originates in the central nervous system. They occur more often in women than in men, and rare in children. Most meningiomas occur in the brain. But they can also grow on parts of the spinal cord.

Meningiomas are often slow-growing. As many as 90% are benign (not cancerous). A small number of meningiomas are cancerous. They tend to grow quickly. They also can spread to other parts of the brain and beyond, often to the lungs. Some meningiomas are classified as atypical. These are not considered either benign or malignant (cancerous). But they may become malignant.

Many meningiomas are asymptomatic, producing no symptoms throughout a person's life, and require no treatment other than periodic observation. But the growth of benign meningiomas can cause serious problems. In some cases, such growth can be fatal. Symptomatic meningiomas are typically treated with either radiosurgery or conventional surgery. Historical evidence of meningiomas has been found going back hundreds of years, with some successful surgeries for their removal beginning in the 1800s.

What causes meningioma?

The causes of meningioma are not well understood. Most cases are sporadic, appearing randomly, while some are familial. The only known predisposing factors associated with meningiomas are exposure to radiation, and certain genetic disorders (e.g. neurofibromatosis). Some have reported an association between meningiomas and the site of a previous injury (e.g. head trauma). However, the relationship with previous head injury isn't well understood. Some have suggested that viruses may play some role as well, but this is unsubstantiated at this point.

Some research suggests a link between meningiomas and the hormone progesterone.

Middle-aged women are three times as likely as men to develop a meningioma. Most meningiomas occur between the ages of 40 and 70. They are very rare in children.

Previous Trauma

Meningiomas have been found at the site of previous trauma (such as near a previous skull fracture, scarred dura, or around foreign bodies), but the relationship isn't fully understood.

Radiation

Exposure to radiation has been found to be associated with a higher incidence of meningiomas. For example, survivors of Hiroshima have an increased incidence of these tumors. The more recently developed methods of delivering radiation therapy that use focused beams help to limit unnecessary exposure to areas outside the target, and so are expected to be safer. Patients who have undergone broad radiation treatments in the past should take care to watch for symptoms and monitor themselves for meningiomas. Meningiomas caused by radiation exposure are generally more aggressive.

Genetic Predisposition

Having neurofibromatosis type 2, a rare, inherited (genetic) nervous system disorder. People with neurofibromatosis type 2 often get benign tumors of the nerves throughout the body. The most frequent genetic mutations (~50%) involved in meningiomas are inactivation mutations in the neurofibromatosis 2 gene (merlin) on chromosome 22q.

Other possible genes/loci include:

- AKT1
- MN1
- PTEN
- SMO
- an unknown gene at 1p13

Viruses

There is a possibility that viruses may be related to meningioma formation, but the relationship is not defined.

Risk Factors:

- Exposure to radiation
- Neurofibromatosis type 2
- Previous injury
- Age between of 40 to 70(especially Middle-aged women)

What are the symptoms of meningioma?

Generally speaking, small tumors (e.g., < 2.0 cm) are usually incidental findings at autopsy without having caused symptoms. Larger tumors can cause symptoms depending on the size and location. A meningioma may cause symptoms by pressing on the brain or spinal cord. However, many meningiomas are found incidentally on MRI leading from a patient visit that often has little to do with the meningioma itself. Symptoms, if present, appear slowly and may be slight at first. Symptoms are location dependent, meaning that the symptom corresponds to the part of the brain that the tumor is pushing on.

The most common symptoms are:

- Focal seizures may be caused by meningiomas that overlie the cerebrum.
- Progressive spastic weakness in legs and incontinence may be caused by tumors that overlie the parasagittal frontoparietal region.
- Sylvian tumors may cause myriad motor, sensory, aphasic, and seizure symptoms, depending on the location.
- Increased intracranial pressure eventually occurs, but is less frequent than in gliomas.
- Diplopia (Double vision) or uneven pupil size can be symptoms if related pressure causes a 3rd and/or 6th nerve palsy.

How is meningioma diagnosed?

Meningiomas are rarely diagnosed before they begin to cause symptoms. Sometimes, meningioma is found accidently while having a procedure for another reason. More commonly, meningioma is often not diagnosed until a person starts having symptoms. The neuro-oncologist can use the patient's symptoms as clues to the location of the tumor. In addition to the patient's detailed medical history and physical examination, the following tests may help the doctor diagnose meningioma and find out where it is located.

physical exam

This includes questions about the patient's symptoms, personal and family health history, physical exam, and tests of vision, and reflexes.

neurological exam

This includes questions about the patient's symptoms, personal and family health history, and tests of vision, hearing, balance, coordination, reflexes and ability to think and remember.

Pathological confirmation

Typically a craniotomy is performed if possible. The tumor is removed and examined under a microscope to determine the pathological characteristics of the tissue. The tumor is then given a pathological grade.

Imaging tests

Imaging tests are most useful when the results are combined with the patient's medical history, physical examination, and neurological tests. This combination helps to more accurately find out where the tumor began, and whether or where it has spread. The most common imaging tests used for diagnosing meningioma include:

Computed tomography (CT or CAT) scan

A CT scan takes X-rays of the head from many different angles. A computer then combines these images into a detailed, cross-sectional view that shows any abnormalities or tumors. Sometimes, a contrast medium (a special dye) is injected into a patient's vein to provide better detail. A CT scan is best for finding changes in the skull that can be caused by meningioma, such as hardening of the area near the tumor, which can mean that the tumor has been there for a long time.

Magnetic resonance imaging (MRI)

An MRI uses magnetic fields, not X-rays, to produce detailed images of the body. A contrast medium may be injected into a patient's vein to create a clearer picture. MRI may create more detailed pictures than CT scans and often show changes in the brain caused by the tumor, such as swelling or areas where the tumor has spread. MRI is the preferred method of diagnosing meningioma.

X-ray

An X-ray is a way to create a picture of the structures inside of the body using a small amount of radiation. An X-ray of the head can sometimes help doctors determine the presence and location of meningioma, but is not sufficient to diagnose the type of tumor.

Cerebral angiogram

A cerebral angiogram is a type of X-ray, or series of X-rays, of the head that shows the arteries and veins in the brain. X-rays are taken after a contrast medium is injected into the main arteries of the head. Because a meningioma can block important veins that drain blood from the brain, it is sometimes important to get an angiogram to plan surgery. In addition, there may be abnormal blood vessels that feed the tumor and these can be seen with the angiogram. Sometimes, material is injected into these tumors before surgery to reduce bleeding during surgery.

Positron emission tomography (PET) scan

A PET scan is a way to create pictures of organs and tissues inside the body. A small amount of a radioactive substance is injected into a patient's body. This substance is absorbed mainly by organs and tissues that use the most energy. Because cancer tends to use energy actively, it absorbs more of the radioactive substance. A scanner then detects this substance to produce images of the inside of the body. A PET scan is rarely used for meningioma.

Lumbar puncture (spinal tap)

A lumbar puncture is a procedure in which a doctor uses a needle to take a sample of cerebrospinal fluid (CSF) to look for tumor cells, blood, or tumor markers (substances found in higher than normal amounts in the blood, urine, or body tissues of people with certain types of tumors). CSF is the fluid that flows around the brain and the spinal cord. Doctors generally give an anesthetic to numb the lower back before the procedure. A lumbar puncture is rarely needed in patients with meningioma.

Electroencephalography (EEG)

An EEG is a noninvasive test in which electrodes are attached to the outside of a person's head to measure electrical activity of the brain. Specifically, EEGs are used to detect seizures. Because meningiomas can cause seizures in some patients, EEGs are occasionally needed for patients with this tumor.

Sometimes, meningioma is diagnosed using only the imaging tests above because the location of the tumor may make a biopsy risky.

Stereotactic neurosurgery/Biopsy

A biopsy can be performed by using a needle guided to the tumor with computers and imaging tests (called a stereotactic technique), or it can be done during surgery when the surgeon can look at the tumor directly. Most meningiomas are removed rather than biopsied so surgery for meningioma is usually done by an open craniotomy (surgery where part of the skull is removed to provide access to the brain) instead of with stereotactic techniques.

Though the majority of meningiomas are benign, they can have malignant presentations. Classification of meningiomas are based upon the WHO classification system.

- Benign (Grade I) – (90%) – meningothelial, fibrous, transitional, psammomatous, angioblastic (most aggressive)

- Atypical (Grade II) – (7%) – chordoid, clear cell, atypical (includes brain invasion)
- Anaplastic/malignant (Grade III) – (2%) – papillary, rhabdoid, anaplastic

How is it treated?

Surgery is the most common treatment for a meningioma. If a meningioma is benign and in a part of the brain where neurosurgeons can safely completely remove it, surgery is likely to be the only treatment needed. For some, total resection surgery is all that is needed for treatment, followed by periodic imaging to monitor any recurrence of a tumor.

Doctors may use radiation therapy after surgery for the most malignant meningiomas or when the neurosurgeon cannot completely remove the meningioma. Radiation therapy is also used to treat meningiomas in locations where surgery is not safe.

For a small meningioma that does not cause any significant signs or symptoms, monitoring the tumor without any immediate treatment, called observation, may be an option. If the meningioma does not grow further, the patient may never need treatment.

Treatment overview

In meningioma care, different types of doctors often work together to create a patient's overall treatment plan that combines different types of treatments. This is called a multidisciplinary team. This team may include neuro-oncologists, medical oncologists, radiation oncologists, surgeons, rehabilitation therapists, and other specialists.

People diagnosed with a CNS tumor usually need treatment as soon as possible. The pressure caused by a growing CNS tumor can cause severe symptoms, including a backup of cerebrospinal fluid and problems with blood circulation, which can damage delicate nerves and deprive cells of nutrients.

Descriptions of the most common treatment options for meningioma are listed below, and may include surgery and radiation therapy, and occasionally chemotherapy. Treatment options and recommendations depend on several factors, including the type and grade of the tumor, possible side effects, and the patient's preferences and overall health.

Treating brain and spinal cord tumors can be challenging. Surgery is the most common type of treatment, but it can be difficult if the tumor is near a delicate portion of the brain or spinal cord. The blood-brain barrier, which normally serves to protect the brain and spinal cord from damaging chemicals, also keeps out many types of chemotherapy. Meningioma grows outside the blood-brain barrier, so some drugs do reach these tumors; however, they are very resistant to currently available chemotherapy.

More refined surgeries, a better understanding of the tumors that can be treated with chemotherapy, and precise delivery of radiation therapy have helped more patients with CNS tumors live longer and have a better quality of life.

Active surveillance

Because a grade I meningioma grows slowly, active surveillance may be recommended for some patients. This approach is also called watchful waiting or watch-and-wait. During active surveillance, the tumor is monitored and treatment would begin if it started causing any symptoms or problems. This approach may be used for much older patients or for those with a tumor that was discovered accidently and is not causing any symptoms.

Surgery

Surgery is the removal of the tumor and surrounding tissue during an operation. For meningioma, it is the most common type of treatment and is often the only treatment needed for benign tumors that are able to be completely removed by surgery. For patients with a cancerous tumor or a tumor that cannot be fully removed with surgery, the treatment plan often includes radiation therapy and/or chemotherapy after surgery.

Blocking the blood vessels that feed the tumor may be performed before surgery to reduce bleeding. Surgery to the brain is done by removing part of the skull, a procedure called a craniotomy. After the surgeon removes the tumor, the patient's own bone will be used to cover the opening in the skull.

In addition to removing or reducing the meningioma, surgery can be used to obtain a sample of tumor for analysis under a microscope. The results of the analysis can show if additional treatments, such as radiation therapy, will be necessary.

There have been rapid advances in surgery for brain tumors, including cortical mapping to identify the areas of the brain that control the senses, language, and motor skills and enhanced imaging methods to give surgeons more tools to plan and perform the surgery.

Radiation therapy

Radiation therapy is the use of high-energy X-rays or other particles to kill tumor cells. Doctors may recommend radiation therapy along with surgery to slow the growth of aggressive tumors. A radiation therapy regimen (schedule) usually consists of a specific number of treatments given over a set period of time. Radiation therapy can be given in several ways. External-beam radiation therapy techniques use a machine outside the body to target the tumor. These techniques are becoming better able to direct radiation to the tumor while avoiding healthy tissue. For example, a linear accelerator is a special X-ray machine that moves around the body to direct pencil-thin beams of radiation to the brain tumor at different angles and intensities. This helps to reduce the amount of healthy tissue exposed to the radiation.

Internal radiation therapy or brachytherapy is the use of tiny pellets or rods containing radioactive materials that are surgically implanted in or near the tumor. This approach is only used for meningioma in clinical trials.

The following **external-beam radiation therapy** techniques may be used:

- **Conventional radiation therapy.** In this procedure, where the radiation is directed is determined by features of the brain and skull and by X-rays. When a person's entire brain needs to receive radiation therapy, this technique is appropriate. For more precise targeting, different techniques are needed.

- **Intensity modulated radiation therapy (IMRT).** IMRT is a type of external-beam radiation therapy that can more directly target a tumor, further sparing normal tissue from radiation therapy. In IMRT, the radiation beams are broken up into smaller beams and the intensity of each of these smaller beams can be changed. This means that the more intense beams, or the beams giving more radiation, can be directed only at the tumor. It is most useful to treat a tumor that is near critical parts of the brain, such as the brain stem and areas that control sight.

- **Three-dimensional conformal radiation therapy.** Based on CT and MRI images, a three-dimensional model of the tumor and normal tissues is created on a computer. Beam size and angles are determined that deliver more radiation to the tumor and less to the normal tissue.

- **Stereotactic radiosurgery.** Stereotactic radiosurgery delivers a single, high dose of radiation directly to the tumor and not healthy tissues. It works best for a tumor that is only in one area of the brain and some benign tumors, including most meningiomas. There are many different types of stereotactic radiosurgery equipment, including:
    - A modified linear accelerator, which is a machine that creates high-energy radiation by using electricity to form a stream of fast-moving particles that help kill tumor cells.
    - A gamma knife is another form of radiation therapy that concentrates highly focused beams of gamma radiation on the tumor. A gamma knife can only be used for meningioma in the brain, not meningioma on the spine.
    - A cyber knife is a robotic device used in radiation therapy to guide radiation to the particularly tumors in the brain, head, and neck.

Fractionated stereotactic radiation therapy. Radiation therapy is delivered as directly as stereotactic radiation therapy, but the dose is divided into small, daily doses over several weeks using a relocatable head frame instead of in a single day. This technique is best for tumors close to complex or sensitive structures, such as the optic nerves or brain stem.

Proton radiation therapy. Proton therapy (also called proton beam therapy) is a type of external-beam radiation therapy that uses protons rather than X-rays. At high energy, protons can destroy tumor cells.

With these different techniques, doctors are trying to better target only the tumor and reduce the dose to the surrounding normal tissue. Depending on the size and location of the tumor, the radiation oncologist may choose any of the above radiation therapy techniques. In certain situations, a combination of two or more techniques may be used.

Side effects from radiation therapy may include fatigue, mild skin reactions, upset stomach, and neurologic symptoms. Most side effects go away soon after treatment is finished. Also, radiation therapy is usually not recommended for children younger than five because of the high risk of damaging their developing brains.

There are long term side effects that may occur years after treatment. A person may experience cognitive problems, including memory loss and a slow decline in intellectual performance. If the pituitary gland (a small gland near the brain that releases may hormones that control bodily functions) received radiation, there may be changes in hormonal levels that need to be evaluated by an endocrinologist (a doctor who specializes in hormonal conditions). How severe these side effects are depends on how much radiation was given and where in the brain.

Chemotherapy

Chemotherapy is the use of drugs to kill tumor cells, usually by stopping the tumor cells' ability to grow and divide. Systemic chemotherapy is delivered through the bloodstream to reach tumor cells throughout the body. Chemotherapy is given by a medical oncologist, a doctor who specializes in treating a tumor with medication. A chemotherapy regimen (schedule) usually consists of a specific number of cycles given over a set period of time. A patient may receive one drug at a time or combinations of different drugs at the same time.

The goal of chemotherapy can be to destroy any tumor remaining after surgery, slow the tumor's growth, or reduce symptoms. However, chemotherapy is rarely used to treat meningioma, although researchers are studying this form of treatment. It is also important to keep in mind that a treatment plan may change over time if it is no longer working.

The side effects of chemotherapy depend on the individual and the dose used, but they can include fatigue, risk of infection, nausea and vomiting, loss of appetite, and diarrhea. These side effects usually go away once treatment is finished.

中英文注释

关键词汇

aphasic [ə'fezik] adj. 失语症的

asymptomatic [ə,simptə'mætik; ei-] adj. 无症状的

atypical [, ei'tipikəl,-ik] adj. 非典型的

brachytherapy [,bræki'θerəpi] n. 近距放射治疗

craniotomy [,kreini'ɒtəmi] n. 颅骨切开术

diplopia [di'pləʊpiə] n. 复视

ectroencephalography [i'lektrəuen,sefə'lɔgrəfi] n. 脑电图

meninges [mi'nindʒi:z] n. 脑膜；髓膜；脑脊膜

neurofibromatosis [,njuərəufi,brəumə'təusis] n. 多发性神经纤维瘤

parasagittal [,pærə'sædʒit(ə)l] adj. 旁矢状面的

radiosurgery [,reidiəu'sə:dʒəri] n. 放射外科

resonance ['rezənəns] n. 共振

主要短语

active surveillance 主动监测

arachnoid mater 蛛网膜

cerebral angiogram 脑血管造影

cross-sectional view 横断面视图

dura mater 硬脑膜

exposure to radiation 辐射照射量

increased intracranial pressure 颅内压增高

intensity modulated radiation therapy 调强放疗

lumbar puncture 腰椎穿刺

pia mater 软脑膜

previous injury 旧伤

proton therapy 质子疗法

stereotactic neurosurgery 立体定向神经外科

three-dimensional conformal radiation therapy 三维适形放疗

刘晓东

Section Six: Otolaryngological Disease

第六部分　耳鼻咽喉疾病

Allergic Rhinitis (AR)
变应性鼻炎

What is allergic rhinitis?

Allergic rhinitis (AR) is an inflammatory disease of the nasal mucous membranes. Allergen exposure of allergic individuals results in an IgE-mediated inflammatory response, which is manifested clinically as rhinorrhea, nasal congestion, postnasal drainage, nasal itching, sneezing, and itchy or watery eyes. AR, more commonly referred to as hay fever, is an inflammation of the nasal passages caused by allergic reaction to airborne substances.

Types

AR is the most common allergic condition and one of the most common of all minor afflictions. AR affects up to 20 percent of children and 15 to 30 percent of adolescents in the United States. Antihistamines and other drugs used to treat allergic rhinitis make up a significant fraction of both prescription and over-the-counter drug sales each year.

There are two types of allergic rhinitis: seasonal and perennial. Seasonal AR occurs in the spring, summer, and early fall, when airborne plant pollens are at their highest levels. In fact, the term hay fever is really a misnomer, since allergy to grass pollen is only one cause of symptoms for most children. Perennial AR occurs all year and is usually caused by airborne pollutants in the home and other places. A child can be affected by one or both types. Symptoms of seasonal AR are worst after being outdoors, while symptoms of perennial AR are worst after spending time indoors.

Both types of allergies can develop at any age, although onset in childhood through early adulthood is most common. Although allergy to a particular substance is not inherited, increased allergic sensitivity may be genetic (inherited). While allergies can improve on their own over time, they can also become worse over time.

Demographics

AR affects up to 20 percent of children and 15 to 30 percent of adolescents. Boys are twice as likely to get allergic rhinitis as girls. Half of children develop the condition before age 10, and half after that time. Some regions of the country are more likely to have the pollens that cause AR, so those areas will have more children with the condition. Other risk factors include having a mother with asthma or having asthma oneself, having others in the family with AR, being the oldest in the family, having a family dog, being breast fed for more than a month and having a higher socioeconomic level.

What causes allergic rhinitis?

Allergic rhinitis is a type of immune reaction. Normally, the immune system responds to foreign microorganisms, or particles like pollen or dust, by producing specific proteins, called antibodies. Antibodies are capable of binding to identifying molecules (antigens) on the foreign particle. This reaction between antibody and antigen sets off a series of reactions designed to protect the body from infection. Sometimes this same series of reactions is triggered by harmless, everyday substances. This is the condition known as allergy, and the offending substance is called an allergen.

Like all allergic reactions, AR involves a special set of cells in the immune system known as mast cells. Mast cells, found in the lining of the nasal passages and eyelids, display a special type of antibody called immunoglobulin type E (IgE) on their surfaces. Inside, mast cells store reactive chemicals in small packets called granules. When the antibodies encounter allergens, they trigger release of the granules, which spill out their chemicals onto neighboring cells, including blood vessels and nerve cells. One of these chemicals, histamine, binds to the surfaces of these other cells, through special proteins called histamine receptors.

Interaction of histamine with receptors on blood vessels causes neighboring cells to become leaky, leading to the fluid collection, swelling, and increased redness characteristic of a runny nose and red, irritated eyes. Histamine also stimulatespain receptors, causing the itchy, scratchy nose, eyes, and throat common in allergic rhinitis.

The number of possible airborne allergens is enormous. Seasonal AR is most commonly caused by grass and tree pollens, since their pollen is produced in large amounts and is dispersed by the wind. Showy flowers like roses or lilacs that attract insects produce a sticky pollen that is less likely to become airborne. Different plants release their pollen at different times of the year, so seasonal AR sufferers may be most affected in spring, summer, or fall, depending on which plants provoke a response. The amount of pollen in the air is reflected in the pollen count, often broadcast on the daily news during allergy season. Pollen counts tend to be lower after a good rain that washes the pollen out of the air and higher on warm, dry, windy days.

Virtually any type of tree or grass may cause AR. A few types of weeds that tend to cause the most trouble include the following:

- ragweed
- sagebrush
- lamb's-quarters
- plantain
- pigweed
- dock/sorrel
- tumbleweed

Perennial AR is often triggered by house dust, a complicated mixture of airborne particles, many of which are potent allergens. House dust contains some or all of the following:

- House mite body parts. All houses contain large numbers of microscopic insects called house mites. These harmless insects feed on fibers, fur, and skin shed by the house's larger occupants. Their tiny body parts easily become airborne.
- Animal dander. Animals constantly shed fur, skin flakes, and dried saliva. Carried in the air, or transferred from pet to owner by direct contact, dander can cause allergy in many sensitive people.
- Mold spores. Molds live in damp spots throughout the house, including basements, bathrooms, air ducts, air conditioners, refrigerator drains, damp windowsills, mattresses, and stuffed furniture. Mildew and other molds release airborne spores that circulate throughout the house.

Other potential causes of perennial allergic rhinitis include the following:

- cigarette smoke
- perfume
- cosmetics
- cleansers
- copier chemicals
- industrial chemicals
- construction material gases

What are the symptoms of allergic rhinitis?

Inflammation of the nose, or rhinitis, is the major symptom of AR. Inflammation causes itching, sneezing, runny nose, redness, and tenderness. Sinus swelling can constrict a child's eustachian tube that connects the inner ear to the throat, causing a congested feeling and "ear popping". The drip of mucus from the sinuses down the back of the throat, combined with increased sensitivity, can also lead to throat irritation and redness. AR usually also causes redness, itching, and watery eyes. Fatigue and headache are also common.

How is allergic rhinitis diagnosed?

Diagnosing seasonal AR is usually easy and can often be done without a medical specialist. When a child's symptoms appear in spring or summer and disappear with the onset of cold weather, seasonal AR is almost certainly the culprit. Other causes of rhinitis, including infection, can usually be ruled out by a physical examination and a nasal smear, in which a sample of mucus is taken on a swab for examination.

Along with a runny nose and reddened eyes, other symptoms may include dark circles under the eyes caused by nasal congestion, the "allergic salute" in which a child rubs a hand along the side of the nose, mouth breathing, sleepiness during the day, and learning problems caused by inability to concentrate during school.

Allergy tests including skin testing and provocation testing can help identify the precise culprit, but may not be done unless a single source is suspected and subsequent avoidance is possible. Skin testing involves placing a small amount of liquid containing a specific allergen on the skin and then either poking, scratching, or injecting it into the skin surface to observe whether redness and swelling occurs. Provocation testing involves challenging an individual with either a small amount of an inhalable or ingestible allergen to see if a response is elicited.

Perennial AR can also usually be diagnosed by careful questioning about the timing of exposure and the onset of symptoms. Specific allergens can be identified through allergy skin testing.

How is allergic rhinitis treated?

Avoidance of the allergens is the best treatment, but this is often not possible. When it is not possible to avoid one or more allergens, there are two major forms of medical treatment: drugs and immunotherapy. Always read the package label for directions or consult your doctor or pharmacist before treating children with over-the-counter medications. Children are not small adults, but have different physiology. They are more susceptible than adults to the effects of certain medicines and may have unexpected reactions.

Drugs

Antihistamines. Antihistamines block the histamine receptors on nasal tissue, decreasing the effect of histamine release by mast cells. They may be used after symptoms appear, though they may be even more effective when used preventively, before symptoms appear. A wide variety of antihistamines are available.

Older (first generation) antihistamines often produce drowsiness as a major side effect. Such antihistamines include the following:

- Diphenhydramine (Benadryl and generics). May be used for children age 2 and up, depending on the type of delivery (capsule, liquid).
- Chlorpheniramine (Chlor-trimeton and generics). May be used for children age 6 and up.
- Brompheniramine (Dimetane and generics). May be used for children age 2 and up.
- Clemastine (Tavist and generics). May be used for children age 12 and up.

Newer antihistamines (second generation) that do not cause drowsiness are available by prescription or over-the-counter include the following:

- Loratidine (Claritin). May be used for children age 2 and up.
- Cetirizine (Zyrtec). May be used for children age 2 and up.
- Fexofenadine (Allegra). May be used for children age 6 and up.
- Azelastin HCl (Astelin). May be used for children age 5 and up.

Decongestants. Decongestants constrict blood vessels to counteract the effects of histamine. Nasal sprays are available that can be applied directly to the nasal lining and oral systemic preparations are available. Decongestants are stimulants and may cause increased heart rate and blood pressure, headaches, and agitation. Use of topical decongestants for longer than several days can cause loss of effectiveness and rebound congestion, in which nasal passages become more severely swollen than before treatment.

Topical corticosteroids. Topical corticosteroids reduce mucous membrane inflammation and are available by prescription. Allergies tend to become worse as the season progresses because the immune system becomes sensitized to particular antigens and can produce a faster, stronger response. Topical corticosteroids are especially effective at reducing this seasonal sensitization because they work more slowly and last longer than most other medication types. As a result, they are best started before allergy season begins. Side effects are usually mild, but may include headaches, nosebleeds, and unpleasant taste sensations. However, a larger skin surface area to body weight ratio may make children more susceptible to adrenal gland problems such as growth retardation and delayed weight gain. Topical corticosteroids administration to children should be limited to the least amount possible to achieve therapeutic effect.

Mast cellstabilizers. Cromolyn sodium prevents the release of mast cell granules, thereby preventing release of histamine and the other chemicals contained in them. It acts as a preventive treatment if it is begun several weeks before the onset of the allergy season. It can be used for perennial AR as well. Cromolyn sodium is so low in side effects that it is recommended for children as young as two years of age.

Immunotherapy

Immunotherapy, also known as desensitization or allergy shots, alters the balance of antibody types in the body, thereby reducing the ability of IgE to cause allergic reactions. Immunotherapy is preceded by allergy testing to determine the precise allergens responsible. Injections involve very small but gradually increasing amounts of allergen, over several weeks or months, with periodic boosters. Full benefits may take up to several years to achieve and are not seen at all in about one in five patients. Individuals receiving all shots will be monitored closely following each shot because of the small risk of anaphylaxis, a condition that can result in difficulty breathing and a sharp drop in blood pressure. Allergy shots can be given to children as young as five years.

Alternative Treatment

Alternative treatments for AR often focus on modulation of the body's immune response, and frequently center around diet and lifestyle adjustments. Chinese herbal medicine can help rebalance a person's system, as can both acute and constitutional homeopathic treatment. Vitamin C in substantial amounts can help stabilize the mucous membrane response. For symptom relief, western herbal remedies including eyebright (Euphrasia officinalis) and nettle (Urtica dioica) may be helpful. Bee pollen may also be effective in alleviating or eliminating AR symptoms.

Prognosis

Most children with AR can achieve adequate relief with a combination of preventive strategies and treatment. While allergies may improve over time, they may also get worse or expand to include new allergens. Early treatment can help prevent an increased sensitization to other allergens.

Prevention

Reducing exposure to pollen may improve symptoms of seasonal AR. Strategies include the following:
- staying indoors with windows closed during the morning hours, when pollen levels are highest
- keeping car windows up
- avoiding uncut fields

- learning which trees are producing pollen in which seasons, and avoiding forests at the height of pollen season
- washing clothes and hair after being outside
- cleaning air conditioner filters in the home regularly
- using electrostatic filters for central air conditioning

Moving to a region with lower pollen levels is rarely effective, since new allergies often develop in children.

Preventing perennial AR requires identification of the responsible allergens.

Mold spores:

- keeping the house dry through ventilation and use of dehumidifiers
- using a disinfectant such as dilute bleach to clean surfaces such as bathroom floors and walls
- having heating/air conditioning ducts cleaned and disinfected
- cleaning and disinfecting air conditioners and coolers
- throwing out moldy or mildewed books, shoes, pillows, or furniture

House dust:

- vacuuming frequently, and changing the bag regularly (Use a bag with small pores to catch extra-fine particles.)
- cleaning floors and walls with a damp mop
- installing electrostatic filters in heating and cooling ducts, and changing all filters regularly

Animal dander:

- avoiding contact if possible
- washing hands after contact
- vacuuming frequently
- keeping pets out of the child's bedroom, and off furniture, rugs, and other dander-catching surfaces
- having pets bathed and groomed frequently

中英文注释

关键词汇

allergen ['ælədʒ(ə)n] n. 过敏原

antihistamine [ænti'histəmin; -mi:n] n. 抗组胺剂, 抗组胺药

asthma ['æsmə] n. 哮喘, 气喘

chlorpheniramine [ˌklɔːfə'niərəmiːn] n. 氯苯吡胺, 扑尔敏

decongestant [diːk(ə)n'dʒest(ə)nt] n. 解充血药, 减充血剂

diphenhydramine [difen'hidrʌmən] n. [药] 苯海拉明

granule ['grænjuːl] n. 颗粒

pollen ['pɒlən] vt. 给…传授花粉；n. [植] 花粉

sneezing ['sniːzɪŋ] n. 打喷嚏；v. 打喷嚏（sneeze 的 ing 形式）

主要短语

allergic rhinitis　变应性鼻炎

alternative treatment　替代疗法

eustachian tube　咽鼓管

house dust　室内尘埃

house dust mite　尘螨

mast cell　肥大细胞

mast cell stabilizers　肥大细胞稳定剂

nasal itching　鼻痒

perennial AR　常年性变应性鼻炎

provocation testing　激发试验

runny nose　流涕

seasonal AR　季节性变应性鼻炎

topical corticosteroids　外用皮质类固醇激素

张海利　王斌全

82

Chronic Suppurative Otitis Media (CSOM)

慢性化脓性中耳炎

What is CSOM?

Chronic suppurative otitis media (CSOM) is the result of an initial episode of acute otitis media and is characterized by a persistent discharge from the middle ear through a tympanic perforation. It is an important cause of preventable hearing loss, particularly in the developing world.

Chronic suppurative otitis media is a persistent inflammation of the middle ear lasting six weeks or more and characterised by recurrent persistent discharge from the ear. The discharge usually occurs through a persistent perforation of the eardrum.

A form of chronic otitis media can occur without perforation of the drum when the middle ear fills with fluid without active infection (glue ear). Discharge may also occur through a drainage tube (grommet), surgically inserted to drain the persistent fluid from the middle ear.

What causes CSOM?

Acute otitis media results from a bacterial infection entering the ear from the throat and is characterised by pus forming in the middle ear, sometimes associated with bleeding. The ear drum may or may not perforate but if it does the perforation tends to heal spontaneously in the majority of cases. Recurrent acute otitis media or delay in healing following an acute attack may lead to persistent perforation of the eardrum and chronic suppurative otitis media.

Other causes of inflammation such as injury or allergy may also affect the middle ear and together all causes of middle ear inflammation are collectively referred to as "Otitis Media".

What are the symptoms of CSOM?

The main symptom of chronic suppurative otitis media is of persistent or frequently recurring discharge from the ear. The discharge is usually purulent (consisting of pus) and may have an offensive smell.

Pain may occur but is less significant than in acute otitis media and there may be no pain. Perforation of the eardrum is present and it is this that allows the pus from the middle ear to escape into the external ear canal. The perforation reduces the amplifying effect of the eardrum and hearing may be impaired.

In severe cases chronic infection can disrupt the chain of ossicles with more profound effect on hearing. Generally there is no significant systemic general illness unless fresh infection superimposes on the chronic inflammation when fever and malaise may occur.

Infection spreading into the cellular passages of the mastoid bone may cause acute mastoiditis and this can spread into the bone itself causing osteomyelitis.

Chronic suppurative otitis media can be associated with a condition called cholesteatoma where growth of granular inflammatory tissue adds to the obstruction within the middle ear cavity and delays healing. Cholesteatoma may also invade local structures including the surrounding bone with destruction of the bony structure. Some patients may experience tinnitus.

Spread of infection into the inner ear can result in damage to the auditory sensory organ (cochlea) and cause labyrinthitis. More serious complications can occur from spread of infection through the skull causing meningitis or cerebral abscess.

● Perforation of the ear drum (tympanic membrane)

Perforation associated with infection results from a build up of pus and fluid within the middle ear causing the drum to bulge and then burst. The eardrum can also be perforated by trauma from a piercing injury, a blow to the head or "barotrauma" where sudden changes of air pressure also can cause bulging and rupture of the membrane. Barotrauma results from the sudden the increase of air pressure in an explosion, or from sudden changes in atmospheric pressure as can occur in diving or air travel. The latter effects can be avoided by regularly "decompressing" the middle ear by swallowing or blowing against a closed nose and mouth to force open the eustachian tube.

Perforation can occur at several locations within the membrane:

● Marginal perforation occurs when the membrane separates along its edge from the bony rim to which it is attached.
● Central perforation occurs when a gap appears within the main membrane but a rim of tissue remains intact and not separated from the bone.
● Attic perforation occurs in a very small part of the membrane that is high up in the cavity immediately above the attachment of one of the ossicles.

Formation of cholesteatoma secondary to the healing process is more commonly associated with attic and marginal perforation.

- Tinnitus

Tinnitus is a recurrent or persistent noise perceived in the absence of any stimulation by sound (ringing in the ears). It is a subjective experience, which can neither be observed by another person nor measured.

The noise perceived might be described as a buzzing, ringing, hissing, whistling or roaring sound which may vary in intensity and with time. It may be continuous or intermittent and may be synchronous with the pulse beat.

Tinnitus can accompany any disorder of the ear including simple problems such as wax or foreign body in the external ear canal. It commonly occurs in association with inner ear disease or sensorineural damage to the ear. It may also accompany the effects of general systemic diseases and has been recognised as a feature in cardiovascular disease, hypothyroidism and anaemia. It can result from the toxic effect of some substances, particularly drugs that are toxic to the inner ear (ototoxic) such as aspirin, quinine and some antibiotics (particularly streptomycin).

How is CSOM treated?

Chronic suppurative otitis media may be treated initially with antibiotics to clear any persistent infection. Longer-term use of antibiotic eardrops has been shown to reduce the amount of pus discharging from the ear in adults. However surgical repair of the eardrum (tympanoplasty) provides a more permanent solution.

For children with recurrent otitis media with no perforation a drainage tube (grommet) may be inserted to help clear residual fluid from the middle ear.

Adenoids or tonsils may need to be removed if they are obstructing the opening of the eustachian tube in the throat.

Management of hearing loss and assessment and treatment of tinnitus forms part of the treatment strategy of the condition.

Prognosis

Chronic suppurative otitis media generally responds well to treatment although this may have to be continued over several months. Significant complications of acute or chronic suppurative otitis media include brain abscess or infection in the temporal bone of the skull but these occur in only a very small number of cases.

The overall prognosis for all forms of otitis media is excellent.

中英文注释

关键词汇

barotrauma [ˌbærəˈtrɔːmə] n.（耳）气压伤

cholesteatoma [ˌkɔləstiəˈtəumə] n.胆脂瘤

labyrinthitis [ˈlæbərinˈθaitis] n.内耳炎；[耳鼻喉]迷路炎

mastoiditis [ˌmæstɒiˈdaitis] n.乳突炎

ossicle [ˈɒsik(ə)l] n.[解剖]小骨，听小骨

osteomyelitis [ˌɒstiəumaiiˈlaitis] n.骨髓炎

otitis [ə(ʊ)ˈtaitis] n.[耳鼻喉]耳炎

tinnitus [ˈtinitəs] n.耳鸣

tympanoplasty [ˈtimpənəˌplæsti] n.中耳整复术

主要短语

acute otitis media　急性中耳炎

cerebral abscess　脑脓肿

chronic suppurative otitis media(CSOM)　慢性化脓性中耳炎

ear drum　耳鼓膜

eustachian tube　咽鼓管

glue ear　胶耳

mastoid bone　乳突骨

offensive smell　臭味

sensorineural damage　感觉神经（感音神经）损害

the chain of ossicles　听骨链

tympanic perforation　鼓膜穿孔

张海利　王斌全

83   Meniere's Syndrome
梅尼埃综合征

What is Meniere's syndrome?

Meniere's syndrome is a disorder of the inner ear that can affect hearing and balance to a varying degree. It is characterized by episodes of vertigo, low-pitched tinnitus, and hearing loss. The hearing loss is fluctuating rather than permanent, meaning that it comes and goes, alternating between ears for some time, then becomes permanent with no return to normal function. It is named after the French physician Prosper Ménière, who, in an article published in 1861, first reported that vertigo was caused by inner ear disorders. The condition affects people differently, it can range in intensity from being a mild annoyance to a lifelong disability.

What causes Meniere's syndrome?

Meniere's syndrome is idiopathic, but it is believed to be linked to endolymphatic hydrops, an excess of fluid in the inner ear. It is thought that endolymphatic fluid bursts from its normal channels in the ear and flows into other areas, causing damage. This is called "hydrops". The membranous labyrinth, a system of membranes in the ear, contains a fluid called endolymph. The membranes can become dilated like a balloon when pressure increases and drainage is blocked. This may be related to swelling of the endolymphatic sac or other tissues in the vestibular system of the inner ear, which is responsible for the body's sense of balance. In some cases, the endolymphatic duct may be obstructed by scar tissue, or may be narrow from birth. In some cases there may be too much fluid secreted by the stria vascularis. The symptoms may occur in the presence of a middle earinfection, head trauma, or an upper respiratory tract infection, or by using aspirin, smoking cigarettes, or drinking alcohol. They may be further exacerbated by excessive consumption of salt in some patients. It has also been proposed that Meniere's symptoms in many patients are caused by the deleterious effects of a herpes virus. Herpesviridae are present in a majority of the population in a dormant state. It is suggested that the virus is reactivated when the immune system is depressed due to a stressor such as trauma, infection, or surgery (under general anesthesia). Symptoms then develop as the virus degrades the structure of the inner ear.

Meniere's syndrome affects about 190 people per 100,000. Recent gender predominance studies show that Meniere's tends to affect women more often than men. Age of onset typically occurs in adult years, with prevalence increasing with age.

What are the symptoms of Meniere's syndrome?

Meniere's often begins with one symptom, and gradually progresses. However, not all symptoms must be present to confirm the diagnosis although several symptoms at once is more conclusive than different symptoms at separate times. Other conditions can present themselves with Meniere's -like symptoms, such as syphilis, Cogan's syndrome, autoimmune disease of the inner ear, dysautonomia, perilymph fistula, multiple sclerosis, acoustic neuroma, and both hypo- and hyperthyroidism.

The symptoms of Meniere's are variable, not all sufferers experience the same symptoms. However, so-called "classic Meniere's" is considered to have the following four symptoms:

- Attacks of rotational vertigo that can be severe, incapacitating, unpredictable, and last anywhere from minutes to hours, but generally no longer than 24 hours. For some, prolonged attacks can occur, lasting from several days to several weeks, often causing the sufferer to be severely incapacitated. This combines with an increase in volume of tinnitus and temporary, albeit significant, hearing loss. Hearing may improve after an attack, but often becomes progressively worse. Nausea, vomiting, and sweating sometimes accompany vertigo, but are symptoms of vertigo, and not of Meniere's.
- Fluctuating, progressive, unilateral (in one ear) or bilateral (in both ears) hearing loss, usually in lower frequencies. For some, sounds can appear tinny or distorted, and patients can experience unusual sensitivity to noises.
- Unilateral or bilateral tinnitus.
- A sensation of fullness or pressure in one or both ears.

Some may have parasympathetic symptoms, which aren't necessarily symptoms of Meniere's, but rather side effects from other symptoms. These are typically nausea, vomiting, and sweating which are typically symptoms of vertigo, and not of Meniere's. Vertigo may induce nystagmus, or uncontrollable rhythmical and jerky eye movements, usually in the horizontal plane, reflecting the essential role of non-visual balance in coordinating eye movements. Sudden, severe attacks of dizziness or vertigo, known informally as "drop attacks", can cause someone who is standing to suddenly fall. Drop attacks are likely to occur later in the disease, but can occur at any time. and in some cases chest pain.

How is Meniere's syndrome diagnosed?

Doctors establish a diagnosis with complaints and medical history. However, a detailed otolaryngological examination, audiometry, and head MRI scan should be performed to exclude a vestibular schwannoma or superior canal dehiscence which would cause similar symptoms. Some of the same symptoms also occur with benign paroxysmal positional vertigo (BPPV), and with cervical spondylosis (which can affect blood supply to the brain and cause vertigo). There is no definitive test for Meniere's, it is only diagnosed when all other causes have been ruled out. If any cause had been discovered, this would eliminate Meniere's syndrome, as by its very definition, as an exclusively idiopathic disease—it has no known cause.

How is Meniere's syndrome treated?

Several environmental and dietary changes are thought to reduce the frequency or severity of symptom outbreaks. It is believed that since high salt diets cause water retention, it can lead to an increase (or at least preventing the decrease) of fluid within the inner ear, although the relationship between salt and the inner ear is not fully understood. High-salt intake is thought to alter the concentrations of fluid in the inner ear and Meniere's episodes could be accelerated by high-salt binges. Recommended salt intake is often around one to two grams per day. One source recommends taking two grams of potassium or more daily.

Additionally, patients may be advised to avoid alcohol, caffeine, and tobacco, all of which can aggravate symptoms of Meniere's. Many patients will have allergy testing done to see if they are candidates for allergy desensitization, as allergies have been shown to aggravate Meniere's symptoms.

Both prescription and over-the-counter medicine can be used to reduce nausea and vomiting during an episode. Included are antihistamines such as meclozine or dimenhydrinate, trimethobenzamide and other antiemetics, betahistine, diazepam, or ginger root. Betahistine, specifically, is of note because it is the only drug listed that has been proposed to prevent symptoms due to its vasodilation effect on the inner ear.

The antiherpes virus drug acyclovir has been used with some success to treat Meniere's syndrome. The likelihood of the effectiveness of the treatment was found to decrease with increasing duration of the disease, probably because viral suppression does not reverse damage. Morphological changes to the inner ear of Meniere's sufferers have also been found in which it was considered likely to have resulted from attack by a herpes simplex virusIt was considered possible that long term treatment with acyclovir (greater than six months) would be required to produce an appreciable effect·

on symptoms. Herpes viruses have the ability to remain dormant in nerve cells by a process known as HHV Latency Associated Transcript. Continued administration of the drug should prevent reactivation of the virus and allow for the possibility of an improvement of symptoms. Another consideration is that different strains of a herpes virus can have different characteristics which may result in differences in the precise effects of the virus. Further confirmation that acyclovir can have a positive effect on Meniere's symptoms has been reported.

Studies done over the use of transtympanic micropressure pulses have indicated promise with patients who had not been previously treated by gentamicin or surgery. Other studies suggest less clear results and propose that micropressure devices are simply placebos.

Surgery

If symptoms do not improve with typical treatment, more permanent surgery is considered. Unfortunately, because the inner ear deals with both balance and hearing, few surgeries guarantee no hearing loss. Nondestructive surgeries include those which do not actively remove any functionality, but rather aim to improve the way the ear works. intratympanic steroid treatments involve injecting steroids (commonly dexamethasone) into the middle ear in order to reduce inflammation and alter inner ear circulation. Surgery to decompress the endolymphatic sac has shown to be effective for temporary relief from symptoms. Most patients see a decrease in vertigo occurrence, while their hearing may be unaffected. This treatment, however, does not address the long-term course of vertigo in Meniere's syndrome, and may require repeated surgery.

Conversely, destructive surgeries are irreversible and involve removing entire functionality of most, if not all, of the affected ear. The inner ear itself can be surgically removed via labyrinthectomy although hearing is always completely lost in the affected ear with this operation. Alternatively, a chemical labyrinthectomy, in which a drug (such as gentamicin) that "kills" the vestibular apparatus is injected into the middle ear can accomplish the same results while retaining hearing. In more serious cases surgeons can cut the nerve to the balance portion of the inner ear in a vestibularneurectomy. Hearing is often mostly preserved, however the surgery involves cutting open into the lining of the brain, and a hospital stay of a few days for monitoring would be required. Vertigo (and the associated nausea and vomiting) typically accompany the recovery from destructive surgeries as the brain learns to compensate.

Physiotherapy

Physiotherapists also have a role in the management of Meniere's disease. In vestibular rehabilitation, physiotherapists use interventions aimed at stabilizing gaze, reducing dizziness and increasing postural balance within the context of activities of daily living. After a vestibular assessment is conducted, the physiotherapist tailors the treatment plan to the needs of that specific patient.

The central nervous system (CNS) can be re-trained because of its plasticity, or alterability, as well as its repetitious pathways. During vestibular rehabilitation, physiotherapists take advantage of this characteristic of the CNS by provoking symptoms of dizziness or unsteadiness with head movements while allowing the visual, somatosensory and vestibular systems to interpret the information. This leads to a continuous decrease in symptoms.

Although a significant amount of research has been done regarding vestibular rehabilitation in other disorders, substantially less has been done specifically on Meniere's disease. However, vestibular physiotherapy is currently accepted as part of best practices in the management of this condition.

Prognosis

Meniere's syndrome usually starts confined to one ear, but it often extends to involve both ears over time. The number of patients who end up withbilateral Meniere's is debated, with ranges spanning from 17% to 75%.

Some Meniere's syndrome sufferers, in severe cases, may end up losing their jobs, and will be on disability until the disease burns out. However, a majority (60%~80%) of sufferers will not need permanent disability and will recover with or without medical help.

Hearing loss usually fluctuates in the beginning stages and becomes more permanent in later stages, although hearing aids and cochlear implants can help remedy damage. Tinnitus can be unpredictable, but patients usually get used to it over time. Meniere's syndrome, being unpredictable, has a variable prognosis. Attacks could come more frequently and more severely, less frequently and less severely, and anywhere in between. However, Meniere's is known to "burn out" when vestibular function has been destroyed to a stage where vertigo attacks cease.

中英文注释

关键词汇

antiemetic [ˌæntiiˈmetik] n. 止吐药

audiometry [ˌɔdiˈɑmətri] n. [耳鼻喉]听力测定；[耳鼻喉]听力测验法，听力学检查

betahistine 倍他司汀（药名）

diazepam [dai'æzipæm] n.［药］安定，地西泮

dysautonomia [dis,ɔ:tə'nəumiə] n. 家族性自主神经异常

idiopathic [,idiə(ʊ)'pæθik] adj. 先天的；自发的，特发的

labyrinthectomy [,læbərin'θektəmi] n.［耳鼻喉］迷路切除术

physiotherapist [,fizio'θɛrəpist] n. 理疗家；理疗医师，物理治疗师

syphilis ['sifilis] n.［性病］梅毒

vertigo ['vɜ:tigəʊ] n. 晕头转向，［临床］眩晕

主要短语

acoustic neuroma 听神经瘤

benign paroxysmal positional vertigo (BPPV) 良性阵发性位置性眩晕

cervical spondylosis 颈椎病

low-pitched tinnitus 低调耳鸣

multiple sclerosis 多发性硬化

otolaryngological examination 耳鼻咽喉科检查

perilymph fistula 外淋巴瘘

vestibular schwannoma 前庭神经鞘瘤

张海利　王斌全

Obstructive Sleep Apnea Hypopnoea Syndrome (OSAHS)

84.

阻塞性睡眠呼吸暂停低通气综合征

What is the OSAHS?

Obstructive Sleep Apnea Hypopnoea Syndrome (OSAHS) refers to a disorder in which there are breaks or pauses in a person's breathing during sleep. Most people who have OSAHS also snore, but not all snorers have OSAHS. People who suffer from OSAHS breathe shallowly or stop breathing for short periods while sleeping. This can happen many times during the night. It results in poor sleep leading to excessive sleepiness during the day. Because these events occur during sleep, a person suffering from OSAHS is often the last one to know what is happening. In deep sleep, the muscles of the throat relax. Normally this doesn't cause any problems with breathing. In OSAHS, complete relaxation of the throat muscles causes blockage of the upper airway at the back of the tongue. Normal breathing then slows or stops completely. Such an episode is called an apnea. During an apnea, people with OSAHS make constant efforts to breath against their blocked airway until the blood oxygen level begins to fall. The brain then needs to arouse the person from deep relaxed sleep so that the muscle time returns, the upper airway then opens and breathing begins again. Unfortunately when a person with OSAHS falls back into deep sleep, the muscles relax once more and the cycle repeats itself again and again overnight. In OSAHS, the apnoeas can last for several seconds and in severe cases the cycle of apnoeas and broken sleep is repeated hundreds of times per night. Most sufferers are unaware of their disrupted sleep but awaken unrefreshed, feeling sleepy and in need of further refreshing sleep.

Who gets OSAHS?

Whilst OSAHS is more common in overweight middle-aged males who snore, it can also affect females, although female hormones and a difference in throat structures may protect women until the menopause. It is estimated that between 11,000 and 22,000 people in Northern Ireland, aged between 30~64, have OSAHS. Narrowing of the back of the throat and the upper airway can also contribute to the risk of getting

OSAHS, even in people who are not overweight or middle-aged. In such people a small jaw, enlarged tongue, big tonsils and big soft palate help to block the upper airway in deep sleep, making OSAHS more likely to occur. Several of these problems can be present in any person at the same time. The use of alcohol, sleeping tablets and tranquillisers prior to sleep relaxes the upper airway muscles and make OSAHS worse. Alcohol can also reduce the brain's response to an apnoea which in turn leads to longer and more severe apnoeas in people who would otherwise have only mild OSAHS and who would otherwise only snore.

What are the symptoms of OSAHS?

Most people with OSAHS snore loudly and breathing during sleep may be laboured and noisy. Sleeping partners may report multiple apnoeas which often end in deep gasping and loud snorting. Sufferers may report waking for short periods after struggling for breath. Symptoms are often worse when lying on the back in deepest sleep. Although a person with OSAHS may not be aware of the many arousals from deep sleep, they suffer from poor quality sleep in spite of long periods of time spent in bed. Such people wake feeling that they haven't had a full refreshing night's sleep. They report difficulty maintaining concentration during the day, have a poor memory, and suffer from excessive daytime sleepiness. At first an OSAHS sufferer may be sleepy only when seated and relaxed, e.g. watching TV, but eventually sleepiness becomes so severe that car accidents and accidents in the workplace occur. Other symptoms of OSAHS include morning headache, nocturia, depression, short temper, grumpiness, personality change and impotence in males, leading to loss of interest in sex.

What are the consequences of untreated OSAHS?

The most serious potential consequences of untreated OSAHS are road traffic accidents and accidents at work because of sleepiness. Untreated OSAHS is associated with a six-fold increase in the risk of such accidents. Patients may also experience difficulties with concentration due to tiredness, increased irritability and depression. There is evidence that patients with OSAHS have an increased risk of high blood pressure and may have a slightly increased risk of angina, heart attacks and strokes. Because OSAHS significantly increases the risk of road traffic accidents, patients must not drive if experiencing excessive daytime sleepiness. Patients must inform the DVLA in Swansea following a diagnosis of the condition. In most cases, the DVLA are happy to allow car drivers to continue driving once they are established on a successful therapy.

How is OSAHS assessed?

When a person is suspected to have OSAHS, their doctor will ask questions about waking and sleeping habits and will make a physical examination. Reports from the sleeping partner or household member about any apnoeas are extremely helpful. Referral to hospital to arrange an overnight sleep study (which is usually then carried out at home after a demonstration at hospital) will probably be required to confirm the diagnosis of OSAHS and to allow its severity to be measured. Occasionally a patient may have to be admitted overnight to hospital for further tests. None of these procedures are uncomfortable or painful.

How is OSAHS treated?

The simplest treatment is to lose weight. This is best done by cutting down on all foods, especially fatty foods, sweet things and alcohol. Alcohol within six hours of bedtime should be avoided as it contributes to OSAHS symptoms. If these measures are not enough, the best form of treatment is continuous positive airway pressure (CPAP) therapy in which a gentle flow of air is applied through the nose at night keeping the pressure in the throat above atmospheric pressure and stopping the throat narrowing to prevent breathing pauses and snoring. Another form of treatment includes gumshield-like devices (mandibular repositioning devices) which attempt to keep the airway clear by moving the jaw forward. This is less effective than CPAP and not appropriate for all patients.

中英文注释

关键词汇

apnoea [æp'niə] n. 窒息，无呼吸；呼吸暂停

grumpiness n. 坏脾气

jaw [dʒɔ] n. 下颌

menopause ['menəpɔːz] n. 绝经

nocturia [nɔk'tjuəriə] n. 夜尿

snore [snɔː] vi. 打鼾

throat [θrəʊt] n. 喉

tonsils ['tansl] n. 扁桃体

tranquilliser ['træŋkwilaizə] n. 镇静剂

主要短语

Obstructive Sleep Apnea Hypopnoea Syndrome (OSAHS) 阻塞性睡眠呼吸暂停低通气综合征

positive airway pressure (CPAP) 气道正压通气
short temper 脾气暴躁
soft palate 软腭

张海利　王斌全

85

What is sinusitis?

Sinusitis is inflammation of the paranasal sinuses. It can be due to infection, allergy, or autoimmune issues. Most cases are due to a viral infection and resolve over the course of 10 days.

Classification

Sinusitis is defined as an inflammation of the mucous membrane that lines the paranasal sinuses and is classified chronologically into several categories:

- acute rhinosinusitis — a new infection that may last up to four weeks and can be subdivided symptomatically into severe and non-severe.
- recurrent acute rhinosinusitis — four or more separate episodes of acute sinusitis that occur within one year.
- subacute rhinosinusitis — an infection that lasts between four and 12 weeks, and represents a transition between acute and chronic infection.
- chronic rhinosinusitis — when the signs and symptoms last for more than 12 weeks.
- acute exacerbation of chronic rhinosinusitis — when the signs and symptoms of chronic rhinosinusitis exacerbate, but return to baseline after treatment.

All these types of sinusitis have similar symptoms, and are thus often difficult to distinguish. Acute sinusitis is very common. Roughly ninety percent of adults have had sinusitis at some point in their life.

Acute

Acute sinusitis is usually precipitated by an earlier upper respiratory tract infection, generally of viral origin. If the infection is of bacterial origin, the most common three causative agents are Streptococcus pneumoniae, Haemophilus influenzae, and Moraxella catarrhalis. Until recently, Haemophilus influenzae was the most common bacterial agent to cause sinus infections. However, introduction of the H. influenza type B (Hib) vaccine has dramatically decreased H. influenza type B infections and now non-typical H. influenza (NTHI) are predominantly seen in clinics. Other sinusitis-causing bacterialpathogens include Staphylococcus aureus and other streptococcispecies, anaerobic bacteria and, less commonly, gram negative bacteria. Viral sinusitis typically lasts for 7 to 10 days. whereas bacterial sinusitis is more persistent. Approximately 0.5% to 2% of viral sinusitis results in subsequent bacterial sinusitis. It is thought that nasal irritation from nose blowing leads to the secondary bacterial infection.

Acute episodes of sinusitis can also result from fungal invasion. These infections are typically seen in patients with diabetes or other immune deficiencies (such as AIDS or transplantpatients on immunosuppressive anti-rejection medications) and can be life threatening. In type I diabetics, ketoacidosis can be associated with sinusitis due to mucormycosis.

Chemical irritation can also trigger sinusitis, commonly from cigarette smoke and chlorine fumes. Rarely, it may be caused by a tooth infection.

Chronic

Chronic sinusitis, by definition, lasts longer than three months and can be caused by many different diseases that share chronic inflammation of the sinuses as a common symptom. Symptoms of chronic sinusitis may include any combination of the following: nasal congestion, facial pain, headache, night-time coughing, an increase in previously minor or controlled asthma symptoms, general malaise, thick green or yellow discharge, feeling of facial 'fullness' or 'tightness' that may worsen when bending over, dizziness, aching teeth, and/or halitosis. Each of these symptoms has multiple other possible causes, which should be considered and investigated as well. Unless complications occur, fever is not a feature of chronic sinusitis. Often chronic sinusitis can lead to anosmia, a reduced sense of smell. In a small number of cases, acute or chronic maxillary sinusitis is associated with a dental infection. Vertigo, lightheadedness, and blurred vision are not typical in chronic sinusitis and other causes should be investigated.

Chronic sinusitis cases are subdivided into cases with polyps and cases without polyps. When polyps are present, the condition is called chronic hyperplastic sinusitis; however, the causes are poorly understood may include allergy, environmental factors such as dust or pollution, bacterial infection, or fungus (either allergic, infective, or reactive). Non-allergic factors, such as vasomotor rhinitis, can also cause chronic sinus problems. Abnormally narrow sinus passages, such as having a deviated septum, can impede drainage from the sinus cavities and be a contributing factor.

Chronic rhinosinusitis represents a multifactorial inflammatory disorder, rather than simply a persistent bacterial infection. The medical management of chronic rhinosinusitis is now focused upon controlling the inflammation that predisposes patients to obstruction, reducing the incidence of infections. However, all forms of chronic rhinosinusitis are associated with impaired sinus drainage and secondary bacterial infections. Most individuals require initial antibiotics to clear any infection and intermittently afterwards to treat acute exacerbations of chronic rhinosinusitis.

A combination of anaerobic and aerobic bacteria, are detected in conjunction with chronic sinusitis. Also isolated are Staphylococcus aureus (including methicilin resistant S.aureus) and coagulase-negative Staphylococci and Gram negative enteric organisms can be isolated. Typically antibiotic treatment provides only a temporary reduction in inflammation, although hyperresponsiveness of the immune system to bacteria has been proposed as a possible cause of sinusitis with polyps (chronic hyperplastic sinusitis).

Attempts have been made to provide a more consistent nomenclature for subtypes of chronic sinusitis. The presence of eosinophils in the mucous lining of the nose and paranasal sinuses has been demonstrated for many patients, and this has been termed eosinophilic mucin rhinosinusitis (EMRS). Cases of EMRS may be related to an allergic response, but allergy is not often documented, resulting in further subcategorization into allergic and non-allergic EMRS.

A more recent, and still debated, development in chronic sinusitis is the role that fungus plays in this disease. Fungus can be found in the nasal cavities and sinuses of most patients with sinusitis, but can also be found in healthy people as well. It remains unclear if fungus is a definite factor in the development of chronic sinusitis and if it is, what the difference may be between those who develop the disease and those who remain free of symptoms. Trials of antifungal treatments have had mixed results.

What causes sinusitis?

Factors which may predispose someone to developing sinusitis include: allergies; structural abnormalities, such as a deviated septum, small sinus ostia or a concha bullosa; nasal polyps; carrying the cystic fibrosis gene, though research is still tentative and prior bouts of sinusitis, because each instance may result in increased inflammation of the nasal or sinus mucosa and potentially further narrow the nasal passageways. Both smoking and second hand smoke are associated with chronic rhinosinusitis. Maxillary sinusitis may also be of dental origin and constitutes a significant percentage (about 20% of all cases of maxillary sinusitis) given the close proximity of the teeth and the sinus floor. The cause of this situation is usually a periapical or periodontal infection of a maxillary posterior tooth, where the inflammatory exudate has eroded through the bone superiorly to drain into the maxillary sinus. Once an odontogenic infection involves the maxilary sinus, it is possible that it may then spread to the orbit or to the ethmoid sinus. Complementary tests based on conventional radiology techniques and modern technology may be indicated. Their indication is based on the clinical context.

Chronic sinusitis can also be caused indirectly through a common but slight abnormality within the auditory or Eustachian tube, which is connected to the sinus cavities and the throat. This tube is usually almost level with the eye sockets but when this sometimes hereditary abnormality is present, it is below this level and sometimes level with the vestibule or nasal entrance. This almost always causes some sort of blockage within the sinus cavities ending in infection and usually resulting in chronic sinusitis.

Pathophysiology

It has been hypothesized that biofilm bacterial infections may account for many cases of antibiotic-refractory chronic sinusitis. Biofilms are complex aggregates of extracellular matrix and inter-dependent microorganisms from multiple species, many of which may be difficult or impossible to isolate using standard clinical laboratory techniques. Bacteria found in biofilms have their antibiotic resistance increased up to 1000 times when compared to free-living bacteria of the same species. A recent study found that biofilms were present on the mucosa of 75% of patients undergoing surgery for chronic sinusitis.

What are the symptoms of sinusitis?

Headache/facial pain or pressure of a dull, constant, or aching sort over the affected sinuses is common with both acute and chronic stages of sinusitis. This pain is typically localized to the involved sinus and may worsen when the affected person bends over or when lying down. Pain often starts on one side of the head and progresses to both sides. Acute and chronic sinusitis may be accompanied by thick nasal discharge that is usually green in color and may contain pus (purulent) and/or blood. Often a localized headache or toothache is present, and it is these symptoms that distinguish a sinus-related headache from other types of headaches, such as tension and migraine headaches. Infection of the eye socket is possible, which may result in the loss of sight and is accompanied by fever and severe illness. Another possible complication is the infection of the bones (osteomyelitis) of the forehead and other facial bones – Pott's puffy tumor.

Sinus infections can also cause inner ear problems due to the congestion of the nasal passages. This can be demonstrated by dizziness, "a pressurized or heavy head", or vibrating sensations in the head. Other symptoms of sinusitis include bad breath and Post-nasal drip.

Recent studies suggest that up to 90% of "sinus headaches" are actually migraines. The confusion occurs in part because migraine involves activation of the trigeminal nerves, which innervate both the sinus region and the meninges surrounding the brain. As a result, it is difficult to accurately determine the site from which the pain originates.

Additionally, nasal congestion can be a common result of migraine headaches, due to the autonomic nerve stimulation that can also cause tearing (lacrimation) and a runny nose (rhinorrhea). A study found that patients with "sinus headaches" responded to triptan migraine medications, but stated dissatisfaction with their treatment when they are treated with decongestants or antibiotics. People with migraines do not typically have the thick nasal discharge that is a common symptom of a sinus infection.

Complications

The close proximity of the brain to the sinuses makes the most dangerous complication of sinusitis, particularly involving the frontal and sphenoid sinuses, infection of the brain by the invasion of anaerobic bacteria through the bones or blood vessels. Abscesses, meningitis, and other life-threatening conditions may result. In extreme cases the patient may experience mild personality changes, headache, altered consciousness, visual problems, seizures, coma, and possibly death.

Sinus infection can spread through anastomosing veins or by direct extension to close structures. Contiguous spread to the orbit may result in periorbital cellulitis, subperiosteal abscess, orbital cellulitis, and abscess. Orbital cellulitis can complicate acute ethmoiditis if anterior and posterior ethmoidal veins thrombophlebitis enables the spread of the infection to the lateral or orbital side of the ethmoid labyrinth. Sinusitis may extend to the central nervous system, where it may cause cavernous sinus thrombosis, retrograde meningitis, and epidural, subdural, and brain abscesses. Orbital symptoms frequently precede intracranial spread of the infection. Other complications include sinobronchitis, maxillary osteomyelitis, and frontal bone osteomyelitis. Osteomyelitis of the frontal bone often originates from a spreading thrombo-phlebitis. A periostitis of the frontal sinus causes an osteitis and a periostitis of the outer membrane, which produces a tender, puffy swelling of the forehead.

The diagnosis of these complication can be assisted by noting local tenderness and dull pain, and can be confirmed by CT and nuclear isotope scanning. The most common microbial causes are anaerobic bacteria and S. aureus. Treatment includes performing surgical drainage and administration of antimicrobial therapy. Surgical debridement is rarely required after an extended course of parenteral antimicrobial therapy. Antibiotics should be administered for at least 6 weeks. Continuous monitoring of patients for possible intracranial complication is advised.

How is sinusitis diagnosed?

Acute

Bacterial and viral acute sinusitis are difficult to distinguish. However, if symptoms last less than 10 days, it is generally considered viral sinusitis. When symptoms last more than 10 days, it is considered bacterial sinusitis. At this point 30% to 50% of cases are bacterial. Imaging by either Xray, CT or MRI is generally not recommended unless complications develop. Pain caused by sinusitis is sometimes confused for pain caused by pulpitis (toothache) of the maxillary teeth, and vice versa. Classically, the increased pain when tilting the head forwards separates sinusitis from pulpitis.

Chronic

For sinusitis lasting more than 12 weeks a CT scan is recommended Nasal endoscopy, and clinical symptoms are also used to make a positive diagnosis. A tissue sample for histology and cultures can also be collected and tested. Allergic fungal sinusitis (AFS) is often seen in people with asthma and nasal polyps. In rare cases, sinusoscopymay be made.

Nasal endoscopy involves inserting a flexible fiber-optic tube with a light and camera at its tip into the nose to examine the nasal passages and sinuses. This is generally a completely painless (although uncomfortable) procedure which takes between five to ten minutes to complete.

How is sinusitis treated?

Conservative

Nasal irrigation may help with symptoms of chronic sinusitis. Decongestant nasal sprays containing for example oxymetazoline may provide relief, but these medications should not be used for more than the recommended period. Longer use may cause rebound sinusitis. Other recommendations include applying a warm, moist cloth to the affected areas several times a day; drinking sufficient fluids in order to thin the mucus; and inhaling low temperature steam two to four times a day.

Antibiotics

The vast majority of cases of sinusitis are caused by viruses and will therefore resolve without antibiotics. However, if symptoms do not resolve within 10 days, amoxicillin is a reasonable antibiotic to use first for treatment with amoxicillin/ clavulanate being indicated when the person's symptoms do not improve after 7 days on amoxicillin alone. Antibiotics are specifically not recommended in those with mild/ moderate disease during the first week of infection due to risk of adverse effects, antibiotic resistance, and cost.

Fluoroquinolones, and a newer macrolide antibiotic such as clarithromycin or a tetracycline like doxycycline, are used in those who have severe allergies to penicillins. Because of increasing resistance to amoxicillin the 2012 guideline of the Infectious Diseases Society of America recommends amoxicillin-clavulanate as the initial treatment of choice for bacterial sinusitis. The guidelines also recommend against other commonly used antibiotics, including azithromycin, clarithromycin and trimethoprim/sulfamethoxazole, because of growing drug resistance.

A short-course (3–7 days) of antibiotics seems to be just as effective as the typical longer-course (10–14 days) of antibiotics for those with clinically diagnosed acute-bacterial sinusitis without any other severe disease or complicating factors. The IDSA guideline suggest five to seven days of antibiotics is long enough to treat a bacterial infection without encouraging resistance. The guideline still do recommend children receive antibiotic treatment for 10 days to two weeks.

Corticosteroids

For unconfirmed acute sinusitis, intranasal corticosteroids have not been found to be better than placebo either alone or in combination with antibiotics. For cases confirmed by radiology or nasal endoscopy, treatment with corticosteroids alone or in combination with antibiotics is supported. The benefit however is small.

There is only limited evidence to support short treatment with oral corticosteroids for chronic rhinosinusitis with nasal polyps.

Surgery

For chronic or recurring sinusitis, referral to an otolaryngologist specialist may be indicated, and treatment options may include nasal surgery. Surgery should only be considered for those patients who do not experience sufficient relief from optimal Medication.

Maxilliary antral washout involves puncturing the sinus and flushing with saline to clear the mucus. A 1996 study of patients with chronic sinusitis found that washout confers no additional benefits over antibiotics alone.

A number of surgical approaches can be used to access the sinuses and these have generally shifted from external approaches to intranasal endoscopic ones. The benefit of Functional Endoscopic Sinus Surgery (FESS) is its ability to allow for a more targeted approach to the affected sinuses, reducing tissue disruption, and minimizing post-operative complications.

Another recently developed treatment is balloon sinuplasty. This method, similar to balloon angioplasty used to "unclog" arteries of the heart, utilizes balloons in an attempt to expand the openings of the sinuses in a less invasive manner. The utility of this treatment for sinus disease is still under debate but appears promising.

For persistent symptoms and disease in patients who have failed medical and the functional endoscopic approaches, older techniques can be used to address the inflammation of the maxillary sinus, such as the Caldwell-Luc radical antrostomy. This surgery involves an incision in the upper gum, opening in the anterior wall of the antrum, removal of the entire diseased maxillary sinus mucosa and drainage is allowed into inferior or middle meatus by creating a large window in the lateral nasal wall.

中英文注释

关键词汇

amoxicillin [ə,mɑksi'silin] n. 阿莫西林；羟氨苄青霉素

anaerobic [,æneə'rəubik] adj. [微]厌氧的

anastomose [ə'næstəməuz] vt. 使吻合

clarithromycin 克拉霉素

doxycycline 强力霉素

eosinophil [,i:ə(ʊ)'sinəfil] adj. 嗜伊红的；n. 嗜曙红细胞；嗜伊红血球嗜酸性粒细胞

fluoroquinolones 喹诺酮类

halitosis [,hæli'təusis] n. 口臭

immunosuppressive [,imjunəusə'presiv] adj. 免抑制疫力的；抑制免疫力的

ketoacidosis [,ki'təuæsi'dəusis] n. 酮症酸中毒

placebo [plə'si:bəu] n. 安慰剂

polyp ['pɒlip] n. 息肉

tetracycline [,tetrə'saikli:n] n. 四环素

主要短语

coagulase-negative staphylococci 凝固酶阴性的葡萄球菌

functional endoscopic sinus surgery (fess) 功能性鼻窦内窥镜手术

gram negative enteric organisms 革兰阴性肠道微生物

haemophilus influenzae. 流感嗜血杆菌

macrolide antibiotic 大环内酯类抗生素

maxillary sinusitis 上颌窦炎

orbital cellulitis 眼眶蜂窝组织炎

streptococcus pneumoniae 肺炎链球菌

sphenoid sinuses 蝶窦

张海利　王斌全

Section Seven: Oral Disease

第七部分　口腔疾病

86

Acute Pulpitis

急性牙髓炎

What is acute pulpitis?

Pulpitis is the consequence that dental caries progress through dentinal tubules into the pulp cavity. Then various Irritants, include bacterial by-products, disintegrating elements of carious dentin, chemicals from food, can arrive at pulp (blood vessels, lymphatic vessels, twig nerves) and make direct injury to the pulp, arising ache or other troubles.

Acute Pulpitis is the acute phase of the pulpitis.

What causes acute pulpitis?

Bacterial causes

Bacteria and their by-products are the main causes of the pulpitis. When deep caries, severeabrasion, direct trauma or medical factors, destroyed the structural integrity of enamel and cementum, bacteria can osmotic into the pulp cavity through the exposed dentinal tubules, pulp, periodontal pocket, and blood vessels, cause the infection of pulp.

Physical causes

Acute trauma and chronic occlusal trauma can make blood vessels through the apical foramen contused and disconnected. Consequently, the blood supply to pulp is stopped, the putrescence and infection happen to the pulp.

The heat produced by grinding the tooth body when we prepare the cavity, polishing restorations, and water coolant we drink, may make the temperature of oral cavity sharp changes, resulting in pulp hyperaemia and infection.

There's evidence indicate that pulp changes can happened when amalgam was condensed into fresh cavities prepared with highspeed drill.

Chemical causes

Some filling materials and bases, such as hydroxybenzene, have chemical insult that can cause pulp infection.

Immunological causes

There are also many lymphatic vessels in Pulp. Immunocompetent cells, immunoglobulins, and complement factors have been identified in inflamed pulpal tissues. Both the humoral and cellular responses occur in the pulp.

What are symptoms of acute pulpitis?

Excruciating acute toothache is the notable characteristic of the acute pulpitis. The ache have following specialties:

The pain, often spontaneous, last half an hour and lighten for several to decades minutes normaly. And often become more poignant in night. This excruciating acute toothache usually be excited by hot or cold stimulating food or drink, and can diffuse to neighboring anatomic part.

In clinical oral examination we often can find deep interproxima cavities, approaching or achieved pulp chamber. Or a restoration impinging on the pulp chamber of the decayed tooth. Sometimes, we can detect a deep periodontal pocket existing around the tooth, Which bottom has arrived at the apical of root.

Exploration with a probe can arose violent ache, and detect a minute pulpal exposure of chamber.

Tooth with acute pulpitis is sensitive to the thermal test. The effect of stimulation often bring a lingering pain in which the patient clearly feels that the pain is still exist several seconds after stimulus being removed. The involved tooth is hypersensitive to the electric pulp test at incipient stage and while not at advanced stage.

Tooth with acute pulpitis is sensitive to vertical knock at advanced stage.

How is acute pulpitis diagnosed?

According to the notable characteristic, excruciating acute toothache, and the results of thermal test, electric pulp test, vertical knock test, we can drawn an conclusion easily.

How is it treated?

Acute pulpitis should be done endodontic treatment.

Emergency Treatment

● Open pulp chamber and make drainage.

The pressure in pulp chamber of acute pulpitis tooth is higher than usual, because the chamber is full of the infection effusion. And the nerve in pulp chamber, without theca, will produce excruciating acute ache stimulated by the high pressure.

We can drill a hole at the top of the pulp chamber, then the infection effusion will effuse, the pressure will reduce, and the excruciating acute ache will be abate. Or we can do a pulpectomy after a local anesthesia directly, and put an amicrobic tampon of hydroxybenzene.

● Antibiotics and Analgesics.

Using antibiotics by the numbers to treat the swelling caused by pulpitis, is aid to drainage. Patients with systemic signs (hyperpyrexia, feeble, ague) or spreading infections should eat antibiotics. Sometimes, the analgesics is necessary when patients can not bear the excruciating acute ache.

Root canal therapy (RCT)

Rct is the next step treatment after emergency treatment. Contemporaneity dentistry deems that root canal therapy, restorative and prosthetic treatment are integral treatment procedure. Rct now is almost thepronoun of endodontic treatment, and usually it follow the below procedures.

● Root canal preparation
  ■ Unclose the roof and access to the pulp chamber space.
  ■ Cleanup the infected pulp tissues in the pulp chamber and root canals.
  ■ Scale the length of every root canals with special guage and special metallic needle.
  ■ Make every root canals inner-diameter more wider and shapes of root canals more smooth with different diameter enlarge needles, and swash the root canal with physiological saline and 1%-3% aquae hydrogenii dioxidi.
● Intracanal antisepsis
  ■ Antisepsis with medicine. Put medicine tampons at the entrance of root canals, or fill the root canals with medicine paper points or medicine cotton twists, then seal them in the root canals. The medicine must have no stimulation to the periapical tissues, and have powerful osmotic force, durative antisepticise function, and easy to use. This measure is often used in our daily clinical treatment. The popular intracanal dressing of choice is calcium hydroxide. Although not characterized as an antiseptic, many evidence have proved that calcium hydroxide to be an effective antimicrobial agent.
  ■ Electrolysis treatment. This measure is leading medicine ions into root canals, and make antisepsis. Its efficacy is 3times to medicines.
  ■ Microwave and laser also be used to disinfect the root canals. Laser intracanal irradiation may be used in this procedure, due to temperature rise. Several studies have evaluated the effectiveness of lasers in sterilizing root canals. In this sense, lasers are being used as a coadjuvant tool in endodontic therapy, for bacterial reduction, and to modify the root canal surface.
● Root canal obturation

Root canal obturation is filling the root canals with special pasta and gutta-percha points. It's aim is making the root canal system be sealed well, avoiding the bacteria enter the root canal system and reinfects tissues. After the root canal preparation and the Intracanal antisepsis treatment, if no rational symptom, no sensitive to percussion, no bad smell, no substantive exudant, we can fill the root canals.

中英文注释

关键词汇

ague ['eigjuː] n. 寒战

amalgam [ə'mælgəm] n. 汞合金

amicrobic ['æmaikrəʊbik] adj. 无菌的

cementum [si'mentəm] n. 牙骨质

coadjuvant ['kəʊdʒjʊvənt] adj. 辅助的

contuse [kən'tuːz] vt. 撞伤，挫伤

drainage ['dreinidʒ] n. 引流

effusion [i'fjuːʒn] n. 渗出物

electrolysis [i,lek'trɒləsis] n. 电解

excruciating [ik'skruːʃieitiŋ] adj. 折磨人的，极痛苦的

exudant [igz'juːdənt] n. 渗出物

feeble ['fiːbl] adj. 虚弱的，乏力的

humoral ['hjuːmərəl] adj. 体液的

hydroxybenzene ['haidrɒksibenziːn] n. 酚

hyperaemia [haipə'miːdiə] n. 充血

hyperpyrexia [,haipəpai'reksiə] n. 高热

immunoglobulin [,imjʊnəʊ'glɒbjʊlin] n. 免疫球蛋白

insult [in'sʌlt] n. 损伤

irritant ['iritənt] n. 刺激物

obturation [ɒbtjʊ'reiʃən] n. 封闭

odontoblast [ɒ'dɒntɒblaːst] n. 成牙本质细胞

osmotic [ɒz'mɒtik] adj. 渗透性的

pasta ['pæstə] n. 糊剂

periapical [piə'raiəpikl] adj. 根尖周的

permeate ['pɜːmieit] vt. 渗透

poignant ['pɔinjənt] adj. 剧烈的

pulpectomy [pʌl'pektəmi] n. 牙髓摘除术

pulpitis ['pʌl'paidis] n. 牙髓炎

tampon ['tæmpɒn] n. 棉球

theca ['θiːkə] n. 鞘

主要短语

acute pulpitis 急性牙髓炎

aquae hydrogenii dioxidi 双氧水

by-products 副产品

calcium hydroxide 氢氧化钙

cotton twists 棉捻

dentinal tubules 牙本质小管

gutta-percha point 牙胶尖

immunocompetent pulpal exposure 穿髓孔

lymphatic vessels 淋巴管

paper points 纸尖

periodontal pocket 牙周袋

physiological saline 生理盐水

pulp cavity 牙髓腔

sensitive to percussion 叩痛

severeabrasion 重度磨耗

twig nerves 末梢神经

王晓飞

87 Chronic Periodontitis

慢性牙周炎

What is chronic periodontitis?

Periodontitis is the chronic infective disease that happened to the periodontal tissues (gingiva, periodontal ligament, alveolar bone), and caused by the microorganism in bacterial plaque, exists on the surface of tooth. It can result in the periodontal infection, periodontal pocket formed, absorbing of alveolar bone. At last, the tooth destroyed by periodontitis has to be pulled out. Chronic periodontitis, its used name is adult periodontitis or chronic adult periodontitis. It is the most common periodontitis, accounted for 95% approximately. It caused by the spreading of long existed chronic gingivitis to the deep periodontal tissues. Many dentists think the chronic gingivitis as the initial stage of the chronic periodontitis in clinic.

What causes chronic periodontitis?

The main cause of chronic periodontitis is dental plaque, which caused by bad teeth cleaning and increasing of salivary viscosity etc. Many other factors, such as dental calculus, food impaction, bad restorations and so on, can increase the retention of dental plaque. When the numbers and the toxicity of microorganism in dental plaque increase, or the defense ability of our body is reduced, the subgingival plaque will breed many Porphyromonas gingivalis, Actinobacillus actinomycetem comitans, bacteroides forsythus, and spirochete etc. They can destory the collogen, make the junctional epithelium proliferates towards root direction. Then the periodontal pocket formed, absorbing of alveolar bone happened. Chronic gingivitis develops to the chronic periodontitis.

What are symptoms of chronic periodontitis?

Main symptoms

Chronic gingivitis is the initial stage of the chronic periodontitis. In this stage, the lesion is usually limited to the free gingiva and the papillae gingiva. The color of gingiva becomes to bright red or kermesinus. Attached gingiva becomes swollen and haematose. Papillae gingivas' shape becomes blunt and hypertrophic, its' surface becomes bright, stippling disappeared. Gently touching the gingiva can make it bleeding. The patients usually visit dentist for bleeding, caused by brushing teeth or biting hard food. The depth of gingival sulcus can be more than 3mm, and false periodontal pocket is formed.

If we don't treat the lesion of gingiva well, and the patients don't clean teeth well, the gingivitis will progress to chronic periodontitis deeply ulteriorly. In this stage, all teeth is encroached on normally, only few patients have a set of teeth (anterior teeth) or separate tooth been implicated. Active stagealternates with resting stage. The course of chronic periodontitis can last more than ten years or even several decades. A great deal of dental calculus on the surface of teeth, defferent degrees of gingivitis exist at the same time. When dentist detect the periodontal pocket, it is easy to bleed or fester spilling over. In an early phase, the periodontal pockets appear and the alveolar bone is absorbed slightly, so teeth are not loose. In an advanced phase, deep periodontal pockets will be formed, the alveolar bone is absorbed seriously, teeth become loose. Patients usually feel lacking strengh when biting, or ache. Acute peridental abscess may even happen rapidly.

Chronic periodontitis is divided into 3 degrees, depend on the depth of periodontal pockets, the degree of attachment loss of connective tissue and the absorbed degree of alveolar bones.

- Mild degree: Gingiva is infected and bleed when examined with a probe. The depth of periodontal pocket less than or equal to 4mm. Attachment loss is 1mm to 2mm. The absorption of alveolar bone is limited to the height of one third of root length, displayed in X-ray picture.

- Moderate degree: Gingivitis exists and bleed in probing, purulence can be find in periodontal pocket, its' depth is less than or equal to 6mm. Attachment loss is 3mm to 4mm The absorption of alveolar bone exceeds the height of one third of the root length, and less than half of the root length. Tooth is slightly loose. Root furcation of multirooted teeth is infected mildly.

- Serious degree: Gingivitis is obvious and peridental abscess is formed. Periodontal pockets' depth is more than 6mm. Attachment loss is equal or greater than 5mm. We can see, in in X-ray picture, that the absorption of alveolar bone exceeds the half of the root length. Root furcation of multirooted teeth is infected obviously. Tooth is loose clearly.

Concomitnta symptoms

In the terminal of chronic periodontitis, besides the four characters (periodontal pocket, gingivitis, absorption of alveolar bone and loosening of tooth), there are many below concomitnta symptoms existing at the same time.

- Tooth displacement. Because of the high of alveolar bone is reduced and teeth is loose, abaxial bite force make the tooth displace from its' primary position.
- Food impaction. The apertures will appear between the loose teeth, the food will be filled into the apertures by the bite force and squeeze of cheek muscles.
- Secondary occlusal trauma. It is indicated that abaxial bite force will destory the normal structure of periodontal tissues and the patient feels biting ache.
- Root is exposed. With the absorption of alveolar bone and descending of the high of dental process, the root is exposed little by little. Patients usually feel teeth loose and sensitive to the hot or cold foods.
- Acute peridental abscess. When the defense ability of our body is reduced, and chronic periodontitis is not treat in time, acute peridental abscess may happen rapidly. Local swelling or ache, and systemic symptoms such as ardent fever, headache and lacking in strength will come forth.
- Retropulpitis. When the bottom of the periodontal pocket access the apical of root, the bacteria can infect the pulp then arose the pulpitis through the root canal.
- Kakostomia. Bad smell usually appears in the mouth of the chronic periodontitis patient. This is caused by the metabolin of a large number of microorganism living in periodontal pockets.

How is chronic periodontitis diagnosed?

Through the attentive enquiry about the history of disease, serious examination and symptoms, we can make the diagnosis of chronic periodontitis.

How is chronic periodontitis treated?

After making a definite diagnosis, and according to the severity of the state of chronic periodontitis, we can set down the treatment plan and estimate its' prognosis.

Chronic periodontitis is elicited by bacteria by and large. Therefore, the treatment plan must have a primarily anti-infectious nature. Reduction or clearing up the infection results for the most part from mechanical treatment of affected teeth and root surfaces as well as the gingival soft tissue. For special patients that have constitutional symptoms, local inunction of external use medicine or systemic medications such as take antibiotics orally and intravenouslly guttae, are necessary. Alterable risk factors must be avoided as far as possible.

Treatment measures

- Control dental plaque. We can make patients know their distribution area of dental plaque with plaque disclosing agent. Then we can teach patients right and efficient teeth cleaning ways or advice them use electric toothbrush. The final aim is reducing the surfaces adhered by dental plaque to less than the 20% of teeth surfaces.

● Wipe off dental calculus. The calculus supragingival can be wipe off by sonic teeth scaling drastically. Subgingival calculus can be remove by subgingival teeth scaling. We can also scrape off the infected cementums exposed in periodontal pockets, where many endotoxin get together. So the surface of root becomes smooth and the gingiva can adhere to it again. Teeth scaling is the basical method to treating chronic periodontitis.

● One to two months later, after the basical periodontal treatment, the patient should see dentist again to reexamine. If the periodental pocket, depth is more than or equal to 5mm, still be detected, we may need to consider surgical ways. Periodontal surgical operation is to incise the gingiva, expose the root surface and root furcation entirely, then wipe off the dental calculus and granulation tissues drastically, modify the shape of gingiva and alveolar bone under direct vision. In some severe circumstances, we have to cut off the root or do bone grafting.

● The loose teeth can be fixed by steel wire or resin splinting, modify and establish balanced.

● occluding relation, make loose teeth become more stable gradually, resume masticatory function.

● Pull out the too loose teeth and nonreserve value teeth as early as possible. Otherwise, these teeth may lead to the diffusion of infection.

Total treatment requires consideration of systemic aspects, including the possibility of interaction of periodontal disease with other diseases, systemic adjuncts to local treatment, and special precautions in patient management necessitated by systemic conditions.

Diabetes mellitus, anemia, or alimentary canal diseases may disturb the coalescence of periodontal tissues. These diseases should be treat and control actively. Smoking also affect the peripheral circulation of periodontal tissues.

It may also entail consideration of function aspects for the establishment of optimal occlusion relationships for the entire dentition.

All these aspects are embodied in a master plan, which consists of a rational sequence of dental procedures that includes periodontal and other measures necessary to create a well-functioning dentition in a healthy periodontal environment.

In principle, the course of periodontitis therapy is similar for all forms of the disease, and is administered in stage or phase of varying duration, depending on the extent and severity of the disease.

However, the details of individual therapy may be dramatically different. These details are dependent on the type of disease, the patient's own desires, patient age, financial circumstances and not least, the preference of the individual clinician.

中英文注释

关键词汇

coalescence [kəʊə'lesns] n. 愈合

collogen [kɒləd'ʒen] n. 胶原

endotoxin [ˌendəʊ'tɒksin] n. 内毒素

haematose [hiːmɑː'təʊs] adj. 充血的

hypertrophic [ˌhipə'trɒfik] adj. 肥大的

kakostomia [kei'kɒstəmiə] n. 口臭

kermesinus ['kɜːməzinəs] n. 暗红色

proliferate [prəˌlifə'reit] vi. 增殖

purulence ['pjʊərʊləns] n. 脓液

retropulpitis [retrɒ'pʌlpitiːz] n. 逆行性牙髓炎

scaling ['skeiliŋ] n. 洁治术

spirochete ['spaiərəkiːt] n. 螺旋体

stippling ['stipliŋ] n. 点彩

viscosity [vi'skɒsəti] n. 黏稠度

主要短语

actinomycetem comitans　放线杆菌

alimentary canal　消化道

alveolar bone　牙槽骨

attached gingiva　附着龈

attachment loss　附着丧失

bacteroides forsythus　福氏类杆菌

bone grafting　植骨

concomitnta symptom　伴发症状

connective tissue　结缔组织

dental calculus　牙结石

dental process　牙槽突

diabetes mellitus　糖尿病

false periodontal pocket　假性牙周袋

free gingiva 游离龈
gingival sulcus 龈沟
granulation tissue 肉芽组织
junctional epithelium 结合上皮
mild degree 轻度
multirooted teeth 多根牙
papillae gingiva 龈乳头
peridental abscess 牙周脓肿
periodontal ligament 牙周韧带
periodontal tissues 末梢循环
porphyromonas gingivalis 牙龈卟啉单胞菌
resin splinting 树脂夹板
root furcation 根分叉

王晓飞

Dental Caries

龋　　病

What is dental caries?

Dental caries, usually we called tooth decay, is one of the most common oral diseases in humankind. Generally, it is the key factor that cause the tooth pain and tooth head body breakage, in almost every race populations.

Dental caries is an infectious microbiological disease, it generally can make partial dissolution and destruction of the calcified tissues of the toothbody. It is a chronic disease, its process is the mineralized tissues of the teeth, include enamel, dentine, and cementum, be affected by the microorganisms fermentable carbohydrases elements in our diet. Then, it can induce to the disintegration of the organic material, and make demineralization of the mineral part of teeth ultimately. After the damage of the dentine, is the bacterial invasion, pulp necrosis and the infection be spreaded into the periapical tissue. Subsequently, pain and tooth decay will appear.

White-spot lesion, appeared on the enamel, is the first sign of dental caries. It can be often detected with the naked eye. Hardly, dental caries is self-limiting, so we must treat it in time to avoid boring oppressive pain and the destruction of the tooth.

What causes dental caries?

A famous theory, about what causes dental caries in its procession, is four correlative factors theory. The four factors are bacteria, diet, host and time. The theory was presented in the 1960s in a model of overlapping circles.

Bacteria

The bacteria in oral is usually exist in dental plaque. Streptococcus mutans and lactobacilli are the main breeds, and play important roles in the development of dental caries. They can live in acidic environment cozily, and richly stimulated by sucrose, and produce great amounts of acids to destruct the tooth body.

Diet

Cookies, cake, bread, beverage and many other our favored foods are belong to carbohydrate, they are the necessary elements that the bacteria to produce acids initiate demineralization depend on. So, the teeth cleaning is very important to us, especially for yang kids. We must do it at least two times a day, after waking up and just before sleep.

Host

Host include teeth and oral environment. The dental plaque, adhered to the surface of the teeth body, is the home of the bacteria in our mouth. Teeth are usually marinated in the saliva, its buffering capacity and flow rate can help us to neutralize and clear the acids produced by bacteria.

Time

Anythings' development need time, as well as the acids produced by bacteria need enough time to make the teeth be demineralized. Dental caries lesions may take several months to come into being, not one night.

What are symptoms of dental caries?

Color Changes

At the initial stage of enamel caries, mineral loss cannot be detected with a probe, small opaque malm colour spots on dried clean teeth surfaces is the main colors change, we called "white spot lesion". It can be diagnosed to smooth surface enamel caries only by sharp eyes before the cavitation has appeared. If the caries happened to the root surface, the discolored areas, will be located in parts that close to the gingival edge, and smaller than enamel white spot. If it not be well stopped, it will encircle the tooth finally. Colors of the initial lesion is diversiform, from yellowish or light brown, through midbrown to almost black. Caries in pits and fissures is difficult to detected. Usually, penetrating eyes are used to detect the discoloration and cavitation, while bitewing radiograph is used to occlusal caries, especially the caries lesion spread into the dentine.

As the lesion developing, the area of colors changing will break down and form a cavity finally. Bacterial plaque will be formed on the wall of cavity, and be protected by teeth cleaning or dental flows. Likely, the dental caries destruction is progressing, in fact, it is a feint.

Yellowish or light brown discoloration usually can be seen at softened area of an acute caries destruction part. Brownish area usually can be detected in a chronic caries teeth.

Shape Changes

Ordinarily, when we refer to dental caries, we are associated with teeth cavity. In fact, according to the above words, at the initial stage of dental caries there is no shape change. In the developing of the dental caries lesion, different depths and different shapes cavity begin to happened.

Smooth surfaces lesion and fissures lesion are different in shape, the reason is the different anatomy framework between fissure and the direction of the enamel prisms. Both of two lesions are cone shaped, but the surface lesions' base of the cone is at the enamel surface, while the fissure lesions' base is at the enamel-dentine junction. Enamel lesion spread is guided by prism direction, but the fissure lesion become more wider when it approaches the dentine.

When lesion arrives at the enamel-dentine junction, it will develop laterally along the junction to the dentine on a wider front. The actual lesion area is larger than us anticipation from examination of the enamel solely. The apparent destruction of enamel caries only partly contribute to the cavity developing, more contribution is from the lesion progressing to the soft infected carious dentine underneath it.

Pain

The stimulated pain, produced by pressure from food tamped in cavity, and soup, icecream and other hot or cold foods, are often make trouble for patients, when the dental caries lesion reached on the dentine.

Usually, we think the dentine and the pulp are different tissues. In fact dentine is produced by differentiated pulpal odontoblasts, then they should be think as the one and the same unit. The stimulated pain is the pulpal odontoblasts' immediately responding to the stimulation. Accordingly, dentine is a vital, highly mineralized tissue that can respond to the temperature or mechanical stimulation as long as the pulp remains alive.

How is dental caries diagnosed?

Several ways and means can be used to examine the dental caries.

Visual Examination

The discolored area and cavities in the tooth body can be seen by our eyes at first hand. Its' a simple and effective mean, can be done by patient himself or dentist.

Probe Examination

This is a unique way, dentists use a special shape probe to detecting the rigidity of tooth tissues and the depth of cavities in every surface of tooth. If probe arose the pain, it indicate that the lesion of dental caries have been reached the dentine through the enamel.

Radiographexamination

Bitewing radiograph is a effective clinical examing way used to detect lesions that are hidden from a careful clinical visual examination, when an adjacent tooth prevents the dentist from seeing an approximal lesion. Radiograph picture is also good at estimating the depth of the genuine lesion, permeating the superficies.

According to the history, symptoms and the results of above clinical examinations, we can make the diagnoses.

How is it treated?

Depend on different dental caries, we can treat it in different way.

Fissure Sealant

There is abundant evidence make clear that shallow fissure is not easy to get dental caries for its' capable of selfcleaning. While deep fissure is difficult to be cleaned well, if it remains sealed, caries will do not progress ulteriorly.

Fissure sealant is a effective way to protect normal tooth structure from being destroyed. Adhesive light cure resin or lightly filled resin is used to penetrate the fissures and prevent plaque accumulation on the occlusal surface. Some times we don't need to cut the tooth indeed, so it is easy to be accepted by young kids for indolence.

Treatment procedures include cleaning, isolation, etching, sealant application and ling curing.

Operative Management

When the dental caries has been destructed deeply, formed a cavity, operative management need to be done to restore the destroyed part.

Operative management include 4 steps:

Cavity Preparation

This procedures include abrading the the destructed infected dental tissues, and forming someshape cavity that filling material can be kept in it firmly.

Isolation

Filling material need a relatively dry environment to be kept firmly. Usually, we use cotton wool rolls, a saliva ejector, suction tube and rubber dam to isolate the tooth from saliva.

Cavity sealers and bases

Cavity sealers are some materials, providing a protective coating to the walls of the prepared cavity and a barrier to the leakage at the interface of the restorative material and the walls.

Cavity bases materials are use to replace lost dentine. Zinc oxide-eugenol, zinc phosphate cements and glass ionomers are used as bases for different restorative materials.

Filling restorative materials

Filling restorative materials into the prepared cavity to seal the cavity and not allow leakage of bacteria between the filling and the tooth. The final purpose is to resume the figure and the function of the destructed tooth. Therefore, restoration materials should have enough rigidity, ductibility and plasticity. Resin, glass ionomers and silver-amalgam are in common used in clinical.

中英文注释

关键词汇

hases ['beisi:z] n. 垫底剂

carbohydrate [ka:bə'haidreit] n. 碳水化合物

cementum [si'mentəm] n. 牙骨质

dentine ['denti:n] n. 牙本质

ductibility [dʌkti'biləti] n. 延展性

indolence ['indələns] adj. 无痛的

lactobacilli [læktəbəsi'li:] n. 乳酸杆菌

malm [ma:m] n. 白垩土

microbiological [,maikrəu,baiə'lɒdʒikl] adj. 微生物的

necrosis [ne'krəusis] n. 坏疽

occlusal [ə'klu:səl] adj. 咬合面的

plasticity [plæ'stisəti] n. 可塑性

resin ['rezin] n. 树脂

saliva [sə'laivə] n. 唾液

sealers ['si:ləz] n. 封闭剂

主要短语

buffering capacity　缓冲能力

bitewing radiograph　咬合片

cotton wool rolls　棉棒

dental caries　龋病

fermentable carbohydrases　发酵酶

flow rate　流动速率

glass ionomers　玻璃离子

periapical tissue　根尖周组织

pulpal odontoblasts　牙髓成牙本质细胞

silver-amalgam　银汞合金

streptococcus mutans　变形链球菌

zinc phosphate　磷酸锌

zinc oxide-eugenol　氧化锌酚剂

王晓飞

89 Recurrent Aphthous Ulcer
复发性阿弗他溃疡

What is recurrent aphthous ulcer?

Recurrent aphthous ulcer (RAU), we also call it recurrent oral ulceration (ROU) or recurrent aphthous stomatitis (RAS) in clinician, is painful lesions that occur within the oral cavity, and one of the most common oral mucosa diseases seen among patients. Its' case rate is 20% or so. Because burning pain, which can be caused on eating, swallowing and speaking, is one of the obvious symptoms of recurrent aphthous ulcer. So the scientist name it use the term "aphthous", derived from a Greek word "aphtha", which means burning pain in Greek.

RAU presents as recurrent, multiple, small, round, or ovoid ulcers, with circumsc-ribedmargins, having yellow or gray floors and are surrounded by erythematous haloes. Periodicity, relapse and self-limitation are three characters of recurrent aphthous ulcer. Epidemiological research show that, RAU is inclined to afflict women more than men and people less than 40 years and present first in childhood or adolescence.

What causes recurrent aphthous ulcer?

The Predisposing factors of RAU are very complex, it may be multifactors. The genetic factors, immune system reactions, physical trauma, stress, microbiologic, nutritional and other factors have been presented by now. Individual difference is very evident. The etiopathogenesis of this disease is yet unclear. So still have no uniform point of view about the pathogeny of RAU.

Genetics

A genetic predisposition for the development of aphthous ulcer is strongly suggested as about 40% of patients have a family history and these individuals develop ulcers earlier and are of more severe nature. Various associations with HLA antigens and RAS have been reported. These associations vary with specific racial and ethnic origins.

Trauma

Trauma to the oral mucosa due to abnormal biting, sharp tooth, dental treatments, local anesthetic injections and tooth brush injury may predispose to the development of recurrent aphthous ulceration. mechanical injury may aid in identifying and studying patients prone to RAU.

Immune factors

The pathogenesis of RAU involves a predominantly cell-mediated immune response in which tumor necrosis factor, or TNF, play a major role. The immunopathogenesis probably includes cell-mediated responses, involving T cells and TNF-production by these and other leukocytes. Other cytokines such as interleukin, or IL-2, IL-10, and natural killer, or NK, cells activated by IL-2 play a important role in RAU. Other studies show that abnormal humoral immunity response and abnormal autoimmunity response may be also associated with RAU.

Tobacco

Several studies reveal negative association between cigarette smoking, smokeless tobacco and RAU. Possible explanations given include increased mucosal keratinization; which serves as a mechanical and protective barrier against trauma and microbes. Nicotine is considered to be the protective factor as it stimulates the production of adrenal steroids by its action on the hypothalamic adrenal axis and reduces production of tumor necrosis factor alpha (TNF-α) and interleukins 1 and 6 (IL-1 andIL-6). Nicotine replacement therapy has been suggested as treatment for patients who develop RAU on cessation of smoking.

Drugs

Certain drugs have been associated with development of RAU, these include angiotensin converting enzyme inhibitor captopril, gold salts, nicorandil, phenindione, phenobarbital, and sodium hypochloride. NSAIDS such as propionic acid, diclofenac, and piroxicam may also cause oral ulceration similar to RAU.

Hematinic deficiency.

Deficiencies of iron, vitamin B12, and folic acid predispose development of RAU. Deficiencies of these hematinics are twice more common in these individuals than controls. Contrary findings in various studies relating the association of hematinic deficiency and RAU have been explained as due to varying genetic backgrounds and dietary habits of the study population.

Stress

Stress has been emphasized as a causative factor in RAU. It has been proposed that stress may induce trauma to oral soft tissues by parafunctional habits such as lip or cheek biting and this trauma may predispose to ulceration. A more recent study shows lack of direct correlation between levels of stress and severity of RAU episodes and suggests that psychological stress may act as a triggering or modifying factor rather than etiological factor in susceptible RAU patients.

Hormonal changes

Conflicting reports exist regarding association of hormonal changes in women and RAU. Studies state association of oral ulceration with onset of menstruation or in the luteal phase of the menstrual cycle. Mc Cartan et al. established no association between RAU and premenstrual period, pregnancy, or menopause in 1992.

Sodium lauryl sulfate - containing toothpast

An increased frequency in the occurrence of RAU has been reported on using sodium lauryl sulfate (SLS)-containing tooth paste with some reduction in ulceration on use of SLS-free tooth paste. However, because of the widespread use of SLS-containing dentifrice, it has been proposed that this may not truly predispose to RAU.

Gluten sensitive enteropathy/celiac disease, inflammatory bowel disease

Gluten sensitive enteropathy (GSE) is an autoimmune inflammatory disease of small intestine that is precipitated by the ingestion of gluten, a wheat protein in susceptible individuals. It is characterized by severe malnutrition, anemia, abdominal pain, diarrhea, aphthous oral ulcers, glossitis, and stomatitis. RAU may be the sole manifestation of the disease. The use of gluten-free diet in the improvement of RAU is considered uncertain. It has been suggested that evaluation for celiac disease may be appropriate for RAU patients. Inflammatory bowel diseases such as Crohn's disease and ulcerative colitis may present with aphthous-like ulceration.

Oral streptococci

Oral streptococci have been considered as microbial agents in the pathogenesis of RAS. They have been implicated as microorganisms directly involved in the pathogenesis of these lesions or as agents which serve as antigenic stimuli, which in turn provoke antibody production that cross-react with oral mucosa. It has been suggested that L form of α-hemolytic streptococci, Streptococcus sanguis, later identified as Streptococcus mitis was the causative agent of this disease.

What are symptoms of recurrent aphthous ulcer?

RAU is characterized by recurrent bouts of solitary or multiple shallow painful ulcers, at intervals of few months to few days in patients. RAU has been described under three different clinical variants as classified by Stanley in 1972.

- **Minor Aphthous Ulcer (MiAU).** MiAU is the most common variant, constituting 80% of RAU. The ulcers are small and scarce in number1 to 5 everytime. Every ulcer is isolated, round or oval, clearly defined. Ulcers vary from 2 to 4 mm millimetres in size. It is most commonly seen in the nonkeratinized mucosal surfaces like labial mucosa, buccal mucosa, and floor of the mouth. When

MiAU in active stage, red, yellow, sunken and pain are four characters of it. The center of it is sunken, its' basement is soft. A 1mm wide red hematodes circle around them. Accidental membranae cover the surface of every ulcer. Burning pain is obvious, and disturbs the speaking, biting and mood of patients. Ulcers heal within 10–14 days without scarring.

- **Major aphthous ulcer (MjAU).** MjAU is also known as periadenitis mucosa necrotica recurrens or Sutton's disease. It affects about 10% –15% of patients. Appearing after puberty, the prodrome is more intense and the ulcers are deeper, exceed 1 cm in diameter, and longer lasting (weeks to months) than minor aphthous ulcer. Most common sites of involvement are lips, soft palate, and throat. Fever, dysphagia, malaise, and scarring may occur.

- **Herpetiform ulcer (HU).** Herpetiform ulceration is characterized by recurrent crops of multiple ulcers. It accounts for 5% of cases. may be up to 100 in number. These are small in size, measure 2–3 mm in diameter. Lesions may coalesce to form large irregular ulcers. These ulcers last for about 10 –14 days. Unlike herpetic ulcers, these are not preceded by vesicles and do not contain viral infected cells. These are more common in women and have a later age of onset than other clinical variants of RAU.

How is recurrent aphthous ulcer diagnosed?

The diagnosis must be based on the periodicity, relapse and self-limitation history, symptoms and careful clinical examination. Possible systemic association with RAU must be ruled out, especially in cases where there is sudden development of ulceration in adulthood. Large, deep and long history ulcer, we should make a biopsy to nail down it's RAU or oral cancer.

How is recurrent aphthous ulcer treated?

There is no enough evidence about the etiopathogenesis of RAU by now, so all treatment can only attempt to restrain symptoms. Aims of treatment are easing the pain when ulcers happen, and to help them to heal as soon as possible. Any treatment can't prevent RAU from recurring. Treatment is symptomatic, the goal being to decrease symptoms, reduce ulcer number and size, and increase disease-free periods. The best treatment is that which will control ulcers for the longest period with minimal adverse side effects. The treatment method should be determined by disease severity, the medical history of patient, the frequency of flare-ups and the patient's ability to tolerate the medication. In all predisposing factors and treat any such factors, where possible, before introducing more specific therapy.

Topical Treatment

In patients with poor oral hygiene, professional help from a dental hygienist should be considered once ulcers heal.

A number of different treatments exist for aphthous ulcers including:anesthetics agents, antiseptics, anti-inflammatory agents, steroids.

Topical steroids, when used for a short period, have a very safe profile and should be the first line of treatment for recurrent oral stomatitis. In addition, oral medicine specialists may administer intralesional injections of a corticosteroid such as betamethasone, dexamethasone or triamcinolone to enhance or boost the local reponce, thus allowing for shorter systemic treatment.

Topical application of 5% amlexanox oral paste has been also shown to increase the healing rate and provide greater pain relief.

Those that exist showed that chlorhexidine gluconate mouthwashes and topical corticosteroids both can reduce the severity and duration of RAU.

Systemic Treatment

Patients with systemic diseases and nutritional deficiencies should be referred to appreciate health-care specialists.

In the majority of patients, symptomatic relief of RAU can be achieved with topical corticosteroids alone, with other immunomodulatory topical agents or by combination therapy. For those patients who present with major and herpetiform RAU, local and /or systemic corticosteroids, antibiotics, antiviral, and oral suspensions of tetracycline or nystatin have been recommended. In patients with recalcitrant RAU, a short course fo systemic corticosteroid therapy may be required, never exceeding more than 50mg per day for five days. This course of treatment is best left to a physician or oral medicine specialist. If corticosteroids are used, patients should be monitored for yeast superinfection.

Its pathogenesis remains unknown, and there are no diagnostic tests available. Diagnosis, therefore, is made on clinical ground alone. several factors-such as trauma, diet and stress are known to trigger the disease. The most important role of the HCP is to identify underlying precipitating factors and try to eliminate them. Furthermore, it is essential to educate the patient regarding the nature of this condition, especially the fact that RAU is not a contagious condition, as often is thought, and that it is not caused by the herpes simplex virus.

Given its painful presentation and inflammatory nature. RAU responds quite well to the use of topical or systemic anti-inflammatory drugs, particularly corticosteroids. Since the advent of high-potency topical steroids, most patients with RAU can be managed this way. However, early intervention is the key.

中英文注释

关键词汇

amlexanox ['æmliksənɒks] n. 氨氯地平

anesthetic [ˌænəsˈθetik] adj. 麻醉的，麻木的

angiotensin [ˌændʒiɑʊˈtensən] n. 血管紧缩素

antiseptic [ˌæntɪˈseptik] n. 杀菌剂，消毒剂

autoimmunity [ɔːtəˈʊimjuːniti] n. 自体免疫

betamethasone ['beitəˈmeθəˌsəʊn] n. 倍他米松

captopril [kæpˈtɒpril] n. 甲巯丙脯酸

celiac ['siːliˌæk] adj. 腹部的，腹腔的

chlorhexidine [klɔːˈheksidain] n. 洗必太，双氯苯双胍己烷

contagious [kənˈteidʒəs] adj. 有传染性的；传染病的

cytokine [ˌsitəˈkin] n. 细胞因子，细胞素

dexamethasone [deksəˈmeθəzəʊn] n. 地塞米松

diarrhea [ˌdaiəˈriə] n. 痢疾

diclofenac [diklɒfeˈnæk] n. 双氯芬酸

dysphagia [disˈfeidʒiə] n. 吞咽困难

epidemiological [ˌepiˌdiːmiəˈlɒdʒikl] adj. 流行病学的

erythematous [ˌeriˈθiːmətəs] adj. 红斑的

etiopathogenesis [iːtiəpæθəˈdʒenisis] n. 发病原理，诱病因素

fematinic [ˌheməˈtinik] n. 补血药

glossitis [glɒˈsaitis] n. 舌炎

gluconate ['gluːkəʊneit] n. 葡（萄）糖酸盐

hemolytic [hiːˈmɒlitik] adj. 溶血的

herpetic [hɜːˈpetik] adj. 疱疹的

herpetiform [hɜːˈpetifɔːm] adj. 疱疹样的

hormonal [hɔːˈməʊnl] adj. 激素的，荷尔蒙的，生理的

hygiene ['haidʒiːn] n. 卫生

hypothalamic [haipəʊθəˈlæmik] adj. 下丘脑的

keratinization [kerətinaiˈzeiʃən] n. 角质化

menstruation [ˌmenstruˈeiʃn] n. 月经，行经，月经期间

mitis ['miːtis] n. 可锻铁

necrosis [neˈkrəʊsis] n. 坏疽

nicorandil [niˈkɔːrændil] n. 尼可地尔（药名）

nystatin ['nistətin] n. 制霉菌素

pathogeny [pəˈθɒdʒini] n. 发病机理

periadenitis [piəraiæ'denaitis] n. 腺周炎

phenindione [fi'nindaiəʊn] n. 苯茚满二酮

phenobarbital [ˌfiːnə'bɑːbitæl] n. 镇静安眠剂，苯巴比妥

piroxicam [paiərɒksi'kæm] n. 吡罗昔康

predisposition [ˌpriːdispə'ziʃn] n. 易感体质

prodrome ['prəʊdrəʊm] n. 前驱症状

relapse [ri'læps] n. 复发

sanguis ['sæŋgwis] n. 血液

scarring [skɑːriŋ] n. 瘢痕

streptococci [ˌstreptə'kɒkai] n. 链球菌（streptococcus 的名词复数）

superinfection [sjuːpərin'fekʃən] n. 重复感染，双重感染

triamcinolone [ˌtraiəm'sinələʊn] n. 氟羟泼尼松龙

vesicle ['vesikl] n. 泡，小泡；痘；水疱

主要短语

accidental membranae 伪膜

adrenal steroid 肾上腺素类固醇

adverse side effect 不良副作用

cell-mediated immune 细胞免疫

etiological factor 病因

folic acid 叶酸

gluten sensitive enteropathy 麸胶敏感性肠病

gold salt 氯金酸钠

herpes simplex virus 单纯疱疹病毒

humoral immunity 体液免疫

individual difference 个体差异

inflammatory bowel disease 肠炎

luteal phase 黄体期

menstrual cycle 月经周期

modifying factor 修饰因子

predisposing factor 发病因素

propionic acid 丙酸

recurrent aphthous stomatitis (RAS) 复发性阿弗他性口腔炎

recurrent aphthous ulcer (RAU) 复发性阿弗他性溃疡

recurrent oral ulceration (ROU) 复发性口腔溃疡

self-limitation 自限性

small intestine 小肠

sodium lauryl sulfate　十二烷硫酸钠
streptococcus mitis　轻型链球菌
ulcerative colitis　溃疡性结肠炎

王晓飞

90 — Recurrent Parotitis
复发性腮腺炎

What is recurrent parotitis?

Recurrent parotitis is defined as recurrent parotid inflammation, generally associated with non-obstructive sialectasis of the parotid gland. Also known as juvenile recurrent parotitis, this disease is characterised by recurring episodes of swelling and/or pain in the parotid gland, usually accompanied by fever and malaise. It usually affects children, but may persist into adulthood.

It is a rare condition, and its aetiology remains an enigma. Its natural history is variable, and in adults more aggressive intervention is often needed. In addition, there is no satisfactory explanation for its usual tendency to resolve spontaneously after puberty. All this has resulted in considerable uncertainty concerning its appropriate management.

What causes recurrent parotitis?

Its cause remains unknown despite several studies. Though the affected glands demonstrate sialectasis of the distal ducts, there seems to be no element of obstruction in most cases. Several theories of causation have been put forward over the years.

Traditionally, ascending infection from the oral cavity has been considered the primary event, with sialectasis being a secondary change. Some scientists proposed that the recurrent episodes of parotid swelling was the end result of a sequence of events:

- There is first a low grade inflammation of the gland and duct epithelium, possibly caused by a low salivary flow rate due to dehydration and debility.
- This results in distortion and stricturing of the distal ducts, and metaplasia of the duct epithelium.
- The metaplasia results in excessive mucus secretion.

These changes, along with possibly a further reduction in salivary flow rate, then predispose to recurrent parotid inflammations.

A reduced salivary flow rate may result from glandular damage caused by the primary infection. However, it may be a primary factor as well. Several workers showed low salivary flow rates, and the significant finding was that the flow rate was reduced in even the unaffected glands in patients. This suggests that those with low salivary flow rates might be predisposed to suffer from repeated ascending infections. This relation to salivary flow rates could also explain the familial tendency that has been reported.

The histological picture includes lymphocytic infiltration around the intralobular ducts, and Patey and Thakray proposed that this lymphocytic infiltration damages the duct wall reticulum, allowing extravasation of secretions into the gland parenchyma, and thus exacerbating the inflammation.

The fragmentation of connective tissue supporting the intralobular ducts was also implicated in the production of the characteristic punctate sialectasis. The dye used for sialography ruptured the already weakened duct walls, producing the appearance of punctate sialectasis. This theory therefore neatly explained the presence of sialectasis in the absence of demonstrable distal obstruction.

The situation, however, is not as simple. Punctate sialectasis is seen in totally asymptomatic glands of affected individuals in up to 70% of cases. Further, detailed histopathological studies have confirmed the presence of duct dilatation and cystic cavities associated with a chronic inflammatory process. And more recently, ultrasonography consistently revealed hypoechoic areas that corresponded to the punctate sialectases demonstrated by sialography. It therefore would appear that the sialectases are actually present, and are not merely artefacts produced by the radio-opaque dye.

As long ago as 1945, Hamilton Bailey proposed the presence of a congenital abnormality of the ductal system, and drew a parallel with bronchiectasis. He pointed out that bronchiectasis could be congenital as well as acquired, and in both cases, the end result was secondary infection of the bronchioles and alveoli. He has been subsequently supported by others.

According to this argument, punctate dilatation of the small distal ducts results in stasis and ascending infection, giving rise to the recurrent acute attacks. Though no evidence has so far emerged in favour of a congenital abnormality, it is still possible that genetic factors may prove important.

Given this state of incomplete knowledge, he present consensus is towards a multifactorial approach. Thus Kono and Ito concluded hat the sialectasis is both the cause and the result of recurrent parotitis. Their histological studies detected dilated cavities consistent with true sialectasis, as well as a few areas of extravasated dye which mimicked sialectasis on he sialogram. Similarly, a detailed study of clinical, radiological, immunological, bacteriological, and histological findings in 20 affected children concluded that the cause was probably a combination of a congenital malformation of portions of the salivary ducts and infections ascending from the mouth after dehydration of the affected children.

However, it must also be acknowledged that juvenile recurrent parotitis can occasionally occur without sialectasis.

One child has suffered repeated attacks of parotitis secondary to repeated chewing of the Stenson's duct orifice.

Many associations have been proposed in the past; these include immunodeficiency, allergy, upper respiratory infections, mumps, etc. None of these, however, has been conclusively shown to have any bearing on this disease. Many other scientists proposed an autoimmune origin, but the self limiting nature of recurrent parotitis and the absence of detectable autoantibodies makes this unlikely. There have been reports of sensitivity to upper respiratory tract infections; these infections may set off attacks of sialadenitis merely by causing dehydration in a child with sialectasis.

The higher rate of secretion in the submandibular gland compared with the parotid gland may protect it from infections. Also, the submandibular gland secretion is relatively richer in mucus, which has antiseptic properties. In fact, no report was found in the literature implicating the submandibular gland.

What are symptoms of recurrent parotitis?

Recurrent parotitis presents as a recurrent painful swelling during mastication and/or swallowing. The disease usually starts in a child between 3 and 6 years of age, but earlier and later occurrence has been observed. Some scientists followed up 20 children and the age of onset in their series ranged from 3 months to 16 years.

Most studies report a sex distribution favouring males. Seventy two percent of patients were male in the series of 25 patients. However, few doctors found from a study of 68 patients, of whom 26 were children, that the sex distribution was equal in childhood, and actually affected females more than males (7.5:1) in patients where the onset of symptoms was after the age of 16 years.

The symptoms are usually unilateral; when bilateral, the symptoms are more prominent on one side. In a series of 25 patients, symptoms were unilateral in 18 patients and bilateral in seven patients (28%).

The number of attacks vary individually, with attacks every three to four months being the commonest pattern. Attacks tend to occur one to five times a year. The frequency rate peaks during the first year at school, but otherwise remains fairly constant for each individual until puberty. After puberty, the symptoms usually subside, and may disappear completely. Two possible ways by which this spontaneous recovery might occur: total atrophy with consequent lack of symptoms, or regeneration of the gland from surviving ductal system. However, there are also persistent cases. The actual proportion of 'persisters' is debatable, though most researchers agree that the numbers are small.

The painful swelling is usually associated with fever. There is typically an absence of pus despite the pyrexia and malaise, though doctors noticed a few drops of mucopurulent secretion on palpating the parotid gland. The swelling lasts from several days to two weeks, and resolves spontaneously, independent of any treatment.

How is recurrent parotitis diagnosed?

We can draw the diagnosis according to the age, it usually affects children and may persist into adulthood. And also can accord to the characteristic history and symptoms that recurring episodes of swelling and/or pain in the parotid gland, usually accompanied by fever and malaise, and careful clinical examination. The results of more aggressive accessory examination are also useful too.

Sialography

The mainstay of diagnosis is sialography, though its role is now becoming secondary to ultrasonography. In 1971, Hemenway classified sialectasis into (a) large duct sialectasis, due to obstruction of the main duct, and (b) small duct/punctate/terminal sialectasis, in which there are multiple small round opacities at the termination of the smaller ducts. Later, Gates and Noyek et al reviewed the classification of punctate sialectasis, and further classified this into (a) pruned tree appearance—in the early stages, the ducts are stretched, tapered, and decreased in number; (b) punctate sialectasis— the peripheral ducts demonstrate punctate dilatation <1 mm diameter, and the intraglandular ductal system is stretched and tapered; (c) globular sialectasis—the ducts are between 1 mm and 2 mm in size and they may be partially non-visualised or irregular, giving rise to a 'mulberry pattern' fruit laden tree appearance; (d) cavitatory sialectasis—coalescence of cystic lesions produces a cavitatory appearance; (e) destructive sialectasis—there is a bizarre pattern of pooling, possibly with stones in the gland. The typical changes in recurrent parotitis are punctate and globular sialectasis, which are scattered throughout the gland; cavitatory and destructive sialectasis are not seen.

These changes are usually bilateral even if the presentation is unilateral. Some clinically symptomless glands are demonstrated sialectasis. The lesions were however smaller and fewer in the symptom-free glands. On the other hand, sialographic changes are not always bilateral, as had been previously believed. These changes tend to diminish and sometimes disappear after the disease becomes quiescent.

In glands with sialectasis, peripheral intraglandular ducts are invisible, indicating that the changes affect the peripheral parts of the ductal tree. The main ducts may be affected as well. However, the presence of main duct dilatation did not influence the clinical course of these patients, as had previously been proposed. Other findings on sialography include acinar and ductal atrophy, with impaired glandular function.

Digital Subtraction Sialography

This has been recommended as superior to conventional sialography for the recognition of inflammatory changes and chronic sialolithiasis.

Ultrasonography

Ultrasonography consistently revealed hypoechoic areas that corresponded to the punctate sialectases demonstrated by sialography. Ultrasonography as the primary investigation for diagnosis, in addition to follow up. Ultrasonography less sensitive than the digital subtraction sialography and ultrasonography, It is possible that improvements in radiological skills and equipment may have now rendered ultrasonography as reliable as sialography.

Duct dilatation having been already revealed by ultrasonography, the role of sialography would be to rule out duct stenosis or obstruction. If, on the other hand, ultrasound reveals a solid mass, computed tomography or magnetic resonance imaging is indicated. If the ultrasonography reveals no abnormality, sialography is performed only if symptoms recur.

Cytology

Salivary smears of normal children are acellular. In contrast, saliva in the presence of sialectasis revealed large amounts of granulocytes, some lymphocytes, and in about 50% of cases, bacteria. The bacteria were mixed, and included aerobic and anaerobic cocci.

Histology

Dilated interlobular ducts with lymphocyte infiltration in the surrounding tissues is seen; the lymphocytes tend to form lymphoid follicles. The duct epithelium shows hyperplasia and metaplasia, with a pseudostratified cylindric pattern being common.

How is recurrent parotitis treated?

Uncertainty about its aetiology has hampered the development of a universally accepted treatment strategy for this condition. The problem is compounded by the rarity of this disease and its uncertain natural history.

Treatment of the acute episode aims to deliver relief of symptoms and to prevent damage to the gland parenchyma. Analgesics and antibiotics have been found to be rapidly effective in relieving the pain and swelling. Penicillin is considered adequate, as the infecting agent is not usually a staphylococcus. Most workers agree in practice, but many question whether antibiotics really change the natural course of the disease, and wonder if resolution of symptoms could merely reflect the natural progression of this disease. In addition to antibiotics and analgesics, other treatments include sialagogic agents to increase salivary flow, warmth and massage, and duct probing. The treatment seems to be effective, however, and may help by clearing the plugs of mucus and cells that form in the acute phase. Steroids may reduce swelling, but will not prevent recurrences.

Prevention of recurrences is difficult, but preventing dehydration and prescribing a prophylactic course of penicillin during winter may help.

The treatment of repeated attacks is more difficult, and several different methods have been tried.

Radiotherapy

This was used for several years, despite it being considered useless by several researchers more than 30 years ago. In fact, the literature contains virtually no evidence in favour of this method of treatment, and yet radiotherapy was being used as the sole treatment at several centres. Its popularity probably rested on its perceived efficacy in reducing the mortality from acute bacterial parotitis.

Ductligation

This has been used successfully by many doctors, recommend it as a simple and effective treatment, though at least one study had described varying results.

Parotidectomy

Parotidectomy has always been the gold standard for obtaining permanent relief. With this operation, however, one is faced with the risk of facial nerve injury; this is especially relevant in recurrent parotitis, where repeated infections result in fibrosis of the gland.

Tympanic Neurectomy

This procedure has recently been recommended as an effective procedure, with good results in 70% cases. Its aim is to destroy secretomotor fibres to the parotid gland thus abolishing/reducing its secretion. The authors recommend extensive interruption of the secretomotor fibres by thoroughly drilling into the hypotympanum and below the basal turn of the cochlea. Nerve regeneration and incomplete sectioning are probably responsible for the early and late failures; it is therefore necessary that the procedure is performed by an experienced otologist.

Other Methods

Various other treatment options have been studied. Intraductal tetracycline instillation as an effective, low risk treatment. They hypothesised that tetracycline produced acinar atrophy.

Some studies found that performing a sialographic study itself resulted in significant improvement of symptoms. The hypothesis was that improvement resulted as a result of the flushing, dilating, and antiseptic actions of the iodine containing dye.

Finally, the fact that many patients seem to recover spontaneously has led researchers to support a conservative approach. About 56% adults and 64% children recovered with only symptomatic treatment, over a five year period. Symptoms may be disappeared by the age of 22 in 23 of 25 patients. A conservative approach therefore is recommended for children, with more aggressive treatment being reserved for the 40% adults and 4% of children whose symptoms persist or worsen.

中英文注释

关键词汇

alveoli [ˌælvi'əʊliː] n. 肺泡

analgesic [ˌænəl'dʒiːzik] n. 止痛剂

atrophy ['ætrəfi] n. 萎缩

artefact ['ɑːtifækt] n. 假象，人为

bacteriological [bæk,tiəriə'lɒdʒikl] adj. 细菌学的

bronchiectasis [brɑŋki'ektəsis] n. 支气管扩张

cochlea ['kɒkliə] n. 耳蜗

debility [di'biləti] n. 衰弱，功能低下

dehydration [ˌdiːhai'dreiʃn] n. 干燥，脱水

episodes ['episəʊdz] n. 发病期

epithelium [ˌepi'θiːliəm] n. 上皮

exacerbate [ig'zæsəbeit] vt. 加剧，恶化

fragmentation [ˌfrægmen'teiʃn] n. 分裂，破碎

follicles ['fɔlikəlz] n. 小囊滤泡

granulocytes [g'rænjʊləsaits] n. 颗粒性白细胞

histopathologica [ˌhistəʊpæθə'lɒdʒikəl] n. 组织病理学

hypoechoic [hai'pəʊkɔik] n. (超声) 低回声的

hypotympanum ['haipəʊtimpənəm] n. 鼓室下部

infiltration [ˌinfil'treiʃn] n. 渗透

juvenile ['dʒuːvənail] n. 青少年

malaise [mə'leiz] n. 不舒服

metaplasia [ˌmetə'pleiʒə] n. 化生，组织变形

mucopurulent [mjuːkəʊ'pjʊərʊlənt] n. 黏液性及脓性

mumps [mʌmps] n. 腮腺炎

non-obstructive ['nɒnəbstr'ʌktiv] adj. 非梗阻性的

onset ['ɒnset] n. 发作

otologist [əʊ'tɒlədʒist] n. 耳科医生

palpate [pæl'peit] vt. 触诊

parenchyma [pə'reŋkimə] n. 软组织，实质

parotid [pə'rɒtid] n. 腮腺

parotitis [ˌpærə'taitis] n. 腮腺炎

pseudostratified [sʲuː'dəʊst'rætifaid] adj. 假复层的

puberty ['pjuːbəti] n. 青春期

pyrexia [pai'reksiə] n. 发热

secretomotor [si'kriːtəʊ'məʊtə] adj. 促进分泌的

sialagogic [ˌsaiələ'gɔdʒik] adj. 催涎的

sialectasis [saiə'lektəsis] n. 涎管扩张

sialogram [sʲəlɒg'ræm] n. 涎管 X 线造影片

sialography [saiə'lɒgrəfi] n. 涎管造影术

sialolithiasis [saiæləli'θaiəsis] n. 涎石病

staphylococcus [ˌstæfilə'kɒkəs] n. 葡萄球菌

stricture ['striktʃə(r)] n. 狭窄，紧束

tetracycline [ˌtetrə'saiklin] n. 四环素

主要短语

antiseptic properties 防腐消毒性能

congenital abnormality 先天性异常

congenital malformation 先天畸形

cystic cavity 囊腔

distal ducts 末梢导管

duct dilatation 导管扩张

familial tendency 家族遗传倾向

gland parenchyma 腺实质

histological picture 组织切片

intralobular ducts 小叶间导管

mucus secretion 黏液分泌

punctate sialectasis 点状腺管扩张

recurrent parotitis 慢性腮腺炎

salivary smears 唾液涂片检查

self limiting nature 自限性

spontaneous recovery 自愈

submandibular gland 下颌下腺

王晓飞

Section Eight: Skin Disease

第八部分　皮　肤　疾　病

91

Acne
痤　疮

What is acne?

Acne at its most basic is a disorder of the pilosebaceous unit, or what is commonly called the hair follicle or pore. According to the American Academy of Dermatology, it is the most common skin disorder in the United States. Acne vulgaris, as common acne is known, is classified as a chronic inflammatory disease of the skin.

Acne is characterized by the presence of pimples or "zits", blackheads, and whiteheads. It chiefly affects the face, neck, chest, back, and/or upper arms of sufferers. Rarely you will find acne in other areas of the body. Acne varies in development from very mild to extremely severe.

What causes acne?

Acne appears when a pore in our skin clogs. This clog begins with dead skin cells. Normally, dead skin cells rise to surface of the pore, and the body sheds the cells. When the body starts to make lots of sebum, oil that keeps our skin from drying out, the dead skin cells can stick together inside the pore. Instead of rising to the surface, the cells become trapped inside the pore.

Sometimes bacteria that live on our skin, p. acnes, also get inside the clogged pore. Inside the pore, the bacteria have a perfect environment for multiplying very quickly. With loads of bacteria inside, the pore becomes inflamed (red and swollen). If the inflammation goes deep into the skin, an acne cyst or nodule appears.

Acne often first appears during puberty, when there is a surge of androgen hormones within the body. Androgens stimulate the sebaceous glands, creating an oilier complexion and one more prone to breakouts.

Most dermatologists agree androgen hormones significantly influence acne development. In addition to puberty, women may see considerable hormonal fluctuations are during menstruation, pregnancy, menopause and perimenopause. During these life phases, acne is most likely to develop or flare up.

Other factors that contribute to acne development include oily cosmetics, comedogenic skin care or hair care products, certain drugs such as steroids and estrogen medications. Acne tends to run in families. If your parents had acne at any point in their lives, your chance of developing acne is higher.

What are signs and symptoms of acne?

Acne signs

Many people think that acne is just pimples. But a person who has acne can have any of these blemishes:

- Blackheads.
- Whiteheads.
- Papules.
- Pustules (what many people call pimples).
- Cysts.
- Nodules.

Acne appears on the face in all of the kinds above, but it can appear on other areas of the body. Acne can appear on the back, chest, neck, shoulders, upper arms and buttocks.

Acne symptoms

Acne can cause more than blemishes. Studies show that people who have acne can have:

- Low self-esteem: Many people who have acne say that their acne makes them feel bad about themselves. Because of their acne, they do not want to be with friends. They miss school and work. Grades can slide, and absenteeism can become a problem because of their acne.
- Depression: Many people who have acne suffer from more than low self-esteem. Acne can lead to a medical condition called depression. The depression can be so bad that people think about what it would be like to commit suicide. Many studies have found that teens who believe that they have "bad" acne were likely to think about committing suicide.
- Dark spots on the skin: These spots appear when the acne heals. It can take months or years for dark spots to disappear.
- Scars (permanent): People who get acne cysts and nodules often see scars when the acne clears. You can prevent these scars. Be sure to see a dermatologist for treatment if you get acne early — between 8 and 12 years old. If someone in your family had acne cysts and nodules, you also should see a dermatologist if you get acne. Treating acne before cysts and nodules appear can prevent scars.

Who gets acne?

If you have a bad case of acne, you may feel that you are the only one. But many people have acne. It is the most common skin problem in the United States. About 40 to 50 million Americans have acne at any one time.

Most people who have acne are teenagers or young adults, but acne can occur at any age. Newborn babies can get acne. Men and women get acne. Some women get acne when they reach middle age.

How does acne develop?

Acne occurs when oil and dead skin cells become trapped within the hair follicle, creating a plug within the pore. This plug of dead cells and oil is called a comedo. Blackheads and whiteheads are examples of non-inflamed comedoes.

As the breakout progresses and bacteria invade, the follicle wall may rupture within the dermis, creating inflammation and redness. Inflamed blemishes vary in severity depending on the damage to the follicle wall and the amount of infection present. Severe cases of acne may lead to deeper lesions and cysts.

Most people with acne have a number of non-inflamed lesions, or comedones. However, not every acne sufferer necessarily suffers from inflamed breakouts.

How do dermatologists diagnose acne?

To diagnose acne, a dermatologist will first examine your skin to make sure you have acne. Other skin conditions can look like acne. If you have acne, the dermatologist will:
- Grade the acne. Grade 1 is mild acne. Grade 4 is severe acne.
- Note what type, or types, of acne appear on your skin.

How do dermatologists treat acne?

Today, there are many effective acne treatments. This does not mean that every acne treatment works for everyone who has acne. But it does mean that virtually every case of acne can be controlled.

People who have mild acne have a few blemishes. They may have whiteheads, blackheads, papules, and/or pustules (aka pimples). Many people can treat mild acne with products that you can buy without a prescription. A product containing benzoyl peroxide or salicylic acid often clears the skin. This does not mean that the acne will clear overnight.

Despite the claims, acne treatment does not work overnight. At-home treatment requires 4-8 weeks to see improvement. Once acne clears, you must continue to treat the skin to prevent breakouts.

If you have a lot of acne, cysts, or nodules, a medicine that you can buy without a prescription may not work. If you want to see clearer skin, you should see a dermatologist. Dermatologists offer the following types of treatment:

Acne treatment that you apply to the skin: Most acne treatments are applied to the skin. The dermatologist may call this topical treatment. There are many topical acne treatments. Some topicals help kill the bacteria. Others work on reducing the oil. The topical medicine may contain a retinoid, prescription-strength benzoyl peroxide, antibiotic, or even salicylic acid. The dermatologist will determine what the patient need.

Acne treatment that works throughout the body: Medicine that works throughout the body may be necessary when you have red, swollen types of acne. This type of treatment is usually necessary to treat acne cysts and nodules. The dermatologist may prescribe one or more of these:

- Antibiotics (helps to kill bacteria and reduce inflammation).
- Birth control pills and other medicine that works on hormones (can be helpful for women).
- Isotretinoin (the only treatment that works on all that causes acne).

Procedures that treat acne: the dermatologist may treat the acne with a procedure that can be performed during an office visit. These treatments include:

- Lasers and other light therapies: These devices reduce the p. acnes bacteria. Your dermatologist can determine whether this type of treatment can be helpful.
- Chemical peels: The patient cannot buy the chemical peels that dermatologists use. Dermatologists use chemical peels to treat 2 types of acne — blackheads and papules.
- Acne removal: The dermatologist may perform a procedure called "drainage and extraction" to remove a large acne cyst. This procedure helps when the cyst does not respond to medicine. It also helps ease the pain and the chance that the cyst will leave a scar. If you absolutely have to get rid of a cyst quickly, the dermatologist may inject the cyst with medicine.

Outcome

Waiting for acne to clear on its own can be frustrating. Without treatment, acne can cause permanent scars, low self-esteem, depression, and anxiety.

To avoid these possible outcomes, dermatologists recommend that people treat acne. When the skin clears, treatment should continue. Treatment prevents new breakouts. The dermatologist can tell the patient when he no longer need to treat acne to prevent breakouts.

中英文注释

关键词汇

blemish ['blemiʃ] n. 污点，缺点，瑕疵

comedo ['kɒmidəʊ; kə'mi:dəʊ] n. 粉刺

cyst [sist] n. 囊肿

dermis ['dɜ:mis] n. 真皮

estrogen ['estrədʒən] n. 雌激素

menopause ['menəpɔ:z] n. 绝经（期）

menstruation [menstru'eiʃ(ə)n] n. 月经期

nodule ['nɒdju:l] n. 结节

perimenopause [,peri'menəupɔ:z] n. 围绝经期

pilosebaceous [pailəusi'beiʃəs] adj. 毛囊皮脂的

pimple ['pimp(ə)l] n. 丘疹

plug [plʌg] n. 栓子

pore [pɔ:] n. 毛孔

puberty ['pju:bəti] n. 青春期

pustule ['pʌstju:l] n. 脓疱

retinoid ['retinɒid] n. 维甲酸

sebum ['si:bəm] n. 皮脂

zit [zit] n. 青春痘

主要短语

acne vulgaris 寻常痤疮

benzoyl peroxide 过氧化苯甲酰

birth control pill 避孕药丸

comedogenic skin 易生黑头粉刺的皮肤

follicle wall 毛囊壁

hair follicle 毛囊

non-inflamed comedone 非炎症性的粉刺

oily cosmetic 油性化妆品

p. acne 痤疮丙酸杆菌

salicylic acid 水杨酸

sebaceous gland 皮脂腺

skin clog 皮肤阻塞

刘宏业

92

Herpes Zoster
带 状 疱 疹

What is herpes zoster?

The varicella-zoster virus (VZV) is a single virus that causes two diseases. The primary VZV infection, also known as chickenpox, typically occurs during childhood. However, VZV infection persists for the infected individual's lifetime, and viral latency subsequently develops along the spinal cord in dorsal root ganglia. Later in life, the virus reactivates—usually in a dermatomal distribution—causing the secondary infection known as herpes zoster, which is also called shingles.

Some illnesses and medical treatments can weaken a person's immune system and increase the risk. These include:
- Cancer.
- HIV/AIDS.
- Some cancer treatments, such as chemotherapy or radiation.
- Medicine taken to prevent rejection of a transplanted organ.
- Cortisone when taken for a long time.

How is varicella-zoster virus transmission?

The primary mode of VZV transmission is via airborne particles. Thus, a child can spread the infection by simply coughing or breathing. In a typical household, there is an 85% risk of transmission of chickenpox to a susceptible sibling. The infection is characterized by fever, malaise, and the typical diffuse rash. The average time from virus exposure to development of the rash is 14 to 15 days, though the time can be as short as 10 days or as long as 20 days. The child or young adult becomes infectious approximately 48 hours before the onset of vesicle eruption and may remain infectious for 4 to 5 days after vesicle eruption. Approximately 10% of patients older than 15 years are considered susceptible for primary VZV infection.

What are clinical manifestations of herpes zoster?

- The warning: An area of skin may burn, itch, tingle, or feel very sensitive. This usually occurs in a small area on 1 side of the body. These symptoms can come and go or be constant. Most people experience this for 1 to 3 days. It can last longer.

- Rash: A rash then appears in the same area.
- Blisters: The rash soon turns into groups of clear blisters. The blisters turn yellow or bloody before they crust over (scab) and heal. The blisters tend to last 2 to 3 weeks.
- Pain: It is uncommon to have blisters without pain. Often the pain is bad enough for a doctor to prescribe painkillers. Once the blisters heal, the pain tends to lessen. The pain can last for months after the blisters clear.
- Flu-like symptoms: The person may get a fever or headache with the rash.

As previously mentioned, herpes zoster is the consequence of the primary VZV infection reactivating after a period of dormancy in the dorsal root ganglia. Herpes zoster is characterized by a unilateral vesicular eruption in a dermatomal distribution, with thoracic and cranial and cervical distributions being the most common. Localized herpes zoster is contagious from the time of rash eruption until the time of lesion crusting. The rate of transmission of herpes zoster infection is lower than that of primary VZV infection. The rash may be accompanied by unbearable itching, altered sensitivity to touch, or allodynia (ie, pain at the site provoked by innocuous stimuli). Pain may also be felt before the rash develops. In some cases, patients experience the allodynia, pain, itching, and burning without a rash ever developing—a condition known as zoster sine herpete. Initially, the rash is erythematous and maculopapular, but it progresses to take the form of coalescing clusters of clear vesicles containing high concentrations of VZV. The rash typically lasts 7 to 10 days and fully heals within 2 to 4 weeks. However, permanent scarring and altered pigmentation occur in some cases. If the infection does not resolve after the acute phase, complications, such as postherpetic neuralgia (PHN), may develop.

What are complications of herpes zoster?

Postherpetic neuralgia is a common and potentially debilitating complication of herpes zoster that is difficult to manage. It is characterized by pain or dysesthesia that persists after resolution of the rash. Postherpetic neuralgia occurs in 10% to 18% of patients with herpes zoster, and the risk for development of this complication increases with advancing age. The severity of pain in PHN ranges from mild to excruciating, and it can be constant, intermittent, or triggered by such stimuli as clothes touching the skin. The pain associated with herpes zoster or PHN may last for a few minutes or occur as chronic pain. The duration of PHN has been found to be inconsistent, ranging from 30 days to 6 months or longer after rash onset. In some cases, the pain persists for years. Postherpetic neuralgia adversely affects the patient's quality of life as a result of its potential to interfere with sleep, work, and other activities of daily living, leading to social withdrawal and depression.

How is herpes zoster diagnosed?

A diagnosis of herpes zoster is often made based on the localization and morphologic characteristics of the rash. The varicella-zoster virus can be collected from lesions and identified using tissue culture, but this is a time-consuming process, and false-negative results may occur because viable virus is difficult to obtain from cutaneous lesions. Polymerase chain reaction (PCR) can be used to detect the DNA of VZV from collected lesion material. However, this technique is not widely available. PCR can be used to positively identify VZV DNA in patients' blood before symptoms manifest. Thus, PCR has potential application as a diagnostic tool for identifying patients who are in the prodromal phase of herpes zoster and patients who have zoster sine herpete, allowing these individuals to receive treatment before rash and nerve damage develop.

Direct fluorescent antibody staining of VZV-infected cells obtained by scraping the base of the lesion is a rapid and sensitive method for diagnosis of herpes zoster. This technique is useful for evaluation of atypical skin lesions to guide early treatment decisions.

How is it treated?

Without treatment, the rash clears in a few weeks. Dermatologists, however, strongly recommend treatment. Without it, many people get pain, numbness, itching, and tingling that can last for months — or years.

It is best to get treatment immediately. Treatment can include:

- Pain relievers to help ease the pain: The pain can be very bad, and prescription painkillers may be necessary.
- Anti-viral medicine: This medicine may be prescribed when a doctor diagnoses shingles within 72 hours of the rash first appearing. The earlier anti-viral treatment is started, the better it works. Anti-viral medicines include famciclovir, valacyclovir, and acyclovir. These can lessen the pain and the amount of time the pain lasts.
- Nerve blocks: Given for intense pain, these injections (shots) contain a numbing anesthetic and sometimes a corticosteroid.
- Corticosteroids: To lower swelling and pain, some patients may get corticosteroid

pills with their anti-viral medicine. This treatment is not common, because it can make the rash spread.

Treatments for pain after the rash clears: Certain anti-depressants, pain relievers, anesthetic creams and patches, and anti-seizure medicines can help.

中英文注释

关键词汇

acyclovir [ei'saikləviə(r)] n. 阿昔洛韦

allodynia [æl əu'diniə] n. 痛觉异常

anesthetic ['ænis'θetik] n. 麻醉剂

atypical [ei'tipikəl] adj. 不典型的

chickenpox ['tʃikin,pɔks] n. 水痘

lesion ['liːʒən] n. 皮损

malaise [mæ'leiz, -'lez] n. 不舒服

numbness ['nʌmnis] n. 麻木

rash [ræʃ] n. 皮疹

shingles ['ʃiŋglz] n. 带状疱疹

viable ['vaiəbəl] adj. 可行的, 能养活的, 能生育的

主要短语

direct fluorescent antibody staining 直接免疫荧光

dorsal root ganglia 背根神经节

false-negative 假阴性

nerve blocks 神经阻滞

polymerase chain reaction (PCR) 聚合酶链反应

postherpetic neuralgia (PHN) 带状疱疹后遗神经痛

prodromal phase 前驱期

the earlier……the better…… 越早越好

varicella-zoster virus (VZV) 水痘 - 带状疱疹病毒

zoster sine herpete 无疹型带状疱疹

刘宏业

93

Leucoderma

白 癜 风

What is leucoderma?

Leucoderma is also known as vitiligo. Leucoderma is the most common chronic depigmentation disorder or hypopigmentation disorder affecting 1-2% of the world population. It includes the loss of functioning melanocytes which causes the appearance of white patches on the skin. These white patches tend to become progressive with time. Any location on the body can be affected and the people with leucoderma have white patches in many areas of the body. The disorder affects all the races and both the sexes equally; however, it is more noticeable in people with dark skin.

Although leucoderma is usually not harmful medically and causes no physically pain, its emotional and psychological effects can be devastating. Infact, in India, those with the disease, especially women, are sometimes discriminated against in marriage. Developing leucoderma after marriage can be ground for divorce. Regardless of person's race and culture, white patches of leucoderma can affect emotional and psychological well-being and self-esteem. People with leucoderma can experience emotional stress, particularly if the condition develops on the visible areas of the body (such as face, hands, arms and feet) or on the genitals. Adolescents, who are particularly concerned about their appearance, can be devastated by widespread leucoderma. Some people who have leucoderma feel embarrassed, ashamed, depressed or worried about how others will react.

What types can leucoderma be divided into?

Leucoderma can be classified into two two types.

● **Bilateral (or Generalized)**

Bilateral or Generalized Leucoderma can begin at any age and tends to progress intermittently over the life of the patient. It produces depigmentation which is remarkably symmetrical in distribution. A patch on the right side of the body is matched by a patch in a similar location on the left side of the body. The entire body can depigment although it rarely does so.

- **Unilateral (or Segmental)**

Unilateral or Segmental Leucoderma commonly begins in childrens and young adults and progresses for a limited period, usually 1-2 years, and then remains static for the rest of the life of the individual. It affects just one side of the body contrast to Bilateral Leucoderma, the distribution is asymmetrical on the skin.

Who gets leucoderma?

Millions of people worldwide have leucoderma. Nearly half get it before they reach 21 years of age. Most will have leucoderma for the rest of their lives. It is very rare for leucoderma to disappear. Leucoderma occurs about equally in people of all skin colors and races. About half the people who get leucoderma are male and half are female.

The risk of getting leucoderma increases if a person has:

- A close blood relative who has leucoderma.
- An autoimmune disease, especially Hashimoto's disease (a thyroid disease) or alopecia areata (causes hair loss).

What causes leucoderma?

Leucoderma develops when cells called melanocytes (meh-lan-o-sites) die. These cells give our skin and hair color. Scientists do not completely understand why these cells die. One type of leucoderma, non-segmental (bilateral) leucoderma, may be an autoimmune disease. An autoimmune disease develops when the body mistakes a part of itself as foreign. If the body mistakes these cells as foreigners, it will attack and kill these cells. Studies suggest that the other type of leucoderma, segmental leucoderma, has a different cause. This type seems to develop when something in the body's nervous system goes awry.

How is leucoderma diagnosed?

If the dermatologist suspects that you have Leucoderma, the dermatologist will:

- Review your medical history, and may ask specific questions such as whether anyone in your family has leucoderma.
- Perform a physical exam, looking carefully at the affected skin.

You also may need a blood test to check the health of your thyroid gland. People who have leucoderma often have an autoimmune thyroid disease. A blood test will tell whether your thyroid is healthy. If you have thyroid disease, treatment can successfully control it.

How do dermatologists treat leucoderma?

There are many treatment options. The goal of most treatments is to restore lost skin color. Here are some key facts about treatment options The type of treatment that is best will depend on the preference, overall health, age and where the leucoderma appears on the body.

No medical treatment (use cosmetics to add lost color):
- Cosmetic options include makeup, a self-tanner and skin dye.
- Offers safe way to make leucoderma less noticeable.
- Often recommended for children because it avoids possible side effects from medicine.
- Drawbacks: Must be repeatedly applied, can be time-consuming, takes practice to get natural-looking result.

Medicine applied to the skin:
- Several different topical (applied to the skin) medicines can repigment the skin.
- Prescribed for small areas.
- The most commonly prescribed medicine is a potent or super-potent topical corticosteroid. About half, 45 percent, of patients regain at least some skin color after 4 to 6 months.
- A topical corticosteroid may be combined with another medicine to improve results.
- Topical medicine works best in people with darkly pigmented skin.
- Topical medicines are most effective on certain areas of the body, such as the face. They are least effective on the hands and feet.
- Not all topical medicines should be used on the face.
- Drawbacks: These medicines have possible side effects, so patients must be carefully monitored. A possible serious side effect of using of a topical corticosteroid for a year or longer is skin atrophy. This means the skin becomes paper thin, very dry and fragile.

Light treatment:
- Uses light to repigment the skin.
- Patient may sit in a light box or receive excimer laser treatments.
- Light box used to treat widespread Leucoderma; laser used to treat small area.
- Works best on the face; least effective on hands and feet.
- Effective for many patients; about 70 percent see results with excimer laser.
- Results can disappear. About half, 44 percent, see results disappear within 1 year of stopping treatment. After 4 years, about 86 percent lose some color

restored by treatment.

- May cause patients with darkly pigmented skin to see areas of darker skin after treatment, but treated skin usually matches untreated skin within a few months.
- Requires a time commitment. Patients need 2 to 3 treatments per week for several weeks.
- May be combined with another treatment such as topical corticosteroid.

PUVA light therapy:

- Uses UVA light and a medicine called psoralen to restore skin color.
- Psoralen may be applied to the skin or taken as a pill.
- Can treat widespread Leucoderma.
- About 50 percent to 75 percent effective in restoring pigment to the face, trunk, upper arms and upper legs.
- Not very effective for the hands or feet.
- Time-consuming, requiring treatment at a hospital or PUVA center twice a week for about 1 year.
- Psoralen can affect the eyes, so this treatment requires eye exams before starting treatment and after finishing treatment.
- To help prevent serious side effects, patients need to be carefully monitored.

Surgery:

- May be an option when light therapy and medicines applied to the skin do not work.
- For adults whose Leucoderma has been stable (not changed) for at least 6 months.
- Not for children.
- Not for people who scar easily or develop keloids (scars that rise above the skin).
- Different surgical procedures available. Most involve removing unaffected skin or skin cells and placing where need pigment.
- Can be effective for 90 percent to 95 percent of patients.
- Possible side effects include failure to work, cobblestone-like skin and infection.

Unconventional treatment:

- Some vitamins, minerals, amino acids and enzymes have been reported to restore skin color in people who have Leucoderma.
- Most have not been studied, so there is no evidence to support these treatments and no knowledge of possible side effects.
- Ginkgo biloba, an herb, has been studied in a clinical trial. Results from this trial indicate that the herb may restore skin color and stop Leucoderma from worsening.

- In the ginkgo biloba trial, 10 patients given ginkgo biloba had noticeable or complete return of skin color. Two patients taking the placebo (contains no active ingredient) also had noticeable or complete return of skin color.
- Because some patients taking the placebo regained their skin color, more study is needed.

Depigmentation:

- This treatment removes the remaining pigment from the skin.
- Very few patients opt for this treatment.
- Removing the rest of the pigment leaves a person with completely white skin.
- It may be an option for an adult who has little pigment left and other treatment has not worked. Removing the remaining pigment can be an effective way to get one skin color.
- To remove the remaining color requires you to apply a cream once or twice day. This cream gradually removes color from the skin.
- Depigmentation can take 1 to 4 years.
- Once treatment is finished, some people see spots of pigment on their skin from being out in the sun. To get rid of these spots, you can use the cream that removed your remaining skin color.

Outcome

It is not possible to predict how a patient will respond to treatment. It is important to keep in mind that no one treatment works for everyone. Results can vary from one part of the body to another. Combining two or more treatments often gives the best results.

Can a child with leucoderma be treated?

Yes, but some treatments are not appropriate for children. The following may be an option for a child:

- Medicine applied to the skin.
- PUVA that uses psoralen applied to the skin. PUVA therapy that uses the psoralen pill is usually not recommended until after 12 years of age. Even then, the risk and benefits of this treatment must be carefully weighed.
- For children with extensive Leucoderma, a dermatologist may recommend narrowband UVB light treatments.

Are researchers looking for more effective treatment?

Yes. They are studying the genes involved in Leucoderma. Researchers believe that by identifying all of the genes involved in Leucoderma, they will learn what destroys the cells that give skin its color. With this knowledge, it should be possible to develop better treatments. One of the key goals of this research is to develop a treatment that will permanently stop the skin from losing color.

中英文注释

关键词汇

cosmetic [kɒz'metik] n. 化妆品

depigmentation [di:pigmən'teiʃən] n. 色素脱失

enzyme ['enzaim] n. 酶

fragile ['frædʒail] adj. 脆弱的

genital ['dʒenitl] n.adj. 生殖器（的）

hypopigmentation [ˌhaipəuˌpigmən'teiʃən] n. 色素减退

keloid ['ki:lɔid] n. 瘢痕疙瘩

leucoderma [lju:kəu'də:mə] n. 白癜风

melanocyte ['melənəuˌsait] n. 黑色素细胞

placebo [plə'si:bəu] n. 安慰剂

psoralen ['sɔ:rələn] n. 补骨脂素（一种光敏感性药物）

scar [skɑ:] n. 疤痕

self-esteem [ˌselfi'sti:m] n. 自尊，自重

主要短语

alopecia areata 斑秃，局限性脱发

amino acid 氨基酸

autoimmune disease 自身免疫性疾病

clinical trial 临床实验

cobblestone-like skin 鹅卵石样皮肤

excimer laser 准分子激光

ginkgo biloba 银杏

Hashimoto's disease 桥本氏病，慢性甲状腺炎（淋巴性甲状腺肿）

nervous system 神经系统

PUVA 补骨脂素联合使用 A 波段紫外线（UVA）暴露疗法

skin atrophy 皮肤萎缩

thyroid gland 甲状腺

topical corticosteroid 局部用皮质类固醇类激素

刘宏业

94

Psoriasis
银屑病(牛皮癣)

What is psoriasis?

Psoriasis is a medical condition that occurs when skin cells grow too quickly. Faulty signals in the immune system cause new skin cells to form in days rather than weeks. The body does not shed these excess skin cells, so the cells pile up on the surface of the skin and lesions form.

Psoriasis is not infectious but it is a very complex medical condition. In fact, the medical community is not certain on what actually happens during the development of psoriasis. Scientists only knew that the immune system as well as the genes has key roles in the development of such. In studying the latter, the medical experts were able to determine that people with psoriasis had T cells that mistakenly trigger reaction at the skin level. T cell is a white blood type which fights viruses and bacteria. Such reaction appears to lie on the person's DNA. Psoriasis sufferers inherit psoriasis-causing genes. There are actually several genes that are involved in the development of psoriasis one of which is the PSORS1. This gene regulates the immune system's capacity to combat infections. Having strep throat is actually one of the triggers of psoriasis. Nevertheless, the triggers to psoriasis are not necessarily universal hence one psoriasis sufferer's trigger may not be the trigger for another sufferer's condition.

Anyone having the 'right mix' of genes can develop psoriasis. In the US alone, there are about 7.5 million people who are suffering from psoriasis and approximately 150,000 cases are added annually. Psoriasis develops among males as well as females and in any age. However, it was reported that majority of the sufferer saw the first sign of psoriasis when they are 15 to 30 years old though they often mistook for something else. Caucasians are more prone of developing psoriasis compared to other races. It would be important to know that approximately 75% of the sufferers start to live with psoriasis before they hit the age of 40. Some sufferers reported the onset of their psoriasis when they reach the age of 50. This is more so when the psoriasis runs in the blood. While family increases the risk of psoriasis, this doesn't guarantee that a family member will suffer from the condition.

What causes psoriasis?

Psoriasis is not contagious. You cannot get psoriasis from touching someone who has psoriasis, swimming in the same pool, or even intimate contact. Psoriasis is much more complex.

So complex, in fact, scientists are still studying what happens when psoriasis develops. We know that the person's immune system and genes play key roles. In studying the immune system, scientists discovered that when a person has psoriasis, the T cells (a type of white blood cell that fights unwanted invaders such as bacteria and viruses) mistakenly trigger a reaction in the skin cells. This is why you may hear psoriasis referred to as a "T cell-mediated disease".

This reaction activates a series of events, causing new skin cells to form in days rather than weeks. The reason T cells trigger this reaction seems to lie in our DNA. People who develop psoriasis inherit genes that cause psoriasis. Unlike some autoimmune conditions, it appears that many genes are involved in psoriasis.

Scientists are still trying to identify all of the genes involved. One of the genes that has been identified is called PSORS1 (SORE-ESS-1). This is one of several genes that regulates how the immune system fights infection.

Scientists also have learned that not everyone who inherits genes for psoriasis gets psoriasis. For psoriasis to appear, it seems that a person must inherit the "right" mix of genes and be exposed to a trigger. Some common triggers are a stressful life event, skin injury, and having strep throat. Many people say that that their psoriasis first appeared after experiencing one of these. Triggers are not universal. What triggers psoriasis in one person may not cause psoriasis to develop in another.

Who gets psoriasis?

People worldwide develop psoriasis. In the United States, nearly 7.5 million people have psoriasis and about 150,000 new cases are diagnosed each year. Studies indicate that psoriasis develops about equally in males and females. Research also shows that Caucasians develop psoriasis more frequently than other races. A study conducted in the United States found the prevalence was 2.5% in Caucasians and 1.3% in African Americans.

A family history of psoriasis seems 4o increase the risk of developing psoriasis. It is important to know that a family history of psoriasis does not guarantee that someone will develop psoriasis.

When do people get psoriasis?

Psoriasis can begin at any age, from infancy through the golden years. There are, however, times when psoriasis is most likely to develop. Most people first see psoriasis between 15 and 30 years of age. About 75% develop psoriasis before they turn 40. Another common time for psoriasis to begin is between 50 and 60 years of age.

What are the signs and symptoms of psoriasis?

The lesions vary in appearance with the type of psoriasis. There are five types of psoriasis: Plaque psoriasis, guttate psoriasis, pustular psoriasis, inverse psoriasis, and erythrodermic psoriasis. About 80% of people living with psoriasis have plaque (plak) psoriasis, also called "psoriasis vulgaris." Plaque psoriasis causes patches of thick, scaly skin that may be white, silvery, or red. Called plaques (plax), these patches can develop anywhere on the skin. The most common areas to find plaques are the elbows, knees, lower back, and scalp (scalp psoriasis).

Psoriasis also can affect the nails. About 50% of people who develop psoriasis see changes in their fingernails and/or toenails. If the nails begin to pull away from the nail bed or develop pitting, ridges, or a yellowish-orange color, this could be a sign of psoriatic arthritis. Without treatment, psoriatic arthritis can progress and become debilitating. It is important to see a dermatologist if nail changes begin or joint pain develops. Early treatment can prevent joint deterioration.

How do dermatologists treat psoriasis?

Currently, there is no cure for psoriasis. However, there are many treatment options that can clear psoriasis for a period of time. Each treatment has advantages and disadvantages, and what works for one patient may not be effective for another. Board-certified dermatologists have the medical training and experience needed to determine the most appropriate treatments for each patient.

There are several forms of psoriasis, and each form has unique characteristics that allow dermatologists to visually identify psoriasis to determine what type, or types, of psoriasis is present. Sometimes a skin biopsy will be performed to confirm the diagnosis.

To choose the most appropriate treatment method, dermatologists consider several factors:

- Type of psoriasis
- Severity (the amount of skin affected)
- Where psoriasis is located
- Patient's age and medical history
- Effects psoriasis has on patient's overall physical and emotional well-being

Types of Treatment

Psoriasis treatments fall into 3 categories:

- Topical (applied to the skin) – Mild to moderate psoriasis
- Phototherapy (light, usually ultraviolet, applied to the skin) – Moderate to severe psoriasis
- Systemic (taken orally or by injection or infusion) – Moderate, severe or disabling psoriasis

While each of these therapies is effective, there are also drawbacks.

Some topicals are messy and may stain clothing and skin. Phototherapy can require 2 to 5 weekly visits to a dermatologist's office or psoriasis clinic for several weeks. Many of the systemic medications have serious side effects and must be combined or rotated with other therapies to maximize effectiveness and minimize side effects. Research is being conducted to find therapies that provide safe, effective, easy-to-use treatment options that provide long-term relief.

Does psoriasis affect quality of life?

For some people, psoriasis is a nuisance. Others find that psoriasis affects every aspect of their daily life. The unpredictable nature of psoriasis may be the reason. Psoriasis is a chronic (lifelong) medical condition. Some people have frequent flare-ups that occur weekly or monthly. Others have occasional flare-ups.

When psoriasis flares, it can cause severe itching and pain. Sometimes the skin cracks and bleeds. When trying to sleep, cracking and bleeding skin can wake a person frequently and cause sleep deprivation. A lack of sleep can make it difficult to focus at school or work. Sometimes a flare-up requires a visit to a dermatologist for additional treatment. Time must be taken from school or work to visit the doctor and get treatment.

These cycles of flare-ups and remissions often lead to feelings of sadness, despair, guilt and anger as well as low self-esteem. Depression is higher in people who have psoriasis than in the general population. Feelings of embarrassment also are common.

Knowledge is power

As psoriasis is a life-long condition, it is important to take an active role in managing it. Learning more about psoriasis, seeing a dermatologist to discuss treatment options, and developing a healthy lifestyle can help people live life to the fullest.

中英文注释

关键词汇

Caucasians [kɔːˈkeiziən] n. 高加索人；白种人
contagious [kənˈteidʒəs] adj. 感染性的；会蔓延的
infectious [inˈfekʃəs] adj. 传染的；传染性的；易传染的

itching ['itʃiŋ] n. adj. 发痒

lesion ['liːʒ(ə)n] n. 损害；身体上的伤害；功能障碍

nail [neil] n. 指甲

nuisance ['njuːs(ə)ns] n. 麻烦事

phototherapy [ˌfotə'θɛrəpi] n. 光疗

psoriasis [sɒ'raiəsis] n. 银屑病

scalp [skælp] n. 头皮

trigger ['trigə] n. vt. 触发；危险因素

ultraviolet [ʌltrə'vaiələt] n. 紫外线辐射

主要短语

board-certified 通过资格验证的

erythrodermic psoriasis 红皮病型银屑病

flare-ups （疾病的）骤然发作

guttate psoriasis 点滴状银屑病

inverse psoriasis 反向性银屑病

lower back 下背

nail bed 甲床

pile up 堆积

plaque psoriasis 斑块状银屑病

pustular psoriasis 脓疱性银屑病

'right mix' of genes 恰当的组合基因

side effect 不良反应

skin biopsy 皮肤活体组织检查

strep throat 链球菌性咽炎

T cell-mediated disease T 细胞介导的疾病

刘宏业

95

Urticaria
荨　麻　疹

What is urticaria (hives)?

If you are one of the people, who easily get rashes upon sudden changes in temperature, when eating certain food or taking some medications, it should not be a cause for alarm. You may have a common condition known as urticaria. Urticaria, also known as hives, hives are pale red swellings of skin "wheals" that occur in groups on any part of the skin. Urticaria is the medical word for hives. Each hive lasts a few hours before fading without trace. New areas may develop as old areas fade. They can vary in size from as small as a pencil eraser to as large as a dinner plate and may join together to form larger swellings. Hives are usually are itchy, but may also burn or sting.

Hives are formed by blood plasma leaking out of small blood vessels in the skin. This is caused by the release of a chemical called histamine. Histamine is released from cells called "mast cells" which lie along the blood vessels in the skin. Allergic reactions, chemicals in foods, or medications can cause histamine release. Sometimes it's impossible to find out why hives are forming.

Hives are very common — 10-20 percent of the population will have at least one episode in their lifetime. Hives usually go away within a few days to a few weeks. Occasionally, a person will continue to have hives for many years.

When hives form around the eyes, lips or genitals, the tissue may swell excessively. Although frightening, the swelling usually goes away in less than 24 hours.

Who gets hives?

Hives are common. Anyone can get them.

What causes hives?

An allergic reaction can trigger hives. Things that trigger commonly trigger an allergic reaction include:
- Foods: Fruits (especially citrus fruits), milk, eggs, peanuts, tree nuts, and shellfish.

629

- Medicines.
- Insect bites and stings.
- Animals.
- Pollen.
- Touching something to which you are allergic, such as latex.
- Allergy shots.

Other causes of hives are:

- Infections, including colds and infections caused by some bacteria or fungi.
- Some illnesses, including a type of vasculitis, lupus, and thyroid disease.
- Exposure to sun (solar urticaria), heat, cold, or water.
- Exercise.
- Stress.
- Pressure on the skin, such as from sitting too long.
- Contact with chemicals.
- Scratching the skin.

Acute Urticaria

Hives lasting less than six weeks are caused by "acute urticaria". With this type of hives, the cause can usually be found. The most common causes are foods, drugs or infections. Insect bites and internal disease may also be responsible. Other causes can be pressure, cold, and sunlight.

Chronic Urticaria

Hives lasting more than six weeks are called "chronic urticaria". The cause of this type of hives is usually much more difficult to identify than that of acute urticaria. In patients with chronic urticaria, the cause is found in only a small number of patients. Your doctor will need to ask many questions in an attempt to find the possible cause. Since there are no specific tests for hives, testing will depend on your medical history and a thorough examination by your dermatologist. Routine blood tests are of little or no value.

Foods

The most common foods that cause hives are nuts, chocolate, fish, tomatoes, eggs, fresh berries and milk. Fresh foods cause hives more often than cooked foods. Food additives and preservatives may also be the problem. Hives may appear within minutes or up to two hours after eating, depending on where the food is absorbed in the digestive tract.

Drugs

Almost any prescription or over-the-counter medication can cause hives. Some of those drugs include antibiotics, pain medications, sedatives, tranquilizers, and diuretics.

Antacids, vitamins, eye and ear drops, laxatives, vaginal douches, or any other non-prescription item can be a potential cause of hives. If you have an attack of hives, it's important to tell your doctor about all of the preparations that you use to assist in finding the cause.

Infections

Many infections can cause hives. Colds are a common cause in children.

Physical Urticarias

Hives can be caused by sunlight, cold, pressure, vibration, or exercise. Hives due to sunlight are called solar urticaria. This is a rare disorder in which hives from within minutes of sun exposure on exposed areas and fade within one to two hours. Hives due to the cold are more common. These appear when the skin is warmed after exposure to cold. If the cold is over large areas of the body, large amounts of histamine may be released which can produce wheezing, flushing, generalized hives, and fainting. A simple test for this type of hives can be done by applying an ice cube to the skin.

These hives can form after firmly stroking or scratching the skin "dermatographism". It affects about 5 percent of the population. Most people with this condition are otherwise healthy. These hives can also occur along with other forms of urticaria. If it is present along with hives, finding and eliminating the cause usually clears the dermatographism. Otherwise, it may last for months or even years.

What are signs and symptoms of hives?

The most common signs (what you see) of hives are:

- Slightly raised, pink or red swellings on the skin.
- Welts that occur alone or in a group, or connect over a large area.
- Skin swelling that subsides or goes away within 24 hours at 1 spot but may appear at another spot.

As for symptoms (what you feel), hives usually itch. They sometimes sting or hurt.

Some people always get hives in the same spot or spots on their body. These people often have a trigger (what causes the hives). Every time they are exposed to that trigger, they get hives.

Your dermatologist may call this type of hives fixed, which means not moving. Fixed hives may happen when a person takes a certain medicine (fixed drug eruption) or gets too much sunlight (fixed solar urticaria).

How do dermatologists diagnose hives?

When a patient has hives on the skin, a dermatologist can often make the diagnosis by looking at the skin. Finding the cause of hives, however, can sometimes be hard.

This is especially true for hives that have been around for more than six weeks.

To find out what is causing your hives, your dermatologist will review your health history, ask questions, and do a physical exam. You may need the following tests:

- Allergy tests (on the skin or blood tests).
- Blood work (to rule out an illness or infection).
- A skin biopsy.

To perform a skin biopsy, the dermatologist removes a small piece of affected skin so that it can be examined under a microscope.

How do dermatologists treat hives?

For a mild or moderate case of hives, the most common treatment is a non-sedating (does not cause drowsiness) antihistamine. Antihistamines relieve symptoms like itching.

If you have chronic hives, your dermatologist may prescribe an antihistamine. You should take this medicine every day to prevent hives from forming. There are many antihistamines on the market. Some make you drowsy, and some do not. No one antihistamine works for everyone. Your dermatologist may combine an antihistamine with other medicines to control the hives.

- Other medicines that are prescribed to treat hives include:
- Cortisones (for short-term use only because of side effects with long-term use).
- Dapsone, an antibacterial.
- Other medicines that fight inflammation (redness and swelling).

Ask your dermatologist about possible side effects (health problems that can result from the medicines).

For some cases of hives or angioedema, you may need an injection of epinephrine (shot of adrenaline).

A hive often will go away in 24 hours or less, but bouts can last longer.

Outcome

A few people have chronic hives (lasting more than six weeks). Sometimes chronic hives go away on their own — often within a year. For others, hives can come and go for months or years. Children may outgrow the allergies that cause their hives.

For most people, hives are not serious. In some people, though, hives may be a sign of an internal disease. Others can get a severe swelling with hives known as angioedema. If you have hives and trouble breathing or swallowing, get emergency care right away.

The best remedy for hives is to try to avoid whatever triggers them.

中英文注释

关键词汇

angioedema [ˌændʒiəui'di:mə] n. 血管性水肿

antacid [æn'tæsid] n. 抑酸药

antihistamine [ænti'histəmin; –mi:n] n. 抗组胺药

cortisone ['kɒ:tizəun] n. 可的松

dapsone ['dæpˌsəun] n. 氨苯砜

diuretic [ˌdaijʊ(ə)'retik] n. 利尿药

drowsy ['draʊzi] adj. 昏昏欲睡的

epinephrine [ˌepi'nefrin; –ri:n] n. 肾上腺素

faint [feint] n. 晕厥

flush [flʌʃ] n. v. 脸红

fungi ['fʌŋgi:] n. 真菌

histamine ['histəmi:n] n. 组胺

itchy ['itʃi] adj. 发痒的

latex ['leiteks] n. 乳胶

laxative ['læksətiv] n. 泻药

lupus ['lupəs] n. 狼疮

pale [peil] adj. 苍白的

prescription [pri'skripʃən] n. 处方

sedatives ['sɛdətivz] n. 镇静剂

sting [stiŋ] n. 刺痛

tranquilizer ['træŋkwilaizə] n. 镇定剂, 抗焦虑药

urticaria [ˌɜ:ti'keəriə] n. 荨麻疹; 风团

vasculitis [ˌvæskjʊ'laitis] n. 血管炎; 结节性脉管炎

vibration [vai'breiʃən] n. 震动, 振动

wheals [hwil] n. 水疱

wheeze [wi:z] n. 哮喘, 喘息

主要短语

allergic reaction 变态反应

allergy shot 脱敏针

allergy test 变态反应试验

blood plasma 血浆, 血清

insect bites 昆虫咬伤

internal disease 内科疾病

leak out　泄露，露出
over-the-counter medication　非处方用药
solar urticaria　日光性荨麻疹
vaginal douche　阴道灌洗液

刘宏业

Section Nine: Ophthalmic Diseases

第九部分　眼科疾病

96 · Age-related Macular Degeneration
老年性黄斑变性

What is age-related macular degeneration?

Age-related macular degeneration is the leading cause of permanent blindness in the elderly. It is a bilateral disease, the average age of visual loss in the first eye being 65 years, with about a 12% incidence of involvement of the second eye each year. About 60% of patients are therefore legally blind in both eyes by the time they reach their seventieth birthday.

What causes age-related macular degeneration?

The exact cause is unknown, but the incidence increases with each decade over age 50. Other associations besides age include race (usually Caucasian), sex (slight female predominance), family history, and a history of cigarette. The disease includes a broad spectrum of clinical and pathologic findings that can be classified into two groups: nonexudative ("dry") and exudative ("wet"). Although both types are progressive and usually bilateral, they differ in their manifestations, prognosis, and management. The more severe exudative form accounts for approximately 90% of all cases of legal blindness due to age-related macular degeneration.

What are symptoms of age-related macular degeneration?

Nonexudative Macular Degeneration

Nonexudative age-related macular degeneration is characterized by variable degrees of atrophy and degeneration of the outer retina. retinal pigment epithelium, Bruch's membrane and choriocapillaris. Of the ophthalmoscopically visible changes in the retinal pigment epithelium and Bruch's membrane, drusen are the most typical. Drusen are discrete, round, yellow-white deposits of variable size beneath the pigment epithelium and are scattered throughout the macula and posterior pole. With time, they may enlarge, coalesce, calcify and increase in number. In addition to drusen, clumps of pigment irregularly dispersed within depigmented areas of atrophy may progressively appear throughout the macula. The level of associated visual impairment is variable and may be minimal.

Exudative Macular Degeneration

Although patients with age-related macular degeneration usually manifest nonexudative changes only, the majority of patients who experience severe vision loss from this disease do so from the development of subretinal neovascularization and related exudative maculopathy. Serous fluid from the underlying choroid can leak through small defects in Bruch's membrane, causing focal detachment of the pigment epithelium. Additional fluid may lead to further separation of the overlying sensory retina, and vision usually decreases if the fovea is involved. Retinal pigment epithelial detachments may spontaneously flatten, with variable visual results, and leave a geographic area of depigmentation at the involved site.

In growth of new vessels from the choroid into the subretinal space is the most important change that predisposes patients with drusen to macular detachment and irreversible loss of central vision. These new vessels grow in a flat cartwheel or sea-fan configuration away from their site of entry into the subretinal space.

Although some subretinal neovascular membranes (SRNVMs) may spontaneously regress, the natural course of subretinal neovascularization in age-related macular degeneration is toward irreversible loss of central vision over a variable period of time. The sensory retina may be damaged by long-standing edema, detachment, or underlying hemorrhage. Furthermore, a hemorrhagic detachment of the retina may undergo fibrous metaplasia, resulting in an elevated subretinal mass called a disciform scar. This elevated fibrovascular mound of variable size represents the cicatricial end stage of exudative age-related macular degeneration. It is usually centrally located and results in permanent loss of central vision.

How is age-related macular degeneration diagnosed?

● **Clinical features**

Nonexudative Macular Degeneration

It is by far the most common type of AMD. It typically causes a gradual mild to moderate impairment of vision over several months or years. This type of AMD is either due to a slow and progressive atrophy of the RPE and photoreceptors or follows collapse of an RPE detachment. Clinically, dry AMD is characterized by sharply circumscribed circular areas of atrophy of the RPE associated with varying degrees of loss of the choriocapillaris. During the late stages the larger choroidal vessels become prominent within the atrophic areas and pre-existing drusen disappear.

Exudative Macular Degeneration

This type is also sometimes referred to as 'neovascular' AMD. Although it is less common than the non-exudative type, its effects on vision are frequently devastating.

In contrast to patients with non-exudative AMD in whom visual impairment is gradual, those with exudative type may lose all central vision within a few days. Exudative AMD may occur in isolation or in association with non-exudative AMD. Two important features of exudative AMD are detachment of the RPE and choroidal neovascularization.

● **Fluorescein angiography**

RPE 'window' defect: The associated atrophy of the RPE (Retinal Pigment Epithelium) overlying drusen gives rise to increased background choroidal fluorescence, which appears early in the angiogram as multiple hyperfluorescent spots. FA may also reveal lesions that are not apparent ophthalmoscopically.

Staining: Drusen may retain fluorescein dye for abnormally long periods of time after most of it has emptied. The actual dimensions of the hyperfluorescent areas seen 20 minutes after dye injection are the same as during the early stages of dye transit. This phenomenon indicates that fluorescein molecules have not leaked but have merely adhered to the lesions.

Leak: The new vessels within the subretinal neovascular membranes (SRNVMs) fill in a 'lacy' pattern during the very early phase of dye transit, fluoresce brightly during peak eye transit (20-30 seconds after injection), and then leak with 1-2 minutes. The fibrous tissue within the membrane then stains with dye and leads to late hyperfluorescence. In eyes with associated detachments of the RPE, the SRNVM fluoresces brighter than the detachment and appears to leak as the angiogram progress.

How is it treated?

Nonexudative Macular Degeneration

There is no generally accepted means of preventing of this type of macular degeneration. A combination of oral antioxidants and zinc is modestly effective in preventing progression of macular drusen to advanced macular degeneration. Laser retinal photocoagulation may have a beneficial effect on drusen but has not yet been shown to improve visual outcome. Most patients with macular drusen never experience significant loss of central vision; the atrophic changes may stabilize or progress slowly. However, the exudative stage may develop suddenly at any time, and in addition to regular ophthalmic examinations, patients are given an Amsler grid to help monitor and report any symptomatic changes.

Exudative Macular Degeneration

In the absence of subretinal neovascularization, no medical or surgical treatment of serous retinal pigment epithelial detachment is of proved benefit. If a well-defined extrafoveal (≥200μm from the center of the foveal avascular zone) subretinal neovascular membrane is present laser photocoagulation is indicated. Angiography defines the precise location and borders of the neovascular membrane, which is then completely ablated by heavy confluent laser burns. Photocoagulation destroys the overlying retina as well but is worthwhile if the subretinal membrane can be halted short of the fovea.

Krypton laser photocoagulation of juxtafoveal (<200µm from the center of the foveal avascular zone) subretinal neovascularization is recommended in nonhypertensive patients. In eyes with predominantly classic subfoveal neovascularization, the use of intravenous verteporfin and photodynamic therapy is beneficial. At this time the effectiveness of parenteral interferon, retinal radiation, or submacular surgery has not been proved. The potential benefit of other modalities, including antiangiogenesis agents and transpupillary thermotherapy, is currently under study.

中英文注释

关键词汇

angiogram ['ɔnjir'grəm] n. 血管造影片

antiangiogenesis [ænti:əngi':oʊdʒenəsis] n. 血管生成抑制

antioxidants [ænti:ɒk'sidænts] n. 抗氧化剂

choriocapillaris [kɔ:ri:əʊ'keipiləris] n. 脉络膜毛细血管

choroid ['kɔːɔid] n. 脉络膜

drusen [d'ru:zn] n. 玻璃膜疣

extrafoveal [ekstrɑ:foʊ'vi:l] adj. 中心凹外的

fibrovascular [faibroʊ'væskjələ] adj. 纤维血管组织的

maculopathy ['mækjʊloʊpəθi] n. 黄斑病变

metaplasia [metə'pleiʒə] n. 转化，化生，组织变形

neovascular [ni:əʊ'væskjələ] adj. 新生血管性

neovascularization ['ni:oʊvæskjʊlərai'zeiʃən] n. 新生血管化

ophthalmoscope [ɔf'θælməskəupikəli] n. 眼底镜

photocoagulation [foʊtoʊkoʊ'ægjə'leiʃən] n. 激光光凝治疗

retina ['rɛtnə] n. 视网膜

submacular [sʌb'mækjʊlə] adj. 黄斑下的

subretinal ['su:britinəl] adj. 视网膜下的

transpupillary [trænsp'ju:piləri] adj. 经瞳孔的

verteporfin [vɜ:ti'pɔ:fin] n. 维替泊芬（光增敏药）

zinc [ziŋk] n. 锌

主要短语

age-related macular degeneration　老年性黄斑变性

amsler grid　阿姆斯勒方格表

Bruch's membrane　布鲁赫膜（玻璃膜）

extrafoveal subretinal neovascularization　中心凹外型新生血管

fluorescein angiography　荧光血管造影

foveal avascular zone　中心凹无血管区

hyperfluorescent spots　强荧光点

juxtafovealsubretinal neovascularization　旁中心凹型新生血管

nonexudative ("dry") and exudative ("wet")　非渗出性和渗出性（干性和湿性）

retinal pigment epithelium　视网膜色素上皮细胞

subfoveal subretinal neovascularization　中心凹下型新生血管

subretinal neovascular membranes　视网膜下新生血管膜

李春晖　高　妍

97 Age-related Cataract
老年性白内障

What is age-related cataract?

Age-related cataract is the lens opacify gradually in older adults, its morbidity rises obviously with increasing age.

Age-related cataract is the main cause of blindness and visual impairment throughout the world. With the general aging of the population, the overall prevalence of visual loss as a result of lens opacities increases each year. Cataracts are believed to be the cause of blindness in more than 15,000,000 people worldwide, and this number is expected to reach 40,000,000 by the year 2025 in the absence of new or more efficiently delivered intervention.

There are three main types of aged-related cataracts: nuclear, cortical, and posterior subcapsular. In many patients, components of more than one type are present.

What causes age-related cataract?

Age-related cataract is a very common cause of visual impairment in order adults. In cross-sectional studies the prevalence of cataracts is 50% in people between the ages of 65 and 74, it increases to 70% in those over the age of 75.

The pathogenesis of age-related cataracts is multifactorial and of not completely understood. As the lens ages, it increases in weight and thickness and decreases in accommodative power. As new layers of cortical fibers are formed concentrically, the lens nucleus undergoes compression and hardening (nuclear sclerosis). Crystallins (len proteins) are changed by chemical modification and aggregation into high-molecular-weight protein. The resulting protein aggregates cause abrupt fluctuations in the refractive index of the lens, scatter light rays, and reduce transparency. Chemical modification of nuclear lens proteins also produces progressive pigmentation. The lens takes on a yellow or brownish hue with advancing age. Other age-related changes in the lens include decreased concentrations of glutathione and potassium, increased concentrations of sodium and calcium, increased hydration.

What are symptoms of age-related cataract?

Decreased Visual Acuity

A cataract is clinically relevant if it causes a significant decrease in visual acuity, and different types of cataract may have different effects on visual acuity. Posterior subvascular cataracts of even mild degree can severely reduce visual acuity; near acuity is often decreased more than distance acuity, possibly because of accommodative miosis. Nuclear sclerotic cataracts, in contrast, are often associated with good near acuity and poor distance acuity. Patients with cortical cataracts tend to maintain good visual acuity until the visual axis is compromised by cortical spokes, which generally does not occur until late in the cataract progression. However, a solitary cortical spoke occasionally affects the visual axis early.

Glare

Cataract patients often complain of increased glare, which may vary in severity from a decrease in contrast sensitivity in brightly lighted environments to disabling glare in the daytime or with oncoming car headlights or similar lighting conditions at night. This complaint is particularly prominent with posterior subcapsular cataracts but is also common with cortical cataracts. Glare is less characteristic of nuclear sclerosis. Many patients tolerate moderate levels of glare with little difficulty, and the presence of this symptom by itself does not mandate surgical treatment.

Myopic Shift

The development of cataract may increase the dioptric power of the lens and commonly causes a mild to moderate degree of myopia. Presbyopic patients find their need for reading glasses is diminished, as they experience so-called second sight. As the optical quality of the lens deteriorates, this temporary advantage is lost. The phenomenon is not characteristic of either cortical or posterior subcapsular cataracts. Asymmetric development of lens-induced myopia may produce significant symptomatic anisometropia, prompting consideration of cataract surgery.

Monocular Diplopia

Occasionally, nuclear changes are localized to the inner layers of the lens nucleus, resulting in a refractile area in the center of the lens. Such an area may best be seen within the red reflex by retinoscopy or direct ophthalmoscope. This type of cataract occasionally results in monocular diplopia, which cannot be corrected with spectacles, contact lenses, or prisms.

How is age-related cataract diagnosed?

Nuclear Cataracts

Some degree of nuclear sclerosis and yellowing is considered physiologically normal in adult patients past middle age. In general, this condition interferes only minimally with visual function. An excessive amount of sclerosis and yellowing is called a nuclear cataract, and it causes a central opacity. The degree of sclerosis, yellowing, and opacification is evaluated with a slit-lamp biomicroscope and by examining the red reflex with pupil dilated.

Nuclear cataracts tend to progress slowly. They are usually bilateral but may be asymmetric. Nuclear cataracts typically cause greater impairment of distance vision than of near vision. In the early stages the progressive hardening of the lens nucleus shift in refraction, or lenticular myopia. In some cases the myopic shift transiently enables presbyopic individuals to read without spectacles, a condition referred to as second sight. Occasionally, the abrupt change in refractive index between the sclerotic nucleus and the cortex of the lens can cause monocular diplopia. Progressive yellowing of the lens causes poor hue discrimination, especially at the blue end of the visible light spectrum. Photopic retinal function may decrease with advanced nuclear cataract. In very advanced cases the lens nucleus becomes opaque and brown and is called a nuclear cataract.

Histopathologically, nuclear cataracts are characterized by homogeneity of the lens nucleus with loss of cellular laminations.

Cortical Cataracts

Changes in the ionic composition of the lens cortex and subsequent changes in hydration of the lens fibers lead to cortical opacification. Cortical cataracts are usually bilateral but are often asymmetric. Their effect on visual function varies greatly, depending on the location of the opacification relative to the visual axis. A common symptom of cortical cataracts is glare from intense focal light sources, such as car headlights. Monocular diplopia may also result. Cortical cataracts vary greatly in their rate of progression; some cortical opacities remain unchanged for prolonged periods, while others progress rapidly.

The first visible signs of cortical cataract formation shown by the slit-lamp biomicroscope are vacuoles and water clefts in the anterior or posterior cortex. Separation of cortical lamellae by fluid may be observed. Wedge-shaped opacities, often called cortical spokes or cuneiform opacities, form near the periphery of the lens, with the pointed end of the opacities oriented toward the center. The cortical spokes appear as white opacities when viewed with the slit-lamp biomicroscope and as dark shadows when viewed by retroillumination. The wedge-shaped opacities may enlarge and coalesce to form large cortical opacities. As the lens continues to take up water, it may swell and become an intumescent cortical cataract. When the entire cortex from the capsule to the nucleus becomes white and opaque, the cataract is said to be mature.

A hypermature cataract occurs when degenerated cortical material leaks through the lens capsule, leaving the capsule wrinkle and shrunken. A morgagnian cataract occurs when further liquefaction of the cortex allows free movement of the nucleus within the capsular bag.

Histopathologically, cortical cataracts are characterized by hydropic swelling of the lens fibers. Globules of eosinophilic material are observed in slitlike spaces between bens fibers.

Posterior Subcapsular Cataracts

Posterior subcapsular cataracts are often seen in patients younger than those presenting with nuclear or cortical cataracts. Posterior subcapsular cataracts are located in the posterior cortical layer and are usually axial. The first indication of posterior subcapsular cataract formation is a subtle iridescent sheen in the posterior cortical layers visible with the slit lamp. In later stages granular opacities and a plaquelike opacity of the posterior subcapsular cortex appear.

The patient often complaints of glare and poor vision under bright lighting conditions; the posterior subcapsular cataract obscures more of the pupillary aperture when miosis is induced by bright lights, accommodation, or miotics. Near visual acuity tends to be reduced more than distance visual acuity. Some patents experience monocular diplopia. Slit-lamp detection of posterior subcapsular cataracts can best be accomplished through a dilated pupil. Retroillumination is also helpful.

How is it treated?

No medical treatment has been proven conclusively to delay, prevent, or reverse the development of cataracts in adults. Aldose reductase inhibitors, which block the conversion of glucose to sorbitol, have been shown to prevent sugar cataracts in animals. Many anticataract agents are under investigation, including sorbitol-lowering agents, aspirin, glutathione-raising agents, and antioxidant vitamins C and E.

A careful refraction to improve spectacle distance and reading correction can reduce the functional visual impairment in many patients. Increased ambient illumination and increased spectacle add are also helpful for reading. Pupillary dilation may improve visual function in patients with small axial cataracts by allowing light to pass through the more peripheral portions of the lens. These approaches may be temporarily effective until cataracts progression causes additional symptoms.

When cataract development to a certain extent, operation treatment is a must choice. At present, there are mainly two kinds of operation mode: Extracapsular Cataract Extraction (ECCE) and Phacoemulsification.

中英文注释

关键词汇

anisometropia [ænisoʊˈmetroʊpir] n. 屈光参差

aspirin [ˈæsprin] n. 阿司匹林

calcium [ˈkælsiəm] n. 钙

eosinophilic [ˌiːəˌsinəˈfilik] adj. 嗜酸粒细胞的

glare [glɛr] n. 眩光

glucose [ˈgluˌkos] n. 葡萄糖

glutathione [ˌglutəˈθaiˌon] n. 谷胱甘肽

hydration [haiˈdreiʃn] n. 水和作用

hydropic [haiˈdrɒpik] adj. 水肿的

hypermature [haipəməˈtjʊr] adj. 过熟期的

intumescent [ˌintjuːˈmesənt] adj. 膨胀的

lenticular [lenˈtikjələ] adj. 晶状体的

miosis [maiˈoʊsis] n. 瞳孔缩小

multifactorial [ˌmʌltifækˈtɔriəl] adj. 多因素的

pathogenesis [ˌpæθəˈdʒɛnisis] n. 发病机理

photopic [foʊˈtɒpik] adj. 明视觉，适应光的

potassium [pəˈtæsiəm] n. 钾

presbyopic [prezbiˈːɒpik] n. 远视眼的，老花眼的

retinoscopy [ˌretnˈɒskəpiː] n. 视网膜镜检查

retroillumination [riːtrɔiˈluːmineiʃn] n. 后部反光照相法

sclerosis [sklɔˈrosis] n. 硬化症

sodium [ˈsodiəm] n. 钠

sorbitol [ˈsɔːbəˌtoʊl] n. 山梨醇

主要短语

aldose reductase 醛糖还原酶

nuclear cataract 核性白内障

capsular bag 晶状体囊袋

cortical fibers 皮质纤维

cross-sectional 代表性的

dioptric power 屈光度

direct ophthalmoscope 直接检眼镜

extracapsular Cataract Extraction (ECCE) 囊外白内障摘除术

miotics 扩瞳剂

monocular Diplopia 单眼复视

morgagnian cataract 过熟期白内障

myopic Shift 近视移动（近视化）

nuclear, cortical, and posterior subcapsular (cataract) 核性，皮质性，和后囊下（白内障）

phacoemulsification 超声乳化

pupillary aperture 瞳孔直径

red reflex 红光反射

slit-lamp biomicroscope 裂隙灯显微镜

李春晖　高　妍

98

Diabetic Retinopathy
糖尿病视网膜病变

What is diabetic retinopathy?

Diabetic retinopathy is one of the leading causes of blindness all over the world. The view that chronic hyperglycemia of diabetes mellitus is the major determinant of diabetic retinopathy is supported by the observation that retinopathy in young people with type I (insulin-dependent) diabetes does not occur for at least 3-5 years after the onset of this systemic disease. Similar results have been obtained for type II (non-insulin-dependent) diabetes, but in such patients the time of onset and therefore the duration of disease are more difficult to determine precisely. It is recommended that patients with type I diabetes mellitus be referred for ophthalmologic examination within 3 years after 3 years after diagnosis and reexamined on at least an annual basis. Type II diabetic patients should be referred for ophthalmologic examination at the time of diagnosis and reexamined at least annually. As diabetic retinopathy can become particularly aggressive during pregnancy, any diabetic woman who becomes pregnant should be examined by an ophthalmologist in the first trimester and at least every 3 months thereafter until parturition.

What causes diabetic retinopathy?

Diabetic retinopathy (DR) is essentially a microangiopathy affecting the retinal precapillary arterioles, the capillaries, and the venules. However, larger vessels may also become involved. The retinopathy has features of both microvascular occlusion retinopathy has features of both microvascular occlusion and leakage. Despite long and extensive research, the pathogenesis of DR is still a matter for much speculation.

Microvascular occlusion
- Thickening of the capillary basement membrane—this is a well-documented histopathological change in diabetics.
- Capillary endothelial cell damage and proliferation.
- Changes in red blood cells leading to defective oxygen transport.
- Increased stickiness and aggregation of platelets.

The most important consequence of retinal capillary non-perfusion is retinal ischaemia which, in turn, causes retinal hypoxia. Initially, the non-perfused area is located in the midretinal periphery. The two main effects of retinal hypoxia are the formation of arteriovenous shunts (communications) and neovascularization.

Microvascular leakage

The cellular elements of retinal capillaries are of two type: endothelial cells and pericytes (mural cells). The tight junctions of the endothelial cells constitute the inner blood-retinal barrier as they prevent the passage of large molecules across the vessel wall. The pericytes, which are wrapped around the capillaries, are thought to be responsible for the structural integrity of the vessel wall itself. In normal healthy individuals, there is one pericyte to each endothelial cell. In diabetic patients, there is a reduction in the number of pericytes which is thought to be responsible for distension of the capillary wall and disruption of the blood-retinal barrier leading to leakage of plasma constituents into the retina. Microaneurysms are saccular pouches which may form as a result of local capillary distension. They may either leak or become thrombosed.

The two consequences of increased vascular permeability are haemorrhage and retinal oedema. The latter may be diffuse or localized.

What are symptoms of diabetic retinopathy?

Microaneurysms

These are located in the inner nuclear layer of the retina and are the first clinically detectable lesions of DR, appearing as small round dots, usually located temporal to the macula. They vary in size from 20 to 200µm in diameter and, when coated with blood, they may be indistinguishable from dot haemorrhages.

Haemorrhages

The clinical appearance of haemorrhages depends on their location within the retina. 'Dot' and 'blot' haemorrhages originate from the venous end of the capillaries and are therefore located within the compact middle layers of the retina. Flame-shaped haemorrhages, which originate from the more superficial precapillary arterioles, follow the course of the retinal nerve fibre layer.

Hard exudates

These are located between the inner plexiform and inner nuclear layers of the retina. They vary in size, have a yellow waxy appearance with relatively distinct margins, and are frequently distributed in a circinate pattern peripheral to areas of chronic focal leakage. The centres of rings of hard exudates usually contain microaneurysms.

Retinal oedema

This is due to increased permeability of the retinal capillaries and is characterized by retinal thickening. Macular oedema is the most common cause of visual impairment in patients with background DR. Initially, the oedema is located between the outer plexiform and inner nuclear layers. Later it may involve the inner plexiform and nerve fibre layers, until eventually the entire thickness of the retina may become oedematous.

Neovascularization

This is the hallmark of preproliferative diabetic retinopathy (PDR). New vessels may proliferate on the optic nerve head, along the course of the major temporal vascular arcades. The new vessel starts as endothelial proliferations arising from veins. The mesenchyme from which the new vessels are derived is also the source of fibroblasts which envelop the vessels forming a fibrovascular epiretinal membrane. Initially, the fibrous component is difficult to detect ophthalmoscopically, but later it becomes more opaque and obivious.

How is diabetic retinopathy diagnosed?

In terms of both prognosis and treatment, it is useful to divide diabetic retinopathy into nonproliferative and proliferative categories.

Nonproliferative Diabetic Retinopathy

Diabetic retinopathy is a progressive microangiopathy characterized by small vessel damage and occlusion. The earliest pathologic changes are thickening of the capillary endothelial basement membrane and reduction of the number of pericytes. With progressive microvascular occlusion, sign of increasing ischemia may be superimposed on the picture of background retinopathy and produce the clinical picture of preproliferative diabetic retinopathy. The most typical findings of the retinal veins, and irregular segmental dilation of the retinal capillary bed (intraretinal microvascular abnormalities).

Proliferative Diabetic Retinopathy

The most serve ocular complications of diabetes mellitus are associated with proliferative diabetic retinopathy. Progressive retinal ischemia eventually stimulates the formation of delicate new vessels that leak serum proteins profusely. Neovascularization is frequently located on the surface of the disk and at the posterior edge of the peripheral zones of "nonperfusion". Iris neovascularization, or rubeosis iridis, can also result.

The fragile new vessels proliferate onto the posterior face of the vitreous and become elevated once the vitreous starts to contract away from the retina. If the vessels bleed, massive vitreous hemorrhage may cause sudden visual loss.

Fluorescein angiography: The use of fluorescein sodium as contrast agent, fast injected from the forearm vein, when sodium fluorescein into the fundus with blood flow, through the fundus camera with a set of color filter, shooting fluorescence form blood vessels, to see the visual process with dynamic cycle, fine structure in order to realize the fundus vascular and micro cycle changes.

FFA (Fundus Fluorescein Angiography) can display the extent of diabetic retinopathy, help us to develop a reasonable treatment plan.

How is it treated?

Nonproliferative Diabetic Retinopathy

Focal argon laser burns are applied to individual microvascular malformations and centres of hard exudate rings. The spot size is between 50 and 200 μm with a duration of 0.1 second or less, with sufficient power to obtain definite whitening around the microaneurysm or leakage site.

Proliferative Diabetic Retinopathy

Argon laser panretinal photocoagulation (RPR) is usually indicated in proliferative diabetic retinopathy. Patients at greatest risk of significant visual loss are those with preretinal or vitreous hemorrhage or neovascularization of the disk. Panretinal photocoagulation can significantly reduce the chance of massive vitreous hemorrhage and retinal detachment in these patients by causing the regression and, in some cases, the disappearance of new vessels.

Some of the serious complication of PDR just described can be treated by pars plana vitrectomy. This is a closed microsurgical technique by which intraocular tissue is removed through a small incision in the pars plana with an automated suction-cutting device, while maintaining the intraocular pressure at a normal or slightly elevated level. With early vitrectomy for severe vitreous hemorrhage and proliferative diabetic retinopathy, good vision may be restored or maintained.

中英文注释

关键词汇

arteriovenous [ɑr,tirio'vinəs] adj. 动静脉的

haemorrhage ['heməridʒ] n. 出血

histopathological [,histoupæθə'lɒdʒikəl] adj. 组织病理学说的

hyperglycemia [,haipəglai'simiə] n. 高血糖症

intraretinal [intrəretinəl] adj. 视网膜内的

ischaemia [i'skiːmiə] n. 缺血

mesenchyme ['mezənkaim] n. 间质

microaneurysm [maikrounjur'rizəm] n. 微动脉瘤

microangiopathy ['maikrouændʒi'ɒpəθi] n. 微血管病

microvascular ['maikroʊ'væskjələ] adj. 毛细血管的
ophthalmologic [ɒfθælmɒ'lədʒik] adj. 眼科学的
pericyte [peri:'sait] n. 周细胞
plexiform ['pleksə,fɔːm] adj. 丛状的
precapillary [pri:kə'piləri] adj. 前毛细血管的
preproliferative [pri'prə,lifə'reitiv] adj. 增殖前的
venule ['venju:l] n. 小静脉

主要短语
diabetic retinopathy (DR) 糖尿病视网膜病变
fibrovascular epiretinal membrane 纤维血管性视网膜前膜
fluorescein angiography 荧光血管造影
hard exudates 硬性渗出
insulin-dependent 胰岛素依赖性
macular oedema 黄斑水肿
nonproliferative diabetic retinopathy 单纯性（非增殖性）糖尿病视网膜病变
panretinal photocoagulation (RPR) 全视网膜光凝
pars plana 睫状体平坦部
pars plana vitrectomy （经睫状体平坦部）玻璃体切割术
proliferative diabetic retinopathy (PDR) 增殖性糖尿病视网膜病变
rubeosis iridis 虹膜红变（虹膜上新生血管）

李春晖 高 妍

99

Glaucoma

青　光　眼

What is glaucoma?

Glaucoma refers to a group of diseases that have in common a characteristic optic neuropathy with associated visual field loss for which elevated intraocular pressure (IOP) is one of the primary risk factors.

In most individuals the optic nerve and visual field changes in glaucoma are determined by both the level of the IOP and the optic nerve axons' resistance to pressure damage. Other factors also seem to predispose the optic nerve axons to damage. Although progressive changes in the visual field and optic nerve are usually related to increased IOP, in cases of normal-tension, or low-tension, glaucoma the IOP remains within the normal range. In most cases of glaucoma the IOP is too high for proper functioning of the optic nerve axons, and lowering the IOP will stabilize the damage. In cases involving other pathophysiologic mechanisms that may affect the optic nerve, progression of optic nerve damage may continue despite lowering of IOP.

The primary glaucomas, by definition, are not associated with known ocular or systemic disorders that cause increased resistance to aqueous outflow. The primary glaucomas usually affect both eyes and may be inherited. Conversely, the secondary glaucomas are associated with ocular or systemic disorders responsible for decreased aqueous outflow. The diseases that cause secondary glaucoma are often unilateral, and familial occurrence is less common.

What causes glaucoma?

Many hereditary and genetic influences are known to be factors in primary open-angle glaucoma. Whereas the prevalence of glaucoma is 1.5%-2.0% in the general population, 10%-15% of first-degree relatives of individuals with primary open-angle glaucoma are likely to develop the disease. In addition, other factors including IOP, size of the optic disc cup, outflow facility, angle configuration, and steroid responsiveness are least in part influenced by heredity.

Both autosomal recessive and autosomal dominant modes of inheritance of open-angle glaucoma have been described in the literature. Adult-onset primary open-angle glaucoma is most consistent with an autosomal recessive transmission, which is also perhaps polygenic (involving more than one gene) and multifactorial (environmental and other nongenetic factors may influence the phenotypic manifestations). Autosomal dominant inheritance is characteristic of juvenile-onset open-angle glaucoma.

Angle-closure glaucoma develops because apposition of the iris to the trabecular meshwork blocks the drainage of aqueous humor. Conceptually, the mechanisms of angle-closure glaucoma fall into two general categories: those that push the iris forward from behind and those that pull it forward into contact with the trabecular meshwork.

Pupillary block, with forward bowing of the iris, is the most frequent cause of angle-closure glaucoma. The flow of aqueous from the posterior chamber through the pupil is impeded, and this obstruction causes aqueous to build up behind the iris. This trapped aqueous forces the iris to bow forward against the trabecular meshwork. This sequence is the mechanism for primary papillary block associated with acute, subacute, and chronic angle-closure glaucoma.

Angle-closure glaucoma may also occur without papillary block. The lens-iris diaphragm can be pushed forward by a tumor or other space-occupying lesion. In addition, the lens-iris diaphragm may come forward when the ciliary body swells and rotates about its insertion into the scleral spur.

What are symptoms of glaucoma?

Open-angle glaucoma

Primary open-angle glaucoma is usually insidious in onset, slowly progressive, and painless. Because central visual acuity is relatively unaffected until late in the disease, visual loss generally progresses without symptoms.

Angle-closure glaucoma

Acute angle-closure glaucoma is characterized by a sudden onset of severe blurring followed by excruciating pain, halos, and nausea and vomiting. Patients are occasionally thought to have acute gastrointestinal disease. Other findings include markedly increased intraocular pressure, a shallow anterior chamber, a steamy cornea, a fixed, moderately dilated pupil, and ciliary injection.

There are recurrent short episodes of unilateral pain, redness, and blurring of vision associated with halos around lights in subacute angle-closure glaucoma. Attacks often occur in the evenings and resolve overnight. Examination between attacks may show only a narrow anterior chamber angle.

Patients with chronic angle-closure glaucoma may never develop episodes of acute rise in intraocular pressure but form increasingly extensive peripheral anterior synechiae accompanied by a gradual rise in intraocular pressure. These patients present in the same way as those with primary open-angle glaucoma, often with extensive visual field loss in both eye. Occasionally, they have attacks of subacute angle closure.

How is glaucoma diagnosed?

Tonometry

Tonometry is measurement of intraocular pressure. The most widely used instrument is the Goldmann applanation tonometer, which is attached to the slitlamp and measures the force required to flatten a fixed area of the cornea. The normal range of intraocular pressure is 10-21mmHg. A single normal reading does not rule out glaucoma. In primary open-angle glaucoma, up to 25% of affected individuals will have a normal intraocular pressure when first measured. Conversely, isolated raised intraocular pressure does not necessarily mean that the patient has primary open-angle glaucoma, since other evidence in the form of a necessary for diagnosis. If the intraocular pressure is consistently elevated in the presence of normal optic disks and visual fields, the patient may be observed periodically as a glaucoma suspect.

Gonioscopy

The anterior chamber angle is formed by the junction of the peripheral cornea and the iris, between which lies the trabecular meshwork. The configuration of this angle has an important bearing on the outflow of aqueous whether it is wide, narrow, or closed. The anterior chamber angle width can be estimated by oblique illumination with a penlight or by slitlamp observation of the depth of the peripheral anterior chamber, but it is best determined by gonioscopy, which allows direct visualization of the angle structures. If it is possible to visualize the full extent of the trabecular meshwork, the scleral spur, and the iris processes, the angle is open. Being unable to see only Schwalbe's line means that the angle is closed.

Optic Disk Assessment

The normal optic disk has a central depression—the physiologic cup—whose size depends on the bulk of the fibers that form the optic nerve relative to the size of the scleral opening through which they must pass. In hyperopic eyes, the scleral opening is small, and thus the optic cup is small; the reverse is true in myopic eyes. Glaucomatous optic atrophy produces specific disk changes characterized chiefly by loss of disk substance—detectable as enlargement of the optic disk cup—associated with disk pallor in the area of cupping. Other forms of optic atrophy cause widespread pallor without increased disk cupping.

Visual Field Examination

Regular visual field examination is essential to the diagnosis and follow-up of glaucoma. Glaucomatous field loss is not in itself specific, since it consists of nerve fiber bundle defects that may be seen in other forms of optic nerve disease; but the pattern of field loss, the nature of its progression, and the correlation with changes in the optic disk are characteristic of the disease.

How is it treated?

Open-angle glaucoma

Most ophthalmologists initiate treatment if the IOP is consistently higher than 30 mmHg, because of the high risk of optic disc damage. If the clinician elects to treat solely on the basis of IOP, care must be taken that the risks of therapy do not exceed he risk of the disease. Furthermore, in patients without demonstrated damage, lowering the IOP of a patient with normal optic discs and visual fields from the 40s into the 20s might be satisfactory. Additional factors that contribute to the decision to start ocular hypertensive therapy include the desires of the patient, reliability of visual fields, availability for follow-up visits, and ability to examine the optic disc.

Angle-closure glaucoma

The definitive treatment for acute closure is either laser iridotomy or surgical iridectomy. Mild attacks may be broken by cholinergic agents (pilocarpine 1%-2%), which induce miosis that pulls the peripheral iris away from the trabecular meshwork. However, when the IOP is quite elevated (e.g., above 40-50 mmHg), the papillary sphincter may be unresponsive to miotic agents alone. The patient should be treated with some combination of a topical beta-adrenergic antagonist; alpha$_2$-adrenergic agonists; an oral, topical, or intravenous carbonic anhydrase inhibitor; and a hyperosmotic agent. This treatment is used to reduce IOP to the point where the miotic agent will constrict the pupil and open the angle. Peribulbar anesthesia, globe compression, and surgical paracentesis have also been described to treat acute angle-closure glaucoma.

Laser iridotomy is the treatment of choice in subacute angle-closure glaucoma.

To chronic angle-closure glaucoma, even if miotics and other agents lower IOP, iridotomy is necessary to relieve the papillary block. Without iridotomy, closure of the angle progresses and becomes irreversible. For most chronic angle-closure glaucoma patients, iridotomy with or without chronic use of ocular hypotensive medication will control the disease; for others, subsequent filtering surgery or laser trabeculoplasty to the remaining open angle will be required. No clinical test can reliably determine whether or not an iridotomy alone will control the disease for an individual patient. However, since laser iridotomy is a relatively low-risk procedure compared to other surgical procedures, it should be performed before a more invasive or risky operative procedure. Individuals with extensive peripheral anterior synechiae and IOP following acute closure may be helped by argon laser gonioplasty.

中英文注释

关键词汇

aqueous ['eikwiəs] n. 房水

autosomal [ɔːtə'soʊməl] adj. 常染色体的

gastrointestinal [gæstroʊin'testinl] adj. 胃肠的

glaucoma [glaʊ'koʊmə] n. 青光眼

glaucomatous [glɔː'koʊmətəs] adj. 青光眼的

gonioplasty [gəʊnaiəʊp'læstai] n. 前房角成形术

gonioscopy [gəʊniːəʊs'kɒpi] n. 前房角镜检查

iridotomy [iri'dɒtəmi] n. 虹膜切开术

miotic [mai'ɒtik] n. 缩瞳剂

paracentesis [pærəsen'tiːsis] n. 穿刺放液术

pilocarpine [pailoʊ'kaːpiːn] n. 匹鲁卡品；毛果芸香碱

polygenic [pɒli'dʒenik] adj. 多基因的

slitlamp [slit'læmp] n. 裂隙灯

tonometry [toʊ'nɒmitri] n. 张力测定法

trabeculoplasty [treibek'jʊləplæsti] n. 小梁成形术

主要短语

alpha$_2$-adrenergic agonists α2 受体激动剂

angle-closure glaucoma 闭角型青光眼

anterior synechiae 虹膜前粘连

beta-adrenergic antagonist β 受体阻滞剂

carbonic anhydrase inhibitor 碳酸酐酶抑制剂

chronic angle-closure glaucoma 慢性闭角型青光眼

ciliary body 睫状体

ciliary injection 睫状充血

globe compression 眼球按摩

goldmann applanation tonometer 压平眼压计

gonioynechialysis 房角分离术

hyperosmotic agent 高渗剂

intraocular pressure (IOP) 眼内压

ocular hypotensive medication 降眼压治疗

open-angle glaucoma 开角型青光眼

peribulbar anesthesia　球周麻醉
schwalbe's line　Schwalbe 线
scleral spur　巩膜突
the optic disc(disk) cup　视盘视杯
the physiologic cup　生理凹陷
the primary glaucoma　原发性青光眼
trabecular meshwork　小梁网
visual field examination　视野检查

李春晖　高　妍

100

Retinal Detachment
视网膜脱离

What is retinal detachment?

Retinal detachment does not result from a single, specific disease; rather, it is the end result of numerous disease processes in which subretinal fluid is present. These include congenital malformations, metabolic disorders, traumatic changes, and vascular diseases.

There are three types of retinal detachments, which are rhegmatogenous, exudative, and tractional. The three types of retinal detachments are not mutually exclusive. For example, cases of malignant melanoma have been seen in which the associated retinal detachment had a retinal break. A more common example is proliferative vitreoretinopathy, which exhibits both rhegmatogenous and traditional features. However, excluding the section on differential diagnosis, the scope of this monograph is limited to rhegmatogenous retinal detachments. Accordingly, throughout the monograph, the term retinal detachment refers to the rhegmatogenous type, unless another type is specifically mentioned.

Rhegmatogenous detachments are the most common. They are caused by a break in the retina through which fluid passes from the vitreous cavity into the subretinal space. Rhegmatogenous detachments are sometimes referred to as primary or idiopathic detachments. The break can be identified preoperatively in more than 90% of cases, but occasionally the presence of a minute, unseen break must be assumed.

Exudative, or serous, detachments are due to an associated process, such as tumor or an inflammation, that has produced subretinal fluid without a retinal break.

Tractional detachments occur when pathologic vitreoretinal adhesions mechanically pull the retina away from the pigment epithelium. The most common causes include proliferative diabetic retinopathy, cicatricial retrolental fibroplasia, proliferative sickle retinopathy, and penetrating trauma.

What causes retinal detachment?

Rhegmatogenous retinal detachment

Rhegmatogenous retinal detachment (RD) affects about 1:10000 of the population each year and is bilateral in about 10% of cases. The retinal breaks responsible for RD are caused by an interplay between vitreoretinal traction and an underlying weakness in the peripheral retina (predisposing degeneration). The relatively high prevalence of retinal breaks (5%) in the general population suggests that there are still unknown factors associated with RD.

Traditional retinal detachment

Traditional retinal detachment is most commonly due to proliferative diabetic retinopathy, proliferative vitreoretinopathy, retinopathy of prematurity, or ocular trauma. The typical tractional retinal detachment has a more concave surface and is likely to be more localized, usually not extending to the ora serrata. The tractional forces that actively pull the sensory retina away from the underlying pigment epithelium are caused by a clinically apparent vitreal, epiretinal, or subretinal membrane consisting of fibroblasts and of glial and retinal pigment epithelial cells.

Exudative retinal detachment

Exudative RDs are much less common than either rhegmatogenous or tractional RDs. They are caused by subretinal disorders which damage the RPE and thereby allow the passage of fluid derived from the choroid into the subretinal space.

What are symptoms of retinal detachment?

The symptoms of retinal detachment include flashes of light, floaters, visual field defect, decreased visual acuity, metamorphopsia, and, very rarely, defective color vision.

The perception of light flashes, or photopsia, is due to the production of phosphenes by pathophysiologic stimulus of the retina. The retina is stimulated by light but is also capable of responding to mechanical disturbances. In fact, the most common cause of light flashes is posterior vitreous detachment.

The most significant cause of floaters is vitreous hemorrhage, and the characteristic numerous tiny black dots may be followed in a few hours by "cobwebs" as the blood forms irregular clots.

Awareness by the patient of a visual field defect or shadow is the first symptom of retinal detachment. Detachments anterior to the equator have no effect on the visual field and cannot be demonstrated with perimetry. Detachments posterior to the equator can be demonstrated by perimetry, but patients rarely notice a field defect until the detachment encroaches on the posterior pole.

When the retinal detachment involve the foveal, it can make the decreased central visual acuity.

How is retinal detachment diagnosed?

An obvious detachment is recognizable by the marked elevation of the retina. The retina appears opaque, its blood vessels are relatively dark, it may lie in folds, and the detached retina may undulate. A shallow, slightly elevated detachment of the retina can be more difficult to diagnose. Stereopsis afforded by the binocular indirect ophthalmoscope enhances recognition and proper evaluation of the characteristics unique to each detachment. It is helpful to examine the normal attached retina, then compare with the adjacent area in question for any changes in retinal transparency that may suggest detachment.

With fundus biomicroscopy, a shadow of the retinal vessels is cast on the pigment epithelium. A small degree of shadow formation may be found in the normal retina, but prominent separation between the retinal vessel and its underlying shadow is the clue to a shallow detachment. The detached retina may assume an "orange- appearance peel," which is best seen when the choroid. If a shallow detachment in the periphery is suspected, scleral indentation usually enables visualization of the subtle retinal separation.

How is it treated?

Prior to surgery, the physician must counsel the patient, write appropriate preoperative orders, and manage existing complications. An informed patient is apt to be more cooperative and ultimately better reconciled to the therapeutic outcome.

Scleal buckling or pneumatic retinopexy are the two most popular and effective surgical techniques for the repair of rhegmatogenous retinal detachment. Each procedure requires careful localization of the retinal break and treatment with cryotherapy or laser in order to create an adhesion between the pigment epithelium and the sensory retina. With scleral bucking surgery, the retinal break is mounted on sclera indented by an explant. The scleral indentation can be achieved by a variety of techniques and materials, each of which has inherent advantages and disadvantages. Pneumatic retinopexy which may be performed with vitrectomy surgery, involves the intraocular injection of air or an expandable gas in order to tamponade the retinal break while the chorioretinal adhesion forms. An overall reattachment rate of 90% is reported; however, the visual results are dependent on the preoperative status of the macula. If the macula is involved in rhegmatogenous tetinal detachment, the likelihood of complete visual recovery is diminished.

The primary treatment of tractional tetinal detachment is vitreoretinal surgery and may involve vitrectomy, membrane removal, scleral buckling, and injection of intraocular gas or silicone oil.

Inflammatory detachments are usually treated medically. Some serous detachments, such as choroidal hemangioma, respond to photocoagulation. Radiation therapy is often used for detachments secondary to metastatic tumors.

中英文注释

关键词汇

chorioretinal ['kɔːriəritinəl] adj. 脉络膜视网膜的

cobwebs ['kɔbˌwebz] n. 蜘蛛网

congenital [kən'dʒɛnitl] adj. 先天性的

exudative [ig'zjuːdətiv] adj. 渗出性的

foveal ['fəuvil] n. 黄斑中心凹

glial ['glaiəl] adj. 神经胶质的

hemangioma [hiːˌmændʒi'oumə] n. 血管瘤

idiopathic [ˌidir'pæθik] adj. 特发性的

malformations [ˌmælfɔːr'meiʃns] n. 畸形

metabolic [ˌmetə'bɒlik] adj. 代谢性的

metamorphopsia [metəmɔː'fɒpsir] n. 视物变形

pathophysiologic [pæθəfizir'lɒdʒik] n. 病理生理的

perimetry [pə'rimətri] n. 视野测量

phosphene ['fɒsfiːn] n. 光幻视：无可见光时闭眼所产生的视觉感受

photopsia [fou'tɒpsir] n. 闪光幻觉

proliferative [prəˌlifə'reitiv] adj. 增殖的

rhegmatogenous [redʒ'mətədʒenəs] adj. 孔源性的

retinopathy [ˌretn'ɒpəθiː] n. 视网膜病

subretinal ['suːbritinəl] adj. 视网膜下的

tractional [træk'ʃənəl] adj. 牵引性的

vitrectomy [vi'trektəmi] n. 玻璃体切除术

vitreoretinal ['vitriəretinəl] adj. 玻璃体视网膜的

主要短语

binocular indirect ophthalmoscope　间接检眼镜

cicatricial retrolental fibroplasia　瘢痕性晶状体后纤维增生症

fundus biomicroscopy　眼底镜检查

malignant melanoma　恶性黑色素瘤

ora serrata　锯状缘

pneumatic retinopexy　气体填充术

proliferative diabetic retinopathy 增殖性糖尿病视网膜病变
proliferative sickle retinopathy 镰状细胞增殖性视网膜病变
proliferative vitreoretinopathy 增殖性玻璃体视网膜病变
retinal detachment 视网膜脱离
retinopathy of prematurity 早产儿视网膜病
scleal buckling 巩膜扣带术
vitreal, epiretinal, or subretinal membrane 玻璃体,视网膜或视网膜下增殖膜

李春晖　高　妍

effective for kidney cancer than for other types of cancer, chemotherapy is used when other types of treatment do not work well.

If surgery can't remove your kidney cancer, your doctor may suggest another option to help destroy the tumor.

中英文注释

关键词汇

abdomen ['æbdəmən] n. 腹部；下腹；腹腔

cancerous ['kænsɚrəs] adj. 癌的；生癌的；像癌的

cryotherapy [ˌkraio'θɛrəpi] n. 冷冻疗法

incision [in'siʒən] n. 切口；切割；切开

lymphoma [lim'fomə] n. 淋巴瘤

metastasize [mə'tæstəsaiz] vi. 转移

sibling ['siblin] n. 兄弟姊妹

spine [spain] n. 脊柱，脊椎

swelling ['swɛlin] n. 肿胀；膨胀；adj. 膨胀的；肿大的；突起的；v. 肿胀；膨胀

主要短语

adrenal gland 肾上腺

anti-angiogenic agent 抗血管生成剂

arterial embolization 肾动脉栓塞

bone pain 骨痛

Gerota's fascia 吉氏筋膜，肾周筋膜

interferon alpha 干扰素 α

interleukin-2 白细胞介素 -2

intravenous pyelogram (IVP) 静脉肾盂造影

kidney cancer 肾癌

multikinase inhibitor 多激酶抑制剂

prescription drug 处方药

radiation oncologist 放射肿瘤医师放射肿瘤学家

radical nephrectomy 根治性肾切除术

radiofrequency ablation 射频消融

shortness of breath 气促；呼吸浅短

simple nephrectomy 单纯性肾切除

targeted therapy 靶向治疗

tyrosine kinase inhibitor 酪氨酸激酶抑制剂

茹 峰 王东文

- Partial nephrectomy removes the cancer in the kidney along with some tissue around it. This procedure is used for patients with smaller tumors (less than 4 cm) or in those patients in which a radical nephrectomy might hurt the other kidney.

You can survive with just a part of one kidney as long as it is still working. If the surgeon removes both kidneys or if both kidneys are not working, you will need a machine to clean your blood (dialysis) or a new kidney (kidney transplant). A transplant is possible if your cancer was found only in your kidney and a donated kidney is available.

If surgery can't remove your kidney cancer, your doctor may suggest another option to help destroy the tumor.

- Cryotherapy uses extreme cold to kill the tumor.
- Radiofrequency ablation uses high-energy radio waves to "cook" the tumor.
- Arterial embolization involves inserting material into an artery that leads to the kidney. This blocks blood flow to the tumor. This procedure may be done to help shrink the tumor before surgery.

Biologic therapy for kidney cancer

This therapy uses your immune system to fight cancer by boosting, directing, or restoring your body's natural defenses. Substances for biologic therapy are made by your body or in a lab. Examples of biologic therapy for metastatic kidney cancer include interferon alpha or interleukin-2.

Targeted therapy for kidney cancer

This therapy uses drugs or other substances to find and target cancer cells without harming normal cells. One type of targeted therapy is anti-angiogenic agents. These keep blood vessels from feeding a tumor, causing it to shrink or stop growing. Another type of targeted agent is known as multikinaseinhibitors or tyrosine kinase inhibitors. These oral drugs block an enzyme pathway that allows cancer cells to grow. A third type of targeted therapy is known as m-TOR inhibitors. There are two of these drugs available, one oral and one by IV. They block a pathway that allows blood vessels to help tumor cells grow. Each of these drugs has a unique place in the management of advanced kidney cancer.

Radiation therapy for kidney cancer

Often used to help with symptoms of kidney cancer or in patients who cannot have surgery, this treatment uses high-energy X-rays or other types of radiation to kill cancer cells or halt their growth. External radiation therapy sends radiation to the cancer from a machine outside the body.

Chemotherapy for kidney cancer

This therapy uses drugs to kill cancer cells or stop them from multiplying. Less